THINKING ABOUT
CRIMINAL JUSTICE
IN CANADA

SECOND EDITION

KARLA O'REGAN
SUSAN REID

 ▪ Toronto, Canada ▪ 2017

Emond Montgomery Publications Limited
1 Eglinton Avenue East, Suite 600
Toronto ON M4P 3A1
http://www.emond.ca/highered

Printed in Canada.
Reprinted December 2018.

We acknowledge the financial support of the Government of Canada.   Canadä

Emond Montgomery Publications has no responsibility for the persistence or accuracy of URLs for external or third-party Internet websites referred to in this publication, and does not guarantee that any content on such websites is, or will remain, accurate or appropriate.

Publisher: Mike Thompson
Director, development and production:
    Kelly Dickson
Senior editor, production: Jim Lyons
Production supervisor: Laura Bast
Developmental editor: Sarah Fulton
Permissions editor: Lisa Brant

Copy editor: Claudia Forgas
Typesetter and text designer: Peggy Issenman
Proofreader: Cindy Fujimoto
Indexer: Belle Wong
Cover designer: Nicole Gaasenbeek
Cover image: bjdlzx/iStock

Library and Archives Canada Cataloguing in Publication

Thinking about criminal justice in Canada / [edited by]
Karla O'Regan, Susan Reid. — Second edition.

Includes bibliographical references and index.
ISBN 978-1-77255-240-9 (softcover)

1. Criminal justice, Administration of—Canada—Textbooks.   I. O'Regan, Karla, editor   II. Reid, Susan, 1958-, editor

HV9960.C2T55 2017   364.971   C2017-900398-4

Brief Contents

Contents

PART FIVE   Youth Justice

Preface

Since the publication of the first edition of this book, there have been a number of significant developments in criminal justice. Canada has introduced assisted dying legislation, debated the decriminalization of marijuana, and enacted the first *Victims Bill of Rights*. The first edition of *Thinking About Criminal Justice in Canada* asked students to think of themselves as key players in the conversations that these kinds of social and legislative changes create. There is much evidence to suggest that today's youth have taken up this challenge, using social media and technology to engage in community mobilization and political activism in unprecedented ways. The 2017 World Women's March is a good example. Estimated to have had more than 3.3 million protestors in attendance in the United States alone, the Women's March was the single largest international protest in world history. It took place in more than 673 locations, on all seven continents, and engaged a large cohort of young people who are not afraid to make their voices heard. As one poster held by a young activist at the March read: "Sorry for the inconvenience—we are trying to change the world."

Our own approach to writing this textbook has been an attempt to bring this spirit of transformative conversation into our classrooms.

Rather than leave students with the impression that they are surrounded by experts whose knowledge of the theory and practice of criminal justice far surpasses their own knowledge, we want to imbue students with a sense of responsibility for the world around them and add their voice to the important debates and challenges that they will face today and in the future. When confronted with real-world applications, students are likely to use the learning strategies and problem-solving skills that they have practised. This book engages students to explore, test, compare, and defend multiple points of view on an issue and questions their own preconceived ideas about the way that these issues might be resolved. It asks them to put critical reflection into practice. "What Do You Think?" discussion boxes appear throughout the chapters, prompting students to make a habit of asking themselves key questions about the material they are learning. How should the overrepresentation of Indigenous people in Canada's prisons be addressed? What strategies should be developed to combat the increased risks of cyber-based crime or the rise in hate-based violence in the wake of the 2016 US election? *What do you think?*

In the first edition, we noted that these kinds of inquiries are one of the reasons that criminal justice is so well situated within the liberal arts. The development of a habit of life-long learning can help students begin to question the vision of society they may have inherited, enabling them to move beyond the role of passive observers and into positions of active learners. This is often a necessary transition in the day-to-day work of criminal justice professionals where decisions can become routinized, leaving out important reflections and opportunities for review and assessment. Effective criminal justice policy must avoid myths and unsubstantiated beliefs about what works and how crime happens. Looking for evidence to support claims requires a commitment to learning—to posing the question *why* and the hypothetical *what if*.

This philosophy of transformative teaching and learning forms the backbone of this book. We have also aimed to improve the book's reputation as a "teachable text." This edition features all new issue-themed case studies, revised "What Do You Think?" discussion boxes, and additional in-class exercises. Continuing the tradition of the first edition, a number of chapters have been authored by criminal justice practitioners, which brings to students an applied perspective on the core curriculum. Supporting statistics, anecdotal news stories, and relevant research are presented in Sidebar boxes, and are meant to encourage students to consider some of the more tangential or analytical questions that are raised in the material. We hope these features prompt thoughtful discussion for you and your students.

Acknowledgments

We have loved the experience of teaching with a book we have written together and for our own students. This book is once again dedicated to them. They continue to inspire us and bring deep meaning to the work that we do.

The team at Emond Publishing were invaluable and improved this text at every stage of its development. We are particularly grateful to Mike Thompson for guiding this ship to port with such patience and compassion, and thank the rest of the dedicated editorial team for being so committed to the project: Sarah Fulton, Laura Bast, Claudia Forgas, and Cindy Fujimoto.

We and Emond wish to thank the following people for reviewing the project at various stages and offering their feedback and suggestions: Joshua Barath, Georgian College; Alison Dunwoody, University of Alberta; Carolyn Gordon, University of Ottawa; Doug King, Mount Royal University; Andreas Tomaszewski, Mount Royal University; Lance Triskle, Georgian College; and Brian Young, Camosun College.

Finally, we acknowledge the patience, enthusiasm, and insights offered by our contributing authors, as well as the consistent support of our families and friends, particularly our colleagues at St. Thomas University. We feel incredibly fortunate to make a living doing what we love in an environment that is deeply committed to undergraduate teaching.

Karla O'Regan and Susan Reid

Additional Resources

For information on accessing the teaching resources available to instructors who have chosen this book for their courses, visit the For Instructors tab on the book's website, **www.emond.ca/CJ2e**. These resources include PowerPoint slides, a test bank, and more. Contact your Emond Publishing representative for more information.

About the Authors

Gail Anderson is a professor in the School of Criminology and co-director of the Centre for Forensic Research at Simon Fraser University.

Jane Barker is an associate professor and chair of the School of Criminology and Criminal Justice at Nipissing University.

Rebecca Bromwich has been a practising Ontario lawyer since 2003. She is director of the Conflict Resolution Program at Carleton University. She has a PhD from Carleton, and an LLM and LLB from Queen's.

Tom Deakin is a full-time professor in the Centre for Justice Studies at Loyalist College in Belleville, Ontario. Prior to assuming this role, Tom was a probation and parole officer for several years. He also briefly worked as a residential counsellor in an open custody youth facility.

Leanne Fitch has been the chief of police for the Fredericton Police Force since 2013, and is a graduate of the Ontario Police College. She holds both a bachelor and masters degree from the University of New Brunswick.

Claire Goggin is an associate professor in the Department of Criminology and Criminal Justice at St. Thomas University, Fredericton.

Kouri Keenan is a research consultant and PhD candidate in the School of Criminology at Simon Fraser University.

Karla O'Regan is a lawyer and an associate professor in the Department of Criminology and Criminal Justice at St. Thomas University, Fredericton.

Susan Reid is a full professor in the Department of Criminology and Criminal Justice at St. Thomas University, Fredericton, and director of the Centre for Research on Youth at Risk.

Ron Roesch is a professor in the Department of Psychology and director of the Mental Health, Law, and Policy Institute at Simon Fraser University.

Stephen Schneider is an associate professor in the Department of Sociology and Criminology at Saint Mary's University.

Graham Stewart was the executive director of The John Howard Society of Canada until his retirement in 2007.

D. Scharie Tavcer is an associate professor in the Department of Economics, Justice, and Policy Studies at Mount Royal University.

Canada's Criminal Justice System: An Overview

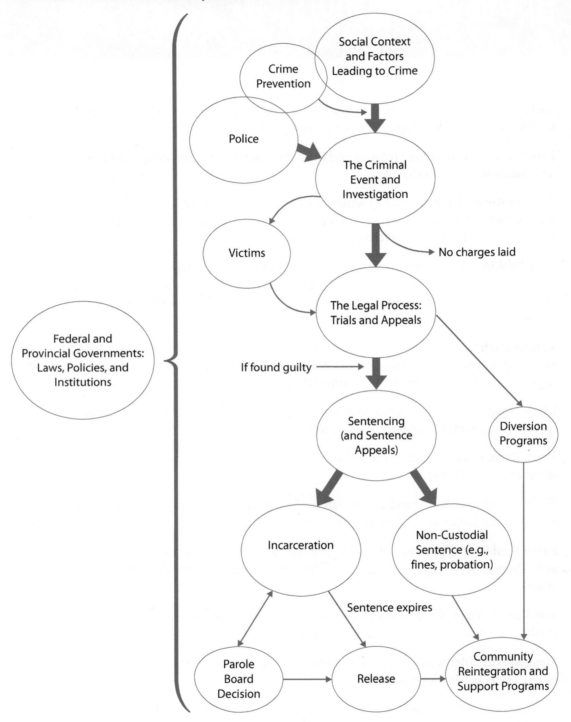

PART ONE

Introduction

You Be the Judge

Karla O'Regan

After hearing about a case involving a violent crime, it is easy to reach a quick conclusion about whether the sentence the judge delivered was fair. Cases of violent crime often create discussion about the value and meaning of a number of important principles such as justice, mercy, vengeance, shame, punishment, and public safety. The goal of this text is to help you think about these principles and other key considerations of Canada's criminal justice system more earnestly, and critically, and by the time you reach the end, we hope, a bit differently! This case study provides you with an opportunity to test your own beliefs about the criminal justice system. Read the following description of a real criminal offence committed in Canada, including information about the victim and the offender. What sentence would you give? What would be your reasons? At the end of the text, you'll have an opportunity to revisit this case to see whether your opinion or reasons have changed.

Please note: This case, as well as some others described in this text, involves a violent offence. Many of the facts are disturbing and should be approached with sensitivity and respect.

A small group of Mushuau Innu youth from Natuashish head out on a hunting expedition in Labrador.

The Offence

On the night of the offence, Matt was riding his bicycle along the town's main road when he met Robbie walking with some friends. Robbie called Matt a "child molester" and indicated that he wanted to fight him. Robbie then removed his jacket and handed it to one of his friends. Matt rode his bicycle into Robbie and the two began to fight. Bystander evidence at trial suggested that Robbie swung at Matt, but missed. Matt then punched Robbie in the face and ran. Robbie chased after Matt and grabbed him by the head. Matt then turned and stabbed Robbie in the left side of his chest with what he claimed was a pocket knife (although no weapon was recovered by police). Robbie was taken to hospital and was admitted for more than two weeks, during which time he underwent surgery. The nurse testified that the wound in Robbie's chest was round and "sufficiently large to be able to put four to five centimetres of [her] little finger into it," leading the trial judge to believe the weapon had been a screwdriver (*R v Dicker*, 2013, para. 15). Matt was arrested and found guilty at trial of aggravated assault and breach of probation.

The Victim

Robbie and Matt were both from the same small town and knew each other fairly well. Robbie had been in a relationship with Matt's sister, with whom he had children. Despite this family connection, Matt and Robbie had a history of fighting and did not get along. A couple of months before the offence, the two had been involved in a heated argument, and although it did not escalate into a physical fight, Robbie did threaten to "give [Matt] a beating" the next time he saw him. Two weeks before the offence, the two were involved in a physical fight outside the town's general store. According to the testimony of the store manager, Robbie threw the first punch, hitting Matt in the chest. Matt then hit Robbie in the face. Robbie then knocked Matt onto the ground, and Matt scrambled to his feet and ran off. The next time they saw each other was the night of the offence.

At Matt's trial, Robbie submitted a victim impact statement. It read, in part:

> Since that night I still have nightmares he is trying to hurt me in my dreams. I was in the hospital for 2 weeks, and they found, he put in 2 stab wounds.[1] They had to put a tube inside me, and to this day I still have chest pains. We had to pay for my partner Beverly to travel to see me when I was in hospital. She stayed [at home] but had to travel every day. Since this happened I went to treatment and I still go to meetings once a week. It was very scary, my family did not know if I would survive and I was very scared to die also. I know this has changed my life forever. (*R v Dicker*, 2013, para. 160)

At the sentencing hearing, the court took note of the seriousness of the wound Matt had inflicted, particularly given its location in the left side of the victim's chest. The judge recognized that while some of Matt's actions could be understood as self-defence, the amount of force he used against Robbie was "excessive." The judge also commented on the importance of finding a sentence that would not only deter Matt from committing further offences, but would also send a message to the community, particularly its young men, that this kind of behaviour is unacceptable.

The Offender

At the time of the offence, Matt was 20 years old. He is a member of the Mushuau Innu First Nation and lives in a small and remote part of Labrador. The community was established as part of a "relocation" project in 2002, when the government moved people out of the nearby community of Davis Inlet as a result of widespread health and social problems, including contaminated water sources, severe levels of domestic violence, alcoholism, substance abuse, and suicide—with more than one quarter of the community's population reporting that they had attempted to end their own lives (Power, 2015). The community gained national attention when a video was released in 1993 of a group of six children (aged 11 to 14) sniffing gasoline in an unheated shack and declaring that life was not worth living. Follow-up reports indicated that inhalant abuse was rampant in the community, with 154 of the town's 169 youths reporting having engaged in solvent abuse, some as young as eight years old. Sixty of these youths reported gas-sniffing on a daily basis.

As a teenager, Matt was falsely accused of having sexually assaulted a group of six young girls. The investigation went on for a long time, and Matt was forced to live outside the community and away from his friends and family for more than a year. This experience had a very negative effect on his life. Criminal charges were laid against him, and the early proceedings of a trial had begun before the RCMP received information that established the allegations were untrue. This case was well known in Matt's community and often resulted in him being bullied. When asked about the stabbing, Matt testified that people were threatening him all the time and that he carried a pocket knife "for protection." He argued that he stabbed Robbie in self-defence.

Matt has a lengthy criminal record, with 16 prior convictions, most of which were for break-and-enter charges and breaches of court orders. One conviction was for assault. For almost all of these offences, Matt was a youth. None of these convictions involved jail time; all of them resulted in periods of probation. While in custody for the aggravated assault charge, Matt incurred additional charges for assaultive behaviour in the pre-trial correctional centre.

English is not Matt's first language. He learned Innu-aimun first in his home. During his childhood, his parents drank heavily, and he witnessed frequent incidents of domestic violence. He struggled in school and was held back a grade, eventually dropping out and leaving school in grade eight. He has had one serious relationship, from which he also has a young daughter. He has struggled with problems with alcohol and domestic violence and has not been able to maintain steady employment.

At the time of sentencing, Matt had applied for a treatment program at a healing lodge and submitted a letter offering him a custodial job with his First Nation upon his release. His sister also submitted a letter of support, indicating that Matt could live with her when released. Matt expressed remorse about stabbing Robbie and, when asked during sentencing about his plans for the future, indicated that he would like to finish school and possibly coach hockey.

While awaiting his sentence, Matt served 66 days in jail. At the time of his offence, he was on probation for a prior conviction (break and enter) and had been ordered to keep the peace and be of good behaviour. He indicated strong emotional ties to his community and his indigenous heritage.

The *Criminal Code* allows for a maximum period of 14 years' imprisonment for the offence of aggravated assault and a maximum period of four years' imprisonment for the offence of breach of probation. In this case, the Crown requested a sentence of six years in prison. The defence recommended a suspended sentence (with a period of probation).

What Do You Think?

1. What sentence would you give Matt in this case? Why? What factors would you take into account when deciding on this sentence?
2. What importance (if any) do you give to the socio-economic context of Matt's background or community? What central principles guide your decision?
3. What do you hope your sentence will accomplish?

SUGGESTED FURTHER READINGS

Burns, A. (2006). Moving and moving forward: Mushuau Innu relocation from Davis Inlet to Natuashish. *Acadiensis, 35*(2), 64–84.

REFERENCES

Power, P. (2015, March 6). A decade after the people of Davis Inlet were relocated, they are still hunting demons. *Globe and Mail.* Retrieved from http://www.theglobeandmail.com/news/national/hunting-demons/article23331533/.

R v Dicker (2013), 280 CRR (2d) 68 (Nfld Prov Ct).

Studying Criminal Justice

LEARNING OUTCOMES

After reading this chapter, students will be able to:

- Describe the differences and similarities between criminology and criminal justice.
- Recognize the key players within the criminal justice system and outline their roles and responsibilities.
- Identify the three subfields of criminal justice studies and the ways each fits within and is informed by the liberal arts tradition.
- Understand the factors that influence how crime is defined and reported, including the role of the media, police practices, and the general public's sense of safety.
- Characterize the core theoretical models of criminal justice and explain how these models inform criminal justice policy.
- Be familiar with key terms in criminal justice studies and policy.

CHAPTER OUTLINE

Introduction

Cases like the one that opened this text reveal the complexity of the criminal justice system and the challenges inherent in its study. No doubt there were many disagreements among your colleagues about the appropriate sentence for Matt and the reasons for it. Working through these debates is a key component of the criminal justice profession and the many different agencies, institutions, and stakeholders it involves. These differences of opinion are also why studying criminal justice can be such an interesting endeavour. There is always more than one side to a story. Crime is, after all, an aspect of social life. Some theorists, such as the French sociologist Émile Durkheim, have argued that crime is a necessary part of human societies and their development. It exists in all civilizations regardless of political leadership, financial circumstances, geography, religious belief, cultural history, demographic composition, language, or levels of industrialization— although, as this text will discuss, each of these factors can influence how much crime there is and how it is dealt with.

Criminology and Criminal Justice: Liberal Arts Endeavours

Understanding how much crime there is, on the one hand, and determining how to address it, on the other, is a good way to think about the difference between criminology and criminal justice. Criminology is interested in *how* and *why* crime happens, while criminal justice is concerned with what to do about criminal activity once it has occurred. Those are, of course, simplistic definitions of both fields and it is important to keep in mind that criminology and criminal justice rely on the work and expertise of each other. Criminology, for example, wants to know more about "the criminal mind" and the factors that motivate an offender to commit illegal acts. Research in this area often relies on psychology, biology, sociology, and the studies that emerge from criminal justice experts about existing offenders and their treatment programs. In the same way, criminal justice scholars are sometimes interested in how to rehabilitate an offender in prison or how to help her reintegrate into a community after release. This challenge is made easier with the help of studies by criminologists that aim to learn more about what motivates people to commit crimes in the first place and how an offender's community can play a role in the prevention, commission, and control of crime.

A Vancouver Police officer interacts with the public. Strong verbal communications skills, empathy, applied ethics, and critical thinking are essential to a successful career in criminal justice.

The cooperative work of criminologists and criminal justice professionals can also be witnessed by examining the central aims of each discipline. The purpose of the criminal justice system is the prevention and control of crime while maintaining and promoting justice. These objectives require knowing a lot about how crime happens and how society feels about it. How should police priorities be determined? What kinds of activities should be illegal? What does just punishment look like? Criminologists are often engaged in research that helps provide some answers to these questions, using scientific methods to explain the interactions of law-making, law-breaking, and the reactions of society to these processes. Criminal justice studies are sometimes housed in political science or sociology departments, given the discipline's interest in studying social control and the various ways it is exercised in defining and responding to criminal behaviour.

It is not surprising that criminal justice professions are often staffed by those with a background in the liberal arts. Williams and Robinson (2004, p. 379) suggest that liberal arts education "has at its center four practices that distinguish it from other kinds of learning: critical thinking, continuing examination of life, encounters with difference, and the free exchange of ideas." These practices help develop key skill sets that are of particular use in the criminal justice field. A 2015 survey of more than 200 criminal justice practitioners found that when asked to rate the skill sets that were most important for success within the profession, strong verbal communication and applied ethics were the most highly ranked, with an emphasis on awareness of racial and gender issues within the criminal justice system (Jones & Bonner, 2016). Criminal justice majors have also been found to score high in intrapersonal intelligence, which, as Tripp and Cobkit (2013) suggest, "indicates a high level of reasoning and an understanding of others' feelings" (p. 482). Moreover, many professionals within the field report that their degrees in criminal justice have improved not only their competency at work but also their ability to excel in higher-level functions. In a 2007 study among American police officers, participants "expressed great support for the degree's ability to improve not only legal and justice system understanding, but more importantly their ability to communicate, analyze, administrate, and engage in human relations" (Carlan, 2007, p. 616).

Skills in applied reasoning and an appreciation for the social and cultural contexts of human relations are even more important when we consider Williams and Robinson's (2004) suggestion that most criminal justice texts ignore issues crucial to the very foundation of all criminal justice processes. In particular, relations of power, **ideology**, politics, and the manipulation of the law through lobbying by special interest groups are areas often left underexplored. The liberal arts encourage a more critical approach to the study of the criminal justice system and its agencies, where it is essential to debunk the dominant myths of crime and criminal justice. This text encourages this kind of approach, using ideology as a framework for understanding both the intended and unintended consequences of a crime policy or program. The utility of ideology as a method of gaining a more critical understanding of the criminal justice system is further explored throughout this chapter.

ideology
A system of beliefs or assumptions about the correct or proper order of things, particularly with respect to morality and political arrangements; a value system that shapes a person's position on specific issues.

SIDEBAR

The Bard Prison Initiative: Liberal Arts in Prison

Want to keep people out of prison? Give them a liberal arts education. This was the answer Max Kenner proposed when he established the Bard Prison Initiative—an organization that helps offer liberal arts education classes to prisoners in the United States. Male and female offenders enroll in academic programs that lead to degrees from Bard College in New York. The organization comprises people who, in the words of its mission statement, "share the view that a liberal education can transform the lives of individual students, and our public institutions, in ways that far exceed the prevailing responses to crime, punishment, and the need for change" (Bard Prison Initiative, n.d.).

The Bard Prison Initiative began as an idea Kenner had while he was an undergraduate student at Bard College. The US Congress had just revoked college funding for prisoners, resulting in the termination of most prison education programs. Kenner, having recently discovered the value of his own liberal arts education, became determined to see it shared with those behind bars. What began as one course offered to 18 inmates is now a nationwide program offered in more than nine states with an annual budget of $2.5 million. As of 2015, almost 350 inmates have earned degrees through the program. Moreover, graduates of the program are significantly less likely to return to prison than their degree-less counterparts. In comparison to the U.S. national average, where about two-thirds of released offenders commit another offence (67.8 percent within three years and 76.6 percent within five years), only 4 percent of all graduates of the initiative's program have returned to prison (Qin, 2015).

For many participants, this outcome is due to the nature of studying the liberal arts. As one graduate remarked, "While at Bard, I learned that freedom was something much different than just a physicality, a space of physical existence. Freedom had a lot do with your ability to think. Freedom had a lot to do with your ability to communicate with others. To see the world in a different view" (Cohen, 2011).

Criminal Justice: Areas of Study and Key Players

Given its mandate of *responding to* crime, the field of criminal justice can be defined as the study of the many institutions and agents that are involved in the investigation of criminal activity, the enforcement of the criminal law, and the correctional arm of the state.

These agencies can be broadly understood to fall within one of three principal areas of criminal justice work—namely, policing, the criminal court system, and corrections. This text is organized around these three subfields of specialization, the first of which is the work of the various policing services in Canada and their affiliated organizations, including municipal, regional, provincial, and federal levels of policing. Policing discussions also centre around the concept of community-based policing, specialized forces such as the Aboriginal Policing Directorate, surveillance and investigative teams, as well as the forensic science services used by police throughout the country.

A second area of criminal justice work centres on criminal law and its procedures. This field of study involves the work of many court-based personnel, including lawyers, judges, and their research teams (comprising paralegals, legal secretaries, and law clerks). It is also an area interested in the work of court services personnel, including bailiffs, registrars, jury attendants, and court reporters, as well as criminal justice professionals who provide services and support to victims and witnesses, such as victim services organizations and social workers, and court-appointed personnel, such as **duty counsel** and child-protection workers.

duty counsel
A lawyer paid by the government to provide legal advice and services to individuals who come to court unrepresented.

A third area of criminal justice work is also one of its largest fields of research: corrections. It focuses on the procedures and institutions of imprisonment in terms of the assessment, treatment, rehabilitation, and reintegration of offenders. Correctional officers, security personnel, and prison administration workers (such as the warden or superintendent of the institution) are key players in this criminal justice field. The work of post-incarceration personnel, such as parole officers, drug and alcohol abuse counsellors, and mental health workers, is also of interest to criminal justice scholars of corrections, as is the policy work of both government and non-government officials and organizations that study the prison experience. Community-based work among criminal justice professionals that does not take place in jail, court, or prison is also a part of the corrections area and includes halfway house counsellors, attendance centre program personnel, educational consultants, youth workers, probation officers, and group home workers, as well as diversion, extrajudicial, or alternative measures co-coordinators.

It is also important to mention the programs that are operated within the community that aim to prevent crime through both voluntary groups (e.g., crime prevention associations, Neighbourhood Watch groups) and other non-governmental organizations (e.g., John Howard Society, Elizabeth Fry Society, St. Leonard's Society). These programs and agencies provide assistance to the more formal state-run institutions under the direction of a broad base of community volunteers and provide additional services to prevent and reduce crime and harm in our communities.

This list of agencies is far from exhaustive , but it should give you some indication of the wide variety of work that is conducted within the criminal justice system and the exciting opportunities that such diversity creates for those who, like you, have chosen criminal justice as a field of study.

How Do We Come to Know What We Know About Crime and Criminal Justice?

The appeal of criminology and criminal justice courses may lie in the fascination that people have with the subject matter, but it is perhaps further enhanced by the popularity of the many dramas that explore issues of crime and justice, such as *Law and Order*, *Criminal Minds*, *Quantico*, *Blue Bloods*, and *CSI*. Many of us are subject to a daily barrage of images about crime and disorder through news media, television, and Internet sources. Crime constitutes a constant and significant portion of the total news portrayed on radio and television, and in the print media. Both the news and entertainment industries are notorious for consistently taking the least common crime or criminal justice event and making it appear to be the most common crime or justice image. Such practices can make anyone *seem* like an instant authority on crime, but all too often the image of crime portrayed in popular media is based more on stereotypes than empirical evidence. This image influences the beliefs we have about crime, which can impede our ability to see things differently or find alternative solutions to a problem. Consumers of a steady diet of crime and criminal justice images from the media have been subjected to a vocabulary of force, where police are portrayed as crime "fighters" in the "war" on crime. As a result, a student entering a course in criminal justice may hold beliefs that crime must be "fought" rather than treated, prevented, reduced, or solved. Students who do not learn about how laws are made may not appreciate that they are imperfect and incomplete, but not impartial. Learning how law can be biased, representing the interests of some over others, is a key step in understanding the present realities of Canada's criminal justice system and its challenges. Similarly, considering the principles of sentencing after a crime has been committed and the subsequent purposes of punishment allows a more critical analysis of the population of offenders that are incarcerated in Canada. Releasing offenders from carceral settings back into our communities is also an area of critical concern with respect to the public misinformation regarding the success of offenders upon release through parole provisions. As students of criminal justice study, these areas will be considered as you further delve into the chapters in this text.

Thinking Critically About the Issues

In asking you to think critically about the issues in this text, we want you to embark on a process of reasonably deciding what to do and/or believe while considering what sources, images, ideas, and arguments helped you reach these positions. We want you not only to be able to assess your own and others' arguments but also to be able to construct good arguments when the issues being presented are controversial. Criminal justice scholars should always be striving to create counterarguments and examples that require empirical evidence or support while remaining sensitive to their own biases and values. Thinking critically about the issues requires a commitment to open-mindedness and fairness, empathy for others' positions, openness to self-criticism, and an appreciation of the value of looking at criminal events from multiple points of view. It may mean a change in some of the beliefs you already have about crime and how it should be addressed, and this kind of shift is not always easy to undertake. As Mark Twain once suggested, "Education consists mainly of what we have unlearned," and when it comes to society's reactions to and treatments of criminal activity, one might say there is a great deal of unlearning to do.

Sherman (1981), in his work on preparing criminal justice professionals, suggested that "the business of criminal justice is forcing people to do what they do not want to do, on the basis of threat of pain, physical harm or, in those countries which still have capital punishment, death" (p. 17). Few commentators on the criminal justice system and even fewer students of criminal justice think about the social and ethical responsibilities of this task before becoming involved with the system themselves. When they do encounter the system, Sherman suggested, the result is a "substantial reality shock" (p. 18). We all have a responsibility to act thoughtfully in our support for public policies within the realm of crime prevention and control, including when we elect our government leaders. Thinking through several viewpoints of the implications of a proposed change to the criminal law or a government agenda to "crack down" on crime is an important task in assessing the value of any given criminal justice practice. Moreover, the media often gets it wrong, leaving the uncritical observer to get it wrong too. As Gendreau, Goggin, Cullen, and Paparozzi (2002, p. 366) have noted:

> [P]ublic opinions are woefully inaccurate and, not surprisingly, tend to be aligned with the "get-tough" orientation of the media. Thus, the public mistakenly believes that prisons (the harsher the better) deter criminal behaviour, that parole rates and parole violations are far too high, that Canada's incarceration rates are lower than those of other countries and our sentencing policies are soft on crime, recidivism rates are sky high, and violent crime is epidemic.

One of the purposes of this text is to help you dispel the myths about crime and criminal justice so as to be able to critically evaluate criminal justice policies in light of competing views about the nature of crime, the methods of intervention, and the possible intended and unintended outcomes of various interventions.

As we have noted, the police, the courts, and the state's correctional arm are the principal areas of focus in criminal justice studies. This is not only a reflection of how our current system *responds* to crime but also how it *defines* crime. It is important to keep in mind how the choices of lawmakers and government officials can influence which behaviours are targeted and by whom. The history and structure of Canada's police systems, courtrooms, and correctional institutions inform us about how the criminal justice system is organized as well as its underlying assumptions. Remember, however, that established approaches are not the only ways of responding to crime. Many alternative approaches to policing or to determining punishments for offenders are explored in criminal justice studies each year (some of which are discussed in upcoming chapters).

Implementing criminal justice policy in policing, criminal law, or corrections requires an understanding that focusing on one form of crime control will affect the quality of life not only of the targeted segment of the population but also of the population as a whole. If any one method is used exclusively, it will have limited returns, so we must be mindful of the need to consider alternative processes. Through a systematic practice of recognizing our own beliefs and being open to the insights of others, we have an opportunity to explore the beliefs that might marginalize others and to consider all sides of an often conflicting array of proposed solutions. This text therefore encourages the study of criminal justice as an inquiry into not simply the *how* of criminal justice, but more importantly, the *why* of the law, police, courts, and corrections.

How Much Crime Is There? Debunking the Myths

Crime and society's response to it are frequent features in news media reports, leaving many issues of policing, the court system, and the correctional system open to public scrutiny. As Gendreau et al. (2002) have noted, public opinion often gets the facts wrong, but even well-informed editorials tend to focus on the failure of the system to keep citizens safe or the injustice of an offender getting off on a "technicality." Few of these opinions take into account the complexity of the system, and while this oversight is understandable given the breadth of issues involved in any case or criminal event, it can easily lead to widespread misconceptions. Consider, for example, the public perception of **crime rates**.

SIDEBAR

Crime Rate

The *crime rate* is a measure of how much crime is known about for any given region or population. It is calculated by adding up all of the criminal incidents that have been reported to the police and dividing by the population (i.e., the rate per every 100,000 persons). In Canada, these data are taken from the Uniform Crime Reporting (UCR) Survey, which collects information filed by police departments across the country about the number of crimes reported, the number of criminal charges that were laid, how these were addressed (e.g., were they "cleared" or solved by police?), as well as the age and gender of the offenders. Because it does not include information about any crimes that were not reported, the crime rate is only one indicator of how much crime really occurs.

Despite politicians' frequent claims to the contrary, the national crime rate in Canada has been falling steadily for the past several decades, and in 2014 it was at its lowest recorded level since 1969 (Statistics Canada, 2015). In 2014 alone, the crime rate dropped 3 percent from the previous year, representing the eleventh consecutive decrease in police-reported crime in Canada. In 2015, there was a slight increase (3 percent), with 5,198 incidents per 100,000 population; however, the rate was comparable to 2013 (5,194 incidents per 100,000). As Figure 1.1 shows, 2015 was the first year that the crime rate increased since 2003 (Allen, 2016).

Among the crimes reported in 2015, 604 were homicides, which increased by 83 from 2014. The 2015 homicide rate (1.68 per 100,000 population) was the highest rate since 2011, but it was still below the average for the previous decade (1.72 per 100,000 population) (Allen, 2016). While the number of homicides increased by 15 percent in 2015, the number of murders still only accounted for less than 1 percent of all violent crimes. The attempted murder rate also increased in 2015, with 144 more than the previous year. As Figure 1.2 shows, the homicide rate and the attempted murder rate fluctuate from year to year with no clear pattern. This kind of fluctuation affects the public's understanding of violent crime.

There is also a misconception that homicides and other violent crimes are more prevalent in large cities. The statistics for 2015 reveal in fact that the incidence of homicide was below the national average (1.68 per 100,000 population) in two of Canada's

FIGURE 1.1   Police-Reported Crime Rates, Canada, 1962–2015

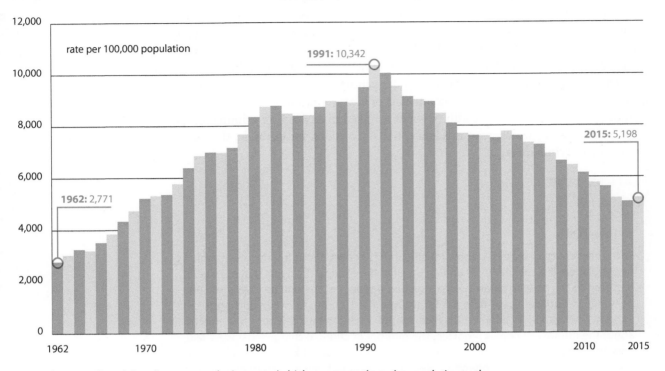

In 2015, Canada's police-reported crime rate (which measures the volume relative to the population size) was up by 3 percent from the previous year, the first increase since 2003.

Source: Allen (2016, chart 3).

three largest cities: in Toronto it was 1.35 per 100,000 population, and in Montreal it was 1.16 per 100,000 population (Allen, 2016). In 2015, Brantford, Ontario recorded no homicides. Does that mean that Brantford is the safest city in Canada? Not necessarily. Given how the crime rate is calculated, the increase of even one homicide in a region can dramatically increase the overall rate. For example, Nova Scotia showed a 100 percent increase in the rate of homicide in 2015, going from 6 homicides in 2014 to 12 homicides in 2015. However, Regina, which has the highest rate of 3.3 homicides per 100,000 population, only showed a 57 percent increase, going from 5 homicides in 2014 to 8 homicides in 2015. Toronto, by comparison, had a total of 82 murders, the same as reported in 2014. It is important to remember that while murder is a very serious event, it is not commonplace.

The crime rate, which measures the overall volume of police-reported crime, counts all offences equally, so that one incident of bicycle theft is counted the same as one incident of homicide. As such, the crime rate tends to be driven by high-volume, less-serious offences, such as minor thefts and mischief rather than the more violent offences people often imagine when they hear the word "crime." In order to have a better understanding of the more serious crimes in Canada, the Crime Severity Index (CSI) was introduced in 2006. In addition to the volume of crime reported to the police, the CSI also gives a weight to each offence based on the average sentences handed down by the courts. The more serious the average sentence, the higher the weight for the offence on the CSI. As a result, in the calculation of the sum of the weighted offences (divided by the population),

FIGURE 1.2   Police-Reported Attempted Murder and Homicide Rates, Canada, 1984–2015

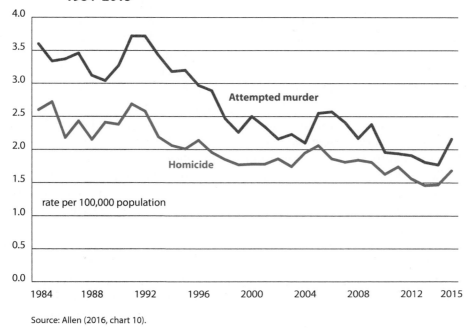

Source: Allen (2016, chart 10).

FIGURE 1.3   Police-Reported Crime Severity Index and Crime Rate, Canada, 1998–2015

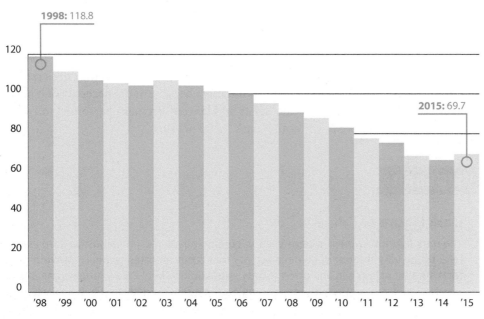

In 2015, Canada's police-reported crime severity index (which measures the volume and severity of crime) was up by 5 percent from the previous year, the first increase in the index in 12 years.

Source: Allen (2016, chart 10).

the more serious offences such as homicide will have a greater impact on changes in the index from year to year (Wallace, Turner, Babyak, & Matarazzo, 2009). As reported by Statistics Canada, in 2015 the CSI increased by 5 percent over the previous year, and this change was due to slight increases in fraud, break and enter, robbery, and homicide (Allen, 2016). The compatibility between the crime rate and the CSI data for 2015 suggests that crime has increased, albeit marginally (see Figure 1.3).

Many factors can affect people's experience of crime, including race, gender, region, and socio-economic status. These factors can contribute to heightened levels of victimization among certain groups, even amid consistently declining crime rates. Following the 2014 RCMP report, *Missing and Murdered Aboriginal Women: A National Operational Overview*, Statistics Canada began working with police to collect data on the Indigenous identities of homicide victims. The results are staggering. In 2014, Indigenous people accounted for 5 percent of the Canadian population as a whole, and yet almost a quarter (23 percent) of all homicide victims and a third (32 percent) of all those accused of homicide were Indigenous people (Miladinovic & Mulligan, 2015). The 2014 homicide rate was six times higher for Indigenous people than for non-Indigenous people (7.20 per 100,000 population as compared with 1.13 per 100,000 population), and Indigenous people were ten times more likely to be accused of a homicide than non-Indigenous people.

These findings point to the importance of examining crime rates from many vantage points, as well as including alternate sources of data to provide a fuller picture of what crime is occurring and how it is experienced. These considerations are particularly important for learning more about unreported crime.

Unreported Crime: The Dark Figure

The crime rate is only one indicator of how much crime is happening in Canada. In addition to police-reported crimes, learning more about self-reported crimes (from victim surveys such as the General Social Survey) provides an overview of how Canadians feel in terms of their sense of personal safety and their satisfaction with the police. Self-report studies are particularly useful given their ability to provide data on crimes that are not reported to police and thus omitted from national measurements of the crime rate. We can never really know how much crime is out there because of the necessity of it having to be reported, which leads criminologists and law enforcement personnel to refer to this unknown amount of crime as the "dark figure of crime."

SIDEBAR

Dark Figure of Crime

The *dark figure of crime* is a term used in criminology and criminal justice studies to refer to the vast amount of criminal activity that is not reported to police, leaving the total amount of crime in any given society impossible to know. How much crime goes unreported is thought to vary, depending on the offence. For example, sexual assault is believed to have the lowest reporting rate of any criminal offence, estimated to be less than 6 percent. This means that of every 100 sexual assaults that occur, the criminal justice system only ever learns about six of them, leaving the remaining 94 incidents within the dark figure of crime.

The General Social Survey (GSS), which began in 1985 and runs every five years, is one of the largest sources of data about unreported crime. It polls a sample of the Canadian population (sample size (n) = 25,000) aged 15 years and older living in Canada and asks a series of questions aimed at learning more about (1) changes in the living conditions and well-being of Canadians over time by gathering data on social trends and (2) current or emerging issues in Canadian society. Currently, the GSS collects data in six theme areas that represent different aspects of Canadians' lives (see Table 1.1).

TABLE 1.1   Current General Social Survey Themes

Caregiving and care receiving	The types of help received and provided for long-term health and aging conditions; the impact of providing care on the caregiver (e.g., health, socio-economic); and the number of houses with wheelchair accessibility
Families	Family structures and experiences (e.g., marriages, divorces, childbirths, adoptions); and organization and decision-making within households
Time use	Unpaid work; non-market production; commuting experiences; daily activities; and time pressures
Social identity	Identification with and participation in national, ethnic, geographical, or cultural groups; shared values; political activities; and social integration
Giving, volunteering, and participating	Levels of community involvement; compassion toward others; volunteer activities; charitable giving patterns; and online group participation patterns
Victimization	Experiences with reported and unreported crimes; spousal/family abuse; instances of cyberbullying and stalking; use of victims' services; crime prevention measures; and perceptions of the criminal justice system

Source: Statistics Canada (2013).

When collecting data under the victimization theme, the GSS asks about experiences with three types of crime, making up eight specific offences: violent victimization (sexual assault, robbery, physical assault); theft of personal property; and household victimization (break and enter, motor vehicle theft, theft of household property, and vandalism). In 2014, 5.6 million respondents to the survey reported that they or someone in their household had been the victim of at least one of these criminal incidents in the preceding 12 months (Perreault, 2015). This is a little less than one in five Canadians (aged 15 or older) and represents a decrease from the self-reported victimization rate in 2004 when the rate was greater than one in four. According to the data from the GSS, fewer than one-third (31 percent) of these incidents were reported to the police in 2014, down slightly from 2004 (34 percent).

In total, Canadians reported 6.4 million crimes in 2014 (Perrault, 2015). About 34 percent consisted of theft of personal property, and 22 percent were a form of physical assault. Theft of household property was reported among 12 percent of respondents, followed by sexual assault (10 percent), vandalism (9 percent), break and enter (7 percent), motor vehicle theft (4 percent), and robbery (3 percent). Most notably, the majority (65 percent) of reported incidents in 2014 were non-violent.

The 2014 GSS included a new question about sexual assaults that had taken place because the victim had been "drugged, intoxicated, manipulated or forced in ways other than physically" (Perreault, 2015). These incidents accounted for 9 percent of all sexual assaults reported on the GSS, with 71 percent involving "sexual touching" and 20 percent involving the use of force. In total, the 2014 GSS reported a rate of sexual assault at 22 incidents per 1,000 people—a slightly lower rate than in 2010, when the rate was 24. Interestingly, when the data from the new question is removed, the 2014 rate drops to 20 incidents per 1,000 people.

Despite their ability to provide some insight into the dark figure of crime, self-report studies depend on respondents' honesty, understanding of the questions posed and particular definitions of crime, and the interpretation of personal experiences. Would most GSS respondents be aware that there are three levels of sexual assault?[2] Would each respondent interpret the new question's focus on non-physical manipulation or force in the same way? How might each respondent read and understand the GSS question about "unwanted sexual touching"? Variations in respondent understanding have an effect on how the rate of sexual assault (and the other crimes reported in the GSS) is understood by criminal justice researchers and professionals and can alter how crime-control policies are developed.

Crime Rates Versus Fear of Crime

Some critics have pointed out that commentary about the falling crime rates is couched in elitism and that the criminologists and scholars who criticize the government for promoting a tough-on-crime agenda are divorced from the reality of crime in their lives. Ian Lee (2011), writing for the Macdonald-Laurier Institute, an Ottawa social policy think tank, has suggested the following:

> [A]ffluent, older privileged people in … any community with average incomes three or four or five times the Canadian income average, have little existential experience with crime … . [T]his suggests that governments need to adopt outreach programs to inform those privileged Canadians, who perhaps do not understand the lived reality of many Canadians, of the data and the relationship between the data, the concerns and fears of many Canadians, and the public policy initiatives undertaken to address those real concerns of ordinary Canadians. (pp. 17–18)

When we look at the Statistics Canada data that Lee (2011) makes reference to, we find that the largest majority of Canadians (93 percent) reported feeling satisfied with their personal safety and that this feeling has been a continuing trend (1999, 91 percent; 2004, 94 percent). Similarly, when respondents were asked about specific situations (e.g., walking alone in their neighbourhood at night), 90 percent reported feeling safe and about 83 percent said they were not at all worried when they were home alone at night. About 58 percent of those who used public transportation reported that they were also not concerned for their safety when waiting for or using these services after dark (Brennan, 2011).

Why, then, amid declining crime rates and an increased sense of safety among Canadians, are "get-tough" approaches to crime still so prevalent? Criminologist Julian Roberts (2007) has suggested that the reporting practices of the mass media have a significant influence on public attitudes and beliefs about crime. News reports tend to

focus on violent offences (despite their rarity) while paying less attention to declining crime rates in general, leading more Canadians to believe that violent crime is on the rise. The influence of the mass media might explain why, despite the statistics that suggest Canadians are generally feeling safer, there continues to be seemingly widespread support for the federal government's tough-on-crime policies. A 2014 public opinion poll revealed that more than 63 percent of Canadians supported increased penalties for those found guilty of serious offences (Angus Reid Global, 2014). A 2009 public opinion poll showed overwhelming support for the federal government's proposed changes to mandatory minimum sentencing, including 72 percent of Canadians being in favour of eliminating the "faint hope clause" and 91 percent supporting a mandatory two-year jail term for anyone caught selling drugs at or near a school (Angus Reid Strategies, 2009).

SIDEBAR

Faint Hope Clause

Canada's *faint hope clause* is found in s 745.6 of the *Criminal Code*. It provides persons convicted of the country's most serious offences (i.e., murder or high treason) and who have been sentenced to life imprisonment without the eligibility for parole the opportunity to apply for parole after they have served 15 years of their sentence. It is not permitted in cases where persons have committed more than one murder. It is called the "faint hope" clause because of how few applications made under this clause have been successful: about 10 percent since its inception in 1976 (Jenish, 1997). Following amendments to the *Criminal Code* in March 2011, the faint hope clause became unavailable to anyone whose offence was committed after December 2, 2011.

Although these polls suggest strong public support for the use of increased punishment to address crime, criminologist Anthony Doob has argued that these polls need to be looked at carefully to gain an accurate picture of public opinion. In the first instance, Doob (2011) warns that many of the questions asked in these polls concern matters that most Canadians are not in a position to be sufficiently informed about:

> [E]very five years or so, Statistics Canada asks members of the public … , "In general, would you say that sentences handed down by the courts are too severe, about right or not severe enough?" Unfortunately, one of the alternative responses that is not offered or recorded is the quite reasonable, "How the [expletive deleted] am I supposed to know? You folks don't make these data available to anyone." Canadians, instead, are compliant with the Statistics Canada interviewer and generally offer an opinion on something for which [adequate] systematic information does not publicly exist. Only about 9% of Canadians in the 2004 survey refused to venture an opinion on an issue—sentence severity—that is essentially unknowable by any Canadian. (pp. 281–282)

The nature of the questions asked in opinion polls can also greatly impact results. Consider opinion polls that show public support for mandatory minimum sentences. These polls tend to ask Canadians only whether they *like* or *want* mandatory minimum sentences. When asked in a poll in 2005 whether judges should have flexibility in sentencing, 74 percent of respondents agreed that judges should be allowed to hand down a sentence that fell *below* the mandatory minimum (Roberts, Crutcher, & Verbrugge, 2007). Doob (2014) argues that this finding demonstrates that while Canadians "may say that they like mandatory minimum penalties, given a choice they would like these penalties *not* to be mandatory" (p. iii). Now consider the government's repeal of the faint hope clause. Public opinion poll data showed that this decision was widely supported by Canadians, yet Doob points to data collected on the outcomes of "faint hope" hearings (showing that over 80 percent of applications were successful) to suggest that "those members of the public having the closest first-hand knowledge of the working of this [former] provision—jurors in Section 745.6 'faint hope' hearings—seem to have been overwhelmingly sympathetic with prisoners' proposals to reduce parole ineligibility times" (p iii). In the areas of counting crime and determining how best to respond to it, it is clear that an individual's political and ideological perceptions influence the questions that are asked and the way the data are interpreted. The same is true when we consider who should "count" as a criminal.

Who Are the "Criminals"?

By definition, a *criminal* is anyone who has been convicted of a crime. Contrary to public opinion, of the many individuals who come in contact with Canada's criminal justice system, the smallest group are those convicted and sentenced to a term in prison. After a person commits a crime, the crime must be reported and investigated before an arrest (if any) can be made. The arrest, as you will learn throughout the course of this text, represents only the beginning of a criminal prosecution. Many decisions by police, lawyers, probation officers, judges, and juries will affect whether a conviction for the crime will occur or, after conviction, what type of sentence will be imposed. There is far more crime than the number of sentences served would suggest. This is because, as cases move through the criminal justice system, various factors affect whether they will continue to the next stage. Many cases are dropped long before they reach the sentencing phase, let alone a sentence of incarceration. This funnelling process is known in criminal justice circles as **attrition** and is estimated in recent Statistics Canada data to be about 4 percent in Canada, meaning that if 100 crimes were reported to police over the year (which would be very low!), only 4 of these would result in a sentence of imprisonment.

attrition
The filtering process that criminal cases undergo as they move through the criminal justice system.

SIDEBAR

The Crime Funnel

The *crime funnel*, also known as *attrition*, refers to the reduction of cases as they make their way through the various parts of the criminal justice system. A small percentage of the total number of cases investigated by police results in conviction, and even fewer end in a custodial sentence. Attrition is greatest at several key points within this funnelling process, including the following:

1. The victim's decision to report the crime to police

2. The police investigation and decision process with respect to whether the allegation is credible or supported by sufficient evidence (i.e., "founded")

3. Discussions between police and Crown prosecutors and their joint discretion to lay a charge

4. The criminal prosecution of an accused, including any pre-trial and trial procedures that can affect whether a case goes forward

5. The judge or jury's decision in reaching a guilty verdict or the entering of a plea from the accused

6. The determination of an appropriate sentence

The number of cases decreases at each of these attrition points.

Figure 1.4 illustrates the crime funnel for 2014. Although more than 2 million crimes were reported to police in Canada that year, criminal charges were laid in just over half of the cases (1,071,314). Of these cases, only 360,640 resulted in a finding of guilt (including both conviction and guilty pleas), with approximately 23 percent (82,764) of those resulting in a custodial sentence (Maxwell, 2015).

There are several decision points where members of the formal criminal justice system are relied on to make choices that will impact the flow of cases through the system. As you will read throughout the chapters in this text, the police officer has discretion in terms of arrest, laying a charge or diverting the individual to alternative measures that are sanctioned by the state. At this point of the funnel, some cases are referred to community supports that are seen to be a better alternative than proceeding by way of the formal machinery of the criminal justice system. Further, as you will learn in the criminal law and criminal procedure chapters (Chapters 6 and 7), lawyers for the Crown and the defence make arguments that either support the charge as laid or negate it based on case law precedent (judge-made law) or procedural law as outlined both in the *Criminal Code* and the *Canadian Charter of Rights and Freedoms*. Assuming that the case before the court is tried and the individual is found guilty, another decision point occurs with respect to the most suitable sentence for the guilty offender. The host of theoretical issues

FIGURE 1.4   The Crime Funnel

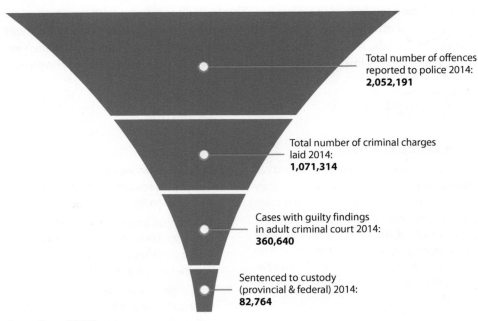

Total number of offences
reported to police 2014:
2,052,191

Total number of criminal charges
laid 2014:
1,071,314

Cases with guilty findings
in adult criminal court 2014:
360,640

Sentenced to custody
(provincial & federal) 2014:
82,764

Source: Maxwell (2015).

that are related to the principles of sentencing will be elaborated on in Chapter 8. At this point, let us consider the sentencing provisions in s 718 of the *Criminal Code*:

> 718. The fundamental purpose of sentencing is to protect society and to contribute, along with crime prevention initiatives, to respect for the law and the maintenance of a just, peaceful and safe society by imposing just sanctions that have one or more of the following objectives:
>
> (a) to denounce unlawful conduct and the harm done to victims or to the community that is caused by unlawful conduct;
>
> (b) to deter the offender and other persons from committing offences;
>
> (c) to separate offenders from society, where necessary;
>
> (d) to assist in rehabilitating offenders;
>
> (e) to provide reparations for harm done to victims or to the community; and
>
> (f) to promote a sense of responsibility in offenders, and acknowledgment of the harm done to victims or to the community.

The principle of restraint on the use of punishment is underscored in s 718.2 (passed in 1996), which indicates that all "available sanctions other than imprisonment that are reasonable in the circumstances should be considered for all offenders."

Many students of criminal justice studies seek employment working in the field of corrections either in provincial detention or correctional centres, federal penitentiaries, or community-based corrections. As we consider the options available for correctional intervention, it is important to consider the field of **penology**. Unlike those responsible for implementing correctional procedures, the practitioners—penologists—are concerned with practices, laws, and procedures shaping punishment and their effectiveness.

Penology

Penology is the multidisciplinary study of the justifications of penalties and social sanctions that seek to understand broader questions concerning who we punish, for what offence, when, and why. The penologist seeks to understand the deployment of penalties within their social, historical, economic, and political contexts.

The crime funnel serves as a good example of what the study of criminal justice is like. We often begin with broad-based concerns or topics, but must narrow them in order to reach a fuller understanding and effect any change. This is particularly the case when what some criminologists refer to as the "social context" of crime is considered. This perspective views the social conditions in which crime takes place (e.g., the existence of inequality or discrimination) as central to understanding how crime is treated by the criminal justice system, including how crime and criminals are defined.

Could You Identify the Criminals in Canada Today?

As some of the studies discussed in this chapter have argued, it is important to think critically about how crime rates and statistics about Canada's criminal population are both calculated and understood. Critical thinking involves asking questions about who is being "counted" as a criminal and at what point in the crime-funnel offenders are situated. Identifying who is a criminal is not always as simple as it seems. Although the term *criminal* brings to mind an image of a person behind bars, a 2015 newspaper editorial declared that on "any given day, Canada has more innocent people in prison than guilty ones" (Editorial, 2015). This result is due to the high number of people who are denied bail while awaiting trial—a problem the Supreme Court of Canada addressed in 2016 in *R v Jordan*. But who are the people most often arrested and convicted of criminal behaviour?

In his book *Who Are the Criminals?*, John Hagan (2010) argued that the question of who criminals are is largely determined by the highly political context of criminal justice policies, where elected leaders "advocate and implement definitions of crime and causal arguments to suit ideological preferences, placate fears, and serve electoral needs" (p. 3). Similarly, Jeffrey Reimen, in his classic book *The Rich Get Richer and the Poor Get Prison* (1979), noted how laws protect the interests of the world's wealthy by defining crime in ways that target society's poor while avoiding the criminalization of corporate, or "white collar," activities. Hagan's historical analysis of US crime policy drew attention to this differential targeting of criminal activity, noting a lax approach to what he refers to as "suite crime" (i.e., **white-collar crime**) and a harsh approach to street crime (e.g., common assault, break and enters). This point illustrates that, in addition to how crime is defined, the ways in which crime is addressed within the criminal justice system are also subject to multiple forms of bias and discrimination, where some social statuses and races experience privileged treatment at the expense of others. For example, Reimen (1979) observed:

See Chapter 7 for more information on bail, the *Jordan* case, and an accused's Charter right to be tried within a reasonable time.

For the same criminal behavior, the poor are more likely to be arrested; if arrested, they are more likely to be charged; if charged, more likely to be convicted; if convicted, more likely to be sentenced to prison; and if sentenced, more likely to be given longer prison terms than members of the middle and upper classes. (p. 112)

A more recent study conducted on the various points of attrition in the US system of justice showed that male and black offenders were more likely to be arrested, convicted, and face sentences of imprisonment than any other type of offender, "leading to a [prison] population that becomes less representative of the total offender population throughout the crime funnel" (Charette & van Koppen, 2016).

SIDEBAR

White-Collar Crime

White-collar crime is a term that was coined initially by sociologist Edwin Sutherland in 1939 to refer to the illegal and fraudulent activities of corporate executives, business personnel, and other persons of high social status that are committed for the purposes of financial gain. These crimes are typically committed during the course of one's employment, and while not considered directly violent, they can have violent consequences, as was the case with the 2001 Enron scandal. In an effort to increase the demand for electricity (and thereby increase profits), Enron traders instructed power plant operators in California to shut down for extended periods of time, creating an electricity shortage. The resulting blackouts experienced in California during some of its warmest months led to mass droughts and severe health problems, and, in some instances, death among the young and elderly (Eichenwald & Richtel, 2002).

Crime Funnel or Crime Net?

Critiques like Reiman's suggest the possibility of a different perspective on the crime funnel. You will recall that the crime funnel suggests that only some criminal behaviour comes to the attention of the police and the courts, and that a great number of cases are dealt with outside the formal criminal justice system. Therefore, a certain amount of "editing out of crimes" takes place as cases proceed through the funnel.

Another way of discussing this phenomenon is what has been referred to as the "crime net." Brannigan (1984) suggested that the crime-net model brings out features of the criminal justice system that are not considered in the crime-funnel approach. The police act as "fishers" seeking criminals, but when taking out their crime "nets" must decide where to go and what fish to catch. This approach suggests that not all people who commit offences are selected for prosecution. Picture the wide but finely meshed nets used by shrimping boats. The nets are widely cast, picking up many fish and sea life of all sizes; yet, many of these nets include an "escape hatch" for larger fish, directing the smaller fish toward the back of the net through a grid that large fish cannot enter. This analogy of a fishing net illustrates how "big fish" may be able to get away from the net that is put out by the police because of the way it is designed, whom it is aiming to catch, and who falls outside their interest.

This social structural approach draws attention to the overrepresentation of some members of society within our prisons, while rich and powerful members who commit equally heinous offences "swim away." It also helps illustrate how the act of defining some activities and not others as "crimes" results in different types of "criminals." The regulation of employment safety standards or the determination of the maximum number of hours in a working day, for example, hardly seems related to criminal justice; however, the exploitation of workers and their impoverished socio-economic conditions has resulted in far more deaths than all of the world's serial killers put together. The Union Carbide disaster in Bhopal, India in 1984 is a sad but effective example. Considered the world's worst industrial catastrophe, the plant's unsafe working conditions resulted in a gas leak that killed an estimated 25,000 people, severely injuring and deforming more than 550,000 others. No time in prison has been served by anyone following this incident (Sarangi, 2012).

Clearly, definitions of crime, perceptions about who is a criminal, and opinions about how to address criminal activity depend on an individual's ideological perspective. For instance, attrition in the criminal justice system might be viewed as a "loss" or a "gain," just as crime rates might be understood to be "high" or "low," depending on what activities are considered criminal. Thinking through your own ideological perspective (as well as those of others) is key for critical criminal justice analyses. The same is true when you are considering how best to intervene in the lives of those who come in conflict with the law. Given the difficulty of understanding how much crime there is in society and who should "count" as a criminal, it seems predictable that it will be difficult to agree on the best way to deal with those individuals who formally enter the criminal justice system. Ongoing debate surrounds whether it is better to treat the underlying individual and social factors that lead to crime or to make offenders pay for their crimes through punishment, denunciation, and retribution.

> **What Do You Think?**
>
> Think back to your decision about the appropriate sentence for the offender in the opening case study. On which side of the crime-control debate would your punishment best fit? Were you most motivated by an interest in treating the "social context" of Matt's crime? Or, were you concerned primarily with the principles of denunciation or retribution? Would a mandatory minimum sentence have made things better or worse for you as a judge in Matt's case?

What Works? The Debate About Crime Control Versus Rehabilitation

Over the years, the pendulum in Canada has swung from left to right in terms of criminal justice policy for those who come in conflict with the law. At the height of the rehabilitative era, when the focus was on individualized treatment, the federal government focused its budget on assessment, treatment, and rehabilitation. Some critics of this approach argued that rehabilitation did not reduce **recidivism**; this position was reinforced by the release of a widely read article, "What Works?—Questions and Answers About Prison Reform" by Robert Martinson (1974), which in essence argued that when it comes to addressing crime in the prison system, "nothing works." Martinson (1979) later clarified this position, stating that it was not the specific treatment programs designed for rehabilitating offenders that had the greatest predictive effect on recidivism, but rather the *conditions* under which these programs were delivered (p. 254). A similar conclusion had been reached by proponents of an effective treatment and intervention for offenders known as "what works" (Gendreau, Little, & Goggin, 1996). This literature has argued that empirical evidence demonstrates that placing low-risk, low-need offenders in inten-

recidivism
Relapsing into criminal behaviour after treatment and/or sentencing within the criminal justice system. Most simply, it can be thought of as "reoffending."

sive "rehabilitation" programs can do more harm than good. Such intensive treatments should be reserved for those offenders who pose serious threats to the larger society. This finding has led some criminologists to suggest that doing nothing at all (radical non-intervention) is sometimes a more effective way of rehabilitating offenders and reducing crime than using the machinery of the criminal justice system. According to this argument, the more intervention and labelling of offenders who are at low risk to reoffend, the more likely it is that the net of social control will be widened. Rather than having fewer offenders within the system, the criminal justice processing and subsequent labelling of those who are at a low risk to reoffend serves to increase the number of offenders coming into the system.

SIDEBAR

Net Widening

Net widening is a term used to describe the effects of providing alternatives to incarceration that deal with offenders outside the court system in order to reduce the numbers of people going to court, and ultimately entering correctional systems. Such alternative measures (known as *diversion*) serve to cast a wider criminal justice net. Rather than decreasing the number of offenders in custody, net widening has increased the total number of offenders under the control of the state.

Webster and Doob (2015, p. 308) note that criminal justice policies until 2006 focused on a set of values that sought to enhance civil liberties for individuals who came into contact with the criminal law, moderation in the severity of criminal punishment, a reaffirmation of restraint in the use of imprisonment, and a focus on offender rehabilitation and reintegration. Webster and Doob suggest that the Conservative government usurped these traditional Canadian moral values and put in place criminal justice polices more like those of the United States. Rather than considering crime as determined by social factors, the focus of Canadian policy-makers has been on offenders making a rational choice to commit crime. These "bad" individuals have been considered not only "beyond hope or redemption but also unworthy of compassion or even tolerance" (p. 314). Through changes to the law on parole and the creation of harsher sanctions (including the possibility of the revocation of citizenship for those individuals with dual citizenship if they are convicted of certain crimes), Webster and Doob (2015) argue that criminal justice policy in Canada has reflected exclusionary tactics that elevate the value of imprisonment and view offenders as "lesser" individuals who have "forfeited their claims to full citizenship" and are "fittingly outlawed from society" (p. 315). Gerber and Jackson (2016) have further elaborated on the ideological basis of punitive attitudes based on political ideologies held by partisan politicians.

These debates highlight the complex challenges involved in determining not simply what crime is but also how best to respond to it. Part of the work of criminal justice scholars is to devise models for approaching these topics in a critical, fair, and thoughtful way. This issue will be revisited after a look at some theoretical models that are useful in considering criminal justice policy and its underlying ideologies.

The Ideology of Criminal Justice: Theoretical Models

Earlier in this chapter, we defined the term *ideology* and spoke about the importance of understanding the values that drive the development and explanation of criminal justice. Political belief systems serve as the basic foundation for both law and its reform. Given that law is the basis for our criminal justice system, criminal justice operations cannot be understood without examining the role that ideology plays in writing and implementing the legislation and policies that shape our system of justice. Williams and Robinson (2004, p. 385) suggested that public policy is influenced by ideology and by stereotypes of criminals as much as, if not more than, by an understanding of the underlying causes of crime and the immediate situations that bring it about. In order to move beyond these stereotypes and debunk these myths, it is important to have some way of bringing together a framework to understand these various competing belief systems.

Herbert Packer (1964) developed a systematic way to conceptualize the influence of ideology on criminal justice systems. He referred to criminal justice as a paradox, characterized by a gulf between how police, courts, and corrections *ought* to behave, and how they actually behave in practice. Packer identified two main models of criminal justice that fall on either side of this gulf, which is commonly referred to as the "punishment–treatment dichotomy."

Crime control is largely concerned with assuring the public that crime will not be tolerated and that, once it has been discovered, it will be severely *punished*.

The *welfare model* stresses the importance of looking after the needs of the offender in order to ensure that the individual's problems are *treated* so that more crime will not occur in the future.

The crime-control model is based on the philosophy of **deterrence**, while the welfare model is primarily based on the tenets of **rehabilitation** and a medical model of treatment.

rehabilitation
The treatment of offenders in order to prevent future criminal activity; a planned intervention that targets some aspect of the offender that is thought to cause the offender's criminality (e.g., attitude, cognitive processes, social relationships, and employment).

SIDEBAR

Deterrence

Deterrence is a philosophical approach to crime that focuses on what forms of punishment are necessary to prevent crime from happening. It has two forms: specific and general. Specific deterrence seeks to punish the individual offender just enough to stop her from committing any future crimes. The assumption is that the offender will have learned the consequences of crime and will choose not to suffer them again. General deterrence seeks to punish offenders severely enough that the general population will choose not to commit crime. This approach aims to make an example of the offender so as to teach everyone the "costs" of crime.

In addition to these two theoretical models, other considerations have been adopted and codified over the years. A variation on the crime-control model has emerged that adds a measure of accountability for human fallibility. Known as the *justice model*, it still focuses on the protection of society through deterrence principles, but it also suggests that there may be human errors in the discovery and subsequent finding of guilt for those accused of criminal conduct. As such, the justice model focuses on making sure that punishments are not only severe enough to deter crime but also applied equally and fairly to everyone. Therefore, this approach focuses on the crime and not the individual who commits it, arguing that the criminal justice system should not apply differential treatment in any circumstances. Not surprisingly, the justice model is a strong proponent of mandatory minimum sentences.

Similarly, with respect to the treatment model of intervention, a great deal of work in the criminological literature has pointed to the strong positive correlation (link) between poverty and crime. This link has led many researchers to emphasize the need to consider the impact of external socio-demographic factors, known as the **root causes of crime**. The *community change model* focuses on these root causes to suggest that the lack of access to resources and the disadvantages experienced by some members of society form the basis for the underlying factors leading to the commission of crime. From this perspective, all members of the community have a responsibility for the ongoing prevention and rehabilitation of individuals who come in conflict with the law (Reid & Reitsma-Street, 1984).

root causes of crime
Social factors in our societies, cultures (family values), economy, and systems that are more likely to lead an individual to commit crime. Examples include peer influence, poverty, unemployment, poor neighbourhoods, and poor literacy.

Based on some of the tenets of the community change model is the approach commonly referred to as "restorative justice." Restorative justice is a model that fits within the treatment approach to crime, emphasizing the importance of healing those relationships that have been broken by conflict and crime. Viewed through this lens, crime is understood as a violation of people and their relationships, and a disruption of the peace of the community as opposed to being simply an offence against the state or an injury suffered solely by the victim. Restorative justice encourages the participation of victims, offenders, and the community in finding solutions that will achieve reconciliation and restore harmony. It also recognizes that sometimes the use of measures outside the criminal justice system (e.g., victim–offender mediation, circle sentencing) is the best response to the crime. Further, the restorative justice approach focuses on the importance of engaging the community in a meaningful dialogue about what the most suitable way of repairing the harm done might be. This model aims to involve all those affected by the crime in its solution, and to work toward a mutually beneficial resolution for the victim and offender that will ensure that the offender understands how his or her behaviour has affected others (Reid & Zuker, 2005).

A comparison of the approach of each of these models is found in Table 1.2.

We will be asking you to think about these ideological underpinnings throughout the remainder of this text. By including an analysis of the historical development of the structures and processes of the criminal justice system and an examination of the

What Do You Think?

How do you think the case study that opened this text might fit within these theoretical models? Was Matt's behaviour made worse by the system or was his "criminal mind" simply beyond aid? Here, in the consideration of an actual case, the links between criminal justice theory and criminal justice practice become evident. How does your sentence fit within the punishment–treatment dichotomy identified by Packer? Do you view Matt's criminal career as an inevitable aspect of his personality and his choices? Or does the criminal justice system have a role to play in perpetuating Matt's criminal attitude and activities?

TABLE 1.2   A Comparison of Theoretical Models

	Restorative justice	Community change	Welfare	Justice	Crime control
Main tenet	When a crime is committed, it has an impact not only on the victim and the offender, but on the wider community as well.	Society is responsible for the promotion of the welfare of its citizens and must work to prevent crime and delinquency.	The treatment needs of the individual offender and his or her family must be attended to.	Interference with an individual's freedom is limited and procedures for criminal justice matters are based on consent by all parties as much as possible.	It is the responsibility of the state and the courts to maintain order in society.
Crime causation (free will vs. determinism)	All citizens have a role to play in the prevention of crime and repair of the harm done when a crime is committed.	Behaviour is seen as being determined by life consequences (e.g., poverty, lack of opportunity, social structure).	Behaviour is seen as being determined by social/psychological forces.	Freely determined: an individual chooses to commit offences.	Freely determined: an individual chooses to commit offences.
Individual or collective response	Collective: families, victims, and the community are involved to the greatest extent possible in rehabilitation, community safety initiatives, and holding offenders accountable.	Focus is on collective society rather than on the individual offender as being responsible for criminal conduct.	Individual: focus is on criminal conduct as being part of other social events affecting the individual, who needs rehabilitation and/or treatment (family dysfunction, alcohol/substance abuse, victim of family violence).	Individual: focus is on the repression of crime, but with a recognition that there is a high probability of error in informal fact finding (i.e., legal safeguards are needed to protect individual liberty and rights).	Collective: repression of criminal conduct through punishment, denunciation, and individual and general deterrence.
Criminal justice response	The individual is required to face the personal harm that his or her offending behaviour has done to the victim and the wider community; restitution, victim–offender mediation, and community service form part of the restoration of the victim, the offender, and the community.	Focus is on changing social processes that lead persons to engage in criminal conduct and to improve the quality of life for all citizens.	Focus is on evaluation of the whole individual and his or her life circumstances; the person is brought to court to be aided and assisted.	Focus is on formal adversarial system of justice; key is the protection of rights for the public and accused, legal safeguards, due process rights (e.g., right to a lawyer, right to appeal, and right to legal representation at all stages of proceedings).	Focus is on a screening process that diverts the innocent out of the courts (i.e., only the guilty go to court); no need for legal safeguards.

Source: Reid and Zuker (2005).

nature of the behaviour of criminals and the legislators, professionals, and others who manage the system, we believe that you will be equipped with the tools to reconsider any of your deeply held assumptions and beliefs about crime, and be open to new ideas and evidence.

Conclusion

Although the contributors to this text have expertise within their respective criminal justice fields, it is important to remain inquisitive about what you read, keeping in mind that many different sides exist to each story. In a number of places throughout the text, you will be asked to stop and "take a sidebar" in order to think critically about specific events, theories, or approaches to crime and punishment. Each part in this text opens with a case study, profiling a particular criminal event or case in Canadian history. Some of these cases may be familiar to you. Perhaps you will read them and immediately form an opinion about the people and events described. Try to take note of these initial thoughts and trace any changes or developments in these first impressions that may occur as you read the chapters that follow the case studies. Ideally, we would like you to leave this text thinking differently from when you first opened it up. The next time you hear a news story about an arrest or investigation, or about the government's latest "war" on crime or drugs, we hope you will be able to engage in the debate in a more informed fashion, with the perspectives you encountered in this text helping you to form your own criminal justice mind.

The expression "take a sidebar," which is picked up in the Sidebar boxes throughout this text, comes from the practice among lawyers to discuss legal issues with the judge "on the side" of the bar. It is what happens when counsel are asked to approach the bench.

Crime is always featured prominently in the news media, and is often very sensational. The old saying "if it bleeds, it leads" still very much applies to journalism today and demonstrates the priorities of most news organizations. The media play a central role in shaping the public's attitudes toward crime, but critical thinkers know they must look beyond sensational headlines and examine the evidence in order to properly understand the issues.

IN-CLASS EXERCISE

Understanding the Differences Between Criminology and Criminal Justice

How well do you understand the differences between criminology and criminal justice? Discuss these two related disciplines in small groups and, using a table like the one below, fill in a few of the key areas of concern or major types of activity found in each field. When you have finished, compare your answers with those of a neighbouring group. Did you miss any? Do you disagree with anything your colleagues wrote? What types of research interests or activities did not fit as neatly into the table as others? Why do you think this might be?

Criminology	Criminal Justice

DISCUSSION QUESTIONS

1. Take a moment to revisit your decision with respect to the case study that opened this text. Which of the five models of criminal justice discussed in this chapter best represents the goals you had when sentencing Matt? Does your determined sentence reflect more than one of the models? In which ways? Are there any models that clearly do not fit your sentence or that case? Why or why not?

2. Think about the issue of attrition of cases through the criminal justice system. Which analogy—the crime funnel or the crime net—do you think best defines why some people end up in jail while others do not? How might these analogies help to explain the overrepresentation of some groups in Canada's prison system? Compare your answers with those of a colleague. What are your major areas of agreement? Where do your assessments differ?

3. Given how much crime is left unreported, how helpful are national crime rates in gaining a picture of what crime occurs in Canada? Do you see value in victimization and self-report surveys like the General Social Survey? What other methods might help criminologists learn more about the *dark figure of crime*? How does knowing that so much unreported crime exists inform your views on what Canada's approach to crime prevention should be?

NOTES

1 The medical record confirmed that there was only one stab wound.
2 The three levels of sexual assault are as follows:

Sexual assault level 1: Any form of touching that is of a sexual nature that is performed without the consent of the complainant. The severity of the offence is determined by the part of the body touched, the nature of the contact, the situation in which it occurred, and any words or gestures that accompanied the act. This touching can range from an unwanted kiss to forced penetration and is found in s 271 of the *Criminal Code*.

Sexual assault level 2: Occurs when a person is sexually assaulted by someone who
- uses a weapon or threatens to use a weapon (imitation or real);
- threatens to cause harm to a third person (friend, family member, or children);
- causes bodily harm to a third party; or
- commits the assault with any other person—multiple assailants (s 272(1)).

Sexual assault level 3: Occurs when a person brutally beats, wounds, maims, disfigures, or endangers the life of someone during an assault (aggravated sexual assault, s 273(1)).

SUGGESTED FURTHER READINGS

Adler, J. (2014). The amazing results when you give a prison inmate a liberal arts education. *Smithsonian*. Retrieved from http://www.smithsonianmag.com/innovation/amazing-results-when-you-give-prison-inmate-liberal-arts-education-180953041/?no-ist=&page=1.

Boyce, J. (2015, July). Police-reported crime statistics in Canada, 2014. *Juristat, 35*(1). Retrieved from http://www.statcan.gc.ca/pub/85-002-x/2015001/article/14211-eng.pdf.

Brannigan, A. (1984). Crimes, courts and corrections: An introduction to crime and social control in Canada. Toronto: Holt Rinehart and Winston.

Bureau of Justice Statistics. (2014, April 22). Recidivism of prisoners released in 30 states in 2005: Patterns from 2005 to 2010. Retrieved from http://www.bjs.gov/index.cfm?ty=pbdetail&iid=4986.

Kivanç, J. (2015, November). Thunder Bay takes Regina's title of Canada's murder capital. *Vice*. Retrieved from http://www.vice.com/en_ca/read/thunder-bay-takes-reginas-title-of-canadas-murder-capital.

Perkel, C. (2015, November). Aboriginal people make up 5 per cent of Canada's population—but nearly a quarter of its murder victims. *National Post*. Retrieved from http://news.nationalpost.com/news/canada/aboriginal-people-make-up-5-per-cent-of-canadas-population-but-nearly-a-quarter-of-its-murder-victims.

Scott, D. (2008). *Penology*. London: Sage.

Statistics Canada. (2016). General Social Survey—Victimization. Retrieved from http://www23.statcan.gc.ca/imdb/p2SV.pl?Function=getSurvey&SDDS=4504.

Toronto Police Service. (2017). TPS crime statistics. Retrieved from http://torontopolice.on.ca/statistics/ytd_stats.php.

REFERENCES

Allen, M. (2016). Police-reported crime statistics in Canada, 2015. *Juristat, 36*(1). Catalogue No. 85-002-X. Retrieved from http://www.statcan.gc.ca/pub/85-002-x/2016001/article/14642-eng.pdf.

Angus Reid Global. (2014, August 12). Six-in-ten Canadians support legalizing marijuana, but say it's not a top justice priority. Retrieved from http://angusreidglobal.com/wp-content/uploads/2014/08/ARG-Marijuana-Opinions2.pdf.

Angus Reid Strategies. (2009, June 26). Canadians endorse federal anti-crime proposals.

Bard Prison Initiative. (n.d.). Mission statement. Retrieved from http://bpi.bard.edu

Brennan, S. (2011). *Canadians' perceptions of personal safety and crime, 2009.* Ottawa: Minister of Industry. Retrieved from http://www.statcan.gc.ca/pub/85-002-x/2011001/article/11577-eng.pdf.

Carlan, P. (2007). The criminal justice degree and policing: Conceptual development or occupational primer? *Policing: An International Journal of Police Strategies & Management, 30*(4), 608–619.

Charette, Y., & van Koppen, V. (2016). A capture-recapture model to estimate the effects of extra-legal disparities on crime funnel selectivity and punishment avoidance. *Security Journal, 29*(4), 561–583. doi:10.1057/sj.2015.30.

Cohen, T. (2011). College-in-prison for inmates serving life sentences. *Morningside Review.* Retrieved from http://morningsidereview.org/essay/college-in-prison-for-inmates-serving-life-sentences/.

Criminal Code of Canada, RSC 1970, c C-34.

Doob, A.N. (2011). The unfinished work of the Canadian Sentencing Commission. *Canadian Journal of Criminology & Criminal Justice, 53*(3), 279–297.

Doob, A.N. (2014). Research on public confidence in the criminal justice system: A compendium of research findings from *Criminological Highlights.* Paper presented at the Sixth Annual Reinventing Criminal Justice Symposium, Ottawa, ON. Retrieved from http://criminology.utoronto.ca/wp-content/uploads/2013/09/PublicConfidence-Doob-ICCLR-11Dec2013.pdf.

Editorial: Most of Canada's prisoners have never been convicted of anything. Why are they in jail? [Editorial]. (2015, July 17). *Globe and Mail.* Retrieved from http://www.theglobeandmail.com/opinion/editorials/most-of-canadas-prisoners-have-never-been-convicted-of-anything-why-are-they-in-jail/article25559599/.

Eichenwald, K., & Richtel, M. (2002, October 12). Enron trader pleads guilty to conspiracy. *New York Times,* C-1.

Gendreau, P., Goggin, C., Cullen, F.T., & Paparozzi, M. (2002). The common sense revolution and correctional policy. In J. McGuire (Ed.), *Offender rehabilitation and treatment: Effective programs and policies to reduce re-offending* (pp. 359–386). Chichester, UK: John Wiley & Sons.

Gendreau, P., Little, T., & Goggin, C. (1996). A meta-analysis of the predictors of adult offender recidivism: What works! *Criminology, 34,* 575–607.

Gerber, M.M., & Jackson, J. (2016). Authority and punishment: On the ideological basis of punitive attitudes towards criminals. *Psychiatry, Psychology and Law, 23*(1), 113–134.

Hagan, J. (2010). *Who are the Criminals? The politics of crime policy from the age of Roosevelt to the age of Reagan.* Princeton, NJ: Princeton University Press.

Jenish, D'A. (1997). Faint hope: Background. *Canadian Encyclopedia.* Retrieved from http://www.thecanadianencyclopedia.ca/en/article/faint-hope-background/.

Jones, H., & Bonner, H.S. (2016). What should criminal justice interns know? Comparing the opinions of student interns and criminal justice practitioners. *Journal of Criminal Justice Education, 27*(3), 381–409.

Lee, I. (2011). *Myths & urban legends concerning crime in Canada*. Ottawa: Macdonald-Laurier Institute. Retrieved from http://www.macdonaldlaurier.ca/files/pdf/Ian_Lee_March_2011.pdf.

Martinson, R. (1974, Spring). What works?—Questions and answers about prison reform. *Public Interest*, 22–54.

Martinson, R. (1979). New findings, new views: A note of caution regarding sentencing reform. *Hofstra Law Review, 7*, 243–258.

Maxwell, A. (2015, November). Adult criminal court statistics in Canada, 2013/2014. *Juristat, 35*(1). Retrieved from http://www.statcan.gc.ca/pub/85-002-x/2015001/article/14226-eng.pdf.

Miladinovic, Z., & Mulligan, L. (2015, November). Homicide in Canada, 2014. *Juristat, 35*(1).

Packer, H. (1964). Two models of the criminal process. *University of Pennsylvania Law Review, 113*(1), 1–68.

Perreault, S. (2015). Criminal victimization in Canada, 2014. *Juristat, 35*(1). Retrieved from http://www.statcan.gc.ca/pub/85-002-x/2015001/article/14241-eng.htm.

Qin, Y. (2015, July 9). Want to keep ex-cons from returning to prison? Give them a liberal arts education. *Washington Post*. Retrieved from https://www.washingtonpost.com/posteverything/wp/2015/07/09/want-to-help-prisoners-stay-out-of-jail-teach-them-to-speak-chinese/.

R v Jordon, [2016] SCJ No 27 (QL).

RCMP. (2014). *Missing and murdered Aboriginal women: A national operational overview*. Retrieved from http://www.rcmp-grc.gc.ca/wam/media/460/original/0cbd8968a049aa0b44d343e76b4a9478.pdf.

Reid, S.A., & Reitsma-Street, M. (1984). Assumptions and implications of new Canadian legislation for young offenders. *Canadian Criminology Forum, 7*(1), 1–19.

Reid, S.A., & Zuker, M.A. (2005). A conceptual framework for understanding youth justice in Canada. In K. Campbell (Ed.), *Youth Justice in Canada*. Toronto: Pearson.

Reimen, J.H. (1979). *The rich get richer and the poor get prison: Ideology, class and criminal justice*. Boston: Allyn and Bacon.

Roberts, J. (2001). *Fear of crime and attitudes to criminal justice: A review of recent trends, 2001–02*. Ottawa: Public Works and Government Services Canada.

Roberts, J. V., Crutcher, N., & Verbrugge, P. (2007). Public attitudes to sentencing in Canada: Exploring recent findings. *Canadian Journal of Criminology and Criminal Justice, 49*(1), 75–107.

Sarangi, S. (2012). Compensation to Bhopal gas victims: Will justice ever be done? *Indian Journal of Medical Ethics, 9*(2), 118–120.

Sherman, L.W. (1981). *The study of ethics in criminology and criminal justice curricula*. Chicago: University of Illinois.

Statistics Canada. (2013). General Social Survey: An overview, 2013. (Ottawa: Minister of Industry, 2013. Retrieved from http://www.statcan.gc.ca/pub/89f0115x/89f0115x2013001-eng.pdf.

Statistics Canada. (2015, July 22). Police-reported crime statistics, 2014. *The Daily*. Retrieved from http://www.statcan.gc.ca/daily-quotidien/150722/dq150722a-eng.htm.

Tripp, T., & Cobkit, S. (2013). Unexpected pathways: Criminal justice career options in the private sector. *Journal of Criminal Justice Education, 24*(4), 478–494.

Wallace, M., Turner, J., Babyak, C., & Matarazzo, A. (2009). *Measuring crime in Canada: Introducing the Crime Severity Index and improvements to the Uniform Crime Reporting Survey*. Ottawa: Statistics Canada. Retrieved from http://www.statcan.gc.ca/pub/85-004-x/85-004-x2009001-eng.htm.

Webster, C.M., & Doob, A.N. (2015). US punitiveness "Canadian style"? Cultural values and Canadian punishment policy. *Punishment & Society, 17*(3), 299–321.

Williams, E.J., & Robinson, M.B. (2004). Ideology and criminal justice: Suggestions for a pedagogical model. *Journal of Criminal Justice Education, 15*(2), 373–392.

Crime Prevention

LEARNING OUTCOMES

After reading this chapter, students will be able to:

- Provide a broad definition of *crime prevention*.
- Understand the fundamental differences between crime prevention and the criminal justice system.
- Describe the core characteristics of crime prevention.
- Understand dominant crime prevention strategies and how they seek to address criminal behaviour.
- Understand the institutions through which crime prevention strategies are delivered.
- Discuss recidivism prevention strategies, particularly social problem-solving approaches, and how they compare and contrast with crime prevention.

MINI CASE STUDY

The Chicago Area Project

In the 1920s, in an attempt to explain the onset of deviant and delinquent behaviour, sociologists at the University of Chicago began to examine the impact of local social conditions and neighbourhood characteristics on young people. Their analysis of where "delinquents" lived in Chicago showed a concentration in inner-city areas characterized by low rent and physical deterioration. These "zones of transition" also experienced a rapid turnover of the local population, a high level of ethnic diversity, economic deprivation, and weak local social institutions. These conditions led to a chronic problem of what the University of Chicago researchers—later known as the *Chicago School*—called "social disorganization," which, in turn, undermined local social cohesion, informal social control, and the positive socialization of children and youth. The researchers argued that as a result of this social pathology, children and young people were ineffectually socialized, giving rise to delinquency (Shaw & McKay, 1942; Shaw, Zorbaugh, McKay, & Cottrell, 1929). This "ecological theory of crime" would revolutionize the field of criminology, which up to this point almost exclusively blamed individual pathology for criminal and deviant behaviour.

On the basis of their work, the Chicago School sociologists formulated the "urban village model." This community-based approach to social development emphasizes initiatives that promote strong, cohesive, and well-functioning communities that positively engage, supervise, and socialize young people as a means to ameliorate crime and delinquency problems at the local level. This model was realized through the Chicago Area Project (CAP), which began in the 1930s to address the problems of juvenile delinquency in some of the poorest neighbourhoods in the city. CAP provided recreational programs for children and youth, began outreach work with delinquent youth, and worked to improve conditions in the neighbourhood. The Chicago School's legacy for crime prevention is expansive and includes highlighting the centrality of local communities in preventing crime, delinquency, and other local social problems; the importance of local collective action, and community organizing and empowerment; the need for strong local institutions (e.g., families, schools, the labour market); and the need to address the root causes of crime through community and social development initiatives. CAP still exists today and continues to work toward improving the quality of life in Chicago neighbourhoods, with particular emphasis on solving problems faced by young people and their families. According to the CAP website, "the original mission of CAP has not changed since its inception: to work toward the prevention and eradication of juvenile delinquency through the development and support of affiliated local community self-help efforts, in communities where the need is greatest."

Similar to Chicago, Toronto has begun revitalizing neglected neighbourhoods such as Regent Park (shown above) with improved design and community programs for youth. See also the Career Profile box on page 53.

The underlying philosophy of CAP is as follows:

> [R]esidents must be empowered through the development of community organizations so that they can act together to improve neighborhood conditions, hold institutions serving the community accountable, reduce antisocial behavior by young people, protect them from inappropriate institutionalization, and provide them with positive models for personal development. (Chicago Area Project, n.d.)

Today, CAP and its many community-based affiliate groups are involved in a wide range of initiatives, such as recreational and sports programs (including summer camps) for children and young people, neighbourhood development projects, mentoring, job training and employment services, after-school tutoring, youth counselling, and alternative justice programs that divert young offenders away from the courts.

What Do You Think?

1. On the basis of this case study, what factors do you believe the Chicago School researchers would argue are most responsible for crime and disorder in socially disorganized neighbourhoods?

2. Is the social disorganization model relevant to Canada? If your answer is yes, conduct some research to identify local communities in Canada that may fit this theory. In addition, identify community crime prevention initiatives in this country that are similar to CAP.

3. How do you think the police and other criminal justice agencies might traditionally respond to "socially disorganized" communities? How do these approaches differ from the ones implemented by the Chicago School?

4. CAP has proven to be particularly influential in the field of crime prevention. Why do you think this is the case?

5. Despite the leading role that Chicago has played in developing and implementing innovative community-based crime prevention programs, it continues to be one of the most violent cities and has one of the highest homicide rates in North America. Identify the challenges that programs such as CAP face when attempting to deal with violence in large urban centres in North America.

Introduction

Although there is no universally accepted definition of *crime prevention*, it can be broadly defined as any pre-emptive intervention intended to block or reduce the risk of a criminal act occurring in a particular time and place or the onset of criminal behaviour within an individual. This broad definition is purposeful, for it reflects the breadth of the crime prevention field, in both theoretical and applied terms. A number of philosophies, strategies, programs, and practices could be classified as "crime prevention." This definition acknowledges the unfinished debate among scholars over the conceptual parameters that should be applied to crime prevention to distinguish it from traditional criminal justice approaches to crime.

Indeed, crime prevention is distinguished from the criminal justice system in several ways: through its proactive nature in dealing with crime (usually before it occurs), the central role played by private citizens and communities, and the reliance on institutions and strategies that often fall outside the criminal justice system. Notwithstanding its distinction as an "alternative approach to the more traditional responses to crime," Welsh and Farrington (2012) contend that crime prevention should nonetheless be "considered the fourth pillar of crime reduction, alongside the institutions of police, courts, and corrections" (p. 3).

The aim of this chapter is to provide an overview of crime prevention, with particular emphasis on contrasting its unique conceptual underpinnings and approaches with those of the criminal justice system.

Crime Prevention Versus the Criminal Justice System

The contemporary field of crime prevention arose as a critique of and an alternative to the criminal justice system. In particular, the traditional "cops, courts, and corrections" approach is seen as being insufficient to control or deter acts that threaten public safety. According to the proponents of crime prevention, the criminal justice system is unable to cope with the actual quantity of crime, and it fails to identify many criminal offenders and bring them to justice, to rehabilitate those offenders who are identified, and to address the root causes of crime and criminality (Canada, 1993, p. 1).

In theory, crime prevention is contrary to the criminal justice system in many respects, including the following:

- It is inherently proactive, not reactive.
- It is based on rigorous scholarship into crime causation, while recommended and applied strategies are frequently guided by evidence-based best practices (in contrast to the criminal justice system, which, generally speaking, is not considered an evidence-based best practice in controlling crime).
- It uses a problem-oriented approach that stresses the gathering of information to assess the causes of a crime problem and employs flexibility through solutions that are individualized for specific circumstances and generally fall outside the criminal justice system. Some common examples of problem-oriented solutions to specific crime problems include helping local drug dealers find legitimate jobs, redesigning parking lots to make it harder to steal cars, or implementing a Neighbourhood Watch program to deter break-and-enters.
- It puts responsibility for safer communities primarily in the hands of private non-state actors (neighbourhood residents, community groups, the private sector), although emphasis is placed on partnerships between state and non-state actors.
- Greater emphasis is placed on "informal" social control (which is carried out by private actors) as opposed to "formal" social control (which is exercised by the state).
- It focuses mainly on potential offenders (at-risk individuals) and potential victims, rather than on those who have already committed a crime.
- When it does target offenders, recidivism prevention strategies emphasize social problem-solving measures (e.g., therapy, education, employment) and not traditional punitive sanctions (e.g., imprisonment).
- It targets not only crime but also fear, disorder, and public incivility.

Each of these distinguishing characteristics is detailed below. Table 2.1 summarizes the differences between crime prevention and the criminal justice system.

TABLE 2.1   A Comparison of Crime Prevention and the Criminal Justice System

	Crime prevention	Criminal justice system
Timing	Proactive	Reactive
Approach	Predict, assess, and intervene	Intervene (no real prediction)
Response	Problem-oriented (wide range of appropriate solutions)	Narrow range of solutions
Lead responsibility	Citizenry	State
Partnerships and collaboration	Partnerships and collaboration fundamental and extensive	Limited partnerships between criminal justice agencies and non-state actors
Organizations providing services	Community groups, NGOs, schools, public health, social welfare agencies	Police, public prosecutors, correctional facilities, parole boards, legislative branches
Control	Informal social control	Formal social control
Scope	Criminal act, criminality (causes), disorder, incivilities, fear	Criminal act
Targets	Victim (and offender)	Offender
Setting	Natural: Home, school, or community	Artificial: State institution
Primary goal	Improved functioning	Control of individuals

Source: Author, with contributions from Greenwood (2006, p. 15).

Proactive Strategies

One critique of the criminal justice system is that it is overwhelmingly reactive when it comes to combating crime and does not have the capacity to proactively address the root causes of crime. The most fundamental characteristic of crime prevention, by contrast, is that it is proactive; it strives to anticipate and prevent crime either by reducing the opportunity for a criminal act to occur in a particular time or place, or by addressing the root causes of criminal behaviour. Proactive crime prevention strategies are epitomized by crime prevention through social development (CPSD), which comprises social problem-solving interventions that primarily cater to children and youth who are at risk of future delinquent and criminal behaviour. Common social problem-solving crime prevention interventions include training parents to create a more loving and nurturing environment for children, providing remedial support for youth who are at risk of dropping out of high school, or delivering treatment programs to people who may commit crimes because of substance abuse problems.

What Do You Think?

1. What are some similarities between the criminal justice system and crime prevention?

2. For high-crime neighbourhoods, what traditional criminal justice approaches do you believe best complement crime prevention strategies?

3. What kinds of informal social control do you think might be effective in addressing the problems within a high-crime neighbourhood?

Evidence-Based Approach

The field of crime prevention emphasizes interventions that are evidence based. The implications of this approach are twofold. First, many dominant crime prevention strategies are informed by rigorous theories of and research into the causes behind criminal behaviour and criminal acts. Second, specific crime prevention strategies are frequently guided by evidence, gathered through research, around what has been shown to work in preventing and controlling crime and criminal behaviour. This evidence-based approach is contrasted with punitive criminal justice measures, which are generally not supported by research as effective interventions to prevent, deter, or control crime (Benforado, 2015).

IN-CLASS EXERCISE

Evidence-Based Crime Prevention

The evidence-based approach to crime prevention is well represented at the American National Institute of Justice's "Crime Solutions" website: www.crimesolutions.gov. This website is dedicated to highlighting best practices in the field of crime prevention, based on rigorous research and project evaluations. Identify at least one crime prevention strategy listed on the website and examine how its interventions (1) adhere to one or more theories or explanations of criminal behaviour, and (2) reflect an evidence-based best practices approach.

Problem-Oriented Approach

According to Cherney (2006), "a core component of crime prevention good practice" is a "problem-solving methodology" (p. 1). This approach to crime control encompasses three components: (1) an *analytical process*, whereby the scope and nature of a (potential) crime problem or criminal behaviour is predicted and assessed by collecting and analyzing relevant information (which includes identifying and separating out the causes of the problem from the symptoms and aggravating factors); (2) an intervention that is *crafted specifically for the problem being addressed* (which includes determining the most appropriate institutions through which interventions can be delivered); and (3) consideration of *a wide range of alternative and flexible solutions* in anticipation of or reaction to a crime risk or onset of criminal behaviour (recognizing the highly individualized nature of each risk). This flexible, problem-oriented methodology contrasts with the "cookie-cutter" approach of the criminal justice system, which relies on the same set of strategies (arrest, prosecute, punish) despite the divergent circumstances of many criminal acts and offenders.

FIGURE 2.1   The Players in Crime Prevention

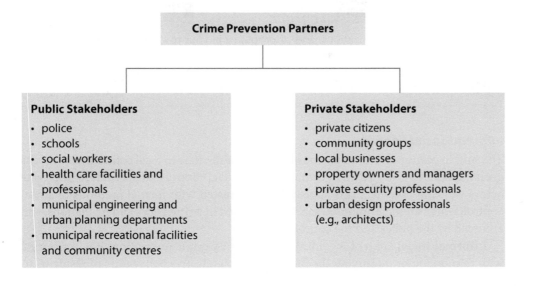

The Central Role of Private Actors and Partnerships

The criminal justice system is symptomatic of a state-imposed, top-down, formal approach to social problem-solving: the government defines the problem (through laws and legislation), then takes responsibility for addressing the problem (through the enforcement of criminal laws by police, prosecutors, the judiciary, correctional facilities, parole agencies, etc.).

By contrast, crime prevention is based on a bottom-up approach, which in turn assumes that private citizens play a major role in maintaining order in a free society and should therefore accept some responsibility for the prevention of crime, criminality, and disorder problems. This idea results in the responsibility for crime prevention being partially transferred from the state to the citizenry.

That said, the state still plays a major role in crime prevention, beyond its traditional criminal justice responsibilities. Crime prevention is thus ultimately a shared responsibility between private and public actors. A hallmark of crime prevention initiatives is that they should be planned and implemented as partnerships between government (public) agencies and other key (private) stakeholders (community groups, private sector businesses, etc.). In addition to police, other government agencies, professionals, and services that are important players in crime prevention include schools, social workers, publicly funded health care facilities and professionals, municipal engineering and urban planning departments, as well as municipal recreational facilities and community centres, to name just a few. The public and private stakeholders in crime prevention are presented in Figure 2.1.

IN-CLASS EXERCISE

Local Actors in Crime Prevention

Identify institutions, organizations, and/or programs in your town or city that play a role in addressing the root causes of criminal behaviour. As part of a class discussion, describe the role they play (and specific programs they implement) in addressing factors that put children and youth at risk of future criminal or delinquent behaviour.

Informal Social Control

The shift in crime prevention responsibilities from the state to local communities means greater emphasis is placed on informal forms of social control that are exerted by private actors working together. This approach is contrasted with formal methods of social control, which are state-imposed sanctions codified in written laws and regulations, and enforced by the police and the courts.

informal social control
The development, observance, and enforcement of local norms for appropriate public behaviour (Greenberg & Rohe, 1986, p. 80).

   Informal social control is central to community crime prevention. It is concerned with reinforcing or modifying the individual and collective behaviours of residents to produce or strengthen a local social environment that can regulate itself, including the prevention of criminal, delinquent, disorderly, and uncivil behaviour. Informal social control is based on customs, common agreement, or social norms. In the neighbourhood context, it refers to the observance and enforcement of implicit local rules for behaviour that is consistent with, and supportive of, the values, standards, and tolerance levels of a particular neighbourhood (Wilson, 1975, p. 24). Informal social control is said to restrict crime and disorder through a vigorous enforcement of local norms and standards by the legitimate users of a particular space, in particular a residential neighbourhood. The activities involved in such community-based enforcement include training residents to identify and report suspicious people or activities; confronting suspicious people; and undertaking local group–based structured activities, such as Neighbourhood Watch or citizen patrols (Greenberg, Rohe, & Williams, 1985; Rosenbaum, 1988; Rosenbaum & Schuck, 2012).

Focusing on Potential Victims and Offenders

The criminal justice system is overwhelmingly focused on offenders—catching them, charging them, prosecuting them, sentencing them, punishing them, and, to a lesser extent, rehabilitating them. The field of crime prevention is also directly concerned with offenders through strategies that attempt to reduce opportunities for them to commit crimes in a particular time and place. However, it tends to pay more attention to the potential victim or target. Situational crime prevention strategies are geared toward protecting people and places from victimization, and the planning and implementation of these interventions are often carried out by the very people who are at risk of becoming victims. Attention is also shifted from the offender to the *potential* offender; this focus is the hallmark of social developmental approaches to crime prevention that seek to address the factors that place children and youth at risk of (future) delinquency and criminality.

   As detailed later in this chapter, offenders have begun to receive more attention in the field of crime prevention through evidence-based recidivism prevention strategies, especially those that emphasize social problem-solving measures that address the causes of (chronic) criminal behaviour. The increased attention placed on recidivism prevention is due to research demonstrating that (1) immediate intervention after a young person has come into formal contact with the criminal justice system for the first time is important to stem future criminal offending (Wilson & Howell, 1993); and (2) a disproportionate amount of crime is carried out by a relatively small group of chronic (recidivist) offenders (Farrington et al., 2006; Prime, White, Liriano, & Patel, 2001; Wikström, Oberwittler, Treiber, & Hardie, 2012). Recidivism prevention is influenced by CPSD and relies heavily on social problem-solving strategies to address the root causes of criminal behaviour in order to help the individual desist from his or her criminal lifestyle. Thus, like CPSD generally, recidivism prevention reflects the importance within the field of crime prevention of putting the offender at the forefront of problem-solving initiatives. Common social problem-solving recidivism prevention strategies include helping an offender complete school or a job-training program; obtain a job; get out of a gang; or receive substance abuse treatment.

Targeting Criminality, Fear, Disorder, and Public Incivility

As discussed above, CPSD is very much focused on addressing the root causes of criminal and delinquent behaviour. It contrasts with the criminal justice system, which was never created to address the root causes of criminality (although corrections-based treatment and rehabilitation do attempt to prevent recidivism, as will be discussed in Chapter 9).

Moreover, crime prevention interventions do not simply address crime; in some cases, they are meant to provide individuals and communities with the education, tools, power, and collective security to alleviate fear of crime (see Chapter 1 for further discussion of the fear of crime).

Certain crime prevention theories and strategies also advocate a focus on disorder and incivility, which are not criminal or illegal acts as defined by the law, but can contribute to local instability that may invite more serious crime problems. Lab (2016) indicates that two types of factors comprise incivility in an area: physical factors ("the deterioration of buildings, litter, graffiti, vandalism, and abandoned buildings and cars") and social factors ("public drunkenness, vagrancy, groups of loitering youths, harassment [such as begging and panhandling], and visible drug sales and use") (p. 19). Such factors may be addressed by mobilizing and organizing neighbourhood residents, which includes promoting a level of informal social control. Some situational crime prevention and law enforcement strategies emphasize **zero tolerance** (sometimes called *order maintenance policing*) toward incivility and disorder problems in the belief that such enforcement might help alleviate factors that encourage more serious crime problems (Sousa & Kelling, 2014; Thacher, 2014; Wilson & Kelling, 1982).

The Goals of Crime Prevention

Greenwood (2006, pp. 12 and 13) distinguishes between the ultimate goals of criminality prevention and the criminal justice system. He implies that the main role of the criminal justice system in helping to produce a civil and orderly society is the "control of individuals" (offenders, in particular, although it can be argued that the state's social control function also targets the broader public through the general deterrence effect of criminal laws, enforcement, and punishment). By contrast, CPSD—through its targeting of at-risk children and youth and emphasis on social problem-solving, community

zero tolerance

A disciplinary approach that advocates automatic punitive responses to all types of disorder and crime problems, no matter how minor, with the intention of eliminating undesirable conduct through punishment and deterrence. For example, fighting in school means an automatic suspension. Also sometimes called *order maintenance policing.*

cohesion, and strong local institutions (e.g., schools, families, communities)—is ultimately geared toward the improved functioning of the individual.

Dominant Crime Prevention Approaches

Crime prevention strategies can be divided into six broad categories:

1. Crime prevention through social development
2. Situational crime prevention
3. Crime prevention through environmental design
4. Community crime prevention
5. Community and problem-oriented policing
6. Recidivism prevention

Crime Prevention Through Social Development

CPSD encompasses interventions that target the root causes of criminal behaviour. Research shows that many chronic offenders come from some type of negative social environment during their childhood and adolescence, which can include poverty, parental neglect and abuse, exposure to violence, poor schooling, or poor role models. Children and youth who are at risk of future criminal offending may also suffer from personal **risk factors** such as hyperactivity, impulsivity, anger management problems, learning disabilities, or psychological disorders (Farrington, 2007; Tanner-Smith, Wilson, & Lipsey, 2015). The underlying premise of CPSD is that risk-focused interventions implemented during childhood and the teen years can alleviate factors that may lead to future delinquent, criminal, and anti-social behaviours. According to Welsh and Farrington (2010), the basic idea of risk-focused criminality prevention is simple: "Identify the key risk factors for offending and implement prevention methods designed to counteract them. There is often a related attempt to identify key **protective factors** against offending and to implement prevention methods designed to enhance them" (p. 9).

risk factors
Factors that increase the risk of criminal or delinquent behaviour.

protective factors
Positive conditions, influences, or interventions that can increase the health and well-being of children and families by counteracting risk factors.

A central institution through which social problem-solving approaches to crime prevention are delivered is the family. The family is crucial in promoting or hindering the future criminal behaviour of a child. Child development is highly influenced by various family characteristics and practices; for example, parent–child relationships, discipline, family mental health, neglect or abuse, and family history of substance abuse or criminal behaviour (Wright & Beaver, 2015). As a result, a primary focus of social problem-solving approaches to crime prevention is to strengthen high-risk family environments by helping develop and support good parenting skills, while addressing problems and negative behaviours experienced by parents that can affect their children (e.g., poverty, substance abuse, aggression). Social problem-solving interventions also cater directly to at-risk children by increasing their personal resilience through, for example, mentoring, remedial education, psychological counselling, social and life-skills development, and recreational activities. (See Chapter 12 on youth justice for more on risk and protective factors.)

MINI CASE STUDY

Strengthening the Spirit: Oskâyi Kiskinotahn—Building a Comprehensive Response to Family Violence in Indigenous Communities

Strengthening the Spirit is a treatment program for Indigenous families at high risk of domestic violence (National Crime Prevention Centre, 2014). Sponsored by the HomeFront Society for the Prevention of Domestic Violence in Calgary, the program was delivered in the Siksika Nation, Tsuu Tina First Nations, and Morley First Nations communities in Alberta from February 2009 to September 2012.

This culturally appropriate treatment program was designed to reduce the incidence of domestic violence and child abuse by fostering the healing and wellness of families through an innovative combination of interventions shown to have worked in the past (e.g., counselling) and by invoking the culture, identity, traditions, and symbols specific to the First Nations' communities served.

As stated in the project evaluation report, appeals to the indigenous culture and identity of participating families was central to the success of Strengthening the Spirit. "The whole experience of colonization, forced assimilation and cultural genocide among Aboriginal peoples has come to be described as historical trauma and intergenerational trauma, all of which continues to be a major contributing factor to the prevalence of family violence among Aboriginal peoples" (HomeFront, 2012, p. 12).

Strengthening the Spirit included programming for both adults and children. A total of 193 men and women participated in the treatment group sessions, with most being women (65 percent). The majority of participants were between 18 and 39 years of age.

Counselling sessions for groups of between 8 and 10 male and female perpetrators and victims of domestic violence were held both on and off reserve in the Calgary area. The sessions included clinical counselling and addictions treatment and were delivered over the course of 12 to 18 weeks. In all, 34 group counselling sessions for adults were held: 10 for men and 21 for women.

The group counselling sessions adhered to a cognitive behavioural approach that began with a discussion of basic concepts (e.g., domestic violence, its causes, effects, and how it can be avoided). They were then followed by games, crafts, role-playing, and exercises that reinforced the concepts learned. These techniques were bolstered by customs and practices indigenous to the First Nations communities served, such as the medicine wheel, sweat lodges, and smudging.

Moderating the group sessions were trained community facilitators who were from the First Nations' communities. A clinical psychologist was assigned to each pilot site to help with training and supervision. Twenty-four Elders from the First Nations communities were involved in program development by ensuring their culture and traditional practices were integrated into the program interventions.

An evaluation of the Strengthening the Spirit project indicated some positive impacts on recidivism rates for the adult participants. Among the 47 percent who did complete the treatment groups, there was a 6 percent self-reported rate of reoffending, compared with a rate of 34 percent among those who did not complete the program.

Group programming was also available for children (aged 5 to 12 years) affected by exposure to family violence at home. Twelve sessions were to be delivered to participating children and facilitated by Strengthening the Spirit mentor trainers. Unfortunately, according to the project evaluation report, "the children's treatment groups were challenged by the demand for child care; programming for youth beyond age 12 years; and lack of referrals from the community/organization for group facilitators. The Strengthening the Spirit Mentor Trainers could not maintain a safe adult/child ratio to continue the children's groups. Therefore, they were offered sporadically and yielded little to no data" (HomeFront, 2012, p. 14).

criminogenic
Producing or tending to produce crime or criminal behaviour.

Schools are second only to families in significance as a crime prevention institution. First and foremost, education is a critical protective factor in offsetting **criminogenic** conditions. The most important role that schools can play is to teach kids to read, write, compute, and think. Like families, schools also provide young people with an environment that is critical to their positive socialization and the development of basic social competencies. Many innovative approaches to school culture and education have been introduced in recent years that can also help deter criminality insofar as such innovations promote learning, attendance, a positive and inclusive school environment, completion of high school, and pro-social behaviour among high-risk students. According to Gottfredson, Cook, and Na (2012), best practices in school-based crime prevention include the following:

- customizing academic programs to the needs of each student
- developing more interactive and experiential teaching practices
- providing alternative curricula for struggling students
- allowing students more say in a school's policies
- providing rewards for academic achievement and consistent attendance
- providing programs that foster important social competencies and life skills that can prevent future criminality
- fostering a school climate that promotes inclusiveness while condemning bullying and other forms of harassment

In recent years, schools have also become a vehicle through which programs are delivered to reduce specific criminogenic risk factors such as aggression, bullying, violence, negative peer pressure, substance abuse, and gang involvement.

Research through the years has shown the following CPSD interventions to be effective in reducing criminogenic risk factors among children and youth (https://www.crimesolutions.gov; Lab, 2016, pp. 165–176; Sherman, 1997; Sherman, Farrington, Welsh, & MacKenzie, 2006, pp. 22–164; Schneider, 2014, pp. 126–165).

Within the home:

- frequent home visits to infants (ages 0–2) by trained nurses and other professionals, which can reduce child abuse and other injuries to infants
- preschool and weekly home visits by teachers to children under age 5, which can reduce arrests when the children are older
- parent skills training in family management practices to provide an appropriate environment for children, which can reduce aggression, hyperactivity, and other problem behaviours (bullying, hitting, stealing, and lying) among children
- cognitive behavioural family counselling and therapy, which can reduce aggression, impulsivity, substance abuse, delinquency, criminality and other anti-social behaviours among adolescents

Within the school:

- clarifying and communicating norms about behaviour through rules, reinforcement of positive behaviour, and school-wide initiatives (such as anti-bullying campaigns), which can reduce crime, delinquency, bullying, and substance abuse among students

- life, social competency, and coping skills training (emphasizing capacities such as stress management, critical thinking, problem solving, self-control, and emotional intelligence), which can reduce delinquency, criminality substance abuse, and certain mental health problems
- training or coaching at-risk youth in thinking skills (using rewards-based behaviour modification techniques), which can reduce substance abuse
- innovative classroom management and instructional initiatives (such as grouping students into smaller units for cooperative learning or using flexible and intensive instruction methods for underachieving or disruptive students), which can reduce substance abuse and delinquency
- dropout prevention programs, which can reduce criminal and delinquent behaviour and incarceration, such as alternative schools (which cater specifically to struggling students), tutoring and mentoring by university students, receiving high school credit for attending job-training programs, and completing high school credits while incarcerated in a correctional facility

Within the community:

- community-based mentoring by Big Brothers Big Sisters, which can reduce substance abuse and violent behaviour during adolescence and lead to greater pro-social behaviour in adulthood
- enriched preschool programs, which can reduce problem behaviours among children from high-risk environments
- community-based, supervised after-school recreation programs, which can reduce substance abuse, academic problems, and juvenile crime and delinquency in the immediate area

Situational Crime Prevention

Situational crime prevention (SCP) involves the management, design, or manipulation of the immediate physical and human environment so as to remove or reduce opportunities for specific types of crimes. In particular, SCP operates on three hypotheses about crime:

1. Most criminal acts require the coming together of motivated offenders and potential victims at a particular time and place (for this reason, situational measures focus on making places safer and more secure).
2. Many types of crime—property crime, in particular—are opportunistic; that is, offenders take advantage of certain opportunities they perceive can be exploited within a particular physical (and human) environment (for this reason, situational measures attempt to reduce opportunities for criminal acts to take place). For example, offenders who break into homes often take advantage of a number of opportunities to avoid getting caught, such as breaking in during the day (when most people are at work), gaining access through unlocked windows or doors, hiding behind large trees or shrubs, and targeting homes that have back alleys (which facilitate an undetected entry and escape).

3. Criminal behaviour involves a rational decision-making process whereby the offender weighs the advantages and disadvantages of a specific criminal act (this being the case, offenders can be deterred from committing crimes) (Clarke, 1997; Clarke & Cornish, 1985; Cohen & Felson, 1979).

Each of these hypotheses draws attention to one of the most important assumptions underlying SCP: human behaviour is affected by the immediate physical environment. Within the context of crime and its prevention, this means that specific settings can create opportunities for an illegal act to occur by transforming one's thoughts or inclinations into a criminal act. "The theory of crime settings rests on a single principle: that easy or tempting opportunities entice people into criminal action" (Felson & Clarke, 1998, pp. 1 and 2).

etiological theories of crime
Theories dealing with the causes of crime.

Based on this **etiological theory of crime**, the essential characteristic of SCP is that it concentrates on reducing the *opportunity* for a criminal act to occur at a particular time and place. Because SCP strategies intervene directly in the opportunistic portion of the criminal process, SCP solutions are restricted to variables that can be manipulated in the context of the relationship between people and their physical environment. SCP approaches to reducing criminal opportunities have been grouped into five categories (Clarke, 1997; Cornish & Clarke, 2003):

1. Increasing the effort needed by the offender to commit a crime by making the targets of crime harder to get at or otherwise hindering the commission of crime

2. Increasing the risks to the offender, whether real or perceived, of detection and apprehension
3. Reducing the rewards to the offender, which in some cases may involve removing the targets of crime altogether
4. Removing people's excuses to commit crimes
5. Reducing provocations—for example, reducing frustration and stress, avoiding disputes, reducing emotional arousal, and neutralizing peer pressure

Crime Prevention Through Environmental Design

environmental design
Fashioning and developing the physical and built landscape, most often in an urban or suburban setting.

Crime prevention through **environmental design** (CPTED) is a situational approach that advocates the proper design and use of a physical space as well as the built environment (houses, buildings, landscapes, streets, parks, and entire neighbourhoods) to reduce the opportunity for crime. CPTED incorporates opportunity-reduction strategies that are both direct (modifying the built environment to prevent crime) and indirect (modifying the environment to stimulate residents to assume greater responsibility over their neighbourhood). Designing the physical and spatial environment of a neighbourhood to promote residents' responsibility and vigilance includes increasing residents' ability to see their surroundings so that they can detect suspicious people (through large windows and front porches on homes) and fostering their integration into and commitment to the neighbourhood (e.g., by building attractive public spaces such as parks or playgrounds), among other measures.

Crime Prevention Through Environmental Design Strategies

CPTED guidelines such as the following are commonly used to reduce the opportunity for crime at a particular time and place:

- implementing target hardening, including locking doors and windows and using fences and security gates
- applying entry control mechanisms, such as computerized pass cards or apartment building entrance intercoms
- limiting the number of entry and exit points in a neighbourhood
- implementing "intentional" surveillance techniques and technology, such as convex mirrors, security cameras, and raised cashier kiosks
- maximizing "natural surveillance" by legitimate users through certain building designs (such as locating windows so they overlook sidewalks and parking lots) and interior and exterior lighting (stressing bright white lights)
- designing buildings and/or pruning ground-level planting to minimize potential hiding or entrapment areas
- promoting the legitimate use of public spaces (encouraging "eyes on the street") by building attractors such as parks, playgrounds, wide sidewalks, and community gardens
- designing spaces to promote social interaction and cohesion among residents
- keeping surrounding areas clean, well maintained, graffiti-free, and attractive to prevent a perception of neglect by potential offenders

BEFORE **AFTER**

Source: Peel Police.

IN-CLASS EXERCISE

Assessing Safe and Unsafe Design Spaces in Your Neighbourhood

Walk around your neighbourhood and take photos of physical space and built characteristics that you believe increase the opportunity for a crime to occur. Also take photos of physical space and built characteristics that you believe decrease the opportunity for a crime to occur. Bring these images to class to share with your colleagues, discussing how some designs adhere to SCP and CPTED principles, while others do not.

Community Crime Prevention

Community crime prevention (CCP) can be divided into the community defence model and the community development model. Both share one element essential to CCP: the existence of a socially cohesive collective of residents who join together to prevent and control crime. While some may view the neighbourhood as simply the area in which situational or social developmental crime prevention programs are implemented, the sociological concept of community in and of itself forms the heart of a distinct crime prevention philosophy and institution. Some have argued that the loss of the socially cohesive neighbourhood has contributed to crime and disorder within advanced Western societies (Forrest & Kearns, 2001; Wirth, 1938). Accordingly, the effectiveness of community-based crime prevention efforts often depends on the extent to which local social cohesion, or a sense of community, exists within a particular locale.

Particularly important to CCP, according to Sampson, Raudenbush, and Earls (1997), is **collective efficacy**, a concept that combines social cohesion with informal social control and is defined as "the linkage of mutual trust and the willingness to intervene for the common good" (p. 919), as well as the realization of "common values and the ability of groups to regulate their members according to desired principles" (Crawford, 1999, p. 518).

The community defence model is geared toward preventing criminal opportunities by organizing local residents to keep a watchful eye out for suspicious activities or individuals. The theory behind this approach is that the implementation of community safety programs will mobilize residents around a shared control over private and public spaces. The crime prevention program that has become universally associated with the community defence model is Neighbourhood Watch.

collective efficacy
The willingness of individuals in a neighbourhood to work together toward a common goal, such as crime control.

SIDEBAR

Neighbourhood Watch

Also called *Block Watch* or *Crime Watch*, this structured program involves a group of neighbours organized to prevent crime and disorder problems within a residential neighbourhood or apartment building. Residents are trained to keep an eye out for suspicious individuals or activities and to call police when such circumstances are spotted.

The community development model promotes the physical, social, and socio-economic development of a neighbourhood, which can include organizing residents, economic development, beautification projects, **gentrification**, and other types of physical development.

A community development approach is said to help prevent crime in a number of ways:

- by addressing physical dilapidation and disorder problems that can contribute to a downward spiral of communities and may invite more serious crime problems
- through the nurturing of local social cohesion and informal social control
- through social and economic development that addresses local criminogenic risk factors

gentrification
The changes that result when middle-class or upper-middle-class individuals acquire and upgrade property in low-income and working-class neighbourhoods.

Community and Problem-Oriented Policing

For police agencies, the philosophy and strategies of crime prevention are realized predominately through community policing and problem-oriented policing (see Chapter 3 for further discussion of policing strategies). The theory of community policing has a number of profound implications for the delivery of policing services. Its goal is much more than to simply enforce laws; community policing is about contributing to the broader safety, security, and health of a community. It advocates that police agencies and their individual members forge a strong partnership with local communities, empowering citizens and neighbourhoods to help prevent crime. The community policing mandate, as it reflects the broader goals of community crime prevention, is to support citizen-based initiatives and reinforce the informal social control mechanisms of the local community (Wilson & Kelling, 1982). By extension, community policing requires the police agency and its members to be accountable to the communities they serve. For Friedmann (1992), a police service must be seen as a part of, not separate and isolated from, the public. Community policing recognizes that the police cannot impose a lasting order on a community from the outside; instead, the police are one of many resources to which a community can turn to help solve local problems.

In theory, community policing bestows greater responsibility, autonomy, and discretion on front-line constables (Skolnick & Bayley, 1988). It may also often involve establishing community policing stations in neighbourhoods. The composition of a police agency committed to community policing should also better reflect the demographic and social makeup of the communities it serves (Leighton, 1991, p. 10).

Community policing involves a problem-oriented approach that encourages police, in partnership with residents and other partners, to address the causes and facilitators of local crime problems in order to prevent such problems from emerging, continuing, or worsening. A problem-solving approach means that police seek out solutions that are most appropriate to the problem, which often entails alternatives to the criminal justice system (Goldstein, 1987, p. 15). As Sherman and Eck (2006) put it, "Where the core concept of community policing was community involvement for its own sake, the core concept for problem-oriented policing was *results*: the effect of police activity on public safety, including (but not limited to) crime prevention" (p. 299).

What Do You Think?

Identify a high-crime neighbourhood in the town or city you live in that has used a community development approach. What initiatives were implemented? To what extent do these approaches adhere to the community development model described above? What further community development initiatives do you believe are needed in this neighbourhood?

The Role of Social Media in Local Crime Prevention Organizing

Much has been written about the role of social media in mobilizing people to support certain causes, such as the election of Barack Obama as president of the United States and the anti-government movement during the "Arab Spring." No doubt social media—including Facebook, Twitter, Instagram, blogs, and websites—have revolutionized the art and science of communicating with, educating, and mobilizing people. Social media are effective communication and organizing tools because they can reach a multitude of people in real time, provide a central "meeting place," and facilitate an inclusive and interactive conversation among like-minded people. Police now use social media not only to communicate with their constituents but also to identify offenders, anticipate criminal acts, and even operate undercover operations (e.g., police posing as teenagers to lure sexual predators).

A few tips for the police and the public on using social media to prevent or respond to crime are as follows:

- Set up a Facebook group dedicated to a particular crime prevention group or activity (e.g., Neighbourhood Watch).
- Provide important updates on ongoing crime prevention projects and activities, or simply communicate crime prevention tips through social media.
- Educate young people through social media on how to use it and the Internet safely and securely (i.e., how not to victimize others or be victimized).
- Use social media to solicit feedback from community members on current crime prevention projects and initiatives.
- Send out "tweetalongs" (through Twitter) that communicate to others activities undertaken during a particular crime prevention event (e.g., a citizen patrol, local safety audit, a youth event).
- On social media, post photos of local sites where there is a particular need for safe design improvements.

- Communicate criminal acts that have immediately or recently taken place or organize an urgent community safety initiative (e.g., to find a lost child) through social media.
- On social media, post photos, videos, or descriptions of criminal offenders in the act to help identify them.
- Monitor social media accounts to anticipate a particular crime or to identify an offender (who may deliberately or inadvertently make a post that could tip the police or the public).

CAREER PROFILE

Elizabeth Byrnes

Superintendent Elizabeth Byrnes is the unit commander of 51 Division of the Toronto Police. Her challenging division includes Regent Park, an area undergoing a massive revitalization project designed in part to make the neighbourhood safer.

How did you become interested in policing?
My father, sister, and two brothers-in-law were police officers. As a teenager, I worked two summers in Toronto parks as part of a youth-in-policing initiative. I constantly heard, "You must want to join the police too," but I hadn't seriously considered that. During my second year of university, I decided that I didn't want a traditional Monday-to-Friday job, and policing seemed like a natural fit for me.

How did you become the unit commander of 51 Division?
A lot of my opportunities came because of timing. I took opportunities and made the most of them. Good work and a good attitude got me noticed, and got me other opportunities. I followed a path of investigative gender-based violence as an investigator in the Sexual Assault Squad, and eventually became unit commander of the Sexual Assault/Sex Crimes Unit. I worked for former chief Bill Blair, which was a great learning opportunity, and helpful during promotional processes, where he was a key decision-maker. I moved from Sex Crimes to our Communications 9-1-1 Centre, to a smaller Division and, from there, to one of the largest, most challenging Divisions in the city: 51 Division.

What are some of your most important duties? Is there a typical day?
I manage a large workforce by understanding and knowing the people. I deal with personnel and human resource issues—everything from PTSD and substance abuse to ensuring there are sufficient officers to do the work, and business process changes to allow them to work better.

What are the most challenging and the most rewarding aspects of your job?
The most challenging issue is competing interests within and outside the police service, and managing expecta-

tions that come along with that. The community expects the police to be able to deal with many issues that are outside our skill set, training, mandate, and staffing abilities.

What are some of the biggest challenges facing 51 Division, and how will the revitalization ease some of these difficulties?
Regent Park is an amazing community. Historically, neighbourhood residents have always looked out for each other. While the revitalization has brought many new, modern residences, it seems to have created some disruption to that sense of neighbourhood, in some ways resulting in divisions along ethnic lines. Regent Park is not the busiest area in the Division, but we have seen significant violence aligned along gang affiliations that still exist in the area.

How will the revitalization affect the relationship between the community and the police?
I think the relationship between our officers and the community has improved in the last three years, mainly because of the Regent Park Neighbourhood Officer program. That program dedicates four officers to the Regent Park Neighbourhood. These officers are very involved with the schools, community agencies, and youth in the area. Over time, we hope there will be increased interaction between residents from all socio-economic groups within that same community space.

Recidivism Prevention

Recidivism prevention is increasingly viewed as a key pillar in crime and violence prevention strategies, policies, and programs. This is due in part to statistics and research that show a small number of adolescent and young adult offenders are responsible for a disproportionate amount of crime and violence (Farrington et al., 2006; Prime et al., 2001; Wikström, et al., 2012). Moreover, many of these serious and chronic offenders do not desist from offending once they are caught and/or released from custody (Sedlak & Bruce, 2010).

Recidivism prevention is concerned with helping juvenile and adult offenders desist from criminal and violent behaviour. Initiatives to prevent reoffending are diverse and can include traditional criminal justice control approaches (surveillance, deterrence, punishment), restorative justice programs (such as the Strengthening the Spirit program described in Mini Case Study "Strengthening the Spirit: Oskâyi Kiskinotahn"), developmentally based social problem-solving interventions (counselling, skills-building, education, and employment programs), or a combination of any of the above (Lipsey, 2009).

Traditionally, efforts to prevent reoffending have been pursued through the use of punitive criminal justice sanctions—specifically, the incarceration of chronic offenders. However, research has consistently shown the *absence* of a strong correlation between punishment or the threat of punishment, on the one hand, and a lower level of recidivism on the other (Lipsey, 2009; MacKenzie, 2006; Petrosino, Turpin-Petrosino, & Guckenburg, 2010; Sedlak & McPherson, 2010; Wilson, MacKenzie, & Mitchell, 2008).

Lipsey's review of the literature on recidivism prevention concluded that interventions embodying "therapeutic" philosophies, such as counselling, cognitive behavioural treatment, and skills training "were more effective than those based on strategies of control or coercion—surveillance, deterrence, and discipline" (Lipsey, 2009, pp. 143–144).

MINI CASE STUDY

Preventing Recidivism Through Multi-Systemic Therapy

Multi-Systemic Therapy (MST) is one example of a cognitive behavioural intervention for chronic, violent, or substance-abusing young offenders. The overarching goal of MST is to eliminate criminal and other types of anti-social behaviour in both the short term and the long term by addressing the multiple determinants of such behaviour through a multi-modal, therapy-based approach.

Within the context of MST, criminal and violent offending is viewed as having many causes; therefore, interventions focus on the multitude of factors influencing anti-social behaviour. The specific treatment used is also dependent on the needs of the young person; it may include interventions that target the at-risk individual, his or her family, peers, school, community, or a combination thereof. Indeed, a multi-systemic therapeutic approach is an example of a "social ecological" model of crime prevention (and health care) that views individuals as part of a network of interconnected social systems (the family, peers, school, neighbourhood, social media networks, etc.). This social system (and its individual components) is viewed as the optimal platform through which problematic behaviours of a young offender can be addressed within the context of a therapeutic approach. Leveraging a nurturing local social network to help treat offenders very much counters the "social disorganization" of some neighbourhoods that University of Chicago sociologists argue creates the preconditions for delinquent and criminal behaviour in the first place (Shaw & McKay, 1942).

MST aims to promote changes in a juvenile offender by recognizing and addressing those social, environmental, and personal risk factors that are influencing the youth's problematic behaviour. As such, an MST intervention is comprehensive and can include the following:

- improving parental discipline practices, relationships between the parents and the youth, and the overall family environment
- decreasing the youth's association with deviant peers
- treating any behavioural, mental health, or academic problems
- getting the youth involved in sports or other positive recreational activities
- developing a strong social support network

While the MST approach attempts to mobilize all local resources to help treat a young person, the family is the primary locus for the intervention. As such, an important component of MST is to provide parents with the skills and resources needed to raise pro-social teenagers.

In a meta-analysis of studies examining MST treatments, Doran, Luczak, Bekman, Koutsenok, and Brown (2012) concluded that there exists "a strong evidence base" indicating that MST is effective for substance-abuse disorders and delinquent, aggressive behaviour. It also produces more positive family functioning and a reduction in criminal offending compared with individual therapy. In addition, MST "is more effective and cost-effective than hospitalization or incarceration" (p. 755).

MST is just one of many social problem-solving approaches to recidivism prevention that have been shown to work. Essential to preventing recidivism is the creation of positive, alternative opportunities to crime: in particular, education, job training, and employment. Social problem-solving approaches are particularly pertinent to those who have been incarcerated because, according to Lockwood, Nally, Ho, and Knutson (2012), "research has consistently revealed that released offenders, if unemployed and uneducated, would likely become recidivist offenders" (pp. 380–381).

Lockwood and colleagues (2012) identified numerous studies showing that vocationally oriented prison education programs "greatly enhanced access to a variety of job sectors for released offenders and that there was lower recidivism for those who were employed" (pp. 381–382). Some of the key components of a corrections-based vocational training and placement program include the following: "(1) working individually with inmates to identify vocational interests and aptitudes, (2) developing individual plans of study for improving vocational skills, (3) providing the identified training as well as other needed services, and (4) helping inmates secure postrelease employment" (Lattimore, Dryden-Witte, & Baker, 1990, p. 5).

Private Policing/Security and Crime Prevention

As emphasized throughout this chapter, the state no longer assumes sole responsibility for crime control or public safety, nor can public law enforcement agencies claim they are the exclusive source of policing services. The private policing and security sector has grown so dramatically in the postwar years that it is now considered the principal tool of crime and loss prevention in many private commercial and industrial spaces. In recent years, private policing and security firms have also increasingly been engaged in policing public spaces, including residential neighbourhoods.

As with crime prevention programs and resources, the growth of private policing reflects the widespread acknowledgment of the limitations of public police agencies and the criminal justice system in identifying and controlling crime and ensuring public safety, especially in a proactive manner. The demand for a highly diverse range of policing and security services now outstrips that which can be supplied by the state.

The private policing and security sector is extensive and diverse. The Canadian Association of Chiefs of Police (1997) categorizes the sector into five levels, ranging from the rudimentary to the complex: (1) static guards (property security, access control, loss prevention); (2) enhanced security services (active crime prevention, limited patrol, by-law enforcement on contract to a local authority); (3) private investigators (general civil investigations); (4) corporate security (security protection of complex operations and prevention of crime against corporations, internal investigation, etc.); and (5) forensic investigation (specialized fraud and other financial investigations). This section is primarily concerned with the first two levels and the role they play in crime prevention in public spaces.

Like public police, private policing and security firms respond to crime in both a proactive and reactive manner. From a proactive perspective, private police are said to prevent or deter crime through their highly visible presence and their related surveillance function (either directly or through closed-circuit video cameras).

A number of studies have examined the extent to which private security firms prevent criminal acts from occurring in public spaces. Armstrong and Carson (1994) found that the use of a private security firm within a public housing community in Texas resulted in a significant decrease in the number of trespassers, burglaries, and disturbances. One of the reasons this private security initiative was successful was that the around-the-clock presence of guards in the community helped prevent and deter crimes, unlike public police that had a largely reactive and intermittent presence in the community (usually only in response to a call for service). Similarly, Walsh, Donovan, and McNicholas (1992) concluded that the Starrett Public Housing community in Brooklyn, New York had a low crime rate as a result of the presence of private security officers (who had full police powers and worked closely with the New York City Police Department). Residents surveyed for this research reported feelings of safety and security, which they attributed to a highly proactive, preventive approach to policing, including foot patrols. The consistent visibility of security personnel was in fact the greatest single factor in influencing residents' perception of safety, according to the researchers. In addition, the private policing personnel were not considered outsiders but rather an integral part of the community. The results of their research led the authors to contend that private security can be "an effective crime prevention factor."

In his ethnographic case study research into the use of security guards by a residential neighbourhood in Britain, Noaks (2000) surveyed residents ("subscribers") who reported a high degree of satisfaction with the crime prevention aspects of the private security service:

> Survey results showed that the crime prevention role was a priority for subscribers, in particular an enhanced physical presence from private guards on the streets. This is borne out by the fact that 74% of subscribers saw the presence on the streets provided by private security as the most important thing that they did in the locality ... When asked what private security had to offer in the area, subscribers most commonly referred to regular patrols (23%) and a deterrent to crime (23%). (p. 148)

Overall, Noaks (2000) reported that "92% of subscribers to the service were either satisfied or very satisfied with the job that private security was doing in the neighbourhood" and the most common reason for this satisfaction was "a lack of trouble in the area" (pp. 150–151).

In his analysis of five studies that assessed the crime prevention effectiveness of adding security guards to parking lots, Eck (2002, p. 266) found that "four showed reductions in car-related crimes," while one found no improvement. Eck noted that while these studies suggest auto thefts and thefts from automobiles "might be prevented by increasing people who watch lots" (p. 266), other research suggests that security guards may be ineffective at controlling thefts from vehicles. Moreover, Eck could not find any studies that examined whether security guards prevented violence against people using parking facilities. He concluded, "because of the mixed results of the evaluations, we do not know if guards or security attendants prevent crimes in parking lots" (p. 266).

Notwithstanding the positive contributions that private security may make to crime prevention and community safety, Finegan (2013) succinctly summarized some of the problems that have accompanied the growing privatization of policing. These problems include poorly trained personnel, lack of regulations and laws governing the private security sector, abuse of powers (private firms are not bound by the constitutional restraints that public police are subject to), and a lack of accountability to the public or government (instead, security personnel are more accountable to company executives).

Conclusion

The field of crime prevention encompasses a wide array of strategies that are delivered through a society's most basic institutions by a range of government agencies and private actors, including those whose mandate is tangential to crime. These include daycare facilities, schools, social welfare agencies, community centres, substance abuse clinics, neighbourhood associations, youth drop-in centres, employment training agencies, and health care facilities, to name just a few. As Sherman (1997, p. 1) wrote, "most crime prevention results from the web of institutional settings of human development and daily life."

While the crime prevention institutions and strategies described in this chapter have been listed separately, the impact and success of each are maximized when they are applied in a coordinated and complementary fashion. In other words, "schools cannot succeed without supportive families, labour markets cannot succeed without well-policed safe streets, and police cannot succeed without community participation in the labor market" (Sherman, 1997, p. 5).

This observation underscores the importance of a comprehensive approach to crime prevention, especially in disadvantaged, high-crime neighbourhoods, where residents are often confronted with myriad problems that can give rise to and facilitate crime and criminal behaviour. A comprehensive approach to crime prevention, according to the National Crime Council of Ireland (2003), must aim to reduce crime by

- reducing the opportunities to commit crime;
- promoting social inclusion and reducing the socio-economic, educational, societal, and environmental factors that can leave children and young people "at risk" of engaging in criminal activities;
- reducing recidivism through the reintegration of young and adult offenders into the community in a planned and supportive way, involving training and education, skills development, and personal support; and
- providing appropriate interventions through an interagency/partnership approach where knowledge, expertise, and best practice are shared to the maximum. (p. 20)

Most crime problems or criminogenic preconditions cannot be solved through spur-of-the-moment, arbitrary actions based on gut feelings or common sense. What is most required is a problem-oriented approach that relies on rigorous information collection and analysis and the application of strategies that have been proven to work in reducing, preventing, or controlling crime (while ensuring these strategies are appropriate to each individual setting).

Specifically, a systematic approach to crime prevention and community safety includes the following:

- putting together a plan that entails researching and understanding targeted crime problems (and their causes and aggravating factors) within a particular setting;
- understanding the environment in which the problems are taking place;
- identifying and mobilizing community members and other key partners;
- developing a strategy to address the identified problems (and their causes);
- implementing the strategy;
- sustaining the strategy;
- monitoring and evaluating the strategy; and
- making any necessary modifications.

DISCUSSION QUESTIONS

1. How would you define crime prevention? Do you believe it should be defined broadly or narrowly? Should it be defined by its methods or its consequences? What parameters would you apply to a definition of crime prevention?

2. Do you believe that the design of physical space and the built environment can actually affect people's behaviour in those places? Do you believe that certain architectural and urban designs can motivate people to assume more interest in the safety of their neighbourhood?

3. What are some of the most successful approaches to improving the root causes of criminal and violent behaviour?

4. Some have argued that police services should not simply focus on law enforcement, but should also help address a wide range of problems, including those that give rise to crime and criminality. Yet the multi-agency approach that is advocated by community policing means that police officers can rely on other professionals who may be better suited to address such causal problems. Within the context of this multi-agency approach to community policing, do you believe that police should stay focused on what they do best (enforcing the laws, responding to calls for service, arresting offenders) and allow their partners to focus on the social problems that give rise to crime? Or do you think officers should engage in problem-oriented policing involving tasks that fall outside their law enforcement mandate? Explain your answer.

SUGGESTED FURTHER READINGS

International Centre for the Prevention of Crime. (2008). *Compendium of crime prevention practices to inspire action across the world*. Montreal: Author.

Lab, S.P. (2010). *Crime prevention approaches, practices, and evaluations* (7th ed.). New York: Anderson.

Schneider, S. (2014). *Crime prevention: Theory and practice* (2nd ed.). Boca Raton, FL: CRC Press.

Sherman, L.W., Farrington, D.P., Welsh, B.C., & MacKenzie, D.L. (Eds.). (2006). *Evidence-based crime prevention* (Rev. ed.). London: Routledge.

Welsh, B.C., & Farrington, D.P. (Eds.). (2012). *The Oxford handbook of crime prevention*. Oxford: Oxford University Press.

REFERENCES

Armstrong, D., & Carson, G. (1994). The use of private security in public housing: A case study. *Journal of Security Administration, 17*(1), 53–60.

Benforado, A. (2015). *Unfair: The new science of criminal injustice*. New York: Crown Publishing Group.

Canada. (1993). *Crime prevention in Canada: Toward a national strategy—Twelfth report of the Standing Committee on Justice and the Solicitor General*. Ottawa: House of Commons Canada.

Canadian Association of Chiefs of Police. (1997). *The private security sector in Canada: A discussion paper*. Ottawa: Author.

Cherney, A. (2006, May). Problem-solving for crime prevention. *Trends and Issues in Crime Prevention, 314*. Retrieved from http://www.aic.gov.au/media_library/publications/tandi _pdf/tandi314.pdf.

Chicago Area Project. (n.d.). About Chicago Area Project. Retrieved from http://www.chicagoareaproject.org/about-us.

Clarke, R.V. (1997). Introduction. In R.V. Clarke (Ed.), *Situational crime prevention: Successful case studies* (2nd ed., pp. 2–43). Albany, NY: Harrow and Heston.

Clarke, R.V., & Cornish, D.B. (1985). Modeling offenders' decisions: A framework for policy and research. In M. Tonry & N. Morris (Eds.), *Crime and justice: An annual review of research* (Vol. 6, pp. 147–185). Chicago: University of Chicago Press.

Cohen, L.E., & Felson, M. (1979). Social change and crime rate trends: A routine activity approach. *American Sociological Review, 44*, 588–608.

Cornish, D.B., & Clarke, R.V. (2003). Opportunities, precipitators, and criminal decisions: A reply to Wortley's critique of situational crime prevention. In M.J. Smith & D.B. Cornish (Eds.), *Theory for practice in situational crime prevention* (pp. 41–96). Monsey, NY: Criminal Justice Press.

Crawford, A. (1999). Questioning appeals to community within crime prevention and control. *European Journal on Criminal Policy and Research, 7*, 509–530.

Doran, N., Luczak, S. Bekman, N., Koutsenok, I., & Brown, S. (2012). Adolescent substance use and aggression: A review. *Criminal Justice and Behavior, 39*, 748–769.

Eck, J. (2002). Preventing crime at places. In L.W. Sherman, D.P. Farrington, B.C. Welsh, & D.L. MacKenzie (Eds.), *Evidence-based crime prevention* (pp. 241–294). London: Routledge.

Farrington, D. (2007). Childhood risk factors and risk-focused prevention, In M. Maguire, R. Morgan, & R. Reiner (Eds.), *The Oxford handbook of criminology* (pp. 602–640). Oxford: Oxford University Press.

Farrington, D., Coid, J., Harnett, L., Jolliffe, D., Soteriou, N., Turner, R., & West, D. (2006). *Criminal careers up to age 50 and life success up to age 48: New findings from the Cambridge Study in Delinquent Development*. London: Home Office.

Felson, M., & Clarke, R.V. (1998). *Opportunity makes the thief: Practical theory for crime prevention* (Police Research Series Paper 98). London: Home Office.

Finegan, S. (2013). Watching the watchers: The growing privatization of criminal law enforcement and the need for limits on neighborhood watch associations. *University of Massachusetts Law Review, 8*, 88–134.

Forrest, R., & Kearns, A. (2001). Social cohesion, social capital and the neighbourhood. *Urban Studies, 38*(12), 2125–2143.

Friedmann, R.R. (1992). *Community policing: Comparative perspectives and prospects*. New York: St. Martin's Press.

Goldstein, H. (1987). Toward community oriented policing: Potential, basic requirements, and threshold questions. *Crime and Delinquency, 33*(1), 6–30.

Gottfredson, D.C., Cook, P.J., & Na, C. (2012). Schools and prevention. In B.C. Welsh & D.P. Farrington (Eds.), *The Oxford handbook of crime prevention* (pp. 269–287). Oxford: Oxford University Press.

Greenberg, S.W., & Rohe, W.M. (1986). Informal social control and crime prevention in modern urban neighborhoods. In R.B. Taylor (Ed.), *Urban neighborhoods: Research and policy* (pp. 79–118). New York: Praeger.

Greenberg, S.W., Rohe, M., & Williams, J. (1985). *Informal citizen action and crime prevention at the neighborhood level: Synthesis and assessment of the research*. Washington, DC: US Department of Justice, National Institute of Justice.

Greenwood, P.W. (2006). *Changing lives: Delinquency prevention as crime-control policy*. Chicago: University of Chicago Press.

HomeFront. (2012, December 21). Final process evaluation report (Unpublished).

Lab, S.P. (2016). *Crime prevention: Approaches, practices, and evaluations* (9th ed.). New York: Routledge.

Lattimore, P.K., Dryden-Witte, A., & Baker, J.R. (1990). Experimental assessment of the effect of vocational training on youthful property offenders. *Evaluation Review, 14*(2), 115–133.

Leighton, B. (1991). Visions of community policing: Rhetoric and reality in Canada. *Canadian Journal of Criminology, 33*(3/4), 485–522.

Lipsey, M.W. (2009). The primary factors that characterize effective interventions with juvenile offenders: A meta-analytic overview of effective interventions. *Victims and Offenders: An International Journal of Evidence-Based Research, Policy, and Practice, 4*(2), 124–147.

Lockwood, S., Nally, J.M. Ho, T., & Knutson, K. (2012). The effect of correctional education on postrelease employment and recidivism: A 5-year follow-up study in the State of Indiana. *Crime & Delinquency, 58*(3), 380–396.

MacKenzie, D.L. (2006) *What works in corrections: Reducing the criminal activities of offenders and delinquents.* New York: Cambridge University Press.

National Crime Council of Ireland. (2003). *A crime prevention strategy for Ireland: Tackling the concerns of local communities.* Dublin: The Stationery Office. Retrieved from http://www.drugsandalcohol.ie/5469/1/NCC_Crime_prevention_strategy.pdf.

National Crime Prevention Centre. (2014). Strengthening the Spirit—Oskâyi Kiskinotahn: Building a comprehensive response to family violence in Aboriginal communities. *Building the Evidence: Project Summaries* (PS-2014-02). Retrieved from https://www.publicsafety .gc.ca/cnt/rsrcs/pblctns/strngthnng-sprt/strngthnng-sprt-eng.pdf.

Noaks, L. (2000). Private cops on the block: A review of the role of private security in residential communities, *Policing and Society, 10*(2), 143–161.

Petrosino A., Turpin-Petrosino, C., & Guckenburg. S. (2010). *Formal system processing of juveniles: Effects on delinquency.* Philadelphia: Campbell Systematic Reviews.

Prime, J., White, S., Liriano, S., & Patel, K. (2001). Criminal careers of those born between 1953 and 1978. *Home Office Statistical Bulletin, 4/01.*

Rosenbaum, D.P. (1988). Community crime prevention: A review and synthesis of the literature. *Justice Quarterly, 5*, 323–395.

Rosenbaum, D.P., & Schuck, A.M. (2012). Comprehensive community partnerships for preventing crime. In B.C. Welsh & D.P. Farrington (Eds.), *The Oxford Handbook of Crime Prevention* (pp. 226–246). Oxford: Oxford University Press.

Sampson, R.J., Raudenbush, S.W., & Earls, F. (1997). Neighborhoods and violent crime: A multilevel study of collective efficacy. *Science, 277*, 918–923.

Schneider, S. (2014). *Crime prevention: Theory and practice* (2nd ed.). Boca Raton, FL: CRC Press.

Sedlak, A., & Bruce, C. (2010, December). Youth's characteristics and backgrounds: Findings from the Survey of Youth in Residential Placement. *OJJDP Bulletin.*

Sedlak, A., & McPherson, K. (2010, May). Conditions of confinement: Findings from the Survey of Youth in Residential Placement. *OJJDP Bulletin.*

Shaw, C.R., & McKay, H.D. (1942). *Juvenile delinquency in urban areas.* Chicago: University of Chicago Press.

Shaw, C.R., Zorbaugh, H., McKay, H.D., & Cottrell, L.S. (1929). *Delinquency areas.* Chicago: University of Chicago Press.

Sherman, L.W. (1997). Thinking about crime prevention. In L.W. Sherman, D. Gottfredson, D. MacKenzie, J. Eck, P. Reuter, & S. Bushway (Eds.), *Preventing crime: What works, what doesn't, what's promising* [Report to the United States Congress] (pp. 1–31). Washington, DC: National Institute of Justice.

Sherman, L.W., & Eck, J. (2006). Policing for crime prevention. In L.W. Sherman, D.P. Farrington, B.C. Welsh, & D.L. MacKenzie (Eds.), *Evidence-based crime prevention* (Rev. ed., pp. 295–329). London: Routledge.

Sherman, L.W., Farrington, D.P., Welsh, B.C., & MacKenzie, D.L. (Eds.). (2006). *Evidence-based crime prevention* (Rev. ed.). London: Routledge.

Skolnick, J.H., & Bayley, D.H. (1988). *Community policing: Issues and practices around the world*. Washington, DC: US Government Printing Office.

Sousa, W., & Kelling, G. (2014). Order maintenance policing. In G. Bruinsma & D. Weisburd (Eds.), *Encyclopedia of criminology and criminal justice* (pp. 3349–3357). New York: Springer.

Tanner-Smith, E., Wilson, S.J., & Lipsey, M.W. (2015). Risk factors and crime. In F. Cullen & P. Wilcox (Eds.), *The Oxford handbook of criminological theory* (pp. 89–114). Oxford: Oxford University Press.

Thacher, D. (2014). Order maintenance policing. In M.D. Reisig & R.J. Kane (Eds.), *The Oxford handbook of police and policing* (pp. 122–147). Oxford: Oxford University Press.

Walsh, W.F., Donovan, E.J., & McNicholas, J.F. (1992). Starrett Protective Service: Private policing in an urban community. In G.W. Bowman, S. Hakim, & P. Seidenstat (Eds.), *Privatizing the United States justice system: Police, adjudication, and corrections services from the private sector* (pp. 157–177). Jefferson, NC: Mcfarland & Co.

Welsh, B.C., & Farrington, D.P. (2010). *The future of crime prevention: Developmental and situational strategies* (Document No. 237329). Washington, DC: National Institute of Justice. Retrieved from https://www.ncjrs.gov/pdffiles1/nij/grants/237329.pdf.

Welsh, B.C., & Farrington, D.P. (2012). Crime prevention and public policy. In B.C. Welsh & D.P. Farrington (Eds.), *The Oxford handbook of crime prevention* (pp. 3–20). Oxford: Oxford University Press.

Wikström, P-O., Oberwittler, D., Treiber, K., & Hardie, B. (2012). *Breaking rules: The social and situational dynamics of young people's urban crime*. Oxford: Oxford University Press.

Wilson, D.B., MacKenzie, D.L., & Mitchell, F.N. (2008). *Effects of correctional boot camps on offending*. Oslo: Campbell Collaboration Systematic Review.

Wilson, J. (1975). *Thinking about crime*. New York: Academic Press.

Wilson, J., & Kelling, G. (1982, March 31). Broken windows. *Atlantic Monthly*, 29–38.

Wilson, J.J., & Howell, J.C. (1993). *Comprehensive strategy for serious, violent, and chronic juvenile offenders. Program summary*. Washington, DC: Office of Juvenile Justice and Delinquency Prevention, U.S. Department of Justice.

Wirth, L. (1938). Urbanism, migration and tolerance: A reassessment. *American Sociological Review, 56*, 117–123.

Wright, J.P., & Beaver, K. (2015). Parenting and crime. In F. Cullen & P. Wilcox (Eds.), *The Oxford handbook of criminological theory* (pp. 40–65). Oxford: Oxford University Press.

PART TWO

Policing

Vancouver's Odd Squad: Community Policing in Practice

Karla O'Regan

Members of Vancouver's Odd Squad.

Policing is a demanding profession that requires its members to act quickly and effectively in a diverse range of situations, many of which are stressful, uncertain, and dangerous. Moreover, as society changes, so too must the police. Finding new and improved ways to address crime is a constant challenge for the police and often requires officers to take on unexpected roles. For example, the police in the early 1900s performed many of the tasks of today's social services agencies, such as operating soup kitchens, helping the unemployed find work, and allowing police stations to be used as night shelters (Palmiotto, 2011).

Developing strong ties with the community continues to be an effective crime prevention strategy for the police. Studies have shown that when the police are more visible in a community, residents feel safer and hold more positive attitudes toward law enforcement (Reisig & Kane, 2014). Establishing stronger ties to the community also improves the willingness of people to report crimes to the police, helping law enforcement agencies to know more about what is happening in their communities.

Indeed, the efforts of one police squad to learn more about the community they patrolled helped to raise awareness and further an investigation into Canada's worst serial killer, Robert Pickton.

While working in Vancouver's Downtown Eastside—a neighbourhood sometimes referred to as Canada's "poorest postal code"—police officer Al Arsenault began to take photos of his "beat" and the residents he met while out on patrol. After sharing the photos with his fellow officers, he was asked by Constable Toby Hinton if the pictures could be used in the drug education presentations he was offering in schools. Together with five other officers, Arsenault and Hinton formed the "Odd Squad"—a non-profit organization that produces drug awareness videos with footage taken by officers while on patrol. The organization's first film, *Through a Blue Lens* (National Film Board of Canada, 1999), profiled the lives of six Downtown Eastside residents who suffered from substance abuse, homelessness, and poverty. The documentary was shot with a video camera that was purchased using funds donated by each of the officers, and it has since been shown in 22 countries around the world. In fact, the National Film Board of Canada cites *Through a Blue Lens* as its most successful documentary to date (Cameron, 2007).

The Odd Squad has since produced more than 15 documentaries, and the original equipment it used to gather the footage for *Through a Blue Lens* is now housed in the Vancouver Police Museum. When asked about how the initiative got started, Arsenault notes that the project was a collaborative effort with the neighbourhood residents themselves in response to seeing local young people engaged in drug abuse:

> [W]e we got tired of seeing kids coming to the Downtown Eastside and get[ting] hooked on drugs. The addicts would want to kick their ass out of the skids … . Then we'd [all] stand around talking about it later, "don't you hate seeing kids down here?" "Yeah me too, what can we do, you know?" "Well hey, we're doing these lectures in schools about drug abuse and the conditions down here … and I'm sure you can speak to it better than us because you're living this." (England, 2004, p. 299)

Aside from accomplishing its initial aims of raising awareness about drug addiction among youth, the Odd Squad's efforts also served to facilitate relationships and establish trust between the police and the community. As Darlene Rowley, a resident featured in *Through a Blue Lens*, remarked, "I had just overdosed on cocaine and had been running through the streets of the Downtown Eastside. If it weren't for Al Arsenault and Toby Hinton, I wouldn't be alive today. They saved my life that night" (Smith, 2001). The Odd Squad officers also reported a significant shift in their own perceptions of the community and its residents as a result of the project. At one point in *Through a Blue Lens*, Constable Hollingsworth tells viewers that when he first began his patrols in the neighbourhood, he viewed its residents as "just all addicts, hypes and trash; garbage essentially. Just a waste of society's monies and taxpayers' dollars." His participation in the Odd Squad changed that. "But when you get to know a little bit about these people and their stories you can't help but have compassion for them. These people have mothers and fathers that love them just like we love our children" (England, 2004, p. 304).

One of the greatest strengths of community policing is the creation of circumstances like these, in which the police and the people they protect can develop empathy for each other. In order to solve crimes, address social problems, and strengthen public safety, police need the public's cooperation—something studies have shown they are far more likely to get when they are trusted by citizens and show an interest in what citizens have to say (Reisig & Kane, 2014). The Odd Squad is a good example of a police team that was able to garner this cooperation. Journalist Stevie Cameron, while reporting on the Robert Pickton case, noted that amid rising numbers of missing women in Vancouver's poorest neighbourhoods, the police were frequently criticized for not caring enough—but the Odd Squad stood apart. "Not all the police officers I knew were indifferent to the women I worked with," Cameron wrote. "Al Arsenault and Toby Hinton functioned more like advocates for marginalized women than beat cops" (Cameron, 2007, p. xix). After the body of April Reoch, an Indigenous woman featured in *Through a Blue Lens*, was discovered in a city dumpster, the Odd Squad led more than 200 people through the streets of Vancouver to attend her funeral, at which Constable Arsenault delivered her eulogy. The story was covered by the *Vancouver Sun*, which resulted in increasing public awareness about the more than 60 women missing from the Downtown Eastside. Vancouver's mayor at the time, Philip Owen, attended the funeral and was prompted into action, offering a $100,000 reward for information leading to Reoch's killer (Vancouver Police Department, 2010).

Information began to pour in, leading police to request a search warrant for Robert Pickton's farm. At the farm, police discovered human remains that matched the DNA of many of the missing women. Forensic teams were sent out to the farm to excavate and search for further evidence. Their discoveries more aptly resembled a horror film than reality. Severed hands and feet, jaw bones, and skulls were found buried, in freezer buckets, and decomposing in garbage pails. Forensic evidence also suggested that Pickton had used his butchering equipment on the farm to dispose of bodies, grinding them with pork meat, in some cases, for resale, and in other instances, for use as pig feed. The forensic investigation of the Pickton farm took more than two years, encompassed a huge geographical area, concerned itself with the deaths of almost 50 victims, and involved the interviewing of more than 1,000 witnesses, making it the largest forensic inquiry in Canadian history. Pickton was initially charged with 27 counts of first-degree murder, and in December 2007 he was convicted by a jury for 6 counts of second-degree murder. Shortly after, he was sentenced to 25 years in jail with no possibility for parole—the maximum available sentence.

Although the missing women investigation and the arrest of Robert Pickton were the result of many people's efforts, the community relationships made possible by the Odd Squad cannot be underestimated. As Cameron (2007) noted, April Reoch's murder might have been left unsolved. "April, too, might have been declared a missing woman, and the man who murdered her likely would not have been brought to justice. But April's situation was different. She knew Al and Toby" (p. xx).

The chapters in this part will demonstrate that finding ways for the police to know their communities better is not a new idea. As Chapter 3's discussion of policing history shows, it is in keeping with many of the founding principles of community policing that were outlined by the "father of policing," Sir Robert Peel. Much like the social services performed by the police at the turn of the 20th century, community-based policing strengthens relationships on both sides of the "thin blue line"—something that benefits everyone. This point was made explicit by Justice Wally Oppal, former attorney general and appellate court judge for British Columbia, who authored the Independent Commission of Inquiry into Policing in British Columbia and the Missing Women Commission of Inquiry in 2010 in response to Pickton's crimes. When asked what the police could do better, he answered: "[T]hey have to adopt more of a community-based policing approach. They have to get outside of their police buildings and their cars and interact more with the public. It is good for the police and it is good for the public" (Parent, 2014, p. 105).

What Do You Think?

1. Although Vancouver's Odd Squad follows a contemporary approach to policing, in what ways do its community-based policing strategies reflect the principles of policing established by Sir Robert Peel? (See "Sidebar—Sir Robert Peel's Nine Principles of Policing" in Chapter 3.) In what ways do its community-based policing strategies differ from those principles?

2. Some commentators critiqued the methods used by the Odd Squad to gather video footage because of the extreme vulnerability of the documentary's participants. What specific kinds of problems do you think these critiques were concerned with? How might these problems be related to the issues the Supreme Court of Canada raised about "Mr. Big" sting operations? (See "Mini Case Study—Nelson Lloyd Hart" in Chapter 4.)

3. Watch *Through a Blue Lens* at the National Film Board of Canada's website. In the documentary, what specific police strategies (discussed in Chapter 3) did the Odd Squad engage in? What legal powers (e.g., to arrest, to search) did officers exercise?

SUGGESTED FURTHER READING

Vancouver Courier. (2012, June 29). Odd Squad out to make a difference. *Vancouver Courier*. Retrieved from http://www.vancourier.com/news/odd-squad-out-to-make-a-difference-1.389853.

REFERENCES

Cameron, S. (2007). *The Pickton file*. Toronto: Knopf Canada.

England, J. (2004). Disciplining subjectivity and space: Representation, film and its material effects. *Antipode, 6*(2), 295–321.

National Film Board of Canada (Producer), & Mannix, V.A. (Director). (1999). *Through a Blue Lens* [Documentary]. Canada. Retrieved from https://www.nfb.ca/film/through_a_blue_lens/.

Palmiotto, M.J. (2011). *Community policing: A police-citizen partnership*. New York: Routledge.

Parent, R. (2014). Interview of Judge Wally Oppal, Queens Council, Supreme Court of British Columbia. In D.K. Das, C. Roberson, & M.M. Berlin (Eds.), *Trends in the judiciary: Interviews with judges across the globe* (pp. 97–116). London: CRC Press.

Reisig, M.D., & Kane, R.J. (2014). *The Oxford handbook of police and policing*. (New York: Oxford University Press).

Smith, C. (2001, March 29). Police board asked to review Odd Squad. *Georgia Straight*. Retrieved from http://www.mapinc.org/drugnews/v01/n568/a03.html?2191.

Vancouver Police Department. (2010). *Missing women investigation review*. Vancouver: Author. Retrieved from http://www.cbc.ca/bc/news/bc-100820-vancouver-police-pickton-investigation-review.pdf.

Policing History, Organization, and Operations

LEARNING OUTCOMES

After reading this chapter, students will be able to:

- Describe significant events in the history of policing.
- Describe the current three-tier structure of the Canadian police.
- Understand the importance of police governance and accountability.
- Better appreciate the reality and complexity of policing in the 21st century.
- Describe contemporary community policing and general police operations.

CHAPTER OUTLINE

Introduction

Writing and research about Canadian policing has been notoriously lacking for decades.[1] Policing literature and police practices from the 18th to 21st centuries have been influenced largely by experiences in European countries and the United States. The objective of this chapter is to provide a uniquely *Canadian* perspective of policing, albeit a brief one. The ability to do so is credited to the growing contributions by academics and practitioners from across the country and beyond who have focused their research attention on the distinctively democratic model of policing that exists in Canada, particularly since the 1990s.

This chapter will begin with the origins of policing, which are rooted in Europe, and trace policing's arrival on the east coast of Canada and its expansion westward, across the country. You will read about the introduction of community policing in the mid-1980s and its evolution to a **contemporary community policing** model in the 21st century. Readers should come to realize that the **thin blue line** view of policing and the stereotypical television crime-fighter image represent the antithesis to the democratic principles that make Canadian policing a treasured model worldwide. Democratic principles remain tied to the foundation of public policing envisioned by Sir Robert Peel of London, England in 1829, and are entrenched in the *Canadian Charter of Rights and Freedoms*. The challenge of modern policing in Canada is to maintain our democratic

contemporary community policing
The police and community working together to identify, prioritize, and solve local crime and disorder issues that impact the quality of life in neighbourhoods and business districts. It embraces the concept of policing through crime prevention, and community safety and well-being from holistic and root cause perspectives.

thin blue line
A symbolic representation of the police as a protective barrier between the general public and its crime and violence.

principles by adhering to Sir Robert Peel's vision of public service, while being nimble and strategic to effectively meet the standards and expectations for public and officer safety in an increasingly complex world. The changing nature of crime and police responsibilities in this century is well described by the Council of Canadian Academies (2014):

> Enabled by information technology and the increasing mobility of people, goods and knowledge, crime is becoming more complex, more "a-spatial" and potentially more harmful. There is a growing mismatch between the increasing threat and reality of a-spatial crimes and the continued organizational emphasis on jurisdiction-based police responses. … Police services are increasingly responding to social problems for which they have limited training and resources. Demand is being influenced by an older, more diverse, and digitally savvy population; in addition, the policing of people with mental illness or in crisis is increasingly recognized as a country-wide issue. (p. 14)

In short, the fast-paced complexities of our world are creating new pressures for transformational change in policing and require greater collaboration with multiple stakeholders to maintain safe and secure communities.

A Snapshot of the History of Policing

The need for order maintenance and protection of life and property has existed ever since people began to gather in groups and acquire property of their own. The field of Canadian policing has experienced many changes over the centuries and is primarily rooted in practices established long ago in Western Europe.

The origins of policing can be traced back to tribal customs of self-policing where retribution for violating the established norms and values was both an individual and a collective responsibility. The primary aims of self-policing were to protect life, to protect the property that was needed to sustain life, and to ensure survival of the group or tribe. As early as 1000 BCE in China, rulers of the Chou Dynasty were known to codify laws that governed their increasingly complex society. These laws were enforced by military authority, signalling for the first time a shift from a self-policing and tribal policing model to a centralized police authority that relied on legitimate military means to enforce those laws. This system evolved similarly elsewhere as reflected many centuries later by the establishment of Greek **kin police** and the **vigiles** of the Roman Empire, who assisted with order maintenance in their early cities and states around 450 BCE.

In medieval Europe, long before the Industrial Revolution, appointed persons were expected to collect taxes, protect peace, and enforce laws of the land for the monarchy of the day. Noblemen of the country similarly hired men to perform duties on their behalf in order to preserve their wealth and order. The commoners, however, had no such means and therefore relied on one another for protection of persons and property. Villages at that time maintained order through a system known as *the hue and cry*. Simply stated, when a hue and cry was issued that a wrong had been committed, it was incumbent on "every fit and able man" to assist in the pursuit and apprehension of the violator.

By the Middle Ages, as early as 1035, the **frankpledge system** was established to strengthen peacekeeping efforts. Under this system, all men between the ages of 15 and 60 had to enlist in groupings of ten families called **tithings** for keeping peace and order. Citizens would report crimes to their tithing and respond to their hue and cry to assist. The elected tithingman became the spokesperson for the group and the community, and

kin police
Adherents of an informal system of mutual protection wherein law enforcement fell to the citizenry who were responsible for their tribe, family, or kin.

vigiles
Watchmen and firefighters in ancient Rome.

frankpledge system
A system of law enforcement in medieval England in which all men who were not part of the nobility were formed into groups and bound by a sworn pledge to ensure each other's good conduct.

tithings
Among the common citizens of Anglo-Saxon England, groups of ten families who were collectively responsible for each other's behaviour.

was also responsible for collecting fines and demanding bail. As villages and populations expanded, the tithing system evolved into networks of ten groups of tithings who were together led by a "hundredman." The hundreds were later combined to form shires (counties and parishes) and were led by officials referred to as "shire-reeves" (sheriffs). The shire-reeves "were appointed by the King to represent his interests and uphold the authority of the Crown. The shire-reeve was invested with considerable military, civil, and judicial powers and made periodic visits to each hundred to ensure that the system of local policing was operating properly" (Griffiths, Parent, & Whitelaw, 2001, p. 5).

The British **watch and ward** system was established under the *Statute of Westminster* in 1285. It "affirmed the principle of local responsibility for policing," whereby an appointed constable would organize the men of the town to serve on a roster basis for protection and enforcement purposes (Cooper, 1981, p. 38). By the mid-1300s, a justice of the peace was established, and the role of constable was expanded to include serving warrants and taking prisoners into custody. The watch and ward system proved effective for hundreds of years, slowly evolving according to community needs. As time passed, however, and with the "advent of urbanism and a more affluent middle class, a practice developed whereby those who could afford to do so hired others, at minimum rates, to substitute for them on the watch roster ... [G]radually, more and more citizens began hiring others until the quality of the watch degenerated, and in many cases, became almost meaningless" (Cooper, 1981, p. 38). This practice, coupled with a growing population and soaring crime rates in England and other countries, signalled the need for policing reform. In 1750 England, a small group of constables and ex-constables called the Bow Street Runners were introduced for the sole purpose of apprehending criminals in a particularly troubled area of London. The concept (initiated by police reformer and magistrate Henry Fielding) expanded, and by the 1800s it included both foot and horse patrol and nine similar organizations established throughout London (Seagrave, 1997, p. 15).

Between 1750 and 1820, the Industrial Revolution was well underway and the population in London doubled, bringing with it a plethora of social ills, crimes, disorder, and public health issues. All of these factors combined to emphasize the need, once again, for policing reform. The first organized police force in English history was established by Sir Robert Peel in London in 1829 when he introduced the *Metropolitan Police Act* (Weiner, 1976, p. 8). The Act created the police office at Scotland Yard, which began under the supervision of Charles Rowan, a former military man, and Richard Mayne, a barrister of law (Seagrave, 1997, p. 17). The organizational structure adopted for the police force was based on a military format that prevails to this day. Similarly, police structures are still referred to as paramilitary operations. The initial philosophy of policing was based on nine principles that guided the English **bobby** for generations (Manning, 1977, p. 76). Primarily, Sir Robert Peel claimed that the police were powerless without the approval, cooperation, and support of the public, and that the police themselves were merely citizens empowered by the people. By 1830, the police force had grown from a complement of 100 men to more than 3,000, and by the 1850s "every borough and county in England was required to develop its own police force" (Seagrave, 1997, p. 17).

Peel's strategy for reform, based on his principles of police–community cooperation and accountability, was a philosophical approach that influenced the trend of policing for many decades afterward.

watch and ward
Continuous vigilance by constables by night (watch) and day (ward).

bobby
A British slang word (like *peeler*) for policeman, in reference to Sir Robert Peel.

Sir Robert Peel's Nine Principles of Policing

1. To prevent crime and disorder as an alternative to their repression by military force and by severity of legal punishment.

2. To recognize always that the power of the police to fulfill their functions and duties is dependent on public approval of their existence, actions and behaviour, and on their ability to secure and maintain public respect.

3. To recognize always that to secure and maintain the respect and approval of the public means also the securing of the willing cooperation of the public in the task of securing observance of laws.

4. To recognize always that the extent to which the cooperation of the public can be secured diminishes, proportionately, the necessity of the use of physical force and compulsion for achieving police objectives.

5. To seek and preserve public favour, not by pandering to public opinion, but by constantly demonstrating absolutely impartial service to law, in complete independence of policy and with regard to justice and injustices of the substance of individual laws; by readily offering individual service and friendship to all members of the public without regard to their wealth or social standing; by ready exercise of courtesy and friendly good humour; and by ready offering of sacrifice in protecting and preserving life.

6. To use physical force only when the exercise of persuasion, advice and warning is found to be insufficient to obtain public cooperation to an extent necessary to secure observance of law to restore order; and to use only the minimum degree of physical force which is necessary on any particular occasion for achieving a police objective.

7. To maintain at all times a relationship with the public that gives reality to the historic tradition that the police are the public and the public are the police; the police being the only members of public who are paid to give full-time attention to the duties which are incumbent on every citizen, in the interests of community welfare and existence.

8. To recognize always the need the for strict adherence to public executive functions, and to refrain from even seeming to usurp the powers of the judiciary or avenging individuals or the state, and from authoritatively judging guilt or punishing the guilty.

9. To recognize always that the test of police efficiency is the absence of crime and disorder and not the visible evidence of police action in dealing with them. (Seagrave, 1997, p. 17)

The History of Policing in Canada

Little is known about early policing activities in Canada, and historians debate where and when the first organized system of policing was established. Some claim that the first police officer appeared on the streets of Quebec in 1651, while others claim that the early settlers of New France introduced organized policing in the late 1700s (Kelly & Kelly, 1976, p. 1).

The earliest recorded forms of policing are captured in various historical accounts. For example, sheriffs were recorded as working in the parish of Fredericton, New Brunswick in 1785 (Forward, 2016, p. 18). The commonly held belief is that formalized policing in British North America began in the east and was modelled after the watch and ward system in England, but little more is known about the development of early municipal police departments. Records also exist indicating that areas settled by the French were more influenced by traditional French systems and led by captains of the militia, and that other areas, such as the port cities of St. John's, Newfoundland and Halifax, Nova Scotia were influenced by fishing admirals, navy, and militias. In 1826, Kingston, Ontario appointed its first full-time paid constable; and in 1835 the city of Toronto replaced its night watch with six full-time constables. A clear trend toward formalized paid policing was emerging in an effort to manage labour and property issues, drunkenness, crime, disorder, and the apprehension of criminals.

With increasing industrialization, urbanization, and modernization of cities in North America, there emerged a greater need for social control, public order, and crime prevention. By 1848, for example, Fredericton's burgeoning police force saw the establishment of paid special constables allocated throughout town wards to maintain order and peace. During this time, constables primarily dealt with the clash between Catholics and Protestants; illegal sales; trading and consumption of liquor; and riotous behaviour. The Saint John Police Force was established in 1849 and initially operated under the supervision of the police magistrate. In 1856, it was placed under the control of a chief of police (Saint John Police Museum, n.d.).

In Upper Canada, an Act of Parliament was passed in 1859 that "created boards of commissioners of police, consisting of the Mayor, the recorder or county judge and a police magistrate," practices that came to be followed elsewhere. Also in 1859, "the governments of the provinces of Canada required that each city and incorporated town have a chief of police and at least one and possibly more constables, paid by the municipality" (Higley, 1984, p. 29). When Canada was officially declared a nation in 1867, the *British North America Act* empowered the federal, provincial, and municipal governments with the responsibilities of criminal law, thus creating a "three tiered system of policing" (Cooper, 1981, p. 40). The first known form of federal policing was the Dominion Police, which was instituted one year after Confederation.

In 1870, the provincial police force of Sûreté du Quebec was formed, and in 1871 so too was the Newfoundland Constabulary. Both entities were established to provide policing to populated areas across their regions. By the early 1900s, "all the changing demands of rapidly expanding cities such as spatial complexity, growing crime rates, riotous disorder, [and] ethnic and racial tensions" created a need for a more organized form of policing (Harring, 1991, p. 253). In 1909, the Ontario Provincial Police was established to address growing concerns in railway and mining camps and other security concerns along the border between the United States and Canada. In 1920, the North West Mounted Police merged with the Dominion Police to officially establish a truly federal police organization known as the Royal Canadian Mounted Police (RCMP).

After the Second World War, policing entered the professional era with increased emphasis on paramilitary structures and depersonalization of service, as well as technology and mobility. Improved communications systems with radios, telephones, and computers, and the introduction of cars and advanced scientific resources were important forces that reshaped policing. Accordingly, society's demands for rapid response to calls for police service, increased efficiency, and police accountability were natural expectations of this period (Johnson, 1992, p. 4; Lundman, 1980, p. 61; Norris, 1973, p. 37). The professional era changed the service style and direction of local police organizations by removing the familiar "street-corner beat cop" and replacing him with motorized patrols. Officers of the professional era soon became strangers in the community, viewed only from a distance, travelling in police cars from street to street and from call to call. "Professional" police officers, it seemed, were preoccupied with law enforcement, report writing, clearance rates, and statistics rather than engaging with the citizens they were sworn to serve and protect (Johnson, 1992, p. 4). In a classic study of policing, *Varieties of Police Behavior*, Wilson (1969) contended that rapid response to calls for police service, law enforcement, and police omnipresence were the ultimate means the police could apply to reduce the public's fear of criminal victimization and secure police professionalism. The final "ingredient" for professionalism was public and administrative accountability through the use of "uniform crime reports." These crime statistics became the "report card of a police agency," with emphasis placed on "capturing stats and data." The police, it appeared, were losing interest in the humanistic aspect of their job and were gaining a reputation as "one-dimensional crime-fighters" (Braiden, 1985, p. 12). Indeed, the professional era stressed centralized control and optimal use of technology, distancing the police from the people.

During this period, the Canadian model of policing was becoming insular and remote from the community, a critical change that led to the development of a new **police subculture**. While this transition enhanced **esprit de corps** within policing circles as police drew into themselves, it pulled them away from the citizenry. Eventually, community influence over police procedures and objectives, as envisioned by Sir Robert Peel, was removed from the hands of the people. Localized policing was no longer "explicitly determined by community decisions" and was largely ungoverned by political authorities (Wilson, 1969, p. 230). From this transition, we saw a change emerge in the thin blue line view of policing, which had once signified the police as a protective barrier between the public and its violence. Instead, for many officers it came to signify an "us versus them" mindset, and the all-powerful phenomenon of police loyalty crept into Canadian policing. This phenomenon led to increasing concerns about corruption in the public policing model, lack of accountability, and inefficiencies in dealing with rising crime rates.

police subculture
Values, beliefs, and approaches to policing shared by members of the profession.

esprit de corps
A spirit of loyalty and enthusiasm among members of a group for the group.

For a contemporary perspective on the thin blue line metaphor, see "Sidebar—The Thin Blue Thread."

The Current Structure of Canadian Police Organizations

Statistics Canada provides a good explanation of the range of policing responsibilities of Canadian police agencies:

> The work performed by police to ensure public safety encompasses a broad spectrum of tasks related to law enforcement, crime prevention and reduction, assistance to victims, maintenance of public order and emergency response. Police workload can be broken down into four general categories: citizen-generated calls for service, officer-initiated enforcement activities, crime prevention and reduction strategies, and administrative duties. (Statistics Canada, 2012a, p. 7)

Public policing in Canada comprises three tiers, reflecting the three tiers of government: federal, provincial, and municipal. The federal government provides national policing through the RCMP, and the RCMP's services are also contracted out to the territories as well as certain provinces and municipalities across the country. There are only three provincial police agencies: the Ontario Provincial Police, Sûreté du Quebec, and the Royal Newfoundland Constabulary. In provinces without a provincial police agency, the RCMP is contracted to serve as the provincial police. Each province is responsible for designating municipal (city) police departments to serve its communities.

Constable Rayan Najjar of the Blood Tribe Police Service in Alberta and a local teenager.

First Nations communities are policed through various police services, including the RCMP, tribal and band police services, and contracts with provincial police or municipal agencies. In all, 57 First Nations police services are located across British Columbia, Alberta, Saskatchewan, and Manitoba; 11 in Ontario; and 37 in Quebec ("First Nations Police," n.d.). St. Mary's First Nation in Fredericton, New Brunswick and Membertou First Nation in Cape Breton, Nova Scotia are the only two communities that rely solely on police services provided through quadripartite (four-party) agreements with the local municipality in which their communities are located.

Municipal and Provincial Policing

Municipal (city) police officers constitute the largest number of police officers in Canada. Currently, 154 municipal police organizations exist in Canada (www.canadianpoliceservices.com). The highest concentration occurs in Ontario, which includes 58 city/urban police services and five university police services. The roles and structures of municipal police services are largely influenced by the provincial government and operate under legislation commonly known as the *Police Act*. Municipal police services vary in size, reflecting the needs of their jurisdiction; they can range from small departments of six town police to medium-sized departments of 100 or more, to large metropolitan and regional police services with staff members in the thousands (e.g., Peel Regional Police, Toronto Police Service, and Vancouver Police Department).

The three provincial police forces provide services for core daily functions in areas not served by either the RCMP or municipal police forces. Most often, these areas include rural communities and small towns. Canada's expansive geography ensures that these police forces face challenges in meeting a wide range of community needs. The Royal Newfoundland Constabulary is distinct from the provincial police in Ontario and Quebec

FIGURE 3.1   Organizational Structure of Waterloo Regional Police Service, 2014

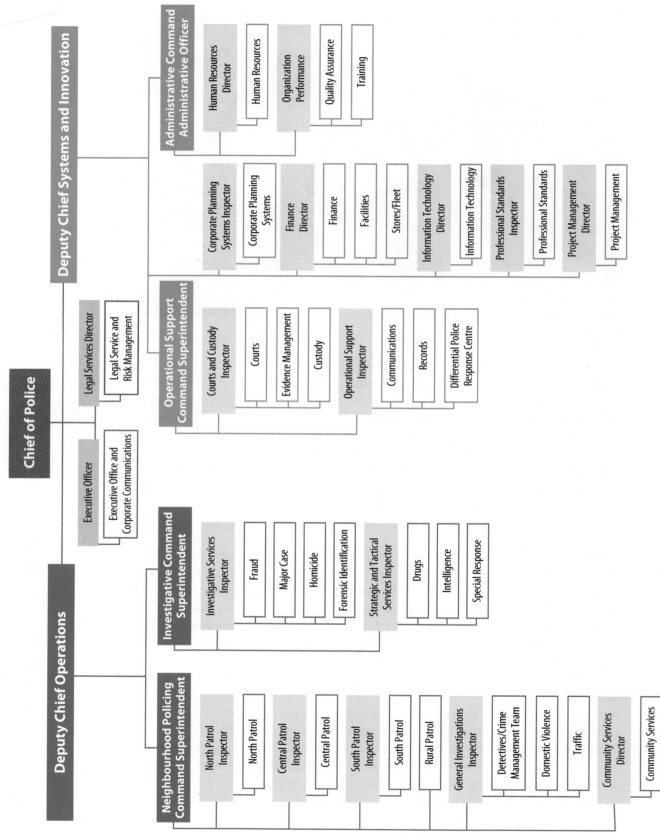

because it is primarily dedicated to providing police services to St. John's, a thriving urban area, while the RCMP is largely responsible for policing the rest of Newfoundland and Labrador, including various Inuit and First Nations communities. Conversely, in Quebec and Ontario, the RCMP pursue only specific federal statute matters, such as customs and excise, and leave rural and First Nations responsibilities to the provincial police services and/or First Nations police services and various municipal agencies.

Both provincial and municipal police services share similar mandates within their respective areas of responsibility, although their governance and reporting structures may vary. Staffing size, budget, areas of specialization, and capital resource equipment correspond with the size of their jurisdictions and the breadth of their expected duties.

As police organizations stem from a paramilitary foundation, command-and-control systems remain part of their primarily top-down hierarchical structure. Figure 3.1 presents an example of a modern municipal organizational structure for a police service (the Waterloo Regional Police Service). It outlines the hierarchical structure from chief of police to operations and administrative divisions (which include constables and civilian staff). It also illustrates the variety of specialized services offered by that police service. Such organizational charts also exist for other police agencies, including the RCMP, provincial police services, and First Nations police services.

Some police organizations have attempted to flatten the traditional hierarchical structure of police services to increase line officer autonomy and encourage the use of **problem-oriented policing** skills. This change in police culture allows front-line officers more discretion to build solutions with external partners in keeping with the philosophy of contemporary community policing. While officers have discretionary powers in the traditional response model, the move to encourage police throughout the **rank and file** to have greater autonomy has threatened the sense of security of some supervisors and leaders who have been educated in and shaped by the command-and-control system of a paramilitary hierarchy.

problem-oriented policing
A proactive policing strategy whereby police focus on the problems that form the basis of crime.

rank and file
A term used in military and paramilitary organizations to denote the general membership of the organization as set apart from the commanders and leaders.

Federal Policing

As the federal police service of Canada, the RCMP reports to the minister of Public Safety. The RCMP is led by the top commanding officer (the commissioner) who has the command-and-control position overseeing the force. The RCMP operates in some capacity in all provinces and territories under the authority of the *Royal Canadian Mounted Police Act* (*RCMP Act*) and enforces laws throughout Canada under the authority of Parliament. Through policing agreements, the RCMP provides various police services to the territories and 180 municipalities in all provinces except Ontario and Quebec. The modern organizational structure of the RCMP includes 15 provincial and territorial divisions, including its training depot in Regina, Saskatchewan and its national headquarters in Ottawa. Table 3.1 shows the actual

TABLE 3.1 Composition of RCMP Membership, as of September 2015

Commissioner	1
Deputy commissioners	7
Assistant commissioners	26
Chief superintendents	58
Superintendents	179
Inspectors	348
Corps sergeants major	1
Sergeants major	1
Staff sergeants major	13
Staff sergeants	812
Sergeants	1,923
Corporals	3,377
Constables	11,491
Special constables	55
Public servants	6,331
Total	**28,461**

Source: Royal Canadian Mounted Police (2016).

police strength of the RCMP and the composition and hierarchy of its membership as of September 2015.

Each division of the RCMP is alphabetically designated (e.g., "B" Division) and managed by a commanding officer at local headquarters. The RCMP provides a range of services from front-line patrol and criminal investigations up to and including national security. Its specialized functions include criminal intelligence services, Internet crime services, explosive disposal services, police dog services, air and marine services, and emergency response teams. It also performs the iconic RCMP Musical Ride for audiences across Canada and around the globe. Additionally, the RCMP oversees the National Police Services (NPS) that are provided within the Canadian justice field to other agencies at the expense of the federal government. Essentially, the RCMP's role is to ensure that special services are provided and shared by the NPS's programs, which include the Canadian Police Information Centre (CPIC), Criminal Intelligence Service Canada (CISC), Forensic Science and Identification Service (FS&IS), the Violent Crime Linkage Analysis System (ViCLAS), the National Sex Offender Registry, and the Canadian Police College (CPC) (Royal Canadian Mounted Police [RCMP], n.d.).

Other Agencies and Resources

When discussing the composition of the policing and security landscape in Canada, it is important to note that the responsibility for community safety and well-being does not lie solely with the public police. In addition to the three tiers of public policing, there are two railway police services: Canadian National (CN) Police Service and Canadian Pacific (CP) Police Service. Moreover, Ontario and British Columbia have **transit police** services. As well, over the past 30 years, the number of private security agencies has increased steadily. According to Statistics Canada, "while security guards differ [from police] in terms of training, accountability, and service to the public, they are also involved in maintaining order, providing assistance, and responding to emergencies" (Hutchins, 2015, p. 16).

It is estimated that private security personnel outnumber public police officers by a ratio of almost 2 to 1 (Canadian Broadcasting Corporation [CBC], 2013). Growth in the private security industry continues to outpace growth in the public police. In 1991 the number of private security positions in Canada was estimated at 80,000, but by 2013 this number had risen to approximately 140,000 (CBC, 2013; Hovbrender, 2011; Li, 2008). In 2013, by contrast, the number of public police officers in Canada was 69,250 (Hutchins, 2015, p. 23). See Figure 3.2.

transit police
Specialized police officers or special constables tasked exclusively with maintaining law and order on public transit such as trains, ferries, and buses.

SIDEBAR

Private Security Personnel

Private security personnel have the same "arrest and detain" powers as an ordinary citizen. While they perform some duties with regard to property protection that are similar to those of the public police, they are often paid by an employer to tend to security needs that are not in the public interest realm, such as controlling property and access to property. Private security personnel are generally paid less than police officers and do not require the same standard of training and education as police officers.

FIGURE 3.2   Police and Private Security Personnel in Canada, 1991–2013

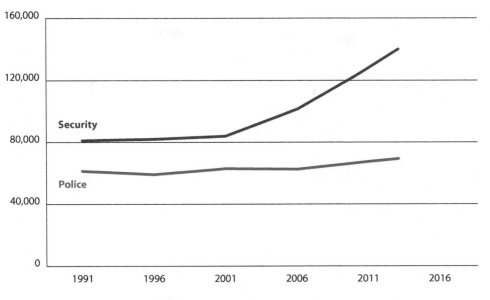

Sources: Hovbrender (2011); Li (2008); Statistics Canada (2009a, 2009b, 2012a, 2012b, 2016).

All police services include a component of civilian (non-police) employees who work in administrative and certain operational capacities, depending on the size of the organization. For example, civilian employees assist with clerical functions, records management, front-desk duties, crime analysis, and crime prevention programs. Statistics Canada reported that in 2014 there were "28,409 civilians employed by police services across Canada, representing 29% of total personnel. In other words, police services employed 2.4 police officers for every one civilian employee" (Hutchins, 2015, p. 3). The civilianization of police officer positions maximizes uniform visibility by freeing up officers to return to more public-facing roles. The Vancouver Police Department estimated that reclassifying 19 police positions as civilian positions would save approximately $600,000 per year, or 0.3 percent of operating expenditures (Council of Canadian Academies, 2014, p. 97). Research does caution, however, that staffing non-core police functions with civilians does limit the opportunity for an officer to return to work in a reduced capacity while recovering from an injury or awaiting the results of a lengthy officer misconduct investigation. For this reason, researchers suggest that it is important to separate the discussion of duty to accommodate from civilianization. When we focus on the idea of the right person for the right job, ferret out the requisite skill set required for a particular job, and save temporary assignments for temporary absences, the conversation becomes clearer. Notably, a trend is developing whereby higher paid, highly specialized civilian positions are in some cases surpassing the need for traditional police positions. The practice of civilianization continues to be viewed by some, especially in unionized police environments, as a threat to the status quo of traditional policing, and integrating civilians into the hierarchy of the police's command-and-control organizational structure remains limited to specific non-core police functions.

Civilianization

Civilianization is the process of transferring non-core police functions from police officers to civilian employees. Civilianization allows police officers to focus on front-line duties and responsibilities that require their highly trained skill set and powers of arrest. For example, clerical support staff could take on data-entry work in the exhibit room, a qualified crime analyst could be hired to assist in intelligence-led policing duties, and commissionaires could provide cellblock security.

Civilianization at the Highest Level

In 2007, the RCMP civilianized its top commanding officer position when the federal government appointed Commissioner William Elliot to lead the force. He was the first commissioner to be in this position without any military or policing background. His commission ended in 2011. Many felt that the attempt to clean up problems in the RCMP by bringing in an "outsider" and civilianizing the position failed.

What Do You Think?

1. Why did the federal government appoint a non-police commissioner? What might have been the government's rationale?
2. What would be some predictable internal reactions?
3. How would the public react to such an appointment?
4. Why might this experiment have failed?
5. What are the dangers of civilianizing top leadership roles in the RCMP? What are the benefits?

Philosophical and Organizational Change

Since the early 1980s, long-standing police traditions and practices, and the police subculture have been challenged by new ideology. Police forces across North America were prompted to re-evaluate their service styles, pressing police leaders in Canada to decide whether the "police should remain a creature of statute, insular and inward looking, or serve the needs of the community" (Braiden, 1985, p. 3). As you have learned so far in this chapter, policing is ever-evolving and continually influenced by a number of internal and external variables. Policing in Canada has, as with many organizations, evolved in an attempt to accommodate the changing needs and demands of society. As a result, from the early 1980s to the mid-1990s, several organizations introduced and experimented with a service style known as community-based policing (or community policing).

While the concept of community-based policing has become almost synonymous with modern policing, it has been interpreted in different ways. Many have opposing views about whether it represents a return to a fundamental style of policing as advocated by Sir Robert Peel in 1829 or is merely an extension of the former crime prevention and public relations model of the early 1970s.

The term *community-based policing* was used primarily in the 1980s and 1990s to reflect a change in policing philosophy. It focused on the police and the community working together to identify and prioritize law enforcement needs and to solve problems in local crime and disorder. It was a way of partnering to improve the quality of life in neighbourhoods, to be proactive in preventing problems, to reduce fear of crime, and to encourage mutual ownership for community safety.

In 1982, the Metropolitan Toronto Police made organizational changes to facilitate community-based policing by decentralizing districts, introducing community officers, increasing foot patrols, and establishing two experimental mini police stations (Green & Mastrofski, 1988, p. 182). In 1985–86, the Fredericton Police Force implemented its first storefront office in a subsidized housing development in an attempt to bring the police and the community closer together to reduce police calls for service and improve the quality of life for area residents and business owners. In 1985, Halifax changed to a decentralized system of policing and increased community orientation through "zone policing" (Clairmont, 1990), and in 1987 the Victoria Police Department in British Columbia established community police stations in various areas throughout the city, demonstrating cooperative efforts between the police, citizens, and ancillary agencies (Walker et al., 1992).

One of the most researched community-based efforts in Canada in the late 1980s and 1990s involved the Edmonton Police Service. In 1987, Edmonton identified community policing as a departmental objective rooted in the "principle that policing must be based within the community rather than the criminal justice system" (Chacko & Nancoo, 1993, p. 311). Subsequently the Neighbourhood Foot Patrol Program (NFPP) was developed and implemented in 21 areas of the city. The main objectives of the NFPP were to reduce repeat calls for service, improve public satisfaction with the police, increase job satisfaction within the organization, increase reporting of crime, and solve community problems (Chacko & Nancoo, 1993, p. 313). In their evaluation of this program, Hornick, Burrows, Phillips, and Leighton (1991) concluded that foot patrol officers "were viewed as more helpful, polite, able to resolve conflict and understand feelings, and prone to provide follow-up material than motor patrol constables" (p. 69). The Edmonton NFPP is an example of a successful strategic effort in community-based policing. The Edmonton Police Service has invested heavily in in-house evaluations of its NFPP model and has participated in extensive external evaluations and follow-up studies by various academic-based institutions and the Police Executive Research Forum based in Washington, DC (Griffiths et al., 2001, p. 183).

In 1990, the RCMP announced its strategic action plan for the implementation of community-based policing nationwide. This announcement appeared to signal a new way forward. At the time, there was significant pressure for change at the RCMP that required police leaders to rethink traditional ideologies and operational strategies and to re-examine how they would deploy their resources. Police leaders encouraged their officers and the public to "buy in" to a new way of doing business. In keeping with this new philosophy, RCMP managers and members alike were required to let go of customary centralized power and authority both internally and externally. In general, the RCMP was expected to change its insular crime-fighting image, established in the professional era, to one of a community partner, willing to listen to the people in matters of public safety. Community-based policing was viewed as a significant paradigm shift that emphasized greater police accountability to the public, operational dependence, information sharing, problem solving, and proactive efforts. In 1993, the Solicitor General of Canada described this new model as a dramatic change:

> In this model, the public plays an influential part in the development of policy, designs of policing strategies and, when appropriate, participates actively in the implementation of those strategies. The ultimate goal is that this cooperative partnership between the community and the police will achieve peace and security. (Chacko & Nancoo, 1993, p. 8)

While the philosophical change to community policing was real, the traditional hierarchical structures of policing remained a barrier to the full adaptation of associated new practices. When analyzing the complex process and outcomes of a change in policing, it is necessary to understand the internal and external relationship dynamics that influence how the police conceptualize, legitimize, and respond to change. The community, governing bodies, and legislators must also be willing to engage in the process. The community and political response to changing police practices, whether positive or negative, will in some way influence the direction of the police organization and, subsequently, how the rank and file fulfill their roles and attach legitimacy to their work. Fitch (1995) described this relationship as a *social system tapestry*: a police organization has an interdependent relationship with the external environment (or community) in which it operates, and successful organizational change requires the cooperation and engagement of all of those affected. Policing is truly a reciprocal relationship between citizenry and those assigned to carry out duties in the public's best interest.

Police Governance and Accountability

Based on the fact that police officers are vested with a great deal of authority and power—including the right to use force (including lethal force) and to suspend a person's fundamental right to freedom—so too are they held to a higher level of account for their actions. The *Police Act* of each province governs the public expectations of the police. The *RCMP Act* governs the RCMP's expectations in a standardized fashion, regardless of the province RCMP officers work in. The *Canadian Charter of Rights and Freedoms* and Canada's *Criminal Code* are additional legislation under which the police operate, specifically around the use of force, search and seizure, and the powers of arrest and detention. Individual police organizations, whether they be municipal, provincial, or federal, also have reams of administrative policies and routine and standing operating procedures. Police officers can be held criminally and civilly accountable for their wrongdoings and are subject to the standards of discipline outlined in their provincial or federal policing legislation. It is the objective adherence to laws and procedures and the application of fair processes, integrity, transparency, and accountability that will uphold the public's trust and confidence in the public police during the most difficult of times.

Code of Conduct for Municipal and Provincial Police in Ontario

The code of conduct for all Ontario municipal police agencies and the Ontario Provincial Police is detailed in Ontario Regulation 268/10. In summary, it states that a chief of police or other police officer commits misconduct if he or she engages in any of the following:

- discreditable conduct
- insubordination

- neglect of duty
- deceit
- breach of confidence
- corrupt practice
- unlawful or unnecessary exercise of authority
- damage to clothing or equipment
- consuming drugs or alcohol in a manner prejudicial to duty

Canadian Policing in the 21st Century

According to Statistics Canada (2016), the actual number of police officers working across the country in 2015 was 68,777 (see Table 3.2). Of this number, 50,790 were working either for municipal (city) or provincial police agencies, and the remaining 17,987 were employed by the RCMP (Mazowita & Greenland, 2016, p. 16). These data indicate a rate of police strength of 192 police officers per 100,000 population, which is a decrease of 0.9 percent from the previous year. In 2014, the police–population ratio in Canada was 14 percent lower than in the United States and many other "peer countries"; in fact, Canada "reported the fourth lowest rate of police strength in 2012," followed by Denmark, Norway, and Finland (Hutchins, 2015, pp. 6–7).

It is important to distinguish between actual police strength and authorized police strength. Actual police strength is the number of police officers employed at a particular time, whereas authorized police strength is the number of positions that police forces are authorized to fill during a fiscal or calendar year. This distinction is significant for police leaders tasked with delivering police services and fulfilling local policing mandates. The difference between actual police strength and authorized police strength is largely attributable to unfilled vacancies due to long-term sickness, maternity/parental leaves, suspensions, retirements, or resignations. Canada's authorized police strength for 2014 (the latest data available) was 71,457 positions (Hutchins, 2015).

Operating expenditures for police services in Canada in 2014–15 totalled $13.9 billion (Mazowita & Greenland, 2016). The challenge for police leaders and governments is to determine the most effective and efficient use of both human resources (police and civilian staff) and capital resources (equipment) to optimize public safety. Since the 2008 global financial crisis, public institutions have been increasingly under pressure to find efficiencies in operating and managing their budgets. Police organizations have not been exempt from these pressures, and a considerable amount of research has been directed at the rising cost of public safety and the economics of policing and community safety (see www.publicsafety.gc.ca).

The core police functions in any police organization remain focused on emergency response, crime prevention, incident response, order maintenance, preserving the peace, investigation, crime and harm reduction, traffic investigations, and traffic enforcement.

TABLE 3.2 Police Officers, by Province and Territory, 2011–2015

	2011	2012	2013	2014	2015
Canada	**69,424**	**69,505**	**69,250**	**68,806**	**68,777**
Newfoundland and Labrador	935	926	917	895	889
Prince Edward Island	244	247	232	236	226
Nova Scotia	1,914	1,934	1,895	1,884	1,855
New Brunswick	1,377	1,364	1,344	1,290	1,278
Quebec	15,802	15,977	16,002	16,194	16,011
Ontario	26,387	26,255	26,359	26,148	26,205
Manitoba	2,593	2,706	2,691	2,646	2,602
Saskatchewan	2,306	2,298	2,306	2,294	2,286
Alberta	6,696	6,787	6,899	6,990	7,155
British Columbia	8,952	8,887	8,856	8,672	8,678
Yukon	122	119	132	135	130
Northwest Territories	197	199	192	192	201
Nunavut	130	125	128	119	131
Royal Canadian Mounted Police (RCMP) Headquarters and Training Academy	1,769	1,681	1,297	1,111	1,130

Source: Statistics Canada (2016).

In order to meet expectations, officers are required to be level headed, intelligent, ethical, skilled, competent decision-makers, and physically and mentally fit. These characteristics need to be balanced with compassion, adaptability, and resilience in order for officers to survive in the policing world of the 21st century.

In the words of the Council of Canadian Academies, "Canada's traditional model dominated by generalist patrol officers may be increasingly ill-suited to deal with the challenges of evolving crime, the complexity of the justice system, the diversity of Canadian society, and the landscape of a safety and security web" (Council of Canadian Academies, 2014, p. 97).

Police leaders are realizing that the generalist police concept of the "jack-of-all-trades" officer is insufficient in the 21st century. We also know from past experience that the insular crime-fighter model has its limitations. While the police cannot be all things to all people all of the time, as a 24/7 public service the police have become, by default, the resource to call, day or night, in a variety of troubling circumstances. Our changing public safety landscape requires the officers of today to be extra-vigilant, educated, adaptable, skilled, and competent as they attend to everything from barking dog complaints to national security and terrorism threats. The police must continue to abide by the principles of community policing and, at the same time, negotiate a few contemporary twists.

Generalists

A generalist is a front-line officer who is expected to have a wide range of community resources, skills, and connections to prevent, respond to, and intervene in a variety of calls for service. The generalist will often supply police specialists with timely information in an effort to help solve more complex matters that require specifically trained skill sets. An example might be a knowledgeable generalist working in a neighbourhood who points crime analysts, detectives, and forensic identification officers in the direction of a local prime individual known for break-and-enters in a specific area.

Due to the changing nature of crime and the complexity of policing requirements, there has been a steady move toward embracing the notion of a safety and security web (Council of Canadian Academies, 2014, pp. 36–37). The web comprises non-police organizations that interact with one another and the police to address matters of safety and security. The police, their community partners, and strategic stakeholders are realizing that they need to work together to proactively understand emerging risks based on intelligence-led policing and predictive analysis (analyzing data by statistical software and techniques to predict future crime trends). In this sense, contemporary community policing is a way of doing business to address a broad range of 21st-century issues, from vandalism to terrorism. It can be effectively used to quell seniors' fear of crime, to intervene and prevent youth radicalization, or to disrupt the cycle of violence in intimate partner relationships. In 2016, during the opening remarks at the World Safety Organization conference, the keynote speaker aptly noted that we must "act early, act on time, and act together." This sentiment is reflected in police work being done across Canada that is based on collaborative efforts, information sharing, prevention, and timely intervention.

Figure 3.3 highlights four key strategic areas that can and should collaborate when complex issues (e.g., cybercrimes and calls for service involving mental health issues) arise in the community. As an example of a potential resource-saving strategy, formal agreements between police services and other agencies are increasingly being used to provide people in crisis situations with faster assistance from the necessary health services (Council of Canadian Academies, 2014, p. 104). Properly trained mental health workers can provide timely assessment and de-escalation techniques and advise police on appropriate and successful response and interventions.

FIGURE 3.3 Contemporary Community Policing Model for Collaboration

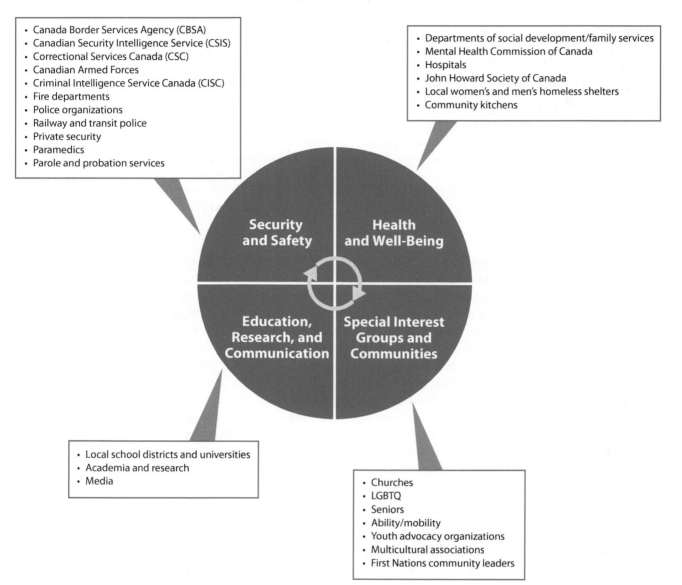

- Canada Border Services Agency (CBSA)
- Canadian Security Intelligence Service (CSIS)
- Correctional Services Canada (CSC)
- Canadian Armed Forces
- Criminal Intelligence Service Canada (CISC)
- Fire departments
- Police organizations
- Railway and transit police
- Private security
- Paramedics
- Parole and probation services

- Departments of social development/family services
- Mental Health Commission of Canada
- Hospitals
- John Howard Society of Canada
- Local women's and men's homeless shelters
- Community kitchens

Security and Safety

Health and Well-Being

Education, Research, and Communication

Special Interest Groups and Communities

- Local school districts and universities
- Academia and research
- Media

- Churches
- LGBTQ
- Seniors
- Ability/mobility
- Youth advocacy organizations
- Multicultural associations
- First Nations community leaders

Safety and Security Web

The safety and security web is a source of specialized knowledge, skills and resources that can assist police in responding to internal and external trends and challenges in policing. The changing nature of threats requires police to work with a range of actors: for example, national and international security institutions, in the case of terrorism threats and transit authorities and other first responders in the case of environmental threats. (Council of Canadian Academies, 2014, p. 141)

Contemporary Community Policing

Contemporary community policing involves various methods of policing. It is not about the delivery of several unrelated programs or initiatives; instead, it is about how each element interacts with and weaves among others, addressing a variety of public safety and social disorder issues. In 2013, Philadelphia Police Commissioner Charles Ramsey was quoted as saying that we need to move from the thin blue line mentality to a "thin blue thread" mentality, using the metaphor of a fabric that comprises many threads working together. In Ramsey's words, "the profession of policing is still based on the principles of Sir Robert Peel, and yet our profession changes and reflects the values, social structure, technology advancements, and political demands of the times" (Wyllie, 2013). Here you can see a recurring theme noted earlier in this chapter (Fitch, 1995), where we argued that the *social system tapestry* of policing is fundamental to successful policing. We simply cannot abandon the critical importance of the interdependency of human and capital resources in our effort to preserve the peace and maintain social order.

SIDEBAR

The Thin Blue Thread

Philadelphia Police Commissioner Charles Ramsey said something really quite interesting: he challenged the metaphor of the thin blue line separating good and evil—separating law-abiding citizens from the dangerous and violent criminals who intend to do harm. He stated: "The problem with being a line is that you're separate and apart from those two things. You're really not a part of either side. I like to think—and as I've gotten older and more mature in this job, I've come to see—a more accurate metaphor, in my opinion. It is one in which the police are seen as a thread woven thorough the communities we serve—a thread that helps hold those communities together, creating a tapestry that reinforces the very fabric of democracy" (Wyllie, 2013).

Community Policing Models and Strategies

Commonly used methods in contemporary community policing include problem-solving models and programs (such as those focused on priority and prolific offenders), crime mapping and data analysis, intelligence-led policing, crime prevention through environmental design, and crime prevention through social development. Contemporary community policing places significant emphasis on prevention, intervention, and crime and harm reduction, but this emphasis is not to be mistaken for a "soft-on-crime approach," as enforcement and investigation remain integral to effective policing. In community policing, technology has become a double-edged sword: while technology provides the police with tools to fight crime, collect and track intelligence, and share information, it also provides criminals with ways of committing crime that continually present new challenges for police.

The SARA Model

One notable community policing problem-solving model is SARA (Scanning—Analysis—Response—Assessment), which was developed by Eck and Spelman in 1987 to "operationalize problem-oriented policing" (Hudy as cited in O'Regan & Reid, 2013, p. 72). The SARA model has been used by numerous North American agencies since the mid-1990s. Based on this model, police begin by "Scanning" to determine whether a problem really exists. Next, they engage in "Analysis" to learn everything possible about the problem (what is happening, when, where, and how). Then, they apply a customized "Response" to the problem. Last, police undertake an "Assessment," evaluating the effectiveness of their response by looking at the process they followed and reviewing whether the problem was solved or mitigated.

The CAPRA Model

In the mid-1990s, the RCMP developed a community policing problem-solving model called CAPRA.[2] It took conventional models like SARA one step further by incorporating all of the critical elements of modern policing, including both community-oriented and problem-oriented elements. CAPRA combines the traditional skills of acquiring and analyzing information (Acquiring and Analyzing Information) and responding professionally to a public safety issue (Response) with the new requirements of client service (Clients—Direct & Indirect), public accountability (Partnerships), and continuous learning (Assessment). Each component of the model asks police to answer key questions to ensure that the process is fully addressed, as the following sections show. The model is typically presented as a series of concentric circles (see Figure 3.4), reinforcing the idea that police need to continuously seek additional information, adapt, redefine, respond, assess, adapt responses, and reassess. Also, the circular design focuses on the need to keep clients and partnerships in mind at all times. CAPRA is more than just a problem-solving model in that it provides an operational framework from which to provide policing services.

FIGURE 3.4   CAPRA Model

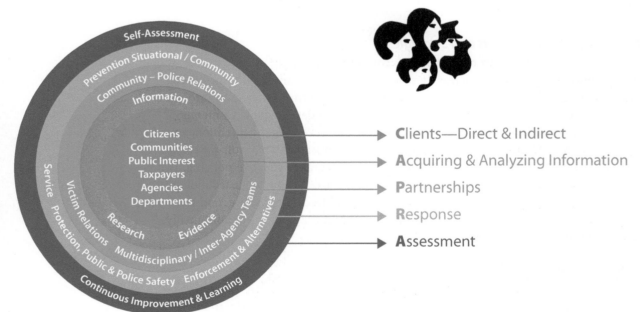

Clients

Who are my direct clients in this situation?

What are their needs, demands, and expectations?

Who are my indirect clients in this situation?

What are their needs, demands, and expectations?

Clients are the people police interact with when delivering their services as well as the people who receive these services. They are at the centre of the model because all policing is done in response to clients' needs, demands, and expectations. As well, problems are defined in light of clients' needs.

As a result, police are required to understand their clients' perspectives and respond to the needs of all those they interact with. Even suspects and prisoners are considered to be clients, since police have a professional obligation to treat them with respect for human dignity and, when necessary, to protect their well-being. Clients are involved, as appropriate, in generating and selecting response options, developing action plans to implement the selected options, and assessing the service provided.

There are two types of clients:

1. *Direct clients:* Those whom police interact with at various points in their service delivery or investigations. Examples of direct clients are complainants, victims, witnesses, suspects, and prisoners.
2. *Indirect clients:* Those not directly involved in an incident or its investigation, but who have an interest in its outcome either because of the way it was handled or because of the association of the incident to similar incidents. Examples of indirect clients are the public, other government agencies or departments, and interest groups.

A client component is not found in any other policing model. CAPRA is unique because it teaches police that the public interest is best understood and served by learning about and working with direct clients and the community, appreciating their needs and interests.

Acquiring and Analyzing Information

What do I already know that will help me to deal with this situation?

What do I need to know that will help me to deal with this situation?

Acquiring and analyzing information is essential to continuously assessing risk during an incident, gathering critical evidence, solving a crime, apprehending a suspect, and presenting a thorough case to ensure the fair outcome of a situation, whether through the judicial system or alternative means. When engaged in preventive problem solving, the more information police have and the better the analysis in consideration of clients' perspectives, the more likely police are to define the problem appropriately, based on the clients' needs, and to arrive at a mutually agreed on response or solution to the problem. Information is acquired from various sources, such as clients and partners, and through research. Research can be as simple as conducting computer checks on a suspect or as complex as crime mapping and geographical profiling.

Partnerships

Who can help me to deal with this situation?

Partners are anyone within the organization (e.g., Police Dog Services, Forensic Identification Section), other government departments or agencies (e.g., Emergency Medical Services, Child and Family Services), or the community (e.g., church pastor, scientist) who can assist police in providing better-quality and more timely service. Establishing and maintaining partnerships on an ongoing basis provides several benefits:

1. It develops the trust needed to know that partners will be available when required.
2. It ensures that police are aware of all existing potential partners so that the best information or assistance is available to clients as soon as possible.
3. It builds contingency plans so that when assistance is required, it is immediately available.
4. It ensures clients receive assistance and follow-up through volunteers when police have to attend to other priorities.

Response

What is my primary responsibility?

What is the public interest, and how is it best served in this situation and in this set of circumstances?

Which client(s) should get priority at various stages of an incident?

Four types of responses are available to police:

1. *Service:* Assisting the public and referring them to appropriate partners.
2. *Protection (public and police safety):* Protecting the public, victims, and those affected by their victimization in partnership with community agencies and experts.
3. *Enforcement and alternatives:* Laying charges and proceeding through the judicial system so that offenders are held accountable is, at times, in the public's best interest. At other times, non-enforcement measures (such as restorative justice) are appropriate.
4. *Prevention (situational/community):* Preventing incidents (offences or problems) from occurring or escalating through intervention, proactive problem-solving, and education.

Police must determine what their primary responsibility is in terms of how the public interest is best served in a particular situation, keeping in mind two things: that elements from more than one of these responses may need to be implemented in order to address all the needs and interests of the client, and that the ideal response can change over the course of an investigation or incident.

Assessment

How could my partners and I have handled that better?

What should we do differently next time?

Did we consult victims and other community members who were affected by the problem?

Did we examine any trends?

Are there any lessons learned that could be shared?

Police must assess their performance in order to continuously improve the quality of their service. They must also monitor incidents and detect patterns in partnership with their clients to solve problems and prevent similar situations from occurring.

The CAPRA model is an operational application of the RCMP's vision and mission. It combines the RCMP's commitment to communities and clients, problem solving in partnership, and continuous learning. The CAPRA model helped to define the competencies necessary for effective community policing. It is taught as part of the recruit training course standard with the RCMP and has been adopted in some form or another by many police agencies and academies across the country. The CAPRA model demonstrates the way in which police officers are expected to treat those with whom they come into contact and how best to assess and address their needs.

CAREER PROFILE

Christine Hudy

Christine Hudy manages the Training Program Support and Evaluation (TPSE) for the RCMP in Regina. She designs and develops the curriculum for the Cadet Training Program.

How did you first become interested in criminal justice and policing?
While working at the University of Regina, I had the opportunity to teach a workshop to a class composed entirely of RCMP officers and civilian employees. As we chatted about criminal justice, policing, and training, I became fascinated by those disciplines and the innovative instructional design approaches being used to develop the Cadet Training Program. I joined the RCMP six months after that workshop!

How did you reach your current position?
I developed a passion for adult education, distance education, instructional design, and educational technology by working at Parkland Regional College and the University of Regina in Saskatchewan early in my career. This experience brought me to the RCMP Academy in Regina, where I became the first instructional designer hired in TPSE. I have now been given the opportunity to manage TPSE, which has evolved into a unit of 15 staff who design and develop curriculum for the RCMP's full scope of induction training.

Describe a typical day for you. What are some of your most important duties?
What I love about my job is that there is no such thing as a typical day. This is the nature of policing and police training. I have two duties I consider most important. First, I provide guidance and support to the teams in TPSE. Second, I often liaise with the other stakeholders on base impacted by the ongoing changes to training. I constantly remind myself of the great responsibility we have to ensure our police officers receive the best training possible so they can provide safe and effective policing service.

What are the most challenging and most rewarding aspects of your job?
Like most other professions, policing undergoes constant and rapid change. Keeping training up to date is challenging and requires us to respond quickly. Nonetheless, it is a tremendous honour to be part of an organization with the history and reputation that the RCMP has, and I am very proud to play a role in "creating" Mounties who go out across our great country and serve the Canadian public.

What are some of the most important skills cadets learn at the training academy?
The most important skill cadets learn is critical thinking. Policing is an increasingly complex and demanding profession, and no two calls are the same. We not only teach cadets the knowledge and skills they will need as police officers, but also teach them the processes for dealing with policing situations. Ultimately, we want our police officers to critically examine every situation so they can make ethical decisions and take appropriate action.

What are some of the unique challenges of being a national police force? How does this impact how cadets are trained?
Being a national police force means that our officers must be prepared to work in diverse settings. We have outlined a set of common competencies that define the standards of performance and behaviour required for a general duty police officer, regardless of where he or she will be working. After cadets graduate from the RCMP Academy, they enter the next phase of training, the Field Coaching Program, at their first detachment. During this six-month period, they build on the knowledge and skills acquired in the Cadet Training Program while performing policing duties under the mentorship of an experienced officer.

Recruitment and Changing Standards

An important focus for police leaders looking to optimize public safety dollars is to seek new ways to recruit, train, and deploy employees. Police candidates who do not possess core values such as integrity, compassion, professionalism, and respect, and who are inadequately trained, are more likely to make poor decisions that will result in *Police Act* complaints or criminal allegations. The cost of poor or inadequate recruiting and training practices are extremely high, ranging from Charter violations, use-of-force lawsuits, discreditable conduct charges, corruption, unlawful arrests, and illegal detention, to name a few. For example, an officer who does not fully understand his or her lawful powers of arrest, and search and seizure may unintentionally violate the rights that provide for a citizen's freedom from unlawful detention and search. The overall damage to the reputation of one's organization and loss of public trust and confidence in the policing profession erodes the ability of the police to do their job effectively.

Prior to the 1970s, provincial and municipal police recruit training was sporadic; officers were hired based on physical strength and general character and went to work without standardized training and, in some cases, with minimal education. As public expectations for professional service rose, so too did the demand for better recruitment processes, qualifications, and training. Police recruitment standards are essentially consistent across Canada. At a minimum, the applicant is required to have a high school diploma, have a clean criminal background, have Canadian citizenship or landed immigrant status, be at least 19 years of age, be physically and mentally fit, be of good character with good references, and have an active driver's licence. Some agencies and academies require that the applicant have completed a one- to two-year police foundation course prior to acceptance. Over the last 30 years, police recruits increasingly have some university courses, a college diploma, and/or undergraduate and graduate degrees prior to applying for recruitment. The selection process typically includes physical and aptitude testing, written examinations, psychological testing, and, in all provinces except New Brunswick and Ontario, a polygraph examination as part of ethics and integrity testing. Recruit training varies across the country, with some recruits graduating from the Ontario Police College, École nationale de police du Québec, or the Atlantic Police Academy. Some larger municipal agencies (e.g., Calgary Police Service) have their own recruit training programs. The RCMP provides its recruits with basic training at the "Depot" Division in Regina.

Once a recruit has been accepted into a training program, he or she will undertake a combination of courses that focus on academic learning, and functional and technical skill development. Field experience is gained through an on-the-job training period where the recruit is paired with a **coach officer**. Functional, technical, and core competency training cover topics such as report writing, criminal law, use-of-force techniques, firearms and driver training, physical fitness, communication, community policing, investigation, de-escalation techniques, role-playing, and court testimony. Training includes a blend of classroom learning, hands-on, e-learning, and repetitive practice. Adherence to lawful order, chain of command, team building, and peer support are often intertwined in the learning environment and reinforced through traditional paramilitary exercises such as drills, parade marching in formation, and group discipline. Once a recruit is a successful graduate of basic training from an accredited police institution and begins employment, he or she is typically paired with a training officer or coach officer for a period of time.

coach officer
An experienced officer who works with a new constable, also called a *field training officer*.

The foundational recruit training is the beginning of a career-long journey of continuous learning that is required in modern policing. In-service training opportunities are provided throughout an officer's career to ensure that he or she maintains core policing skills in areas such as firearms proficiency, first aid, use-of-force and de-escalation techniques, case law, and cultural competency. Specialized courses (e.g., forensic identification, cybercrime, accident reconstruction, explosive disposal, police service dog handling, polygraph, and incident command) are also available through police academies, the Canadian Police College, the RCMP, universities, and colleges.

Policing and Mental Health Challenges

Since the late 20th century, the area of mental health has produced new challenges for both front-line and administrative policing.

In the 1980s, a trend to de-institutionalize people with severe mental illness created an influx of police calls involving mental health issues in communities across the country. De-institutionalization alone was not problematic, but the lack of housing and support services available to successfully integrate this vulnerable population into local communities created enormous challenges. What followed were a number of high-conflict and high-profile incidents between police and people with varying degrees of mental illness. Unfortunately, police were largely untrained and unprepared to deal with these complex issues. Efforts have since been made, and continue to be made, to improve the outcomes of these interactions through community partnership, training, and collaboration. In fact, the Canadian Association of Chiefs of Police has partnered with the Mental Health Commission of Canada in a strategic effort to improve a nationwide community policing response and intervention approach aimed at reducing conflict and tragedy in these often challenging calls for service involving this vulnerable segment of our population.

Over the past ten to 15 years, society has more openly acknowledged that mental illness can affect anyone. This understanding has impacted policing with respect to employee wellness and compensation cases. The incidence of reported post-traumatic stress disorder (PTSD) has increased in policing, which is a clear departure from the old culture where police officers were expected to "suck it up" and not buckle from the weight of witnessed trauma compounded over time and through exposure to significantly abnormal events. From an administrative perspective, the issues associated with mental illness have brought police agencies under intense external scrutiny for mishandled calls for service, and they have caused internal staffing challenges in terms of accommodating those suffering from workplace-related illness.

Technology

Technological advances produce both new opportunities and challenges in policing. While rapidly changing technology has provided the police with new tools, so too have these advantages been made available to others to use for criminal purposes. Just as modernized transportation had an impact on the speed at which criminals could physically travel from one policing jurisdiction to another, so too has information technology changed the dynamic of policing and created new frontiers for crime. The rapid mobilization of criminals between jurisdictions that was experienced with the advent of trains, cars, and planes from the late 18th to 20th centuries pales in comparison to the rapid mobilization of criminals online. No longer does a person need to be on the scene to commit a crime, and yet they can inflict damage with the stroke of a key or a voice-activated device. Information technology has created a new "a-spatial" dimension in the reality of everyday policing. Traditional crimes such as fraud, sexual exploitation, threats, harassment, youth radicalization, and terrorism, for example, are amplified and made more complex through the use of technology. Consequently, a shift toward a "pan-government" approach to policing is taking place in recognition of the long reach of cybercrime and the complexity of cybersecurity. Freed from geographical boundaries, police agencies are facing unparalleled challenges for which they remain all too commonly ill-prepared to prevent, intervene, or respond effectively. Aggravating this reality is the lack of robust and current legislation in Canada related to cybercrime.

Over and above the technological implications related to crime and criminal investigation, consider the impact of both traditional and social media on the public's perception of policing: because police officer's actions are so easily recorded and shared, policing attitudes and officer behaviour are undeniable. As noted earlier in this chapter, the issue of governance and accountability are critically important to maintaining the public's trust and confidence in the police. Various forms of media provide the public with minute-by-minute accounts of events as they unfold. On one hand, this provides for greater transparency and accountability of policing, and on the other it has created opportunities for individuals to intentionally or unintentionally perpetuate misinformation. The implications of technology in and on policing is the subject of great interest and controversy, covering a broad array of issues.

> **What Do You Think?**
>
> 1. If you were an officer, what would you consider to be the dangers and advantages of policing in the age of social media?
>
> 2. As an officer, would you post about your personal life online (e.g., have a Facebook page)? Why or why not?
>
> 3. Are police organizational policies on the use of social media important?
>
> 4. How can social media be used lawfully for investigations?
>
> 5. What role do social media play in contemporary community policing?

Conclusion

As you have read in this chapter, policing has a long history and tradition of professional practice. The policing strategies discussed in this chapter are built on this foundation. It is critical going forward that governments, community leaders, and police organizations conduct meaningful internal and external evaluations and gap analyses to identify critical risk areas that Canadian police agencies are unable to effectively address alone. The changing nature of crime underscores the reality that modern policing is about far more than just the number of officers and calls for service. Frank conversations and explorations of civilianization, specialization, training, safety and security webs, and human resource management will continue to be of pressing importance as policing continues to evolve in the 21st century.

DISCUSSION QUESTIONS

1. Sir Robert Peel covered a number of areas in his nine principles. In the context of today's policing environment, are there any other principles you would add?
2. Police agencies always have continued public support and approval as a goal. What challenges do you see in the early stages of this century that pose a threat to achieving this goal?
3. An increasing number of police operations depend on covert (or secretive), coercive, and deceptive techniques. These techniques can range from using unmarked police cars to catch speeding drivers to having undercover operatives pose as heroin drug dealers. When are such practices justifiable? Is there a time when they are not? (For a detailed example, jump ahead to Chapter 4's discussion of "Mr. Big" operations.)

NOTES

1 This brief chapter of policing is not written from an average perspective. The author is a veteran police officer of 32 years' service in the profession and is currently serving as a chief of police. The views presented are her own and not reflective of her police organization or her employer.
2 The section on the CAPRA model is adapted from Chapter 3 of the first edition of this text, by Christine Hudy, with permission.

SUGGESTED FURTHER READINGS

Police Sector Council, http://www.policecouncil.ca.
Sheehan, D., & Oosten, R. (2006). *Behind the badge: History of the RCMP "Depot" Division.* Regina: Centax Books.

REFERENCES

Braiden, C. (1985). *Bank robberies and stolen bikes: Thoughts of a street cop.* Ottawa: Minister of Solicitor General.

Canadian Broadcasting Corporation. (2013, November 10). Surge in private security raises concerns over rights. *CBC News.* Retrieved from http://www.cbc.ca/news/canada/surge-in-private-security-raises-concerns-over-rights-1.1335730.

Chacko, J., & Nancoo, S. (1993). *Community policing in Canada.* Toronto: Canadian Scholars Press.

Clairmont, D.J.. (1990). *To the forefront: Community-based zone policing in Halifax.* Ottawa, ON: Canadian Police College.

Cooper, H.S. (1981). The evolution of Canadian police. In W.T. McGrath & M.P. Mitchell (Eds.), *The police function in Canada.* Agincourt, ON: Methuen.

Council of Canadian Academies. (2014). *Policing Canada in the 21st century: New policing for new challenges.* Ottawa: Author.

First Nations Police. (n.d.). Retrieved from http://www.canadianpoliceservices.com/firstnations_police.html.

Fitch, L.J. (1995). *Reviving the peeler: A case study of organizational change and community-based policing* (Unpublished master's thesis). University of New Brunswick, Fredericton.

Forward, G.J. (2016). *The origins and evolution of policing and criminal justice in Fredericton, New Brunswick: 1785–1916* (Thesis). University of New Brunswick, Fredericton.

Green, J.R., & Mastrofski, S. (1988). *Community policing: Rhetoric or reality?* New York: Praeger.

Griffiths, C.T., Parent, R.B., & Whitelaw, B. (2001). *Community policing in Canada.* Nelson Thompson Learning.

Harring, S.L. (1991). *Policing a class society: The experience of American cities 1865–1983.* New Brunswick, NJ: Rutgers University Press.

Higley, D.D. (1984). *O.P.P.: The history of the Ontario Provincial Police force.* Toronto: The Queen's Printer.

Hornick, J.P., Burrows, B.A., Phillips, D.M., & Leighton, B. (1991). An impact evaluation of the Edmonton Neighbourhood Foot Patrol Program. *Canadian Journal of Program Evaluation, 6*(1), 47–70.

Hovbrender, A. (2011). *Situational analysis of the private security industry and national occupational standards for security guards, private investigators and armoured car guards.* Ottawa: Police Sector Council.

Hutchins, H. (2015). Police resources in Canada, 2014. *Juristat, 36*(1). Catalogue No. 85-002-X. Retrieved from http://www.statcan.gc.ca/pub/85-002-x/2015001/article/14146-eng.pdf.

Johnson, R. (1992). *Back to the Basics. Community and Aboriginal Policing Bulletin, April:*1-11.

Kelly, W., & Kelly, N. (1976) *Policing in Canada.* Toronto: MacMillian.

Li, G. (2008). Private security and public policing. *Juristat, 28*(10). Catalogue No. 85-002-X. Retrieved from http://www.statcan.gc.ca/pub/85-002-x/2008010/article/10730-eng.htm.

Lundman, R.J. (1980). *Police and policing: An introduction.* New York: Holt, Rinehart and Winston.

Manning, P.K. (1977). *Police work: The social organization of policing.* Cambridge, MA: MIT Press.

Mazowita, B., & Greenland, J. (2016). Police resources in Canada, 2015. *Juristat, 36*(1). Catalogue No. 85-002-X. Retrieved from http://www.statcan.gc.ca/pub/85-002-x/2016001/article/14323-eng.pdf.

Norris, D.F. (1973). Police community relations. Lexington, MA: Lexington Books.

O'Regan, K., & Reid, S. (2013). *Thinking about criminal justice in Canada.* Toronto: Emond Montgomery.

Royal Canadian Mounted Police. (n.d.). National Police Services (NPS). Retrieved from http://www.rcmp-grc.gc.ca/sps/nps-snp-eng.htm.

Royal Canadian Mounted Police. (2016). Organizational structure. Retrieved from http://www.rcmp-grc.gc.ca/about-ausujet/organi-eng.htm.

Ruddell, R., & Jones, N.A. (2014). The economics of Canadian policing five years into the great recession. Regina: Collaborative Centre for Justice and Safety.

Saint John Police Museum. (n.d.). History of the Saint John Police Force. Retrieved from http://saintjohnnbpolicemuseum.webs.com/history.htm.

Seagrave, J. (1993, November 13–17). Listening to what people say: Implementation and evaluation of community consultative groups. *RCMP Gazette, 55*(11).

Seagrave, J. (1997). *Introduction to policing in Canada.* Scarborough, ON: Prentice-Hall.

Statistics Canada. (2009a). Table 1: Police officers, private investigators and security guards Canada 1991, 1996, 2001, and 2006. Retrieved from http://www.statcan.gc.ca/pub/85-002-x/2008010/article/10730/tbl/tbl1-eng.htm.

Statistics Canada. (2009b). Table 1: Trends in police personnel and expenditures, Canada, 1962 to 2009. Retrieved from http://www.statcan.gc.ca/pub/85-225-x/2009000/t001-eng.htm.

Statistics Canada. (2012a). Police resources in Canada, 2012. (Ottawa: Minister of Industry, 2013). Retrieved from http://www.statcan.gc.ca/pub/85-225-x/85-225-x2012000-eng.pdf.

Statistics Canada. (2012b). Table 2: Police officers by province/territory, 2010. Retrieved from http://www.statcan.gc.ca/pub/85-225-x/2010000/t002-eng.htm.

Statistics Canada. (2016). Police officers, by province and territory [2011–2015]. Retrieved from http://www.statcan.gc.ca/tables-tableaux/sum-som/l01/cst01/legal05a-eng.htm.

Walker, S.G., Walker, C., & McDavid, J. (1992). *The Victoria community police stations: A three year evaluation*. Ottawa: Minister of Supply and Services.

Weiner, N.L. (1976). *The role of the police in urban society: Conflicts and consequences*. Indianapolis. Bobbs-Merrill.

Wilson, J.Q. (1969). *Varieties of police behavior*. Cambridge, MA: Harvard University Press.

Wyllie, D. (2013). IACP 2013: Commissioner Charles Ramsey envisions a thin blue thread. *PoliceOne.com*. Retrieved from http://www.policeone.com/police-products/police-technology/articles/6531959-IACP-2013-Commissioner-Charles-Ramsey-envisions-a-thin-blue-thread/.

Policing and the Law

LEARNING OUTCOMES

After reading this chapter, students will be able to:

- Discuss the impact of the *Canadian Charter of Rights and Freedoms* on police powers.

- Distinguish between police detention and arrest, and discuss the powers of police to detain and arrest suspects.

- Understand the distinction between custodial and non-custodial interrogation techniques.

- Understand the common law powers and statutory powers relating to search and seizure in Canada.

- Consider the importance of use of force as an option to resolve conflict and understand the legal provisions for police use of force.

- Understand the National Use of Force Framework and identify the factors that guide police in determining how to respond to a situation.

- Discuss police accountability and the complaints process models used to investigate allegations of police wrongdoing.

Introduction

In Canada, a number of legislative frameworks define the roles, powers, and responsibilities of the police. In general terms, police officers act on behalf of the government and society to prevent criminal activity, detect and apprehend criminals, preserve the peace, enforce laws, respond to emergencies, assist victims of crimes, and assist in the prosecution of offenders. Indeed, we all rely on the police to maintain law and order and keep us safe.

However, a conflict arises in our **adversarial system** of criminal justice between the legal mandate of the police to maintain order and the values and processes that exist in a democracy. For years, Canadians have attempted to balance the competing imperatives of crime control and due process without compromising the rights of the accused and the integrity of the administration of justice. We have sought to preserve basic procedural fairness to accused persons without unduly limiting society's interest in solving crimes and convicting the guilty. Without question, this debate will continue into the future.

adversarial system
System of justice in which cases are argued by two opposing sides, the prosecution and the defence, both of which are responsible for fully and forcefully presenting their respective positions; cases are heard and decided by an impartial judge.

The aftermath of terror: Cathy Cirillo (left) at the memorial for her son, Corporal Nathan Cirillo, killed by an extremist Islamic sympathizer. Above right, mourners gather near the Quebec City mosque where a white supremacist murdered Muslims at prayer in January 2017.

As you may recall from Chapter 1, the authors identify five competing models of criminal justice, or normative value positions: crime control, welfare, justice, community change, and restorative justice models. On January 20, 2015, the federal government introduced the *Anti-terrorism Act, 2015* (Bill C-51), an omnibus security bill. The proposed amendments in Bill C-51 sought to expand the powers of Canada's spy agency, the Canadian Security Intelligence Service (CSIS), and give the RCMP new powers to combat the growing threat of terrorism. The then-governing Conservatives, under the leadership of Prime Minister Stephen Harper, said the measures contained in the bill were necessary to prevent or mitigate threats to national security and keep Canadians safe. Recently, the government of Canada has been particularly concerned about the radicalization and recruitment of foreign fighters abroad. Certain terrorist organizations—such as the so-called Islamic State (ISIS)—have been able to recruit an unprecedented number of men and women from the West, including Canada. Moreover, these extremist groups have been particularly adept at inspiring terrorist acts around the world.

The Harper government tabled its anti-terror legislation following the lone-wolf attacks in October 2014 on Warrant Officer Patrice Vincent in Saint-Jean-sur-Richelieu, Quebec, and Corporal Nathan Cirillo in Ottawa. Bill C-51 would bring about significant changes to Canadian legislation, including the *Criminal Code* and the *Canadian Security Intelligence Service Act*. The most notable amendments contained in the legislation include the following:

1. A new criminal offence was created for knowingly promoting or encouraging someone to carry out terrorist attacks against Canadians. The bill also criminalized the dissemination of terrorist literature and propaganda.
2. Law enforcement agencies were given the authority to arrest someone without a warrant based on suspicion that the individual might engage in or promote an act of terrorism.

3. The government's "no-fly" list was expanded to include Canadians planning to travel abroad to join extremist groups, such as ISIS. The bill also gave security officials the power to revoke passports from suspected extremists.

4. Judges were given the authority to order the removal of terrorist propaganda from the Internet.

5. Law enforcement officials were given the authority to detain a terror suspect in preventive detention without charge for a period of up to seven days.

6. Information-sharing provisions would allow law enforcement and national security agencies to access Canadians' personal and confidential information without their knowledge or consent, as long as the information is related to national security.

7. CSIS was given the authority to actively disrupt suspected terror plots, including "interference with the economic or financial stability of Canada or its infrastructure."

8. Some court proceedings (such as immigration hearings) would be allowed to be sealed at any point in the process in order to protect sensitive and classified information.

Bill C-51 sparked a firestorm of criticism across the political spectrum. Many security experts have argued that the legislation is overly broad and could jeopardize fundamental rights and freedoms, such as the right to privacy, freedom of expression, and of peaceful assembly (i.e., the ability to protest). Moreover, the legislation greatly expands the powers and mandate of CSIS, but lacks sufficient oversight to hold CSIS accountable.

Although highly controversial, Bill C-51 came into force on June 18, 2015. In July 2015, both the Canadian Civil Liberties Association (CCLA) and the Canadian Journalists for Free Expression (CJFE) launched a constitutional challenge against it, saying that some provisions in the new law threaten Canadians' rights to privacy, freedom of expression, and due process.

Newly elected Prime Minister Justin Trudeau said his government would repeal certain parts of the anti-terrorism law and introduce new legislation that balances civil liberties with public safety. In September 2016, the Liberal government announced it would hold public consultations to seek Canadians' input regarding amendments to Bill C-51 before implementing any changes to the current law.

Criminal law is far from static. Whether a result of law that has developed through court decisions (i.e., common law) or legislative changes made by federal and provincial governments, the legal landscape in Canada is forever changing. Consequently, police powers are constantly evolving. The introduction in 1982 of the *Canadian Charter of Rights and Freedoms* has undoubtedly affected the way police officers carry out their law enforcement mandate. This chapter will examine the impact of the Charter on the following powers that the police exercise in the course of their duties:

- detention and arrest
- search and seizure
- use of force

What Do You Think?

Which of the models of criminal justice (see Chapter 1) does Bill C-51 fit into? Do you agree with the legislative changes it has brought about? Do you think they will help prevent terrorism in Canada?

Police Powers to Detain and Arrest
Charter Considerations

The enactment of the Charter has had a profound impact on the legal powers of the police and has placed limits on what officers can do when investigating crime. Two sections of the Charter are particularly important when considering the concepts of arrest and detention. First, s 9 prohibits state agents, usually police, from arbitrarily detaining or imprisoning individuals. This means that police must have a valid reason for detaining or imprisoning someone. Second, everyone who has been arrested or detained has the right under s 10(a) to be informed of the reasons for the detention or arrest, while s 10(b) entitles persons to be informed of their right to legal counsel and to retain and instruct counsel without delay.

SIDEBAR

Key Sections of the Charter Relating to Detention and Arrest

Detention or imprisonment
   9. Everyone has the right not to be arbitrarily detained or imprisoned.
Arrest or detention
   10. Everyone has the right on arrest or detention
      (a) to be informed promptly of the reasons therefor;
      (b) to retain and instruct counsel without delay and to be informed of that right; and
      (c) to have the validity of the detention determined by way of *habeas corpus* and to be released if the detention is not lawful.

Detention

Contrary to popular belief, an arrest is not the first contact accused persons have with the criminal justice system. Police officers in Canada can detain, question, and search a suspect for investigative purposes before making an arrest. Historically, this authority has not always existed, because the common law has been restrictive in granting powers to police. For example, police did not have the right to detain an individual, only to arrest a person if the officers had reasonable grounds to do so. In more recent years, however, the courts have acknowledged that a natural consequence of the general duties of police officers is the power to enforce the law. This means that the police have the ability to use force—in detaining, searching, and arresting persons suspected of criminal activity. The police power to detain for investigative purposes has its origins in the *ancillary powers doctrine.*

The Ancillary Powers Doctrine

The *ancillary powers doctrine* is the process through which new police powers can be created by way of common law (also known as case law or precedent). Common law is developed by judges through decisions of the courts rather than through legislative action by Parliament. When delineating the police powers of investigative detention, the Supreme Court of Canada, in *R v Mann* (2004), stated that the common law should reflect "current and emerging societal needs and values" (para. 17). The Supreme Court held that police officers may detain a person for investigative purposes, provided that a clear connection exists between the person to be detained and a recent or ongoing criminal offence (para. 34).

What Do You Think?

Do you think that judges should be allowed to create police powers, or should such substantive changes to the law be enacted by Parliament and enshrined in statute?

At what point is an individual detained within the meaning of the Charter? "Detention" includes a broad range of encounters between police officers and members of the public. Nevertheless, police cannot be said to detain within the meaning of the Charter every suspect they stop for investigative purposes. While an individual who is stopped is being detained in the sense that he or she is "delayed" or "kept waiting," it is important to note that the constitutional rights recognized by ss 9 and 10 are not engaged unless the delay involves significant physical or psychological restraint; the police are not prohibited from interacting with members of the public. However, the situation becomes fundamentally different once police have specific grounds to connect an individual to a crime. Once there is a link between the person stopped and a recent or ongoing criminal offence, the encounter becomes an investigative detention (*R v Mann*, 2004). According to the Supreme Court of Canada in *R v Therens* (1985), a detention occurs when a police officer "assumes control over the movement of a person by a demand or direction which may have significant legal consequence and which prevents or impedes access to counsel" (para. 49). Correspondingly, the duty to inform an individual of his or her s 10(b) Charter right to retain and instruct counsel is triggered at the outset of an investigative detention. Such detentions are to be brief, and they do not impose an obligation on the suspect to answer questions posed by the police (*R v Mann*, 2004, para. 45).

IN-CLASS EXERCISE

Detention or Not?

Consider the following scenario, respond to the questions that follow, and discuss your answers (and reasons for them) as a class:

Ally Walken and her dog, Spot, are out for their daily walk around the neighbourhood. A police officer approaches Walken and tells her that there has been a series of break-ins in the community and that the police are investigating. A second patrol car arrives during the encounter. One of the officers asks Walken if she has seen anything unusual or suspicious, and requests that she produce some identification.

1. Is this scenario an example of a detention within the meaning of the Charter?
2. Is Ally Walken being detained for investigative purposes?
3. What if, during the initial questioning of Walken, officers receive information by radio that includes a detailed description of the suspect and the description matches the appearance of Walken? In this context, is there a legitimate reason for the officers to exercise police investigative powers?

Arrest

The authority police have to make an arrest is granted under different legislation, including federal statutes such as the *Criminal Code* and *Controlled Drugs and Substances Act*, as well as provincial laws such as motor vehicle statutes (e.g., Ontario's *Highway Traffic Act*). Police officers can make an arrest under various circumstances, including to prevent the commission of a criminal offence, to compel the attendance of the accused in court, and to end an offence against public order, such as causing an unnecessary disturbance (i.e., breach of the peace). An **arrest** occurs when a police officer assumes control over the movement of a person by a demand or direction.

When can a police officer make an arrest? If an arrest is justified, and if time permits, the officer can seek an **arrest warrant** by swearing an **information** in front of a justice of the peace (or a judge) alleging that a criminal offence has been committed. If the justice of the peace agrees that there are "reasonable grounds to believe that it is necessary in the public interest," a warrant will be issued directing the police to apprehend the person named in the warrant and bring that individual before a justice of the peace as soon as practicable. Once the warrant has been issued, s 29 of the *Criminal Code* requires that the arresting officer give notice to the named person of the existence of the warrant, advise of the reason for it, and produce it if requested, if it is feasible to do so.

Police officers are exposed to a variety of situations, sometimes requiring them to act quickly. To illustrate: a police officer may observe a suspect committing a criminal act, such as robbery. In an instance such as this, it is not reasonable for the officer to go to a justice of the peace before swearing the information. Is it possible for the police to make an arrest without a warrant?

According to s 495(1) of the *Criminal Code*, police officers are granted the authority to arrest without a warrant

- a person who has committed an indictable offence or who, on reasonable grounds, they believe has committed or is about to commit an indictable offence;
- a person whom they find committing a criminal offence; or
- a person in respect of whom they have reasonable grounds to believe that a warrant of arrest or committal is in force within the territorial jurisdiction in which the person is found.

arrest
Taking or keeping of a person in custody by legal authority, especially in response to a criminal offence.

arrest warrant
A document signed by a judge or a justice of the peace authorizing a police officer to apprehend a specific person for a specified reason and bring that person before a justice of the peace.

information
A written complaint, sworn under oath by a citizen or more typically a police officer, alleging that the accused has committed a specific criminal offence.

Section 495(2) imposes a duty on police officers not to arrest a person without a warrant for three types of offences: those found in s 553 of the *Criminal Code*, hybrid offences, and those punishable on summary conviction. If, however, the officer has reasonable grounds to believe that an arrest is necessary in the public interest for these types of offences, the officer can make an arrest in order to

- establish the identity of the person,
- secure or preserve evidence of or relating to the offence, or
- prevent the continuation or repetition of the offence or the commission of another offence.

A police officer is also authorized to arrest an individual if the officer believes that the person will fail to appear in court.

What are reasonable grounds for making an arrest? In *R v Storrey* (1990), the Supreme Court of Canada ruled that the arresting officer must subjectively have reasonable and probable grounds on which to base an arrest without a warrant. That is, a police officer must believe that he or she has the grounds to arrest. Further, the grounds for arrest must be justifiable from an objective point of view. This means that a reasonable person standing in the shoes of the officer would also believe that grounds for arrest exist, but those grounds need not amount to a ***prima facie*** case for conviction before making the arrest.

As Griffiths (2013, p. 142) pointed out, in the case of an arrest or an investigative detention, an important threshold in the criminal justice process is crossed. Upon arrest or detention, the police are required to inform a suspect promptly under s 10(a) of the Charter of the reasons the person is being arrested, and they must advise the person under s 10(b) that he or she has the right to retain and instruct counsel without delay. The latter section imposes the following duties on state authorities when they detain or arrest a suspect (*R v Bartle*, 1994):

1. The duty to inform persons of their right to counsel without delay as well as the existence and availability of legal aid and duty counsel;
2. The duty to provide detainees with a reasonable opportunity to exercise their right; and
3. The duty to desist from questioning until that reasonable opportunity has been exercised.

Additionally, officers are required by common law to inform detainees of legal aid and duty counsel programs (*R v Brydges*, 1990), as well as the existence of a 24-hour 1-800 (toll-free) telephone number that detainees can access to get preliminary legal advice (*R v Bartle*, 1994). State authorities are permitted to forgo the second and third duties in urgent and dangerous circumstances. Notably, the person being detained can always relinquish the rights guaranteed by s 10(b) of the Charter, although in *Bartle* the Supreme Court of Canada stated that the standard for **waiver** will be high, especially in circumstances where the alleged waiver has been implicit. If the detainee invokes his or her right and is reasonably diligent in exercising that right, there is a duty on the police to provide the detainee with a reasonable opportunity to contact counsel and to refrain from eliciting evidence until the individual has done so. Failure by the police to fulfill their duties under s 10 could result in evidence obtained subsequently being excluded under s 24(2) of the Charter.

prima facie
Legal presumption meaning "on the face of it" or "at first sight." It refers to a matter that appears to be self-evident from the facts. The term denotes evidence that, unless contested, would be sufficient to prove a particular fact in issue; the evidence need not be conclusive.

waiver
The giving up of a right; it may be done expressly, or it may be implied from the circumstances.

The Toronto G20 Summit: Lawful Exercise of Police Powers or Unlawful Exercise of Authority?

In June 2010, police in Toronto arrested or detained more than 1,000 people during the G20 summit. Most of them were held in "inhumane conditions" at a makeshift detention centre located inside a shuttered film studio in Toronto's Leslieville neighbourhood. The largely peaceful protest against the G20 summit quickly turned violent when a group of rogue demonstrators broke off from the main protest march to confuse police. Several dozen protesters engaged in acts of vandalism, including torching police vehicles and smashing store windows. Fully equipped riot police were quickly deployed to provide security. They responded with pepper spray, tear gas, rubber bullets, and force to control the protesters. Police also used a controversial crowd control tactic known as "kettling" to surround and arrest hundreds of protesters. However, police also rounded up hundreds of peaceful protesters, journalists, and innocent bystanders in the process. Several hundred were held in the pouring rain and cold for more than four hours, while some were randomly carted off to the detention centre. Most of the people arrested or detained were released without charge.

In the weeks and months that followed, Toronto police came under intense public and media scrutiny for their handling of the G20 summit. Numerous civil rights groups alleged that the police had violated civil liberties, made unlawful arrests, and used excessive force on protesters. In August 2014, the Ontario Court of Appeal certified two class-action lawsuits alleging civil rights abuses by the police during the G20 summit. The province's top court emphasized that "the police cannot sweep up scores of people just in the hope that one of the persons captured is a person who they believe is engaged in criminal activity" (*Sherry Good v Toronto Police Services Board*, 2014, para. 49).

What Do You Think?

1. Were protesters arbitrarily detained and/or arrested in violation of their rights under s 9 of the Charter? Do you think the mass detentions and/or arrests were justified under s 1 of the Charter?

2. Should the police have allowed detainees the opportunity to speak to a lawyer? Did the police infringe on their rights under s 10(b) of the Charter?

Under what circumstances can a police officer enter a private dwelling to arrest some-one? In *Eccles v Bourque et al.* (1975), the Supreme Court of Canada held that police officers could enter a private dwelling to make an arrest pursuant to an arrest warrant. Two decades later, Canada's highest court ruled in *R v Feeney* (1997) that, absent **exigent circumstances**, police officers are prohibited from entering private dwellings without authorization. In response to this decision, Parliament introduced what is now s 529.3 of the *Criminal Code*, which permits police officers to enter a private dwelling without a warrant for the purpose of arresting a suspect in exigent circumstances. According to s 529.4(3), officers must announce their presence before entering, unless they have rea-sonable grounds to believe that the announcement would place someone in imminent danger of bodily harm or result in the loss of evidence.

exigent circumstances
Situations in which people are in imminent danger of bodily harm or death, in which there is risk of imminent loss or destruction of evidence, or in which a suspect will escape.

Police Questioning of Suspects

Investigation is a fundamental duty in policing. Police officers may ask questions as part of the investigative process. They may seek out information from various persons, including suspects, witnesses, and victims of crime. The police interview is an investiga-tive technique used in law enforcement to search for and gather information that will assist in an investigation. More specifically, the purpose of investigative interviewing is to collect evidence to mount a successful prosecution (e.g., eyewitness description of the offender).

SIDEBAR

Police Street Checks

The practice of "carding"—also referred to as street checks—is a policing strategy used to investigate general criminal activity and gather information for intelligence pur-poses (Ontario Ministry of Community Safety and Correctional Services, 2016). A street check occurs when a police officer arbitrarily stops a citizen on the street and requests personal identification and information, whether or not the person is part of an on-going police investigation (Marin, 2015, para. 1). Any identifying information—includ-ing a description of the individual, gang affiliation, known associates, and race—is then stored in a police database for possible future use. Police street checks have been common practice in Toronto and other cities across Ontario, including Brampton, Mississauga, London, and Hamilton. Law enforcement agencies insist that street checks help detect and prevent crime. The practice has proven to be particularly effective in policing high-crime areas, or "hot spots," and has resulted in a number of high-profile arrests (see Warmington, 2015, for specific examples).

Opponents argue that the practice of performing street checks on citizens not under investigation is unconstitutional, and that it unfairly and disproportionately targets racial minorities, straining community–police relations (this disproportionality is why the practice is also referred to as **racial profiling**). Data collected from street checks by the Toronto Police Service between 2003 and 2008 showed that black males aged 15 to 24 represented 8 percent of the Toronto population, yet they were stopped and documented nearly three times more often than white males of the same age (Rankin, 2010). Analysis of crime data in other cities showed similar results; for ex-ample, in Ottawa (Larocque, 2015), and Mississauga and Brampton (Grewal, 2015). Notwithstanding, the police insist they are targeting neighbourhoods plagued by high

racial profiling
The act or tendency of law enforcement officers and others to consider people suspicious or more likely to commit crime based on the colour of their skin or their ethnicity.

crime rates—which are predominantly made up of racial minorities—with a proactive investigative technique.

In 2015, the Ontario government announced new regulations ending the controversial practice of random and arbitrary police street checks. As of January 1, 2017, the new rules will require police to tell anyone subjected to a street check why they are being stopped, and that they have a right to not provide any identifying information. Officers must also keep a detailed record about each transaction; failing to do so will be a code of conduct violation. In addition, Ontario's street check regulations establish new training, data management, reporting, and independent oversight requirements to strengthen transparency and increase accountability. See the Ontario Ministry of Community Safety and Correctional Services website for more information on the new regulations (www.mcscs.jus.gov.on.ca/english/Policing/StreetChecks.html).

What Do You Think?

1. Should police have the ability to stop and question people without a legitimate investigative purpose? Are street checks a form of arbitrary detention that is contrary to s 9 of the Charter?

2. Does the practice of street checks violate the right to equal treatment under the law that is protected by s 15 of the Charter?

3. Do you agree with the new regulations on street checks enacted by the Ontario government? Explain your answer.

4. Do the new regulations hinder the police's ability to proactively investigate suspicious and/or criminal activity?

People protesting against racial profiling in front of police headquarters in Toronto.

Non-custodial Interviewing

Investigative interviewing is of fundamental importance to police work. The purpose of a police interview is to gather information from various parties—including complainants, victims, witnesses, and suspects—about a crime under investigation. There are no laws preventing police from interacting with members of the public. Police can approach individuals and ask questions at any time. Police questioning can occur in an informal setting, such as on the street or in other public places, or at one's home or place of work. Police may also ask individuals to voluntarily come to the police station to give a statement. At this stage, the person being interviewed is not officially considered a suspect in the crime being investigated. That is, the interviewee is not in police custody and so is not considered to be under arrest or in detention. He or she is not required to answer questions and is free to leave at any time. However, any statements made during the course of an investigative interview can potentially be used as evidence later on.

Custodial Interviewing and Interrogation

Suspect interviews typically occur while a person is being detained, or after an arrest has been made. Formal interviews generally take place at a police station, and it is standard practice to electronically record all interactions between police officers and the suspect. A person in police custody has the right to speak to a lawyer and the right to remain silent when being questioned by police. While police must be respectful of an individual's Charter rights, they are still permitted to question a suspect as part of their duty to investigate alleged crimes (*R v Singh*, 2007). The suspect does not have to answer any questions or give a statement to police; however, anything the suspect says during a police interview may be given in evidence later on at trial.

The criminal law limits the ways in which police are permitted to question suspects. The confessions rule provides that "no statement made out of court by an accused to a person in authority can be admitted into evidence against him unless the prosecution shows, to the satisfaction of the trial judge, that the statement was made freely and voluntarily" (*R v Hodgson*, 1998, para. 12). The primary purpose of the confessions rule is to guard against the risk of unreliable confessions (*R v Oickle*, 2000). It also protects the right against self-incrimination and "regulates state conduct to protect basic fairness in the criminal process" (*R v Hart*, 2014, para. 175). In *R v Oickle* (2000), the Supreme Court of Canada held that to determine voluntariness, a court must consider a number of relevant factors, including (1) threats or promises, (2) oppression, (3) the operating mind requirement, and (4) police trickery (paras. 48–67). If a confession is involuntary for any of the preceding reasons, it is inadmissible as evidence in court.

During the police interview, a suspect may be questioned first in a non-confrontational, non-accusatory manner so that the interviewer can establish rapport and gather both investigative and behavioural information from the interviewee (Gudjonsson, 2012, p. 467; Snook & House, 2008, p. 10). The purpose of an interview is "to elicit as much reliable and accurate information as possible by providing the interviewee with an opportunity to give an uninterrupted, personal account of the event or events being investigated" (Snook, Eastwood, Stinson, Tedeschini, & House, 2010, p. 209). The investigative interview can help police determine whether there is sufficient evidence that an individual has committed a crime. It can also help police assess an individual's verbal and non-verbal behaviour, identify whether a suspect is truthful or deceptive, or, potentially, clear an individual suspected of wrongdoing. If the suspect is deceptive or uncooperative during the interview, investigators may resort to other types of interview methods, such as interrogation, to further their investigation.

The goal of police interrogation is to elicit a confession or admission from a criminal suspect using a range of psychological methods that are confrontational, manipulative, and suggestive (Drizin & Leo, 2004, p. 910). Unlike the police interview, interrogation is an accusatory, guilt-presumptive process. It is used when police are confident the suspect is involved in the crime being investigated. Police interrogation is "stress-inducing by design—structured to promote a sense of isolation and increase the anxiety and despair associated with denial relative to confession" (Kassin et al., 2010, p. 6). Interrogators routinely use trickery and deceit during interrogations, such as lying to a suspect, presenting fabricated or false evidence, and using implied threats and coercion, to encourage a confession (Gudjonsson, 2003). To illustrate, police may lie about the existence of incontrovertible evidence of the suspect's guilt (e.g., eyewitness identification, fingerprints, DNA evidence) in order to persuade the suspect to confess, even if no such evidence exists. In addition, interrogators may offer sympathy, provide moral justification for the alleged crime, offer face-saving excuses, or downplay the pending consequences of confessing.

SIDEBAR

Interrogation Versus Non-Coercive Information Gathering

Today, the Reid Technique is the most influential and widely used police interrogation procedure in North America. It is a nine-step process designed to wear down a suspect's psychological resistance to confess. To be sure, the Reid Technique is a highly effective method of eliciting confessions from guilty suspects. Critics, however, argue that this method of interrogation is psychologically coercive and can lead to false confessions (Davis & O'Donohue, 2003; Drizin & Leo, 2004; Gudjonsson, 2003; Kassin, 2006; Kassin et al., 2010; Redlich & Meissner, 2009). It seems counterintuitive to think that an innocent person would ever confess to a crime he or she did not commit. Yet exonerations through post-conviction DNA testing have revealed that police-induced false confessions are among the leading causes of wrongful conviction. According to the Innocence Project (n.d.), approximately 25 percent of innocent defendants later exonerated by DNA evidence made false confessions or gave false incriminating statements to police.

In light of concerns raised by accusatorial interrogation methods, law enforcement agencies in Canada, the United Kingdom, New Zealand, Norway, and elsewhere have adopted a non-coercive, information-gathering approach to investigative interviewing known as PEACE (Preparation and Planning, Engage and Explain, Account, Closure, and Evaluate). Unlike coercive psychological interrogation methods, this model focuses on developing and maintaining rapport with interviewees, active listening, explaining the allegation(s) and the seriousness of the offence(s), and allowing interviewees to provide an account without interruption. Only when suspects have offered their perspective are they questioned by police and given the opportunity to clarify and explain any inconsistencies, discrepancies, or contradictions in that account (Hartweig, Meissner, & Semel, 2014, p. 216). Investigators are not permitted to lie to suspects or employ deception (e.g., lying about evidence) during an interview or interrogation. Under the PEACE model of interviewing, the emphasis is on fact-finding (i.e., checking the accuracy of the account) rather than obtaining a confession. A review of the existing empirical literature suggests that information-gathering approaches are as effective as accusatorial interrogation methods in obtaining confessions from criminal suspects. Moreover, they significantly reduce the likelihood of false confessions because innocent suspects are not subjected to psychologically coercive tactics (Meissner et al., 2014).

Non-custodial Interrogation Techniques

"Mr. Big" Operations

Since the early 1990s, police in Canada have sometimes used what is known as the "Mr. Big" technique to obtain confessions from persons suspected of murder or other serious crimes. The premise is to make the target (the suspect) believe he (or she) is being recruited into the ranks of a large, highly sophisticated criminal organization. This technique involves a group of specially trained undercover police officers posing as organized crime figures working under the direction of "Mr. Big"—the boss of the criminal organization. (See "Mini Case Study—Nelson Lloyd Hart.")

Undercover police officers initiate contact with the target and attempt to recruit him to join the ranks of their criminal organization. Officers gradually cultivate a friendly relationship with the target and gain the person's trust and confidence. The target is invited to participate in apparent illegal activity with the undercover officers, such as smuggling stolen goods, money laundering, or stealing vehicles. Sometimes, staged acts of violence are used to demonstrate what happens to individuals who betray the criminal organization and its members.

The operation culminates with a meeting, akin to a job interview, between the target and Mr. Big. The target is told that he must come clean about his past to continue as a member in the organization, as his criminal history—including the current murder investigation—could bring unwanted police attention to the group. Once a confession is obtained, the target is arrested and charged with a crime.

Mr. Big operations are typically employed in homicide cases that have gone cold. The technique has been highly successful in obtaining confessions and has secured convictions in hundreds of cases (*R v Hart*, 2014, para. 4). By 2008, the Mr. Big technique had been used in more than 350 cases across Canada. In 75 percent of these operations, the person of interest has been charged with, or cleared of, a crime, while the remaining 25 percent remain unsolved. Of the cases prosecuted, more than 95 percent have resulted in convictions (Keenan & Brockman, 2010, p. 23). The technique has also uncovered incriminating evidence, such as the body in a homicide investigation (as in the case of *R v McCreery* [1998]). Such discoveries help "in the generally positive assessment of the technique and in arguably avoiding false confessions" (Quigley, 2015, p. 2).

However, the Mr. Big technique is not without controversy. The procedure's ingenuity is also its Achilles' heel. In *R v Hart* (2014), the Supreme Court of Canada identified three major problems associated with Mr. Big operations: (1) the risk of false confessions and subsequent wrongful convictions; (2) prejudice to the accused; and (3) the potential for police misconduct. The Supreme Court also noted that the law, as it was then, provided insufficient protection to persons who confessed during Mr. Big operations. To address these concerns, Canada's top court created a new common law rule of evidence that presumes confessions obtained through Mr. Big stings are inadmissible, unless the Crown can demonstrate otherwise.

Nelson Lloyd Hart

On the morning of August 4, 2002, Nelson Lloyd Hart took his three-year-old twin daughters, Karen and Krista, to Little Harbour Park on Gander Lake, where both girls drowned. There were no witnesses. Hart initially told investigators that Krista had accidentally fallen in the lake, but that he did not jump in to help her because he could not swim. Despite having a functioning cellphone in his car, Hart said he panicked and drove 11 kilometres to his home in Gander, passing a hospital, to get his wife, who also could not swim. When Hart's wife asked where Karen was, he claimed to have forgotten her at the dock. The couple raced back to the lake, where they found both children floating in the water. By the time first responders arrived, Karen was dead and Krista was unconscious. The next day she was taken off life-support and died.

Hart's unusual behaviour cast a dark cloud of suspicion over him. When questioned by detectives, Hart maintained Krista and Karen's tragic deaths were accidental. But two weeks later, Hart claimed that he had had an epileptic seizure on the wharf and did not know how the girls ended up in the lake. He said he lied to police because he was afraid he would lose his driver's licence. (Hart's licence had been suspended several times due to his epilepsy.)

Investigators were convinced Hart was guilty, but there was insufficient evidence to lay charges. Eventually, the case went cold. However, two years later the RCMP initiated a Mr. Big sting operation, drawing Hart into a make-believe world of organized crime. Surveillance conducted on Hart, who had a grade-five education, revealed that he was socially isolated, unemployed, poor, and relying on food banks, and the operation was tailored accordingly. Undercover officers provided Hart with a job that often allowed him to stay in luxury hotels and dine in expensive restaurants. He was paid more than $15,000 for transporting supposedly illegal goods, and had a lifestyle that he could only have dreamt about. Over time, he also came to view the undercover officers as his "best friends" and referred to them as his "brothers."

The operation drew to a close when Hart was told that he could earn up to $25,000 if he participated in an upcoming "big deal." The catch was that he would be required to meet with the purported crime boss, "Mr. Big," who had the final say on Hart's membership in the criminal organization. Hart was told that Mr. Big could use his influence and connections to make his legal problems go away. After initially denying he killed Krista and Karen, Hart eventually told the crime boss that he pushed the three-year old girls off the wharf because he feared Child Protection Services was planning to give Hart's brother custody of his children. Three days later, Hart took Mr. Big to the scene of the crime and re-enacted how he had pushed his daughters into the water. Both confessions were secretly videotaped. Based on this evidence, a jury later found Nelson Hart guilty of two counts of first-degree murder, and he was sentenced to life in prison with no chance of parole for 25 years.

Hart appealed and, in 2012, the Newfoundland and Labrador Court of Appeal overturned his murder conviction and sentence, concluding that two confessions used as evidence at his trial were obtained in breach of his right to silence under s 7 of the Charter. The court ruled, however, that a third confession was admissible and ordered a new trial.

Ultimately, in 2014, the Supreme Court of Canada, in a unanimous ruling, upheld the appeal court decision. The Supreme Court found that the financial and social inducements offered to Hart raised serious doubts about the reliability of his statements to undercover police officers. In addition, the ruling noted Hart's confession

was inconsistent with the known facts and lacked sufficient independent corroboration. The Supreme Court
concluded, "these confessions are not worth the risk they
pose" and that "it would be unsafe to rest a conviction
on this evidence" (*R v Hart*, 2014, para. 146). Lacking evidence, the Crown dropped the charges, and Hart was
released from prison.

What Do You Think?

1. Should the police be permitted to use deceit in order to obtain a confession? Is the Mr. Big technique
   ethical? Why or why not?

2. Do you agree with the Supreme Court of Canada's
   decision in the *Hart* case? Did Nelson Hart get away
   with murder?

Search and Seizure

As early as the 17th century, the common law has recognized the importance of, and
has placed a high value on, the security and privacy of the home (*Semayne's Case*, 1604).
Since the introduction of the Charter, "the emphasis on privacy in Canada has gained
considerable importance" (*R v Feeney*, 1997, para. 42). Both common law and statutory
powers authorize the police to search individuals and places and to seize evidence for the
purposes of prosecution. Section 8 of the Charter provides that all Canadians have the
right to be secure against unreasonable search or seizure. Such protection was first considered by the Supreme Court of Canada in *Hunter et al v Southam Inc* (1984). Mr. Justice
Dickson, writing for a unanimous court, said that the protection entrenched in s 8 of
the Charter is very broad in its scope and is intended to prevent unjustified state intrusions into the privacy of individuals. In other words, it prohibits unreasonable searches.

Constitutional Minimum Standards

The court established what are known as "constitutional minimum standards"—a framework within which to evaluate the constitutionality of legislation authorizing search
warrants. Unauthorized searches (without a search warrant or wiretap authorization)
are generally and presumptively unreasonable under s 8 of the Charter. Where it is feasible, and if there is time to do so, police officers need to satisfy the following minimum
requirements:

- have prior authorization (e.g., a search warrant or wiretap authorization) (*Hunter
  et al v Southam Inc*, p. 160);
- have authorization from a person who is capable of acting judicially—that is, in
  a neutral and impartial manner (e.g., justice of the peace or judge) (p. 162); and
- have reasonable grounds to believe, sworn upon oath by the individual seeking
  the authorization, that an offence has been committed and that there is evidence
  to be found at the place of the search (p. 168).

The standard is high. There must be a "credibly based probability"—that is, the items
sought are likely to be found—rather than mere suspicion. It is important to note that
if a search is authorized by law (through a search warrant, wiretap authorization, or
exemptions under common law or legislation), it still has to be carried out in a reasonable manner.

information to obtain a search warrant (ITO)
A document prepared and sworn by the person seeking a search warrant (usually a police officer) specifying the offence alleged, the place(s) to be searched, and the specific item(s) to be seized.

Search by Warrant: Criminal Code

The general authority for issuing search warrants is found in s 487 of the *Criminal Code*.[1] Before issuing a warrant, a justice (i.e., a provincial court judge or justice of the peace) must be satisfied that there are reasonable grounds to believe that evidence with respect to the commission of an offence will be found at the place of the search. The details that must be provided to the justice are set out in an **information to obtain a search warrant (ITO)**. The test in reviewing a decision to issue a warrant is whether "there was reliable evidence that might reasonably be believed on the basis of which the authorization could have issued" (*R v Morelli*, 2010, para. 40). The Supreme Court of Canada's decision in *Morelli* made clear that courts will not tolerate misleading or incomplete ITOs. Lastly, s 29(1) of the *Criminal Code* states that everyone who executes a warrant must have it with him or her "where it is feasible to do so, and to produce it when requested to do so." This statutory provision complements the rights afforded to persons upon arrest or detention under s 10 of the Charter.

Special Warrant Provisions

DNA Evidence

What is the scope of the law regarding the taking of bodily substances for DNA analysis? Prior to the 1995 amendments to the *Criminal Code*, the search and seizure of bodily samples was not authorized by either statutory or common law. Therefore, police officers used the "scavenger method" to obtain DNA samples by searching for discarded tissues and cigarette butts (Brockman, 2015, p. 176). As noted in *R v Stillman* (1997), police cannot take hair samples, dental impressions, or buccal (cheek) swabs without prior judicial authorization. These types of searches are deemed to be highly invasive and contravene the principles of fundamental justice pursuant to s 7 of the Charter (*R v Stillman*, 1997, para. 51). Special provisions now exist for obtaining forensic evidence: blood samples are covered in s 256 of the *Criminal Code*, while DNA and bodily impression warrants are found in ss 487.04 to 487.091.

Electronic Surveillance

The interception of our private communications by means of electronic surveillance is also covered under our right not to be subjected to unreasonable search and seizure. Police officers must obtain prior judicial authorization either under s 184.2 of the *Criminal Code*—to intercept communications with the consent of one of the parties (participant surveillance)—or under s 186—to intercept private communications without the consent of either party (third-party surveillance). In the latter context, judicial authorization is sought by an application made under s 185 and is accompanied by an affidavit—a written statement of facts sworn under oath. Under s 186(1), before the authorization is granted, the affiant—usually a police officer—must demonstrate what is referred to as "investigative necessity." The requirements of s 186(1) coincide with the constitutional requirements under s 8 of the Charter (*R v Unger*, 1993). Failure to comply with these requirements would render the interceptions (communications) unlawful.

If an application to obtain the authorization fails to demonstrate that a warrant is a necessary part of the police investigation, or if the evidence disclosed in the officer's affidavit filed in support of the request is falsified, evidence obtained as a result could be excluded pursuant to s 24(2) of the Charter. If authorization is properly obtained, it must, as with a search warrant, be reasonably executed and must be done in a reasonable manner (*R v Joseph*, 2000, p. 136).[2]

Search Without Warrant: Legislation and Common Law

Some searches authorized by legislation or common law are considered reasonable under s 8 of the Charter and can be conducted without authorization (no need for a search warrant). Numerous statutory powers allow for warrantless searches. Section 117.02 of the *Criminal Code* authorizes a peace officer to conduct a warrantless search of persons, vehicles, or any place or premises other than a dwelling house for weapons or ammunition "where the conditions for obtaining a warrant exist but, by reason of exigent circumstances, it would not be practicable to obtain a warrant." Warrantless searches or entries into private dwellings are permitted in limited exigent circumstances (see s 529.3 of the *Criminal Code* and s 11(7) of the *Controlled Drugs and Substances Act*). To illustrate, police officers are authorized to forcibly enter a private dwelling in response to an emergency 911 call. They have a duty to find out the reason for the call and have the power, derived as a matter of common law from their duty, to enter the dwelling to verify that there is in fact no emergency (*R v Godoy*, 1999, para. 23). Lastly, it should be noted that numerous provincial statutes and other federal statutes allow for search and seizure without authorization.

Search During Investigative Detention: No Fishing Expeditions

As explained earlier, the Supreme Court of Canada in *Mann* (2004) found that the police have the authority to detain persons for investigative purposes. The majority held that a lawful detention for investigative purposes must be "reasonably necessary on an objective view of the totality of the circumstances, informing the officer's suspicion that there is a clear nexus between the individual to be detained and a recent or on-going criminal offence" (para. 34). The Supreme Court also considered the extent to which police officers could search a person held in an investigative detention. According to Mr. Justice Iacobucci, for the majority, "Where a police officer has reasonable grounds to believe that his or her safety or that of others is at risk, the officer may engage in a protective pat-down search of the detained individual" (para. 45). While a pat-down search incidental to an investigative detention may be justified, this common law power does not authorize a "fishing expedition"; the police cannot go through pockets to obtain evidence. As previously discussed, police must advise the individual of the reason for the detention, as well as the person's rights under s 10 of the Charter. Following on the heels of the *Mann* case, several Supreme Court of Canada judgments have drawn a clear distinction between detention and arrest. It is important to understand the difference between an arrest and investigative detention because the extent of police search powers will vary according to the type of search being carried out.

Police Safety Searches

More recently, the Supreme Court of Canada has used the ancillary powers doctrine to grant police officers the authority to conduct "safety searches" (i.e., search for weapons), provided the search is reasonably necessary in the circumstances. A "safety search" is a search conducted by police officers on individuals who are not detained or arrested, and are undertaken to ensure the safety of the police and the public (Skolnik, 2016, p. 238). In *R v MacDonald* (2014), Canada's highest court clarified the legal threshold for lawful "safety searches." The majority held that the police have the power to conduct this type of search where the officer has reasonable grounds to believe that a suspect is armed and is an imminent threat to public or officer safety. Mr. Justice LeBel cautioned that a search cannot be justified on the basis of a hunch or general safety concerns (para. 41).

Technique for Investigating Marijuana Grow Operations

The police are not permitted to carry out fishing expeditions or illegal searches in order to gather evidence to obtain a search warrant. For example, in *R v Kokesch* (1990), the police conducted a **perimeter search** of the accused's property on the basis of a suspicion that he was growing marijuana, but without reasonable and probable grounds for believing that narcotics would be found on the premises prior to conducting the perimeter search.

perimeter search
A search of the outside of a dwelling and its surroundings; it is used as a method of acquiring sufficient information on which to base a search warrant application to search inside the dwelling.

The Supreme Court of Canada found that the warrantless search of the yard violated s 8 of the Charter, and the evidence was accordingly excluded under s 24(2). Likewise, the Supreme Court has also found that the "knock on" technique constitutes a search and violates s 8 as well (*R v Evans*, 1996). This tactic involves a police officer approaching a dwelling and knocking on the door in hopes that when the occupant opens it, sufficient evidence (i.e., olfactory, or smell) will be immediately apparent to support an arrest or an application for a warrant. The knock-on technique goes beyond that which is authorized by law and is now considered an illegal search. Warrantless searches of the accused's garbage (placed at the end of the driveway) were, however, allowed by the Supreme Court in *R v Patrick* (2009), provided that the police did not have to trespass into the "airspace" of the property owner to do so.

Searching Incident to Arrest

Another warrantless search that is allowed at common law is a search incidental to arrest; that is, the power of a police officer to search a person who is taken into custody (and the immediate surrounding area) without warrant. Police officers do not need reasonable grounds to conduct this type of search, but they first need reasonable grounds to make the arrest. In other words, for the search to be lawful, the arrest itself must be lawful. A search incidental to arrest is not mandatory and must be for a valid purpose, such as to secure or preserve evidence, ensure the safety of the officer or the suspect, and prevent escape (*Cloutier v Langlois*, 1990, p. 186). The search cannot be conducted in an abusive fashion and must be carried out in a reasonable manner. In *R v Golden* (2001), the Supreme Court of Canada in a 5 to 4 majority held that, if a search incident to a lawful arrest involves a strip search, the police must have "reasonable and probable grounds justifying the strip search in addition to reasonable and probable grounds justifying the arrest" (para. 99).

Plain View Doctrine

The police also retain the common law power to seize items under the plain view doctrine. In the context of search and seizure, this doctrine provides that objects discernible by a police officer who is legally in a position to observe them can be seized without a search warrant and are admissible as evidence. To illustrate, if a police officer lawfully stops a motorist for a traffic violation (e.g., speeding) and, while approaching the vehicle, sees a firearm on the back seat, the police officer has reasonable grounds to search inside the vehicle and seize the firearm, even though that offence has nothing to do with the traffic violation. Additionally, while the law related to search and seizure prevents unjustified state intrusions into the privacy of individuals, s 489(2) of the *Criminal Code* allows police officers who are executing a search warrant to seize evidence of an offence that is not mentioned in the warrant. It is not a power to search, but rather a power to seize items in plain view.

Consent Searches

Police officers are authorized to conduct warrantless searches when an individual voluntarily consents to the search, thereby waiving the constitutional protections afforded them. Fairness demands that the individual appreciates the potential legal consequences of agreeing to the search. The person consenting must truly understand that the police may use anything uncovered in a search in a subsequent prosecution. In *R v Wills* (1992), the Ontario Court of Appeal provided the following guidelines for establishing whether voluntary consent was given (para. 69):

- there was consent, expressed or implied;
- the person had the authority to give the consent;
- the consent was voluntary and was not the product of police oppression, coercion, or other external conduct, which negated the freedom to choose;
- the person was aware of the nature of the search being requested;
- the person was aware of his or her right to refuse to permit the police to engage in the search; and
- the person was aware of the potential consequences of giving the consent.

In essence, the consent must be real and voluntary. The person searched must have sufficient awareness to have waived constitutional rights against search and seizure. The degree of awareness of the consequences of the waiver of the s 8 right required of an accused in a given case will depend on its particular facts. The Supreme Court of Canada later approved of these guidelines for consent in *R v Borden* (1994).

Police Use of Force

In recent years, the use of force by Canadian police officers has attracted considerable media and public attention. Several incidents involving police wrongdoing have been featured prominently in headline news stories, including those in which individuals have died while in police custody and where deadly force was used. The high-profile shooting of Sammy Yatim on a Toronto streetcar by Constable James Forcillo in 2013 (which resulted in Forcillo receiving a precedent-setting sentence of six years in prison), is one very notable recent example (see *R v Forcillo* (2016) for more information on this case).

Since most people have little direct contact with the criminal justice system, popular media and journalistic reports are a fertile source of information and education on topics such as police use of force. Indeed, these reports of police wrongdoing are sensationalized and often critical of the actions of the police. Sometimes, such incidents of police wrongdoing/misconduct warrant close scrutiny and censure; other times, however, the allegations are without foundation. As Walma and West (2001) observed, "public scrutiny

The death of Sammy Yatim from shots fired by Constable James Forcillo was captured by a citizen bystander and widely seen on social media.

always enjoys the benefit of hindsight, sober reflection, and in some cases additional information" (p. 59). It is important to keep in mind that police officers can quickly find themselves in dangerous and unpredictable situations and have little time to assess a threat or possible threat, determine an appropriate response, and defuse the situation.

Nevertheless, these narratives undoubtedly have an effect on public attitudes toward the police, the criminal justice system, and government more generally. Moreover, negative perceptions of the police and the use of force to resolve conflict have eroded public confidence in the administration of justice. This damage has placed a burden on the integrity, prestige, and reputation of the law enforcement profession. To illustrate, a 2012 Ipsos Reid poll showed that public confidence in the RCMP had dropped significantly, compared with a similar poll that was done in 2007 (Boswell, 2013). This poll followed on the heels of several well-publicized scandals involving Canada's national police force. The tragic death of Robert Dziekański at Vancouver International Airport (see "Mini Case Study— Robert Dziekański" later in this chapter), which was captured on amateur video, resulted in an international outcry against the use of lethal force by police and provoked considerable debate about the use of conducted energy weapons (CEWs). The Dziekański case also led to widespread concern over the conflict of interest present in police investigating themselves, and whether officer-related incidents of death or serious harm can be investigated in an impartial way. The topic of police investigating police, as well as policy reform in this area (e.g., establishment of independent, civilian-led investigative agencies), will be addressed later in this chapter. Illustrating the dynamic nature of public opinion, a more recent poll conducted by the Angus Reid Institute (2014) reported an increase in public confidence in the RCMP and other police forces, from 38 percent in 2012 to 67 percent in 2014. However, the RCMP faces new challenges with recent rulings on a class-action lawsuit concerning sexual harassment within the force, as well as the issue of RCMP mishandling of cases of missing and murdered Indigenous women.

Influences on the Use of Force

The **use of force** is a defining feature of the police, and officers are granted the authority to use force, including deadly force, to assist them in their broad law enforcement mandate (i.e., crime control and public order) (Bittner, 1970; Manning, 1977). Although it is fundamental to police work, the level of force employed should be guided by the principles of proportionality, necessity, and reasonableness. If a police officer uses excessive force in the course of his or her duties, it could amount to a violation of the suspect's right to life, liberty, and security of the person under s 7 of the Charter. If an agent of the state (e.g., a police officer) violates an individual's rights and freedoms guaranteed under the Charter, the accused may seek a remedy under s 24(2) or in civil court.

According to Murphy and McKenna (2007, p. 5), a number of situational, structural, and symbolic qualities are unique to police work, such as danger, risk, authority, and conflict. Police officers are exposed to a variety of scenarios while carrying out their enforcement duties that range from rather benign to highly charged, risky, and potentially dangerous situations. When an officer responds to an incident, he or she is continuously assessing the risk to determine the appropriate level of intervention. If the use of force is necessary, the level of force should correspond to the level of resistance by the individual.

Significantly, no system of laws or regulations prescribes how police officers should react in every possible scenario they might encounter in the field. Therefore, **discretion** plays a vital role in policing and permeates all aspects of the job. Decision-making responsibilities with respect to the use of force are important for the resolution of problems and disputes. Prominent factors influencing a police officer's discretion to take action include legal factors such as the seriousness of the crime and the strength of the evidence, as well as non-legal factors such as social class, sex, age, the characteristics of the neighbourhood, and the demeanour of the individual. As the seriousness of a police incident increases, the amount of discretion an officer can exercise decreases correspondingly. Indeed, police officers exercise a considerable amount of discretion in how to best resolve situations, and do so with little oversight or accountability for the decisions they make (MacAlister, 2012, p. 2).

use of force
The amount of effort required by police to compel compliance by an unwilling subject.

discretion
The decision-making process and judgment police officers use when determining how best to deal with a situation they encounter. Other branches of the criminal justice system, including the courts and corrections, also have discretionary powers that can influence the outcome of cases.

MINI CASE STUDY

Robert Dziekański

In October 2007, Robert Dziekański, a 40-year-old construction worker, emigrated from Poland to join his mother, Zofia Cisowski, in Kamloops, British Columbia. He arrived at the Vancouver International Airport on October 13, 2007, following a long flight. He and his mother had arranged to meet at the baggage carousel in the international terminal. Unbeknown to either of them, the baggage area for international arrivals was a secured area where his mother was not allowed to enter. Dziekański was eventually cleared through a primary customs inspection by a Canadian border services officer and referred to the cus-

toms secondary area for further processing, which is standard procedure for someone who does not speak English and is immigrating to the country. For the next six hours, however, Dziekański's whereabouts remained unclear, although he was seen several times wandering around the customs and baggage area for international arrivals. Dziekański was eventually escorted by another border services officer to the immigration secondary area after having completed a secondary customs examination. Once Dziekański's immigration procedures were done, he wandered back and forth between the public area of the international arrivals terminal and the International Reception Lounge.

For reasons that have not been adequately explained, Dziekański remained in the international arrivals area for almost 12 hours, growing increasingly confused and visibly agitated. Among other things, he was fatigued from the flight and anxious to see his mother, who was waiting for him in the public waiting area. Speaking no languages other than Polish, he was unable to communicate effectively with bystanders and airport security personnel, and efforts to calm him down were unsuccessful. He threw a wooden table against a set of glass doors in the International Reception Lounge and smashed a computer. Four RCMP officers arrived on the scene and moved into the secure area where Dziekański was holed up. One officer quickly used a conducted energy weapon five times against Dziekański, who, after being subdued and handcuffed, died shortly thereafter.

Although provincial Crown prosecutors decided not to lay charges against the police officers involved in the incident, the BC government established a commission of inquiry and appointed Thomas Braidwood, a former appeal court justice, to head up the commission. The first phase of the inquiry (see Braidwood, 2009) examined the police use of conducted energy weapons, and the second phase (see Braidwood, 2010) focused on the circumstances surrounding the death of Dziekański. From the first report came numerous recommendations, including appropriate training and retraining on the proper use of CEWs, restricting their use to circumstances where a suspect's behaviour is imminently likely to cause bodily harm, and avoiding the repeated deployment of a CEW on a suspect in a single encounter. Additionally, Mr. Justice Braidwood suggested that the RCMP be required to comply with the policies and procedures with respect to CEWs applicable to provincially regulated law enforcement agencies.

In his second report, released in June 2010, Mr. Justice Braidwood was critical of the conduct of the police officers involved, suggesting that the tragic outcome could have been prevented. He recommended the establishment of an independent, civilian-based investigative agency to investigate police-involved deaths and incidents causing serious harm. In October 2011, the BC legislature introduced amendments to the *Police Act*, creating an Independent Investigation Office (IIO).

What Do You Think?

1. Were the officers' actions proportional, necessary, and reasonable in the circumstances? Explain your answer.

2. Do you feel that the use of force in this context was excessive? Explain your answer.

Justifications for the Use of Force

Unquestionably, police have a duty to administer and enforce the law. As alluded to in the introduction, this duty entails, among other things, investigating alleged offences, apprehending offenders, and protecting life and property. It is reasonable that police officers should be granted special powers to use force, including deadly force, in meeting these obligations. The authority to use force comes from a number of sources, including the common law and various statutes (e.g., the *Criminal Code*, provincial and territorial police acts, and firearms regulations). The duties of the RCMP also originate from common law and are set out in s 18 of the *Royal Canadian Mounted Police Act*. This Act states, among other things, that it is the duty of its members (i.e., peace officers) to engage in "the apprehension of criminals and offenders and others who may be lawfully taken into custody."[3]

The primary legal justification for the use of force, however, is found in s 25(1) of the *Criminal Code*:

> Every one who is required or authorized by law to do anything in the administration or enforcement of the law ... is, if he acts on reasonable grounds, justified in doing what he is required or authorized to do and in using as much force as is necessary for that purpose.

This provision is fairly broad and complicated. Section 25(1) creates a legal justification for individuals, including police officers, to use as much force as is necessary in the administration and enforcement of the law provided that their actions are required or authorized and they act on reasonable grounds. Notably, s 25(3) places a limit on the powers granted in s 25(1) by prohibiting force intended or likely to cause death or grievous bodily harm unless the officer has an **objectively reasonable** belief that the amount of force used is necessary for self-protection, or for safeguarding another person under the officer's protection, from death or grievous bodily harm.

However, s 25(4) permits the police to use force that is intended or likely to cause death or grievous bodily harm to prevent a suspect from fleeing a lawful arrest (with or without a warrant), provided that all of the following requirements of the provision are met:

- The arrest must be lawful.
- The offence must be serious enough that the person could be arrested without warrant.
- The officer must reasonably believe the force is necessary to protect the officer or others from "imminent or future death or grievous bodily harm."
- The escape cannot be prevented by "reasonable means in a less violent manner."

Criminal offences for which no arrest warrant is required or for which a warrantless arrest is legal include the following:

- indictable offences
- persons escaping from lawful arrest
- persons whom a police officer finds committing a criminal offence

Although s 25 of the *Criminal Code* authorizes the police to use force, including lethal force, police officers who use force that is objectively excessive—that is, not reasonable under the circumstances—are subject to criminal liability under s 26. If the actions of the officer are found to be unreasonable or excessive, he or she may be criminally charged with assault pursuant to s 265. Similarly, if a police officer causes the death of a person in circumstances that are found not to meet the requirements of s 25(3), (4), or (5), that officer may be charged with homicide.

Indeed, police officers are justified in using force if they act on reasonable grounds and use only as much force as is necessary. Notwithstanding that fact, the use-of-force provisions found in s 25 of the *Criminal Code* are problematic because it is difficult to ascertain how much force is "reasonable" or "necessary." In an effort to clarify the level of force that is appropriate in the possible scenarios officers might encounter in the field, various police agencies have developed a "use-of-force model" to help guide them. The use-of-force model serves as a standardized guideline, and it outlines the various actions to consider in situations requiring the use of force.

objectively reasonable
Where a person's thoughts or actions, measured by the "objective standard" used in courts to establish criminal responsibility, are deemed to be those that a reasonable person would have in a similar situation.

Models of Police Use of Force

As you read the following, it is important to keep in mind that models are simplified ways of explaining complex processes, such as police use of force.

In Canada, models depicting use of force by police officers first appeared in the 1980s. While they proved helpful for training purposes, many concerns arose from their use, including the number of models in existence, inconsistent vocabulary/terminology, and varying approaches to the use of force by police agencies. As noted by Hoffman, Lawrence, and Brown (2004), these earlier models were generally rigid and represented a linear, progressive decision-making process. Linear models were based on the assumption that all situations were unidirectional, following a path from soft approaches to intermediate weapons, culminating with use of lethal force. Research and experience demonstrate, however, that a linear approach does not reflect the dynamic nature of real-life police situations as effectively as the appropriate use-of-force response options do (p. 3).

Given the criticisms associated with linear models, law enforcement agencies subsequently developed new models that took into account the situations police officers encounter in their day-to-day activities. In 1993, Ontario developed the Ontario Use of Force Options Model, which "integrated both force options and a generic decision-making process summarized as 'assess-plan-act'" (Hoffman et al., 2004). The success of the Ontario model prompted a number of other provinces and the RCMP to follow suit.[4] In April 1999, 65 use-of-force experts and trainers from Canada and the United States were brought together at the Ontario Police College to develop the National Use of Force Framework. The Canadian Association of Chiefs of Police (CACP) endorsed this national initiative in November 2000 as a framework from which law enforcement agencies across Canada could develop sound procedures and protocols for their own use-of-force standards (Braidwood, 2009, p. 94).

The National Use of Force Framework presented in Figure 4.1 is a standardized approach to conflict situations and represents the process by which an officer assesses, plans, and responds to a given situation.[5] Unlike a unidirectional linear model, this framework provides an element of proportionality between the situation and the police response. As discussed above, earlier models did not reflect the true nature of many real-life situations and assumed that police incidents progressed directly from minimal force to lethal force. In reality, situations may not follow this progression at all (MacAlister, 2010). For example, a situation may start out extremely violently without any buildup. Others may start out intensely, but de-escalate to where persons involved become cooperative. For this reason, unidirectional linear models have been criticized for requiring an officer to move through the incremental progression one step at a time. They are also viewed as limiting the tactical options available to an officer when responding to a particular level of resistance/threat exhibited by a suspect. Moreover, unidirectional linear models restrict an officer's ability to de-escalate a given situation and resort to lower-level force options even though the circumstances have been reassessed.

The National Use of Force Framework focuses on the dynamic nature of a police situation and recognizes that unique factors influence the officer's risk assessment. For example, some situations will require the use of little or no force to resolve a conflict (i.e., verbal commands and the proximity of a police officer will suffice), whereas police control of combative situations may require complete incapacitation of the subject (i.e.,

FIGURE 4.1   National Use of Force Framework

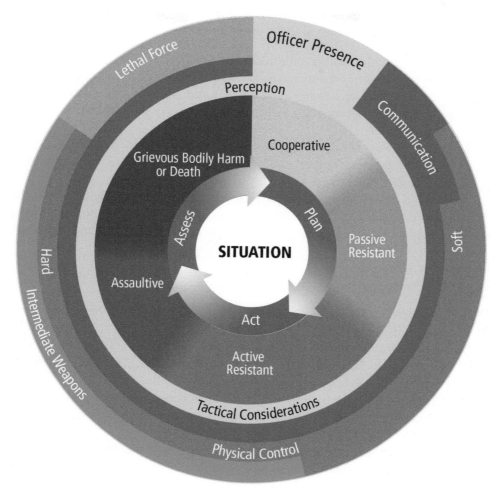

The officer continuously assesses the situation and acts in a reasonable manner to ensure officer and public safety.

deadly force) (Alpert, Dunham, & MacDonald, 2004, p. 475). Because each situation is unlike another, it is important for police to scrutinize situations on a case-by-case basis.

The assessment process is continuous and helps "explain how a behaviour (and response option) can change from cooperative to assaultive (or from communication to lethal force) in a split-second without passing through any of the other behaviour or force options" (Hoffman et al., 2004). Assessing how to respond to an incident requires that officers consider three factors: the situation, the subject's behaviour, and the officer's perceptions and tactical considerations. These factors guide the officer in determining whether to escalate, de-escalate or, when possible, to disengage from an incident. What follows is a brief examination of the key components of the National Use of Force Framework.

A. The Situation

When an officer responds to an incident, he or she must address at least six different situational conditions (Braidwood, 2009, pp. 96 and 97):

1. *Environment:* the weather, time of day, location, and physical position.
2. *Number of subjects:* the number of subjects compared with the number of officers.
3. *Perception of subject's abilities:* the subject's size, strength, and emotional state; proximity to weapons; and whether the subject is under the influence of drugs and/or alcohol.
4. *Prior knowledge of subject:* the subject's criminal history and reputation.
5. *Time and distance:* the level of threat to public safety, availability of cover, imminent arrival of backup, and ability to increase the distance.
6. *Potential attack signs:* possible physical behaviours that may give clues as to the subject's intentions (e.g., ignoring the officer, aggressive verbalization, refusing to comply with a lawful request, invasion of personal space, and hiding or fleeing).

B. Subject's Behaviour

Subject behaviours are divided into five categories:

1. *Cooperative:* the subject is compliant and responds positively to the officer's verbal commands.
2. *Non-cooperative:* the subject is non-compliant with the officer's lawful requests or commands. There is little or no physical resistance (e.g., failure to follow directions, refusal to leave the scene, taunting police officers).
3. *Resistant:* the subject actively resists an officer's lawful direction and uses non-assaultive physical action to resist or escape an officer's control (e.g., attempting to escape custody by fleeing).
4. *Combative:* the subject exhibits active and hostile resistance to an officer's lawful requests and attempts, threatens, or applies physical force with the intent to cause injury or resist (e.g., kicking, punching).
5. *Showing the potential to cause grievous bodily harm or death:* the subject's behaviour is threatening, and the officer reasonably believes the subject's actions are intended to, or likely to, cause grievous bodily harm or death to the public or the officer (e.g., use of a firearm or knife).

C. Officer's Perceptions and Tactical Considerations

Five categories of force response options are available to police officers. The objective of the use-of-force model is to guide officers in their assessment of the situation, select a level of force that is appropriate to the circumstances, and to act in a reasonable manner to ensure officer and public safety. Given the dynamic nature of any situation, the use-of-force options selected may change at any point.

1. *Officer presence:* the presence of an officer, or visible signs of authority such as a uniform or marked police car, may change a subject's behaviour.
2. *Communication:* verbal and non-verbal communication may be used to control and/or resolve the situation.

3. *Physical control:* this force option means any physical technique, not involving the use of a weapon, used to gain control. "Soft" techniques include joint locks, restraining techniques, and handcuffing. "Hard" techniques include empty-hand strikes such as punches, kicks, and strategic application of pressure (e.g., choke hold).
4. *Intermediate weapons:* they are less lethal weapons (not intended to cause serious injury or death), including impact weapons (e.g., police baton, Taser) and aerosols (e.g., tear gas, pepper spray).
5. *Lethal force:* this force option involves the use of any weapons or techniques that are intended to, or are reasonably likely to, cause grievous bodily harm or death.

Although police officers are guided by the philosophy that the most successful police intervention is the one that results in the least amount of harm, police-related incidents involving the use of force "are typically dynamic, rapidly evolving, and often extremely violent in nature" (Butler & Hall, 2008, p. 142).

Police Wrongdoing and Accountability

For years, various accountability and complaints process models have been employed in different jurisdictions around the world to investigate alleged police wrongdoing. As Table 4.1 illustrates, they range from marginal independence to complete independence by non-police agencies (MacAlister, 2012, p. 158). Throughout most of Canada, such allegations have historically been investigated by other police officers. These investigations have typically been conducted by Internal Affairs or Professional Standards units within the police organization directly involved in the alleged wrongdoing—with investigative oversight by police officers from a neighbouring agency on occasion.

TABLE 4.1   Investigating Alleged Police Wrongdoing

Internal	Investigations carried out by officers from within the same agency
Quasi-internal	Investigations carried out by the same agency with investigative oversight by officers from another police agency
Hybrid-quasi internal	Investigations carried out by police from a nearby police agency
Hybrid	Investigations carried out by police from a nearby police agency under civilian oversight and/or control
Hybrid-quasi-external	Investigations carried out by a civilian-led agency using seconded police
Quasi-external	Investigations carried out by a civilian agency using seconded and civilian investigators
External	Investigations carried out by a civilian agency that is led and staffed by non-police civilians

Source: MacAlister (2010).

Such was the case with the RCMP until 2010, when the agency announced a new national policy directive that would see all serious police-related incidents forwarded to outside agencies (Royal Canadian Mounted Police [RCMP], 2010).

What Do You Think?

Should police agencies investigate the actions of their own members? Do you agree with the underlying philosophy that police officers are in the best position to judge the actions of other officers in the field? Are police officers able to conduct impartial and neutral investigations into misconduct of their own?

Today, this internal investigative process remains prevalent among municipal police agencies in Quebec, New Brunswick, Prince Edward Island, and Newfoundland and Labrador (MacAlister, 2012, p. 158).

The underlying philosophy behind self-investigations is that police officers are the only persons who have the requisite expertise to undertake such investigations. This argument, however, has been shown to be problematic. In 2007, Paul E. Kennedy, then chair of the Commission for Public Complaints Against the RCMP, initiated an inquiry into public concerns regarding the impartiality of RCMP members conducting criminal investigations into the activities of other RCMP members in cases involving serious injury or death. The commission analyzed a total of 28 randomly selected cases alleged to have resulted in sexual assault, serious injury, or death between 2002 and 2007, taking into account the following criteria:

- conduct
- policy compliance
- timeliness
- line management
- level of response

In its final report, *Police Investigating Police: Final Public Report*, the commission found that more than two-thirds of the cases were handled inappropriately (Kennedy, 2009, p. 69). Although the commission recommended legislative, policy, procedural, and structural changes to improve criminal investigations into RCMP members, it fell short of proposing a genuine independent civilian investigation model. Instead, the commission recommended that other police agencies be used to investigate cases of police-involved deaths and other serious injury cases. The RCMP accepted these recommendations in early 2010 (RCMP, 2010).

The notion of police investigating themselves undoubtedly gives rise to legitimate concerns about conflict of interest, as well as concerns regarding the impartiality of investigators. As Mr. Justice Braidwood noted in his 2010 report:

> Many members of the public perceive that the investigators may allow loyalty to fellow officers to interfere with the impartial investigative process. This perception, even if not justified in a given case, can lead to public distrust and an undermining of public confidence in the police. (p. 411)

Over the past two decades, concerns over a perceived lack of objectivity and legitimacy have led to calls for reform and for the establishment of an independent regulatory framework to investigate incidents of alleged police misconduct. Moreover, in an era of increased accountability, jurisdictions in some provinces have mandated civilian-led agencies to investigate critical incidents of police-related deaths and serious injuries. One of the central features of this regulatory framework is that impartial civilians who are independent of any police service or organization undertake these investigations; it is a civilian-managed and civilian-run process (MacAlister, 2010, p. 37).

In response to concerns about the police investigating themselves, Ontario established the Special Investigations Unit (SIU). In existence since 1989, the SIU is a civilian oversight body charged with investigating incidents involving death and serious injury of members of the public arising in the course of police work. The SIU "seeks to protect the fundamental human rights of all its citizens by ensuring that those charged with enforcing the laws and advancing public safety remain accountable should they violate those rights" (Adams, 2003, p. 9). Similar civilian-led investigative bodies have been established in Alberta (Alberta Serious Incident Response Team), Manitoba (Independent Investigation Unit of Manitoba), and Nova Scotia (Serious Incident Response Team).

British Columbia has witnessed a spate of police-involved shootings and in-custody deaths in recent years. A *Vancouver Sun* investigation found that 48 fatal police shootings took place in British Columbia from 2004 through 2015, equating to approximately four deaths per year (Culbert, 2015). These statistics do not include persons who died in police custody from other means (e.g., self-inflicted death, motor vehicle incident, and use of a conducted energy weapon or other use-of-force option). A number of high-profile cases garnered considerable media attention and public scrutiny, and several government inquiries into police-involved deaths in British Columbia called for the provincial government to establish an independent oversight agency to investigate police-related deaths (Braidwood, 2010; Davies, 2009; Oppal, 1994). In May 2011, Shirley Bond, British Columbia's minister of justice and attorney general, introduced Bill 12 into the Legislative Assembly to amend the *Police Act* in order to create the Independent Investigations Office (IIO) of BC. The agency was established in response to recommendations arising out of the Robert Dziekański and Frank Paul public inquiries (for information about the death of Frank Paul, see Davies [2009]).

The IIO is an independent civilian police oversight agency. At the time of writing, it had 24 investigators, half of whom were formerly police officers. Led by the chief civilian director, the IIO is responsible for investigating all officer-related incidents that result in death or serious harm within the province of British Columbia. The agency's jurisdiction also extends to alleged contraventions of a "prescribed provision" in federal or provincial legislation. The IIO does not have authority to investigate complaints involving police misconduct. Complaints alleging misconduct by municipal police officers are the responsibility of the Office of the Police Complaint Commissioner (OPCC), while the Civilian Review and Complaints Commission for the RCMP (CRCC) reviews complaints made by the public about members of the RCMP. The IIO's overall mandate is to create more accountability, oversight, and transparency in the investigation of police incidents that result in death or serious harm, as well as to enhance public confidence in policing.

The IIO's *Annual Report 2015–2016* (Independent Investigations Office of BC, 2016) noted that, since becoming operational in September 2012, the agency has received 871 notifications of critical incidents and has undertaken a total of 170 investigations. Of the 50 cases referred to Crown counsel for consideration, eight cases (16 percent) resulted in the approval of charges against the involved officers. Of those eight cases, one officer was acquitted, two cases resulted in guilty pleas, and two resulted in a stay of proceedings. In the other three cases, the decisions regarding charge assessment were pending. In 39 cases (78 percent) referred to Crown counsel, charges were not approved against the officers involved. In an effort to ensure transparency and accountability, all case files forwarded to Crown counsel for charge assessment, as well as public reports clearing officers of any wrongdoing, are released on the IIO's website.

Conclusion

The Charter has had a profound effect on our adversarial system of criminal justice. Indeed, the legal rights provisions set out in ss 7 to 14 of the Charter protect individuals from abuses of state power throughout the criminal investigative process, while ensuring fairness during subsequent legal proceedings. Passage of the Charter was a watershed moment in human rights and civil liberties history. It also marked a dramatic transformation in the Canadian legal landscape, with a shift away from crime control and the perceived needs of law enforcement to an emphasis on due process values and the rights of individual citizens. On the one hand, some have argued that the police have become constrained by the Charter, which they consider has limited the powers that police officers require to effectively carry out their law enforcement mandate. On the other hand, others view the Charter as an important system of procedural checks and balances that, among other things, has influenced police decision-making processes and how police officers approach law enforcement more generally. The police are not given carte blanche during criminal investigations, but, as we have seen throughout this chapter, common law authority and statutory provisions grant the police powers to carry out their duties effectively—duties that may include more intrusive investigative techniques where reasonable grounds exist to deploy them.

As Gérald Lafrenière (2001) pointed out in a paper prepared for the Senate Special Committee on Illegal Drugs:

> It is clear that the arrival of the Charter and the individual rights and freedoms that it protects has allowed the courts to play an even greater role in defining permissible boundaries of police conduct. In determining whether police conduct is acceptable, one is generally forced to weigh conflicting interests. First, there are the individual's interests, including the interest of being free from state intrusion. Second, there are the state's interests, including protecting society from crime. Because these interests generally conflict, it can sometimes be difficult to agree on where the line should be drawn in relation to police conduct. (p. 1)

Since the inception of the Charter over 30 years ago, the courts have sought to delicately balance the competing interests of the state and the individual. Doing so has not been easy, as evidenced by the fact that Canada's highest court "has taken inherently conflicting positions in cases that pit police investigative powers against Charter rights" (Stribopoulos, 2005, para. 6). This approach highlights the key issues and tensions inherent in the competing models of criminal justice alluded to in Chapter 1.

There is no doubt that the police require powers to maintain law and order in our society. Both Parliament and the courts have recognized the difficulty in detecting crime, enforcing the law, and protecting society while, at the same time, safeguarding individuals from abuses of state power. The struggle to find a compromise between competing imperatives such as the rights of the individual and the integrity of the administration of justice is sure to continue in years to come.

DISCUSSION QUESTIONS

1. What sections of the Charter have an effect on the law regarding detention and arrest in Canada?
2. Do you think the Harper government's controversial *Anti-terrorism Act, 2015* should be repealed? It has been argued that some of the provisions violate the Charter. Which sections of the Charter are relevant to this argument?
3. On what grounds can a police officer stop an individual for an investigative detention? Provide an example of a situation that might be considered a detention. Also provide an example of circumstances that would not be viewed as a detention for investigative purposes.
4. Under what circumstances can a police officer arrest someone without a warrant?
5. Do you think arbitrary police street checks should be permitted? Is "carding" a legitimate tool to help solve and prevent crime in high-crime neighbourhoods?
6. Why do you think some people might falsely confess to a crime they did not commit?
7. Studies have shown that false confessions are a contributing factor in many wrongful convictions. What do you think could be done to reduce the number of false confessions and increase the number of true confessions?
8. It is garbage day and you have placed your garbage cans at the edge of your residential property for collection. Can a police officer reach a few inches over the property line in order to retrieve items from the cans? Is this a breach of your s 8 Charter right to be secure against unreasonable search or seizure? If the police seize incriminating evidence from your garbage cans, should that evidence be excluded in accordance with s 24(2) of the Charter?
9. Should evidence that has been improperly or illegally seized by the police during a search be automatically excluded from trial?
10. Police officers are authorized to conduct warrantless searches when an individual voluntarily consents to the search. What are the guidelines for establishing whether voluntary consent was given?
11. What is the National Use of Force Framework?
12. What are two criticisms of the unidirectional linear model of the use of force?

NOTES

1 Section 487.1 allows a person seeking a search warrant to obtain one by means of telecommunication where it is impracticable for the peace officer to appear personally to make the application.
2 See Keenan and Brockman (2010) for an analysis of how wiretap authorizations are obtained in undercover operations, such as the "Mr. Big" investigative technique.
3 See *R v LSL*, [1997] SJ No 30 (QL) (QB).
4 The RCMP uses the Incident Management Intervention Model (IMIM), which is similar to the model presented here.
5 In addition, Griffiths (2013) notes how the model "provides police administrators and judicial review personnel with an objective framework for analyzing use-of-force situations" (p. 147).

SUGGESTED FURTHER READINGS

Braidwood, T. (2010). *Why? The Robert Dziekański tragedy.* Vancouver: Braidwood Commission on the Death of Robert Dziekański.

Brockman, J. (2015). *An introduction to Canadian criminal procedure and evidence* (5th ed.). Toronto: Nelson.

Cameron, J. (1996). *The Charter's impact on the criminal justice system.* Scarborough, ON: Carswell.

Canadian Civil Liberties Association. (2015, July 21). *CCLA & CJFE mounting Charter challenge against Bill C-51* [Press release]. Retrieved from https://ccla.org/ccla-and-cjfe-mounting-charter-challenge-against-bill-c-51/.

Davies, W.H. (2009). *Alone and cold: Criminal Justice Branch response—Davies Commission inquiry into the response of the Criminal Justice Branch (B.C.).* Victoria: Davies Commission. Retrieved from http://www.bccla.org/wp-content/uploads/2012/03/2009-BCCLA-Report-Davies-Inquiry-Alone-Cold.pdf.

Griffiths, C.T. (2015). *Canadian criminal justice: A primer* (5th ed.). Toronto: Nelson.

Hoffman, R., Lawrence, C., & Brown, G. (2004). Canada's National Use of Force Framework for police officers. *Police Chief, 71,* 125–141.

Kennedy, P. (2009). *Police investigating police: Final public report.* Ottawa: Commission for Public Complaints Against the RCMP.

Wood, J. (2007). *Report on the review of the police complaint process in British Columbia.* Victoria: Government of British Columbia.

REFERENCES

Adams, G.W. (2003). *Review report on the Special Investigations Unit reforms prepared for the Attorney General of Ontario by the Honourable George W. Adams, Q.C.* Toronto: Ministry of the Attorney General.

Alpert, G.P., Dunham, R.G., & MacDonald, J.M. (2004). Interactive police–citizen encounters that result in force. *Police Quarterly, 7,* 475–488.

Angus Reid Institute. (2014, May 6). Canadian confidence in police, courts sees significant rebound over 2012 sentiment. Retrieved from http://angusreid.org/canadian-confidence-in-police-courts-sees-significant-rebound-over-2012-sentiment/.

Bittner, E. (1970). *The functions of police in modern society.* Washington, DC: Government Printing Office.

Boswell, R. (2013, January 1). Public opinion of scandal-plagued RCMP down "significantly" in past five years: Poll. *National Post.* Retrieved from http://news.nationalpost.com/news/canada/public-opinion-of-scandal-plagued-rcmp-down-significantly-in-past-five-years-poll.

Braidwood, T. (2009). *Restoring public confidence: Restricting the use of conducted energy weapons in British Columbia.* Vancouver: Braidwood Commission on the Death of Robert Dziekański.

Braidwood, T. (2010). *Why? The Robert Dziekański tragedy.* Vancouver: Braidwood Commission on the Death of Robert Dziekański.

Brockman, J. (2015). *An introduction to Canadian criminal procedure and evidence* (5th ed.). Toronto: Nelson.

Butler, C., & Hall, C. (2008). Police/public interaction: Arrests, use of force by police, and resulting injuries to subjects and officers—A description of risk in one major Canadian city. *Law Enforcement Executive Forum, 8,* 141–157.

Canadian Association of Chiefs of Police. (n.d.). National use of force model. Retrieved from https://www.cacp.ca/cacp-use-of-force-advisory-committee-activities.html?asst_id=199.

Cloutier v Langlois, [1990] 1 SCR 158.

Culbert, L. (2015, March 31). Seven killed in B.C. this year in police shootings *Vancouver Sun*. Retrieved from http://www.vancouversun.com/health/seven+killed+this+year+police+shootings/11441774/story.html.

Davies, W.H. (2009). *Alone and cold: Criminal Justice Branch response—Davies Commission inquiry into the response of the Criminal Justice Branch (B.C.)*. Victoria: Davies Commission. Retrieved from http://www.bccla.org/wp-content/uploads/2012/03/2009-BCCLA-Report-Davies-Inquiry-Alone-Cold.pdf.

Davis, D., & O'Donohue, W. (2003). The road to perdition: "Extreme influence" tactics in the interrogation room. In W. O'Donohue, P. Laws, & C. Hollin (Eds.), *Handbook of forensic psychology* (pp. 897–996). New York: Basic Books.

Drizin, S.A., & Leo, R.A. (2004). The problem of false confessions in the post-DNA world. *North Carolina Law Review, 82*(3), 891–1007.

Eccles v Bourque et al, [1975] 2 SCR 739.

Grewal, S. (2015, September 24). Blacks three times more likely to be carded by Peel police than whites. *Toronto Star*. Retrieved from https://www.thestar.com/news/gta/2015/09/24/blacks-three-times-more-likely-to-be-carded-by-peel-police-than-whites.html.

Griffiths, C.T. (2013). *Canadian police work* (3rd ed.). Toronto: Nelson.

Gudjonsson, G.H. (2003). *The psychology of interrogations and confessions: A handbook*. Chichester, UK: John Wiley.

Gudjonsson, G.H. (2012). Investigative interviewing. In T. Newburn, T. Williamson, & A. Wright (Eds.), *Handbook of criminal investigation* (pp. 466–492). Cullompton, UK: Willan.

Hartwig, M., Meissner, C.A., & Semel, M.D. (2014). Human intelligence interviewing and interrogation: Assessing the challenges of developing an ethical, evidence-based approach. In R. Bull (Ed.), *Investigative interviewing* (pp. 209–228). New York: Springer.

Hoffman, R., Lawrence, C., & Brown, G. (2004, October). Canada's national use of force framework for police officers. *Police Chief, 125*.

Hunter et al v Southam Inc, [1984] 2 SCR 145.

Independent Investigations Office of BC. (2016). *Annual report 2015–2016*. Surrey, BC: Author. Retrieved from http://iiobc.ca/wp-content/uploads/2016/11/IIO-2015-2016-Annual-Report-Interactive.pdf.

Innocence Project. (n.d.). False confessions or admissions. Retrieved from http://www.innocenceproject.org/causes/false-confessions-admissions/.

Kassin, S.M. (2006). A critical appraisal of modern police interrogations. In T. Williamson (Ed.), *Investigative interviewing: Rights, research, regulation* (pp. 207–228). Devon, UK: Willan.

Kassin, S.M., Drizin, S.A., Grisso, T., Gudjonsson, G.H., Leo, R.A., & Redlich, A.D. (2010). Police-induced confessions: Risk factors and recommendations. *Law and Human Behavior, 34*, 3–38.

Keenan, K.T., & Brockman, J. (2010). *Mr. Big: Exposing undercover investigations in Canada*. Halifax: Fernwood.

Kennedy, P. (2009). *Police investigating police: Final public report*. Ottawa: Commission for Public Complaints Against the RCMP.

Lafrenière, G. (2001). *Police powers and drug-related offences: Prepared for the Senate Special Committee on Illegal Drugs*. Ottawa: Library of Parliament. Retrieved from http://www.parl.gc.ca/Content/SEN/Committee/371/ille/library/powers-e.htm.

Larocque, C. (2015, July 23). Ottawa police taking heat over street checks. *Ottawa Sun*. Retrieved from http://www.ottawasun.com/2015/07/23/ottawa-police-taking-heat-over-street-checks.

MacAlister, D. (2010). *Police-involved deaths: The failure of self-investigation final report*. Vancouver: British Columbia Civil Liberties Association.

MacAlister, D. (2012). Policing the police in Canada: Alternative approaches to the investigation of serious police wrongdoing. In D. MacAlister (Ed.), *Police-involved deaths: The need for reform* (pp. 158–191). Vancouver: British Columbia Civil Liberties Association.

Manning, P.K. (1977). *Police work: The social organization of policing.* Cambridge, MA: MIT Press.

Marin, A. (2015). *"Street checks and balances": Submission in response to the Ministry of Community Safety and Correctional Services' consultation on proposed Ontario regulation for street checks.* Toronto: Ombudsman Ontario. Retrieved from https://www.ombudsman.on .ca/Files/sitemedia/Documents/OntarioOmbudsman-StreetChecks-EN.pdf.

Meissner, C.A., Redlich, A.D., Michael, S.W., Evans, J.R., Camilletti, C.R., Bhatt, S., & Brandon, S. (2014). Accusatorial and information-gathering interrogation methods and their effects on true and false confessions: A meta-analytic review. *Journal of Experimental Criminology, 10*(4), 459–486.

Murphy, C., & McKenna, P. (2007). *Rethinking police governance, culture and management.* Ottawa: Public Safety Canada. Retrieved from https://www.publicsafety.gc.ca/cnt/cntrng -crm/tsk-frc-rcmp-grc/_fl/archive-rthnk-plc-eng.pdf.

Ontario Ministry of Community Safety and Correctional Services. (2016). Street checks: Final regulations. Retrieved from http://www.mcscs.jus.gov.on.ca/english/Policing/ StreetChecks.html.

Oppal, W.T. (1994). *Closing the gap: Policing and the community—Commission of Inquiry into policing in British Columbia.* Victoria: Queen's Printer.

Quigley, T. (2015, January). Recent developments: Criminal procedure, Part I—A new legal regime for the admissibility of "Mr. Big" confessions. *Carswell's Criminal Law Practice Page Exclusive Feature,* 1–6. Retrieved from http://www.carswell.com/DynamicData/ AttachedDocs/Criminal%20Law%20Practice%20Page/Jan2015/CriminalLawPageExclusive Feature_January2015.pdf.

R v Bartle, [1994] 3 SCR 173.

R v Borden, [1994] 3 SCR 145.

R v Brydges, [1990] 1 SCR 190.

R v Evans, [1996] 1 SCR 8.

R v Feeney, [1997] 2 SCR 13.

R v Forcillo, 2016 ONSC 4850.

R v Godoy, [1999] 1 SCR 311.

R v Golden, 2001 SCC 83, [2001] 3 SCR 679.

R v Hart, 2014 SCC 52, [2014] 2 SCR 544.

R v Hodgson, [1998] 2 SCR 449.

R v Joseph, 2000 BCSC 219, BCJ No 2800 (QL).

R v Kokesch, [1990] 3 SCR 3.

R v LSL, 1991 CanLII 7820, [1991] SJ No 30 (QL) (QB).

R v MacDonald, 2014 SCC 3.

R v Mann, 2004 SCC 52 [2004] 3 SCR 59.

R v McCreery, 1998 CanLII 5055, [1998] BCJ No 1199 (QL) (CA).

R v Morelli, 2010 SCC 8, [2010] 1 SCR 253.

R v Oickle, 2000 SCC 38, [2000] 2 SCR 3.

R v Patrick, 2009 SCC 17, [2009] 1 SCR 579.

R v Singh, 2007 SCC 48, [2007] 3 SCR 405.

R v Stillman, [1997] 1 SCR 607.

R v Storrey, [1990] 1 SCR 241.

R v Therens, [1985] 1 SCR 613.

R v Unger (1993), 83 CCC (3d) 228 (Man CA).

R v Wills (1992), 70 CCC (3d) 529 (Ont CA).

Rankin, J. (2010, February 6). Race matters: Blacks documented by police at high rate. *Toronto Star*. Retrieved from https://www.thestar.com/news/crime/raceandcrime/2010/02/06/race_matters_blacks_documented_by_police_at_high_rate.html.

Redlich, A.D., & Meissner, C.A. (2009). Techniques and controversies in the interrogation of suspects: The artful practice versus the scientific study. In J.L. Skeem, K.S. Douglas, & S.O. Lilienfeld (Eds.), *Psychological science in the courtroom* (pp. 124–148). New York: Guilford Press.

Royal Canadian Mounted Police. (2010, February 4). *RCMP announces new policy on external investigations* [Press release]. Retrieved from http://news.gc.ca/web/article-en.do?m=/index&nid=510769.

Semayne's Case (1604), 5 Co Rep 91a.

Sherry Good v Toronto Police Services Board, 2014 ONSC 4583, 375 DLR (4th) 200.

Skolnik, T. (2016). The suspicious distinction between reasonable suspicion and reasonable grounds to believe. *Ottawa Law Review, 47*(1), 223–249.

Snook, B., Eastwood, J., Stinson, M., Tedeschini, J., & House, J.C. (2010). Reforming investigative interviewing in Canada. *Canadian Journal of Criminology and Criminal Justice, 52*(2), 215–229.

Snook, B., & House, J. C. (2008, November). An alternative interviewing method: All we are saying is give PEACE a chance. *Blue Line Magazine*, 10–12.

Stribopoulos, J. (2005). In search of dialogue: The Supreme Court, police powers and the Charter. *Queen's Law Journal, 31*, 1–74.

Walma, M.W., & West, L. (2001). *Police powers and procedures*. Toronto: Emond Montgomery.

Warmington, J. (2015, November 18). Street checks needed to solve crimes. *Toronto Sun*. Retrieved from http://www.torontosun.com/2015/11/18/street-checks-needed-to-solve-crimes.

Forensic Science and Forensic Psychology

LEARNING OUTCOMES

After reading this chapter, students will be able to:

- Distinguish between evidence with class characteristics and evidence with individual characteristics.
- Understand the difference between crime scene investigators and laboratory forensic scientists.
- Understand how forensic psychologists assess the fitness to stand trial and criminal responsibility of an accused.
- Describe two primary approaches to assessing the risk of recidivism.
- Summarize the interventions used to reduce delinquent behaviour in juveniles.
- Describe the factors that can affect the accuracy of eyewitness identification.
- Describe interrogation techniques used by police.

Introduction

Forensic science and forensic psychology, once only discussed in laboratories, police investigations, and courtrooms, have, due to a proliferation of crime television shows, become household words. The growth in public interest in these disciplines is good, as it is important for the general public to understand how the legal system works. Unfortunately, much of the information provided in television shows is incorrect, or, at the very least, exaggerated. This chapter will explain the basics of forensic science and forensic psychology.

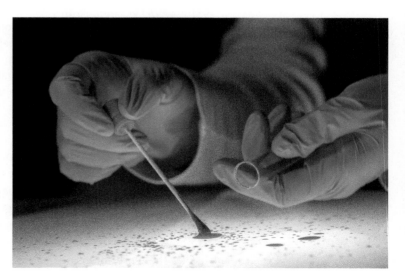

Forensic Science

Forensic science is the application of science to the law. More specifically, it is "the application of science to the criminal and civil laws that are enforced by police agencies in a criminal justice system" (Saferstein, 2015, p. 4).

Note that the pertinent word in *forensic science* is *science* and not *forensic*. In this context, *forensic* means "as applied to the law." Therefore, forensic biology (a subdiscipline of forensic science) is the application of biological theories, techniques, and practices to the law.

Anyone who performs a scientific forensic analysis must be a scientist before he or she can become a forensic scientist. Although television shows often depict a single scientist performing multiple analyses across a range of disparate disciplines, this portrayal is misleading. In reality, each discipline requires very specific and lengthy education and training, and no single person would have the time to become qualified in multiple sciences. As well, the distinction between laboratory scientists, crime scene investigators, coroners or medical examiners and other forensic specialists is often blurred in portrayals on television and in books. In reality, each role involves a very different career path.

Forensic Evidence

trace evidence
Any small piece of evidence that is left behind and/or picked up at a crime scene. This can include just about anything, such as fingerprints, fibres, hair, soil, blood, semen, and paint.

Forensic scientists analyze physical trace evidence. **Trace evidence** refers to all the tiny fragments of our lives that can be picked up or left behind at a crime scene, such as fingerprints, body fluids, hair, footprints, paint, gasoline, glue, gunshot residue, and fibres. One of the most basic principles of forensic science is Locard's exchange principle. Edmond Locard was a pioneer of forensic science and the founder of the first forensic laboratory in Lyon, France in 1910. Locard recognized that when an offender commits a crime, he or she leave traces of him or herself—physical evidence—behind, and also picks up traces from the crime scene and the victim. Because an *exchange* of physical evidence takes place between the offender and the scene, careful analysis can link the scene, offender, and victim.

SIDEBAR

Locard's Exchange Principle

This basic principle of forensic science is over 100 years old. Edmond Locard recognized that every contact involves an exchange of physical materials that can be later analyzed scientifically. For example, an offender enters a residence, rapes a woman on a carpet, and leaves. He takes with him fibres from her carpet and clothing, and hair from her head and pubic region, and he leaves behind fibres from his clothing, head, and pubic hair, as well as semen, skin cells under her fingernails, and hairs from his dog that were on his clothing. Each of these materials can be analyzed and identified. Then the level of significance must be determined to assess the probative value of the evidence.

Many of the analyses performed by forensic scientists, such as identifying and quantifying a substance, are the same as those performed by any other scientist. For example, a chemist working for a gasoline company may analyze a substance in a drilled core sample to determine the presence and grade of gasoline to decide whether it is worth investing in further exploration. A forensic chemist will perform very similar tests to determine whether the stain on a piece of carpet is gasoline and, if it is, of what type and grade. Therefore, forensic scientists are, first and foremost, scientists. However, once the evidence is identified and quantified, the forensic scientist must then determine its significance to a criminal investigation. Evidence is considered to have a range of significance levels, from low to high. This assessment is based on how likely it is that an innocent person or area might also possess such material. For example, imagine that white cotton fibres are found on the victim. A suspect is rapidly identified and is wearing a white cotton T-shirt that has fibres that match exactly with those on the victim. Is this evidence highly significant? No, because although the fibres on the victim and those from the white cotton T-shirt match exactly, the **exhibit** would also match any other white cotton T-shirt, and, no doubt, millions of such T-shirts exist. Such evidence has very little **probative value**. In a different scenario, if a fibre found on the victim was discovered to have come from a sweater made in Mongolia from hand-dyed yak wool, it is likely to be much rarer and therefore more significant. However, it is still not unique, and its level of significance would depend on how many such sweaters were made from that dye lot and also how many were sold in the victim's area.

exhibit
An individual piece of evidence.

probative value
The ability of a piece of evidence to prove or assist in proving something to the trier of fact.

SIDEBAR

Fibres and the Atlanta Child Murderer

Wayne Williams was convicted in 1982 of the murders of two young men in Georgia, but he is thought to be responsible for the deaths of many other young men and children. Although a large body of evidence was used in securing his conviction, one essential part was fibre evidence recovered from 12 murder victims and linked to an unusual carpet in Williams' home (Saferstein, 2011). Carpet fibres are usually not unique, so in order to assess the value of this evidence, police had to determine how common the material was in the general population. They determined that the type of fibre was manufactured by only one company, over only a 12-month period, and that only 16,397 square feet of carpet containing the fibres of that colour were sold in Georgia and the surrounding nine states. It was estimated that only 82 rooms in Georgia would have this carpet. The chance of any residence other than that of Williams having such a carpet in the Atlanta area was calculated to be 1 in 7,792 (Saferstein, 2011). This fact made the fibres quite rare, greatly increasing the level of significance of the evidence.

Certain evidence is considered to have **class characteristics** or be class evidence. That is, the evidence is not unique, but can be associated with a group. Much evidence—for example, paint, fibres, glue, duct tape, and glass—has class characteristics, but it can nevertheless be very valuable. Consider a hit and run where yellow paint chips are left on the victim's clothing. Car paint is specific to a manufacturer, a range of years, and a model of vehicle, and all car paints are stored in databases available to investigators. Therefore, a chemical analysis of the paint type and colour could lead investigators to determine that the paint chip came from a Honda Civic manufactured between 2010 and 2014. Although the paint chip would probably match the paint of many vehicles in an area, it has narrowed the search down to a finite number of vehicles and, perhaps more important, has eliminated every other vehicle on the road. Cars are registered, so a search can be made for people who own such a vehicle in the vicinity of the crime. In particular, those with cars in body shops or with front-end damage can be prioritized.

class characteristics
Characteristics that allow an exhibit to be associated with a group, but not a single source.

Once a possible suspect vehicle is located, other evidence from the vehicle, such as body fluids, may confirm the link between the vehicle and the victim.

trier of fact
Judge and/or jury.

When presenting class evidence to the **trier of fact**, it is vital that the level of significance be included in the forensic science report and testimony. If the examiner states that the evidence is an exact match to something belonging to the suspect, that claim sounds extremely convincing to a jury, but it may be misleading, as the evidence may also be an exact match to many other objects in the courtroom alone (consider, for example, white cotton T-shirt fibres). Therefore, it is imperative that the examiner calculate the mathematical probability (expressed as a ratio) that such evidence might also be found on a random, innocent person; for example, "the chance of anyone else possessing this evidence is 1 in 50,000." When several pieces of evidence have class characteristics and their probability of being found in the general population is known, then these data can be multiplied to determine the probability that a random person would have *all* of the pieces of evidence, making the class evidence more significant. For example, imagine that a suspect has a fibre on his clothing that matches that of the victim's sweater, and the chance that this match could be a random match is 1 in 8,000. In addition, the suspect has a fibre on his clothing that matches that of the blanket on which the victim was assaulted, and the chance that this match could be a random match is 1 in 4,000. Therefore, the chance that a random person might have both fibres on him or her would be 1 in 32,000,000.

individual characteristics
Characteristics that allow an exhibit to be associated with a single source.

Most evidence has class characteristics, but some evidence also possesses **individual characteristics**, which means the evidence can be associated with a single source with a high degree of certainty. Such evidence includes DNA and fingerprints, which are considered to be unique to just one person, except in the case of identical twins (twins who come from the same zygote have identical DNA, but have unique fingerprints). Evidence with individual characteristics is extremely probative.

Forensic Investigations

A forensic investigation involves a diverse group of people, including crime scene investigators and laboratory scientists. If a death is involved, a coroner or medical examiner will examine the body and, if he or she determines that an autopsy is required, will consult a forensic pathologist. As well, a number of other forensic specialists may be involved in a forensic investigation.

Crime Scene Investigation

Contrary to the way such investigations are portrayed on television, in Canada crime scenes are almost entirely processed by sworn police officers, not civilians. These police officers are not general duty officers but highly trained and specialized identification officers (often abbreviated to "ident" or "ident officers"). Before applying for the Identification Section of a police force, police officers must have served several years in general duty and undergone a general aptitude examination for ident. Their training includes extensive course work in many areas such as photography, crime scene examination, and evidence collection, and several years of on-the-job training under the mentorship of a qualified specialist, culminating in a mock trial.

When a crime is identified, although general duty officers may be the first to attend the scene to determine whether a crime has taken place and to secure the scene, ident officers process the scene and identify and collect the evidence. Ident officers must ensure that **continuity of evidence**, or chain of custody, is maintained at all times. By doing so, when an exhibit is presented in court, the ident officer can say exactly where the evidence was located, how it was collected, who has handled it, and how it has been maintained to date to show that the evidence could not have been altered or tampered with at any time. To maintain continuity, anyone handling an exhibit must sign for it and document what was done to it to explain any changes. For example, a dish of ice cream knocked to the floor during the commission of a crime may be found when it is still partially frozen, but will obviously melt and change appearance over time. Before it is collected, the ident officer will document the condition of the ice cream at the time of discovery through notes, sketches, and, most important, photography. Despite the fact that the exhibit will have changed by the time it is examined at the laboratory and discussed in court, the documentation at the scene will show the court the condition of the exhibit at the earlier time, will explain changes that have occurred since, and may be of value in estimating when the dish was knocked to the ground.

Ident officers will document the entire scene with photography, notes, and measurements so that the scene can be recreated later for the trier of fact. All pieces of evidence will be seized and taken for further analyses. Of course, at this time it may not be obvious what is evidence and what is not, so everything will be documented. Ident will liaise between the investigating officers and the forensic laboratories to ensure that the evidence is transported to the laboratory to be analyzed by scientists in the appropriate sections (e.g., biology, chemistry, firearms). However, some types of evidence are analyzed directly by ident officers, including fingerprints, palm prints, and footwear impressions. Some ident officers receive advanced training to analyze blood-spatter pattern evidence. Once the evidence is submitted to the laboratory or analyzed by ident officers, the role of ident officers for that crime scene is over, unless they are called on later to testify in court as to what they did at the scene. Ident officers are specialized crime scene investigators and, while they work closely with the officers assigned to investigate the crime, they do not participate in further investigation of the crime.

Forensic Laboratories

In contrast with those involved in crime scene processing, forensic scientists in laboratories are civilians and not sworn police officers. They do not attend crime scenes but receive evidence from the ident team and analyze it in a laboratory. Their results are then submitted to the police investigating the crime, and they may be asked to testify as expert witnesses. They are unbiased and will objectively and scientifically analyze the evidence. For example, if a jacket with blood on it and DNA samples from two individuals are submitted, scientists in the Biology Section will analyze all three pieces of evidence, obtain DNA profiles, and submit a report stating that the blood on the jacket did or did not match the profile of Subject A or Subject B. The laboratory forensic scientist does not care whether the jacket belonged to the suspect, the victim, or a bystander, nor whether Subject A or Subject B is a suspect or a victim. He or she simply reports the scientific results.

The three main groups of forensic laboratories in Canada are as follows: the Royal Canadian Mounted Police National Forensic Laboratory Services, located in Vancouver, Edmonton, and Ottawa; the Centre of Forensic Sciences, in Toronto and Sault Ste. Marie; and the Laboratoire de sciences judiciaires et de médecine légale, in Montreal.

continuity of evidence
The chronological record of everyone that handles an exhibit and everything that is done to it, such as analyses, from the moment that it is seized to its final disposition. Also called *chain of custody*.

The Start of Forensic Science in Canada

The first forensic laboratory in North America was founded in Montreal in 1914, ten years before America's first crime lab was established and 18 years before the FBI crime laboratory came into existence. It was established by Dr. Wilfred Dérôme, a Canadian pioneer in forensic science. In 1929, J. Edgar Hoover, the first director of the FBI, visited the Montreal laboratory to assist in planning the FBI crime laboratory. The Montreal laboratory is now known as the Laboratoire des sciences judiciaires et de médecine légale and serves as the crime lab for the province of Quebec.

Most laboratory forensic scientists have a bachelor's degree in their discipline, and often a graduate degree, and then enter the laboratory system where they are trained in-house for a further one to two years before they become specialists. This training includes course work and working on files under a mentor scientist, and it culminates in a mock trial. Once qualified as specialists, laboratory forensic scientists continue to undergo further training as new technologies are developed. Although each laboratory is a little different, most have the sections discussed below.

Evidence Management or Case Receipt Section

Evidence collected at the crime scene first enters the laboratory in the Evidence Management or Case Receipt Section. It is here that all evidence is tagged and recorded in a computer monitoring system so that its progress and location through the laboratory can be monitored to maintain continuity and to determine its status at any given time. Some exhibits will only go to one section, while others may go to several sections, depending on the type of evidence recovered.

CAREER PROFILE

Jorge Frasca

Jorge Frasca is a technical operations leader in the Evidence Recovery Unit of the RCMP Forensic Laboratory in Vancouver.

How did you become interested in forensics?
Forensics was never really an interest for me until my wife told me the Royal Canadian Mounted Police (RCMP) was hiring scientists to work in forensics. I put in my application, was eventually hired as a forensic biologist at the RCMP Forensic Laboratory in Vancouver, and have been employed in forensics ever since.

How did you become a technical operations leader?
I began my career as a search technologist in the Evidence Recovery Unit, which is the front-end search, identification, and recovery unit in biology. I quickly gained experience and confidence in the examination of exhibits, recovering and identifying a variety of evidence, and conducting the search of numerous exhibits. I was then promoted to search coordinator and, after two years, to section manager. I enjoyed managing, but was always drawn toward the scientific part of the work. When I had an opportunity to become technical operations leader, I did not hesitate. I have a much more direct involvement with the technical aspects of forensic science, and still work closely with others to manage their training, development, and technical competencies.

What are some of your most important duties? Is there such thing as a typical day for you?
One of the things that I enjoy most about my job is that it is quite varied. Every aspect is important, as they can all impact the quality of the work that is carried out in the laboratory. However, the most important part of my role involves being a coach and mentor in the technical aspects of evidence examination and recovery. As well, being involved in the development of policy and scientific methodology and techniques on behalf of the discipline are very important responsibilities.

What are the most challenging and the most rewarding aspects of your job?
Being a forensic scientist is a somewhat unique experience. My role allows me to develop both scientific and personal skills, and use knowledge gained throughout my career directly in support of high-profile investigations; in some instances, the results of my work can have a very tangible and immediate impact. On a daily basis, I am consulted on complex casework scenarios and challenging examination situations. Being involved in providing factual and objective evidence that can help these investigations is satisfying and rewarding on a personal level.

The most challenging and rewarding part of my job is leading the training and supervision of new forensic scientists. It makes no difference how much experience and knowledge I have gained, passing these skills to understudies and helping them develop can be difficult at times.

Overall, I find it very gratifying to know that my work contributes to the ongoing effort to make our communities safer.

In your opinion, what are some of the greatest contributions of forensic evidence to investigating and solving crimes?
Forensic science can assist criminal investigations by providing physical evidence that links individuals to each other and to crime scenes. It can also help to corroborate a particular scenario, witness statement, and/or sequence of events.

While traditional investigative techniques can put police on the right track, forensic evidence provides factual, unbiased evidence, and can greatly assist in showing whether a theory is correct.

With the advent of DNA profiling, forensic evidence has evolved from "nice to have" evidence to a "must have" in a greater number of investigations, particularly those that are more serious and high profile in nature.

How have the media affected the public's view of forensics?
In my opinion, the focus of the media on forensics is a double-edged sword.

On the one hand, the spotlight has grossly inflated the expectations of forensic evidence, and it places unrealistic expectations on what the science is capable of. The reality is that while forensics can be a very powerful tool, there are certain questions that it will not be able to answer. Forensic scientists need to place more emphasis on education, so that these expectations can be properly balanced.

On the other hand, the publicity has increased the demand on the services that forensic laboratories provide. An increased emphasis on forensics helps push the science forward, and it forces laboratories and scientists to constantly improve their processes and methodology.

In my opinion, the most important effect of the focus of the media on forensics is that it has opened the door for many new scientists to consider pursuing a career in forensic science. An increased demand for positions in forensics has had a positive impact on the quality of personnel that forensic laboratories can draw from.

Evidence Recovery Section

The first step to recovering forensically useful evidence from an exhibit occurs in the Evidence Recovery Section. Search technologists examine the exhibit to locate and recover the evidence itself. For example, a bedsheet may be brought to the lab as an exhibit. The search technologists will use a variety of scientific methods, such as microscopy and chemical tests, to locate potential evidentiary material on the bedsheet. These tests are often **presumptive tests**, which indicate whether materials such as blood or semen may be present. Evidence collected in this section will be sent to the appropriate laboratories for further testing.

Forensic Biology Section

Forensic biologists analyze body fluids such as semen, blood, and tissue. Forensic biologists are involved in the investigation of all sorts of crimes, but primarily those involving interpersonal assault, sexual assault, and murder. Their first job is to identify what the specimen in question is; for example, is the stain semen, saliva, blood, urine, feces, or vomitus? Various presumptive tests will indicate to which group a specimen belongs, then a **confirmatory test** will positively identify it. Next, biologists must determine whether the specimen originates from a human. In the past, once the specimen was confirmed as being from a human, biologists would look at blood groups to determine how common this sample might be in a random population. However, with the advancements in our understanding of DNA profiling, biologists can now individualize an exhibit to a single person.

DNA is the basic building block of life and provides the entire genetic roadmap for all organisms. DNA is organized into chromosomes that are made up of base pairs, or nucleotides, and certain combinations of these nucleotides make up genes that code for proteins, which determine what a cell will become and how it functions. The vast majority (about 99 percent) of DNA is shared by all humans. This genetic similarity makes sense when we consider that we all have the same number of legs, eyes, kidneys, etc., and that one person's organs function in the same manner as another's. Only a very small part of our DNA gives us different appearances from one another. However, this part of our DNA is not involved in DNA profiling. Instead, DNA profiling involves regions of the DNA molecule that do not code for specific functions or features, but instead have no function that we yet understand. What we do know is that certain sections of these regions repeat themselves many times, and the number of repeats is extremely variable among people. This variation is what makes a person's DNA unique. These repeating sections are called short tandem repeats, or STRs. Many areas, or **loci**, in the DNA molecule contain STRs, and it is these regions (not the sequences that make up genes) that are studied and analyzed when a forensic biologist types, or profiles, DNA.

Within the world's population, there are innumerable possibilities for the number of times a particular sequence of nucleotides can repeat itself on a DNA strand in these very variable STR regions. These possibilities become even greater when we consider several areas, each containing different lengths of repeating sequences.

Databases have been established that indicate how common a particular profile is in the general population. Once the biologist has determined the DNA profile of an exhibit, she or he will compare it with the profiles in databases to determine the likelihood that any other person would have the same profile (expressed as a ratio). Loci that are

---

presumptive test
An analysis of a sample that indicates whether a substance (e.g., semen) may be present. This test does not prove that a substance is present, as the test has been subject to false positives. If the test result is positive, further confirmatory tests are required. If the test result is negative, the substance is not present and no further testing is required. Such tests eliminate a large number of substances and narrow down the type of confirmatory test required.

confirmatory test
A test that identifies a substance conclusively. It has no false positives. However, it is often expensive, so presumptive tests are used to focus the confirmatory test required.

locus (pl. loci)
A site on a chromosome, almost like the address of an area of the chromosome.

known to exhibit extreme variability in STRs are chosen, so the chance of someone else having the same DNA profile will be very small. For example, imagine that one locus of a DNA sample is compared with loci in a DNA database, and the results indicate that the chance of anyone else having the same profile is 1 in 150,000. Next, a second locus is compared with loci in the DNA database; let's say the chance of anyone else having the same profile is 1 in 180,000. The chance of anyone else having the same profiles at *both* loci would be 1 in 27,000,000. In practice in North America, 15 different loci are compared and then multiplied so that the chance of anyone else having the same profiles at all loci become astronomical.

DNA databases are affected by relatedness and, therefore, more conservative estimates need to be used when family members are included in the suspect pool. However, as family members originate from the same genetic pools, this fact can be useful in forensic investigations. Of course, one drawback of DNA is that identical twins have identical DNA. At the same time, recent studies have begun to question whether the DNA of identical twins is indeed the same; it is conceivable that one day we may be able to genetically differentiate between such twins.

MINI CASE STUDY

Familial DNA and the Grim Sleeper

Although not yet three decades old, the role of DNA in our criminal justice system is well accepted and understood. In fact, DNA analysis is considered the gold standard in forensic science (Committee on Identifying the Needs of the Forensic Sciences Community, National Research Council, 2009). Many countries have DNA databases that contain DNA profiles of known criminals convicted of specific offences as well as unidentified DNA from crime scenes and victims. However, for forensic evidence to be valuable, it needs to be matched to a comparison sample. DNA alone merely shows us a barcode of genetic information; it does not give us a name. The purpose of DNA databases is to allow investigators to compare DNA from crime scenes and victims to known exemplars. What happens when an offender is not listed in a database? The relatively new and controversial use of familial DNA came to the public's eye recently in the case of "The Grim Sleeper."

In Los Angeles, between 1985 and 2007, the murders of at least ten women, and one attempted murder, were linked by DNA to a single killer, dubbed the "Grim Sleeper" due to an apparent gap of 14 years of inactivity (Augenstein, 2016). Unfortunately, although the DNA of the killer was known, there were no matches in the DNA database, and the killer remained at large.

Although everyone's nuclear DNA is unique (except for identical twins, as mentioned above), family members do have more similar DNA than non-family members because their genetic profiles come from the same genetic pool—that is, their mutual parents and grandparents. In the Grim Sleeper case, investigators searched the DNA database for profiles that showed enough similarity to suggest a familial relationship to the killer, and found such a similarity in Christopher Franklin, who was in the database due to a felony weapons charge. While investigating Christopher Franklin's family, investigators zeroed in on Christopher's father, Lonnie Franklin Jr., aged 57, as a suspect. To clandestinely collect a DNA sample from Lonnie Franklin Jr., an undercover Los Angeles police officer posed as a waiter at a restaurant at which Lonnie Franklin Jr. ate. Several items left behind by the suspect, including plates, cutlery, drinking glasses, and pizza crusts were collected for analysis. Such items are considered abandoned, meaning that a person has no expectation of privacy with them (such as garbage), so they may be collected without a warrant. In this case, DNA from the collected items matched the DNA in the saliva found on the victims, and Lonnie Franklin Jr. was arrested and charged. He was subsequently convicted in May 2016 of ten counts of murder and one count of attempted murder and was sentenced to death (Augenstein, 2016).

What Do You Think?

Although Lonnie Franklin Jr. was convicted because his DNA matched the DNA on the victims, it was familial DNA that led police to him. Without the police looking for family members in the DNA database, he would never have been caught and stopped. Do you think this is an acceptable method for locating a suspect? What possible legal challenges would you anticipate in Canada to using familial DNA in relation to the *Canadian Charter of Rights and Freedoms*?

The development of DNA profiling heralded a new age in criminal investigation. DNA profiling has been used in the conviction and exoneration of many people, and its usefulness has steadily increased as new techniques have been developed to enable scientists to analyze smaller and more degraded samples. However, as DNA profiling becomes more and more specialized, the risks of contamination increase and forensic scientists need to be aware of issues related to mixed samples. Unfortunately, several cases of flawed analyses have recently resulted in wrongful convictions. Therefore, research to improve the science is ongoing.

SIDEBAR

Wrongful Conviction Cases

In 1969, Gail Miller, a 20-year-old nursing student, was found raped and murdered in Saskatoon, Saskatchewan. DNA profiling was unknown at the time, and as a result of a flawed investigation, 17-year-old David Milgaard was wrongly convicted of her murder in 1970. Subsequently, he served 23 years in prison, despite continually protesting his innocence. On July 18, 1997, DNA analyses performed in Britain proved that the semen found on the victim's clothing could not have been Milgaard's, and he was exonerated. The DNA analysis led to the arrest and conviction of Larry Fisher, a serial offender who had been living in Saskatoon at the time.

In 1985, in Queensville, Ontario, Guy Paul Morin was arrested for the rape and murder of Christine Jessop, his nine-year-old neighbour. He was initially acquitted but was retried in 1992, at which time he was convicted. Although DNA profiling existed at this time, it was in its infancy, and because the victim's body had not been discovered for several months, the DNA was too degraded to be analyzed. Later improvements in DNA analysis, including the development of polymerase chain reaction (PCR), which allows an analyst to make large copies of a tiny fragment of DNA, meant that semen samples on the victim's body could now be analyzed. Those analyses established that semen found on Christine Jessop's clothing was not Guy Paul Morin's, and in 1995 he too was exonerated.

Both of these high-profile Canadian cases resulted in Royal Commissions (Kaufman, 1998; MacCallum, 2008), but these cases are not the only examples of wrongful convictions in Canada. The Morin case led to the development of Innocence Canada (formerly the Association in Defence of the Wrongly Convicted), a non-profit organization that advocates for wrongly convicted individuals. At the time of writing, Innocence Canada had secured the exonerations of 21 wrongfully convicted persons (www.aidwyc.org/cases/historical/). Moreover, in both the United States and Canada, the Innocence Project works tirelessly on the exonerations of the wrongfully convicted, with DNA as its most important tool (www.innocenceproject.org).

Many countries have DNA databases that contain DNA profiles of offenders and unidentified DNA from crime scenes and victims. Canada and the United States use CODIS (Combined DNA Index System) software to maintain and run their DNA databases. CODIS has two main indices: the Convicted Offender Index, which contains the profiles of offenders convicted of specific, listed crimes; and the Crime Scene Index, which contains the DNA profile of unknown persons from crime scenes. These indices allow subsequent samples to be matched to other crime scenes and to offenders.

The material commonly referred to as DNA is actually *nuclear DNA*, which is found in the nucleus of all nucleated cells. However, there is a second type of DNA, found in the mitochondria of cells, which is called *mitochondrial DNA* (mtDNA). Mitochondrial DNA is entirely different from nuclear DNA and is not a combination of both parents' genetic material. Instead, it is inherited unchanged from the mother. The mother's egg contains not only genetic material that combines with that of the father's sperm, but also all the other materials that the fetus will require, including mitochondria, the powerhouses of the cell. Although we all have mitochondria in our cells, only females can pass them to their offspring. A person's mitochondrial DNA is, therefore, identical to that of their biological brothers and sisters as well as their mother, their mother's siblings, and their maternal grandmother and her siblings going back throughout the entire matriarchal line. As such, it is not as individual as DNA, but it does link a person to his or her maternal line and can be very useful in mass disaster identifications. Mitochondrial DNA is more resistant to degradation than nuclear DNA and is also found in the hair shaft, whereas nuclear DNA can only be retrieved from a hair when the root follicle is still attached.

Forensic Chemistry/Trace Evidence Section

Forensic Chemistry, or the Trace Evidence Section, involves analyses of paints/polymers, fibres/textiles, gunshot residue, explosives, ignitable liquids, and fire debris, as well as physical matching. Forensic chemists handle a large array of crimes, including burglary, hit and runs, assaults, homicide, arson, and terrorism. First, the forensic chemist must determine what the exhibit is. Presumptive tests can eliminate many substances and help the scientist narrow down the possibilities before a confirmatory test is done. Both qualitative and quantitative tests are performed, first, to determine what substances are present, and second, to determine the percentages of each component. For example, a stain on a carpet could be almost anything, but if tests indicate that it is a type of gasoline, then further tests can be performed to determine the grade and type of gasoline, which can then be linked to a gasoline company, a distributor, and finally the actual gas station to which the product was delivered. Almost all evidence handled by forensic chemists, however, possesses only class characteristics, so determining significance is vitally important. The nature of some types of trace evidence makes it very difficult to show a high level of significance.

Forensic chemists are involved in the analysis of arson and explosions, such as those characteristic of terrorist attacks. Surprisingly, a great deal of valuable evidence is left behind after a fire or explosion, including accelerants or parts of a bomb, such as timers, duct tape, batteries, and explosive materials. Some of these items may have high significance because they are quite rare, but others are very common. For example, many modern homemade bombs, such as those used by Timothy McVeigh in the Oklahoma City bombings in 1995, are based on ammonium nitrate, which is derived from manure.

Forensically, there are two major drawbacks with investigations of crimes involving these devices. First, such evidence is easily washed away when fires are put out. Second, manure could arguably be found almost anywhere, so it has low significance, even if it is found in the home of a suspected bomber. Of course, the location of the manure might impact the level of significance: if it is found on the floor of the kitchen, it could have been brought in on the sole of a shoe, and so has low significance; but if it is found on a dresser in a bedroom, the likelihood of it getting there by chance is low, thereby increasing its significance.

Forensic Toxicology Section

Forensic toxicologists are concerned with identifying drugs and poisons, including alcohol, in body fluids and paraphernalia, and then interpreting their findings in terms of the behavioural and physiological effects on a person. Toxicologists handle a wide range of crimes, including murder, assault, sexual assault, impaired driving, poisonings, product tampering, parole and probation violations, and clandestine laboratories. The two main parts of a toxicological investigation are the analytical stage and the interpretive stage.

The analytical stage involves first selecting the best specimen for analysis, such as blood or urine. When a person takes a drug (whether illicit or therapeutic) or alcohol, the body immediately starts metabolizing the substance and breaking it down into its metabolites, which are then further broken down into their metabolites. The toxicologist will use a range of chemical tests to first presumptively identify the main group into which the substance(s) (e.g., opiates) belongs and then follow with confirmatory tests to identify and quantify it.

Once the parent substance and its metabolites have been identified and quantified, the toxicologist will interpret the results. Interpretation will answer such questions as when the last dose was taken, how much was taken, the mode of delivery (e.g., intravenous, snorting, smoking, ingestion) and the effect it would have had on the person at a specific time. For example, if the person had been a victim of sexual assault, would the person have been conscious at the time the attack occurred, or was the drug one that was likely to induce memory loss?

Toxicological analyses are also valuable as part of an autopsy examination, because they can indicate whether a person's death was related to drugs or alcohol.

Firearms and Toolmarks Section

Firearms and toolmarks examination primarily involves matching a suspect's firearm or tool with a bullet or mark to determine whether the suspect fired the bullet or caused the mark. A tool in this context is any hard object that makes a mark on a soft object. It could be a traditional tool, such as a chisel, but it could also be a boot or the barrel of a gun. Tools and firearms leave both class and individual characteristics on a soft object. Class characteristics include features such as the width and shape of a chisel or the **calibre** of a gun. Tools and firearms also have individual characteristics that are caused by the manufacturing process and also by later use. When a tool or firearm is manufactured, even if it is mass produced, the machinery picks up little bits of metal, dust, and grease in between the production of each unit. These elements can attach to or make minute marks on the tool or firearm as it is made. As a result, each new tool or firearm is slightly different. Individual characteristics are exacerbated when the tool is used or the gun is fired, because each use adds new small scratches and eliminates others.

calibre
The width of a gun barrel before rifling is added.

Firearms are really just advanced tools in that the hard metal barrel, the breech face, firing pin, and extractor all leave marks on the softer metals of the cartridge. When a gun is manufactured, the barrel itself is a solid piece of metal into which a hole is drilled. This drilling process leaves both class and individual characteristics on the inside of the barrel. Most handgun and rifle barrels are then drilled a second time to add **rifling**, which adds further class and individual characteristics. All of these marks will be imparted to the bullet, linking it specifically to that weapon. To determine whether a bullet has been fired from a specific gun, the examiner cannot just compare the gun to the bullet. He or she must compare like with like, so a comparison bullet is fired into a tank of water and then compared under a **comparison microscope** with the suspect bullet. First the class characteristics are examined to see whether they match (if not, the weapon can be eliminated), then the minute individual marks are compared to see whether they also match, individualizing the bullet to the weapon.

Firearm examiners also examine gunshot residue, which is left behind on the hands of a shooter as well as on a target, if it is close. This residue can help in reconstructions to determine who was the shooter and the distances between protagonists.

rifling
Spiral grooves cut into the barrel of a gun that engage the bullet and put a spin on it, so that it flies straight and does not yaw.

comparison microscope
Two light microscopes connected by an optical bridge that allows the examiner to see two separate objects on different stages, in the same field.

Questioned Documents Section

Forensic document examiners compare handwriting and handprinting exhibits with known exemplars in order to determine whether they were written by the same person. Handwriting has both class and individual characteristics. It is considered individualizing if there is a large enough sample of freely and fluently executed writing. A child first learns to write by copying from a book or a teacher's example; gradually, the child begins to write fluently and concentrate more on content than on the formation of letters. Class characteristics form as most children learn from the same type of copybook, and a group will learn from a lone grade one teacher. Nonetheless, handwriting develops individualizing characteristics because everyone has an individual perception of an image and an individual physical makeup that impacts dexterity. Also, handwriting errors in childhood that are not corrected become habit, and children incorporate features of writing from people who are significant in their lives. As well, each person has natural variation within his or her writing, meaning that we do not write the same word the same way each time. Hence, if two signatures are exactly the same, then one of them is a forgery. Forensic document examiners also look at materials and machines that create documents, such as pens, paper, and printers, and analyze documents that have been altered either deliberately or by fire or water.

IN-CLASS EXERCISE

Forensic Document Examination

Write your signature 20 times on a piece of paper. Were any EXACTLY the same? Write a sentence and give it to a friend to copy. What method did he or she use to copy it? Did your friend trace it or just eyeball it? Can you tell that it is a forgery? How? Try to write a paragraph or two and disguise your writing so it looks as though you did not write it. Does it look convincing? Why or why not?

Death Investigations

Coroners and Medical Examiners

Death investigations in Canada originate in the coroners system of England, dating back to 900 when Crowners (later changed to *coroners*) were appointed by the king to investigate death. Crowners examined the body of the deceased, investigated the death, held inquests, and arrested the person believed responsible. Therefore, they held the roles of much of our present criminal justice system. Today, a coroner's duties include the investigation of sudden, unexpected natural or violent deaths. The coroner oversees death investigations under criteria that are defined by each province's *Coroners Act*. Only deaths that occur under the care of a doctor, of a known and expected condition, are excluded. Coroners come from a variety of backgrounds and are not required to be medical doctors (except in Ontario). Coroners investigate all aspects of a death and complete a Judgement of Inquiry for each case. They also possess quasi-judicial powers and, in special cases, may call and preside over an inquest or hearing into the circumstances surrounding a death. An inquest includes a jury, and the coroner may call both lay and expert witnesses to give evidence. The inquest, however, is fact-finding and not fault-finding, and it is conducted to determine the factors about a death, which involves answering five main questions: Who is the decedent? What is the medical cause of death? Where did the person die? When did the person die? and By what means did the person die? Once these five questions are answered, the role of the coroner is to suggest methods to prevent further similar deaths. For example, if a number of vehicular deaths have occurred at a particular intersection, then the coroner may recommend that a traffic light be established at the intersection.

The medical examiner system began in the United States in 1877, and several Canadian provinces have adopted this system (Alberta, Manitoba, Nova Scotia, and Newfoundland and Labrador). In contrast to most coroners, medical examiners are always medical doctors, although usually only the chief and deputy chief medical examiners are forensic pathologists. Medical examiners do not have judicial powers, and inquests are conducted by a separately appointed body. However, the five main questions remain the same, and both coroners and medical examiners are ombudspersons for the dead.

Forensic Pathologists

pathology
The study of disease.

The forensic pathologist is a medical doctor with a specialty in **pathology** as well as further specialization in forensic pathology. Forensic pathologists perform autopsies at the bequest of the coroner or medical examiner to assist in answering the five questions mentioned above and to determine the cause and **manner of death**. They also interpret injury patterns and will reconstruct events leading to injury, which may help in determining manner of death. For example, certain types of injury, such as cuts on the hands and forearms, may suggest that the person was trying to defend himself or herself, or may indicate that the wound was impossible for the decedent to have inflicted on him or herself, ruling out suicide.

manner of death
The classification of death. It can be natural, accidental, suicide, homicide, or undetermined.

Other Forensic Specialists

Several other forensic disciplines are outside the expertise of the police service or crime lab, but may be of value in an investigation. Some scientists in these disciplines may work full-time in the forensic arena, whereas others may work in universities, museums, or private practice and consult to police when a case requires their expertise. They include but are not limited to forensic odontologists, anthropologists, entomologists, botanists, engineers, nurses, and artists. A few of these specialists are discussed below.

Forensic odontologists are dentists who examine the dentition of an unknown decedent and compare it with the dental records of missing persons in order to identify the victim. When an adequate number of teeth are present, a person's dentition is considered to be individualizing. Because teeth are covered with enamel, the hardest substance in the human body, they preserve extremely well, meaning that forensic odontologists are particularly important in mass disasters and terrorist attacks in which large numbers of decedents, often damaged or highly decomposed, need to be identified. Although perhaps 95 percent of the forensic odontologist's job is victim identification, a forensic odontologist may also be involved in bite mark recognition, abuse identification, and civil issues related to dental practice.

Forensic anthropologists are specialists in the human skeleton and its trauma. They are usually involved in cases in which the remains are entirely or partially skeletonized, and they aid the investigation by developing a biological profile that includes the sex, ancestry, age range, height range, and any individualizing features (e.g., previously healed trauma), which will aid in the identification of the decedent. They are trained in analyzing trauma and natural disease processes and

A jawbone is seen through a magnifier used for forensic dentistry. In cases where a body has been badly burned or has decomposed, examining teeth and dental records may offer the only reliable method of identifying a victim.

Blow fly larvae (Diptera: Calliphoridae) feeding in masses on a pig carcass.

are adept at working with damaged and burned bones to reconstruct a skeleton. In the past, forensic anthropologists worked mostly on individual cases, but they have risen to prominence in many mass disaster and genocide investigations in which interpreting the skeletons can provide vital evidence in determining how death occurred.

Forensic entomologists study the insects associated with a body in order to understand many factors about a crime. In particular, they provide an estimate of the minimum time that insects have been colonizing a body. Certain species of insects are attracted to a body immediately after death to lay their eggs. These eggs develop into larvae and progress through their life cycle on the body. As insects are cold blooded, their development is predictable based on species and temperature, so a forensic entomologist can calculate the minimum age of the oldest insects that will, in turn, infer the minimum elapsed time since death. As decomposition progresses, the body becomes less attractive to early colonizing insects and more attractive to later colonizing species, and these species colonize in a predictable sequence, dependent on season, habitat, and geographical region. Local knowledge of colonization sequences can be used to estimate the minimum elapsed time since death over several months or even years. Insects can also indicate the presence and position of wound sites, whether a body has been moved or disturbed after death, and the estimated length of time of neglect in living victims.

Forensic botanists study plants and pollen, which can be very valuable in forensic investigations because plants and plant parts are everywhere in our environment and species are specific to certain seasons and habitats. Furthermore, plants grow at predictable rates, so if plants have grown over a grave or through a skeleton, their presence can indicate a minimum elapsed time since death. Pollen grains are tiny, identifiable, and everywhere, so they will be found at crime scenes, on victims and suspects, and in vehicles. They can be used to include or exclude the season when a crime took place, and to determine where a vehicle has been driven. For example, if a suspect claims that he has not been in the area of a crime scene, an examination of the pollen in his car's air filter can indicate, at least, whether his vehicle was driven in the area of the crime scene, at a particular time of year.

Forensic Psychology

forensic psychology
The application of psychological research, methods, theories, and practices to a task faced by the legal system (Wrightsman & Fulero, 2005, p. 2).

Forensic psychology can trace its roots to Hugo Münsterberg (1863–1916). In his 1908 book *On the Witness Stand*, Münsterberg made a case for greater use of psychological research on such topics as the reliability of eyewitness testimony and false confessions in the courts. Although we now have clear evidence that supports expert testimony on these and many other forensic psychology topics, the research available at the time Münsterberg was writing was methodologically flawed and did not support the claims he was making for greater use of psychology in the legal system. Indeed, John Henry Wigmore, who many consider to be one of the most important legal scholars in American jurisprudence, wrote a satirical law review article in 1909 in which he subjected Münsterberg's claims to a rigorous cross-examination in a mock trial. Of course, Wigmore concluded that Münsterberg greatly exaggerated the contributions that this research could make to the law. This view was shared by most legal scholars at the time, and while some forensic psychology research was conducted into the 1930s, it was mostly unheard of throughout the 1940s and 1950s. Indeed, it was not until the late 1960s that the field of forensic psychology began to form as a distinct discipline, when Jay Ziskin and a small group of psychologists created the American

Hugo Münsterberg.

Psychology-Law Society (AP-LS) and stimulated the development of graduate programs in the United States and Canada to train psychologists as researchers and practitioners in the field of forensic psychology. For example, Simon Fraser University established a Law and Forensic Psychology doctoral program that trains forensic psychologists in both clinical forensic practice and research.

The Roles of Forensic Psychologists

Forensic psychology is a broad discipline in which psychologists engage in both research and clinical practice that can be applied to legal issues. Some forensic psychologists have training in clinical psychology and perform clinical assessments of individuals and may testify in court about those assessments. Others engage primarily in research and may testify in court about the relevance of that research to legal matters. Forensic psychologists are involved in questions that exist at the interface of psychology and law, such as the following:

- Is an accused fit to stand trial, or should he or she be considered not responsible for a criminal offence?
- Can future violence or recidivism generally be predicted?
- What treatments are effective with offenders?
- Do juveniles understand their rights at arrest?
- Are eyewitnesses reliable?
- How should suspects be interrogated?
- How do jurors make decisions about innocence or guilt?

We will consider many of these questions in the remainder of this chapter. For more details about the roles of forensic psychologists, see Roesch, Zapf, Hart, and Connolly (2014).

Fitness to Stand Trial and Criminal Responsibility

The mental state of an accused can be an issue for the courts to consider. Mental disorder is a concern when it interferes with the accused's ability to understand the charges against him or her or the accused's ability to share facts about the case with counsel. These matters relate to an accused's *fitness to stand trial*. Also of concern is whether an accused's mental state at the time of an alleged offence may have prevented him or her from having the requisite mental capacity to form the intention to commit an offence. This matter relates to whether the accused should be considered *not criminally responsible on account of mental disorder*.

Fitness to Stand Trial

In Canada, fitness to stand trial evaluations are conducted on over 5,000 accused each year. Fitness laws were created to ensure that every accused has the ability to participate fully in his or her defence. Accused who do not meet the fitness criteria can be found unfit to stand trial and their legal proceedings are stayed until fitness is restored. Section 2 of the *Criminal Code* defines *unfit to stand trial* as follows:

[U]nable on account of mental disorder to conduct a defence at any stage of the proceedings before a verdict is rendered or to instruct counsel to do so, and, in particular, unable on account of mental disorder to

(a) understand the nature or object of the proceedings,
(b) understand the possible consequences of the proceedings, or
(c) communicate with counsel.

Psychiatrists and psychologists may be asked to evaluate an accused with regard to his or her fitness to stand trial (Viljoen, Roesch, Ogloff, & Zapf, 2003). The evaluation usually involves a diagnostic interview to determine whether the accused has a mental disorder, and, if so, whether that mental disorder impairs the ability to proceed with trial. Evaluators may also rely on forensic assessment instruments developed to assess fitness, such as the Fitness Interview Test—Revised (Roesch, Zapf, & Eaves, 2006), which was developed specifically for use in Canada and provides the evaluator with questions to be asked in 16 different domains relevant to proceeding with a criminal case. Once the evaluator has conducted the complete evaluation, a report to the court is prepared detailing his or her opinions regarding the accused's abilities. If the accused is found fit to stand trial, the criminal case proceeds as usual. If the court finds that the accused is unfit to stand trial, it will order commitment of the accused to a psychiatric hospital or forensic facility for treatment to restore fitness. The most common form of treatment involves the administration of psychotropic medication; however, some hospitals also have treatment programs designed to increase an accused's understanding of the legal process or programs that confront the problems that hinder an accused's ability to participate in his or her defence (Zapf & Roesch, 2011). The majority of accused individuals are restored to fitness within a six-month period and almost all accused are successfully treated within one year.

Criminal Responsibility

While the fitness issue focuses on an accused's mental state at the time of the criminal proceedings, the issue of criminal responsibility, colloquially known as an **insanity defence**, has to do with an accused's mental state at the time of the alleged offence. This is an important distinction. The case of Vincent Li illustrates the fact that an accused can be found fit to stand trial yet still successfully raise a defence of insanity.

Fit to Stand Trial, But Not Criminally Responsible: The Case of Vincent Li
On July 30, 2008, Vince Weiguang Li boarded a Greyhound bus destined for Winnipeg, Manitoba. Approximately 90 minutes later, Mr. Li suddenly produced a large hunting knife and began stabbing his sleeping seatmate, a person who was unknown to him, in the neck and chest. Mr. Li decapitated and displayed his victim's severed head to the other passengers who had gathered outside. Mr. Li continued to dismember the corpse and then proceeded to perform acts of cannibalism. Mr. Li was arrested and charged with second-degree murder. The court ordered an evaluation of his fitness to stand trial. He was subsequently found fit to stand trial and returned to court for trial.

At his trial in 2009, Mr. Li's defence team raised the issue of criminal responsibility, arguing that he was mentally ill at the time of the offence. Psychiatric assessments found that Mr. Li was suffering from schizophrenia, a mental illness in which symptoms such as hallucinations, delusions, and paranoia can be present. The assessment reports

insanity defence
A defence to a crime based on an argument that the individual was not responsible for his or her actions at the time of the crime due to his or her mental state.

For a discussion of how the corrections system handled Vincent Li's case, see the Mini Case Study in Chapter 9.

noted that Mr. Li heard the voice of God, which directed him to move from Edmonton to Winnipeg. The voice had led Mr. Li to believe, under a paranoid delusion, that the deceased victim was a threat to his own life, both before and after the deceased victim's death. The judge agreed that Mr. Li was suffering from a mental disorder and found him not criminally responsible on account of mental disorder. The judge commented that individuals who are profoundly ill do not have the mental capacity to intentionally commit a crime, and added that the goal of criminal law is to punish criminals, not persons who have a mental illness. Mr. Li was remanded to a psychiatric facility for treatment.

NCRMD

In Canada, the insanity defence is known as *not criminally responsible on account of mental disorder* (NCRMD). The legal foundation for NCRMD is the **M'Naghten standard**, which derives from an English murder case from 1843 in which the judgment held that at the time of the offence the accused "was labouring under such a defect of reason, from disease of the mind, as not to know the nature and quality of the act he was doing, or as not to know that what he was doing was wrong" (*M'Naghten's Case*, 1843, p. 722). In Canada, the *Criminal Code* states that "no person is criminally responsible for an act committed or an omission made while suffering from a mental disorder that rendered the person incapable of appreciating the nature and quality of the act or omission or of knowing that it was wrong" (s 16). A careful reading of the Code makes it clear that a mental disorder is a necessary condition for a finding of NCRMD, but it is not sufficient by itself because it must be shown that the mental disorder caused the accused to be unable to appreciate the act or know it was wrong.

The issue of NCRMD is raised only infrequently (in less than 1 percent of criminal cases), and even when it is raised it is rarely successful; only about 25 percent of those referred for evaluation are found by the courts to meet the legal criteria for NCRMD (Livingston, Wilson, Tien, & Bond, 2003).

Forensic psychologists have provided assessment tools to aid in evaluating NCRMD. This type of evaluation is more difficult than a fitness evaluation because the evaluator has to assess an accused's state at the time of the alleged offence rather than his or her current mental state. An accused may have had a psychotic disorder at the time of the offence but may subsequently have been treated with antipsychotic medications, and so does not present psychotic symptoms at the time of the NCRMD assessment. The evaluation usually involves an interview with the accused, a review of relevant records (such as mental health treatment records), as well as the police report. Interviews may be conducted with individuals who know the accused well or who were with the accused at or around the time of the offence. Personality tests, such as the Minnesota Multiphasic Personality Inventory, may also be useful. One test was developed specifically to assess criminal responsibility: Rogers Criminal Responsibility Assessment Scales, or R-CRAS (Rogers, 1984). The R-CRAS has 30 items on five scales that provide measures of patient reliability, organicity, psychopathology, cognitive control, and behavioural control. It provides a useful guide for evaluators to ensure key issues related to assessing criminal responsibility are incorporated into the evaluation.

M'Naghten standard
The historical standard for insanity that allowed a defendant to be acquitted if he or she did not know what he or she was doing or that it was wrong.

What Do You Think?

The insanity defence is a rarely used defence, but its successful use in a highly publicized murder case like that of Mr. Li often generates controversy. Many people think the insanity defence should be abolished. What do you think? What are the arguments for and against the use of this defence?

For more on this issue, see "Insanity Defense" (n.d.).

An accused found NCRMD is subject to one of three dispositions: an absolute discharge, a conditional discharge (living in the community with conditions), or detention in hospital (with or without conditions). The majority of individuals found NCRMD are initially detained in psychiatric hospitals or forensic institutions for a period of confinement and treatment of their mental disorder. Vince Li, who was found NCRMD, was sent to a forensic facility in 2009 but was subsequently allowed to live in a group home before being permitted to resume independent living in the community in February 2016.

Risk Assessment

Assessment of risk for recidivism or future violence is a common task of forensic psychologists. It is the area that has been subject to the most research of almost any forensic psychology topic over the past three decades. **Risk assessments** may be used to assess individuals who are being considered for pre-trial release, for probation or parole, and for many other decisions in both the criminal and civil justice systems.

Violence risk assessment considers the following:

(a) the *nature* of the violence or the types of violence that may occur;
(b) the *severity* or seriousness of the violence;
(c) the *frequency* of the violence or how often violence might occur;
(d) the *imminence* or how soon violence might occur; and
(e) the *likelihood* or probability that violence will occur. (Roesch et al., 2014, p. 73)

Two primary approaches are used to assess risk of recidivism: the actuarial decision-making approach and the structured professional judgment. In an actuarial decision-making approach, the evaluator uses a forensic assessment instrument that was built on research involving large samples (it is quantitative in nature). A researcher developing an instrument using this approach would collect data from a large group of offenders and examine the factors that are most associated with an outcome variable, such as committing a violent crime. The result is a set of items that can be scored for an individual who is being assessed for risk. An example of an actuarial instrument is the Violence Risk Appraisal Guide (VRAG) (Quinsey, Harris, Rice, & Cormier, 2005), which was developed by a group of Canadian psychologists. Items that have been found to be associated with risk of violent recidivism include elementary school maladjustment, history of alcohol abuse, and the psychopathy measure (see the next section for a discussion of psychopathy). Scores on each item are weighted to account for how strongly they are associated with the outcome variable. Once all of the factors are rated, the scores are tallied. The VRAG score table indicates the chances of recidivism as a function of the total score. For example, if an inmate about to be released from prison had a VRAG score of 9, that would correspond to a 44 percent chance of recidivism seven years' post-release and 58 percent ten years' post-release.

The structured professional judgment (SPJ) relies on a selection of risk factors that have been identified in the literature as related to risk of recidivism. An SPJ instrument may include risk factors similar to those found in an actuarial instrument. However, an SPJ instrument also includes an assessment of current clinical functioning and incorporates the formulation of risk management strategies. For example, a person with anger management issues could be referred to an anger management treatment program

---

risk assessment
An assessment approach based on the identification of factors shown to predict future delinquent or criminal behaviour.

as a risk management strategy. Another difference is that although each item in an SPJ instrument is scored, a total score is not obtained. Rather, evaluators consider each of the risk factors and how those risk factors might be managed, and then use their professional judgment to form an opinion about the individual's risk of recidivism. An example of an SPJ instrument is the Historical, Clinical, Risk Management-20, or HCR-20 (Douglas, Hart, Webster, & Belfrage, 2013). The risk factors it considers include prior violence, current violent ideation, symptoms of mental disorder, personal support, and treatment response.

Both actuarial and SPJ approaches perform equally well in predicting violence or recidivism (Skeem & Monahan, 2011), but it is important to keep in mind that these predictions are far from perfect. Risk assessment instruments such as the VRAG and the HCR-20 improve predictions over chance levels, but two types of errors do occur. One error is predicting that someone will be violent who turns out not to be (a false positive), while another occurs when someone who was predicted to be non-violent commits a violent crime (a false negative). Research is ongoing to improve the accuracy of predictive instruments.

Psychopathy

Psychopathy is one of the most robust predictors of future violence. Robert Hare, emeritus professor of psychology at the University of British Columbia, is the world's leading expert on **psychopathy**. He considers three areas when evaluating a person's psychopathic tendencies: the nature of the person's interpersonal relationships, affective involvement, and lifestyle. Interpersonally, psychopaths are grandiose, egocentric, manipulative, and cold-hearted. Affectively, they lack empathy, and are unable to feel guilt and remorse. Moreover, their lifestyle is impulsive and sensation-seeking, and they typically fail to fulfill responsibilities. Professor Hare (2003) created the primary instrument used to assess psychopathy: the Psychopathy Checklist-Revised (PCL-R). It comprises a 20-item scale that assesses the core elements of the psychopathic character. Examples of items on the PCL-R are grandiose sense of self-worth, pathological lying, lack of remorse or guilt, poor behavioural controls, early behavioural problems, impulsivity, and juvenile delinquency. Scoring is based on an interview and a review of file records and collateral information. The maximum score is 40, and a score of 30 or more is indicative of psychopathy. Research shows that about 25 percent of prison inmates meet the criteria for psychopathy, and that psychopathy is effective in predicting both general recidivism (Leistico, Salekin, DeCoster, & Rogers, 2008) and violent recidivism (Walters, 2003).

psychopathy
A personality disorder describing individuals who show a blatant disregard for others, both behaviourally and emotionally.

Juvenile Assessments and Interventions

Juvenile assessments and interventions are a major focus of forensic psychology. Forensic psychologists assist the courts on a number of juvenile-related matters. For example, they help assess a juvenile's understanding and appreciation of arrest rights, evaluate the fitness of a juvenile to stand trial, and suggest interventions that might prevent high-risk youth from offending. Space does not permit a consideration of the range of juvenile assessments and interventions provided by forensic psychologists, so we will limit our discussion to a review of interventions for reducing delinquency.

See Chapter 12 for more information about interventions.

Research has shown that preventive interventions, especially early intervention, can reduce juvenile delinquency, including serious and violent offending (Corrado et al., 2015). Research on juvenile risk assessment has identified many risk markers that can place a youth at high risk of delinquent behaviour (Slobogin & Fondacaro, 2011). This research can inform preventive interventions, which are divided into three levels: primary, secondary, and tertiary.

Primary prevention interventions take place before a problem develops and are directed at a general population rather than specific individuals. The goal is to prevent a problem (such as delinquent behaviour) before it occurs. An example of a primary prevention activity is a media campaign warning of the risks of alcohol use for expectant mothers. It is now well established that use of alcohol or drugs during pregnancy can result in Fetal Alcohol Spectrum Disorders (FASDs), and individuals with FASDs are at a higher risk of juvenile and adult criminality (Streissguth & Kanter, 1997). Thus, if an FASD is prevented, delinquent behaviour resulting from it is eliminated. **Secondary prevention** programs are directed at specific high-risk groups, but the intervention takes place early in a youth's life, before significant problems have developed. An example is the Montreal Preventive Treatment Program, a two-year program aimed at seven- to nine-year-old boys who were identified as having high levels of disruptive behaviour in kindergarten. The program focuses on school-based social skills and parent training (Tremblay, Masse, Pagani, & Vitaro, 1996). Follow-up studies have shown that this type of program reduces the likelihood of delinquent behaviour in the future. **Tertiary prevention** takes place long after delinquent behaviour has occurred, and its goal is to prevent serious offenders from continuing to offend in the future. An example is Multi-Systemic Therapy (MST), which provides high-risk youth with intensive individual, family, and community support, with an average of 60 hours of direct services (Henggeler, Schoenwald, Borduin, Rowland, & Cunningham, 2009).

Expert Testimony

The role of a forensic psychologist who conducts an evaluation of an accused is different from the role of a psychologist providing treatment to a patient. In the latter, the patient is the client, but in the former, the defence, prosecutor, or the court is the client. For court-ordered evaluations, the forensic psychologist must be neutral and not serve as an advocate for either side of the case. Forensic psychologists may be asked to testify regarding their assessment of an accused regarding psycholegal issues such as whether the accused is fit to stand trial, is a risk for future violence, or is not criminally responsible. Forensic psychologists may also serve as general witnesses and testify about research on a forensic psychology area, such as eyewitness testimony or false confessions.

In *R v Mohan* (1994) the Supreme Court of Canada stated that the admission of expert evidence depends on the following four criteria:

1. *Relevance.* Relevance is a matter decided by a judge. In deciding on relevance, the judge may consider whether the evidence is likely to assist the jury in its fact-finding mission, or whether it is likely to confuse and confound the jury.

primary prevention
Interventions that take place before a problem develops; they are directed at a general population rather than specific individuals.

secondary prevention
Interventions directed at specific high-risk individuals; the intervention takes place before more serious problems have developed.

tertiary prevention
Interventions for individuals usually long after the initial problem developed, with the goal of preventing further criminal behaviour.

2. *Necessity in assisting the trier of fact.* An expert's opinion is admissible to furnish the court with scientific information that is likely to be outside the experience and knowledge of a judge or jury. If on the proven facts a judge or jury can form its own conclusions without help, then the opinion of an expert is unnecessary.

3. *The absence of any exclusionary rule.* If evidence has been determined to be inadmissible in prior cases, having it reported by an expert will not make it admissible. For example, if evidence about an accused's bad character has been found to be inadmissible, an expert would not be permitted to introduce this testimony.

4. *A properly qualified expert.* An expert must have the necessary training or experience to have acquired special or peculiar knowledge through study or experience in respect of the matters on which he or she undertakes to testify.

It is important to bear in mind that even though expert evidence is admitted, the weight that it carries in the decision made by a judge or jury may vary. A judge or jury may choose not to consider the evidence at all or only to consider part of it.

Eyewitness Research and Testimony

Eyewitness testimony is often the most compelling evidence offered in a trial. Laboratory research has shown that mock jurors convicted a defendant twice as often when the defendant was identified by a credible eyewitness than when there was no eyewitness identification (Cutler & Penrod, 1995). Loftus (1984) reviewed 347 cases for which eyewitness testimony was the only evidence presented. The accused were convicted in 75 percent of the cases, and over half of the conviction cases had just one eyewitness. When eyewitnesses are accurate, it results in the correct conviction of offenders. However, given the substantial weight placed on eyewitness testimony, *mistaken* eyewitness testimony is concerning. The Innocence Project (2009) presents some compelling reasons for this concern:

- In 38% of the misidentification cases, multiple eyewitnesses misidentified the same innocent person.
- Fifty-three percent of the misidentification cases, where race is known, involved cross-racial misidentifications.
- In 50% of the misidentification cases, eyewitness testimony was the central evidence used against the defendant (without other corroborating evidence like confessions, forensic science or informant testimony).
- In 36% of the misidentification cases, the real perpetrator was identified through DNA evidence.
- In at least 48% of the misidentification cases where a real perpetrator was later identified through DNA testing, that perpetrator went on to commit additional violent crimes while an innocent person was serving time in prison for his previous crime.

Thomas Sophonow

Thomas Sophonow was convicted in 1981 of the murder of a 16-year-old girl who was killed at her workplace in a donut shop in Winnipeg. There was no direct evidence linking him to the murder, and his conviction largely rested on the testimony of an eyewitness. Mr. Sophonow spent four years in prison before he was released on appeal. Subsequently, the Winnipeg Police Department announced that he could not have committed this murder. He was later awarded $2.3 million as compensation for his wrongful conviction.

Recall that Hugo Münsterberg made a case for expert testimony on the reliability of eyewitnesses. Now, over 100 years later, psychological research has uncovered the factors that lead to incorrect identifications and this research has been used to propose changes that can be adopted by police and the courts to minimize the number of false identifications. For example, studies have demonstrated that when a weapon is present, a witness's memory is impaired, in large part because they focus more on the weapon and less on the physical characteristics of the event and the perpetrator (Kramer, Buckhout, & Eugenio, 1990). We also know that people are better at recognizing the faces of members of their own race than they are at recognizing the faces of members of other races (Meissner & Brigham, 2001). The way in which a lineup is conducted can also lead to incorrect identifications. Witnesses may assume that the perpetrator is present and select the individual that most closely approximates the perpetrator. However, research has also shown that if a witness is told that the perpetrator might or might not be present and, therefore, he or she should not feel obligated to make an identification, inaccurate or false identifications can be reduced substantially (Brewer & Palmer, 2010).

Eyewitness research has led to many policy changes. For example, Fisher (2010) developed the **cognitive interview**, which provides guidelines for police interviewers that can minimize contamination of a witness's memory and improve the accuracy of memory retrieval. Wells and colleagues (1998) recommended guidelines for conducting a lineup in order to minimize incorrect identifications. For example, an officer in charge of the lineup or photospread should not know who the suspect is, which avoids the possibility of inadvertent hints or reactions that could lead the witness before the identification takes place.

Forensic psychologists may also be asked to testify as a general expert witness to inform the court about the factors impacting accuracy and the conditions under which mistaken identifications may occur.

Police Investigations and Interrogations

While eyewitness testimony is compelling evidence at trial, so too is a confession by the accused. Most confessions are valid, but sometimes a suspect confesses to a crime he or

cognitive interview
A method of interviewing witnesses to enhance the correct recall of information.

she did not actually commit, as Simon Marshall did (see "Sidebar—Simon Marshall"). The Innocence Project found that over 25 percent of the more than 290 wrongful convictions overturned by DNA evidence in the United States have involved some form of a **false confession**. Why would an innocent person confess to a crime? There are a few reasons. Some individuals, particularly adolescents or those with mental health problems, may be more vulnerable to interrogation tactics. Police deception may also be a factor, as in the use of the "Mr. Big" technique discussed in Chapter 4 (see also Smith, Stinson, & Patry, 2010). Researchers have identified three types of false confessions (Kassin, 2005). A **voluntary false confession** occurs when an innocent person confesses without being prompted by the police. A **coerced-compliant false confession** occurs when a suspect wishes to escape from the stress of the interrogation, to avoid a threat of harm or punishment, or to gain a promised or implied reward such as being allowed to sleep, eat, or make a phone call. (The infamous Central Park jogger case is an example of a coerced-compliant false confession. In that case, five boys were interrogated over lengthy periods, deprived of sleep, and convinced that they would be allowed to go home if they confessed.) A **coerced-internalized false confession** results from highly suggestive interrogations.

false confession
When individuals confess to a crime they did not commit or exaggerate involvement in a crime they did commit.

voluntary false confession
When an innocent person confesses to a crime without being prompted by the police.

coerced-compliant false confession
When a suspect confesses because he or she wishes to escape from the stress of the interrogation, to avoid a threat of harm or punishment, or to gain a promised or implied reward.

coerced-internalized false confession
When a suspect who is coerced, tired, and highly suggestible confesses because the suspect actually comes to believe that he or she committed the crime.

SIDEBAR

Simon Marshall

In 1997, Simon Marshall was convicted in Quebec of 15 counts of rape, based largely on his confession. Marshall, who was diagnosed with borderline personality disorder and an intellectual disability, was released in 2003 after a DNA analysis showed he was in fact innocent. The Quebec government awarded him $2.3 million to compensate for his wrongful conviction.

Many police interrogators in Canada use the Reid Technique discussed in Chapter 4. Kassin and McNall (1991) identified two strategies central to this technique. In **maximization**, the interrogator uses "scare tactics" designed to intimidate a suspect into a confession. This intimidation is achieved by emphasizing or overstating the seriousness of the offence and the magnitude of the charges. False or exaggerated claims about the evidence may be made. In **minimization**, interrogators provide suspects with a false sense of security by offering face-saving excuses, moral justification, blaming a victim or accomplice, or playing down the seriousness of the charges. These tactics do result in valid confessions, but they may also increase the possibility of a false confession, especially with more vulnerable suspects. As discussed in Chapter 4, law enforcement agencies in several countries, including Canada, have begun to adopt an alternative approach to interrogation, called Preparation and Planning, Engage and Explain, Account, Closure, and Evaluate, or PEACE (Bull & Milne, 2004). In this model, interviewers keep an open mind about the innocence or guilt of the suspect and treat all suspects fairly, giving special consideration to vulnerable subjects. One of the primary aims of the PEACE model is to reduce the likelihood of false confessions.

maximization
An interrogation strategy whereby an interrogator uses "scare tactics" designed to intimidate a suspect into a confession.

minimization
An interrogation strategy whereby an interrogator provides suspects with a false sense of security by offering face-saving excuses, moral justification, blaming a victim or accomplice, or playing down the seriousness of the charges to encourage a suspect to make a confession.

Conclusion

This chapter has provided a brief overview of forensic science and forensic psychology. Although forensic science can refer to any science that has a legal role, it primarily refers to science used to analyze evidence (particularly physical evidence) from a crime scene, and most of these analyses are performed by bench scientists in forensic laboratories and by ident officers. In some cases, external experts are consulted when their expertise is required. Forensic science primarily aims to link a suspect to a victim and a crime.

Forensic psychology is a very different type of science. It does not consider physical evidence from a crime scene, but instead looks specifically at the human element. For example, it involves the application of psychological expertise to assessing whether a person is fit to stand trial or is not responsible for his or her actions, predicting an offender's future risk of recidivism, determining whether eyewitnesses are reliable, assisting police with interrogation approaches, and assessing the effectiveness of treatments for offenders. Together, forensic science and forensic psychology are valuable at all stages of criminal justice, from the crime scene to the courtroom and beyond.

DISCUSSION QUESTIONS

1. Go to a hardware store and examine five or six of the exact same hammer, chisel, or screwdriver. Look closely and you will see a vast number of very tiny little scratches. These are individualizing and will be present on the mark left behind by the tool. At home, use a tool of any sort to make a mark in something soft, like wax or cheese. See how many tiny individualizing marks you can see. Make another mark with a similar tool—can you see the differences? Discuss your results.

2. Television shows always portray a subject as much more exciting, dramatic, and glamorous than in real life. For example, in reality, police officers do not spend all day engaged in car chases and dramatic arrests. Instead, they spend a lot of time writing up reports or patrolling streets. Reality, though, would not be nearly as interesting to watch. Why do you think television audiences seem to easily accept the forensic science and forensic psychology they see on television as factual? What are some real-life problems with believing that these television portrayals are accurate?

3. In the past, most convictions were based on eyewitness testimony, while today most convictions are based on science. Both eyewitness testimony and science have led to wrongful convictions. Which source do you think is *less likely* to lead to wrongful convictions, and why?

4. Why might an innocent suspect falsely confess to a crime that he or she did not commit?

5. Should developmental maturity be taken into account when determining punishment for youth who have committed violent crimes? Explain.

6. How does fitness to stand trial differ from the issue of criminal responsibility?

SUGGESTED FURTHER READINGS

Anderson, G.S. (Ed) (2007). *All you ever wanted to know about forensic science in Canada but didn't know who to ask!* Ottawa: Canadian Society of Forensic Sciences. http://www.csfs.ca/wp-content/uploads/2016/05/booklet2007.pdf.

Corrado, R., & Freedman, L. (2011). Risk profiles, trajectories and intervention points for serious and chronic young offenders. *International Journal of Child, Youth and Family Studies, 2*, 197–232.

Desmarais, S.L., & Read, J.D. (2010). After 30 years, what do we know about what jurors know? A meta-analytic review of lay knowledge regarding eyewitness factors. *Law and Human Behavior, 35*, 200–210.

Pakosh, C.M. (Ed.). (2016). *The lawyers guide to the forensic sciences.* Toronto: Irwin Press.

Smith, S.M., Stinson, V., & Patry, M.W. (2010). Confession evidence in Canada: Psychological issues and legal landscapes. *Psychology, Crime & Law, 18*, 317–333.

Zapf, P.A., Golding, S.L., & Roesch, R. (2006). Criminal responsibility and the insanity defense. In I.B. Weiner & A.K. Hess (Eds.), *Handbook of forensic psychology* (3rd ed., pp. 332–363). New York: Wiley.

REFERENCES

Augenstein, S. (2016, June 7). "Grim Sleeper" jury recommends death. *Forensic News Daily*.

Brewer, N., & Palmer, M.A. (2010). Eyewitness identification tests. *Legal and Criminological Psychology, 15*, 77–96.

Bull, R., & Milne, R., (2004). Attempts to improve police interviewing of suspects. In G.D. Lassiter (Ed.), *Interrogation, confessions and entrapment* (pp. 181–196). New York: Kluwer/Plenum.

Committee on Identifying the Needs of the Forensic Sciences Community, National Research Council. (2009). *Strengthening forensic science in the United States: A path forward*. Washington, DC: Committee on Identifying the Needs of the Forensic Sciences Community, National Research Council of the National Academies, The National Academies Press.

Corrado, R., Leschied, A., Lussier, P., & Whatley, J. (2015). *Serious and violent juvenile offenders and youth criminal justice: A Canadian perspective*. Burnaby, BC: Simon Fraser University Publications.

Cutler, B.L., & Penrod, S.D. (1995). *Mistaken identification: The eyewitness, psychology and the law*. Cambridge, UK: Cambridge University Press.

Douglas, K.S., Hart, S.D., Webster, C.D., & Belfrage, H. (2013). *HCR-20 Assessing Risk for Violence V3: Manual and worksheets.* Burnaby, BC: Mental Health, Law, and Policy Institute.

Fisher, R.P. (2010). Interviewing cooperative witnesses. *Legal and Criminological Psychology, 15*, 25–38.

Hare, R.D. (2003). *Manual for the Revised Psychopathy Checklist* (2nd ed.). Toronto: Multi-Health Systems.

Henggeler, S.W., Schoenwald, S.K., Borduin, C.M., Rowland, M.D., & Cunningham, P.B. (2009). *Multisystemic therapy for antisocial behavior in children and adolescents* (2nd ed.). New York: Guilford.

Innocence Project. (2009, July 16). Reevaluating lineups: Why witnesses make mistakes and how to reduce the chance of misidentification. Retrieved from http://www.innocenceproject.org/reevaluating-lineups-why-witnesses-make-mistakes-and-how-to-reduce-the-chance-of-a-misidentification/.

Insanity defense—Is there a need for the insanity defense? (n.d.). Retrieved from http://law.jrank.org/pages/7666/Insanity-Defense-THERE-NEED-INSANITY-DEFENSE.html#ixzz4QZJ5apwf.

Kassin, S.M. (2005). On the psychology of confessions: Does *innocence* put *innocents* at risk? *American Psychologist, 60*, 215–228.

Kassin, S.M., & McNall, K. (1991). Police interrogations and confessions: Communicating promises and threats by pragmatic implication. *Law and Human Behavior, 15*, 233–251.

Kaufman, F. (1998). *Report of the Kaufman Commission on Proceedings Involving Guy Paul Morin: Executive summary.* Ottawa: Ministry of the Attorney General. Retrieved from https://www.attorneygeneral.jus.gov.on.ca/english/about/pubs/morin/morin_esumm.html.

Kramer, T.H., Buckhout, R., & Eugenio, P. (1990). Weapon focus, arousal, and eyewitness memory: Attention must be paid. *Law and Human Behavior, 14*, 167–184.

Leistico, A.M.R., Salekin, R.T., DeCoster, J., & Rogers, R. (2008). A large-scale meta-analysis relating the Hare measures of psychopathy to antisocial conduct. *Law and Human Behavior, 32*, 28–45.

Livingston, J.D., Wilson, D., Tien, G., & Bond, L. (2003). A follow-up study of persons found Not Criminally Responsible on Account of Mental Disorder in Canada. *Canadian Journal of Psychiatry, 48*, 408–445.

Loftus, E.F. (1984). Expert testimony on the eyewitness. In G.L. Wells & E.F. Loftus (Eds.), *Eyewitness testimony: Psychological perspectives* (pp. 273–283). New York: Cambridge University Press.

MacCallum, E.P. (2008). *Report of the Commission of the Inquiry into the Wrongful Conviction of David Milgaard.* Retrieved from http://www.qp.gov.sk.ca/Publications_Centre/Justice/Milgaard/01-Vol1-Intro.pdf.

Meissner, C.A., & Brigham, J.C. (2001). Thirty years of investigating the own-race bias in memory for faces: A meta-analytic review. *Psychology, Public Policy, and Law, 7*, 3–35.

M'Naghten's Case, 8 Eng Rep 718 (1843).

Münsterberg, H. (1908). *On the witness stand.* Garden City, NY: Doubleday.

Quinsey, V.L., Harris, G.T., Rice, M.E., & Cormier, C.A. (2005). *Violent offenders: Appraising and managing risk* (2nd ed.). Washington, DC: American Psychological Association.

R v Mohan, [1994] 2 SCR 9.

Roesch, R., Zapf, P.A., & Eaves, D. (2006). *Fitness Interview Test—Revised: A structured interview for assessing competency to stand trial.* Sarasota, FL: Professional Resource Press.

Roesch, R., Zapf, P.A., Hart, S.D., & Connolly, D.A. (2014). *Forensic psychology and law: A Canadian perspective.* Toronto: Wiley.

Rogers, R. (1984). *Rogers Criminal Responsibility Assessment Scales (R-CRAS) and test manual.* Odessa, FL: Psychological Assessment Resources.

Saferstein, R. (2011). *Criminalistics. An introduction to forensic science* (10th ed.). Upper Saddle River, NJ: Pearson.

Saferstein, R. (2015). *Criminalistics. An introduction to forensic science* (11th ed.). Upper Saddle River, NJ: Pearson.

Skeem, J.L., & Monahan, J. (2011). Current directions in violence risk assessment. *Current Directions in Psychological Science, 20*, 38–42.

Slobogin, C., & Fondacaro, M.R. (2011). *Juveniles at risk: A plea for preventive justice.* New York: Oxford University Press. Smith, S.M., Stinson, V., & Patry, M.W. (2010). Confession evidence in Canada: Psychological issues and legal landscapes. *Psychology, Crime & Law, 18*, 317–333.

Streissguth, A.P., & Kanter J. (Eds.). (1997). *The challenge of fetal alcohol syndrome: Overcoming secondary disabilities.* Seattle: University of Washington Press.

Tremblay, R.E., Masse, L., Pagani, L., & Vitaro, F. (1996). From childhood physical aggression to adolescent maladjustment: The Montreal Prevention Experiment. In R.D. Peters & R.J. McMahon (Eds.), *Preventing childhood disorders, substance abuse, and delinquency.* Thousand Oaks, CA: Sage.

Viljoen, J.L., Roesch, R., Ogloff, J.R.P., & Zapf, P.A. (2003). The role of Canadian psychologists in conducting fitness and criminal responsibility evaluations. *Canadian Psychology, 44,* 369–381.

Walters, G.D. (2003). Predicting criminal justice outcomes with the Psychopathy Checklist and Lifestyle Criminality Screening Form: A meta-analytic comparison. *Behavioral Sciences and the Law, 21,* 89–102.

Wells, G.L., Small, M., Penrod, S.D., Malpass, R.S., Fulero, S.M., & Brimacombe, C.A.E. (1998). Eyewitness identification procedures: Recommendations for lineups and photospreads. *Law and Human Behavior, 22,* 603–647.

Wigmore, J.H. (1909). Professor Münsterberg and the psychology of evidence. *Illinois Law Review, 3,* 399–445.

Wrightsman, L.S., & Fulero, S.M. (2005). *Forensic psychology.* Belmont, CA: Thomson Wadsworth.

Zapf, P.A., & Roesch, R. (2011). Future directions in the restoration of competence to stand trial. *Current Directions in Psychological Science, 20*(1), 43–47.

PART THREE

The Courts

R v Bourque (2014)

Karla O'Regan

A bronze monument in Moncton, New Brunswick memorializes Constables Douglas Larche, David Ross, and Fabrice Gevaudan, who were killed during the 2014 Moncton shootings.

In contrast with other regions around the world, Canada has had very few incidents of mass shootings. Sometimes referred to as "rampage shootings," these events involve the targeted killing of multiple victims by gun violence, often in a public place. In the United States, 47 mass shootings have taken place between 2006 and 2016, with the worst in the country's history taking place in June 2016 in Orlando, Florida (Follman, Aronson, & Pan, 2016). In comparison, Australia has not experienced a mass shooting in 20 years—something that many experts suggest is a direct result of the strict gun control legislation that the country passed in 1996 (Chapman, Alpers, & Jones, 2016).

In the same time frame, Canada has experienced four mass shootings, one of which resulted in "the harshest punishment imposed since the last hanging in 1962" (Taber, 2014). On June 4, 2014, 24-year-old Justin Bourque left his home in Moncton, New Brunswick dressed in full camouflage with two semi-automatic rifles strapped criss-cross on his back. He was also carrying a pump-action shotgun and three boxes of ammunition. Residents phoned police to report seeing Bourque as he walked through his quiet, suburban neighbourhood and into an adjacent wooded area. As one witness reported: "He just had this blank stare on his face, just a dead look in his eyes. He was calm as could be. He was just walking at a steady pace. It wasn't fast. It wasn't slow. He did not waver, not even to avoid a pothole" (McMahon, Friscolanti, & Patriquin, 2014).

Police arrived on the scene and set up a perimeter around the woods and surrounding community and immediately requested that Police Dog Services be dispatched (MacNeil, 2015). As police were directing residents into their homes, Bourque emerged from the woods and was pursued by surrounding officers. He then opened fire on the officers, killing three and severely injuring two others before disappearing into another wooded area. All of the victims were killed within an hour of Bourque having left his home.

Police searched for Bourque for the next 28 hours, during which time a neighbourhood-wide lockdown was ordered in Moncton. Meanwhile, friends and family identified Bourque after neighbourhood residents shared images on social media that they had taken of the shooter earlier that morning. Hundreds of RCMP and police officers from several provinces arrived to assist in the search, including 100 tactical officers, five armoured vehicles, and aircraft from both RCMP and Transport Canada. With the help of infrared cameras that identified the shooter's thermal image from the air, police were able to arrest him at 12:10 a.m. on June 6, 2014.

While in custody, Bourque gave a statement to police in which he admitted to specifically targeting police officers. A number of Facebook posts he had made in the weeks leading up to the attack conveyed a sense of anger and frustration at the Canadian government and its agents. "If we are born poor, we die poor," he posted on February 27. "We live under their reign, under crownless kings. Unless the people take notice, fight, and destroy the 1% the battle for the futur [sic] is lost" (McMahon et al., 2014). Friends and acquaintances who were interviewed after Bourque's arrest remembered his frequent "anti-cop" and "anti-establishment" rants, although all believed he was "a big talker, nothing more" (McMahon et al., 2014).

Murder is considered one of the most serious offences in Canada's *Criminal Code*, and its circumstances can aggravate its severity in the eyes of the law and result in a classification of first-degree murder. As you will learn in Chapter 6, one of the conditions for a first-degree murder conviction is the offender's state of mind: Was the killing planned and deliberate? A homicide can also be classified as first-degree murder based on who the intended victim is, such as a law enforcement officer. The tragic case of the 2014 Moncton shootings included both of these circumstances, resulting in three charges of first-degree murder and two charges of attempted first-degree murder. Bourque pleaded guilty to all five charges.

Aside from the horrific nature of his crimes and the dramatic circumstances of his capture, it was Bourque's prison sentence that garnered the most headlines. First-degree murder in Canada carries a mandatory life sentence, so from the moment he pleaded guilty, Bourque was facing a life behind bars. What marks his punishment as the country's worst since the death penalty, however, is the length of time Bourque must serve before being eligible for parole. Following a 2011 amendment to Canada's *Criminal Code*, judges may now order that the mandatory 25-year period of parole ineligibility for murder convictions be served consecutively in cases of multiple murders. This provision was first used in 2013 in the case of Travis Baumgartner, the former armoured car guard who shot four of his co-workers, killing three of them. He was sentenced to life imprisonment with a period of 40 years of parole ineligibility. Bourque's period of parole ineligibility was set at 75 years (25 years for each first-degree murder conviction), meaning that he will be 99 years old before he can apply for release.

Reaching a sentencing decision is no easy task, particularly when the offence is as tragic, violent, and senseless as the murders in this case. Chapter 8 will discuss the various factors a sentencing judge must consider when punishing an offender, including the principles of deterrence and denunciation—both of which were highlighted by the sentencing judge in Bourque's case. When reaching his decision to impose three consecutive periods of parole ineligibility in *R v Bourque*, Justice David Smith of the Court of Queen's Bench of New Brunswick noted the following:

> The murders were carried out as ambushes so that the first responding officers had no chance. They were killed because they were police officers acting in the line of duty and represented authority in the offender's mind.
>
> The offender displayed such premeditated preparation in the commission of crimes that were so grave and appalling that the sentence must denounce the conduct in the strongest possible manner … . The sentence must also serve as general deterrent giving notice to anyone thinking of similar deeds that society condemns such actions to the extent that no leniency may be expected. (paras. 47, 52)

The shootings and subsequent police hunt for Bourque had a considerable impact on Moncton and its surrounding communities, where violent crime is a rarity. In the year prior to the shootings, for example, there were no reported homicides in Moncton

(Boyce, Cotter, & Perrault, 2014). As Assistant Commissioner Alphonse MacNeil of the RCMP wrote in his independent review of the incidents:

> The evening … was warm and sunny. Children were playing in their yards and on the streets, families were preparing dinner and people were traveling about in their vehicles. No one could have predicted that this bright summer's evening would quickly darken as the tragic events that unfolded would change the lives of many forever. That evening, within 20 minutes, Constables David Ross, Fabrice Gevaudan, and Douglas Larche were murdered, Constables Eric Dubois and Darlene Goguen were wounded, Cst. Martine Benoit survived multiple rounds fired into her police vehicle and several others were exposed to high powered rifle fire. The unthinkable actions of one individual left three families without their husband, son, father, and brother. The RCMP lost three of their own and the community [was] stripped of [its] sense of security. People across New Brunswick and the country were shaken to their core as they tried to make sense of such a senseless tragedy. (MacNeil, 2015)

In the wake of such terror and loss, it is understandable to want to see the offender punished as harshly as possible. The difficulty, however, is that studies conducted by criminal justice scholars and other social scientists show that deterrence-based punishment rarely serves to decrease crime. Rather, in most cases, it increases it. Indeed, Travis Baumgartner's sentence (issued in September 2013) did little to deter Justin Bourque from committing very similar crimes less than nine months later. Moreover, the use of parole eligibility periods has been shown to *decrease* violent behaviour among prison inmates, particularly those serving lengthy sentences. The reduction of violent and anti-social behaviour within prison walls has, in turn, also been shown to reduce reoffending rates among those inmates who *are* released (particularly those who have served lengthy sentences). In this way, parole eligibility also serves to create a safer environment for correctional staff and other inmates.

At his sentencing hearing, Bourque made reference to the widespread harm and suffering his actions had caused, apologizing to the families of the fallen officers. When issuing his sentence, the judge cited a number of psychological factors (some of which were discussed in Chapter 5) which may have contributed to Bourque's crimes; however, as MacNeil's report noted, the events of June 4, 2016 amount to a "senseless tragedy."

All too often, criminal law is tasked with addressing crimes, such as the Moncton shootings, that leave a community searching for answers and struggling to heal. The determination of the presence of the physical (*actus reus*) and mental (*mens rea*) components of a crime is an important stage of the criminal process. Moreover, as Chapter 6 indicates, the presence or absence of these components establishes the criminal defences available to a person accused of a crime. In Bourque's case, no criminal defence was needed because of his guilty plea—an official admission of wrongdoing that the court hears at an accused's arraignment. These and other court processes are discussed in Chapter 7 which, along with the sentencing procedures outlined in Chapter 8, demonstrate the complex process through which offenders are punished for criminal wrongdoing in Canada.

The *Bourque* case renewed debates about the role of punishment in criminal law, including the use and value of parole programs. Early in 2016, Bourque's lawyer reported an intention to file an appeal of his sentence. As this case develops, criminal justice scholars (like yourself!) will need to think critically about the issues and challenges this case raises for criminal law in Canada. They include determining what actions the law should punish and the purpose for which penalties are imposed.

Explore these correctional issues in further depth in Part Four of this text.

What Do You Think?

1. A lot of public debate occurred when Bourque was sentenced, particularly around the imposition of a 75-year period of parole ineligibility. What do you think a judge should have in mind when sentencing an offender? As you read about the Moncton shootings, did you have the same principles of punishment in mind as when you considered what sentence to give Matt in this text's Part One case study? What similarities and differences can you identify in how you would approach these two cases?

2. Should judges use the same framework when sentencing each offender, or are there certain factors that should change how some offenders or types of crimes are punished? After you read through the sentencing principles outlined in Chapter 8, consider how well the sentencing judge in the *Bourque* case addressed them. Do you think the *Bourque* case points to areas in Canada's criminal law that are in need of reform?

3. Social media played a large role in the *Bourque* case. Pictures taken and posted by neighbourhood residents during the incident helped the police identify the offender. However, during its search for Bourque, the RCMP warned residents not to post anything about police movements on social media. The fear was that Bourque was following these posts to learn where the police were and what they were doing. What role should social media have in a police investigation? Should criminal law be used to sanction individuals who compromise police investigations or safety through their use of social media? How might these social media sanctions compare to the use of publication bans (see Chapter 7) in criminal trials?

SUGGESTED FURTHER READINGS

O'Regan, K. (2014, November 3). Justin Bourque's case prompts debate over lengthy prison terms. *CBC News*. Retrieved from http://www.cbc.ca/news/canada/new-brunswick/justin-bourque-s-case-prompts-debate-over-lengthy-prison-terms-1.2821580.

REFERENCES

Boyce, J., Cotter, A., & Perreault, S. (2014, July 23). Police-reported crime statistics in Canada, 2013. *Juristat, 34*(1). Retrieved from http://www.statcan.gc.ca/pub/85-002-x/2014001/article/14040-eng.pdf.

Chapman, S., Alpers, P., & Jones, M. (2016). Association between gun law reforms and intentional firearm deaths in Australia, 1979–2013. *JAMA, 316*(3), 291–299.

Follman, M., Aronson, G., & Pan, D. (2016, September 24). A guide to mass shootings in America. *Mother Jones*. Retrieved from http://www.motherjones.com/politics/2012/07/mass-shootings-map.

MacNeil, A. (2015). Independent review—Moncton shooting—June 4, 2014: Narrative description June 4, 19:18 to June 6, 00:20. Retrieved from http://www.rcmp-grc.gc.ca/en/independent-review-moncton-shooting-june-4-2014#desc.

McMahon, T., Friscolanti, M., & Patriquin, M. (2014, June 15). The untold story of Justin Bourque. *Maclean's*. Retrieved from http://www.macleans.ca/news/canada/untold-story-justin-bourque/.

R v Bourque, 2014 NBQB 237.

Taber, J. (2014, October 31). Moncton RCMP killer Justin Bourque given 75-year sentence without parole. *Globe and Mail*. Retrieved from http://www.theglobeandmail.com/news/national/bourque-sentence/article21397474/.

Criminal Law

LEARNING OUTCOMES

After reading this chapter, students will be able to:

- Understand the historical origins and primary sources of criminal law in Canada.
- Recognize the difference between federal and provincial authority to prohibit acts.
- Define *actus reus* and its components as well as subjective and objective *mens rea*.
- Describe a variety of ways in which a person can be involved in a criminal offence.
- Describe situations when the mere attempt to commit an offence is enough to be considered a crime.
- Be familiar with criminal defences including automatism, mistake of fact, not criminally responsible on account of mental disorder (NCRMD), and intoxication.

Introduction

Law operates as a set of rules for governing human behaviour. Because these rules are derived from community customs and norms, laws can vary tremendously from one society to the next. This is particularly the case with criminal law, given its close association with morality. Although criminal law is normally focused on acts that are just too harmful or dangerous to be permitted in society, it can also serve to prohibit behaviours that the community finds too distasteful, unconventional, or simply annoying. The United States has a wide variety of examples of prohibited acts because each state has its own set of criminal laws, or **penal code**. In the District of Columbia, for instance, it is a federal crime to harass a golfer or tennis player while in any national park.[1] In the state of Massachusetts, putting the national anthem into a dance mix medley comes with a hefty criminal fine.[2] Despite having only one set of criminal laws, Canada has its own fair share of unusual prohibitions. Challenging someone to a duel, for example, is a crime punishable with up to two years in prison,[3] and simply *having* a stink bomb (let alone using one) in a public place could result in six months in prison.[4] These unusual uses of the law seem to support one legal historian's view that in criminal law, "the 'extraordinary' is as much the norm as the ordinary" (Norrie, 2014, p. 9).

penal code
A compilation of the laws that establish a jurisdiction's criminal law; also referred to as a *criminal code*.

One of the more important functions of criminal law is not simply the establishment of a society's definitions of "right" and "wrong," but the development of tools for determining when a (legal) wrong has been committed. This chapter will explore the legal definitions and principles that are used to determine when a criminal offence has occurred. It includes a discussion of both the physical (*actus reus*) and mental (*mens rea*) components of a crime, as well as the different roles a person can play in the commission of an offence. It also examines some of the defences that are available to a person accused of a crime in Canada. This chapter begins with a look at the origins and primary sources of criminal law.

Historical Origins and Primary Sources of Criminal Law

Historically, crime was a conflict between private citizens. For example, stealing a horse or trespassing onto someone's property were viewed as personal injuries and were dealt with through **private prosecutions**. Citizens who felt they had been wronged could launch a criminal trial against the accused person, a legal process resembling a civil lawsuit today. There were, however, penalties for losing one's case.

One of the earliest known examples of a written set of criminal laws is the *Code of Hammurabi*, which dates back to about 1754 BCE. The Code contains laws and corresponding punishments (perhaps one of the most famous being "an eye for an eye"). Among the Code's punishments is a death sentence for anyone who falsely accuses another. Many determinations of guilt based on the Code were reliant on the **ordeal**—a method for seeking an answer from the divine about whether the accused was guilty or not. For example, the "glowing iron ordeal" required that the accused person hold a red-hot iron (or, in some cases, an ember from the fire itself) in a bare hand while walking for a distance. Afterward, the hand would be bandaged and re-examined three days later. If the wound had become infected, the accused was guilty.

private prosecution
A criminal trial or proceeding that is brought by a private citizen, rather than a publicly appointed official (e.g., Crown attorney, public prosecutor).

ordeal
An ancient criminal trial method that involved subjecting the accused to a painful or dangerous test (e.g., holding a hot iron) as a means of seeking an answer from the divine about the accused's guilt or innocence.

Code of Hammurabi

Enacted by Hammurabi, the sixth King of Babylon, in about 1754 BCE, the *Code of Hammurabi* contains 282 laws, each with its own corresponding punishment. Law #2 outlines the procedure for dealing with false accusations, and includes the use of an ordeal for determining the accused's guilt or innocence:

> 2. If anyone brings an accusation against a man, and the accused goes to the river and leaps into the river, if he sinks in the river his accuser shall take possession of his house. But if the river proves that the accused is not guilty, and he escapes unhurt, then he who had brought the accusation shall be put to death, while he who leaped into the river shall take possession of the house that had belonged to his accuser.

This ancient stele depicts Hammurabi (standing) receiving the royal insignia from the god Shamash. The laws are carved into the stone below.

Today (thankfully), far more objective criteria for determining guilt are used in criminal law, and the accused is afforded a number of rights during a criminal trial (many of which are explored in greater detail in Chapter 7). These procedural protections represent one of the most significant developments in criminal law's history—a move away from viewing crime as a private conflict between individuals to understanding it as a public offence against the state. Because crime is viewed as a public offence against the state, criminal cases in Canada are always written as *R v The Accused* (or *The Queen v The Accused*). *R* is the abbreviation for *Regina*, which is Latin for "Queen," and signals that the case is between the state and the accused rather than between the accused and the victim. This is also why public prosecutors are known as *Crown* attorneys. They act on behalf of the government during a criminal trial, representing the interests of the public in a safe and secure society with respected laws.

Criminal law in Canada relies heavily on the laws and traditions of Great Britain. Indeed, the English House of Lords served as the highest court of appeal for Canadians until the 1931 *Statute of Westminster*, which recognized the Supreme Court of Canada as the country's highest legal authority. Although Canada continues to use the English system of **common law**, all of Canada's criminal laws were **codified** (written down) in 1892 with the first *Criminal Code*. Together, the *Criminal Code* and the common law represent the two primary sources of criminal law in Canada.

Statutory Sources and the Division of Powers

Canada's *Criminal Code* is usually the first source mentioned in discussions about where criminal law comes from. This makes sense given that the Code is where the majority of Canada's criminal offences are found. (How these offences are classified and interact with other **statutory** sources of criminal law, such as the *Canadian Charter of Rights and Freedoms* or the *Canada Evidence Act*, are topics addressed in Chapter 7.) A number of other statutes create offences that form part of Canada's criminal law, such as the *Controlled Drugs and Substances Act* and the *Crimes Against Humanity and War Crimes Act*.

common law
Law that is developed by judges when deciding cases, rather than through legislative enactments.

codified
Written down and collected; for example, the *Criminal Code*, which contains a written record of all of Canada's criminal laws, is a codified law.

statutory
Given power by statute, meaning a piece of legislation that is passed by Parliament and becomes law.

Crimes Against Humanity and War Crimes Act

The *Crimes Against Humanity and War Crimes Act* (CAHWCA) is an especially interesting example of a criminal law statute, because it gives domestic legal effect to international criminal law. Under the CAHWCA, Canadian courts are authorized to assume jurisdiction over crimes against humanity, war crimes, genocide, and any other crime recognized under international law, even if the crime took place in another country and did not involve any Canadian citizens—a power referred to as "universal jurisdiction." The CAHWCA also allows courts to assume jurisdiction over international crimes committed within Canada or abroad by Canadian citizens and state officials.

This provision suggests that international law can take its place alongside the common law, statutes, and the Constitution as a source of criminal law in Canada.

In 2009, Désiré Munyaneza, a Rwandan national with permanent resident status in Canada, became the first person charged and convicted under the CAHWCA. After being recognized by members of the Rwandan diaspora in Toronto, Munyaneza was prosecuted in Quebec. The Quebec Superior Court found him guilty of genocide, war crimes, and crimes against humanity during the Rwandan genocide, and sentenced him to life imprisonment with no possibility of parole for 25 years.

These laws are all federal legislation because the power to make criminal law is found in s 91(27) of the *British North America Act* of 1867. Also known as the *Constitution Act, 1867*, this document establishes the legislative powers for each level of government (see "Sidebar—Sections 91 and 92 of the *Constitution Act, 1867*"). Section 91 outlines the areas for which the federal government may enact laws (e.g., Canada's military, currency, and national census), while s 92 dictates the kinds of activities that provincial governments may regulate (e.g., provincial prison systems or property and civil rights within a province). A number of provincial laws resemble criminal law, in that they prohibit behaviour and impose a penalty. Motor vehicle and liquor law offences are good examples. Section 92 of the *Constitution Act, 1867* allows each province to pass laws that establish the rules for driving or the legal drinking age, as well as the penalties for violating these regulations. Although being caught speeding or having sold liquor to a person under the legal drinking age may *seem* like areas of concern for criminal law, they fall under **regulatory offences**, or **quasi-criminal law**.

regulatory offences
Violations of legal rules or guidelines pertaining to legal activities (e.g., drinking). Also known as *quasi-criminal law*.

quasi-criminal law
Regulations and statutes pertaining to legal activities that create offences and penalties that are not enacted under the federal government's criminal law power. (See also *regulatory offences*.)

Regulatory offences differ from criminal law in two important ways. First, regulatory offences generally pertain to activities that are inherently legal (such as operating a motor vehicle). By contrast, criminal law focuses on illegal or prohibited acts. Second, regulatory offences are *not* enacted under the federal government's s 91(27) criminal law power, but instead are made up of a wide variety of regulations and by-laws from all three levels of government. Occasionally, areas of overlap exist between federal and provincial legislation when each level of government has enacted laws aimed at regulating the same behaviour. When this overlap occurs, the principle of **federal paramountcy** recognizes the federal government's legislative power over that of the provinces, declaring the federal law to be valid (and the provincial law to be invalid). This principle requires that there be a direct conflict between the federal and provincial laws in question and that the purpose of the law be one that clearly falls within the federal government's powers in s 91 of the *Constitution Act, 1867*.

federal paramountcy
The principle that when there is a conflict between federal and provincial laws, the federal legislation will succeed and the provincial law will be considered invalid (insofar as it conflicts with the federal law).

For a law to fall under the federal criminal law power in s 91(27) of *Constitution Act, 1867*, it must have three components:

1. A prohibition (meaning the law must forbid or disallow certain conduct);
2. A penalty (which can include a fine or a period of imprisonment); and
3. A criminal public purpose.

ultra vires
Latin for "beyond the power of"; used in law to refer to legislation that is enacted outside the jurisdiction of the governing body that issued it and is, therefore, invalid.

The meaning of a "criminal public purpose" was decided in the *Margarine Reference* case in 1949 when Justice Rand of the Supreme Court of Canada held that to be a valid exercise of s 91(27), the law must be directed toward "some evil or injurious or undesirable effect upon the public" in one of five categories: public peace, order, security, health, and morality (*Reference re Validity of Section 5 (a) Dairy Industry Act*, 1949). Given how broad these purposes are, it is not surprising that conflict occasionally arises between federal criminal law and provincial regulatory offences. The 1983 Supreme Court of Canada case of *Westendorp v The Queen* offers a good example. Westendorp was arrested and found guilty under a municipal by-law in Calgary that prohibited being on the street for the purposes of prostitution. At the Supreme Court, she argued that the law was **ultra vires** (or outside the jurisdiction of) the provincial government, and therefore invalid. Although the Alberta government argued that the law was a valid use of its power to regulate local roadways and traffic (under s 92(10) of the *Constitution Act, 1867*), the Supreme Court found that the law's true purpose was to regulate morality, and would therefore fall under the federal government's power to enact criminal law. This case also involved the legal doctrine of **colourability**, which applies when a government presents a law's purpose as something other than what it is, in order to "colour" it in a way that fits within its jurisdiction. In *Westendorp*, the Supreme Court found the Calgary by-law to be invalid because it was a law aimed at prohibiting and punishing prostitution for reasons of morality (a clear criminal purpose) but was disguised (or "coloured") as being about controlling local traffic for the purposes of fitting within the province's powers under s 92.

colourability

A legal doctrine referring to disguised attempts by a legislature to introduce a law that it does not have the authority or jurisdiction to enact.

SIDEBAR

Sections 91 and 92 of the Constitution Act, 1867

Federal Powers (s 91)

- the national debt (ss 1(a)) and the taxation system (ss 3)
- the regulation of trade and commerce (ss 2) and unemployment insurance (ss 2(a))
- the postal service (ss 5)
- the census and collection of national statistics (ss 6)
- the militia, military, and naval service, and defence (ss 7)
- shipping routes, lighthouses, and navigation (ss 9 and 10)
- quarantine and the establishment of marine hospitals (ss 11)
- the regulation of the sea coast and inland fisheries (ss 12)
- currency (ss 14), banking (ss 15 and 16), and bankruptcy (ss 21)
- patents (ss 22) and copyrights (ss 23)
- indigenous populations and reserve land (ss 24)
- citizenship (ss 25)
- marriage and divorce (ss 26)
- criminal law and procedure (ss 27)

Provincial Powers (s 92)

- provincial taxation system (ss 2)
- the management and sale of provincial lands and timber (ss 5)
- the establishment and management of provincial prisons (ss 6) and hospitals (ss 7)
- the management of municipal institutions (ss 8)
- licensing for shops, taverns, liquor, and gaming (ss 9)
- local roads and highways (ss 10)
- property and civil rights in the province (ss 13)
- the administration of the provincial justice system, including establishing both civil and criminal courts (ss 14)
- the imposition of punishment (by fine, penalty, or imprisonment) as part of the enforcement of any valid provincial law (ss 15)
- generally, all matters of a merely local or private nature in the province (ss 16)

Common Law

The *Westendorp* case is an example of the second major source of criminal law in Canada: judicial decisions. It is typical in discussions of criminal law to see a reference made to the "leading case" on a particular topic—this is the common law system at work. As judges hear cases and interpret the law, new ways of approaching legal issues are developed. When judges consider certain new approaches to be the most useful, they rely on them repeatedly, resulting in changes to criminal law. This is one of the reasons the common law is often referred to as "judge-made law"—the law literally changes with each decision that a judge makes. The common law also has a long and rich history within the tithing and shire-reeve systems of England (as discussed in Chapter 3), where legal disputes were resolved in accordance with local customs and values. As these early legal systems were developed over time, the law became a record of the beliefs and practices that each community held "in common."

Each new criminal case comes to a judge with a unique set of challenges. Researching how other judges have dealt with a similar problem can assist judges in knowing how to handle the case they have at hand. Judges are free to adopt the decisions reached in other cases, or they may choose to resolve the case in an entirely new way, offering a different interpretation of a law or legal requirement. However, where a decision on a legal issue has been reached by a court of higher jurisdiction, all judges in lower courts must follow the higher court's decision. (See Figure 6.1 for an outline of Canada's court structure.) This is the principle of **stare decisis**—a Latin term meaning "the decision before," which requires that judges follow the decisions of relevant cases that have come before them. This practice (also known as "precedent" in legal circles), stems from a central common law principle known as the **rule of law**. This legal principle dates back to the *Code of Hammurabi* and requires that laws be based on established rules rather than secret determinations or the whims of individual leaders or officials. Intrinsic to this principle is a commitment to equality before the law. Regardless of one's social, economic, or political position, the law should be applied equally to everyone.

The rule of law is also the reason why almost all of Canada's criminal offences have been written down (or codified). Codification ensures that laws are not made up or applied randomly. Moreover, citizens can be made aware of what actions are prohibited (and punishable) when criminal offences are recorded and publicized. One of the principles of the rule of law can be found in s 9 of the *Criminal Code*, which states that a person may not be convicted of a common law offence. The only exception to this provision is the common law offence of **contempt of court**. However, a number of common law defences continue to operate in Canada, such as the defences of necessity and duress. Others, such as the defence of intoxication (discussed near the end of this chapter), developed out of the common law but have since been codified.

The Legal Components of a Crime: Actus Reus and Mens Rea

A common law principle that plays a major role in the criminal justice system is that a person is presumed innocent until proven guilty. In Canada, the presumption of innocence is recognized in s 11(d) of the Charter. The presumption of innocence requires the Crown to prove that the accused person is guilty. "Guilt" in criminal law has two

---

For a discussion of the kinds of offences that are tried in each court, see Chapter 7.

stare decisis
Latin for "to stand by things decided"; used in law to refer to the common law principle that judges must respect and follow decisions made by higher courts.

rule of law
The principle that no one is above the law and that each person, regardless of political or economic position, should be subject to the same law (rather than the arbitrary decisions of the powerful).

contempt of court
Canada's only common law offence, it consists of deliberately disobeying a court order or showing disrespect to the court process.

FIGURE 6.1   Hierarchy of Courts

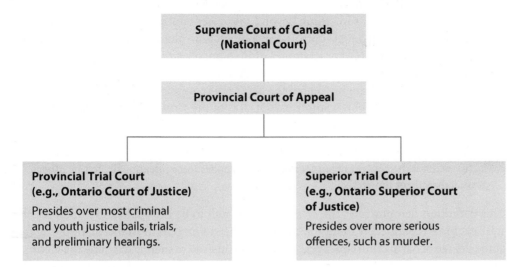

components: a physical one (***actus reus***) and a mental one (***mens rea***). Together, they make up the central consideration of criminal law: moral blameworthiness. Criminal law seeks to punish only those people who have done harmful things on purpose and with sufficient disregard for others. Moral blameworthiness asks the question: Does the person accused of this crime *deserve* to be punished? Is the person *worthy* of blame?

These questions are important. Apart from its punishment, criminal conviction comes with a high degree of social and economic stigma. Offenders are often denied employment and housing on the basis of their prior offences, and research has shown that prisoners suffer from multiple forms of social exclusion. In many cases, the families of offenders are also stigmatized, increasing children's risk of mental illness, substance abuse, and criminal behaviour (Murray, 2007). Before labelling a person a criminal, the law needs to establish that a guilty act was committed with a guilty mind. This requirement is known as the **principle of simultaneity** and serves as the basis for all criminal defences.

Actus Reus

Although usually defined simply as a "guilty act," the *actus reus* involves the consideration of a number of interrelated legal issues. They include the components of the *actus reus*, the role of omissions, and the legal doctrine of causation.

Components of the *Actus Reus*

Criminal offences are defined in the *Criminal Code* to include a statement about what is prohibited (e.g., murder) and what the punishment for that action will be (e.g., life imprisonment). These definitions need to be precise because criminal law is not concerned with every undesirable or offensive action, but only those that cause harm to others. The accused's *actus reus* can therefore be said to comprise the following components: prohibited (voluntary) *conduct* that occurs in certain *circumstances* resulting in harmful *consequences*.

actus reus
Latin for "guilty act"; used in law to refer to the physical acts and circumstances that must be proven to have occurred and been present during the commission of an offence.

mens rea
Latin for "guilty mind"; used in law to refer to the mental state the Crown must prove the accused had during the commission of an offence.

principle of simultaneity
A criminal law requirement that the *actus reus* and *mens rea* occurred at the same time or were part of the same chain of events during the commission of a crime.

All of these components must be proven by the Crown to establish a completed *actus reus*, beginning with the voluntary conduct of the accused. Where the accused's physical actions were the result of something beyond his or her control (such as a car hitting a patch of ice and skidding out of control), the conduct is involuntary and therefore cannot complete the *actus reus*. (Other examples of involuntary actions that negate the *actus reus* are discussed later in this chapter under "Automatism.")

In many instances, changing one of the *actus reus* components can result in a completely different offence. For example, s 265(1)(a) of the *Criminal Code* defines the offence of assault as follows:

> 265(1) A person commits an assault when
> (a) without the consent of another person, he applies force intentionally to that other person, directly or indirectly.

This definition demonstrates the *actus reus* of assault to be the application of direct or indirect force (conduct) without the consent of the victim (circumstances), resulting in some degree of harm (consequences). If, however, instead of merely harming the victim, the consequence of the accused's use of force was the victim's death, the offence would be murder, rather than assault. If the circumstances of the offence were changed to include the use of a gun or knife, the offence would become assault with a weapon. Many other offences (e.g., aggravated assault, sexual assault, assault causing bodily harm) share the conduct component of the *actus reus* (i.e., use of force) but differ in their required circumstances and consequences.

IN-CLASS EXERCISE

Actus Reus Components

Using the following offence descriptions of the *Criminal Code* as a guide, identify the *actus reus* components that the Crown must prove for the offence of public nudity.

> **Nudity**
> 174(1) Every one who, without lawful excuse,
> (a) is nude in a public place, or
> (b) is nude and exposed to public view while on private property, whether or not the property is his own,
> is guilty of an offence punishable on summary conviction.
> **Nude**
> (2) For the purposes of this section, a person is nude who is so clad as to offend against public decency or order.

1. What is the conduct?

2. What are the circumstances?

3. What are the consequences?

Answers to in-class exercises can be found at the end of the chapter.

Omissions

A criminal offence can also be committed when the accused *fails* to do something. In such a case, the required conduct of the *actus reus* is a lack of action, known as an

omission to act. In Canada, a failure to act can amount to criminal conduct only when it can be shown that the accused was under a legal duty to do something in the first place. In some circumstances, this pre-existing legal duty is established by statute. Consider s 215(1)(a) of the *Criminal Code* as an example. It reads as follows:

> 215(1) Every one is under a legal duty
> (a) as a parent, foster parent, guardian or head of a family, to provide necessaries of life for a child under the age of sixteen years;
> (b) to provide necessaries of life to their spouse or common-law partner; and
> (c) to provide necessaries of life to a person under his charge if that person
> (i) is unable, by reason of detention, age, illness, mental disorder or other cause, to withdraw himself from that charge, and
> (ii) is unable to provide himself with necessaries of life.

This **provision** creates a legal duty for parents and guardians of children under the age of 16, as well as married persons and caretakers, to provide their children, spouses, and dependants with the "necessaries of life." Failure to do so is a criminal offence (defined in s 215(2)). This is an example of a circumstance where the conduct component of the *actus reus* is satisfied when the accused does nothing at all. The *Criminal Code* contains a few others, including the duty to assist a police officer (in s 129(b)) and the duty to protect people from falling accidents where the accused has made an opening in ice or excavated a hole (s 263).

However, where no legal duty can be shown to have existed between the accused and the victim, the accused's failure to act does not result in criminal liability. This means that there is no legal duty to rescue in Canada (apart from those created by statute).

Causation

Another important component of the *actus reus* that the Crown must prove in a criminal trial is a connection between the accused's acts and the law's prohibited consequences. This **causal link** between the actions of the accused and the harm suffered by the victim is a central element in establishing criminal responsibility. As was noted earlier, moral blameworthiness is a core principle of Canada's criminal justice system and must precede punishment. Before finding a person guilty, the criminal law requires proof that the accused's actions (or inactions) *caused* the victim's injury (see Figure 6.2).

omission to act
The failure to act in circumstances where there is a legal obligation to do so.

provision
In law, it refers to a specific section of a statute; an article or clause in a piece of legislation.

What Do You Think?

Much debate has surrounded whether a legal duty to rescue should exist in Canadian jurisdictions. Since 1975, one jurisdiction—Quebec—has enacted such legislation. Quebec's *Charter of Human Rights and Freedoms* contains a duty to rescue (or "good Samaritan law" as such a law is sometimes called), requiring all citizens to assist anyone they find in danger, unless doing so would endanger themselves.

1. Should other jurisdictions in Canada enact good Samaritan laws?
2. What are some of the pros and cons of using the criminal law to create a duty to rescue?

causal link
An established connection between an accused's conduct (act or omission) and a prohibited legal consequence; also known as *causation*.

FIGURE 6.2   Elements of the Actus Reus

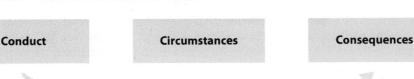

causal link

In many cases, establishing causation in a criminal case is a simple factual matter. If person A fires a gun at person B (who then dies), it is not difficult to say that A's actions were the cause of B's death. As the facts of a case get more complicated, however, establishing a direct causal link between the accused's actions and the harm suffered can become more challenging. Suppose that B suffered a non-fatal wound when shot by A and opted not to seek medical treatment. B later dies as a result of an infection. Can it still be said that A's act of firing the gun *caused* B's death? Is A responsible for B's death? The answer to both questions is "yes." Even though B's decision to leave the wound untreated contributed to the death, B would not have been wounded had A not fired the gun. Moreover, the act of firing a weapon at a person is a dangerous one, and it comes with harmful and foreseeable consequences. When people act in ways that cause preventable harms, criminal law holds them responsible, as the "*R v Maybin* Sidebar" (below) describes.

intervening act
An event or act that occurs between the accused's actions and the victim's injury that is significant enough to break the causal link between the conduct of the accused and the law's prohibited consequence.

SIDEBAR

R v Maybin (2012): Intervening Acts

Some events can interrupt the chain of causation. These **intervening acts** (from the Latin term *novus actus interveniens*, meaning "new intervening act") occur between the accused's actions and the victim's injury and are significant enough to sever the causal link between the conduct of the accused and the prohibited consequence. For this reason, intervening acts are also referred to as "breaking the chain" in English law. To be an intervening act, an event must (1) have a significant impact on the victim's injury or death; and (2) not be a reasonably foreseeable consequence of the accused's actions.

One of Canada's leading cases on the law of intervening acts involves a bar fight in Nanaimo, British Columbia. In October 2006, two brothers, Tim and Matthew Maybin, were playing a game of pool at a local bar when the victim, Michael Brophy, touched one of the balls on the pool table. This action offended Tim Maybin who, helped by his brother, grabbed the victim and violently punched his face and head several times. The victim did not defend himself but fell face-forward onto the pool table. The fight caught the attention of one of the bar's bouncers, who walked over to the pool table and struck the unconscious victim very hard behind his right ear. The two attacks took place within a minute's time. The victim was then carried out of the bar and left, unconscious, on the sidewalk. The police and an ambulance were called and the victim was taken to hospital where he later died due to massive amounts of bleeding in the brain.

Both Maybin brothers and the bouncer were arrested and charged with manslaughter. Although it was clear the victim had died as a result of a blow to the head, it was not clear which blow to the head had actually *caused* his death. Was it the first series of punches thrown by Tim Maybin? Or perhaps the fatal blow to the head was delivered by the bouncer? The trial judge was unable to decide, concluding that there were three possible causes of death: the punches delivered by Tim (with Matthew's help), the bouncer's punch to the back of the victim's head, or a combination of the two. The uncertainty about which act was linked to the victim's death left the judge with enough reasonable doubt to acquit all three accused.

The British Columbia Court of Appeal disagreed and ordered a new trial. The Maybin brothers appealed to the Supreme Court of Canada, but lost. Tim Maybin later pleaded guilty to manslaughter and was sentenced to two years less a day. Both his brother, Matthew, and the bouncer pleaded guilty to assault causing bodily harm.

In its decision to dismiss the appeal, the Supreme Court of Canada ruled that although the bouncer's attack may have contributed to the victim's death, it was not an unforeseeable event and could therefore not be considered an intervening act. Rather, the court argued that by starting a bar fight, the Maybin brothers should reasonably have expected that bar staff security might intervene in a physical manner. The Maybin brothers were obviously responsible for Tim's punches, but because this attack also *caused* the bouncer to attack, the causal link between the Maybins' actions and the victim's death was left intact.

Mens Rea

The principle of moral blameworthiness is also of central concern in the law's consideration of the accused's state of mind. Just as criminal law seeks only to prohibit actions that have caused harmful consequences, it is also interested in punishing only those who have acted with dangerous intentions. The guilty mind (or *mens rea*) is the second substantial component of criminal liability. The importance of this mental element to criminal law was described in the case of *R v Théroux* (1993) by Justice McLachlin (now the Supreme Court of Canada's Chief Justice): "Its function in criminal law is to prevent the conviction of the morally innocent—those who do not understand or intend the consequences of their acts" (p. 17). Criminal offenders are those who have deliberately intended to do harm to others or have acted in circumstances where they knew (or should have known) that harm was likely to occur (such as the Maybin brothers in *R v Maybin*). There are two forms of *mens rea* in criminal law: subjective and objective.

Subjective *Mens Rea*

The form of *mens rea* that is most familiar to people is the subjective one. Subjective *mens rea* focuses on what was actually going on in the accused's mind at the time of the offence. What did the accused *intend* to do? What was the accused thinking when the offence took place? What specific circumstances was the accused aware of when the crime occurred? These questions help determine how criminally responsible the accused should be. The *Criminal Code*'s most serious offences require that the Crown prove the accused *chose* to cause the harm suffered by the victim. Specifically, the Crown must show that at the time of the crime, the accused had one of the following four types of subjective *mens rea*: intention, knowledge, recklessness, or wilful blindness.

Intention

Intention is often explicitly mentioned in the *Criminal Code*'s definition of an offence. Consider the offence of assault as an example. Note how s 265(1)(a) of the *Criminal Code* defines the offence and includes a subjective *mens rea* requirement:

> 265(1) A person commits an assault when
> (a) without the consent of another person, he *applies force intentionally* to that other person, directly or indirectly. [Emphasis added.]

Here, the Code clearly states that the Crown must prove the accused's deliberate *intention* to commit the requisite conduct (application of force) in the required circumstances (without consent) before the accused can be criminally responsible for the prohibited consequences (injury to the victim). The conduct itself is insufficient. The accused's guilt also lies in the choices that drove the conduct in the first place.

SIDEBAR

Intention Versus Motive

It is important to note that in the criminal law, the accused's intention is distinguished from the accused's **motive**. Although popular film and television crime dramas focus a great deal on the offender's reasons for committing a crime, criminal law cares very little about *why* a person may have performed an illegal act. Instead, the focus is on whether the accused *intended* to commit an offence. The motivation behind this intention, while interesting (and often helpful in police investigations), is rarely legally relevant.

Knowledge

Knowledge is another form of subjective *mens rea*. Some offences in the *Criminal Code* require that the accused had knowledge of certain circumstances at the time of the offence. Consider the offence of criminal harassment (s 264(1)) as one example:

> 264(1) No person shall, without lawful authority and *knowing that another person is harassed* or recklessly as to whether the other person is harassed, engage in conduct referred to in subsection (2) that causes that other person reasonably, in all the circumstances, to fear for their safety or the safety of anyone known to them. [Emphasis added.]

SIDEBAR

Criminal Harassment

Section 264(2) of the *Criminal Code* lists a number of actions that are considered criminal harassment when they are committed with the knowledge that they are likely to scare the victim. These acts are as follows:

(a) repeatedly following from place to place the other person or anyone known to them;

(b) repeatedly communicating with, either directly or indirectly, the other person or anyone known to them;

(c) besetting or watching the dwelling-house, or place where the other person, or anyone known to them, resides, works, carries on business or happens to be; or

(d) engaging in threatening conduct directed at the other person or any member of their family.

This offence criminalizes behaviour (such as repeatedly following or watching a person) when it occurs in circumstances that create fear for the victim. This makes the accused's *knowledge* of the victim's fear a key component to the offence. It is certainly a central factor in the accused's moral blameworthiness. An accused who *knows* that his or her actions are scaring the victim is certainly more deserving of punishment than an accused who does not.

Recklessness

It may be hard to imagine a situation where an accused person could engage in the kinds of behaviour that amount to criminal harassment *without* causing fear in the person being watched, followed, or threatened. This is why the *Criminal Code*'s definition of *criminal harassment* makes reference to a third form of subjective *mens rea*: **recklessness**. This mental state belongs to those people who are aware of the risks created by their actions but opt to proceed with them anyway. An example would be a person who drives a car onto a crowded sidewalk. The risk that someone will get hurt is easily foreseeable; therefore, the driver can be said to have acted *recklessly*. In these circumstances, it is the accused's *choice* to act in a way that is likely to cause harm that forms the guilty mind. This knowledge of foreseeable harm is what the law views as punishable.

Wilful Blindness

A related form of subjective *mens rea* is **wilful blindness**. It is present when accused persons can be said to have "shut their eyes" to the risks created by their conduct. As the Supreme Court of Canada noted in the case of *Sansregret v The Queen* (1985), a wilfully blind person is "a person who has become aware of the need for some inquiry [but] declines to make the inquiry because he does not wish to know the truth" (p. 584). Consider someone who purchases cheap merchandise that "fell off the back of a truck." If the person purchases such merchandise in circumstances where it is clear that the items are stolen, the person cannot avoid criminal blameworthiness by simply choosing not to ask where the merchandise came from. The Supreme Court has also defined *wilful blindness* as "deliberate ignorance," and has instructed all lower courts to treat it as equivalent to actual knowledge for the purposes of establishing an accused's mental guilt. In this way, an accused's attempt to avoid having (guilty) knowledge will not create a defence against criminal conviction.

Offences Defined by Specific Mental States

In addition to the various forms of subjective *mens rea*, some offences in the *Criminal Code* are defined by the specific mental states that the accused must have to commit them. The classification of murder in Canadian criminal law is a good example. Section 231(1) of the *Criminal Code* indicates that "murder is first degree or second degree" and section 231(7) provides that "all murder that is not first degree murder is second degree murder." To convict a person of murder, the Crown must be able to prove that the accused intended to cause the death of the victim (or was reckless as to whether the victim might die as a result of the accused's actions). To convict a person of first-degree murder, however, a further form of *mens rea* is needed. As s 231(2) states: "Murder is first degree when it is planned and deliberate." Thus, in addition to establishing a subjective intent to kill, the Crown must also be able to prove that the accused *planned* the victim's death before acting deliberately to carry out that plan.

The meaning of "planned and deliberate" was the subject of the case of *R v Banwait* (2011). The victim was attacked by Banwait and his friends in a parking lot and struck on the head with a number of weapons, including a hammer, a wooden two-by-four, and a metal pipe. He immediately fell into a coma from which he

recklessness
A form of subjective *mens rea* where the accused was aware of the risks created by his or her conduct but chose to proceed in the face of them anyway.

wilful blindness
A form of subjective *mens rea* where the accused deliberately chose not to see the risks created by his or her conduct.

did not awaken, dying in hospital 20 days after the attack. When convicting the accused of first-degree murder, the trial judge noted that a murder is "planned and deliberate" when it is

- "committed as a result of a scheme or plan that has been *previously formulated or designed*"
- "considered, not impulsive"
- "carefully thought out, not hasty or rash"
- "one that the actor has taken the time to weigh the advantages and disadvantages of" (*R v Banwait*, 2010, paras. 50 and 181)

SIDEBAR

First-Degree Murder

Section 231 of the *Criminal Code* outlines the requirements for classifying a murder in the first degree. Although the "planned and deliberate" form of first-degree murder is the most widely known, there are other circumstances in which a murder can take place that will classify it as first degree. These include:

- when the offender received payment for the murder (i.e., a contract killing) (s 231(3))
- when the victim is a police officer, sheriff, warden, or correctional officer, also known as **capital murder** (s 231(4))
- when the murder was carried out at the direction or for the benefit of a criminal organization (s 231(6.1))

- when the victim dies while the accused is committing (or attempting to commit) one of the following crimes:
  - hijacking an aircraft (s 231(5)(a))
  - sexual assault, including with a weapon and causing bodily harm (s 231(5)(b)–(c))
  - aggravated sexual assault ((s 231(5)(d))
  - kidnapping and forcible confinement (s 231(5)(e))
  - hostage taking (s 231(5)(f))
  - criminal harassment (s 231(6))
  - terrorist activity (s 231(6.01))
  - intimidating a justice system participant or journalist (s 231(6.2))

---

capital murder
A homicide where the victim is a peace officer (including police and other law enforcement officers, sheriffs, prison wardens, guards, and correctional officers).

objective liability
Criminal responsibility for having acted in a negligent way; that is, failing to meet the standard of a reasonable person.

Objective *Mens Rea*

In Canada, some crimes do not require proof that the accused had any specific intention to commit the offence. Such offences impose what is known as **objective liability**: criminal responsibility for having behaved in a way that exposes others to unnecessary and preventable harm. Objective *mens rea* is not concerned with what the subjective intention or state of mind of the accused was at the time of the offence. In contrast to subjective *mens rea*, the thoughts or intentions that the accused had while committing the offence are irrelevant. Instead, objective *mens rea* asks what a reasonable person would have known and done in the same circumstances, and the accused's actions are judged in relation to this standard. Where the accused's actions represent a *marked departure* from what a reasonable person would have done in the same situation, objective *mens* *rea* is satisfied. Put simply, objective *mens rea* does not ask the question "What was the accused thinking?" Instead, it asks: "What *should* the accused have been thinking?"

Crimes of negligence, including manslaughter, are examples of offences that require an objective *mens rea*. These offences impose guilt on individuals for showing a disregard for the lives and safety of others; for example, when the accused is engaged in conduct that would be considered dangerous by most people's standards. The use of the reasonable person standard is a way of determining what "most people" would think and do. Although no one is at fault in some accidents, injury or death could have been prevented had the accused been more careful in others. It is the latter situation that objective liability punishes, although it is important to note that objective *mens rea* requires more than mere carelessness. It must be proven that the accused acted in a way that was substantially different from how a reasonable person would have acted in the same circumstances. The accused must be more than forgetful or lacking in consideration. Before criminal punishment can be imposed, the accused must be shown to have been **negligent**, which is understood as failing to take the same care and consideration that any reasonable person would have known to do.

An important component of objective *mens rea* in Canadian criminal law is the **modified objective standard**. This standard allows judges to attribute the knowledge or awareness of the circumstances that the accused had at the time of the offence to the hypothetical reasonable person. The standard is well demonstrated in the tragic case of *R v Vaillancourt* (1995). Vaillancourt was showing a friend how his handgun worked. The gun was loaded, so Vaillancourt opened the magazine of the gun to empty it of bullets. Unfortunately, neither of them were aware that one of the bullets had remained in the gun. Vaillancourt, believing the gun to be unloaded, began to demonstrate the gun to his friend, pulling the trigger four separate times without incident. Vaillancourt then pointed the gun at his friend's head and pulled the trigger a fifth time. Sadly, the gun fired, and the bullet that remained in the magazine killed the victim instantly. Vaillancourt was charged with manslaughter, but the court was unable to establish that he had the requisite objective *mens rea*. The evidence supported the accused's claim that he had honestly believed the gun to be empty. There was no reason to believe he had intended to kill his friend (therefore eliminating the possibility of a charge of murder). It could also not be said that a reasonable person who believed the gun was empty (as Vaillancourt did) would have acted differently. Pulling the trigger of an unloaded gun could not be said to be an "objectively" dangerous act. As a result, Vaillancourt was acquitted.

Modes of Participation: Parties to an Offence

A person can be involved in a criminal offence (and subject to criminal liability) in many ways. In Canada, this concept is known as becoming a **party to an offence** and is outlined in s 21(1) of the *Criminal Code*, which reads:

> 21(1) Every one is a party to an offence who
>   (a) actually commits it;
>   (b) does or omits to do anything for the purpose of aiding any person to commit it; or
>   (c) abets any person in committing it.

negligent
Failing to take proper care when acting; in a criminal law context, it is the marked departure from the standard of a reasonable person.

modified objective standard
The consideration of the accused's personal circumstances and knowledge when assessing whether a reasonable person would have acted differently.

party to an offence
A person involved in a criminal offence and subject to criminal liability.

principal
In law, the person who actually commits the offence in question.

Section 21(1)(a) refers to the role of the **principal** or person who actually commits the offence. The principal is the individual who plays a primary part in the completion of the *actus reus* and *mens rea* of the crime. In a case involving a fatal stabbing, for example, the principal would be the person who wielded the knife.

It is possible for a crime to involve more than one principal offender (sometimes referred to as *joint principal offenders*). The case of *R v Paskimin* (2012) provides a good example. This case involved the stabbing death of an inmate in the Saskatchewan Penitentiary. The victim was attacked by two other inmates during a basketball game and stabbed repeatedly in the chest, neck, and face. Although Paskimin did not commit the stabbing, he held the victim so as to prevent him from getting away. The trial judge determined that Paskimin was a principal to the offence. He had participated in the completion of the *actus reus* of murder and had formed the necessary intent to kill the victim. In the words of the trial judge: "When one holds a victim to prevent him from retreating while another person repeatedly stabs the victim with a homemade knife in the face, chest and back, it is open to conclude, and I do conclude, that Paskimin possessed the requisite intent" (*R v Paskimin*, 2012, para. 29). As a result, Paskimin was convicted of second-degree murder and given a life sentence with no chance of parole for 14 years.

The remaining parts of s 21(1) of the *Criminal Code* refer to those situations where a person can become a party to an offence by providing some form of assistance or encouragement to the principal in committing the crime. Such a person is said to have aided and abetted in the commission of an offence. Although these forms of criminal participation are often cited together, each represents a different role a person can play during the commission of an offence. To **aid** in an offence, a person must provide help or assistance to the principal offender. Standing guard while a person breaks into a store is an example. **Abetting** is an act of encouragement. It involves urging or advising the principal offender during the commission of an offence. Merely being present when a crime is being committed is not enough to amount to aiding or abetting—even if a person does nothing to prevent the offence from being completed. To be guilty of aiding and abetting, a person must actively try to help or encourage the principal offender. Aiders and abettors are charged with (and punished for) the same offence as the principal.

aid
In law, to do something or fail to do something with the purpose of helping another person commit a criminal offence.

abet
To offer encouragement or advice to a person during the commission of a criminal offence.

counsel
In law, to recommend, incite, or repeatedly request that a person commit a criminal offence.

A third and related form of criminal participation is outlined in s 22 of the *Criminal Code*, which states that it is a criminal offence to **counsel** a person to commit an offence. The courts have defined "counselling" as an act of solicitation or incitement. It includes asking or convincing someone to commit an offence with a clear intent to see the crime committed. Section 464 of the Code makes it clear that a person who counsels another person to commit an offence will be guilty of a crime even if that offence is ultimately not committed.

Each of the three preceding modes of participation focuses on the ways a person can become a party to an offence before or during the commission of the crime. A fourth way that a person can participate in a crime is by providing assistance to the offender *after* the offence has been committed. This mode of participation is known as being an **accessory after the fact**. Section 23(1) of the *Criminal Code* is clear about what is involved in this offence, defining an accessory after the fact as "one who, knowing that a person has been a party to the offence, receives, comforts or assists that person for the purpose of enabling that person to escape." This definition applies to people who provide shelter, money, transportation, or other forms of assistance to a person they

accessory after the fact
A person who aids another person they know has committed an offence; assistance includes helping the offender evade capture.

know has committed a crime. A person can also become an accessory after the fact by failing to do something, such as phone the police or provide information as to a fugitive's whereabouts. Remember, too, that criminal law will treat wilful blindness as equivalent to actual knowledge. This means that a person who helps someone, while believing a crime has been committed, cannot avoid becoming an accessory after the fact by failing to find out for sure. The Ontario Court of Appeal remarked on this point in the case of *R v Duong* (1998), noting that "actual suspicion, combined with a conscious decision not to make inquiries which could confirm that suspicion, is equated in the eyes of the criminal law with actual knowledge" (para. 23).

Those who have been a party to an offence are guilty of the same offence as the principal offender. A person who abets a murder will be found guilty of murder and punished in the same way as the person who did the actual killing. Section 23.1 of the *Criminal Code* extends the liability of parties to an offence to circumstances where the principal offender is not convicted. This means that the person who aids, abets, counsels, or acts as an accessory after the fact to an offence can be found guilty, even if the person who he or she assisted is not.

In some criminal cases, parties to an offence engage in behaviour that amounts to many different modes of participation. The chilling case of *R v JF* (2011) provides a good example. J.F., a youth, was friends with two sisters who informed him of their plan to kill their mother and collect on her life insurance policy. The sisters (dubbed the "Bathtub Girls" by the media) told J.F. that they intended to drown their mother in the bathtub, after ensuring that she was heavily intoxicated. Police searched the home computer and found online chat conversations between J.F. and one of the sisters in which J.F. advised the girls to give their mother codeine pills (in the form of Tylenol 3s) in addition to the alcohol because it would "knock [her] right out" (para. 7). The sisters carried through with their plan, drowning their mother in the bathtub after drugging her with codeine-laced drinks. (Autopsy results found codeine levels in the victim's blood that were 3.5 times the medically advised level.) J.F. also offered suggestions on how to create an alibi and what to do should their mother gain consciousness during the attack, signing off with "well good luck—wear gloves!" (Mitchell, 2008).

IN-CLASS EXERCISE

Modes of Participation in Murder

Read through the following transcript of one of the MSN chats that police found in the case of *R v JF* (2011). It takes place between J.F. and one of the sisters (T), who was convicted of the first-degree murder of her mother, less than a week before the killing. Was J.F. a party to this offence? Work in small groups to identify evidence from the transcript below that would support charges against J.F. How many different ways can J.F. be seen to have participated in the mother's murder?

J.F.: your mom gets Tylenol 3's, right?
T: probably
J.F.: seriously, you should include them in the game plan
T: why though? if theyre not necessary
T: u cant possibly make drowning into a suicide
T: but if she like ods in the process
T: lol

J.F.: I'm not talking 20 here

J.F.: I mean like 5

J.F.: they knock you right out

J.F.: well, what happens if she, say, wakes up to see you and [R] holding her underwater … ?

T: were not just gonna be like … hmm … she looks drunk … into the tub!

T: were gonna make sure she cant walk and cant possibly drink anymore

T: and doesnt react to water on her face

T: at ALL

T: and besides, head first, easier to hold down

T: and then just turn her over or sumthin

J.F.: not reacting to water on face and not reacting to lungs filling with water is very different

J.F.: drowning is the single most painful way to die after burning to death slowly …

T: lol yea. … it would suck to drown. …

J.F.: my advice:

J.F.: if she wakes up part way through

J.F.: drag her out of the tub, and pretend that you were helping her

J.F.: even an inch of water in the bottom of your lungs and you'll die withing a few days

T: ahahahha its great how u think we didn't think this through

T: that was discussed:P

J.F.: I'm telling you things that I'm not sure if you KNOW them

T: it depends on how much she like fights back. …

J.F.: I could get movie tickets for an hour before it happens

J.F.: a paper trail

[T suggests this is a waste of money.]

J.F.: wanna go to Jack [Astor]'s afterwards? that'd be a nice celebration dinner

J.F.: like I said, I'm involved this much, I'm willing to help you with any of it [T].

(*R v JF*, 2011, paras. 7 and 35)

Answers to in-class exercises can be found at the end of the chapter.

Modes of Participation: Incomplete Offences

Although the law usually requires that a crime be committed before a punishment is imposed, in certain situations the mere attempt to commit an offence is enough to earn a criminal conviction. For example, consider the case of a murderer who aims a gun at the intended victim, fires, and misses. There are a number of reasons why the law might seek to criminalize the shooter's actions. From the view of moral blameworthiness, it would seem strange to reward the would-be assassin's bad aim. Moreover, the danger created by firing a gun at a person is the same, whether the bullet finds its mark or not. Therefore, it makes sense to penalize attempts to commit an offence from a crime prevention standpoint as well.

Like all offences, criminal attempts have both an *actus reus* and a *mens rea*. The mental element for an attempt is the same as what is required for the completed offence. For example, the *mens rea* for attempted murder is having the intent to kill. Proving that the accused had the intention to complete the offence is a key component of the rationale for criminalizing attempts. Given that by its very nature an attempt involves an incomplete *actus reus*, criminal attempts place a great deal of emphasis on the state of mind the accused had at the time of the attempt.

Criminal law, however, does not punish individuals just for having guilty thoughts. Doing so would violate the principle of simultaneity, discussed earlier. Criminal attempts therefore involve an *actus reus* that, like other offences in the *Criminal Code*, has specific requirements depending on the crime being committed. The overarching principle of criminal attempts is that the accused must go *beyond merely preparing* to commit the offence. Some step in furtherance of the criminal intention must be made. The case of *R v Goldberg* (2014) provides a useful example. Goldberg met a woman online and the two became engaged. He sent a substantial sum of money to her family. The relationship subsequently ended and the woman married someone else. Enraged, Goldberg travelled to the city in which the couple lived and confronted them while carrying a loaded handgun. He pointed the gun at the couple and demanded his money, telling them to "back up." The woman testified at trial that Goldberg had told them that they were "going to die." At one point, the woman's husband tackled Goldberg and the gun discharged. Fortunately, the bullet did not hit anyone, but Goldberg was charged with attempted murder. In its decision to convict Goldberg, the court noted that the *actus reus* for the offence was clearly present. "[I]ndeed it would be difficult to suggest," the court stated, "that confronting [the victims] and pointing the gun, fully loaded and laser-sighted, at them while telling them they were going to die, was 'mere preparation'" (para. 42).

Determining when the accused has done enough to move beyond merely preparing for an offence can be a difficult task. Criminal attempts involve circumstances where the accused has not gone far enough to complete the offence, but has done more than simply plan the crime. As such, the exact requirements for proving the *actus reus* in criminal attempt cases will depend on the details of the offence the accused was preparing to commit and the steps that were taken in furtherance of that aim. The Supreme Court of Canada has suggested that "drawing the line between preparation and attempt" must be done within the context of the facts of each case and is ultimately a matter best "left to common sense judgment" (*Deutsch v The Queen*, 1986, para. 26).

Conspiracy

Another offence in the *Criminal Code* that does not require a completed *actus reus* is **conspiracy**. Much like the criminalization of attempts, the law's prohibition of conspiracies is about protecting the public from future criminal activity. Conspirators do not need to follow through with their criminal plan to be found guilty. Instead, merely agreeing to commit the crime is enough to warrant criminal punishment.

The crime of conspiracy is found in s 465 of the *Criminal Code*. This section only indicates the punishments for committing the offence. The definition of "conspiracy" has been left to the courts to determine. Over time, the offence of conspiracy has been defined by the courts as follows: an agreement between two or more persons to commit a crime.

The agreement to commit a crime is the central component of the offence of conspiracy. As the Supreme Court of Canada noted in the case of *Papalia v R* (1979), "the word 'conspire' derives from two Latin words, 'con' and 'spirare,' meaning 'to breathe together.' To conspire is to agree. ... On a charge of conspiracy the agreement itself is the gist of the offence" (p. 276). This is why the *actus reus* of conspiracy is the agreement itself and the central element of the offence that the Crown must prove to obtain a conviction.

The other component of the offence of conspiracy is that the criminal agreement was reached between two or more people. It may seem a matter of common sense that one cannot conspire with oneself; however, there are at least two circumstances where this principle has had less obvious implications. The first is in cases where the conspirators are a married couple. The common law has historically treated spouses as "one person" and has protected them from having to testify against one another. As a result, to be convicted of conspiracy, a married couple would need to have at least one other co-conspirator

conspiracy
An agreement between two or more persons to commit a criminal offence.

involved in the agreement to satisfy the "two or more persons" requirement. The second is in cases involving undercover police officers who are involved in the conspiracy. In these cases, the officer does not have a real intention to commit a crime and therefore lacks the required *mens rea*.

The penalties for conspiracy vary, depending on the offence committed. Conspiracy to commit murder is punishable with a sentence of life imprisonment. Conspiracy to commit any other indictable offence comes with the same penalty as the offence the conspirators agreed to commit. Conspiracy to commit aggravated assault, for example, would come with the same penalty as the completed offence of aggravated assault (i.e., 14 years' imprisonment).

Defences: Missing Actus Reus Components

As discussed earlier in this chapter, to be convicted of a crime, a person must complete a guilty act while having a guilty mind. The principle of simultaneity is the foundation for many criminal defences. To avoid a criminal conviction, an accused can argue that one of the central components of the crime (i.e., *actus reus* or the *mens rea*) is defective or missing. Two of the criminal defences available to an accused that focus on a missing *actus reus* are automatism and mistake of fact.

Automatism

automatism
A state of impaired consciousness wherein a person's actions are not voluntary.

Automatism is one example of a criminal defence that is based on a defective or absent *actus reus*. As previously noted, the conduct component of the *actus reus* must be a voluntary action. The accused must be shown to have been in control of the behaviour or actions that make up the criminal conduct. In automatism cases, the accused is suffering from an impaired consciousness that prevents voluntary action. As a result, the *actus reus* is not present and the accused is entitled to an acquittal.

Five types of automatism are recognized in criminal law:

- "normal" condition automatism
- external blow automatism
- involuntary intoxication automatism
- self-induced intoxication automatism
- mental disorder automatism

Only the first three of these result in an acquittal for the accused (see Figure 6.3). States of automatism that are caused by voluntary intoxication or a mental disorder are treated under other defence categories (see the discussion in "Defences: Missing Mens Rea Components," below). "Normal" condition automatism (also referred to as "non-insane automatism") refers to states of impaired consciousness that result from something other than a mental disorder. It is referred to as "normal" condition automatism because the cause of the automatism is something that many people might experience. The most common example is sleepwalking, where the accused acts, but without control over those actions. This defence was raised in the strange case of *R v Parks* (1992) (see "Mini Case Study—Murder While Sleepwalking: The Case of Ken Parks"). Another example would be persons who commit offences while under hypnosis, as was the case in *R v Book* (1999).

FIGURE 6.3   Legal Outcomes of Automatism Defences

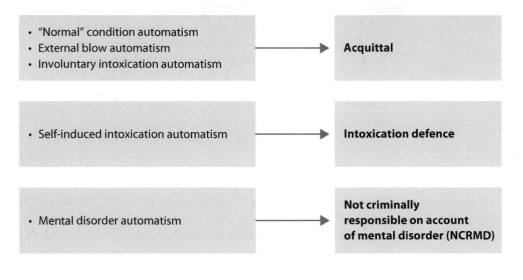

MINI CASE STUDY

Murder While Sleepwalking: The Case of Ken Parks

During the evening of May 23, 1987, Ken Parks was at home with his wife near Toronto. She had worked that day and arrived home at about 10:45 p.m. They talked and each had a non-alcoholic drink. Afterward, his wife went upstairs to bed while Ken decided to watch some television. He fell asleep soon afterward. Sometime later, in the early hours of May 24, he got up from the couch and put on a jacket and running shoes. He took his car keys and the key to his in-laws' home. He left his house, went to the garage where his car was parked, opened the garage door, got into the car and drove to his in-laws' home in Scarborough—a trip of about 23 km. There is no evidence of the exact route he followed to travel this distance, but if he had taken his usual route, it would have involved some travel on Highway 401, a multi-lane, high-speed highway. He would have used its entrance and exit ramps, negotiated approximately six turns, and encountered approximately eight sets of traffic lights.

Parks arrived at his in-laws' home sometime after 2:40 a.m. He drove to an underground parking area, selected a parking space, and parked his car. He then took a tire iron from the trunk of his car and, using a key he had to their home, entered his in-laws' house (which, at the time, would have been in darkness). He went to the kitchen, got a kitchen knife and went to the bedroom in which his mother and father-in-law were sleeping. He straddled his father-in-law in his bed, put his hands around his neck and strangled him until his father-in-law lost consciousness. At some stage, he inflicted cuts to his father-in-law's head and chest. His father-in-law was later hospitalized, but recovered. Ken Parks then stabbed his mother-in-law and brutally beat her with the tire iron (which was later recovered in the bedroom). She died from these injuries.

He then left the house, got into his car, and drove to a nearby police station. He took the knife with him. He arrived at the police station, screaming:

> I just killed someone with my bare hands. Oh my God, I just killed someone; I've just killed two people; My God, I've just killed two people with my hands; My God, I've just killed two people. My hands; I just killed two people. I killed them; I just killed two people; I've just killed my mother- and father-in-law. I stabbed and beat them to death. It's all my fault.

Parks claimed to have "woken up" while driving and remembered the crimes as though they had been a dream. He was immediately arrested and charged with second-degree murder and attempted murder. At his trial, the defence presented medical and expert evidence that Parks was, in fact, sleepwalking when he committed the crimes. The jury accepted this evidence and Parks was acquitted using the defence of automatism. To date, Parks' case is the only instance of the so-called "sleepwalking defence" being successfully used in a murder trial in Canadian legal history.

What Do You Think?

Assuming that Ken Parks was, in fact, sleepwalking when he committed these offences, how should the law address his crimes? In the Parks case, the court examined a number of issues, including the risk that Ken Parks posed to public safety, and his history of mental illness. What other factors should be considered by the court in cases of normal condition automatism? How important is the principle of simultaneity in cases like this one?

External blow automatism results from a physical or psychological trauma that is severe enough to impair the accused's consciousness and cause involuntary actions. One of the leading cases on this issue is *Bleta v R* (1964), in which the accused was involved in a fist fight on a Toronto street. During the altercation, Bleta fell and hit his head on the pavement, resulting in a substantial head trauma. He staggered to his feet and approached the man he had been fighting with (who was now walking away) and stabbed him in the neck. The victim died and Bleta was charged with his murder. At his trial, Bleta argued that he had acted while in a state of automatism caused by his head injury. A number of eyewitnesses (including a police officer) testified that after hitting his head, Bleta appeared "dazed." The doctor who treated him for his head injury also testified that Bleta suffered from amnesia, headaches, and other symptoms consistent with automatism. The Supreme Court of Canada accepted this evidence and acquitted Bleta.

Cases where the accused has ingested drugs or had enough to drink to fall into a state of automatism (sometimes referred to as "blackout drunk") are dealt with differently, depending on whether the intoxication was voluntarily induced. Cases where the accused has become impaired on a *voluntary* basis are addressed using the defence of intoxication (see "Intoxication," below). Where, however, accused persons are not aware that they have taken a drug or did not choose to become intoxicated, this level of voluntariness is not present, and the defence of automatism would apply. The 2013 Ontario case of *R v Weening* provides an example. Weening was a vegetable farmer who drove his produce into the city to sell. On the day of the offence, Weening was involved in an accident involving three other vehicles. The accident had occurred as a result of Weening's erratic driving, which included driving at half the posted speed limit while weaving back and forth across the lanes of traffic. Although Weening had no alcohol in his system, police charged him with impaired driving after he staggered out of his truck and a pill bottle fell to the ground. He admitted to having taken an anti-anxiety pill that had been prescribed by his doctor. He had not been informed by his doctor that the medication might interfere with his ability to operate a motor vehicle. Moreover, although Weening had been taking the medication regularly with no side effects, it was later determined that the pharmacy had issued the wrong dosage, giving Weening 1-mg pills rather than the prescribed 0.5-mg pills. The court found that this accidental doubling of his prescribed dosage had resulted in the accused unknowingly taking more of the medication than he had intended and acquitted him on the basis that Weening's intoxication level (and the ensuing automatism) was not voluntarily induced.

In each case where the defence of automatism results in an acquittal for the accused, it is on the basis that the accused's actions were involuntary. If the accused cannot be said to have been in control of the criminal conduct that occurred, the *actus reus* is not complete.

Mistake of Fact

Another example of a defence that relies on an absence of one of the *actus reus* components is mistake of fact. It applies to those accused who argue that they acted with a mistaken understanding of some kind. In many cases, it is the required *circumstances* of the crime's *actus reus* that are at issue. Assault cases provide a good example. As noted earlier in this chapter, the *actus reus* of assault offences includes the application of force (conduct) without consent (circumstances) that results in harm (consequences). If, however, the accused is operating with a mistaken belief that consent is present, the mistake of fact defence may apply. Where this defence arises most often is in cases of sexual assault, where the accused argues that he acted under the mistaken understanding that the victim was consenting. This defence (sometimes referred to as the "consent defence") requires that the accused prove that the mistake (of believing the victim was consenting) was both honest and based on reasonable steps to ascertain the victim's consent. The accused cannot *assume* that consent is present and then raise the defence of mistake of fact. Instead, he must be able to demonstrate that after a number of positive steps were taken to determine whether the victim was consenting, the accused made the mistake of believing that she was.

Assaults that take place during the context of a sporting event *do* rely on the implicit assumption of consent. By stepping into a boxing ring or onto an ice rink, boxers and players understand that some force will be applied to them. They can thus be said to have consented to a certain degree of force (even if no explicit attempt to gain this consent has been taken by the accused). However, there are instances in which the force used exceeds what would reasonably be expected during the regular course of the sport. In these cases, the accused cannot rely on an assumption that the victim consented. This was the case in *R v McSorley* (2000), where during the course of an NHL professional hockey game, Marty McSorley struck Donald Brashear across the neck with a hockey stick, causing him to fall to the ice and suffer a severe concussion. Although McSorley raised the defence of mistake of fact (arguing that he was operating under the mistaken belief that Brashear had consented to the injury by playing the game), the court determined that the act of hitting a player in the head with a stick went beyond what players could be said to have reasonably consented to when agreeing to play the game. As a result, McSorley was convicted of assault with a weapon (and never played professional hockey again).

Defences: Missing Mens Rea Components

Other criminal defences are available to an accused that focus on an absence of the offence's required mental element, or *mens rea*. This section discusses two of these defences: **not criminally responsible on account of mental disorder (NCRMD)** and intoxication.

Not Criminally Responsible on Account of Mental Disorder

Crimes that are committed by individuals suffering from a mental disorder are examples of offences in which the required *mens rea* is not present. NCRMD (discussed

not criminally responsible on account of mental disorder (NCRMD)
A legal finding that an accused person is not criminally responsible on account of a mental disorder.

in Chapter 5) is applied to those individuals who were suffering from a mental illness or disorder at the time of the offence, preventing them from knowing that what they were doing was wrong. Not every mental condition or illness will satisfy this standard. Instead, only those disorders or abnormal mental states that interfere with an accused's ability to know and understand that what he or she is doing is wrong will trigger an NCRMD inquiry. Like most other defences in criminal law, NCRMD reflects the principle of simultaneity. A person must knowingly or deliberately do something wrong to be convicted of a crime. The case of *R v Oommen* (1994) provides a tragic example. Oommen suffered from a paranoid psychosis that led him to believe that his friend (who was sleeping at his apartment) had been sent to kill him. Fearing for his life, Oommen shot his friend while she lay sleeping, believing that she would kill him if he did not kill her first. Although Oommen was not under the impression that killing was *right*, his delusions did leave him with the impression that the murder was necessary, if not justified in the circumstances (as he believed them to be). As a result, the Supreme Court of Canada found Oommen to be NCRMD.

Contrary to popular belief, when a person is found NCRMD, he or she is neither acquitted nor released from state custody. Instead, the offender is sent before a Review Board that determines what kind of threat to public safety the offender may pose, as well as what treatment options might best serve the individual's needs. In the most serious of cases, the offender is detained in a mental health facility until such time that he or she does not pose a risk to the public. In less serious cases, the Review Board may release the offender with conditions, which can include that the NCRMD individual

- reside in a particular place (e.g., group home);
- abstain from illegal drugs and/or alcohol;
- submit to urinalysis testing for prohibited substances;
- abide by a specified treatment plan;
- report to a designated person (e.g., psychiatrist) on a scheduled basis; and
- refrain from possessing weapons. (Department of Justice Canada, 2006, p. 3)

For more on aggravating and mitigating factors in sentencing, see Chapter 8.

NCRMD cases represent a very small portion of the total number of cases that go through Canada's criminal justice system. In a study of all criminal cases from the years 2005 to 2012, an NCRMD verdict was reached in 1,908 adult cases (Miladinovic & Lukassen, 2014). This number represents less than 1 percent of all adult criminal court cases per year in each of the ten reporting provinces and territories included in the study.

Intoxication

The defence of intoxication has a long and complicated history in criminal law. One of the first cases (*Reniger v Fogassa*) to address the question of whether an intoxicated accused could be guilty of a crime occurred almost 500 years ago! The early English cases show that an accused person's excessive intoxication level was treated as an aggravating factor in criminal sentencing—a tradition that is still used today in Canada for certain offences (e.g., impaired driving). However, where a person's intoxication level is so extreme as to deprive him or her of the ability to formulate a criminal intent, it can result in the absence of the *mens rea* needed for a conviction.

The general rule in Canadian criminal law is that the defence of intoxication is only available to persons accused of an offence that requires a specific form of *mens rea*. These crimes are known as **specific intent offences** and are distinguishable from **general intent offences** in the degree of complex thought or reasoning that is required to satisfy the *mens rea*. A specific intent offence is one where the accused has performed the *actus reus* with a further aim in mind. An example is the offence of murder, given that the accused must be shown to have intended not only to apply force but also to do so with the *specific intent* to cause the victim's death. Contrast this offence with the general intent offence of assault, where the Crown need show only that the accused applied the force intentionally. No further objective needs to have been intended by the accused.

In Canada, the defence of intoxication is only available for crimes of specific intent. The rationale is that an accused's state of drunkenness might interfere with the ability to formulate a complex thought or to think about the intended consequences of an act. However, intoxication is not likely to prevent an accused from forming a general intent.

The distinction between crimes of specific intent and general intent is not always easy to determine. This point was well evidenced in the case of *R v Tatton* (2015), where the accused decided to cook some bacon while in a highly intoxicated state. After putting oil in the pan, Tatton set the burner to "high" and left the house to get a coffee from Tim Hortons. When he returned 20 minutes later, the house was on fire. He was charged with arson, which the trial judge determined was a crime of specific intent, and acquitted him on the basis of the defence of intoxication. On appeal to the Supreme Court of Canada, however, this decision was overturned when it was determined that the trial judge had made an error in classifying arson as a specific intent offence. Arson, according to the Supreme Court, was a crime of *general* intent and therefore the defence of intoxication was *not* available to Tatton.

An exception to this general rule was found in an earlier Supreme Court of Canada case, *R v Daviault* (1994), which involved the sexual assault of an elderly woman who was confined to a wheelchair. The accused was a severe alcoholic and had consumed enough alcohol on the day of the offence to induce a "blackout." He had no memory of the assault. The court ruled that his state of drunkenness was akin to automatism, resulting in an inability to formulate even the most basic of intents. As a result, no *mens rea* could be found and the accused was acquitted.

Understandably, the *Daviault* case created a lot of controversy. Parliament responded by enacting s 33.1 of the *Criminal Code*. This section makes the defence of intoxication unavailable for any offence that involves personal violence, regardless of how intoxicated the accused might be. Notably, as of the time of writing, this section has yet to be challenged under the Charter. There are also occasions where a person may drink to excess or ingest drugs that trigger a psychosis or mental disorder. When a person in this state commits a criminal offence, the offence is treated under the NCRMD defence.

Conclusion

Criminal law involves a consideration of some of life's most challenging questions. What is the nature of "wrong"? What kinds of behaviour should the law prohibit? When is punishment deserved? Because of the complexity of the issues it addresses on a daily basis, criminal law is always under public scrutiny. Decisions about what behaviours should be criminalized and how they should be punished are often the subject of reform and political debate. Understanding the central values that lie at the heart of criminal

specific intent offence
A crime that requires a higher level of thought or reasoning to carry out, such as having knowledge of certain circumstances or an intention to bring about a particular consequence (e.g., murder).

general intent offence
A crime that involves a minimal level of mental activity or a *mens rea* that only pertains to the performance of the illegal act and not a further objective (e.g., assault).

responsibility can enhance both the quality of these discussions and the usefulness of their outcomes. Criminal law must always aim to strike a balance between the rights of the individual and the law's interest in protecting society. In turn, criminal justice scholars must continuously assess how well Canada's criminal law is handling this task.

DISCUSSION QUESTIONS

1. What are some of the advantages of the common law system? Thinking back to the decision you reached when reading this part's opening case study, would it have helped to know how other judges had decided similar cases? Why or why not?

2. How does the modern practice of *stare decisis* relate to the historical systems of policing and criminal law discussed in this and other chapters?

3. Consider the following facts:

   Wayne and Greg are drinking at a bar and begin to argue. The fight escalates, and Wayne throws a beer bottle at Greg. Greg attempts to block the bottle with his arm, but it breaks upon impact, slicing open Greg's forearm. Wayne runs off immediately and Greg decides to wrap the wound with a few napkins and continue drinking. Greg eventually makes his way home and passes out on his couch. The next morning, he wakes up and can barely move his arm. He does not like hospitals, so he decides to just leave the wound alone and hope it gets better. Unfortunately, Greg develops a serious infection and dies.

   Can Wayne be held criminally responsible for Greg's death? Why or why not? Be as specific as you can about your reasons. What legal principles are at play? What defences might Wayne be able to raise?

NOTES

1 See 36 CFR §7.96(b)(3), which reads, in part, "Trespassing, intimidating, harassing or otherwise interfering with authorized golf players, or interfering with the play of tennis players is prohibited."

2 See Massachusetts' Title I, Chapter 264, §9, which reads, in part: "Whoever plays, sings or renders the 'Star Spangled Banner,' or any part thereof, as dance music, as an exit march or as a part of a medley of any kind, shall be punished by a fine of not more than one hundred dollars."

3 *Criminal Code*, RSC 1985, c C-46, s 71.

4 *Ibid*, s 178(b).

SUGGESTED FURTHER READINGS

Greenspan, E.L., & Rosenberg, M. (2010). *Guide to Martin's annual criminal code* (2nd ed.). Toronto: Emond Montgomery.

Roach, K. (2015) *Criminal law* (6th ed.). Toronto: Irwin Law.

Verdun-Jones, S. (2015) *Criminal law in Canada: Cases, questions, and the code* (6th ed.). Toronto: Nelson.

REFERENCES

Bleta v R, [1964] SCR 561.

Department of Justice Canada. (2006). *The Review Board systems in Canada: An Overview of Results from the mentally disordered accused data collection study.* Ottawa: Department of Justice. Retrieved from http://www.justice.gc.ca/eng/rp-pr/csj-sjc/jsp-sjp/rr06_1/rr06_1.pdf.

Deutsch v The Queen, [1986] 2 SCR 2.

Miladinovic, Z., & Lukassen, J. (2014). Verdicts of not criminally responsible on account of mental disorder in adult criminal courts, 2005/2006—2011/2012. *Juristat, 34*(1), Catalogue No. 85-002-X. Retrieved from http://www.statcan.gc.ca/pub/85-002-x/2014001/article/14085-eng.htm.

Mitchell, B. (2008). *The class project: How to kill a mother—The true story of Canada's infamous Bathtub Girls.* Toronto: Key Porter Books.

Murray, J. (2007). The cycle of punishment: Social exclusion of prisoners and their children. *Criminology & Criminal Justice, 7*(1), 55–81.

Norrie, A. (2014). *Crime, reason, and history: A critical introduction to criminal law.* Cambridge: Cambridge University Press.

Papalia v R, [1979] 2 SCR 256.

R v Banwait, 2010 ONCA 869, 265 CCC (3d) 201.

R v Banwait, 2011 SCC 55 [2011] 3 SCR 533.

R v Book, 1999 ABPC 149.

R v Daviault, [1994] 3 SCR 63.

R v Devon Trent Gerald Paskimin, 2012 SKCA 35.

R v Duong, 1998 CanLII 7124, [1998] OJ No 1681 (QL) (CA).

R v Goldberg, 2014 BCCA 313.

R v JF, 2011 ONCA 220, 105 OR (3d) 161.

R v Maybin, 2012 SCC 24, [2012] 2 SCR 30.

R v McSorley, 2000 BCPC 116.

R v Oommen, [1994] 2 SCR 507.

R v Parks, [1992] 2 SCR 871.

R v Tatton, 2015 SCC 33, [2015] 2 SCR 574.

R v Théroux, [1993] 2 SCR 5.

R v Vaillancourt (1995), 105 CCC (3d) 552 (QCCA).

R v Weening, 2013 ONCJ 408, [2013] OJ No 3454.

Reference re Validity of Section 5 (a) Dairy Industry Act, [1949] SCR 1.

Reniger v Fogassa (1550), 75 ER 1 (Exch Ch).

Sansregret v The Queen, [1985] 1 SCR 570.

Westendorp v The Queen, [1983] 1 SCR 43.

Suggested Answers to In-Class Exercises

Actus Reus Components

1. **Conduct:** be naked
2. **Circumstances:** in a public place; or on private property, if exposed to public view
3. **Consequences:** be seen and offend public decency or order

Mode of Participation in Murder

In this case, there is evidence that J.F. acted to both aid and abet the crime of first-degree murder. He offered assistance and encouragement to the sisters and helped them create an alibi after the murder, also making him an accessory after the fact. The Supreme Court of Canada also found J.F. guilty of conspiracy to commit first-degree murder.

Criminal Procedure and Evidence

LEARNING OUTCOMES

After reading this chapter, students will be able to:

- Understand the history and structure of Canada's court system, including some of its specialized courts and tribunals.

- Describe the three types of criminal court jurisdiction.

- Explain the criminal offence classification system and its impact on trial procedures.

- Define the legal requirements for a bail order.

- Understand the role and processes of an arraignment and a preliminary inquiry.

- Be familiar with the jury selection process in Canada, including the nature of challenges for cause.

- Describe the legal test for excluding evidence on the basis of a Charter challenge.

- Recognize the four types of legal privilege and understand how they affect the duty of disclosure.

- Appreciate the role of a *voir dire* in a criminal trial.

Introduction

Criminal procedure is concerned with the rules and processes that must be followed before, during, and after a criminal trial. It addresses how an accused can be brought to court, the rights that he or she has while there, and the various stages of the criminal prosecution and punishment of the accused, should a conviction be reached. It focuses on how criminal courts are structured and what rules must be followed to ensure the accused has a fair trial. It outlines the roles and responsibilities for the courtroom's key players, including Crown and defence counsel, the accused, the judge, the jury, witnesses, and the police.

In contrast to Chapter 6, which focuses on *what criminal law is*, this chapter focuses on *how criminal law operates*. It begins with an overview of Canada's criminal court structure and the three types of jurisdiction that a court must have before an accused's case can be heard. It then examines the *Criminal Code*'s classification of offences and the effect this classification has on trial procedures. This chapter discusses the criminal processes for two stages of an accused's criminal prosecution: pre-trial procedures (the arraignment and preliminary inquiry) and trial procedures (rules of evidence, jury selection, and verdicts). Post-trial procedures (sentencing and appeals) are addressed in Chapter 8. This chapter concludes with a brief discussion of the role of the *Canadian Charter of Rights and Freedoms* in criminal procedure.

Criminal Court Structure

Canada's justice system operates on both federal and provincial/territorial levels. Each court level is responsible for different types of offences, but all courts in Canada fall under the jurisdiction of the Supreme Court of Canada (see Figure 7.1).

FIGURE 7.1   Canada's Court Structure

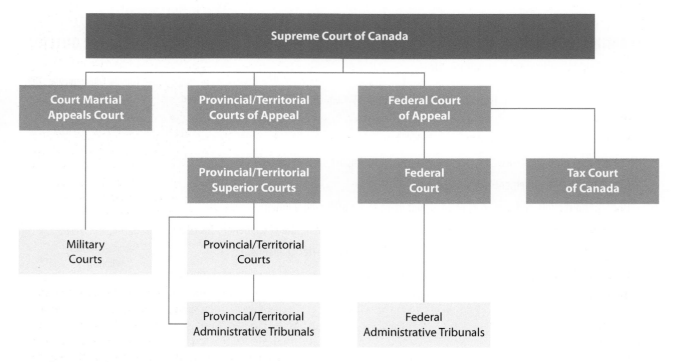

Source: Department of Justice Canada (2015, p. 4).

The Supreme Court of Canada building in Ottawa.

Supreme Court of Canada

The country's highest court is the final avenue of appeal for decisions coming from both federal and provincial or territorial courts of appeal. Prior to 1949, however, decisions of the Supreme Court of Canada could be appealed to the Privy Council in London, England. The famous Persons Case of 1929 took this route (see "Mini Case Study—*Edwards v Attorney General of Canada*: The Persons Case").

MINI CASE STUDY

Edwards v Attorney General of Canada: The Persons Case

One of the most famous cases in Canadian history involved the interpretation of one word in the country's Constitution: "persons." *The British North America Act* (BNA Act) describes who can be appointed to the Senate. It defines the qualifications of a senator to be persons who were at least 30 years of age, lived within the province of appointment, and owned property worth at least $4,000. The BNA Act did not explicitly state that senators also had to be men, but it was written using only the male pronoun (something that is still done in laws today). As such, Canadian courts had always considered only men to be qualified "persons" under the law. This allowed the government to refuse to appoint women senators. "The gentlemen would like nothing better than to have women in the Senate," the government noted, "but the *British North America Act* made no provision for women" (Benoit, 2000).

The question of whether women were "persons" and thus eligible for appointment to the Senate became a national issue in 1928 when the Supreme Court of Canada was asked to determine the matter. The question was brought by Emily Murphy, the first woman ever to be appointed as a judge in Canada. Murphy was appointed in 1916, the same year that women in Canada were first given the right to vote and the right to hold political office (except in Quebec, where women had to wait until 1940 for the right to vote in provincial elections!). Judge Murphy's legal status as a person was raised on her first day in court, when a lawyer objected to her presiding over the case on the basis that she was a woman and therefore not a person. "No decision coming from her court may bind anyone" the lawyer argued (Benoit, 2000). Judge Murphy overruled the objection, but when her appointment to the Senate was later refused on the same grounds, she became determined to see the matter settled once and for all. In 1927, she invited four other prominent activists, Henrietta Muir Edwards, Louise McKinney, Irene Palby, and Nellie McClung to join her in bringing the case to the Supreme Court. Together, they would become known as "The Famous Five."

Sadly, the Supreme Court denied their application on April 24, 1928, declaring that women were *not* legal

The unveiling of a plaque to commemorate the Famous Five in Ottawa, 1938. Among those pictured are Prime Minister William Lyon Mackenzie King (centre) and Mrs. Nellie McClung (far right).

persons and were therefore ineligible to sit in the Senate. This decision was met with great outcry throughout Canada. Mary Ellen Smith, British Columbia's first female Member of the Legislative Assembly (MLA) and the first female Speaker of a legislative assembly in the entire British Empire, poignantly noted: "The iron dropped into the souls of women in Canada when we heard that it took a man to decree that his mother was not a person" (Hughes, 2002, p. 66).

Thankfully, in 1928, the Supreme Court of Canada was not the court of final appeal for the country. The Famous Five took their case across the Atlantic Ocean to Britain's House of Lords and won! On October 18, 1929, Canadian women were declared "persons" by the Lord Chancellor of England. "The exclusion of women from all public offices is a relic of days more barbarous than ours," he declared to a packed courtroom. "The word 'persons' may include members of both sexes, and to those who ask why the word should include females, the obvious answer is why should it not?" (Hughes, 2002, pp. 66–67).

No trials are ever held at the Supreme Court of Canada, nor do any witnesses ever testify before the Supreme Court. Instead, the Supreme Court's nine judges (including one chief justice) hear cases from the country's various appeal courts, which involve only the presentation of legal arguments by lawyers. Occasionally, the federal government (via the Governor General) can ask the Supreme Court to answer a question about the constitutional validity of a piece of legislation. This type of question is known as a **reference** (because the government has "referred" a question of law to the Supreme Court for its opinion). A good example is the *Reference re Same-Sex Marriage* case that was heard by the Supreme Court in 2004. This case asked the Supreme Court to determine whether same-sex marriage could be made legal in Canada. In a unanimous decision, the Supreme Court ruled that the federal government's proposed legislation to make marriage available to all people in Canada was consistent with the Charter and the Constitution.

reference
An application by the Governor General to have the Supreme Court of Canada issue an interpretation of a federal or provincial law, often in relation to its constitutionality.

Supreme Court judges are appointed by the prime minister on the recommendation of the minister of justice. These recommendations are reached in consultation with the chief justice of the Supreme Court and the recently established Independent Advisory Board for Supreme Court of Canada Judicial Appointments. To serve as a judge on the Supreme Court, a person must have been a judge on a provincial or territorial court at the superior or appellate level or a practising lawyer for ten years. All appointees must also be bilingual with a proven track record of superior legal knowledge, skills, and public service. The Supreme Court must include at least three judges from Quebec and traditionally includes three judges from Ontario, two from Western Canada, and one from the Atlantic provinces.

leave to appeal
Permission to bring a case to an appellate court.

Before a case can be heard by the Supreme Court, it must be granted permission (or **leave to appeal**) from a panel of judges of the Supreme Court. There are a number of factors that the Supreme Court considers when determining whether to hear a case, including the case's national significance. If the case will establish an important legal principle or provide an answer to a long-standing legal question, the Supreme Court will grant leave to appeal. In some circumstances, an accused has an automatic right to appeal. In criminal cases, this right exists when a person is acquitted at trial but found guilty at the Court of Appeal or when the Court of Appeal decision is not unanimous.

Federal Courts

The federal court system hears cases involving claims against the government and cases in federally regulated areas, such as immigration and citizenship. The Federal Court of Appeal also reviews the decisions of most federal **tribunals** (including those listed in s 28 of the *Federal Courts Act*, such as the Canada Industrial Relations Board and the Copyright Board). There are also specialized courts within the federal court structure, such as the Tax Court of Canada, which hears disputes between taxpayers and the government, and the Military Court system (that includes the Court Martial Appeals Court of Canada), which hears cases involving disciplinary offences among members of the Canadian Forces.

tribunal
Decision-making body that adjudicates matters that affect a person's legal rights.

Provincial and Territorial Court System

The provincial and territorial court system is the first venue for criminal cases in Canada. There are three court levels in each province/territory:

- provincial/territorial courts
- superior courts
- courts of appeal

Although the power to make criminal law lies with the federal government, the authority to establish courts and determine how they are structured is a provincial matter (see ss 91(27) and 92(14) of the *Constitution Act* in "Sidebar—Sections 91 and 92 of the *Constitution Act, 1867*" in Chapter 6). The provincial authority to organize territorial and provincial courts is why the superior court is known as the Court of Queen's Bench in some provinces (Alberta, Manitoba, New Brunswick, and Saskatchewan) and as the supreme court of the province in others. Nunavut is the only single-level court system in Canada, where the Nunavut Court of Justice serves as both the territorial and superior-level trial court (Department of Justice Canada, 2015).

Provincial/Territorial Courts

In most cases, when a person has to appear in court, he or she will appear in a provincial or territorial court. These courts handle a wide variety of matters, such as traffic and by-law violations, small claims, all family law cases (except divorces), and all but the most serious of criminal cases. Provincial or territorial courts hear all preliminary inquiries (discussed later in this chapter) and house a number of specialized courts, including youth courts, drug treatment courts, and courts that address family violence.

For more about specialized courts, see Chapter 8

Superior Courts

The superior court for each province and territory acts as the first court of appeal for the territorial and provincial courts. The most serious criminal cases are heard at the superior court level, as are all criminal trials with a jury. In some regions, superior courts will travel to remote or rural communities in order to hold court (such as in Matt's case, at the beginning of this book). This practice is common in Nunavut, given how many of its residents live a far distance from Iqaluit, where the provincial courthouse is located. The Nunavut Court of Justice "flies to about 85 percent of all 25 communities" in the territory with "a judge, a clerk, a court reporter, a prosecutor, and at least one defence attorney" and, where possible, an interpreter (Department of Justice Canada, 2015, p. 6).

Most superior courts have a family division to deal with specific family law matters that cannot be addressed in the provincial/territorial courts, such as divorce or the division of property. Other common family law matters, such as child protection, adoption, and custody and access agreements, are normally heard in provincial/territorial courts (depending on the province or territory). Given the overlap of jurisdiction in family law, many provinces have created a unified family court, which hears family matters within both provincial and territorial court and superior court jurisdictions.

Courts of Appeal

Just as the superior court of each province acts as the first court of appeal for provincial and territorial court cases, the Court of Appeal is the first appellate court for cases that come from each province and territory's superior court. The provincial and territorial courts of appeal operate in a similar manner to the Supreme Court of Canada. Cases are not heard without leave to appeal, and provincial or territorial governments can send constitutional questions (reference cases) to their respective courts of appeal for determination. Decisions of the Court of Appeal are binding on all superior and lower courts within the province or territory and are influential to those outside of it.

Criminal Court Jurisdiction

Before a court can hear a case, it must have the authority, or jurisdiction, to do so. In criminal cases, there are three types of jurisdiction: territorial, temporal, and statutory.

Territorial Jurisdiction

The place where the accused commits an offence establishes its territorial jurisdiction. Provincial courts normally only hold criminal trials for offences that have taken place within the province's borders. However, under certain circumstances, a case can be heard outside its territorial jurisdiction. The attorney general that has the territorial jurisdiction to prosecute a case can consent to allow another jurisdiction to take the case, should the accused request this change. This **waiver of charges** can be requested by the accused in relation to any offence other than an offence listed in s 469 of the *Criminal Code* (discussed later in the chapter).

In exceptional circumstances, the Crown or the accused can also request a **change of venue**, which transfers the case to another court within the same province. Such requests are rare, but when there is a reasonable prospect that an accused may not be able to get a fair trial (e.g., because of a lot of negative pre-trial publicity), a court is likely to grant the request. For example, the trial of Paul Bernardo, one of Canada's most notorious serial killers, was moved to Toronto from the smaller community of St. Catharines (where the murders had taken place) on the basis that a local jury would struggle to be impartial.

Temporal Jurisdiction

Temporal jurisdiction refers to the period of time that the state has to bring an accused person to trial. If the Crown takes too long in making its case against the accused, the state can lose its authority to prosecute the offence. The type of offence that the accused is alleged to have committed can affect how much time the Crown has to bring a case to trial. Summary offences, for example, must be prosecuted within six months of the day of the offence. After that time, the court loses jurisdiction to hear the case.

Another way that time limitations affect the prosecution of offences is a result of s 11(b) of the Charter. This section reads as follows: "Any person charged with an offence has the right to be tried within a reasonable time." When the period of time between the date an accused is charged and the date the trial concludes is unreasonable, the court can issue a **stay of proceedings**, which stops the case from going forward. In a 2016 Supreme Court of Canada decision, it was determined that any period longer than 18 months (for cases in provincial or territorial courts) or 30 months (for cases in superior court) would be considered unreasonable, unless the Crown could show the presence of "exceptional circumstances" (*R v Jordan*, 2016).

For more information on how judges use the decisions of higher courts, see the discussion of the principle of *stare decisis* in Chapter 6.

waiver of charges
A court order (applied for by the accused under s 478(3) of the *Criminal Code*) that allows an offence to be tried in a jurisdiction other than the one in which the crime was committed.

change of venue
A court order (applied for under s 599(1) of the *Criminal Code*) that transfers jurisdiction over a case to another court within the province for reasons of prejudice or unfairness to the accused.

stay of proceedings
A court order that suspends (temporarily or permanently, depending on the order) a criminal trial.

An accused may want a speedy trial for a number of reasons. Despite the Charter right to be presumed innocent, being accused of a crime comes with a great deal of social stigma. The accused may have to await trial in custody or, if released, be subject to restrictive conditions and tremendous police scrutiny during the pre-trial investigation. Most important, however, the accused faces the looming threat of criminal punishment while awaiting an uncertain trial and verdict. In recognition of these circumstances and their harmful effects, the criminal law refers to the post-charge period for a person accused of a crime as being a **state of jeopardy**. Section 11(b) of the Charter is meant to protect the accused from being in this state for an unreasonable period of time.

state of jeopardy
The accused's position of being in danger of criminal conviction and punishment.

SIDEBAR

Unreasonable Trial Delay

Although the Charter is often understood as a protection of individual rights, a number of societal interests are also served by its principles. The promise of timely justice in s 11(b) is a good example. The Supreme Court of Canada remarked on the wider values that are served by a speedy trial in *R v Jordan* (2016):

> As the months following a criminal charge become years, everyone suffers. Accused persons remain in a state of uncertainty, often in pre-trial detention. Victims and their families who, in many cases, have suffered tragic losses cannot move forward with their lives. And the public, whose interest is served by promptly bringing those charged with criminal offences to trial, is justifiably frustrated by watching years pass before a trial occurs. ... [T]he right to be tried within a reasonable time is central to the administration of Canada's system of criminal justice. It finds expression in the familiar maxim: "Justice delayed is justice denied." An unreasonable delay denies justice to the accused, victims and their families, and the public as a whole. (paras. 2 and 19)

Statutory Jurisdiction

Statutory jurisdiction is, as one might expect, jurisdiction established by a statute. The *Criminal Code* requires that certain offences be tried only by certain courts. The most serious offences in the *Criminal Code*, for example, (such as murder) can only be heard by a superior court. This requirement grants the superior court **absolute jurisdiction** (also referred to as *exclusive jurisdiction*) over those crimes, which means that provincial and territorial courts cannot hear cases involving those offences. Statutory jurisdiction also has an effect on the procedural rights that are available to an accused, since some trial procedures (e.g., jury trials) are only available in a superior court. Statutory jurisdiction is based on how criminal offences are classified in the *Criminal Code*.

absolute jurisdiction
The exclusive authority of a court to try an offence, established by statute or by the classification of an offence. Also referred to as *exclusive jurisdiction*.

Classification of Offences

The way that an offence is classified in the *Criminal Code* determines many things, including the range of available punishments for the offence as well as what trial procedures and appeal options will apply. As previously noted, the Code also dictates which court has jurisdiction to hear a case and how much time the Crown has to prosecute.

The *Criminal Code* classifies criminal offences into three categories:

- summary conviction offences
- indictable offences
- hybrid (or dual) offences

Classification of Offences in the Criminal Code

punishment provision
The *Criminal Code* section that describes the classification and eligible penalties for an offence. Also referred to as a *charging section*.

How do you identify whether an offence is a summary conviction offence, an indictable offence, or a hybrid offence? A quick look at the *Criminal Code* can give you the answer. The **punishment provision** (also referred to as the *charging section*) for each offence indicates how the crime has been classified. The offence of aggravated assault provides a good example. Section 268(1) of the *Criminal Code* describes the **elements of the offence** of aggravated assault. The offence's classification (in italics in the text that follows) is located in the description of the eligible punishments in s 268(2):

elements of the offence
The components of a crime that a Crown must prove to obtain a conviction; that is, the *actus reus* (guilty act) and *mens rea* (guilty mind).

268(1) Every one commits an aggravated assault who wounds, maims, disfigures or endangers the life of the complainant.
(2) Every one who commits an aggravated assault is *guilty of an indictable offence* and liable to imprisonment for a term not exceeding fourteen years. [Emphasis added.]

Summary Conviction Offences

Summary conviction offences are considered to be the least serious offences in the *Criminal Code*. Examples include a number of property and fraud offences, as well as public nuisance violations, such as vagrancy or trespassing at night. Summary conviction offences are punishable with no more than six months' imprisonment, a maximum fine of $5,000, or both. Only a provincial or territorial court can hear a summary conviction offence. Thus, these offences do not require a preliminary inquiry, and they cannot be tried by a jury.

Indictable Offences

The most common offences in the *Criminal Code* are indictable offences. Although considered more serious than summary conviction offences, the nature of the crimes they cover is diverse, from violent personal offences (e.g., aggravated assault) to fraud and property crimes. Some indictable offences have **mandatory minimum punishments**, while others are punishable with a sentence of life imprisonment (e.g., attempted murder). Unless otherwise stated, indictable offences have a maximum penalty of five years' imprisonment (see s 743 of the *Criminal Code*).

mandatory minimum punishments
Proscribed minimum penalties for certain offences (see Chapter 8 for a full discussion).

There are two subsets of indictable offences, each referred to by the section of the *Criminal Code* in which they are classified: ss 469 and 553.

469 Offences

Section 469 of the *Criminal Code* lists the most serious offences in Canada, including murder, conspiracy, treason, war crimes, and piracy, among others. Superior courts have absolute jurisdiction over 469 offences, which means that no other court can hear cases involving these crimes. Offences listed in s 469 must be tried by a judge and jury, unless both the Crown (speaking for the attorney general) and the accused can agree to a trial by judge alone. These offences represent such serious transgressions of the country's values that they must be judged by representatives of the community as a whole.

553 Offences

Section 553 of the *Criminal Code* lists another set of crimes that are classified as offences of absolute jurisdiction. Only the provincial court has the authority to hear these cases, so trials for these offences do not have a preliminary inquiry or the use of a jury. Offences listed in s 553 are considered to be less serious than the other indictable offences in the Code. Examples include theft or fraud (under $5,000), breach of probation, and public mischief.

Hybrid (or Dual) Offences

Some offences are called hybrid (or dual) offences because they can be prosecuted as either summary conviction offences or as indictable offences, depending on how the Crown decides to proceed. This decision is based on a number of Crown discretionary factors and is made known to the accused either before or at the **arraignment**, when the charges are read in court.

arraignment
A court hearing where the accused is called by name before the court, read the charges he or she is accused of, and asked to submit a plea.

SIDEBAR

Crown Discretionary Factors

When an accused is charged with a hybrid offence, the Crown must decide whether to proceed by summary conviction or by indictment. This determination is made after considering a number of factors, including the following:

- the seriousness of the offence (on alleged facts), including harm done and number of victims
- the accused's criminal record or membership in a criminal organization
- eligible penalties in the event of a conviction
- evidence of witness tampering
- preliminary inquiry procedures and their burden on the victim(s)/witnesses
- the prevalence of the offence in the community
- the public's interest in a trial by jury (Public Prosecution Service of Canada, 2014).

Pre-Trial Procedures

Much of criminal procedure begins when the state first intervenes in the life of an accused. In most circumstances, this occurs when the person is arrested. As discussed in Chapter 4, a number of *Criminal Code* provisions address how the police should conduct an arrest, as well as the conditions under which an accused must be released. Just like a criminal investigation, in a criminal trial, the accused faces the state (and its considerable power) alone. For this reason, it is crucial that certain rights and protections be afforded to the accused so as to "even the playing field." Providing the accused with a right to a lawyer (including the right to be provided a lawyer if the accused cannot afford to hire one) is a good example. Ensuring that the accused has legal representation is a matter normally handled at the first appearance in court.

First Appearance in Court

Once the police make an arrest, depending on the type of offence committed, the accused is either held in custody or released on a **promise to appear** or with a **summons**. An officer can give one of these notices to appear in court at a later date to an accused upon release (provided that the offence is a summary conviction, hybrid, or 553 offence). At the first appearance in court, the court will address the following:

- whether the accused has legal representation
- the Crown's obligation to disclose its case to the accused
- how the accused intends to plead
- the scheduling of the bail hearing (if applicable)
- the scheduling of the arraignment

Accused persons often attend their first appearance in court without having found a lawyer to represent them. In these instances, the accused can receive advice from a **legal aid** lawyer or **duty counsel**, a lawyer hired to work out of the provincial courthouse and offer assistance to unrepresented and low-income clients. Eligibility for legal aid services is based on the financial circumstances of the accused as well as the nature of the legal matter. Only "emergency situations" are covered by legal aid, such as cases involving youths and cases where the accused is facing jail time, deportation, domestic violence, or loss of child custody. A 2015 Statistics Canada survey of legal aid programs across the country showed that subsidized legal services are in great demand. Provincial governments reported receiving nearly 718,000 applications for full legal aid services in 2013–14, but were only able to approve 465,000 (Dupuis, 2015). Data also showed that the cost of delivery for these services is on the rise, with more than $850 million dollars in federal and provincial funding having been spent on legal aid programs in 2014–15 (see Table 7.1). Yet, Chief Justice Beverley McLachlin has remarked on the importance of legal aid, likening it to an essential public service: "We need to think of it in the same way we think of health care or education," she wrote. "The wellbeing of our justice system—and the public's confidence in it—depends on it" (McLachlin, 2002, p. 282).

At the accused's first appearance, the court will also ask the Crown to provide the accused with the details about the alleged offence (including how it plans to proceed if the offence is a hybrid offence). Although the accused's plea is not formally entered until the arraignment, at the first appearance, the court will often ask for an indication of

---

promise to appear

A notice to appear in court on a specified date that is given to an accused (charged with a summary conviction, hybrid, or s 553 offence) upon release by police.

summons

A court order to appear before a judge on a specified date.

legal aid

A collaboratively funded project between the federal and provincial governments to provide legal services to those who cannot afford them.

duty counsel

A lawyer paid by the government to provide legal advice and services to individuals who come to court unrepresented.

TABLE 7.1   The Annual Cost of Legal Aid in Canada, 2010–11 to 2014–15

	2010–11	2011–12	2012–13	2013–14	2014–15
	(thousands of dollars)				
Legal aid service expenditures	619,149	645,328	676,240	665,005	686,337
Criminal legal aid matters	320,420	337,119	358,319	351,608	356,431
Civil legal aid matters	298,729	308,209	317,921	313,397	329,906
Total cost (includes admin. costs)	752,091	779,955	816,864	814,135	850,322

Source: Statistics Canada (2016).

how the accused *intends* to plead. This allows the court to make the necessary arrangements for scheduling the accused's upcoming hearings. If the accused has not already been released, the court will also use the accused's first appearance as an opportunity to schedule a bail hearing.

Bail Hearing

In most criminal cases, the accused will be released on bail unless the Crown can show that she or he should be held in custody. This presumption of release applies to most offences in the *Criminal Code*, with a few notable exceptions, including those offences listed in s 469. For example, a person charged with armed robbery (a regular indictable offence) will not be held in custody unless the Crown can show why the accused should be. However, if a person is charged with one of the Code's most serious offences, found in s 469, a **reverse onus** is placed on the accused at a bail hearing. In other words, the accused will *not* be released on bail unless the defence can convince the court otherwise. It is for this reason that an accused's bail hearing is also known as a **show cause hearing**, because either the Crown or the defence (depending on the offence the accused is charged with) will have to *show cause* for detaining or releasing the accused.

There are three grounds upon which a court can deny bail to an accused. They are outlined in s 515(10) of the *Criminal Code* and are as follows:

(a) to ensure his or her attendance in court;
(b) for the protection or safety of the public; and
(c) to maintain the public's confidence in the justice system.

In determining whether the accused's release will impact the public's confidence in the justice system, the court considers the apparent strength of the Crown's case, the seriousness of the offence (including whether a firearm or excessive violence was used), and what the possible penalties might be, should the accused be convicted.

If the accused is released, the court can order compliance with certain conditions, such as surrendering a passport, maintaining a curfew, abstaining from drugs and alcohol, and/or staying within the geographical jurisdiction. The accused can also be asked for a **recognizance**, which is a sum of money that is deposited with the court and forfeited if the accused does not show up for trial. In some cases, a friend or relative of the accused will agree to pay a sum of money to the court if the accused fails to attend at trial. This person is referred to as a **surety**.

Section 523(1) of the *Criminal Code* requires that bail conditions continue until the end of the accused's trial and, if the accused is convicted, until the accused is sentenced. An accused can request that bail conditions be reviewed and altered if a significant change in his or her circumstances has occurred. Once a person has been convicted, if the defence plans to appeal this conviction, an application can be brought under s 679(3) of the *Criminal Code* for release pending this appeal. When the person has been convicted for a serious offence (such as murder), bail pending appeal is granted only in rare cases (see "Sidebar—Bail Pending Appeal: *R v Oland* (2016)").

reverse onus
A shift in the burden of proof onto the accused; in a bail hearing setting, the requirement that the accused prove why he or she should be released from custody.

show cause hearing
A court hearing to determine whether the accused should be released or held in custody awaiting trial; also known as a *bail hearing*.

recognizance
A sum of money that is deposited with the court upon the accused's release and forfeited should the accused fail to show up for trial.

surety
A person (usually known to the accused) who agrees to pay a certain sum of money to the court if the accused fails to attend at trial.

Bail Pending Appeal: R v Oland (2016)

The issue of bail pending appeal gained national head-lines in the fall of 2016 when Dennis Oland sought re-lease following his conviction of the second-degree murder of his father. The crime was a violent one. The victim, Richard Oland, was found bludgeoned to death in his office in Saint John, New Brunswick, on a warm July evening in 2011. Forensic pathologists estimated that the victim sustained more than 45 wounds to the head and neck, including defensive injuries to his hands. Although no murder weapon was ever found, the nature of the injuries led forensic experts to suggest a drywall hammer had been used in the attack. Blood spatter was found on every wall of the office, and enough force had been used to shatter the victim's skull and eye sockets. Enough blood pooled beneath the victim's body to soak through three layers of flooring, staining the ceiling of an office below.

The Crown's theory was that the accused, the victim's son, had killed his father in a rage, fuelled by emotional and economic stress. The Crown submitted evidence that the two had a difficult relationship and that the accused owed his father more than half a million dollars. After hearing three months of evidence, the jury convicted Dennis Oland of second-degree murder. Oland appealed and sought bail pending the court's review of his con-viction. At the time, only 34 cases (out of 77 applications) of convicted murderers had been granted bail pending appeal in Canadian history (none of which had taken place in New Brunswick). The New Brunswick Court of Appeal denied Oland's request, citing the public's con-fidence in the justice system as the central obstacle:

> In the end, the reasonable member of the public, looking at this dispassionately, would [note] that the offence for which Mr. Oland was convicted ranks among the most serious in the *Criminal Code*, as well as the brutality with which the offence was committed and the trial judge's imposition of a life sentence. ... I am forced to conclude that knowing all this, should Mr. Oland be released in these circumstances, the confidence of the reasonable member of the public in the administration of criminal justice would be undermined. (para. 32)

Dennis Oland leaving court in police custody.

Oland appealed this decision to the Supreme Court of Canada, who heard the case on October 31, 2016. In the interim, the appeal of his conviction was allowed, resulting in his murder conviction being overturned and an order for a second trial. Oland then applied for bail again (this time pending his new trial). As luck would have it, the same judge who had denied his bail pending appeal heard the case. This time, the judge allowed the appeal and granted Oland release awaiting his second trial. Reflecting on the same issue of the public's confi-dence in the justice system, Justice Marc Richard of the New Brunswick Court of Appeal remarked that "any rea-sonable member of the public would understand that Mr. Oland has reacquired the presumption of innocence." As a result, the judge concluded that "the public's con-fidence in the administration of justice would be *under-mined* rather than advanced by detaining Mr. Oland any further" (MacKinnon, 2016; emphasis added).

Oland was released on October 25, 2016 after serving more than ten months in jail. It is estimated that it could take more than two years for his second trial for the murder of his father to conclude.

Arraignment

The image that most people have when thinking about an accused's first day in court is the arraignment. In this court hearing, an accused is called by name and read the charge(s) that she or he has been alleged to have committed before being asked for a plea. The document that lists the charges the accused is facing can take the form of an **information** or an **indictment**. An information is a statement that a person (usually a police officer) makes to a court under oath. As a result, it is more difficult to make changes to an information because it has been sworn. Amendments to an information require a court order. An indictment, however, is not a sworn document. It is presented to the court by the Crown (an act known as **preferring an indictment**) and serves as a statement of the charges the accused faces at trial. It can be changed by the Crown any time before the accused enters a plea.

Entering a Plea

Although "guilty" and "not guilty" are the two most commonly made pleas, s 607(1) of the *Criminal Code* provides for three additional pleas: ***autrefois acquit***, ***autrefois convict***, and pardon. These special pleas are tied to s 11(h) of the Charter, which creates a constitutional protection against being tried for the same offence twice (sometimes referred to as placing the accused in "double jeopardy"). In the case of *autrefois acquit* and *autrefois convict*, the accused must show that she or he has already been acquitted or convicted (and served the sentence) of the same offence. In the case of the plea of a pardon, the accused must show that she or he has been pardoned for the offence.

information
A written complaint, sworn under oath by a citizen, or more typically a police officer, alleging that the accused has committed a specific criminal offence.

indictment
A formal accusation of an offence that is presented to a superior court by the Crown (as an agent of the attorney general) to serve as a statement of the charges at issue in a criminal trial.

preferring an indictment
The Crown's act of presenting or submitting a statement of the charges it is laying against the accused to a superior court judge.

autrefois acquit
The accused has been acquitted of the same *Criminal Code* offence in a prior criminal case.

autrefois convict
The accused has been convicted of the same *Criminal Code* offence in a prior criminal case.

SIDEBAR

Criminal Pardons

Pardons are granted by the National Parole Board to offenders who have completed their sentences and have demonstrated good behaviour after reintegrating into society. A pardon removes the offence from the offender's criminal record. Neither the offence nor the pardon will appear in a search of the Canadian Police Information Centre (CPIC) database. Offenders are not eligible to apply for a pardon until they have been living successfully in their communities for at least five years for summary conviction offences and ten years for indictable offences. Some offenders are *ineligible* for pardons, including the following:

- offenders who have been sentenced to life imprisonment
- offenders who have been convicted of three (or more) indictable offences for which the sentence served for each was two years (or more) of imprisonment
- offenders who committed sexual offences in relation to children (unless the offender was less than five years older than the victim and no violence, intimidation, or coercion was used)

In 2015–16, the Parole Board of Canada reported making 1,977 pardon decisions, granting parole in 82 percent of cases and denying it in 18 percent (Parole Board of

Canada, 2016). Although pardons can be revoked, data suggest that revocation is a rare occurrence. In a study of the Parole Board of Canada's pardon practices between 1970 and 2003, researchers found that of the 291,392 pardons granted in the 33-year period, only 9,280 had been revoked, leading them to conclude that "once an offender is granted a pardon, he or she is almost always successful in his or her 'new life'" (Ruddell & Winfree, 2006, p. 461).

What Do You Think?

Should criminal offenders be able to seek a pardon for their past convictions? What criminal justice ideology does your answer best reflect?

Elections

The other procedural event that takes place at an arraignment is the accused's election. As previously noted, the classification of an offence plays a role in determining which court will have jurisdiction to hear the offence. Some offences fall within the exclusive jurisdiction of the provincial court: that is, summary conviction offences, hybrid offences (where the Crown proceeds summarily), and s 553 offences. Other offences, specifically those listed in s 469, can only be tried by a superior court. In any other case where the offence is *not* one of absolute jurisdiction, the accused has an opportunity to select which court (provincial or superior) will hear the case. This choice is referred to as the accused's **election**. It is available whenever the accused is charged with an indictable offence (not in s 553) or a hybrid offence in which the Crown proceeded by way of indictment (see Figure 7.2).

> **election**
> The accused's choice about which court and trial proceeding will be used; it is available for certain offences only.

When the accused has an election, she or he can select one of the following:

- a trial by judge in provincial court
- a trial by judge in superior court
- a trial by judge and jury in superior court

> **preliminary inquiry**
> A court hearing (held before a trial in a superior court) to determine whether the Crown has sufficient evidence to proceed to trial.

If the accused elects a superior court trial, a **preliminary inquiry** is first held in provincial court, followed by the trial (by judge alone or judge and jury, depending on the accused's choice) in superior court. If the accused elects a provincial court trial, no preliminary inquiry will be held, nor does the accused have the option of a jury trial. As a result, provincial court trials are much shorter than superior court trials—a reason an accused might elect a trial by provincial court. In other cases, however, an accused might want to see a jury determine the matter and would therefore elect a superior court trial.

The attorney general may override the accused's election (under ss 568 and 569 of the *Criminal Code*) to force a jury trial if the offence is punishable by more than five years' imprisonment. This override of the accused's election is sometimes used in cases with more than one accused if they have elected different modes of trial. Overriding the accused's election can ensure that all accused persons are tried before the same court.

FIGURE 7.2   Election Map

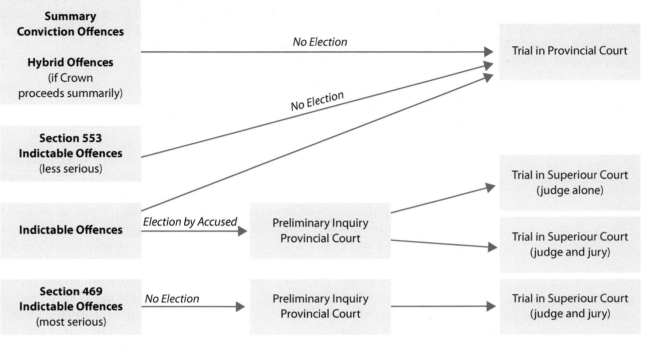

Source: Based on Brockman and Gordon Rose (2011).

IN-CLASS EXERCISE

Elections

Using the election map in Figure 7.2, determine whether an accused would have an election when charged with the following offences:

1. Armed robbery
2. Theft of jewellery valued at $2,000
3. Conspiracy to commit murder

For each offence, answer the following questions:

a. Does the accused have an election?
b. What court(s) has jurisdiction to hear the case, and why?

Answers to in-class exercises can be found at the end of the chapter.

Preliminary Inquiry

The preliminary inquiry is a court hearing that is held in provincial/territorial court when the accused has elected a superior court trial. Its central purpose is to determine whether the Crown has a strong enough case to warrant a full criminal trial. The prosecution presents the evidence to the judge, who determines whether the Crown has a ***prima facie*** case against the accused. In other words, if all of the Crown's evidence were

prima facie
Legal presumption meaning "on the face of it" or "at first sight." It refers to a matter that appears to be self-evident from the facts. The term denotes evidence that, unless contested, would be sufficient to prove a particular fact in issue; the evidence need not be conclusive.

to be believed or taken "at face value," could the accused be found guilty? If the judge can answer this question with a "yes," the accused is ordered to stand trial (also known as a **trial committal**). Although the defence is not required to present any evidence, it may choose to cross-examine the Crown's witnesses and present opposing arguments in order to weigh the judge's decision in the defence's favour.

The preliminary inquiry has three central functions:

- to prevent unnecessary trials
- to serve as a tool of discovery for the defence
- to preserve evidence

In the first instance, the preliminary inquiry is designed to protect both the accused and the public from the costs (financial and emotional) of a frivolous and unnecessary trial. Even when cases are deemed to be strong enough to go to trial, the preliminary inquiry can help to identify weaknesses in the case for each side, prompting more successful plea negotiations or the Crown's withdrawal (or lessening) of the accused's charges.

The preliminary inquiry is also a good opportunity for the accused to learn about the prosecution's case. The state's obligation to provide the accused with all of the information she or he may need in preparing a defence is known as **Crown disclosure**. Failure to provide the accused with full disclosure can amount to a miscarriage of justice and, in serious cases, a stay of proceedings. The Crown's duty to disclose its case to the accused is ongoing, which means that as new evidence is gathered, it must be shared with the defence. The only exception to this rule is evidence that is determined to be **privileged**.

Because so much of the Crown's case is presented during the preliminary inquiry, it can also serve as a way of preserving evidence in the event that a piece of evidence or a witness becomes unavailable (either through death or sickness) at the time of trial. The court can also order a publication ban for the preliminary inquiry (that will continue until the end of the trial), which prevents the news media from reporting on the case. This order is given when the fairness of the accused's trial would be jeopardized by the public learning too many details about the case.

At any point during the preliminary inquiry, the accused can decide to stop the proceeding and go directly to trial. This **consent committal** can happen after the accused has heard enough of the Crown's case and agrees to end the preliminary inquiry and go to trial. Sometimes, the defence uses the preliminary inquiry as an opportunity to hear from a certain witness or test run a cross-examination strategy. After that witness has testified, the accused might enter a consent committal to move the case immediately to trial.

trial committal
An order by a provincial court judge to send an accused to trial, usually issued after a preliminary inquiry.

Crown disclosure
The ongoing legal obligation of the Crown to turn its case (including all evidence and relevant information) over to the accused; this legal right is protected in ss 7 and 11(a) of the Charter, which recognizes the accused's right to make a full answer and defence to a criminal charge.

privilege
A legal doctrine that protects certain pieces of evidence from having to be disclosed to opposing counsel on the basis of a legally recognized relationship of confidentiality.

consent committal
The accused's agreement to proceed to trial; it stops or bypasses the preliminary inquiry.

SIDEBAR

The Doctrine of Privilege

Privilege is a legal right to withhold relevant evidence from opposing counsel. The result is that the withheld evidence cannot be used in a criminal trial. The doctrine of privilege is an exception to the general rule at common law that all relevant information is admissible and allows both the Crown and the defence to hold back evidence that would normally have to be disclosed. Although privilege can interfere with the criminal justice system's pursuit of truth, this value is sacrificed in order to preserve other important policy considerations, such as confidentiality, the protection of informants, and the fostering of certain relationships.

Four types of legally recognized privilege exist in Canadian law:

- *Solicitor–client privilege*—it protects any documents or communications made between a lawyer and a client in the preparation of a legal case.
- *Spousal communications privilege*—it protects a person from having to testify against a spouse about any interactions that took place between them during the marriage; it ends with death or divorce and can be waived (by the spouse, not the accused).
- *Police informer privilege*—it protects the police and the Crown from having to disclose the names and identities of confidential informants.
- *Public interest immunity privilege*—it protects the Crown from having to disclose confidential government documents for reasons of national security; also known as "Crown privilege."

Privilege can also be extended (beyond these four recognized kinds) by successfully arguing to a court that each of the four following conditions (known as the **Wigmore criteria**) are met:

1. That the communications took place with the understanding that they would be confidential
2. That this element of confidentiality is essential to the relationship between the parties
3. That this relationship is one that is in the public interest to see fostered
4. That disclosing the communications will cause greater injury than benefit

The Wigmore criteria are applied on a case-by-case basis, leading some to refer to them as *case-by-case privilege* or *class privilege*.

Wigmore criteria
Four conditions upon which the doctrine of privilege can be extended to relationships outside the recognized forms of legal privilege; also known as *case-by-case privilege* or *class privilege*.

Criminal Trial Procedures

Once the accused has been committed to trial, a date is scheduled for the trial to begin. In some cases, the parties may be required to attend a **pre-trial conference** (in jury trial cases) or a *trial confirmation hearing* (in provincial court cases). At these pre-trial hearings, the Crown and defence each confirm that they are ready to proceed to trial. If either side plans to call an expert witness or bring a Charter challenge, it is required to notify the court at the pre-trial hearing, since the complexity of the case will affect how long the trial can be expected to run. Knowing the estimated length of the trial is an important factor in jury selections.

pre-trial conference
A meeting between the Crown and the accused that takes place before a superior court judge prior to the beginning of a trial; it is referred to as a *trial confirmation hearing* in provincial court cases.

Jury Trials

There is a long history of granting individuals accused of a crime the right to be judged by a community of their peers. The modern day jury system can trace its roots to the frankpledge system at the turn of the second century, when groups of 12 people were

For more on the frankpledge system, see Chapter 3.

selected from a tithing to investigate serious crimes and determine how they should be addressed. In Canada, the right to a jury trial is protected in s 11(f) of the Charter. Anyone charged with an offence that is punishable with five years of imprisonment (or more) is entitled to a trial by jury. This right can be lost, however, if the accused fails to show up for trial (per s 598(1) of the *Criminal Code*).

Jury Eligibility and Exemption

Not everyone is eligible to serve as a juror. The criteria for jury duty is determined by each province and territory, although every Canadian jurisdiction disqualifies people who work within the criminal justice system from serving on a jury (including lawyers, police officers, and corrections officers). Other jury eligibility criteria vary from place to place, but often include a requirement of Canadian citizenship and a clean criminal record.

Eligible jurors may qualify for an *exemption* from jury duty. Much like the jury eligibility criteria, the grounds for exemption from jury service are determined by the provincial and territorial governments and, thus, vary across the country. There are some common grounds of jury duty exemption, however, such as serious personal or financial hardship, caretaking responsibilities for young children, as well as being enrolled in full-time study at a university or college. When a person receives a **juror summons** in the mail, she or he can request to be excused from jury duty by returning it to the court with a letter outlining how she or he meets the grounds for exemption. If the court denies this request, she or he must show up for jury duty on the date in the summons. Failure to do so can result in a conviction for contempt of court and a fine of up to $1,000.

"Alright, I'll go with innocent, too. But can we ask the judge to give him a few weeks of jury duty just in case?"

juror summons
A court order that requires a person to appear before a superior court on a specified day as a member of a jury array or jury panel.

Jury Duty

In order to provide everyone with the right to have a jury trial, the law obligates citizens to serve as jurors. Jury duty can be an onerous form of civil service. As the Supreme Court of Canada remarked in the case of *R v Yumnu* (2012):

> Jurors give up much to perform their civic duty. In some instances, serving on a jury can be a difficult and draining experience. Long trials in particular can take a toll on an individual's personal and professional life. Jury duty is precisely that—a duty. People are not asked to volunteer; they are selected at random and required to serve unless they are otherwise exempted or excused. Once selected, jurors become judges of the facts. Their personal lives at that point are no more relevant than that of the presiding judge. (paras. 41–42)

Jury Selection

Potential jurors are selected from the general population, using a list of people eligible for jury duty known as the **jury roll**. This list is generated from a variety of sources, depending on the jurisdiction. Registered voter lists are a common but imperfect source for jury rolls because they tend to exclude marginalized populations, such as the homeless, the unemployed, the poor, and those groups of people who are often in transition, such as students or new citizens. National census data as well as First Nations Band lists are other sources of the jury roll.

Only a certain number of people from the jury roll will be chosen (or "summoned") from the general population for any given trial. This group is known as the **jury array** (or *jury panel*) and consists of anywhere from 50 to 300 people, depending on the number and type of trials that are scheduled. The Dennis Oland trial (see "Sidebar—Bail Pending Appeal: *R v Oland* (2016)") had a jury panel of more than 5,000 people—a group so large they had to assemble in a Saint John hockey arena during the jury selection, making it the largest jury array in Canadian history.

Once the jury panel has been assembled, the judge will announce the case and the length of time that the trial is estimated to take. The judge will then list the names of everyone involved in the case (including the accused, the lawyers, and the court staff) before asking any members of the array who believe they are unable to serve as a juror on the trial to step forward. Members who come forward might include people who have an undeclared ground of exemption or anyone who has a personal connection or conflict of interest with a person involved in the case. After all ineligible and exempted jurors have been excused from the courtroom, the jury selection process begins. Each member of the array is assigned a juror number, which is put on a **juror card** and placed in a box or rotating drum. A court staff member randomly draws juror cards out of the drum (lottery style), and each juror is called to come forward. This is the last opportunity a person has to voice any inability she or he may have in serving on the jury. If the potential juror is not "challenged" by the Crown or the defence, she or he is sworn in and becomes the first member of the jury. This process continues until at least 12 jurors are selected. In many cases, a judge may select more than 12 people so that there are "spares," should a juror fall ill or otherwise be unable to serve during the trial.

In very rare cases, the jury array may empty before 12 suitable jurors have been found. This situation can arise in cases involving a very violent offence or one that is expected to last many months. If a court runs out of available jurors, it may order the sheriff to immediately summon more people to jury duty in order to replenish the panel. These newly summoned jurors are known as **talesmen** and can be gathered from nearby shopping malls or neighbourhoods (see ss 642(1) and (2) of the *Criminal Code*).

Jury Challenges

As each potential juror is called forth from the array, it is open to the Crown or the defence to "challenge" or object to the selection. Two kinds of challenges can be brought against a potential juror: a peremptory challenge or a challenge for cause. **Peremptory challenges** are granted automatically to each side in a criminal trial and can be used to "veto" the selection of a juror without having to disclose the reason for doing so. The number of peremptory challenges that are available depends on the type of offence the accused is charged with (see Table 7.2).

jury roll
A jurisdiction's list of eligible jurors (from which the jury array or jury panel is summoned).

jury array
The group of persons summoned to court for jury duty from which the jury is selected. It is also referred to as a *jury panel*.

juror card
A ballot that contains the name, address, and occupation of the person summoned to jury duty that is entered into the lottery drum during a jury selection.

talesman
In a jury, a person immediately summoned to court to join a jury panel after the initial array has been exhausted; this person is usually from a place or community near the courthouse.

peremptory challenge
A challenge to a potential juror for which no reason need be provided; it is available to both the Crown and the defence on a limited basis.

TABLE 7.2 Peremptory Challenges

Type of offence	Number of peremptory challenges
High treason or first-degree murder	20
Indictable offences that are punishable with five years' imprisonment (or more)	12
All other offences	4

challenge for cause
A challenge to the choice of a potential juror on the grounds of ineligibility or impartiality.

A **challenge for cause** requires the Crown or the defence to *show cause* why a juror should be excluded. Causes can include a ground of ineligibility (e.g., the potential juror is not a citizen or has been convicted of a criminal offence) or a ground of impartiality (i.e., bias). In the case of impartiality, either side is entitled to pose a question to each prospective juror that asks about the person's ability to judge the evidence in the case without bias, prejudice, or partiality. Canadian cases have allowed challenge for cause questions on the basis of pre-trial publicity as well as racial prejudice (see "Sidebar—*R v Parks* (1993)").

SIDEBAR

R v Parks (1993)

In 1993, the Ontario Court of Appeal heard the case of Carlton Parks, a drug dealer, who was charged with manslaughter following a fatal altercation with a drug user. Parks argued that the victim had attacked him and that he had stabbed him in self-defence. Because Parks was a black Jamaican immigrant and the victim was a white man, Parks' defence lawyer argued that the defence should be allowed to challenge potential jurors for possible racial prejudice. The court agreed, and each potential juror was asked the following question:

> Would your ability to judge the evidence in the case without bias, prejudice or partiality be affected by the fact that the person charged is black and the deceased is a white man?

Racial prejudice remains the most common ground on which courts have allowed challenge for cause questions. Applications for challenges for cause on the basis of a number of other potential biases have all been unsuccessful, including bias against persons with mental illness, the accused's HIV status, her or his participation in the occult, or the type of offence committed (e.g., sexual offences against children, spousal assault).

Jury Deliberations

charge to the jury
The trial judge's instructions to the jury about how the relevant law applies to the case at hand.

After a trial has concluded, the trial judge will provide instructions to the jury about how the relevant law applies to the case at hand. This is known as the **charge to the jury** and, if improperly given, can be a ground for an appeal of the case. Following the charge to the jury, the trial judge dismisses the jury to its deliberations. These deliberations are held in complete secrecy. Jurors are not permitted to discuss the case with anyone (including other jurors) while they are outside of the jury room. In fact, it is a criminal offence in Canada for jurors to disclose any information about what took place during deliberations (per s 649 of the *Criminal Code*). Juries may be **sequestered**, or kept in isolation, during a lengthy trial if real or perceived risk of outside influence exists.

Jury verdicts must be unanimous. If agreement on the verdict cannot be reached by all of the jurors, the result is a **hung jury** and the trial judge must declare a mistrial. This outcome means that a new trial will have to be held before a new jury—a time-consuming and stressful process for everyone involved. For this reason, it is common for trial judges to request juries to "try again" when a unanimous verdict has not been reached.

A mistake in the trial judge's charge to the jury was the reason a new trial was ordered in the Dennis Oland case, discussed in "Sidebar—Bail Pending Appeal: *R v Oland* (2016)."

sequestered
To keep the jury isolated from the public and any news media about the case so as to preserve impartiality.

hung jury
A jury that is unable to reach a unanimous verdict, resulting in a mistrial.

Voir Dire

During a criminal trial, there are times when a judge must determine a legal issue that has an effect on what evidence will be admissible. It is important that the jury not learn about evidence that might later be excluded on the basis of a Charter challenge. As a result, the evidence is heard in a ***voir dire*** in the absence of the jury. The term *voir dire* originates from a Latin oath that jurors were required to take: *verum dicere*, meaning "to speak the truth" or "to say what is true" (Black's Law Dictionary, 2014). At a *voir dire*, the Crown and the defence present arguments about whether a piece of evidence should be excluded, or whether an expert witness will be allowed to testify. The trial judge then determines what the jury will hear when the trial reconvenes. If the accused testifies at the *voir dire*, what she or he says cannot be used as evidence during the trial. Sometimes referred to as a "trial within a trial," the *voir dire* is often held at the beginning of a trial in order to minimize inconvenience to the jury (Brockman, 2015).

voir dire
A court hearing that takes place within a trial in the absence of the jury to determine a legal issue, often the admissibility of evidence.

Burden of Proof

In a criminal trial, it is up to the Crown to prove its case against the accused. This is what is known as the **burden of proof**. The full responsibility for establishing the guilt of the accused rests on the state. This means that the accused does not need to present any defence or call any witnesses. The accused also has the right not to testify. Moreover, the jury is not permitted to draw a guilty inference from the accused's decision not to take the stand. Section 4(6) of the *Canada Evidence Act* provides that the failure of an accused to testify "shall not be made the subject of comment by the judge or by counsel for the prosecution." In other words, a failure to testify cannot be read as evidence of the accused's guilt.

The rationale behind the burden of proof stems from the tremendous power imbalance between the accused and the state. The Crown has the full resources of the police and the attorney general when preparing and prosecuting its case. The accused faces this power alone. As such, the burden is on the Crown to prove the accused's guilt **beyond a reasonable doubt**. This means that a jury does not need to believe the defence's version of events. The "beyond a reasonable doubt" standard is a high one. It requires more than believing the accused is *probably* guilty, but less than an absolute certainty that she or he has committed the offence. If the jury is left with any doubt about the accused's guilt and,

burden of proof
The responsibility to prove the allegations at issue in a trial.

beyond a reasonable doubt
The standard of proof in criminal cases; it requires believing the accused is guilty beyond any doubt that a reasonable person, having heard all of the same evidence, would have.

in their estimation any reasonable person, having heard all the same evidence, would share that doubt, then they must acquit.

Placing the burden of proof on the Crown is also a component of the accused's right to be presumed innocent. This point was explicitly made by the Supreme Court of Canada in the case of *R v Lifchus* (1997) when the court remarked that

> it must be made clear to the jury that the standard of proof beyond a reasonable doubt is … inextricably linked to … the presumption of innocence. The two concepts are forever as closely linked as Romeo with Juliet or Oberon with Titania and they must be presented together as a unit. If the presumption of innocence is the golden thread of criminal justice then proof beyond a reasonable doubt is the silver and these two threads are forever intertwined in the fabric of criminal law. Jurors must be reminded that the burden of proving beyond a reasonable doubt that the accused committed the crime rests with the prosecution throughout the trial and never shifts to the accused. (para. 27)

SIDEBAR

Wrongful Convictions

Of all the mistakes that are possible in a system as large and complex as Canada's criminal justice system, no error is as grievous as sending an innocent person to jail. Although often thought to be a rare occurrence, the development of forensic science (and DNA analysis, in particular) has brought far more wrongful convictions to the forefront of criminal justice studies. Recent scholarship in Canada, the United States, and the United Kingdom has begun to explore these miscarriages of justice, prompting the establishment of a number of governmental inquiries and commissions aimed at identifying the causes and effects of wrongful convictions.

The actual number of wrongful convictions is difficult to determine, although data offered by the Innocence Project, a non-profit organization established in 1993 to help free the wrongfully convicted, suggests that 347 wrongful convictions have been overturned in the United States since 1989 through DNA testing (Innocence Project, 2016). The organization's Canadian branch reports that 21 wrongfully convicted persons have been exonerated in Canada since 1993 (Innocence Canada, 2016). This figure is also supported in the academic literature (Campbell & Denov, 2016). In jurisdictions such as the United States, where capital punishment is still in use, the dangers of using unreliable or false informant testimony are amplified. The Innocence Project reports that of the 347 cases they have successfully been overturned, 20 of the convicted had been serving time on death row. In more than two-thirds (70 percent) of these cases, the accused was a racial minority, with 62 percent being African American. When considered in the context of the overrepresentation of racial minorities in prison and research demonstrating the systemic forms of bias and discrimination that operate in the criminal justice system, these issues become all the more serious.

Criminal Evidence and the Charter

The legal rights found in the Charter play a central role in criminal procedure. Many of the court processes followed during a criminal prosecution exist to protect the accused's constitutionally protected right to a fair trial that has been conducted in accordance with the principles of fundamental justice. For example, if the Crown takes too long to bring an accused to trial, the state can lose its jurisdiction to hear the case because an accused has the right under the Charter "to be tried within a reasonable time" (s 11(b)). The Charter can therefore create a tension in the criminal justice system between **factual guilt** and **legal guilt**. Factual guilt refers to whether the accused is *actually* guilty (or guilty "in fact"). Legal guilt refers to guilt that is provable in court. One of the areas where this tension is most prevalent is the exclusion of evidence due to a violation of Charter rights.

factual guilt
The accused's actual guilt.

legal guilt
The accused's guilt that is provable in a court of law.

MINI CASE STUDY

The Oakes Test

Each time a law or a police action is found to violate a Charter right, the courts must determine whether the violation is "justified" within the meaning of s 1 of the Charter, which reads:

> The *Canadian Charter of Rights and Freedoms* guarantees the rights and freedoms set out in it subject only to such reasonable limits prescribed by law as can be demonstrably justified in a free and democratic society.

This section provides that the rights within the Charter cannot be violated unless the government can offer a sufficiently good reason to do so and, even then, that they do so in the least intrusive way possible. This is what is meant by a "reasonable limit" in s 1.

Shortly after the Charter came into force, the Supreme Court of Canada was asked to define what the words in s 1 meant when David Oakes was arrested by police with eight vials of hashish oil on him. Although Oakes argued that the oil was for his own personal use, the *Narcotic Control Act* at the time contained a provision that allowed police to assume that anyone carrying a narcotic was doing so with the intention of trafficking (i.e., selling it to others). Oakes argued that this provision violated his right to be presumed innocent until proven guilty (s 11(d) of the Charter). The Supreme Court agreed but then had to consider whether this violation could be "justified in a free and democratic society." The steps the Supreme Court took in determining this matter are known as the ***Oakes* test**.

The two-step *Oakes* test is applied each time a Charter right has been violated. All of the parts in each step of the test must be passed in order for the violation to be permissible—that is, to be "justified in a free and democratic society."

***Oakes* test**
The framework used by the courts to determine whether a Charter right violation can be justified under s 1 of the Charter.

Step 1: Determining a "Pressing and Substantial Objective"

The first step of the *Oakes* test asks the following questions:

- What is the reason offered for the right violation?
- What is the objective of the law or action that has infringed the Charter?
- Is it important enough to override the most important rights and freedoms Canada offers?

Assuming that the law or action passes this first step of the test, the court moves on to the second step to examine three specific aspects of the Charter violation:

Step 2: Proportionality

Assuming that the reason for violating the Charter right is important enough, are the measures taken to reach that objective "proportional"? The proportionality test comprises three parts:

- *Rational connection*—Does the law or action that has violated the right make sense? Given the "pressing and substantial" objective offered in Step 1, does the law or action seem like a rational way to achieve it?
- *Minimal impairment*—Does the infringing law or action violate the Charter right as little as possible? Is there another way to achieve the same objective without violating the Charter at all? Or perhaps not as much?
- *Deleterious effects*—What might be the negative consequences of violating this right? Even though the law or action has an objective that is very important, and the means by which the government is trying to achieve it are rational and infringe the Charter as little as possible, are the consequences of allowing the violation of a right too damaging to permit? In other words, do the means ultimately justify the ends?

In the *Oakes* case itself, the court did not actually complete all of the stages of the s 1 analysis. Although the trafficking provision was found to have a pressing and substantial objective, the court found that it could not satisfy the rational connection test. Because the law failed one of the parts of the *Oakes* test, the court did not need to consider the remaining parts to determine that it was unconstitutional.

What Do You Think?

Presume that the rational connection test was passed in the *Oakes* case. How might you decide the remaining two parts (minimal impairment and deleterious effects)? Would a presumption of trafficking pass the *Oakes* test in your court?

Exclusion of Evidence

If police violate any of the accused's Charter rights when investigating a case, the evidence collected may not be admissible in court. Some people might remark that an accused who was acquitted following the exclusion of evidence "got off on a technicality." As frustrating as cases like this can be, it is important to remember that this "technicality" is a Charter right. It is an important safeguard against the significant power that both the Crown and the police wield in the everyday lives of citizens. As noted in Chapter 4, police are able to interrupt day-to-day activities in many ways, whether with a random roadblock set up to check inspection stickers, a pat-down or "frisk" search outside a concert, or entering private homes to make an arrest or conduct a search for evidence. When police perform these functions reasonably, the rights of privacy that they violate are overlooked in the interests of a safe society. When police have overstepped the bounds of their power, however, the law cannot be allowed to benefit from such violations.

Evidence can be excluded under s 24(2) of the Charter, provided that the accused can successfully argue that

- one of her or his rights found within the Charter has been violated;
- the evidence the police found was obtained in a manner that violated that right; and
- the admission of the evidence would bring the administration of justice into disrepute.

The accused must be able to prove *all three* of these factors in order to have the evidence excluded from the trial. To successfully argue that evidence was "obtained in a manner" that violated a Charter right, the accused must be able to demonstrate a connection between the right violation and the gathering of the evidence. For example, if the police conducted a warrantless search of the accused's home by trespassing onto her property and looking in the windows, the accused's right to be protected from unreasonable search and seizure (s 8 of the Charter) would be violated. Any evidence gathered by police while illegally on the accused's property (e.g., anything seen through the windows) would have been obtained as a direct result of the illegal search. As such, this evidence would have been "obtained in a manner" that violated a Charter right. Another way to determine whether evidence was "obtained in a manner" that violated a Charter right is to ask, "Could police have gathered the evidence in any way *other than* the method that violated the Charter right?" If the answer is "no," the evidence can be said to have been obtained in a manner that violated the Charter.

The third part of the s 24(2) exclusion test requires the court to assess whether admitting the evidence at trial would affect the public's confidence in the criminal justice system. Although the public has a general interest in seeing a criminal court determine guilt on the basis of *all* available evidence, when this evidence has been gathered in a particularly violent or offensive manner, excluding the evidence is sometimes necessary to ensure the public does not doubt the justice system's fairness and legitimacy. The case of *R v Golden* (2001) is a striking example (see "Mini Case Study—*R v Golden* (2001)").

In 2009, the Supreme Court of Canada addressed the factors that a court must use when assessing whether the admission of evidence is likely to endanger the public's confidence in the criminal justice system. These factors have since become known as the *Grant* factors, after the Supreme Court case in which they were decided. They include:

1. The seriousness of police conduct that infringed the Charter right
   - Did police act willfully, recklessly, or in good faith?
   - Was the violation deliberate or accidental?

2. The impact of the violation on the public's perception of Charter rights
   - Will the admission of evidence suggest that Charter rights matter very little?
   - What will the admission signal to the population about the value of Charter rights? Will it foster confidence in the system or cynicism?
3. Society's interest in adjudicating a case on its merits
   - Criminal trials aim to seek the truth about what happened. Is this truth-seeking interest better served by admitting the evidence or excluding it?
   - How important is the evidence to the prosecution's case? Is it probative?

After considering these three factors, if the administration of justice would be better served by excluding the evidence, the court will rule it to be inadmissible and the trial will carry on without the jury ever hearing about the excluded evidence.

MINI CASE STUDY

R v Golden (2001)

Ian Golden was a suspected drug dealer who had been under police surveillance. He was being watched by police while he sat in a Subway sandwich restaurant in Toronto in January 1997. After witnessing two people enter the restaurant and apparently take a substance from Golden, police entered the restaurant and placed Golden under arrest for drug trafficking. Following the arrest, police performed a pat-down search of Golden, but found no drugs. Unsatisfied, the police decided to conduct a strip search in the restaurant, pulling Golden's pants down and exposing him from the waist down. A plastic bag was seen protruding from Golden's buttocks, but police were unable to dislodge it. A police officer then retrieved a pair of plastic gloves from the restaurant kitchen (which were used for cleaning the restaurant washrooms and toilets) and used them during a search of Mr. Golden's rectum. During this process, Golden lost control of his bowels—something that was witnessed by onlookers. Police were eventually able to pull out the plastic bag, finding 10.1 grams of cocaine (with an estimated street value of $500 to $2,000).

The cocaine was admitted at Golden's trial, where he was found guilty of trafficking. He appealed to the Ontario Court of Appeal, but lost. It was not until the Supreme Court of Canada heard his case in 2001 (long after Mr. Golden had served his sentence) that the police strip search was deemed to be unreasonable. The Supreme Court remarked that Golden

> was strip searched in a public place, and in a manner that showed considerable disregard for his dignity and his physical integrity, despite the absence of reasonable and probable grounds or exigent circumstances. (para. 116)

Although Golden was *factually* guilty, this guilt would not have been known to police had they not violated his rights to gather the evidence. While the public has an interest in seeing crimes prosecuted, it also has an interest in making sure police deal with the public in fair and responsible ways. In this case, the admission of illegally obtained evidence could lead the public to have *less* confidence in the justice system, rather than more, lending credibility to its exclusion under s 24(2) of the Charter.

Conclusion

Many of the chapters in this text examine the tension in Canada's criminal justice system between the state's interest in protecting the public and each individual's right to privacy and freedom from state intervention. Criminal procedure can be thought of as an enterprise concerned with finding the right balance between these two competing interests. Often, this balance requires the creation and enforcement of protections for the accused—a lone individual who stands against the power of the state. Robert Cover (1986) described the criminal law as a "field of pain and death" where violence is imposed in many ways:

> A judge articulates her understanding of a text and, as a result, somebody loses his freedom, his property, his children, even his life. Interpretations in law also constitute justifications for violence which has already occurred or which is about to occur. When interpreters have finished their work, they frequently leave behind victims whose lives have been torn apart by these organized, social practices of violence. (p. 1601)

It is this violence that the Charter and its criminal procedures are designed to mitigate. As this chapter has discussed, from the moment an accused is arrested, the state has a number of responsibilities. It must hold an arraignment and justify any continued detention of the accused. The Crown must disclose its case so that the accused can make full answer and defence to the charges, and it must be able to prove the accused's guilt beyond a reasonable doubt. The next chapter will examine some of the post-trial processes that a person faces after having been convicted at trial, including the sentencing hearing and the procedures for appealing the decision of the trial judge.

DISCUSSION QUESTIONS

1. Jane, a justice of the peace, has been arrested for accepting a bribe, contrary to s 119 of the *Criminal Code*. She has hired you, a criminal defence lawyer, to represent her. She was arraigned in provincial court two days ago, and pleaded "not guilty." Since that time, she has been held in custody. Jane has expressed an interest in being released on bail, awaiting her trial. What will you need to do to help get Jane out on bail? Jane also wants to know whether she will be able to elect her mode of trial in this case. What will you tell her?

2. Some legal scholars have critiqued the use of the *Oakes* test, suggesting that it is not really a relevant test given how many other balancing and analytical tests the courts use when assessing Charter rights violations. Others argue that the *Oakes* test should not be universally applied to all rights violations but, rather, that different types of Charter rights require different kinds of analyses. Explore this debate on your own and explain whether you agree with these critiques, and why.

3. This chapter suggested that the exclusion of evidence is a good example of the tension within the criminal justice system between factual and legal guilt. Do you agree? Why or why not? How might applications for the exclusion of evidence under s 24(2) of the Charter be understood within the context of the tension between the interests of society in being protected (largely through police investigative powers) and the interests of individual human rights? Should the exclusion of evidence be permitted? Why or why not?

SUGGESTED FURTHER READINGS

Coughlan, S. (2016). *Criminal procedure* (3rd ed.). Toronto: Irwin Law.

Sheehy, E., et al. (2014). *Criminal law & procedure: Proof, defences, and beyond* (5th ed.). Concord: Captus.

Stuart, D. (2016). Learning Canadian criminal procedure (12th ed.). Toronto: Carswell.

Verdun-Jones, S. (2015). *Criminal law in Canada: Cases, questions, and the code* (6th ed.). Toronto: Nelson.

REFERENCES

Benoit, M. (2000). Are women persons? The "Persons' Case." *The Archivist/L'Archiviste, 199.* Retrieved from https://www.collectionscanada.gc.ca/publications/002/015002-2100-e.html.

Black's law dictionary (10th ed.). (2014). n.p.: Thomson West.

Brockman, J. (2015). *An introduction to Canadian criminal procedure & evidence* (5th ed.). Toronto: Nelson.

Brockman, J., & Gordon Rose, V. (2011). *An introduction to Canadian criminal procedure and evidence* (4th ed.). Toronto: Nelson.

Campbell, K.M., & Denov, M. (2016). Wrongful convictions in Canada: Causes, consequences, and responses. In J.V. Roberts & M.G. Grossman (Eds.), *Criminal justice in Canada: A reader* (5th ed., pp. 225–242). Toronto: Nelson.

Cover, R. (1986). Violence and the word. *Yale Law Journal, 95,* 1601–1629.

Department of Justice Canada. (2015). *Canada's court system.* Ottawa: Her Majesty the Queen in Right of Canada. Retrieved from http://www.justice.gc.ca/eng/csj-sjc/ccs-ajc/pdf/courten.pdf.

Dupuis, M. (2015). *Legal aid in Canada, 2013/2014.* Ottawa: Statistics Canada. Retrieved from http://www.statcan.gc.ca/pub/85-002-x/2015001/article/14159-eng.htm.

Edwards v Canada (Attorney General), [1930] AC 124, 1929 UKPC 86.

Hughes, V. (2002) Women in public life: The Canadian Persons Case of 1929. *British Journal of Canadian Studies, 19*(2), 257–270.

Innocence Canada. (2016). Exonerations. Retrieved from https://www.aidwyc.org/cases/historical/.

Innocence Project. (2016). DNA exonerations in the United States. Retrieved from http://www.innocenceproject.org/dna-exonerations-in-the-united-states/.

MacKinnon, B.J. (2016, October 25). Dennis Oland released on bail by N.B. Court of Appeal, pending retrial. *CBC News.* Retrieved from http://www.cbc.ca/news/canada/new-brunswick/bail-hearing-dennis-oland-1.3820067.

McLachlin, B., C.J.C. (2002). Preserving public confidence in the courts and the legal profession. *Manitoba Law Journal, 29*(3), 277–287.

Parole Board of Canada. (2016). Statistics: Parole, pardons and clemency. Retrieved from https://www.canada.ca/en/parole-board/corporate/publications-and-forms/fact-sheets/statistics-parole-pardons-and-clemency.html.

Public Prosecution Service of Canada. (2014). *Public Prosecution Service of Canada deskbook.* Ottawa: Her Majesty the Queen in Right of Canada, represented by the Attorney General of Canada. Retrieved from http://www.ppsc-sppc.gc.ca/eng/pub/fpsd-sfpg/index.html.

R v Golden, 2001 SCC 83, [2001] 3 SCR 679.

R v Grant, 2009 SCC 32, [2009] 2 SCR 353.

R v Jordan, 2016 SCC 27, [2016] SCJ No 27 (QL).

R v Lifchus, [1997] 3 SCR 320.

R v Oakes, [1986] 1 SCR 103.

R v Oland, 2016 CanLII 7428 (NBCA).

R v Parks 1993 CanLII 3383, 84 CCC (3d) 353 (Ont. CA).

R v Yumnu, 2012 SCC 73, [2012] 3 SCR 777.

References re Same-Sex Marriage, 2004 SCC 79, [2004] 3 SCR 698. Ruddell, W., & Winfree, L.T. (2006). Setting aside criminal convictions in Canada: A successful approach to offender reintegration. *The Prison Journal, 86*(4), pp. 452–469.

Statistics Canada. (2016, April 20). Table 258-0007—Legal aid plan expenditures, by type of expenditure, annual (dollars), CANSIM (database). Retrieved from http://www5.statcan.gc.ca/cansim/a26?lang=eng&id=2580007.

Suggested Answers to In-Class Exercise

1. Armed robbery
   a. Yes
   b. Both (until accused elects); a regular indictable offence

2. Theft of jewellery valued at $2,000
   a. No
   b. Provincial; a 553 offence

3. Conspiracy to commit murder
   a. No
   b. Superior; a 469 offence

Sentencing

LEARNING OUTCOMES

After reading this chapter, students will be able to:

- Compare the purpose, principles, benefits, and limitations of sentencing in Canada.
- Understand the sentencing process, including how judges make sentencing decisions.
- Comment on the involvement of victims of crime in the sentencing process.
- Describe the various types of dispositions.
- Describe the grounds for appealing a sentence or a conviction.
- Explain the objectives of Indigenous restorative justice remedies and specialized courts.

CHAPTER OUTLINE

Introduction

The determination of a just and appropriate sentence is a delicate art which attempts to balance carefully the societal goals of sentencing against the moral blameworthiness of the offender and the circumstances of the offence, while at all times taking into account the needs and current conditions of and in the community. (*R v M (CA)*, 1996)

Sentencing in Canada has remained fairly consistent since formalized courts, at both the federal and provincial levels, were established shortly after Confederation in 1867. Once an accused person is convicted (found guilty) of a crime, the court must decide on an appropriate sentence. Sentencing is one of the most challenging and controversial aspects of our justice system. The public has strong opinions about it, the media reports its perspective, and the written law has its framework. In addition to all of that, there are the individuals affected by the crime—victims and offenders—who also have a broad range of religious, social, cultural, and moral values and views that influence their perspectives on sentencing. Regardless of any opinion or belief, a judge must adhere to the sentencing guidelines within the *Criminal Code*.

Principles of Sentencing

Sentencing involves handing out a prescribed punishment to the convicted offender, taking into consideration that an appropriate sentence can deter the individual from committing future crimes, as well as rehabilitate the individual. There are many different types of sentences. Formally called **dispositions**, the different types of sentences can be found attached to each offence within the *Criminal Code*.

Although written in black and white, sentencing raises a number of complicated questions. Should the disposition support Canada's judicial goal of maintaining order in society? Will this disposition deter other potential offenders from committing similar crimes? Does the disposition acknowledge society's support in rehabilitating this offender? Does the disposition **denounce** victimization? Answers to these questions may seem straightforward at first, but, in reality, they are complex. What is an "appropriate" sentence, and who defines it? How can we be certain that a punishment will indeed prevent future crimes? How do we know whether the convicted offender can be rehabilitated? What is the overriding purpose of sentencing—to protect society, or to rehabilitate or punish offenders? Moreover, judges can exercise their discretion for most offences, meaning that although specific disposition parameters are articulated in the *Criminal Code*, judges have options in most cases. Offences for which judges have fewer options are those that have an articulated mandatory minimum term of incarceration. We will discuss this topic later in this chapter.

Aside from all of that, we must acknowledge that regardless of how long or tough sentences may be, in most cases, offenders will eventually get out of prison. This point raises further questions, such as, Did prison prepare the offender to **reintegrate** into and be a productive member of society? What sentencing mechanisms are in place if he or she does not reintegrate into society in a pro-social manner?

Section 718 of the *Criminal Code* clarifies how sentences should be decided and delivered. It lists six principles of sentencing that are intended to guide judges in each sentence they hand down:

(a) to denounce unlawful conduct … ;
(b) to deter the offender and other persons from committing offences;
(c) to separate offenders from society, where necessary;
(d) to assist in rehabilitating offenders;
(e) to provide reparations for harm done to victims or to the community; and
(f) to promote a sense of responsibility in offenders, and acknowledgment of harm done to victims and to the community.

Denunciation Model

Quite simply, at its foundation, the denunciation model puts into practice dispositions that are meant to denounce the offender's conduct in the form of punishment. Also known as the *retributive model*, it maintains that punishment should be equal to the harm done (i.e., equal to the harm on the victim or business) and that offenders should be punished no more or no less severely than their actions warrant. The focus here is on the *crime* committed rather than on any attributes (positive or negative) of the individual offender. For example, John is convicted of assault with a prior history of assault; the denunciation model purports that he should be given the same sentence as Joe, who has also been convicted of assault and has a prior history of assault. However, imagine that John has a history of addiction and is Indigenous and young: Should his sentence take these factors into consideration (mitigating or reducing the sentence)? What if Joe's history includes corporate crimes and Joe is Caucasian and middle-aged? According to the denunciation model, both offenders should be given the same disposition. In theory, it may make sense to base the disposition only on the crime committed—and a judge takes this logic into consideration—but in practice, sentencing is often not based *solely* on the offence.

The denunciation model maintains that while sentences are determinate (will eventually end), they should be shorter rather than longer. For example, advocates of this approach might support a sentence of seven years for assault with a weapon with no opportunity to apply for **parole**. By contrast, supporters of the deterrence or selective incapacitation models, discussed below, would prefer a longer sentence with no opportunity to apply for parole, and supporters of the rehabilitation model would prefer a shorter sentence with mandated treatment and an opportunity to apply for parole.

Think for a moment about the conditions an offender experiences in prison: limited connection to the outside world, shared housing with other (sometimes violent) offenders, restricted freedom, and limited recreation. These conditions may satisfy the public appetite for revenge. However, will depriving a person in this way necessarily develop a "better" person, or might the harsh conditions of prison cause psychological damage to the offender? In what ways might an offender be changed—for better or worse—by prison once he or she is released? Retribution can quench a public thirst for "justice" by imposing harm on an offender as he or she has done on the victim(s), but does retribution work in achieving the goal of a safer society?

Deterrence Model

The concept of **deterrence** plays a key role in sentencing—the objective being to deter not only current offenders from committing future crimes but also potential offenders. This crime-control model is based on protecting society and reforming the offender. Cesare Beccaria (1738–1794) argued that the purpose of law and punishment is to create a better society, not to enact revenge (as in the retributive model). Beccaria believed that law is most effective when the punishment is swift, severe, and certain. However, if the causes underlying an individual's choice to steal, for example, involve factors such as addiction and poverty, it may be that no law would deter him or her from committing that crime again because the root causes (in this case, poverty and addiction) remain. Think about it: the *Criminal Code* has 467 sections of laws and more than ten additional acts, yet every day many of those laws are broken. Why is that? Does deterrence really work?

Many people commit crimes despite being fully aware of the consequences of being caught. Do you think harsher sentences would deter crime, or might they potentially make crime worse?

parole
A type of conditional release from a federal penitentiary such as escorted temporary absence, day parole, full parole, or statutory release. Just because an offender is eligible to apply for parole does not guarantee that it will be granted.

deterrence
Disincentive to commit a crime, controlled by the person's fear or threat of getting arrested and incarcerated.

Laws and dispositions are meant to control deviant behaviour and protect society. In order to achieve these goals, deterrence is understood to fall into two categories: specific and general. *Specific* deterrence is meant to discourage the offender from committing future crimes, while *general* deterrence is meant to discourage all other potential offenders (and the general public) from committing such crimes. That is, if the sentence is severe enough, it will deter others from committing similar criminal acts. As such, proponents of the deterrence model generally favour longer sentences.

What disposition is a suitable deterrent for a particular crime and offender? If the disposition involves incarceration, how long should that sentence be? If a sentence is too lenient, it might send the message that sentencing is not to be feared; in other words, it might fail to deter. If a sentence is too harsh, the message might be that the justice system is excessively punitive, which could, in turn, produce a backlash of more criminal activity. For example, if the minimum sentence of incarceration for armed robbery were ten years in prison (instead of five, for a first offence), armed robbers might decide to kill their victims to reduce their chances of being identified and caught. Further, the various sentencing dispositions also provoke questions about the logic and value behind their creation: Who decides that one crime is more "harmful" than another? For example, a conviction of sexual assault (*Criminal Code*, s 271) does not carry a minimum term of incarceration. That means the judge has discretion to issue a fine or probation instead of a prison sentence. Conversely, a conviction of trafficking in a substance (*Controlled Drugs and Substances Act*, s 5(1)) carries a minimum punishment of imprisonment for one year if certain circumstances (e.g., use of violence or a weapon) are present. This means that when the offence is committed within these circumstances, a judge has no choice but to send the offender to prison.

> ### What Do You Think?
>
> Recall the case study on Matt and Robbie that begins Part One of this text, and the sentence you had suggested for Matt. Try to consider your sentence in terms of deterrence: In what ways, if any, does it reflect specific and/or general deterrence?

Selective Incapacitation Model

The selective incapacitation model is based on the idea that if someone is removed from society, that person will no longer be a threat. The belief is that by removing or restricting an offender's freedom, it makes it almost impossible for him or her to commit another crime. However, while it is true that such an offender would not be able to victimize anyone in society, he or she might victimize a fellow inmate or a member of the correctional staff in the institution. What about when the offender is eventually released? Will he or she stop victimizing people (with or without treatment) then?

While both the selective incapacitation and deterrence models focus on punishing offenders for the express purpose of protecting society, the selective incapacitation model favours much longer sentences. This approach is generally taken with offenders who have lengthy criminal histories. Long prison sentences are considered a good idea because removing habitual or career offenders from society for an extended period is thought to decrease the overall crime rate, and some research supports this thinking (Malsch & Duker, 2012; Vollard, 2012). Further, some research suggests that the cost of incarcerating repeat offenders is offset by public savings elsewhere. Studies by Zedlewski (1983, 1985, 2009) have concluded that for every $1 spent on incarcerating an offender, there is a larger saving to society in terms of social costs (such as insurance premiums for businesses and taxes to pay police).

However, critics believe that justifications for the selective incapacitation model are flawed because they cannot prove the cause–effect relationship between punishing one offender with life imprisonment and reducing the overall rate of various crimes. Further, incapacitating criminals protects society only while the offenders are in prison. The fact is, almost all incarcerated offenders will be released from prison eventually, and some research supports the position that after offenders have served their prison terms, they may actually be more predisposed to committing further crimes (as cited in Clear, 1994), especially if the reasons they committed crimes in the first place have not been addressed.

Rehabilitation Model

The rehabilitation model takes the approach that when offenders are treated in humane ways, they are far more likely to lead crime-free lives once released from prison. In this view, communities, individuals, and the state all have a role in repairing the harm done by an offender's actions. Treatment programs and case management are designed to "correct" the offender's anti-social behaviour and treat his or her personality "flaws" in the hope that what was once learned can be unlearned and that new pro-social coping behaviours can be established. The basis for this approach is rooted in the belief that offenders have many layers—they are not "just" criminals—and that their social and psychological experiences (e.g., lack of education, living in poverty, or enduring child-hood abuse) have influenced their criminal thinking and decision-making. Therefore, treatment is necessary if society wants an offender to be a "changed person" when he or she returns to society. Since every offender is different and his or her accompanying social and psychological issues are different, the type and length of treatment available to offenders should likewise be varied. Advocates of rehabilitation-based sentencing believe that prisons should have a range of programs available to assist the variety of offenders housed within.

A rehabilitation approach, of course, requires a long-term commitment from federal and provincial governments to fund programs and staff. Regardless of which political party is in power, we often hear society debate the merits of investing millions of dollars on rehabilitating offenders. Further, the success of rehabilitation programs is itself the subject of much debate. Many argue against spending valuable resources on programming in prison, while others believe in its inherent value, especially when programs and offender needs are matched effectively (Andrews et al., 1990, p. 400).

> ### What Do You Think?
>
> In the Part One case study, consider the offender, Matt. When the offence occurred, Matt was 20 years old. At this stage in Matt's life, what programs would you recommend that could successfully support his rehabilitation?

Restorative Justice Model

The restorative justice model of sentencing focuses on repairing the various harms that have occurred as a result of a criminal act. This model recognizes that crime causes harm that can be felt by an individual, a business, and/or a community, and that crime is harmful to the victim, the victim's family, the offender, and his or her family as well. The belief is that by repairing this harm—emotional and material—offenders will understand the consequences of their actions and be deterred from committing future crimes, and that the community and its members will be healed and able to collectively continue on without fear. This model is about bringing people together to respond to crime, its causes, and its consequences. It is based on the idea that those responses should not punish the offender, but should instead put conditions in place to restore the victim, offender, and community to the state they were in before the crime occurred, insofar as that is possible.

Maximum punishments for all crimes are supported by proponents of restorative justice, although minimum punishments are not. Instead, judicial discretion is valued and preference is given to a wide range of dispositions that may fit the offender, victim(s), and the community better than incarceration. In other words, for many crimes, sentences such as fines, community service (e.g., repairing the broken store window caused by a break-in), financial compensation to victims, reconciliation (mediation between victim and offender), and apologies (to individuals and the community) are favoured over imprisonment. Our criminal justice system is typically adversarial, but efforts are being made in some cities to include restorative justice methods in dispositions. Specialized courts, discussed later in this chapter, are examples of such efforts.

SIDEBAR

What Are the Numbers for Incarcerated Indigenous People?

Canada's population at the end of 2016 was 36,443,632 (Statistics Canada, 2016a). Data from the 2011 National Household Survey (NHS) showed that 1,400,685 people in Canada had an Aboriginal identity and that this population represented 4.3 percent of the total Canadian population. In comparison, 3.8 percent of the population identified as Aboriginal in the 2006 census, 3.3 percent identified as Aboriginal in the 2001 census, and 2.8 percent identified as Aboriginal in the 1996 census (Statistics Canada, 2013). However, Aboriginal people currently account for 23.2 percent of the total inmate population. Moreover, approximately 3,500 Aboriginal people are in federal penitentiaries on any given day. The overrepresentation of Aboriginal adults was more pronounced for females than males. Aboriginal females accounted for 38 percent of female admissions to provincial/territorial sentenced custody, while the comparable figure for Aboriginal males was 24 percent. In the federal correctional services, Aboriginal females represented 31 percent, while Aboriginal males accounted for 22 percent of admissions to sentenced custody. Aboriginal women offenders comprise 33 percent of the total inmate population under federal jurisdiction (Office of the Correctional Investigator, 2016).

What Do You Think?

Reflect on the statistical realities for Indigenous offenders while considering the models of sentencing previously presented. How might we explain the growing overrepresentation of Indigenous people in our prisons?

How Does a Judge Decide on a Sentence?

Regardless of whether an offender was found guilty by a judge or by a jury, it is the judge (or justice) presiding over the trial who decides on an appropriate disposition. It can include a period of incarceration, a term of probation, a fine, and/or a conditional sentence, or all of these, among others. Ideally, the same trial heard in different courtrooms by different judges should result in the same or similar dispositions. However, in reality, a judicial decision means judicial discretion—the judge who is deciding what an appropriate disposition will be is, of course, a human being. Despite the requirement that all judges be unbiased in their rulings, they are men and women, embedded within society's fabric, who have histories of their own and who are potentially affected by events, opinions, and experiences. Not surprisingly, then, judicial discretion creates disparity. **Disparity** is the notion that differences exist, not necessarily due to intentional prejudice, but as a result of a judge's beliefs and philosophies. Disparity is simply that there are differences between how one judge will sentence an offender compared to how another judge may sentence the same offender. This disparity has caused concern and has led to demands that judicial discretion be controlled. The follow-up question would be, How can that be achieved? Judges must sentence a convicted person according to the terms set out in the *Criminal Code* for that offence, but in many cases, there is leeway.

disparity
A difference or inconsistency in rulings and/or dispositions among judges.

Issues in Sentencing

Judicial Discretion

The Canadian Criminal Justice Association (CCJA) has recommended that sentences "be based on individual contextual factors relating to each offence, rather than legislated minimums that result in ineffective, expensive, and unduly harsh periods of incarceration" (Canadian Criminal Justice Association [CCJA], 2006). In this light, the discretion of individual judges is an important factor. Judicial discretion has been addressed by other legislation throughout the history of Canada's *Criminal Code*. In 1996, Bill C-41 (the *Strengthening Military Justice in the Defence of Canada Act*) came into force, enacting a comprehensive reform of the law of sentencing. It clarified how sentences should be decided and delivered and introduced the six principles of sentencing in s 718 of the *Criminal Code* (discussed earlier in this chapter).

Mandatory Minimum Sentences

In 2012, Bill C-10 (the *Safe Streets and Communities Act*) was enacted. Among other things, it aimed to eliminate judicial discretion and disparity by directing mandatory minimum terms of incarceration for specific offences. Although there is support behind the premise, critics argue that it cannot be ignored that what led Bob to commit an armed robbery could be very different circumstances from what led Sam to commit the same offence (e.g., addiction, being a survivor of abuse, thrill-seeking). If these circumstances are not addressed, the result may be an unduly harsh sentence for one person and an overly lenient sentence for another.

The *Safe Streets and Communities Act* brought together nine smaller bills and is commonly referred to as the Omnibus Crime Bill. It followed a deterrent model in the belief that "getting tough" with harsher sentencing would deter crime. However, as discussed in Chapter 1, statistical evidence shows that violent crime had been steadily decreasing *prior to* the enactment of the *Safe Streets and Communities Act*. The police-reported crime rate, which measures the volume of crime per 100,000 population, continued to decline in 2012, down 3 percent from 2011. After peaking in 1991, the police-reported crime rate has generally declined and, in 2012, it reached its lowest level since 1972 (Boyce, 2015, pp. 4–5).

Currently, 29 offences in the *Criminal Code* carry a mandatory minimum sentence of imprisonment. The majority (19) of these sentences were introduced in 1995, with the enactment of Bill C-68, which focused on crimes of repeat violent offenders and crimes involving firearms. In 2012, the *Safe Streets and Communities Act* added ten more offences.

Currently, mandatory minimum sentences in Canada can be broken down into four principal categories:

1. A mandatory life sentence, imposed upon conviction for treason, first-degree murder, second-degree murder, and manslaughter.
2. Mandatory minimum sentences primarily for firearms offences.
3. Mandatory minimum sentences for repeat offenders.
4. Mandatory minimum sentences for offences when the victim is under age 16.

Several offences carry mandatory minimum terms of incarceration—the theoretical basis of which is deterrence, the protection of society, and denouncing an individual's repeat offending (see Table 8.1). These sentences are "prescribed," which means that a judge has no discretion. Concerns have been raised that mandatory minimums could lead to unfair sentencing in cases where public interest and individual mitigating circumstances could support a more lenient sentence. One well-known example is the Robert Latimer case (see "Mini Case Study—Robert Latimer"). Conversely, some serious crimes carry no mandatory minimum term of incarceration. For example, in the case of an individual convicted of sexual assault (*Criminal Code*, s 271) or sexual assault with a weapon (s 272) where the weapon was not actually used and the victim was over the age of 18, the presiding judge has the discretion to sentence the offender to a term of probation with no incarceration.

What Do You Think?

Should the *Criminal Code* be revised so that sexual assault convictions carry a mandatory minimum term of incarceration? Would doing so reduce the number of sexual assaults?

TABLE 8.1   Mandatory Minimum Sentences Under the Criminal Code

Criminal Code section	Offence	Mandatory minimum sentence
47(1)(4)	High treason	25 years
85*	Using a firearm during the commission of an offence	• 1 year: first conviction • 3 years: subsequent convictions
	Using an imitation firearm during the commission of an offence	• 1 year: first conviction • 3 years: subsequent convictions
92(1)	Possession of a firearm	No minimum • 1 year: second conviction • 2 years less a day or less: subsequent convictions
95	Possession of a prohibited or restricted firearm with ammunition	*Indictable offence:* • 3 years: first conviction • 5 years: subsequent convictions *Summary offence:* No minimum, but 1 year maximum
96	Possession of a weapon obtained by the commission of an offence	*Summary offence:* No minimum, but 1 year maximum
99*	Weapons trafficking with a restricted firearm or with organized crime	• 3 years: first conviction • 5 years: subsequent convictions

Criminal Code section	Offence	Mandatory minimum sentence
100*	Possession for the purpose of trafficking firearms	• 3 years: first conviction • 5 years: subsequent convictions
	Possession for the purpose of trafficking in other cases	1 year
103*	Importing or exporting a prohibited firearm	• 3 years: first conviction • 5 years: subsequent convictions
212(2)†	Living off the avails of child prostitution	2 years
212(2.1)†	Aggravated offence in relation to living off the avails of child prostitution	5 years
220	Criminal negligence causing death	No minimum
	Criminal negligence causing death with a firearm	4 years
237	Infanticide	No minimum, but 5 years maximum
239*	Attempted murder	No minimum
	Attempted murder with a firearm	4 years
	Attempted murder with a restricted firearm and with organized crime	• 5 years: first conviction • 7 years: subsequent convictions
244*	Discharging a firearm with intent to commit indictable offence	4 years
	Discharging a restricted firearm with intent or in relation to organized crime	• 5 years: first conviction • 7 years: subsequent convictions
253	Operation of a motor vehicle while impaired	*Indictable offence:* No minimum, but 5 years maximum *Summary offence:* • $1,000 fine: first conviction • 30 days: second conviction • 120 days: subsequent convictions
	Operation of a motor vehicle while impaired and causes bodily harm	No minimum, but 10 years maximum
	Operation of a motor vehicle while impaired and causes death	No minimum, but 10 years maximum
	Having blood alcohol content over .08%	*Indictable offence:* No minimum, but 5 years maximum *Summary offence:* • $1,000 fine: first conviction • 30 days: second conviction • 120 days, and 18 months maximum: subsequent convictions
254(5)	Failing/refusing to provide a breath sample	*Indictable offence:* No minimum, but 5 years maximum *Summary offence:* • $1,000 fine: first conviction • 30 days: second conviction • 120 days: subsequent convictions

Criminal Code section	Offence	Mandatory minimum sentence
271	Sexual assault	*Indictable offence:* No minimum, but 10 years maximum *Summary offence:* No minimum, but 18 months maximum
	Sexual assault when complainant under 16	*Indictable offence:* 1 year *Summary offence:* 90 days
272*	Sexual assault with a weapon or threat of a weapon, threats to a third party, or causing bodily harm	No minimum, but 14 years maximum
	Sexual assault with a weapon or threat of a weapon, threats to a third party, or causing bodily harm, with a restricted firearm or with organized crime	• 5 years: first conviction, and 14 years maximum • 7 years: subsequent convictions, and 14 years maximum
	Sexual assault with a weapon or threat of a weapon, threats to a third party, or causing bodily harm, with a restricted firearm	4 years, and 14 years maximum
	Sexual assault with a weapon or threat of a weapon, threats to a third party, or causing bodily harm, complainant under age 16	5 years, and 14 years maximum
273*	Aggravated sexual assault	No minimum, but life maximum
	Aggravated sexual assault with a restricted firearm or with organized crime	• 5 years: first conviction, and life maximum • 7 years: subsequent convictions, and life maximum
	Aggravated sexual assault with a restricted firearm	4 years, and life maximum
	Aggravated sexual assault, complainant under age 16	5 years, and life maximum
279*	Kidnapping	No minimum, but 10 years maximum
	Kidnapping with a restricted firearm or with organized crime	• 5 years: first conviction • 7 years: subsequent convictions, and life maximum
	Kidnapping with a restricted firearm	4 years, and life maximum
	Kidnapping, complainant under age 16	5 years, and life maximum
286.3(2)	Procuring under 18 years	5 years, and 14 years maximum
344*	Robbery	No minimum, but life maximum
	Robbery with a restricted firearm or with organized crime	• 5 years: first conviction, and life maximum • 7 years: subsequent convictions, and life maximum
	Robbery with a restricted firearm	4 years, and life maximum
346*	Extortion	No minimum, but life maximum
	Extortion with a restricted firearm or with organized crime	• 5 years: first conviction, and life maximum • 7 years: subsequent convictions, and life maximum
	Extortion with a restricted firearm	4 years, and life maximum

* Can now be sentenced consecutively.
† Repealed, 2014.

MINI CASE STUDY

Robert Latimer

The Robert Latimer case (*R v Latimer*, 2001) is for various reasons one of the most famous in Canadian history. It sparked fierce national debates on the issues of mandatory minimum sentences and euthanasia, sometimes referred to as "mercy killing." Here is a timeline of the case:

- October 1993: Robert Latimer, a Saskatchewan farmer, kills his severely disabled 12-year-old daughter Tracy by placing her in his pickup truck and asphyxiating her with exhaust fumes. He initially tries to hide his actions, but later admits to poisoning his daughter. He is charged with first-degree murder.
- Fall 1994: Latimer admits during his trial that he killed Tracy, but suggests his actions were justified because he wanted to put an end to the chronic pain that she suffered.
- November 1994: Latimer is convicted of second-degree murder. The judge has no choice in sentencing because this offence carries a mandatory sentence of life in prison, and requires offenders to serve a minimum of ten years in jail before applying for parole. Latimer appeals his conviction and the sentence.
- July 1995: The Saskatchewan Court of Appeal upholds the conviction (i.e., the conviction remains).
- October 1995: It is revealed that the Crown prosecutor interfered with the jury by asking them about their beliefs pertaining to religion, abortion, and mercy killing, which leads to a further appeal.
- November 1996: The Supreme Court of Canada hears the appeal.
- February 1997: The Supreme Court of Canada orders a new trial.
- November 1997: The jury in the second trial finds Latimer guilty of second-degree murder and recommends that he be eligible for parole after one year, which goes against the mandatory minimum sentence set out in the *Criminal Code.*
- December 1997: The trial judge gives Latimer a "constitutional exemption" to the mandatory minimum sentence of ten years and imposes a sentence of one year in custody followed by one year to be spent in the community. The Crown appeals this sentence.
- November 1998: The Saskatchewan Court of Appeal sets aside the constitutional exemption and upholds the mandatory minimum sentence.
- February 1999: Latimer appeals to the Supreme Court of Canada.
- January 2001: The Supreme Court upholds Latimer's life sentence with no possibility of parole for ten years.
- December 2010: The Parole Board of Canada releases Latimer on full parole.

What Do You Think?

Should the *Criminal Code* be revised so that judges can consider "constitutional exemptions" to minimum terms of incarceration in certain cases, such as Robert Latimer's? What would be the conditions to grant such an exemption, and what consequences

For recent developments on the legalization of physician-assisted dying, see *Carter v Canada (Attorney General)* (2016) and M. Butler, *"Carter v Canada:* The Supreme Court of Canada's Decision on Assisted Dying" (2015). Both are available online.

might there be to individuals and society as a whole of opening the possibility to such exemptions?

In 2016, the Supreme Court of Canada struck down two of the mandatory minimum sentencing reforms put in place by the *Safe Streets and Communities Act*: those pertaining to drugs (in *R v Lloyd*, 2016) and bail conditions (in *R v Safarzadeh-Markhali*, 2016).

In the case of *R v Lloyd* (2016), the Supreme Court ruled six to three that a mandatory minimum sentence of one year in prison for a drug offence violates the *Canadian Charter of Rights and Freedoms*. In its ruling, the court said that the sentence caught in its net not only the serious drug trafficking that warrants such a sentence but also conduct that is "much less blameworthy" (Harris, 2016).

In the case of *R v Safarzadeh-Markhali* (2016), the Supreme Court unanimously held that a person who is denied bail because of prior convictions will be able to receive enhanced credit for time served before sentencing. On the grounds that pre-trial custody often involves difficult conditions with no programming options, a person denied bail is normally eligible to get 1.5 days of credit for each day spent in pre-sentence custody. In 2009, the former Conservative government introduced sentencing reforms denying the enhanced credit to persons denied bail because of a previous conviction (Harris, 2016).

So far, we have seen that when making a sentencing decision, judges must consider the following:

- the sentencing limits of the summary or indictable offence;
- the seriousness of the crime;
- a sentencing philosophy; and
- whether the offender can be rehabilitated.

Aggravating and Mitigating Circumstances

Before sentencing, judges must also consider whether any other circumstances were present during the commission of the crime or relevant to the offender's criminal lifestyle. Such circumstances may include whether the offender was acting in self-defence, was under the influence of drugs or alcohol, or was in a position of trust over the victim. These aggravating circumstances or mitigating factors may be presented to the judge in a "pre-sentence report" and should be added to the list of factors for the judge's consideration.

Aggravating circumstances can often result in a more severe sentence than would be imposed in a case without such circumstances or in contrast to the average sentence length for a particular offence. This means that despite the general parameters of a disposition (its mandatory minimum and the maximum term listed in the *Criminal Code*), if any one or more of these circumstances were present during the commission of the offence, the judge may choose to increase the sentencing penalty. Such circumstances could be as follows:

What Do You Think?

1. Do you agree with the Supreme Court of Canada's rulings in *R v Lloyd* (2016) and *R v Safarzadeh-Markhali* (2016)?

2. What model of sentencing does each Supreme Court decision follow (i.e., denunciation, deterrence, selective incapacitation, rehabilitation, or restorative justice)?

3. What consequences might these rulings have for individuals and society as a whole?

aggravating circumstances
Factors of the crime or life circumstances of the accused, which may permit the judge to allocate a more severe disposition, including specifying a length of time in prison before the offender is eligible to apply for release.

- The offender was in a position of trust and authority over the victim.
- There was premeditation and planning.
- The offender used force or a weapon.
- There was injury to the victim.
- There was high financial or personal value of the stolen or damaged property or goods.
- The victim was a youth or a vulnerable person, such as a senior citizen or someone with a developmental disorder.

Non-offence factors could also affect the severity of a sentence. An offender with a long criminal record may receive a harsher sentence than a first-time offender for the same offence. The judge would consider how much time had passed since the offender's last conviction (sometimes called the **gap principle**), and whether the offence was committed while the offender was out on bail or on probation, or on some form of conditional release, such as parole. Also weighing against the offender may be whether he or she interfered with the police investigation, lied to the police, escaped from lawful custody, or gave a false identity.

Mitigating circumstances are factors that may make the sentence more lenient. Such circumstances would mitigate a sentence—that is, provide reasonable explanations for how and why the offence occurred. These circumstances are not considered excuses in order to avoid criminal responsibility; they are considered practical elements that speak to the fact that people are fallible, have complex histories, and may be dealing with a variety of issues that can influence their decision-making. Here are some circumstances that might be taken into consideration:

- The accused was acting in self-defence.
- The accused was intoxicated or has a history of addiction.
- There was no premeditation.
- The crime was of financial need rather than greed.
- The accused has mental health issues that may reduce his or her decision-making capabilities.
- The accused is Aboriginal (*Criminal Code*, s 718.2(e)).
- The accused is a senior with a short life expectancy because of a chronic or terminal illness.

Under s 718.2 of the *Criminal Code*, a judge is required to consider several factors when determining an appropriate sentence, and that "sentence should be increased or reduced to account for any relevant aggravating or mitigating circumstances relating to the offence or the offender," without ignoring evidence that the offence was motivated by prejudice, the offender was in a position of trust, or other such factors (see "Sidebar—Determining the Sentence").

---

non-offence factors
Factors that are not directly a part of the offence, but which could impact the type and length of a sentence; for example, whether the offender has a lengthy criminal record or is a first-time offender, or hindered the police investigation.

gap principle
A term used to describe how much time (in days, months, or years) has passed from the offender's last conviction (not arrest) to the current conviction.

mitigating circumstances
Factors of the crime or life circumstances of the accused that may permit the judge to allocate a more lenient disposition in keeping with the parameters outlined in the *Criminal Code*.

Determining the Sentence

The following passage from s 718.2 of the *Criminal Code* presents several considerations that a judge must take into account when determining a sentence:

(a) a sentence should be increased or reduced to account for any relevant aggravating or mitigating circumstances relating to the offence or the offender, and, without limiting the generality of the foregoing,

    (i) evidence that the offence was motivated by bias, prejudice or hate based on race, national or ethnic origin, language, colour, religion, sex, age, mental or physical disability, sexual orientation, or any other similar factor,

    (ii) evidence that the offender, in committing the offence, abused the offender's spouse or common law partner, ... [or] a person under the age of eighteen years,

    (iii) evidence that the offender, in committing the offence, abused a position of trust or authority in relation to the victim, ...

    (iv) evidence that the offence was committed for the benefit of, at the direction of or in association with a criminal organization,

    (v) evidence that the offence was a terrorism offence, ...

    shall be deemed to be aggravating circumstances;

(b) a sentence should be similar to sentences imposed on similar offenders for similar offences committed in similar circumstances;

(c) where consecutive sentences are imposed, the combined sentence should not be unduly long or harsh;

(d) an offender should not be deprived of liberty, if less restrictive sanctions may be appropriate in the circumstances; and

(e) all available sanctions, other than imprisonment, that are reasonable in the circumstances ... should be considered for all offenders, with particular attention to the circumstances of Aboriginal offenders.

Sentencing Terminology

Concurrent sentence: A sentence that allows the convicted offender to serve two or more sentences simultaneously; the total time the offender serves is equal to the longest sentence.

Consecutive sentence: A sentence in which the convicted offender serves two or more sentences one after the other; the total time the offender serves is equal to the total time of the sentences imposed.

Sections 718.01 and 718.02 of the *Criminal Code* state that sentencing for offences involving child abuse, assaulting a police officer, or intimidation of anyone involved in the justice system should also "give primary consideration to the objectives of denunciation and deterrence of such conduct." Section 718.1 requires that the sentence must be proportionate to the gravity of the offence and the degree of responsibility of the offender. This requirement means that the sentence given for an offence should not be extreme—basically, *not* in accordance with an "eye for an eye," but rather that the offence and the sentence must align.

Section 718.2(e) of the *Criminal Code* is another sentencing guideline that addresses the overrepresentation of Indigenous people in Canadian prisons. The Supreme Court of Canada upheld this sentencing section in *R v Gladue* (1999). It stated that where a term of incarceration would normally be imposed, judges must consider the unique circumstances of Indigenous people in deciding whether imprisonment is absolutely necessary. Specifically, judges must consider the following:

- the systemic factors that may have contributed to the criminal behaviour of the Indigenous individual; and
- the specific sentencing procedures and sanctions that may be more appropriate. These may include such things as restorative justice and healing practices (Griffiths & Cunningham, 2003, p. 201).

However, in subsequent cases (e.g., *R v Wells*, 2000), the Supreme Court of Canada held that s 718.2(e) of the *Criminal Code* should not have an impact on the fundamental duty of sentencing—that judges should impose a sentence that is appropriate for the offence and the offender (Griffiths & Cunningham, 2003, p. 202). In other words, judges are not required to be more lenient on Indigenous offenders or to automatically reduce a sentence on the basis of the offender's race. As Justice Iacobucci remarked in *Wells*, "particularly violent and serious offences will result in imprisonment for aboriginal offenders as often as for non-aboriginal offenders" (para. 44). Instead, s 718.2(e) acknowledges that a proportional sentence must be one that is reached "with sensitivity to and understanding of the difficulties aboriginal people have faced with both the criminal justice system and society at large" (*R v Gladue*, 1999, para. 81). This point was reiterated by the Supreme Court of Canada in *R v Ipeelee* (2012).

To learn how the judge who presided over Matt's case (see the Part One case study) used s 718.2(e) in reaching his decision, see the "Conclusion" chapter of this text.

For more on the *Gladue* decision and its implications, see Chapter 11.

SIDEBAR

The Gladue Factors

The Supreme Court of Canada's decision in *R v Gladue* (1999) resulted in a series of guidelines for judges when considering suitable dispositions for Indigenous offenders. Section 718.2(e) of the *Criminal Code* states: "all available sanctions, other than imprisonment, that are reasonable in the circumstances and consistent with the harm done to victims or to the community should be considered for all offenders, with particular attention to the circumstances of Aboriginal offenders." Known as the *Gladue* factors, these guidelines provide judges with a set of considerations that are specific to Canada's Indigenous population in light of the lengthy ramifications of Canada's *Indian Act*. The guidelines take the following into consideration:

- Substance abuse—personally, in the immediate family, extended family, and community.
- Poverty—as a child, an adult, within an offender's family, or community.
- Overt/covert racism—in the community, by family members, strangers, school, or workplace.
- Family—quality of relationships, divorce, family involvement in crime, residential. school attendance of individual or family members, abandonment, etc.
- Abuse—sexual, emotional, physical, and spiritual.
- Unemployment—low income, lack of employment opportunity.
- Lack of educational opportunities.
- Dislocation from an Aboriginal community.
- Group/community experiences of discrimination.
- Foster care or adoption—age, length of time, by non-Aboriginal family. (Maurutto & Hannah-Moffat, 2016, p. 456)

Another important outcome of the *Gladue* decision was the establishment of specialized courts for Indigenous offenders. Known as "*Gladue* courts," these regular criminal courts employ a unique sentencing approach that is assisted by a team of specially trained experts who prepare materials (i.e., a *Gladue* report) to support the judge's application of s 718.2(e) of the *Criminal Code* and the *Gladue* factors.

If requested, a pre-sentence report (PSR) can be prepared by a probation officer to help the judge determine an appropriate sentence for an offender. A PSR gives a history of the offender, not only in the context of the crime, and provides the judge with a better sense of the person he or she is sentencing. Such reports are very often used when sentencing youth offenders. A probation officer's PSR could include the following details:

- information on whether the offender has previous convictions or is a first-time offender
- gang activity or criminal associations
- vulnerability of the victim
- multiple incidents committed during the offence
- use or threatened use of a weapon
- the level of brutality used during the offence
- any employment record
- rehabilitative efforts since the offence was committed
- disadvantaged background
- guilty plea and indications of remorse
- length of time to prosecute or sentence the offender
- overall good character

What Do You Think?

In the Part One case study, many mitigating and aggravating factors were present. If you were the judge in this case, how much weight would you place on these factors when determining a suitable sentence for Matt? Does your sentence change when considering the impact the offence has had on the victim?

The Role of Victims in the Sentencing Process

Judges may invite the victims of a crime to prepare a written statement detailing how the crime has impacted their lives, work, health, and relationships. The parameters of this statement, called a victim impact statement, are set out in the subsections of s 722 of the *Criminal Code*. In 1988, prompted by the UN *Declaration of Basic Principles of Justice for Victims of Crime*, all Canadian ministers of justice agreed to adopt a uniform policy statement of victims' rights that would be used to guide their legislative and administrative initiatives in the area of criminal justice (Canadian Resource Centre for Victims of Crime, 2006).

Throughout any trial process, a victim may be called to the stand as a witness to give testimony in response to questions asked by the Crown prosecutor and by defence counsel, but the victim is not permitted to talk freely. A victim impact statement, therefore, offers victims a sense of ownership, allowing them to tell their side of the story, as we saw in the Part One case study. Victim impact statements may assist the judge in determining an appropriate sentence.

Enacted in 2015, the *Canadian Victims Bill of Rights* increased the justice system's acceptance of victims, the recognition of their rights, and their involvement in the system. Historically, victims have been considered witnesses and are involved in the justice system only to give testimony to what they witnessed. They are not told about trial outcomes, adjournments, or arrest processes, and occasionally they had permission to provide the court with a Victim Impact Statement (which gives the judge information about the effects of the crime). Rarely would a VIS be given much weight. The Victims Bill aims to give victims more information and inclusion in the process and to ensure that their VIS would be considered, by judges, when determining a suitable sentence for the convicted person.

Advocates argue that making victims part of the court system recognizes the impact the crime has had on them (and their families). Therefore, doing so grants them their rightful opportunity to address the court directly and share their personal perspectives. Critics argue that expanding victims' rights challenges the very basis of our adversarial legal system and may bias proceedings. Regardless, the *Canadian Victims Bill of Rights* is now legislated; however, judicial discretion may still interfere with its overall purpose, as in a 2016 case where an Alberta judge would not permit the inclusion of a victim impact statement unless it was read by the victim herself. The *Criminal Code* (s 722) and the *Canadian Victims Bill of Rights* give victims the choice of reading the statement themselves or allocating a representative to do so for them (such as the Crown prosecutor). By law, it is up to the judge to permit its inclusion, but seldom is a victim's choice overruled.

Types of Dispositions

According to the Department of Justice Canada (2016b), 64 percent of criminal cases completed in 2011–12 resulted in a finding of guilt (a percentage that is consistent with results from the preceding decade). The remainder of cases were stayed, withdrawn, dismissed, or discharged (32 percent), acquitted (3 percent), or resulted in some other type of decision (1 percent).

Not Criminally Responsible on Account of Mental Disorder

Recall from Chapter 6 that for a determination of not criminally responsible on account of mental disorder (NCRMD), the court must accept that an accused person committed the criminal act, but that he or she lacked a guilty mind when doing so. As was also discussed in Chapter 6, to convict someone of any offence, the Crown must first prove *two* elements:

1. *actus reus* = Latin for "guilty act." The Crown must provide evidence to prove (beyond a reasonable doubt) that the accused committed the criminal act.
2. *mens rea* = Latin for "guilty mind." The Crown must provide evidence to prove (beyond a reasonable doubt) that the accused intended to commit the criminal act (versus self-defence or an accident, etc.).

> Judges almost always accept such joint submissions from the Crown and defence. It is important to remember that accused persons found NCRMD are convicted, not acquitted.

Reasons that can affect *mens rea* include mental illness or disease, including episodes of psychosis. As outlined in Chapter 5, independent psychologists or psychiatrists are hired to evaluate the accused in terms of both his or her current mental state and his or her mental state at the time of the crime. In Canada, the Crown and defence typically work together on such cases and put a joint submission together for the court. Their submission clearly states that both sides (Crown and defence) acknowledge that the accused committed the guilty act (*actus reus*), but that due to a mental disorder, the accused did not have a guilty mind (*mens rea*) at the time of the offence. If accepted by the judge, the convicted person will serve a period of incarceration in a forensic mental hospital and his or her conditional release will be determined at review board meetings governed by the province's mental health act.

SIDEBAR

A High-Profile Case of Not Criminally Responsible on Account of Mental Disorder

Allan Schoenborn was found NCRMD in the 2008 stabbing and smothering deaths of his children Kaitlynne, ten, Max, eight, and Cordon, five, in Merritt, British Columbia. In 2015, he was granted the right to request escorted outings into the community. However, as at the writing of this text, the Crown was seeking to have Schoenborn designated a high-risk accused (Grant, 2016). NCRMD offenders designated as high risk are held in custody in hospital and cannot be released by a review board until the high-risk designation is removed by a court (Government of Canada, 2014).

Absolute and Conditional Discharges

absolute discharge
A finding of guilt without a conviction. It is imposed when considered to be in the best interests of the accused and not contrary to public interest. Offenders given an absolute discharge cannot be charged and retried for the offence.

When the court imposes an **absolute discharge**, the offender is found guilty of the offence, but is not convicted (meaning that there is no criminal record). The offender cannot be subsequently charged with and retried on the same offence. However, a record is kept of the absolute discharge and can be used against the offender if he or she commits another crime in the future (John Howard Society of Alberta, 1999).

A **conditional discharge** requires the offender to follow certain rules for a specified time period as set out in a probation order. Once that period has passed without the offender breaking any of the rules, the discharge becomes absolute. If the conditions of the probation order are not followed or the offender commits a new offence while on probation, the offender can be convicted of the original offence and sentenced accordingly.

Suspended Sentence

With a suspended sentence, a conviction is entered, but the judge "suspends" the passing of a sentence for a fixed time period, either with or without a probation order. If the conditions of the suspended sentence (or probation order) are not followed or the offender commits a new offence, the offender can be convicted of the original offence and sentenced accordingly.

Fines

A judge has discretion over whether a fine stands alone as a disposition for a conviction or is combined with other types of dispositions, such as probation and/or incarceration.

Any person convicted of an offence (except if the offence has a minimum term of incarceration) can receive a fine (*Criminal Code*, s 734). For summary conviction offences, the maximum fine is $5,000 (s 787); for indictable conviction offences, there is no limit. Judges will also normally impose a 15 percent victim fine surcharge (s 737) or a restitution order (s 738) (John Howard Society of Alberta, 1999). Table 8.2 shows the mean amount of fines imposed in adult criminal courts in relation to guilty verdicts between 2010–11 and 2014–15.

In 2014–15, fines were imposed in 28 percent of adult criminal court cases. In general, fines can range from small amounts for less serious offences to large amounts for more serious offences. In 2014–15, the median amount of fine imposed was $500 (Statistics Canada, 2016b, 2016c).

Restitution

Restitution involves the offender paying a specified sum directly to the victim for expenses resulting from the crime, such as property loss and/or damage. The amount of restitution is equal to the replacement value of the property. In cases where someone is injured, the restitution may cover medical bills and lost income (John Howard Society of Alberta, 1999). The belief is that "repayment" of the harm done needs to occur in order for the accused to "learn" from his or her mistakes. However, many offenders are financially unable to meet the expectations of the restitution order.

conditional discharge
Similar to an absolute discharge, a finding of guilt without conviction. It is imposed when an accused is found guilty for a summary offence with no mandatory minimum punishment, and when it is considered to be in the accused's best interest and not contrary to the public's interest. Conditional discharges are accompanied by rules that must be followed.

TABLE 8.2   Adult Criminal Courts, Guilty Cases by Mean and Median Amount of Fine

	2010–11	2011–12	2012–13	2013–14	2014–15
Count	76,914	69,853	69,408	70,323	58,939
Mean	$1,093	$1,200	$1,129	$1,372	$1,076
Median	$1,000	$800	$800	$800	$500

Source: Statistics Canada (2016c).

Fines, Victim Surcharges, and Restitution Orders

A *fine* is paid by the offender directly to government; the money collected is used to pay for various judicial services and resources. A *victim surcharge* is a monetary penalty paid by an offender to the province or territory where sentencing occurs; the money collected is used to support victims of crime in the jurisdiction. By contrast, a *restitution order* is an order for the offender to pay money directly to the victim(s) of the crime for financial losses incurred as a result of the offender's crime.

Fine Option Program

Offenders sentenced to pay fines may participate in the fine option program, which allows them to pay off their fines through work in the community. They can perform this service in lieu of, or in addition to, the cash payment of fines. The compensation rate is set at provincial minimum wage standards for adults and typically involves some type of community service.

Institutional Fine Option

Offenders who are unable or who refuse to pay a fine may be eligible to "work off" the fine by remaining in a correctional facility. When they have earned enough credits to satisfy the fine, they are released (John Howard Society of Alberta, 1999, pp. 4–5). The period of imprisonment is based on the following calculation:

$$\frac{\text{the unpaid amount of the fine} + \text{the costs \& charges of committing the person to prison}}{\text{(divided by)}\ \text{8 hours per day}} \times \begin{array}{l}\text{the provincial}\\ \text{minimum hourly wage}\end{array}$$

Intermittent Sentence

intermittent sentence
A prison sentence served at designated times (usually weekends), with the offender residing in the community the rest of the time under certain conditions as set out in a probation order.

When a judge sentences an offender to prison for 90 days or less, s 732 of the *Criminal Code* allows the judge to order that the time be served intermittently. An **intermittent sentence** allows the offender to serve the prison sentence at designated times. For example, an offender could serve the prison sentence on weekends so that he or she could still maintain employment during the week to support a family, etc. When not in custody, the offender must comply with the conditions set out in a probation order (John Howard Society of Alberta, 1999, p. 6). If the conditions of the sentence and/or probation order are not followed or the offender commits a new offence, the offender can be sent to prison.

Conditional Sentence

conditional sentence
A prison sentence that is served in the community, under certain restrictions, the primary goal of which is to reduce judicial reliance on incarceration.

A **conditional sentence** is a prison sentence that is served in the community. Time in prison is suspended as long as the offender obeys the rules imposed by the court and is under the supervision of a probation officer. A conditional sentence can be given as an alternative to incarceration for sentences of less than two years, but some offenders are ineligible, such as those convicted of an offence that has a mandatory minimum prison sentence. All conditional sentence orders have mandatory conditions, and they may also include optional conditions (Canadian Bar Association, British Columbia Branch, 2011). Table 8.3 lists mandatory conditions that must be met by those serving conditional sentences, and some common examples of optional conditions that may be required.

TABLE 8.3   Conditional Sentences: Mandatory and Optional Conditions

Mandatory conditions	Optional conditions
Keep the peace and be of good behaviour.	Do not use drugs and/or alcohol.
Appear before the court when required to do so.	Do not own, possess, and/or carry a weapon.
Report to a supervisor/probation officer by a specified date.	Perform community service within a specified time period.
Remain within the jurisdiction.	Attend a treatment program approved by the court.
Notify the court, the supervisor, or the probation officer in advance of any change of name, address, and/or employment.	Do not associate with known criminal contacts.
	Stay a specified distance away from an individual(s) and/or specific location(s).

MINI CASE STUDY

R v Proulx (2000)

R v Proulx (2000) is another key case in Canadian history that has influenced sentencing. Here, the Supreme Court of Canada's judgment pertained to conditional sentences. In this case, after drinking at a party, the 18-year-old accused decided to drive some friends home in a vehicle that was mechanically unsound. He drove erratically for 10 to 20 minutes, sideswiped one car, and crashed into another. One of the passengers in the accused's car was killed, and the driver of the second car was seriously injured. The accused pleaded guilty to dangerous driving causing bodily harm and dangerous driving causing death. The trial judge sentenced him to 18 months in jail. Proulx appealed, resulting in the Manitoba Court of Appeal substituting the jail time with a conditional sentence. Another appeal was submitted, this time by the Crown, which resulted in the Supreme Court restoring the original jail sentence. The Supreme Court explained that the original sentence was not unfit and that the trial judge did not commit any error that would justify overturning the jail sentence in favour of a conditional sentence (Department of Justice Canada, 2011).

What Do You Think?

1. Search your *Criminal Code* to find whether or not there is a mandatory minimum attached to either of those offences.

2. Do you think a conditional sentence should have stood for this conviction?

Probation

probation
A disposition that is served within the community. Probation orders come with mandatory conditions (e.g., regular check-in with a probation officer; keeping the peace) and often additional restrictions and conditions (e.g., avoidance of certain geographical areas; addiction treatment).

Probation is a sentence that is served in the community. A probation order could follow a period of incarceration or it could be used instead of incarceration. While on probation, the convicted person must follow specific conditions set by the judge for a specified time period under the supervision of a probation officer. All probation orders have a set of mandatory conditions and judges have the discretion of adding further optional conditions that may reflect the particular offending behaviour. Offenders who break any of the conditions of their probation order may be charged with breach of probation (*Criminal Code*, s 733.1) and subject to a term of imprisonment of up to two years. (For information on probation in relation to youth, see Chapter 12.)

In 2013–14, probation was the most common disposition imposed in adult criminal court cases, at 43 percent of all guilty cases. This finding includes sentences of probation alone or in combination with other types of sentences. The median length of probation in Canada during this time period was 365 days (Maxwell, 2015).

Imprisonment

Imprisonment involves taking away an offender's freedom and incarcerating him or her in either a provincial or federal correctional facility. The facility the offender is sent to depends on the length of the sentence (two years less a day = provincial jail; over two years = federal penitentiary). Imprisonment is the most serious disposition available in Canada and is intended as a last resort to be used only when a judge considers less restrictive dispositions are not suitable.

SIDEBAR

Terms of Incarceration for Summary and Indictable Conviction Offences

For *summary conviction offences*, the maximum term of incarceration is six months.

For *indictable conviction offences*, the term varies by offence. Some offences have a minimum term and a maximum term of incarceration; others have no minimum term, but have a maximum term of incarceration; and still others carry the maximum sentence possible, which is life imprisonment.

Dangerous Offender Designation

dangerous offender
A designation that can be applied to an offender who has repeat convictions that shows a failure of restraint, a pattern of offending, and a demonstrable likelihood of causing death or injury to another person. If so designated, the sentence of incarceration imposed can be indeterminate.

Under s 753 of the *Criminal Code*, the Crown can apply to designate an individual as a **dangerous offender**. Any person may qualify who is convicted of a serious personal injury offence (e.g., sexual offence, homicide offence); who poses a danger to the life, safety, or physical/mental well-being of others; and who the Crown has established engages in a pattern of repetitive behaviour. Section 753 allows the court to impose on a dangerous offender a sentence of detention in a penitentiary for an indeterminate period of incarceration (i.e., a life sentence) or lesser period.

Long-Term Offender Designation

Section 753.1(1) of the *Criminal Code* describes those offenders who may be subject to a long-term offender application by the Crown, which is any person who meets the following criteria:

(a) it would be appropriate to impose a sentence of imprisonment of two years or more for the offence for which the offender has been convicted;

(b) there is a substantial risk that the offender will reoffend; and

(c) there is a reasonable possibility of eventual control of the risk in the community.

If designated as a long-term offender by the court, the offender will be given a sentence of imprisonment of at least two years, followed by a period of supervision in the community not exceeding ten years (a long-term supervision order).

> **What Do You Think?**
>
> In the Part One case study, did Matt qualify for a dangerous offender designation, a long-term supervision order, or neither?

Appealing a Sentence or a Conviction

> The right to appeal a court's decision is an important safeguard in our legal system because a court could make an error in a trial. (Department of Justice Canada, 2016b)

Once the trial has ended and an accused has been convicted, there is the possibility of an appeal, which can be filed by either the Crown or the defence counsel. The finding of guilt (conviction) or innocence (acquittal) can be appealed, as can the sentence. There must be grounds for appeal, however, that involve questions of law, questions of fact, or both. For example, a convicted person who appeals a conviction must be able to show that there was a procedural error (question of law) in the trial, that evidence presented was not correct (question of fact), or that new evidence was discovered (question of fact) that resulted in the offender being found guilty. A convicted person who appeals a sentence must show that the sentence is too harsh or is unconstitutional (according to the Charter). Most appeals originate from the defence. However, the Crown can also appeal a sentence (if it is considered to be too lenient) or the acquittal of an accused person, although the Crown must first be able to establish that a legal error occurred in the first trial (Griffiths & Cunningham, 2003, p. 167). Figure 8.1 presents the structure of the appeals process in Canada.

Once an appeal has been filed, the convicted person may be released from jail on bail until the appeal is heard or **remanded** into custody while the appeal takes place. A judge must consider whether it is in the best interests of society, the court, and the individual to deny bail. Judges must also consider the merit of the appeal to ensure that frivolous appeals do not take up the court's time.

In Ontario, a review was recently undertaken of the appeals management process. The result was the 2016 guideline "Scheduling and Case Management Guidelines for Criminal Appeals" (Court of Appeal for Ontario, 2016). This guideline sets out specific protocols and time limits that must be adhered to for appeals to be heard in a timely manner and managed efficiently.

For more on the importance of timely processing of cases and appeals, see "Sidebar— Unreasonable Trial Delay" in Chapter 7.

remand
The holding of an accused in custody while the person waits for trial (as opposed to being granted bail, which would allow the individual to live in the community while awaiting trial).

FIGURE 8.1   The Appeal Process in Canada

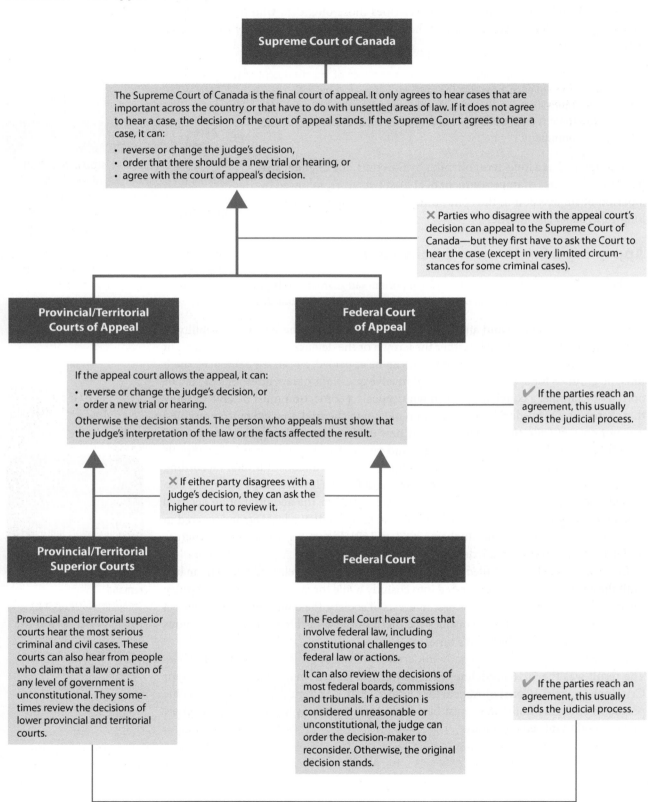

Indigenous Restorative Justice Remedies and Specialized Courts

Indigenous Healing Circles

Indigenous culture reflects a belief that all living things—people, animals, and nature—are interconnected. Circles, being inherently inclusive and non-hierarchical, represent respect, equality, continuity, and interconnectedness. Healing circles—gatherings in which people come together to express themselves as equals—have proven to be a very useful tool for addressing criminal behaviour within Canadian Indigenous communities. They support the process of healing for offenders, victims, and their families, and give people a means to reclaim their cultural traditions. They have also been adopted within criminal justice systems as an alternative or additional sanction to address the harms caused by criminal behaviour to both the offenders and victims. After a finding or an admission of guilt, the court invites interested members of the community to join the judge, prosecutor, defence counsel, police, social service providers, and community elders, along with the offender and the victim, and their families and supporters, in a circle to discuss the offence, factors that may have contributed to it, sentencing options, and ways of reintegrating the offender into the community. The circle allows individuals to work together toward healing, in the belief that that each person has a role and responsibility in that process.

> For more on efforts by Correctional Service Canada to incorporate traditional Indigenous practices into prison practices, see Chapter 11.

What Do You Think?

What place would Indigenous healing circles have in the sentencing of Matt in the Part One case study? How might a healing circle serve the justice needs of Matt's community? What sentencing principles are best served with the use of healing circles?

CAREER PROFILE

Barry Stuart

Judge Barry Stuart, now retired, was the chief judge of the Territorial Court of the Yukon. He pioneered the use of Peacemaking Circles in Canada and is well known for his work with community-based justice processes.

How did you first become interested in restorative justice?
While working in the Papua New Guinea National Planning Office in 1974, I was fascinated by many parts of their informal, village-level justice processes. These processes evolved over many generations, were transparent and inclusive, and they aspired to achieve reconciliation, healing, and peacemaking. Our courts focus on unrealistically narrowly defined legal questions in ways that exclude key people and interests. Our legal processes undermine the relationships needed among all participants to collaboratively find new ways to deal with their differences and generate sustainable relationships and outcomes. In Papua New Guinea, their inclusive, consensus-based, peacemaking processes offered so much more.

How did you become the chief judge of the Territorial Court of the Yukon?
At 16, I set out ten goals for my life. None of them included anything that suggested I might ever be a judge. The two that led me to Yukon were "experience every province before settling down" and "ensure I leave this world a better place than I found it." The latter goal led me to law school. Medicine lost out because too many in my extended family were doctors. I—perhaps foolishly—rebelled against their pressure, thinking law addressed the health of interactions within communities. While teaching law at Dalhousie, I was offered a chance to serve as a Yukon deputy judge. That summer, I fell in love with the Yukon. I agreed to return for two years to serve as their chief judge, and to work with the wonderful people I encountered in communities and in the justice system.

Now that you are retired, how involved are you in restorative justice?

Once involved in it, it seems you are stuck for life working on processes that build relationships of mutual respect, trust, and understanding. I am slightly over 16, not a long way over 60, working on any fronts developing inclusive processes that aspire to build collaborative relationships and safe places for difficult conversations.

Looking back on your career, what are you most proud of? What do you feel has been your biggest impact?

No question, I am most proud that I never gave up, worked hard on my dreams, and never stopped dreaming of what can be done to improve our shared world. But the rest is still a work in progress.

Why is it so important to involve the community in the justice process?

If communities fail to be involved in the hard moral work, we will fail to create the relationships needed to appreciate the strength in our differences, and to build mutual respect and trust. No community—geographical, institutional, or family based—can be more than strangers superficially related unless all voices are respected, engaged, and feel a deep sense of reciprocal connection. A connection that offers opportunities to give and receive in meaningful ways. Restorative processes build community opportunities out of conflict, which generate the connections necessary for healthy communities. Restorative processes are an essential feature of participatory democracy. The health of our families, local communities, indeed of our nation depends on inclusive, peacemaking, consensus-based processes on all levels.

How effective are restorative justice practices in both providing closure to victims and preventing recidivism?

No one process fits all conflicts. The challenge in every case is to fit the best process to the conflict, not to reshape conflicts to fit the process. Some conflicts, some crimes, are not suitable for only restorative processes. With every crime, a very careful triage is needed at every stage to determine what process best serves the interests of the parties and communities, and best realizes the overarching objectives and principles we share.

In all of my experiences, restorative processes are much more effective in providing closure to victims and preventing recidivism, and profoundly better at developing innovative, effective solutions to complex challenges. They are clearly needed to build the collaborative partnerships among all state agencies, and within communities, to heal harm, reconnect victims to their communities, and connect offenders to constructive lives. They are also necessary for community members to become involved in the hard moral work of building community.

Drug Treatment Courts

Drug treatment courts (DTCs) began as a response to large numbers of (non-violent) offenders being incarcerated for drug-related offences and continuing to reoffend due to their underlying addictions. DTCs aim to reduce crimes through court-monitored treatment and community support for those with alcohol and/or drug addictions. The first DTC opened in Toronto in 1998; to date, there are five other such courts in operation in cities across Canada. The principles of DTC recognize that not all criminal behaviour is inherently "malicious," but instead can be a symptom of an individual's addiction. By diverting drug-dependent offenders from the correctional system, more effective measures can be implemented in the belief that future criminal activity will be deterred. Participants must appear regularly in court and successfully complete all ordered sanctions, programming, and treatment. Once the participant gains social stability and demonstrates control over the addiction, either the criminal charges are "stayed" (meaning a judgment is suspended or postponed) or the offender receives a non-custodial sentence (such as house arrest). If unsuccessful, the offender will be sentenced as part of the regular court process (see Chapter 11 for more on offenders who abuse drugs and alcohol).

Domestic Violence Courts

Domestic violence courts have been established in several cities across Canada since as early as 1990. These courts address the nature of domestic or family violence by "providing a more coherent and holistic approach to families involved in both the criminal and family justice systems" (Di Luca, Dann, & Davies, 2014, p. 48). Many unique dynamics exist within the context of family violence, such that a high proportion of victims will often recant their earlier testimony or are reluctant victims and witnesses. Because of these realities, alternatives are needed. Specially trained judges, Crown prosecutors, probation officers, court workers, and defence counsel are assigned to these courts. Together they work with the family involved to create positive solutions for every member of the family.

Conclusion

Sentencing in Canada is one of the most complex and controversial aspects of our criminal justice system. Judges must make crucial decisions that will restrict (or remove) an individual's rights and freedom. Judges make such decisions by considering various aspects of the accused, the case, the offence(s), the context, the victim(s), and more. When issuing a disposition, judges are also guided by the principles in the various theoretical models of sentencing: denunciation, deterrence, selective incapacitation, rehabilitation, and restorative justice. With the 2015 change in our federal government, certain laws are being revised, reversed, and/or reconsidered, including some laws around mandatory minimum sentences. Such changes to our laws are favoured by some and criticized by others. We must wait for the long-term consequences to be revealed in order to make valid judgments. Meanwhile, ongoing issues in the context of sentencing are the overrepresentation of Indigenous people within our correctional system, the growing need for specialized courts, and recognition of the value of the victim's role within the sentencing process.

IN-CLASS EXERCISE

You Be the Judge

Read the case of *R v Archibald* (2012 CanLII 11927 (NLSCTD)). Now, you be the judge! In small groups, present the case to the class. Identify and discuss the mitigating and aggravating factors, as well as the five other elements the judge must consider (*Criminal Code*, s 718, etc.) prior to his disposition. Use the *Criminal Code* and together decide on an appropriate disposition (it may or may not differ from the one imposed). Share your group's decision-making process with the class as a whole. Discuss and debate.

DISCUSSION QUESTIONS

1. What are some of the arguments for mandatory minimum sentences? What are some of the arguments against them? If mandatory minimum sentences (such as those in the *Safe Streets and Communities Act*) had been in place prior to the crime described in the Part One case study, do you think that they may have deterred or prevented the crime?
2. Why do you think so many Canadians support "tough on crime" policies, despite the relatively lower levels of crime today?
3. How do the media influence public opinion on sentencing? How do the media influence decisions made by judges?
4. What are the benefits of victim impact statements? What are the limitations?
5. What aspects of our criminal justice system would you change and why?
6. Compare and contrast the sentencing options of absolute discharge and suspended sentence. When should neither be used?
7. Do you agree with the principle articulated specifically within s 718.2(e) of the *Criminal Code*? What consequences might consideration of this principle have for Indigenous and non-Indigenous offenders as well as society's perception of the criminal justice system?

SUGGESTED FURTHER READINGS

Clayton C. R., Gerald, C., Annamaria, E., & Nader, H. (2012). *Sentencing* (8th ed.). Toronto: LexisNexis.

Turnbull, S. (2016). *Parole in Canada: Gender and diversity in the federal system*. Vancouver: University of British Columbia Press.

REFERENCES

Andrews, D.A., Zinger, I., Hoge, R., Bonta, J., Gendreau, P., & Cullen, F. (1990). Does correctional treatment work? A clinically relevant and psychologically informed meta-analysis. *Criminology, 28*, 393–404.

Boyce, J. (2015, July). Police-reported crime statistics in Canada, 2014. *Juristat, 35*(1). Catalogue No. 85-002-X. Retrieved from http://www.statcan.gc.ca/pub/85-002-x/2015001/article/14211-eng.pdf.

Butler, M. (2015). *Carter v Canada*: The Supreme Court of Canada's decision on assisted dying. Retrieved from http://www.lop.parl.gc.ca/content/lop/ResearchPublications/2015-47-e.html.

Canadian Bar Association, British Columbia Branch. (2011). Conditional sentences, probation and discharges. Retrieved from http://www.cbabc.org/For-the-Public/Dial-A-Law/Scripts/Criminal-Law/203.

Canadian Criminal Justice Association. (2006). Brief to the Standing Committee on Justice, Human Rights, Public Safety and Emergency Preparedness (position paper). Retrieved from https://www.ccja-acjp.ca/pub/en/.

Canadian Resource Centre for Victims of Crime. (2006). Victims' rights in Canada. Retrieved from http://www.crcvc.ca/docs/vicrights.pdf.

Carter v Canada (Attorney General), 2016 SCC 4, [2016] 1 SCR 13.

Clear, T. (1994). *Harm in American penology: Offenders, victims, and their communities*. Albany, NY: State University of New York Press.

Court of Appeal for Ontario. (2016). Scheduling and case management guidelines for criminal appeals. Retrieved from http://www.ontariocourts.ca/coa/en/notices/pd/schedulecriminal.htm.

Department of Justice Canada. (2011). *The changing face of conditional sentencing*. Ottawa: Author. Retrieved from http://www.justice.gc.ca/eng/rp-pr/csj-sjc/jsp-sjp/op00_3-po00_3/op00_3.pdf.

Department of Justice Canada. (2016a). The appeal process in Canada. Retrieved from http://justice.gc.ca/eng/csj-sjc/just/appeal2-appel2.html.

Department of Justice Canada. (2016b). Civil and criminal cases. Retrieved from http://www.justice.gc.ca/eng/csj-sjc/just/08.html.

Di Luca, J., Dann, E., & Davies, B. (2014). *Best practices where there is family violence (criminal law perspective)*. Ottawa: Her Majesty the Queen in Right of Canada, represented by the Minister of Justice and Attorney General of Canada. Retrieved from http://www.justice.gc.ca/eng/rp-pr/cj-jp/fv-vf/bpfv-pevf/bpfv-pevf.pdf.

Government of Canada. (2014, July 11). Coming into force of the *Not Criminally Responsible Reform Act* [Press release]. Retrieved from http://news.gc.ca/web/article-en.do?nid=867529.

Grant, M. (2016, May 16). Not criminally responsible: Why Mathew de Grood is unlikely to be convicted of murder despite killing 5. *CBC News*. Retrieved from http://www.cbc.ca/news/canada/calgary/ncr-matthew-degrood-brentwood-stabbing-1.3583660.

Griffiths, C.T., & Cunningham, A.H. (2003). *Canadian criminal justice: A primer* (2nd ed.). Toronto: Nelson Thomson Canada.

Harris, K. (2016, April 15). Supreme Court strikes down 2 Conservative sentencing reforms. *CBC News*. Retrieved from http://www.cbc.ca/news/politics/supreme-court-sentencing-mandatory-minumums-1.3537150.

John Howard Society of Alberta. (1999). Sentencing in Canada. Retrieved from http://www.johnhoward.ab.ca/pub/old/pdf/C33.pdf.

Malsch, M., & Duker, M.J.A. (2012). *Incapacitation: trends and new perspectives*. Burlington, VT: Ashgate.

Maurutto, P., & Hannah-Moffat, K. (2016). Aboriginal knowledges in specialized courts: Emerging practices in Gladue courts. *Canadian Journal of Law and Society, 31*(3), 451–471.

Maxwell, A. (2015, November). Adult criminal court statistics in Canada, 2013/2014. *Juristat, 35*(1). Catalogue No. 85-002-X. Retrieved from http://www.statcan.gc.ca/pub/85-002-x/2015001/article/14226-eng.pdf.

Office of the Correctional Investigator. (2016). Aboriginal issues. Retrieved from http://www.oci-bec.gc.ca/cnt/priorities-priorites/aboriginals-autochtones-eng.aspx.

R v Archibald, 2012 CanLII 11927 (NLSCTD).

R v Gladue, [1999] 1 SCR 688.

R v Ipeelee, 2012 SCC 13, [2012] 1 SCR 433.

R v Latimer, 2001 SCC 1, [2001] 1 SCR 3.

R v Lloyd, 2016 SCC 13, [2016] 1 SCR 130.

R v M (CA), [1996] 1 SCR 500.

R v Proulx, 2000 SCC 5, [2000] 1 SCR 61.

R v Safarzadeh-Markhali, 2016 SCC 14, [2016] 1 SCR 180.

R v Wells, 2000 SCC 10, [2000] 1 SCR 207.

Statistics Canada. (2013). Aboriginal peoples in Canada: First Nations people, Métis and Inuit: National Household Survey, 2011. Ottawa: Minister of Industry, 2013. Retrieved from http://www12.statcan.gc.ca/nhs-enm/2011/as-sa/99-011-x/99-011-x2011001-eng.pdf.

Statistics Canada. (2016a). Table 051-0005: Estimates of population, Canada, provinces and territories, quarterly (persons), CANSIM. Retrieved from http://www5.statcan.gc.ca/cansim/a26?lang=eng&retrLang=eng&id=0510005&&pattern=&stByVal=1&p1=1&.

Statistics Canada. (2016b). Table 252-0056: Adult criminal courts, guilty cases by type of sentence, annual (number), CANSIM. Retrieved from http://www5.statcan.gc.ca/cansim/a05?lang=eng&id=2520056.

Statistics Canada. (2016c). Table 252-0063: Adult criminal courts, guilty cases by mean and median amount of fine annual (number unless otherwise noted), CANSIM. Retrieved from http://www5.statcan.gc.ca/cansim/a26?lang=eng&retrLang=eng&id=2520063&&pattern=&stByVal=1&p1=1&p2=35&tabMode=dataTable&csid.

Vollard, B. (2012). Preventing crime through selective incapacitation. *The Economic Journal 123*(567), 262–284. doi:10.1111/j.1468-0297.2012.02522.x.

Zedlewski, E.W. (1983). Deterrence findings and data sources: A comparison of the uniform crime reports and the national crime surveys. *Journal of Research in Crime and Delinquency, 20*(2), 262–276.

Zedlewski, E.W. (1985). When have we punished enough? *Public Administration Review, 45,* 771–779.

Zedlewski, E.W. (2009). Conducting cost benefit analyses in criminal justice evaluations: Do we dare? *European Journal on Criminal Policy & Research, 15*(4), 355–364. doi:10.1007/s10610-009-9108-9.

PART FOUR

Corrections

McCann v The Queen (1975):
Solitary Confinement in Canada

Karla O'Regan

My home is hell in one small cell
That no man wants to own,
For here I spend my life condemned
A man the world disowns.

Within these walls that never fall.
The damned all come to know.
The row of cells—the special hell,
Called Solitary Row.

Jack McCann wrote these words about his time in Canada's prison system after having spent a total of 1,471 days in solitary confinement (Jackson, 2015). McCann was serving a 15-year sentence for armed robbery when he escaped from a BC Penitentiary in 1973 to alert a reporter from the *Vancouver Sun* about the conditions in which prisoners were being held in isolation. Known among prisoners as "the hole," solitary confinement is the isolation of inmates in small, barren rooms in complete isolation from the rest of the general prison population. These cells are often lit 24 hours a day and provide inmates with minimal human contact. The following is a description of the administrative segregation cells at BC Penitentiary:

> The cells measured 11 feet by 6½ feet and consisted of three solid concrete walls and a solid steel door with a five-inch-square window which could only be opened from outside the cell. Inside the cell there was no proper bed. The prisoner slept on a cement slab four inches off the floor; the slab was covered by a sheet of plywood upon which was laid a four-inch-thick foam pad. Prisoners were provided with blankets, sheets, and a foam-rubber pillow. About two feet from the end of the sleeping platform against the back wall was a combination toilet and wash-basin. ... There were no other furnishings in the cell. The cell was illuminated by a light that burned twenty-four hours a day. (Jackson, 2015, p. 59)

McCann himself had just spent 754 consecutive days in solitary confinement prior to his escape. When he was recaptured, he was ordered back to solitary, where he remained for almost another year (Jackson, 2015). McCann later organized with other inmates to bring a legal claim against the federal government. They argued that the use of solitary confinement was a violation of their right to be free from cruel and unusual punishment (a right now found in s 12 of the *Canadian Charter of Rights and Freedoms*). The case went all the way to the Federal Court of Canada, where McCann and his co-plaintiffs lost (*McCann v The Queen*, 1975).

The conditions for prisoners in solitary confinement in Canada's correctional system have not changed much since McCann took his case to the Federal Court. Inmates in segregation are housed in small cells with almost no human contact. Cell size varies between institutions; however, in Canada they range from five to seven square metres (Winter, 2015). Prisoners are allowed only one hour of each day outside their cells to shower and exercise or walk in the yard; however, they must do this alone. As one prisoner in solitary reported, "you never get to see the grass or the sun. The only way you know it's raining is by the sound of the rain on the roof" (Jackson, 2015, p. 59).

Canada's correctional system employs two different kinds of solitary confinement: disciplinary segregation and administrative segregation. The conditions in which inmates are housed are the same for each type of segregation. There are only two differences between the two forms of confinement: (1) the reasons for which an inmate can be sent to solitary; and (2) the length of time the inmate will spend there. Disciplinary segregation is used when inmates break prison rules, which can include being disrespectful to a staff member, disobeying a staff member, or engaging in a fight (*Corrections and Conditional Release Act* [CCRA], s 40). Disciplinary segregation is limited to a maximum of 30 days (CCRA, s 44(1)(f)). Administrative segregation has no maximum period. It can be ordered for an indefinite period of time and, according to s 31(1) of the CCRA, it is used "to maintain the security of the penitentiary or the safety of any person by not allowing an inmate to associate with other inmates."

This creates a wide spectrum of reasons for which a prisoner can be sent to administrative segregation. Some of these reasons are arbitrary or insufficient—or so suggest a number of inmates who brought lawsuits against both federal and provincial governments in 2016. They argue that the lack of an independent review process for administrative segregation orders leaves them open to being overused and imposed for punitive reasons (*Canadian Civil Liberties Association v Canada (A.G.)*, 2015). In at least one case, the courts have agreed with this argument. In 2016, an Alberta judge ordered three federal inmates to be released from segregation on the basis that "prison authorities ignored factors around procedural fairness, aboriginal identity and mental-health history before isolating them" (White, 2016).

Not surprisingly, the conditions of extreme isolation that prisoners in solitary confinement experience have been shown to have a number of detrimental effects on their mental and physical health. Insomnia, hallucinations, and self-injury are common among inmates housed in solitary confinement, even for short periods of time. These effects have been found to be worse for young people and those suffering from mental illness. In addition, the longer the period of time spent in isolation, the more severe the effects (*Canadian Civil Liberties Association v Canada (A.G.)*, 2015, para. 25). In the worst cases, prisoners in solitary confinement are driven to extreme forms of self-injury or suicide. As Chris Trotchie, one of the plaintiffs in a lawsuit against the BC government for its use of solitary confinement, describes: "I was abused as a child. And it [solitary] brings that right back. It makes me want to harm myself again. It makes me want to disassociate myself from that state of mind" (Lupick, 2015). McCann gave similar evidence in his Federal Court case, remarking that he had been asked by prison officials to clean up the blood in neighbouring cells after three of his fellow inmates had slashed themselves while in segregation. McCann testified that he had "begged and pleaded to be let out of solitary," to no avail. When a fourth inmate slashed himself, McCann reached his limit and set himself on fire in his cell. He later offered testimony to the Federal Court about his thoughts as he and his cell burned: "I remember watching the space beneath the door get bigger. I thought I could crawl beneath it and be free ... I wanted to get out. I don't care if I die, I never want to go back to that position again" (Jackson, 2015, p. 60). Studies conducted on the use of administrative segregation have found that it does not affect all inmates equally, and that its negative effects can vary depending on a number of factors, such as the length of time an offender spends in segregation and the degree of social and mental isolation the cell conditions create.

The 2015–16 annual report of the Office of the Correctional Investigator of Canada noted that more than one-quarter (26 percent) of all deaths that occurred in custody in 2015–16 took place while the prisoner was in administrative segregation. Moreover, these deaths are disproportionately suffered by members of already marginalized groups. In 77 percent of prison death cases in 2015–16, the inmate had been previously diagnosed with a mental disorder, and in 69 percent of prison death cases, the inmate had at least one prior suicide attempt (Sapers, 2016, p. 25). Further, the groups that are overrepresented in the prison population (including the mentally ill, substance abusers, and Indigenous people) are also overrepresented in solitary confinement. A *Maclean's* article on Adam Capay, a 23-year-old Indigenous inmate who has served more than four years in administrative segregation in an Ontario prison, stated the following:

> Indigenous offenders serve much harder time than anyone else. Indigenous inmates are placed in minimum-security institutions at just half the rate of their non-Indigenous counterparts. They are more likely to be placed in segregation, accounting for 31 per cent of cases; once in isolation, they'll spend 16 per cent more time there. They account for 45 per cent of all self-harm incidents, and one-third of suicides. Nine in 10 are held to the expiry of their sentence, versus two-thirds of the non-Indigenous inmate population. They are more likely to be restrained in prison, to be involved in use-of-force incidents, to receive institutional charges, to die there. (Patriquin, 2016)

Capay was serving a five-month sentence for a series of mischief, theft, and assault charges when he had an altercation with another inmate, who died. Capay was charged with first-degree murder and has been in administrative segregation ever since. His trial has been delayed three times (Porter, 2016). This is a familiar story for many prisoners in solitary confinement. Many inmates first come to jail on a relatively minor offence, but are later sentenced to additional time or placed in segregation as a result of altercations or misconduct in prison.

Some criminologists have argued that the conditions of solitary confinement aggravate this pattern, serving as a cycle or "treadwheel" from which prisoners cannot escape. This is particularly the case for prisoners who are sent to administrative segregation for acts of self-injury (as Chris Trotchie was). Studies have shown that lengthy periods of time spent in segregation can increase an inmate's acts of self-injury (National Institue of Justice, 2016). This means that a prisoner's time in solitary can be lengthened by behaviour caused by the isolation itself. As Jackson (2015) noted:

> [T]he segregation unit is different from the rest of the penitentiary in ways that go beyond the physical differences in the cells, the denial of access to work and hobbies, and the restrictions on exercise. ... In segregation the worst things about prisons—the humiliation and degradation of the prisoners, the frustration, the despair, the loneliness, and the deep sense of antagonism between the prisoners and the guards—are intensified. ... There is a

See Chapter 9 for some of the suggestions that criminologists have made about how to best approach the use of administrative segregation.

perverse symbiotic relationship between guards and prisoners in [solitary]. The guards, by perceiving the prisoners as the most dangerous and violent of men, can justify to themselves the intensity of the surveillance and the rigours of detention. Prisoners, by responding to that perception of dangerousness with acts of defiance, have at least one avenue of asserting their individuality and their autonomy, of manifesting their refusal to submit. (p. 62)

Not all uses of administrative segregation have been found to share these negative consequences, as discussed in Chapter 9. Its long-term use, however, is widely regarded as problematic (National Institute of Justice, 2016). In a 2011 report to the General Assembly of the United Nations, Juan Méndez, Special Rapporteur on Torture, recommended a worldwide ban on the "prolonged use" of solitary confinement (defined as more than 15 days) given the mental and psychological damage it causes. "Considering the severe mental pain or suffering solitary confinement may cause when used as a punishment, during pretrial detention, indefinitely or for a prolonged period, for juveniles or persons with mental disabilities," he wrote, "it can amount to torture or cruel, inhuman or degrading treatment or punishment" (United Nations, General Assembly, 2011, p. 22).

At the time of his case, McCann was thought to have served more time in solitary confinement than any other prisoner in Canadian history (Jackson, 2015, p. 60). Sadly, Canada's use of solitary confinement has since seen many other cases that would challenge this record. In April 2015, the *National Post* reported that "somewhere in Canada is a prisoner who has spent 6,273 consecutive days alone in a cell" (Winter, 2015). That is more than 17 years in isolation.

There have also been many high-profile cases of suicide by inmates confined to isolation for prolonged periods of time. Many of these prisoners were young and Indigenous, such as 22-year-old Edward Snowshoe, who committed suicide in 2010 after spending 162 consecutive days in segregation. Most notable among these deaths is the tragic case of 19-year-old Ashley Smith, which launched a special investigation by the Office of the Correctional Investigator in 2007 on the use of solitary confinement in Canada's prison system. Smith's case was also subject to a coroner's inquest, which resulted in 104 recommendations, including that the use of solitary confinement be limited to no more than fifteen days at a time and that it never be used with inmates who have a history of self-injury or mental illness (*Smith (Re)*, 2013). In its 2015–16 annual report, the Office of the Correctional Investigator noted that very few of these recommendations have been adopted by Correctional Service Canada (Sapers, 2016).

Solitary confinement can pose a problem outside prison walls as well. According to Howard Sapers, the former Correctional Investigator, "it is very difficult, if not impossible, to prepare people for release into the community if you're keeping them locked in a cell for 23 out of 24 hours a day." He added, "the prolonged use of segregation runs counter to the stated goal of Corrections Canada" (Winter, 2015).

Canada is not the only Western country contravening the recommendations of the United Nations on solitary confinement. Early on February 19, 2016, Albert Woodfox was released from a Louisiana state prison after having served more time in solitary confinement than any other person in world history—almost 45 years (more than 16,000 days) (Cole, 2015). He was interviewed for the *New York Times* shortly after his release. The reporter noted:

See the opening case study of Part Five to learn more about Ashley Smith.

When someone is in a cell for four decades he measures things differently: time, certainly, but also freedom. Asked to recall his last trip as a free man, as a 22-year-old on the run to New York, Mr. Woodfox said he did not remember it as a feeling of freedom. True freedom he discovered much later, he said, after years of reading of brave men. "When I began to understand who I was, I considered myself free," he said. "No matter how much concrete they use to hold me in a particular place they couldn't stop my mind."

[Following the interview, Mr. Woodfox] revealed a gift that his brother had given him a few hours earlier to celebrate his first morning as a free man in 45 years: a watch. (Robertson, 2016)

In 2016, the BC Civil Liberties Association and Canadian Civil Liberties Association joined forces with the John Howard Society and the Elizabeth Fry Society to bring lawsuits against the federal government for its use of prolonged solitary confinement. These cases will further the issues raised in *McCann v The Queen* (1975) and provide a post-Charter analysis of solitary confinement. They will also offer an opportunity for Canadians to rethink the role that prisons are meant to play in society. As the chapters in this part will demonstrate, many factors must be considered when balancing the needs of offenders and those of a just and peaceful society. Ironically, the study of imprisonment can often reveal a great deal about what it means to be free.

What Do You Think?

1. Why might it be important for a correctional institution to be able to isolate an inmate from the general prison population for a certain period of time? How might these needs be balanced against the mental and physical well-being of the inmate?

2. For a useful class or study exercise, look up the 2013 coroner's inquest report on the Ashley Smith case (Smith (Re), 2013). At the end of the report, you will find the list of 104 recommendations that the jury made with respect to the mental health care of (female) offenders in Canada's federal prison system. Many of these recommendations pertain to the use of administrative segregation. Read through them and discuss whether any of them address the needs you identified in question one. If they do, how so?

3. Think back to the discussion of the *Oakes* test in Chapter 7. Suppose that the solitary confinement lawsuits brought in 2016 against the federal government for its use of prolonged solitary confinement are successful in establishing a violation of s 12 of the Charter, "the right not to be subjected to any cruel and unusual treatment or punishment." Do you think the government's use of long-term segregation would pass the *Oakes* test? Try to imagine the arguments that the federal government and prisoners' rights organizations would make for and against the prolonged solitary confinement.

4. How might solitary confinement be viewed by each of the criminal justice models examined in Chapter 1 (i.e., crime-control model, welfare model, justice model, community change model, and restorative justice model)? Provide evidence to support each position.

SUGGESTED FURTHER READINGS

British Columbia Civil Liberties Association and the John Howard Society of Canada v Canada (A.G.). (2015, January 19). Vancouver, BCSC, File No. 150415 (Notice of Civil Claim).

Jackson, M. (1983). *Prisoners of isolation: solitary confinement in Canada.* Toronto: University of Toronto Press.

REFERENCES

Canadian Civil Liberties Association v Canada (A.G.). (2015, January 27). Toronto, Ont. Sup. Ct. J., File No. CV-15-520661 (Notice of Application).

Cole, D. (2015, June 16). Albert Woodfox's forty years in solitary confinement. *New Yorker.* Retrieved from http://www.newyorker.com/news/news-desk/albert-woodfoxs-forty-years -in-solitary-confinement.

Corrections and Conditional Release Act, SC 1992, c 20.

Jackson, M. (2015). Reflections on 40 years of advocacy to end the isolation of Canadian prisoners. *Canadian Journal of Human Rights, 4*(1), 57–87.

Lupick, T. (2015, May 14). B.C. inmate sent to solitary confinement for self-harm sues province for rights violations. *Georgia Straight.* Retrieved from http://www.straight.com/news/451876/ bc-inmate-sent-solitary-confinement-self-harm-sues-province-rights-violations.

McCann v The Queen (1975), 68 DLR (3d) 661 (FC).

National Institute of Justice. (2016). Restrictive housing in the U.S.: Issues, challenges, and future directions. Washington, DC: Department of Justice. Retrieved from https://www. ncjrs.gov/pdffiles1/nij/250315.pdf.

Patriquin, M. (2016, November 2). Why Adam Capay has spent 1,560 days in solitary. *MacLean's.* Retrieved from http://www.macleans.ca/news/why-adam-capay-has-spent -1560-days-in-solitary/.

Porter, J. (2016, October 26). First Nations man spends 4 years in solitary confinement in Northern Ontario awaiting trial. *CBC News.* Retrieved from http://www.cbc.ca/news/ canada/thunder-bay/four-years-solitary-1.3821245.

Robertson, C. (2016, February 20). For 45 years in prison, Louisiana man kept calm and held fast to hope. *New York Times.* Retrieved from http://www.nytimes.com/2016/02/21/us/for -45-years-in-prison-louisiana-man-kept-calm-and-held-fast-to-hope.html.

Sapers, H. (2016). *Annual report of the Office of the Correctional Investigator 2015–2016.* Ottawa: Her Majesty the Queen in Right of Canada. Retrieved from http://www.oci-bec.gc.ca/cnt/rpt/pdf/annrpt/annrpt20152016-eng.pdf.

Smith (Re), 2013 CanLII 92762 (Ont OCCO).

United Nations, General Assembly. (2011). Torture and other cruel, inhuman or degrading treatment or punishment: Interim report of the Special Rapporteur of the Human Rights Council on torture and other cruel, inhuman or degrading treatment or punishment (A/66/268). Retrieved from http://solitaryconfinement.org/uploads/ SpecRapTortureAug2011.pdf.

White, P. (2016, August 18). Keeping inmates in isolation is "not reasonable," Alberta judge rules. *Globe and Mail.* Retrieved from http://www.theglobeandmail.com/news/national/ court-ruling-a-rebuke-of-prison-systems-use-of-solitary-confinement/article31462387/.

Winter, J. (2015, April 24). Seventeen years alone in a cell: "Keeping somebody in segregation for that length of time is very hard to justify." *National Post.* Retrieved from http://news.nationalpost.com/news/canada/seventeen-years-alone-in-a-cell-keeping -somebody-in-segregation-for-that-length-of-time-is-very-hard-to-justify.

Institutional and Community Corrections

Introduction

Historically, corrections in Canada involved an exclusive focus on custody, whose purpose was both punishment and penitence; hence, the use of the word *penitentiary* to characterize our first prisons. From the 1835 opening of Kingston Penitentiary through to the 1920s, offender sentencing options consisted of custodial terms supplemented by harsh corporal punishments (e.g., flogging). During the period between the two World Wars, the Canadian penitentiary system experienced sufficient turmoil to warrant the establishment of the Royal Commission to Investigate the Penal System of Canada (Canada, 1938). The task force examined conditions of confinement and made sweeping recommendations for wholesale changes to the prison system by placing greater emphasis on rehabilitation at the expense of punishment. After the Second World War, there was an unparalleled growth in community-based sentencing options (e.g., probation), which now constitute the most common type of sentence ordered by Canadian courts (Reitano, 2016).

The correctional system is responsible for the administration of all judicial sentences. Its principle mandate is the protection of the public, which it aims to achieve through the detention and delivery of rehabilitative programming designed to reduce offenders' anti-social behaviours. The nature and extent of correctional supervision are determined at the time of sentencing. To better understand how this supervision is administered, one must appreciate the duality of responsibility for correctional services as laid out in Canada's founding legislation, the *British North America Act* (BNA Act) of 1867. Under the terms of the BNA Act, the delivery of correctional services is split between federal and provincial/territorial levels of government such that adults (i.e., those 18 years and over) sentenced to two years or more are under the jurisdiction of the federal system, while adults sentenced to two years less a day are the responsibility of the provinces/territories. Provincial and territorial jurisdictions also include the custodial and community supervision of youth as well as all adults and youth held in pre-trial detention or awaiting sentencing (i.e., on remand).

Incarceration Rate

As Figure 9.1 shows, in 2014–15, Canada's incarceration rate, including inmates in both federal and provincial/territorial custody, stood at 114 per 100,000 population (Walmsley, 2015; World Prison Brief, n.d.). This rate compares favourably with that of other Western democracies, such as England and Wales (147 per 100,000), but it is slightly higher than the rates in many European countries (e.g., France: 103 per 100,000; Germany: 78 per 100,000). Of note, the United States has the second-highest incarceration rate in the world (693 per 100,000), in large part due to the toughening of custodial sanctions over the last 30 years.

FIGURE 9.1   Incarceration Rates per 100,000 Population for Selected Countries, 2014–15

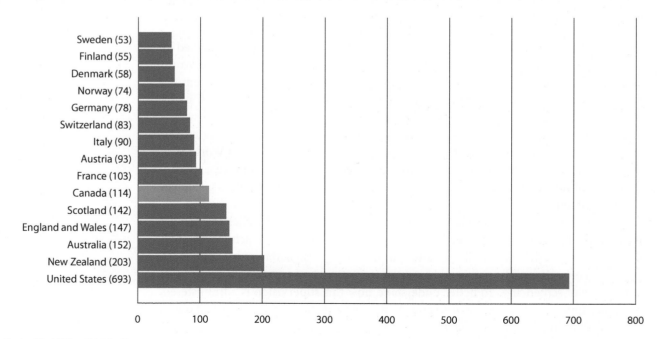

Source: World Prison Brief. (n.d.).

The Federal Correctional System

While the federal and provincial/territorial correctional systems share many characteristics, it is useful to examine the key elements of each separately. The federal system is operated by Correctional Service Canada (CSC), an agency of the federal government whose mandate is established in the *Corrections and Conditional Release Act* (CCRA). The CCRA lays out the policies and directives that are designed to ensure public safety, establish staff responsibility, and manage offender supervision. Under the terms of the CCRA, CSC is responsible for the custody of inmates and their preparation for eventual release through the delivery of rehabilitative programming. CSC is also the agency responsible for supervision of federal offenders in the community (i.e., those on conditional release). Finally, CSC is tasked with ensuring that the public is sufficiently educated regarding the role of CSC, with the goal of balancing the purposes of sentencing with the public's understanding of those purposes.

The Office of the Correctional Investigator (OCI) also operates under the CCRA and investigates complaints from federal offenders regarding "decisions, recommendations, acts or omissions" on the part of CSC (Sapers, 2016, p. 2). In addition, the OCI serves an important purpose in providing an independent investigative and review mechanism to ensure that CSC is held accountable in terms of its legislated mandate. As directed by the CCRA, the OCI is responsible for reviewing all incidents in which offenders experience serious bodily harm or death, including self- or other-inflicted injuries. The OCI submits annual reports of its activities to Parliament, highlighting the current status of its chief areas of concern, including inmate health care; deaths in custody; conditions of confinement; community reintegration; and correctional services for Indigenous and female populations (Sapers, 2016).

Federally, the correctional system is divided into five regions: Atlantic, Quebec, Ontario, Prairie, and Pacific (Correctional Service Canada [CSC], 2016b). Each region includes a Regional Reception Centre, where newly sentenced offenders are assessed prior to transfer to a permanent facility, and a Regional Treatment Centre, which addresses inmates' mental health needs. In addition, CSC maintains community parole offices and community correctional centres within each region.

CSC operates 37 secure custody facilities for male inmates classified as either minimum, medium, maximum, or multi-level security. Each classification level corresponds to the relative degree of supervision and freedom of movement that offenders will experience in custody. The six secure custody facilities for female inmates are all rated as multi-level security. Female facilities were constructed as a result of the recommendations of the Arbour Commission of Inquiry (Canada, 1996) following a violent riot in 1994 at the now-closed Prison for Women at Kingston Penitentiary, during which an all-male riot squad shackled and strip-searched female prisoners.

Types of Facilities

Canada's prisons are of varied ages and reflect the different periods in which they were constructed. For example, Stony Mountain Institution (1877) in Manitoba and Dorchester Penitentiary (1880) in New Brunswick are among Canada's oldest operating prisons and are representative of the post-Confederation penitentiary building boom. Their architectural style reflects the late 19th-century belief that improvements in

Stony Mountain Institution, Manitoba.

Grande Cache Institution, Alberta.

inmate behaviour could be effected through a combined regimen of silence and servitude. Accordingly, most penitentiaries of this period employed a linear or radial design (Johnston, 2000) in which cells were arranged in back-to-back ranges in order to maximize the space available for communal prison labour workshops.

The designs of more recently built custody facilities reflect the changing priorities of the correctional system to enhance offenders' reintegration potential by providing conditions of confinement that mirror living conditions in wider society. As a result, facilities such as Grande Cache Institution (1995) in Alberta or Bath Institution (1972) in Ontario continue to prioritize staff and inmate safety and security using direct observation living units or separate inmate houses. Many of the newer facilities are designed to accommodate the requirements of inmates at multiple levels of security classification and the needs of diverse populations. For example, CSC operates a number of regional Aboriginal Healing Lodges for male and female inmates, which provide offender programming rooted in Indigenous traditions and values.

Offender Population

As of 2014–15, a total of 15,043 inmates were in federal custody (CSC, 2017). An additional 7,915 offenders were being supervised in the community while on conditional release (i.e., parole). In the same period, females accounted for approximately 5 percent of all federal inmates (CSC, 2014b), a rate that is relatively consistent with that of other Western democracies (i.e., United States: 9.3 percent; Australia: 8.0 percent; New Zealand: 6.7 percent; Germany: 5.7 percent; and France: 3.2 percent). By contrast, Indigenous offenders—First Nations people, Métis, and Inuit—accounted for approximately 25 percent of inmates in federal custody (Public Safety Canada, 2016).

Population Profile: 2014–15

During this period, half of all federal offenders (those in custody and in the community) were serving sentences of less than five years. Of these, 22.8 percent were serving sentences of three years or less (Public Safety Canada, 2016). The majority self-identified as Caucasian (60.4 percent) or Indigenous (21.9 percent). In terms of current offences, 49 percent had been convicted of a sexual offence or other violent offence, 20 percent had been convicted of homicide, and 17 percent had been convicted of a drug offence (CSC, 2017). Collectively, 69 percent of offenders were serving time for a violent offence (Public Safety Canada, 2016).

The majority of offenders in custody were classified as medium security (62.9 percent). Approximately 55 percent were between 18 and 39 years of age, with one-quarter (23.5 percent) categorized as "seniors" (i.e., 50 years or older) (Public Safety Canada, 2016).

Almost one-quarter of inmates (23.2 percent) were serving an indeterminate sentence, one whose end date is not fixed by the courts at time of sentencing. There are two types of indeterminate sentences. The first is typically known as a "life sentence," by which an offender is subject to CSC supervision until death, whether in custody or in the community. For example, an offender convicted of second-degree murder receives a life sentence, but the court sets the minimum time the offender must serve before being eligible to apply for parole (i.e., between 10 and 25 years). The second type of indeterminate sentence results from the court declaring an individual a "dangerous offender" (DO). The DO designation is typically reserved for those with an extensive history of violence who are deemed to pose a significant risk to reoffend violently. Application for a DO designation must be submitted by the Crown prosecutor prior to sentencing (Public Safety Canada, 2016).

For an in-depth look at the dangerous offender designation, see Chapter 11.

MINI CASE STUDY

Vincent Li Granted His Freedom

One of the most high-profile murder cases of the last decade became news once again in February 2017 when Vincent Li was given an absolute discharge, nine years after the brutal murder of 22-year-old Tim McLean on a Greyhound bus in 2008.

In March 2009, Li was found not criminally responsible on account of mental disorder (NCRMD) for the gruesome decapitation of McLean, a stranger who had been sitting beside him. In his ruling, Justice John Scurfield wrote, "These grotesque acts are appalling. However, the acts themselves and the context in which they were committed are strongly suggestive of a mental disorder. He did not appreciate the act he committed was morally wrong. He believed he was acting in self defence and that he had been commanded by God to do so."

Li was diagnosed as a schizophrenic who had suffered a psychotic episode that led him to murder McLean. Li was remanded to a secure psychiatric hospital for treatment, and his case was reviewed annually. Psychiatrists determined that Li was responding well to medication, and he was slowly granted more freedom, eventually moving into his own apartment, although he continued to be monitored and was subject to various conditions. These conditions included that he continue to take his medication and receive counselling.

A 1999 Supreme Court of Canada ruling established that review boards must grant an absolute discharge to an offender who is deemed to no longer pose a significant threat to public safety. Li (who has legally changed his name) was given his full freedom, with no criminal record, although there is a police record of his case (known as a "non-conviction record") and his DNA is registered with the national DNA databank. Doctors appearing before the Manitoba Criminal Code Review Board stated that Li had been a model patient and understood that he must continue to take his medication in order to avoid future episodes. The board stated, "[T]he weight of evidence does not substantiate that [Mr. Li] poses a significant threat to the safety of the public." Here is the timeline of Li's treatment:

2009: Found NCRMD
2010: Daily supervised walks on hospital grounds
2011: Unescorted walks on hospital grounds
2012: Short, escorted day trips
2013: Supervised visits to nearby towns and beaches
2014: Moved to an unlocked ward in the hospital; allowed short unescorted trips
2015: Granted release to halfway house (with conditions, including curfew)
2016: Granted conditional discharge (living independently in Winnipeg with conditions)
2017: Granted absolute discharge (living independently in Winnipeg; no conditions)

What Do You Think?

- Do you agree with the board's decision to release Li, based on experts' opinions that he was not likely to act violently again?
- Li's DNA is now in a registry, but since he was considered NCRMD, he therefore has no criminal record. Do you agree with that policy?
- McLean's family proposed the designation "NPA" (not psychologically responsible), which still confers criminal responsibility. Is that a useful solution?

Sources: CTV.ca News Staff (2009); Lambert (2017).

DOs are subject to periodic review by the Parole Board of Canada (PBC), which determines a release date once the offender is no longer regarded as a significant risk to the community. At a minimum, DOs are eligible for day parole after having served four years of their sentence and full parole after having served seven years. As of 2014–15, CSC was responsible for 622 DOs, 94.2 percent of whom were held in custody. The remaining 36 DOs were being supervised in the community. Of note, Indigenous offenders represented 31.5 percent of DOs, while female offenders represented 0.01 percent of DOs (Public Safety Canada, 2016).

Correctional System Costs

In 2014–15, overall expenditures for the federal correctional system were approximately $2.6 billion (CSC, 2017). This sum covered the cost of CSC, the PBC, and the OCI (Public Safety Canada, 2016) and represented a 70 percent increase in expenditures since 2004–5. The increased costs have been due, in part, to the changing nature of offenders and their needs (e.g., senior offenders) as well as the construction or retrofitting of 2,700 cells in 30 facilities since 2013–14, estimated to have cost more than $700 million (Sapers, 2015). The average annual cost of corrections per offender varies depending on the level of institutional security classification, type of offender, and location of service. For example, the annual average cost of minimum, medium, and maximum security facilities for males is $83,182, $101,583, and $156,768, respectively. The comparable cost for females in multi-level facilities averages $219,884 per year. Further, the average annual cost of secure custody, regardless of classification level, is 70 percent more than that of community-based supervision (i.e., $115,310 versus $34,432 per offender, respectively) (Public Safety Canada, 2016).

Entering Federal Custody

What happens when offenders are sentenced to federal custody? See Figure 9.2. Typically, after sentencing, they arrive at a Regional Reception Centre. There, they undergo an extensive battery of assessments to identify their priority risk and need factors. Their relevant security classification is based on three criteria: institutional adjustment, escape risk, and risk to the public should they escape (CSC, 2016a). The results from the intake assessment and security classification assessments are incorporated into the offender's correctional plan, which lays out a risk management strategy for the offender. The correctional plan documents the offender's (1) current offence, accountability, and motivation for change; (2) physical and mental health information; and (3) responsivity factors (e.g., capacity to respond to treatment, and literacy level). It includes the offender's needs with regard to correctional programming and serves as a basis for monitoring ongoing progress in those programs (CSC, 2015; Nafekh, Allegri, Stys, & Jensen, 2009). The correctional plan also includes the timeline for conditional release (i.e., parole), which allows those working with the offender to develop an appropriate supervision strategy to address identified risk and needs and document the offender's progress toward reducing the risk of institutional infractions and post-release recidivism.

FIGURE 9.2   The Process of Entering Federal Custody

Source: Adapted from Nafekh et al. (2009).

This model assumes that the information the CCRA requires CSC to collect to make decisions on the risk assessment and security placement of an offender is available in a timely manner. However, a 2015 Auditor General of Canada's report indicated that risk assessments were being completed in the absence of key information, notably criminal record and court documents. In response to the Auditor General's recommendations, CSC agreed to clarify in policy the minimum documentation required for offender assessments, liaise with other components of the criminal justice system to collect relevant offender information, and update risk assessments as additional information becomes available (Auditor General of Canada, 2015).

IN-CLASS EXERCISE

Offender Risk and Need Assessment

As a federal parole officer, one of your responsibilities is to evaluate offender risk to reoffend. Based on the following descriptors, what level of risk does John, the offender, pose? Consider the offender's needs which, if addressed through treatment, could reduce his risk to reoffend.

John is a 39-year-old first-time federal offender who is serving a three-year sentence for possession of cocaine. During the first six months of his sentence, he has twice been put into disciplinary segregation for institutional misconducts. John has previously served provincial time, during which he attempted unsuccessfully to escape.

John is recently divorced and has had only limited contact in the last two years with his three children: two boys and one girl, all under 12 years of age. John has a grade 10 education and has a sporadic occupational record, having held six different jobs in the two years prior to this incarceration. His social network is quite limited as, due to his repeated incarcerations, his parents and siblings have broken off all contact with him.

John has no known psychiatric history but has received treatment for depression in the past. Although he no longer drinks, John has a long history of alcoholism and has recently been diagnosed with cirrhosis of the liver. He indicates that he is interested in attending Alcoholics Anonymous while he is in custody.

criminogenic risk factors
Characteristics of the offender or his or her circumstances (such as anti-social attitude, anti-social personality, anti-social associates) that increase criminal potential. When these risk factors are reduced through appropriate treatment, the risk for continued criminal behaviour is reduced.

interventions
Strategies, such as treatment programs, job training, or upgrading education that are used to help an offender learn alternatives to criminal behaviour.

The Risk-Need-Responsivity Model

The Risk-Need-Responsivity (RNR) model is the prominent approach in the treatment of offenders in Canada. The RNR model has resulted in not only improvements in the assessment of offenders but also reductions in recidivism for those offenders who participated in treatment programs based on this model (Bonta & Andrews, 2017).] As its name indicates, the three principles underlying the model are offender risk, need, and responsivity (Bonta & Andrews, 2017). The risk principle states that correctional programs will be most effective (i.e., reduce recidivism) if the most intensive levels of programming are directed at moderate and higher risk offenders. The need principle states that the appropriate targets of treatment are **criminogenic risk factors**. These factors are different from the non-criminogenic aspects of the offender or his or her circumstances (such as personal distress or social class), which are not empirically related to criminality. Finally, the responsivity principle states that the most successful **interventions** are those that use treatments known to be effective in changing behaviour (e.g., cognitive-behavioural strategies) and treatment delivery strategies that are sensitive to offenders' individual learning styles (Bonta & Andrews, 2017).

Correctional Treatment

The effectiveness of correctional programs in reducing recidivism by targeting offender risks and needs has been well documented in the empirical literature (Andrews, Bonta, & Hoge, 1990; Andrews, Zinger, et al., 1990; Bonta & Andrews, 2017). CSC provides a series of treatment programs designed to address offenders' correctional, educational, social, and vocational risks and needs. Correctional programs typically address key dynamic criminogenic risk factors such as anti-social attitudes and substance use. Educational and vocational programs target other criminogenic risk factors such as poor education and vocational achievement through academic and literacy skill development. Social programs aid offenders in developing necessary social skills that aim to improve their overall reintegration potential (CSC, 2016d).

Correctional Service Canada's Evaluation of Correctional Programs

A comprehensive review of CSC's programs, including violence prevention programs, sex offender programs, and community maintenance programs, was conducted by CSC's evaluation branch in 2007–8 (Nafekh et al., 2009). The survey involved a large sample of first-time federal offenders (more than 48,000) who had been incarcerated between 1997 and 2007. The inmate sample was divided into two groups: those who had participated in programming and those who had not. The bulk of the respondents were male (95 percent) and, of those, 82 percent were non-Indigenous. The majority of the non-Indigenous sample were housed in medium (62 percent) or minimum (30 percent) security facilities, and their average sentence length (excluding those serving life sentences) was 3.7 years. The outcomes of interest included violent institutional misconducts; non-violent institutional misconducts; substance-related institutional misconducts; release on parole; re-admission for technical revocation; re-admission for new non-violent offence; and re-admission for new violent offence (Nafekh et al., 2009).

In their summary of results, the evaluation authors noted that, with the exception of sex offender programs, some discrepancy existed in referral rates and program participation rates: inmates who were eligible for programs were not being referred, and inmates who were referred to programs did not necessarily attend. Typical reasons for not attending programs included the following: inmate refused (65.4 percent), not enough time to complete the program (36.3 percent), programs not currently available (35.9 percent), or too long a waiting list for programs (18.4 percent) (Nafekh et al., 2009).

At the same time, the evaluation authors reported that inmates who did participate in programs responded to treatment and were more likely to be granted parole, although such participation had little effect in reducing institutional infractions. Post-release outcomes such as technical revocation, violent offences, and non-violent offences, were lower for program participants, especially those who completed the entire program, which suggests that correctional treatment can have long-term benefits. These outcomes were most evident for participants whose treatment program targets consistently matched assessed risk and needs. By contrast, and consistent with research results reported by Bonta and Andrews (2017), poorer outcomes were noted for participants whose program treatment targets did not consistently match assessed risk and needs (Nafekh et al., 2009).

The authors concluded that, in general, the delivery of correctional programming is cost effective in terms of a reduction in the number of days incarcerated through earlier release and more days in the community, post-release. However, they raised concerns about CSC's ability to meet the needs of specific offender subgroups, particularly inmates with mental health needs and learning disabilities, and inmates housed in higher security classification facilities (Nafekh et al., 2009).

Integrated Correctional Program Model

More recently, CSC has begun implementing the Integrated Correctional Program Model (ICPM) for male offenders, which is designed to address multiple risk factors concurrently. The ICPM has three program streams: multi-target programs, sex offender programs, and Indigenous multi-target programs (CSC, 2014a). A key objective of the ICPM is to ensure that offenders have timely access to appropriate levels of programming throughout the course of their sentence. According to a 2015 report by the Auditor General, this objective appears to be being met, although it has not necessarily translated into earlier parole release for offenders in the program (Auditor General of Canada, 2015).

CSC has conducted a preliminary evaluation of the effectiveness of the ICPM, which shows recidivism rates are 10 percent better in the Pacific region, where the ICPM is operational, compared to the Prairie region, where the model has yet to be implemented (Motiuk, 2016).

Beyond the obvious reductions in harm to persons and property brought about by reduced recidivism, a study by Romani, Morgan, Gross, and McDonald (2012) shows significant cost savings as well. They compared the outcomes of three approaches to correctional programming: those that employed traditional criminal **sanctions** (e.g., incarceration and probation), non-RNR treatment programs, and RNR treatment programs. The authors reported that the average cost per 1 percent reduction in recidivism was seven times less for RNR interventions versus non-RNR interventions, and 20 times less for RNR interventions versus traditional criminal sanctions. Further, the effectiveness of RNR programs was consistently greater on average than the effectiveness of either the criminal sanctions or non-RNR program groups. These findings suggest that investment in RNR-based correctional programming is both effective and economical, thereby addressing concerns of both legislators and taxpayers alike.

sanction
A penalty, such as a fine, probation, or incarceration, imposed on a person found guilty of a criminal offence.

Conditional Release

In Canada, the vast majority of federal inmates will eventually be released into the community. As such, one of the main purposes of the correctional system is to maximize inmates' community reintegration potential while minimizing their risk of harm to the public. It aims to do this through a process of graduated release into the community. The governing legislation is the CCRA, whose underlying principle is that risk reduction can best be achieved if offenders are encouraged to participate in programs that address their criminogenic needs while they are still under sentence (i.e., prior to their warrant expiry date). After that point, offenders are no longer legally under the supervision of the correctional system. As such, the CCRA works to ensure that a custodial sentence is used for its intended purpose—helping offenders reduce their risk to reoffend through participation in effective correctional programming. The CCRA also sets out a schedule of conditional release dates—dates at which an offender is eligible to apply for release to the community, while remaining under the supervision of the correctional system.

IN-CLASS EXERCISE

Correctional Services Legislation

Consult the provincial or territorial legislation for adult corrections for your jurisdiction and locate the following elements: the correctional services' mandate and mission statement, the types of services provided by the service, and the expected outcomes for in-custody and community-based treatments delivered by that service.

Provincial and Territorial Correctional Systems

As indicated previously, the provinces and territories are responsible for adult offenders who have been sentenced to two years less a day as well, as for offenders under 18 years of age (this latter population is discussed in Chapter 12). Correctional services in each province and territory are governed by specific legislation and, for the most part, the types of services provided are relatively similar. For example, all provinces and territories operate secure custody facilities for convicted male and female adults and youth, and are responsible for administering community-based sentences.

The provinces and territories are also responsible for the detention of individuals on remand. Individuals on remand include convicted offenders awaiting sentencing, accused individuals awaiting a bail hearing, or those who have been denied bail and are detained prior to or during their trial. The decision to deny bail is based on the following criteria: whether the individual is a flight risk; whether the individual poses a risk of harm to the public; and whether the individual's release may undermine confidence in the administration of justice (Webster, Doob, & Meyers, 2009).

Across all provinces and territories, remand populations have been steadily increasing since 1986 (Johnson, 2003; Kong & Peters, 2008), and remanded offenders currently outnumber sentenced offenders in provincial and territorial custody (Webster et al., 2009). The upward trend in bail remands is the result in part of an increase in the number of charges and court appearances by an accused per case (Webster et al., 2009). For example, in 2007 almost 30 percent of cases in Ontario required three or more court appearances before a decision regarding bail was reached (Webster et al., 2009). This reality sits in contrast with the expectations laid out in bail legislation, which presumes that for the majority of accused, one court appearance should be sufficient for bail determination. As Figure 9.3 shows, remands represented almost 60 percent of offenders in detention in Canada in 2014–15, although rates vary considerably per province and territory (Perreault, 2014; Reitano, 2016; Statistics Canada, 2015). Of note, only Quebec and the Yukon have shown meaningful decreases in the percentage of remands from 2011–12 to 2014–15.

The presence of remands in provincial and territorial jails is having a significant impact on the management of correctional facilities. For example, jails have a limited capacity to absorb additional inmates, particularly inmates who, because of their status, are detained for undefined terms, must be kept separate from sentenced inmates, and have little or no access to correctional programming or other activities (Webster, Doob, & Myers, 2009). The impact of increasing numbers of remands is expected to be amplified by the *Safe Streets and Communities Act* of 2012 (discussed in detail later in the chapter), which is

FIGURE 9.3 **Remands as a Percentage of Total Admissions, 2011–12 to 2014–15**

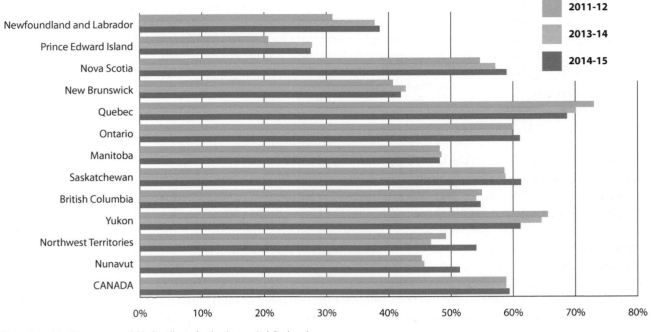

Note: Complete data was unavailable for Alberta for the time period displayed.
Sources: Perreault (2014), Reitano (2016), and Statistics Canada (2015).

projected to increase provincial and territorial correctional populations. The combined consequences of increased numbers of inmates include overcrowding, constraints on conditions of confinement, reduced access to treatment and programming, and increased demands on provincial and territorial budgets. The increase in the number of provincial and territorial inmates is reflected in the cost of correctional services, which was $2.16 billion in 2013–14, an increase of 56.2 percent since 2004–5 (Public Safety Canada, 2016).

Community-Based Sentences

Community-based sentences allow offenders to serve their sentence while living in the community. A community-based sentence serves two primary purposes: (1) it affords the criminal justice system a means of applying a suitable sanction in response to anti-social behaviour; and (2) it affords the criminal justice system a means of applying a suitable sanction without removing the offender from his or her community network and responsibilities (i.e., family, work, school, etc.). From both perspectives, community sanctions are more cost effective than custody and, as a response to less serious offences, are in keeping with the justice system's "least restrictive" principle.

As is the case with the federal correctional system, the overriding priority of provincial and territorial correctional systems is public safety. Provinces and territories work to meet this goal through the provision of a number of community-based sentencing options, including probation, Intensive Support and Supervision Program (ISSPs), conditional sentences, and community service. Provincial and territorial corrections are also supported by a number of non-governmental agencies that provide services and programming for offenders in the community. These include the Salvation Army, St. Leonard's Society, the Elizabeth Fry Society, and the John Howard Society. Collectively, these agencies play an integral role in contributing to the management and treatment of offenders.

A diversity of perspectives exists on the use of community-based sentences. Experienced corrections professionals recognize the benefits of such options, having witnessed first-hand the effect that community-based sentences can have in reducing criminal behaviour. However, victims of crime may feel resentful that an offender is seemingly not being sufficiently "punished" or may feel vulnerable at the prospect of encountering the offender in the community. It is also important to note that community-based sentences provide offenders with an opportunity to apply skills learned through programming in the "real world." This is key to successful reintegration and has been confirmed through research examining the effects of rehabilitation delivered in community versus custody settings (Andrews, Zinger, et al., 1990). This result is further enhanced when community-based programs follow the RNR principles described earlier (Bonta & Andrews, 2017).

Probation

Probation is the most commonly used sentence in Canadian corrections (Reitano, 2016). Between 2004–5 and 2010–11, the number of offenders on probation increased steadily from 92,922 to 101,825, but in 2013–14, the number of offenders on probation had declined to 84,905 (Public Safety Canada, 2016). Probation orders vary in length, but they are no longer than three years. They may be used on their own or in combination with a period of custody (i.e., two years less a day) and/or other community sanctions (e.g., fines, community service). Suspended sentences (whereby an offender's sentence is "suspended" based on the observance of specific conditions) and intermittent sentences (whereby an offender serves a custody sentence at designated times, such as weekends) are also available as probation options. In issuing a probation order, judges consider the following criteria: the nature and degree of seriousness of the offence; the degree of risk to the community posed by the offender; and the offender's specific needs (Weinrath, 2013).

One of the strengths of probation orders is that, in length and scope, they can be relatively tailored to the individual offender. This approach is consistent with the RNR principles, which emphasize that the greatest reductions in recidivism are achieved by targeting the criminogenic risk factors of moderate and higher risk offenders (Bonta & Andrews, 2017). At the same time, there are also standard conditions for all offenders on probation: keep the peace and be of good behaviour; notify the probation officer of changes in circumstances (i.e., address, employment, etc.); and appear before the court as necessary.

Intensive Support and Supervision Programs

ISSPs were first developed in the United Stated in the 1980s as a sentence "in between" custody and probation, one which reflected the more punitive philosophy of the period's correctional climate. The intention was for probation officers to manage smaller caseloads, thereby allowing them to provide more intensive supervision of offenders in the community. In reality, ISSPs, which are often combined with electronic monitoring and/or house arrest, have led to higher revocation rates for technical violations (i.e., breach of probation conditions), but not necessarily higher rates of recidivism. The available research suggests that, in general, ISSPs have not been effective in reducing recidivism

(Aos, Miller, & Drake, 2006; Bonta, Wallace-Capretta, & Rooney, 2000; Petersilia & Turner, 1989). However, their effectiveness does improve when they are paired with evidence-based rehabilitative treatments (Bottos, 2008). Weinrath (2013) has concluded that ISSPs may yet prove useful, but not in the absence of more substantive treatment programs that target higher risk offenders, which is in keeping with Bonta and Andrews's (2017) RNR principles.

Conditional Sentences

First introduced in 1996, conditional sentences were designed to provide the courts with an alternative to custody while continuing to hold offenders accountable for their actions. They are typically used in lieu of custody for offenders who present minimal risk of harm to the public. Conditional sentences impose strict conditions on offenders in the community which, if breached, can lead to the imposition of additional restrictions or a period of incarceration. Recent legislative changes introduced by the *Safe Streets and Communities Act* will see restrictions on the use of conditional sentences as a community-based sentencing option.

Community Service Orders

A community service order is imposed by the court and affords offenders the opportunity to make reparations to communities that have been harmed by their criminal actions. Community service orders generally take the form of an assigned number of hours of volunteer work with local agencies such as food banks, second-hand clothing depots, or community centres.

Pre-Sentence Reports

The key to the success of a community-based sentence is striking a balance between minimizing risk of harm to the public while maximizing offenders' reintegration potential. Pre-sentence reports represent one of the ways in which this balance is reached. For the majority of provincial and territorial offenders, a pre-sentence report is ordered by the judge prior to passing sentence. It is typically prepared by a probation officer and includes details of the offender's background, any mitigating and aggravating circumstances surrounding the offence, as well as details of the offender's social support networks (e.g., family, community), risk and need factors, necessary correctional programming, and any other information that may benefit the judge in reaching an appropriate sentencing decision, as per the *Criminal Code* (s 721).

Current Controversies and Future Concerns

Safe Streets and Communities Act

For more on Bill C-10 (*Safe Streets and Communities Act*), see Chapter 8.

The *Safe Streets and Communities Act*, commonly known as Bill C-10, was proclaimed into law in March 2012. It embodied a number of amendments to nine existing pieces of legislation and effected significant changes to sentencing and parole eligibility, among other corrections issues. Specifically, Bill C-10 expanded the use of mandatory minimum sentences for selected sexual offences (e.g., child pornography, sexual interference; Ricciardelli, 2014) and drug offences (Webster, 2012). In the case of drug offences, Bill C-10 amended the *Controlled Drugs and Substances Act* to include a six-month minimum sentence for those convicted of growing from 6 to 200 cannabis plants, a one-year minimum sentence for drug offences involving violence, and a two-year minimum sentence for drug offences in which the offender used the services of or involved someone under 18 years of age. In addition, increases in inmate populations, especially at the provincial and territorial levels, are anticipated as Bill C-10 restricts the use of conditional sentences and amends the *Youth Criminal Justice Act* such that convicted youth will receive more custodial and adult-level sentences.

SIDEBAR

Two Views on the Safe Streets and Communities Act (Bill C-10)

Rob Nicholson, who was the Conservative government's justice minister when the Act was passed, said:

> These are very reasonable measures. They go after those who sexually exploit children, people in the child pornography business and it goes after drug traffickers. This will be welcomed, particularly by victims, those involved with law enforcement and, as we know, Canadians are supportive of what we are doing in this area … . [T]his sends the message out to people that if you get involved with this kind of activity, there will be consequences. (Cohen, 2012)

Writing in the *Toronto Star*, Trinda L. Ernst (2011) commented:

> Bill C-10 is titled The Safe Streets and Communities Act—an ironic name, considering that Canada already has some of the safest streets and communities in the world and a declining crime rate. This bill will do nothing to improve that state of affairs but, through its overreach and overreaction to imaginary problems, Bill C-10 could easily make it worse. It could eventually create the very problems it's supposed to solve.
>
> Bill C-10 will require new prisons; mandate incarceration for minor, non-violent offences; justify poor treatment of inmates and make their reintegration into society more difficult. Texas and California, among other jurisdictions, have already started down this road before changing course, realizing it cost too much and made their justice system worse. Canada is poised to repeat their mistake.

What Do You Think?

- Do you think most Canadians support "tough on crime" measures, as the justice minister stated?
- Which of the two views above do you agree with, and why?

Federal prison populations are also likely to increase as a consequence of changes to the PBC's decision-making process under Bill C-10. That is, Bill C-10 eliminates the reference in the CCRA to the "least restrictive principle" (i.e., balancing the imperative of maintaining public safety while applying the least restrictive option in terms of offender disposition) in making parole decisions. Bill C-10 also mandates that unsuccessful parole applicants must wait longer to reapply. Finally, more restrictive eligibility criteria for conditional sentences will result in offenders receiving more, and longer, custody sentences.

Collectively, these legislative changes have the potential to significantly increase the population of Canada's prisons, which can lead to overcrowding, a condition which may contribute to increased levels of institutional infractions. Further, it remains to be seen just how governments will afford these projected increases in custody populations.

When Bill C-10 was introduced, the then-Conservative government indicated that the associated costs were in the range of $78.6 million over five years, but it failed to provide any costing analysis (White, 2011). Cost estimates vary, but all are consistent in projecting that the changes created by Bill C-10 will result in the need for additional resources and expenditures across the justice system, including courts, corrections, and community services (e.g., probation). Moreover, most concur that the bulk of the additional resource costs will fall to the provinces and territories. For example, the Office of the Parliamentary Budget Officer estimated that changes to the eligibility criteria for conditional sentences would cost the federal government $8 million, while the cost to provincial governments would be in the order of $137 million (Yalkin & Kirk, 2012). Similarly, the Institut de recherche et d'informations socio-économiques (IRIS), an independent Quebec-based non-profit social policy research organization, assessed the projected cost of additional prison spaces, one of Bill C-10's expected outcomes (Hébert & Michaud, 2011). Their report estimated that construction costs for new spaces would be in the range of $18 billion for federal, provincial, and territorial governments, with approximately $1 billion of that falling to the provinces and territories. Ongoing operational and maintenance costs were estimated to be $1.6 billion annually at the federal level and $2.2 billion annually for the provinces and territories (Hébert & Michaud, 2011). Individual provinces and territories vary in their estimates of the potential impact of the legislation on their budgets ("National Crime Bill," 2012).

Notably, both the Ontario and Quebec governments have stated unequivocally that they will not assume responsibility for any increases to their correctional budgets that result from the introduction of Bill C-10 (Fitzpatrick, 2011; White, 2011). Indeed, critics of the legislation have been vocal in their objections to the changes to correctional policy heralded by the legislation. Eighty-seven witnesses gave testimony to the House of Commons Standing Committee on Justice and Human Rights prior to third reading of the bill, including individuals from professional associations (i.e., Canadian Bar Association, Canadian Psychiatric Association), offender advocates (i.e., Canadian Association of Elizabeth Fry Societies, John Howard Society of Canada, Office of the Correctional Investigator), and academic researchers (i.e., Anthony Doob, PhD, Ivan Zinger, PhD). The legislation also provoked considerable debate beyond the committee level (Iftene & Manson, 2013; Lau & Martin, 2012; Pomerance, 2013; Rudin, 2013; Webster, 2012). Most recently, the Ontario Court of Appeal ruled that mandatory minimum sentences for weapons possession constitute "cruel and unusual punishment" (Canadian Press, 2013).

For the most part, criticisms of Bill C-10 have reflected a general concern regarding (1) the speed with which the "omnibus" legislation was rushed through Parliament, thereby limiting debate (i.e., first reading: September 20, 2011; royal assent: March 13, 2012); (2) the failure of the former Conservative government to consult the extensive empirical record that exists regarding "what works" in controlling crime and reducing recidivism; and (3) the former federal government's cavalier dismissal of the need for detailed and accurate cost estimates of the legislation's impact on federal and provincial budgets.

With the installation of a new federal government in October 2015, Bill C-10 may be revisited. In light of the myriad priorities on its political agenda (i.e., Indigenous reconciliation, climate change, terrorism, and the economy), the Liberal federal government would need to make a concerted commitment to revise and repeal aspects of the bill. Shortly after taking office, Prime Minister Justin Trudeau charged the minister of justice with a wholesale review of the sweeping changes brought about by Bill C-10 (Fine & White, 2015; Trudeau, 2015), although that review has yet to be undertaken.

> ### What Do You Think?
>
> Should reforms or improvements to the criminal justice system be a higher priority for the federal government?

Administrative Segregation

Recall the story of Jack McCann, discussed in the opening case study of Part Four. There is, perhaps, no single corrections issue that has galvanized debate in Canada as has the use of administrative segregation, or solitary confinement, particularly in the last decade. Since the tragic death of Ashley Smith in 2007 (discussed in the opening case study of Part Five), the merits of administrative segregation, the frequency and context of its application, the characteristics of those who experience it, and its functional effects have preoccupied professionals and the general population alike.

As noted earlier in this chapter, administrative segregation is distinct from disciplinary segregation. Disciplinary segregation is an institutional sanction of specified duration that is used in response to inmate misconduct. By contrast, administrative segregation is typically used as a means of removing an inmate who may cause harm to staff and/or other inmates or who is at risk of being victimized by others. Assignment to administrative segregation may be voluntarily or involuntarily.

What does research say about the effects of administrative segregation? Morgan et al., (2016) undertook two meta-analytical reviews to shed light on the matter. Review One included 14 studies published between 2002 and 2016 on predominantly adult male samples in US prisons. It measured the effects of administrative segregation on psychological functioning, and medical, psychophysiological, and behavioural outcomes. Review Two included 19 studies published between 1963 and 2014 on predominantly adult male American (42 percent) and Canadian (42 percent) samples. It measured the effects of administrative segregation on behavioural functioning, physical health, cognitive functioning, mental health, anti-social indicators, and social interaction. Collectively, the two reviews included 209 estimates of the effects of between 2 to 12 months of administrative segregation on inmates in relation to the outcomes noted above.

The results of Review One indicated that the effect of administrative segregation on psychological functioning ranged from weak to moderate. That is, inmates in administrative segregation tended to have slightly higher levels of hostility and anxiety than their non-administrative segregation counterparts. Consistent with that finding, the administrative segregation group also exhibited higher levels of sensory arousal, but there was no difference between the two groups on measures of major mental illness (i.e., psychosis, paranoid ideation, etc.). Nor was there any difference in levels of somatization (i.e., expressions of physical symptoms as a function of mental illness), anger, or cognitive functioning. With respect to behavioural outcomes, the administrative segregation group had a slightly higher post-release recidivism rate than the non-administrative segregation group, but there was no difference between the two groups in the rate of institutional misconducts (Morgan et al., 2016).

The results of Review Two indicated that the effect of administrative segregation on overall behavioural functioning was modest. Moreover, the administrative segregation group had a slightly higher rates of self-injury and recidivism as compared with the non-administrative segregation group (Morgan et al., 2016). Similar negative effects of administrative segregation were reported for physical health as well as cognitive functioning, although few studies were involved in this comparison. The effect of administrative segregation on mental health indices was in the medium range and was largely accounted for by higher levels of anxiety among administrative segregation inmates. This group also scored higher on anti-social indicators, but no differential effect was found on social interaction.

How should we interpret these findings? The results of the two reviews were generally consistent in reporting that the effects of administrative segregation on inmate functioning and behaviour were in the weak to moderate range (Morgan et al., 2016). Further, when study quality was taken into account, the most methodologically rigorous studies produced smaller effect sizes (i.e., weaker relationships outcome) than did studies with poor quality designs.

While the results of the two reviews did indicate a measurable effect of administrative segregation on some outcomes, the findings on the effects of administrative segregation in these reviews cannot be characterized as extremely negative, and certainly not torturous (Grassian, 1983; Scharff-Smith, 2006). Even in the case of increased self-injury in response to administrative segregation, as reported in Review Two, very few studies reported this effect. Moreover, the question of whether inmates who experienced administrative segregation had a history of self-injury prior to their being housed in administrative segregation was not specified. This distinction is important because research indicates that inmates who self-injure are also more likely to have higher rates of institutional misconducts than inmates who do not self-injure (Smith & Kaminski, 2010), which places them at higher risk of being segregated. In addition, as noted by the OCI (Sapers, 2016), the correctional system tends to respond to self-injurious behaviours from a security rather than a mental health perspective. Such policies may contribute to the self-injurious behaviours found among the administrative segregation inmates in these samples.

The findings from the two reviews by Morgan et al. (2016) do not provide licence for an increase in the use of administrative segregation, nor do the research authors recommend such a policy. A key question that the findings raise is whether administrative segregation produces more negative effects than incarceration in general. The studies reviewed by Morgan et al. (2016) suggest that this may not be the case. They reported that, for 8 of 13 outcomes, inmates in administrative segregation did not differ statistically from non-administrative segregation inmates with respect to self-injury, victimization, cognitive functioning, mood-emotion, anger and aggression, psychosis, hypersensitivity and hyperactivity, and social interaction.

Further, reviews of the effects of regular incarceration on inmate functioning (Bonta & Gendreau, 1990; Gendreau & Labrecque, in press; Gendreau & Smith, 2012; Jonson, 2013; Smith, Goggin, & Gendreau, 2002) are consistent with the effects of administrative segregation as reported by Morgan et al. (2016). Morgan et al. (2016) acknowledged the importance of understanding how environmental factors such as prison culture, staff–inmate relations, and overcrowding may affect the kinds of outcomes examined in their reviews. For example, research on general prison conditions indicates that unpredictable regimes in which relations between staff and inmates are characterized as disparaging and demeaning (see Weinrath, 2016) combined with limited (or non-existent) access to effective rehabilitation programming can result in compromised psychological functioning among inmates (Gendreau & Bonta, 1984; Gendreau & Labrecque, in press; Gendreau & Thériault, 2011; Vantour, 1975). Further, offender characteristics (i.e., coping skills, mental health status) may also play a role in responses to administrative segregation.

The present debate about the use of administrative segregation in Canada has sparked calls for its abolition among jurists, offender advocates, and politicians alike (Pate, 2016; Fine & White, 2015; Fine & Wingrove, 2014; Kirkup, 2016). The available evidence, however, does not provide resounding support that administrative segregation has overwhelmingly negative effects (i.e., permanent psychological debilitation). Moreover, there are the practicalities for prison administrators who must deal with potentially dangerous inmates. To that end, additional research is needed to further explain the impact of administrative segregation on inmate behaviour and functioning as well as to provide clarification regarding the clinical considerations of its use.

Some may dismiss the age-old cry for additional research as a convenient way of avoiding taking a stand on a controversial issue. Instead, it is meant to underscore the limited utility of individual studies or small study samples. Recall the two reviews by Morgan et al. (2016), which included only 33 studies. As Hunt (1997) has documented, how we "take stock" of a research area is through repeated studies that can contribute to large-scale meta-analytical reviews of a literature. This process may take more time than many are prepared to wait, but it remains the most useful strategy to arrive at sound conclusions about an issue (Hunter & Schmidt, 1996) and is particularly germane to advancing social policy research.

To that end, Gendreau and Labrecque (in press) offer the following suggestions to researchers regarding the study of administrative segregation:

1. Researchers need to specify the administrative segregation conditions that inmates are experiencing in order to ensure comparative consistency across research studies. For example, in some jurisdictions, inmates in administrative segregation may be more or less deprived of sensory stimulation (i.e., books, TV, social interaction). To verify the effects of administrative segregation, the relative degree of deprivation being experienced needs to be reported. One stumbling block to achieving this goal is the inherent difficulty in conducting research on prison populations. Few jurisdictions have their own research staff, which means that collaboration between correctional agencies and outside researchers is generally required.

2. While most inmates are sent to administrative segregation involuntarily, about one-quarter of Canadian inmates in administrative segregation are there voluntarily (Morgan et al., 2016). Obviously, this status may influence inmates' pre-detention behaviours and/or have differential effects on inmates' responses to administrative segregation. Again, studies should clarify the nature of the inmate samples who experience administrative segregation.

3. More research is needed to understand the characteristics of inmates who may respond poorly to administrative segregation versus those who may not. Preliminary research suggests that the former group includes inmates who are more likely to seek stimulation, be prone to impulsivity, and/or have limited coping skills. With this information in hand, alternate decisions regarding confinement can be made by prison administrators.

Gendreau and Labrecque (in press) also offer the following suggestions to clinicians/administrators regarding the use of administrative segregation:

1. Mentally ill inmates should be diverted from administrative segregation and detained in more suitable circumstances (i.e., prison hospitals) in order to provide an appropriate level of clinical monitoring (i.e., medication management). The available literature provides details regarding the appropriate psychiatric screening tools to use in determining inmates' mental health status (Martin, Colman, Simpson, & McKenzie, 2013; Smith, Gendreau, & Goggin, 2007).
2. Inmates should not be detained in administrative segregation simply because a correctional system lacks more creative responses to inmates' disruptive behaviours. The available literature on predictors of prison misconducts (Gendreau, Goggin, & Law, 1997), the risk measures that are suitable to identify inmates who are prone to such behaviours (Campbell, French, & Gendreau, 2009), and the interventions most effective in reducing institutional infractions (French & Gendreau, 2006) provide direction in that regard. Limiting the number of available administrative segregation spaces and establishing limits on maximum days in administrative segregation will also encourage correctional systems to adopt more effective strategies to deal with inmates' challenging behaviours.

Such policy changes will contribute to more humane conditions for inmates that, coupled with appropriate treatment interventions (Bonta & Andrews, 2017) will, in turn, contribute to improved public safety overall.

Offender Health Needs

In many jurisdictions, an increasing proportion of offenders admitted to prison are reported to have collateral health needs. For example, in a recent survey of correctional services in 13 countries, including Canada (CSC, 2016c), respondents identified mental health needs (61 percent), addictions (61 percent), and physical health needs (56 percent) as significant challenges to their systems (see Figure 9.4). The majority of correctional services (53 percent) noted the need to tailor programming and physical space to meet the mental health needs of inmates and were attempting to do so by expanding partnerships with community agencies, recruiting qualified staff, and incorporating technology (i.e., electronic health records, telehealth services, etc.) in the delivery of some health care services (CSC, 2016c).

With respect to CSC, as of March 2015, 5 percent of the staff in custody facilities were health care workers, 44 percent were correctional officers, 5.1 percent were program staff, and 3.8 percent were parole officers and supervisors (Public Safety Canada, 2016). With the exception of correctional officers and program staff, the proportion of all other

FIGURE 9.4   Proportion of Organizations Facing Challenges and Ongoing Transformation in the Area of Offender Health

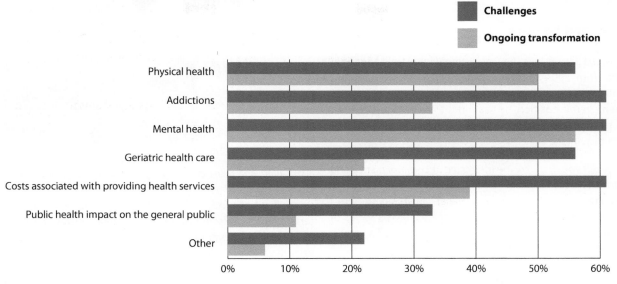

Source: Correctional Service Canada (2016c).

staff, including health care workers, has decreased slightly since 2006. As of March 2015, 0.4 percent of the staff in community supervision were health care workers, 1.6 percent were program staff, and 3.9 percent were parole officers and supervisors. The proportion of health care workers and program staff increased slightly since 2006.

At the same time, recent research by Stewart, Nolan, Sapers, Power, Panaro, and Smith (2015) demonstrates that inmates entering Canadian federal prisons are presenting with significant physical and mental health conditions and at rates exceeding those in the general population. For example, Stewart et al. (2015) reported that between April and September of 2012, 19 percent of 2,273 new admissions self-reported having cardiovascular disease, 15 percent had asthma, and approximately 10 percent had a blood-borne virus (i.e., HIV/AIDS, hepatitis C). In the general Canadian population, 5 percent have cardiovascular disease, 8.5 percent have asthma, (Public Health Agency of Canada, 2016), and approximately 3 percent have a blood-borne virus (Public Health Agency of Canada, 2015). Clearly, offender populations are compromised by both serious chronic and infectious conditions that require treatment while they are under sentence—treatment the CSC is legislated to provide under the CCRA.

CAREER PROFILE

Howard Sapers

Howard Sapers was the Correctional Investigator of Canada from 2004 to 2016. He is now is an independent advisor on corrections reform for the Ontario government. In this position, he examines the use of segregation in prisons and works to improve corrections throughout the province.

How did you first become interested in criminal justice and corrections?
My interest began at Simon Fraser University, where I studied criminology. I was fortunate to have a series of summer jobs and work placements that offered a variety of criminal justice system experiences.

Describe your career path. How did you become the Correctional Investigator of Canada?
I wouldn't say I followed a path. I remained open to new opportunities. My original plan was to go to law school, but other interesting choices came along that were consistent with my values, so I pursued them. Prior to becoming the Correctional Investigator of Canada, I held other positions related to criminal justice, including executive director of the John Howard Society of Alberta and director of the Crime Prevention Investment Fund at the National Crime Prevention Centre.

Describe a typical day for you. What were some of your most important duties?
Days were rarely the same. My time was split between specific functions related to my mandate as an ombudsman—representing my office to the public, media, and Parliament—and fulfilling the role of a senior official within the federal public sector.

What were the most challenging and most rewarding aspects of your job?
Resolving both individual issues and encouraging systemic change. I also found fostering an environment that allows staff to develop and achieve their own goals was very rewarding.

What issues do you feel are most important to address in Canada's prisons? How do these practices and conditions affect recidivism and reintegration?
The number one issue is the growing overrepresentation of Indigenous Canadians in prisons and jails. This is a national human rights issue. Shifting resources to better meet the program, treatment, and vocational needs of offenders and refocusing efforts on community reintegration will have a positive effect on recidivism.

What—if any—changes have you seen in prison conditions since your June 2015 report (Sapers, 2015)? What changes would you still like to see?
Change comes slowly to corrections. Over the last few years, there have been improvements in mental health screening and in culturally appropriate programming for Indigenous offenders, but I have not noted significant positive changes since my 2015 report. Reducing the use of administrative segregation, closing gaps in correctional outcomes for Indigenous offenders, and enhanced approaches for responding to the needs of mentally ill offenders are all priority areas of concern.

It is noteworthy that, of the more than 6,000 complaints processed by the OCI in 2015–16, health care issues (11.9 percent) were of greatest concern to offenders followed by conditions of confinement (11.3 percent) and staff issues (6.4 percent) (see Figure 9.5) (Sapers, 2016). Indeed, the OCI has repeatedly highlighted concerns surrounding offenders' health care needs, particularly mental health care issues, and the provision of appropriate health services in its annual reports (Sapers, 2015, 2016). Further, health care was also a dominant concern for both Indigenous offenders (13.2 percent) and female offenders (11.0 percent). This underscores the need for ongoing monitoring of offender health status and the extent to which the correctional service is meeting those needs. To that point, corrections representatives from the federal, provincial, and territorial governments have recently committed to developing a framework to address offenders' mental health needs through the coordinated delivery of appropriate services (CSC, 2012b).

FIGURE 9.5   Offender Complaints Processed by the Office of the Correctional Investigator, 2015–16

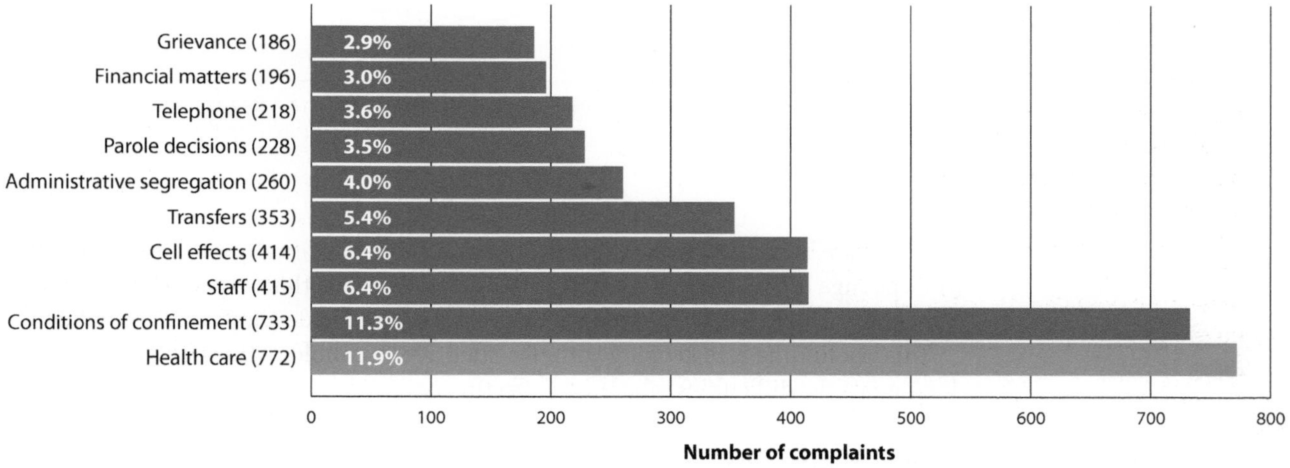

Number of complaints

Indigenous Offenders

By almost every measure, Indigenous offenders are overrepresented in the correctional system (see Chapter 11). They tend to serve more of their sentence than do non-Indigenous offenders prior to their first applications for day parole and full parole. Figure 9.6 presents the day parole and full parole grant rate for federal inmates. As the data indicates, Indigenous inmates are less likely than non-Indigenous inmates to be granted either day or full parole. Indigenous offenders are also more likely than non-Indigenous offenders to serve their sentence to warrant expiry, be classified as maximum security, and be revoked on parole (Sapers, 2016). For many Indigenous offenders, historical marginalization contributes to their correctional experience.

CSC is not unaware of these discrepancies and has developed a policy agenda that aims to provide effective Indigenous programming and address issues relevant to the Indigenous population (CSC, 2012a). A recent audit of the extent to which the service is meeting its objectives indicates that, while an appropriate policy framework is in place, there have been problems ensuring that the implementation and delivery of those policy

FIGURE 9.6   **Federal Parole Grant Rate: Aboriginal Versus Non-Aboriginal Offenders, 2005–6 to 2014–15**

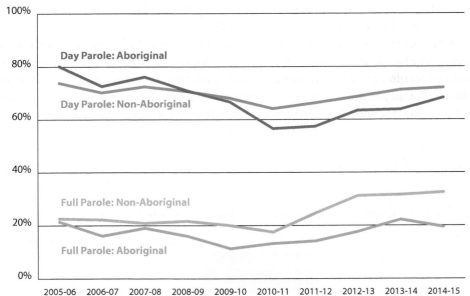

Source: Public Safety Canada (2016).

priorities are being effectively executed (CSC, 2012a). Specifically, the audit found that while change is occurring, it is taking place at a slower rate than expected. Importantly, front-line staff are not as engaged in the process as are the developers of the policy.

This last finding is in keeping with the extensive "technology transfer" literature that documents the difficulties inherent in effecting policy change at the organizational level (Goggin & Gendreau, 2006). A key impediment to successful change is the failure to adequately engage staff. Their "buy-in" requires comprehensive training prior to implementation, periodic "booster" sessions, and ongoing supervision post-implementation. As Borum (2003) noted, "good intentions and good ideas are not sufficient to produce a successful intervention" (p. 129). Ongoing review and monitoring of CSC's Indigenous policy initiative must be given priority by the service.

Vulnerable Populations

The needs of particular offender subpopulations extend beyond their criminogenic characteristics. These subpopulations include senior inmates (i.e., those 50 and over), inmates with Fetal Alcohol Spectrum Disorders (FASDs), and transgender inmates, among others. While their particular needs may differ, they share common concerns regarding support services and protection from other inmates.

Senior inmates may have health conditions that pre-date their incarceration and can present significant challenges to the safe operation of institutional facilities. For example, chronic conditions may require physical supports (i.e., walkers, wheelchairs, etc.) or treatment modalities (i.e., narcotics for pain management) that are difficult to accommodate in a prison context or whose delivery may compromise facility security. Further, such conditions necessarily add to the economic cost of delivering correctional services.

For discussion of the challenges presented to the corrections system by an aging inmate population, see Chapter 11.

Inmates with an FASD require specialized treatments and supports, something that the OCI highlighted in its most recent annual report by suggesting that CSC partner with community agencies who have expertise in this area to better respond to this population (Sapers, 2016).

With regard to transgender inmates, the OCI has noted that CSC's current policy should be updated in order to safeguard their rights and also to be consistent with general legal standards, both domestically and internationally, regarding their treatment, safety, and privacy needs while in custody (Sapers, 2016). We will engage in a more detailed examination of vulnerable prison populations in Chapter 11.

Conclusion

When viewed through the lens of history, Canada's correctional landscape has matured considerably from the monolithic and brutal system first unveiled in the early 1800s. Today's federal, provincial, and territorial correctional services must balance the need to safeguard the public with a mandate to rehabilitate offenders representing diverse populations and presenting with increasingly complex needs. And Canada is obliged to do so while maintaining the highest professional standards in meeting its responsibilities as a signatory to international conventions regarding the detention and treatment of offender populations (e.g., United Nations Office on Drugs and Crime, 2015). Indeed, Canada is generally regarded as a world leader in the management and delivery of correctional services.

That said, one should not be complacent regarding the progress made by Canada's correctional services over the last 200 years. Sustaining such progress requires a rigorous commitment to the goals of furthering public protection through the safe and humane management of offenders, both in custody and in the community. This will entail improved strategies to deal with the needs of subsets of the offender population. For example, the OCI has called for the creation of a Deputy Commissioner for Indigenous Corrections (Sapers, 2016). A related position was created to address the needs of female offenders following recommendations by the Arbour Commission (Canada, 1996). The outcome has been an unprecedented growth in services, programs, and research specific to female offenders in the last 20 years. A similar position focusing on Indigenous offenders could be the catalyst necessary to address more comprehensively the needs of this overrepresented offender population.

Other strategies include enhancing offenders' reintegration potential by further engaging with community agencies who offer support services for offenders. The importance of bridge-building initiatives between custody and community cannot be overstated, as they play a seminal role in reducing offender recidivism and, thereby, enhancing public safety.

Finally, correctional services rely on the contributions of researchers in the area to further our understanding of what works best for whom in particular contexts. For example, prisons that have incorporated the principles of RNR have shown reduced rates of institutional infractions and post-release recidivism as compared with systems that lack an RNR focus. To that end, we must insist that the policies and practices of our correctional services are evidence-based in order that they can best protect the public and provide humane treatment for offenders.

DISCUSSION QUESTIONS

1. How should the provinces and territories best respond to the increased costs of correctional services as a result of Bill C-10? How should they balance the demand for additional custody beds with the provision of community-based services?

2. What position should federal, provincial, and territorial correctional services take regarding the use of administrative segregation? What other means of controlling or safeguarding inmates could these services implement? Should the use of administrative segregation be abolished altogether or are there conditions under which its use could be better controlled? For example, should jurisdictions limit the number of available administrative segregation cells and/or the maximum number of days one can be detained in administrative segregation?

3. Correctional services are increasingly faced with the need to accommodate diverse populations such as senior or transgender offenders. What should the response of the correctional system be to the unique needs of such populations? For example, is it the responsibility of correctional services to provide health care to offenders with age-related acute and/or chronic conditions? What are the implications of providing health aids to older adults in terms of institutional security? How should the needs of vulnerable populations who may require segregation in order to ensure their protection from other inmates best be addressed?

4. The disproportionate incarceration of Indigenous people in Canada is a long-standing concern. Attempts have been made to effect change at the sentencing level (e.g., the *Gladue* decision). What other issues need to be addressed to see a substantive reduction in incarceration rates among Indigenous people?

5. The delivery of effective correctional programming implicitly depends on the adequate risk assessment of offenders' needs. What principles underlie the comprehensive assessment of an offender's risk status?

SUGGESTED FURTHER READINGS

Canadian Association of Elizabeth Fry Societies: http://www.caefs.ca.

Correctional Service Canada: http://www.csc-scc.gc.ca.

Correctional Service Canada. (2008). Speakers binder: Section 5—Overview of the management of offenders. Retrieved from http://www.csc-scc.gc.ca/text/pblct/sb-go/05-eng.shtml.

Correctional Service Canada. (2015). Beyond the fence: A virtual tour of a Canadian penitentiary. Retrieved from http://www.csc-scc.gc.ca/csc-virtual-tour/index-eng.shtml.

Correctional Service Canada. (2015). What happens after sentencing. Retrieved from http://www.csc-scc.gc.ca/vids/htm/whas-eng.shtml.

Corrections and Conditional Release Act, SC 1992 c 20.

John Howard Society of Canada: http://www.johnhoward.ca.

Office of the Correctional Investigator: http://www.oci-bec.gc.ca.

Statistics Canada Juristat: http://www.statcan.gc.ca/pub/85-002-x/index-eng.htm.

St. Leonard's Society of Canada: http://www.stleonards.ca.

REFERENCES

Andrews, D.A., Bonta, J., & Hoge, R.D. (1990). Classification for effective rehabilitation: Rediscovering psychology. *Criminal Justice and Behavior, 17*, 19–52.

Andrews, D.A., Zinger, I., Hoge, R.D., Bonta, J., Gendreau, P., & Cullen, F.T. (1990). Does correctional treatment work? A clinically relevant and psychologically informed meta-analysis. *Criminology, 28*, 369–404.

Aos, S., Miller, M., & Drake, E. (2006). *Evidence-based public policy options to reduce future prison construction, criminal justice costs, and crime rates* (Report No. 06-10-1201). Olympia, WA: Washington State Institute of Public Policy.

Auditor General of Canada. (2015). *Preparing male offenders for release—Correctional Service of Canada* (Report 6). Ottawa: Author.

Bonta, J., & Andrews, D.A. (2017). *The psychology of criminal conduct* (6th ed.). Cincinnati, OH: Anderson.

Bonta, J., & Gendreau, P. (1990). Re-examining the cruel and unusual punishment of prison life. *Law and Human Behavior, 14*, 347–372.

Bonta, J., Wallace-Capretta, S., & Rooney, J. (2000). A quasi-experimental evaluation of an intensive rehabilitation supervision program. *Criminal Justice and Behavior, 27*, 312–329.

Borum, R. (2003). Managing at-risk juvenile offenders in the community: Putting evidence-based principles into practice. *Journal of Contemporary Criminal Justice, 19*, 114–137.

Bottos, S. (2008). *An overview of electronic monitoring in corrections: The issues and implications.* Ottawa: Correctional Service Canada.

Campbell, M.A., French, S., & Gendreau, P. (2009). The prediction of violence in adult offenders: A meta-analytic comparison. *Criminal Justice and Behavior, 36*, 567–590.

Canada. (1938). *Report of the Royal Commission to investigate the penal system of Canada* (Archambault report). Ottawa: Author.

Canada. (1996). *Commission of inquiry into certain events at the Prison for Women in Kingston* (Arbour Commission). Ottawa: Author.

Canadian Press. (2013, November 12). Mandatory minimum sentences for gun crimes ruled unconstitutional. *Globe and Mail.* Retrieved from http://www.theglobeandmail.com/news/national/minimum-sentencing-law-for-gun-crimes-ruled-unconstitutional/article15387142/.

Cohen, T. (2012, March 12). Tories use majority to pass omnibus crime bill. *National Post.* Retrieved from http://news.nationalpost.com/news/canada/contentious-tory-crime-bill-passes-as-countrys-biggest-provinces-voice-concerns-over-costs.

Correctional Service Canada. (2012a). *Audit of the implementation of the Aboriginal corrections accountability framework.* Ottawa: Author.

Correctional Service Canada. (2012b). *Mental health strategy for corrections in Canada.* Ottawa: Author.

Correctional Service Canada. (2014a). *Integrated Correctional Program Model.* Ottawa: Author.

Correctional Service Canada. (2014b). *Research results: Women offenders.* Ottawa: Author.

Correctional Service Canada. (2015). Commissioner's directive 705-6: Correctional planning and criminal profile. Retrieved from http://www.csc-scc.gc.ca/acts-and-regulations/705-6-cd-eng.shtml.

Correctional Service Canada. (2016a). Serving time. Retrieved from http://www.csc-scc.gc.ca/correctional-process/002001-1000-eng.shtml.

Correctional Service Canada. (2016b). Institutional profiles. Retrieved from http://www.csc-scc.gc.ca/institutions/index-eng.shtml.

Correctional Service Canada. (2016c). *International survey of correctional services: Corrections in transformation* (No. SR-16-04). Ottawa: Author.

Correctional Service Canada. (2016d). Offender rehabilitation. Retrieved from http://www.csc-scc.gc.ca/correctional-process/002001-2000-eng.shtml.

Correctional Service Canada. (2017). *CSC statistics: Key facts and figures.* Ottawa: Author.

CTV.ca News Staff. (2009, March 5). Vince Li not criminally responsible for beheading. *CTV News.* Retrieved from http://www.ctvnews.ca/vince-li-not-criminally-responsible-for -beheading-1.375979.

Ernst, Trinda L. (2011). 10 reasons to oppose Bill C-10. *Toronto Star.* Retrieved from https://www .thestar.com/opinion/editorialopinion/2011/11/14/10_reasons_to_oppose_bill_c10.html.

Fine, S., & White, P. (2015, November 13). Trudeau calls for ban on long-term solitary confinement in federal prisons. *Globe and Mail.* Retrieved from http://www .theglobeandmail.com/news/national/trudeau-calls-for-implementation-of-ashley-smith -inquest-recommendations/article27256251/.

Fine, S., & Wingrove, J. (2014, December 11). Retired Supreme Court Justice Arbour slams practice of solitary confinement. *Globe and Mail.* Retrieved from http://www. theglobeandmail.com/news/national/retired-supreme-court-justice-arbour-slams -practice-of-solitary-confinement/article22036544/.

Fitzpatrick, M. (2011, November 1). Quebec will refuse to pay for omnibus crime bill. *CBC News.* Retrieved from http://www.cbc.ca/news/politics/quebec-will-refuse-to-pay-for -omnibus-crime-bill-1.1048561.

French, S., & Gendreau, P. (2006). Reducing prison misconducts: What works! *Criminal Justice and Behavior, 33,* 185–218.

Gendreau, P., & Bonta, J. (1984). Solitary confinement is not cruel and unusual punishment: Sometimes people are! *Canadian Journal of Criminology, 26,* 467–478.

Gendreau, P., Goggin, C., & Law, M. (1997). Predicting prison misconducts. *Criminal Justice and Behavior, 24,* 414–431.

Gendreau, P., & Labrecque, R.M. (in press). The effects of administrative segregation: A lesson in knowledge cumulation. In J. Wooldredge & P. Smith (Eds.), *Oxford handbook on prisons and imprisonment.* New York: Oxford University Press.

Gendreau, P., & Smith, P. (2012). Assessment and treatment strategies for correctional institutions. In J.A. Dvoskin, J.L. Skeem, R.W. Novaco, & K.S. Douglas (Eds.), *Using social science to reduce violent offending* (pp. 157–178). New York: Oxford University Press.

Gendreau, P., & Thériault, Y. (2011). Bibliotherapy for cynics revisited: Commentary on one year longitudinal study of the psychological effects of administrative segregation. (Corrections & Mental Health: An Update of the National Institute of Corrections). Retrieved from http://community.nicic.gov/blogs/mentalhealth/archive/2011/06/21/ bibliotherapy-for-cynics-revisited-commentary-on-one-year-longitudinal-study-of-the -psychological-effects-of-administrative-segregation.aspx.

Goggin, C., & Gendreau, P. (2006). The implementation and maintenance of quality services in offender rehabilitation programmes. In C.R. Hollin & E.J. Palmer (Eds.), *Offending behaviour programmes: Development, application, and controversies* (pp. 209–246). West Sussex, UK: John Wiley.

Grassian, S. (1983). Psychopathological effects of solitary confinement. *American Journal of Psychiatry, 140,* 1450–1454.

Hébert, G., & Michaud, J.-M. (2011). *Coûts et efficacité des politiques correctionnelles fédérales.* Montreal: Institut de recherche et d'informations socio-économiques (IRIS).

Hunt, M. (1997). *How science takes stock: The story of meta-analysis.* New York: Russell Sage.

Hunter, J.E., & Schmidt, F.L. (1996). Cumulative research knowledge and social policy formulation: The critical role of meta-analysis. *Psychology, Public Policy, and Law, 2,* 324–347.

Iftene, A., & Manson, A. (2013). Recent crime legislation and the challenge for prison health care. *Canadian Medical Association Journal, 185,* 886–889.

Johnson, S. (2003). Custodial remand in Canada, 1986/87 to 2000/01. *Juristat, 23*(7).

Johnston, N. (2000). *Forms of constraint: A history of prison architecture*. Chicago: University of Illinois Press.

Jonson, C.L. (2013). The effects of imprisonment. In F.T. Cullen & P. Wilcox (Eds.), *The Oxford handbook of criminological theory* (pp. 672–690). New York: Oxford University Press.

Kirkup, K. (2016, March 10). Prison watchdog calls for end to solitary for mentally ill inmates. *CBC News*. Retrieved from http://www.cbc.ca/news/politics/prison-watchdog-end-to -solitary-mental-health-inmates-1.3485315.

Kong, R., & Peters, V. (2008). Remand in adult corrections and sentencing patterns. *Juristat, 28*(9).

Lambert, S. (2017, February 10). Freedom granted to man who beheaded Greyhound bus passenger. *Toronto Star*. Retrieved from https://www.thestar.com/news/canada/2017/02/10/ freedom-granted-to-man-who-beheaded-passenger-on-greyhound-bus.html.

Lau, J., & Martin, R.E. (2012). *Health impacts of the Safe Streets and Communities Act (Bill C-10): Responding to mandatory minimum sentencing*. Vancouver: School of Population and Public Health, Collaborating Centre for Prison Health and Education.

Martin, M.S., Colman, I., Simpson, A., & McKenzie, K. (2013). Mental health screening tools in correctional institutions: A systematic review. *BMC Psychiatry, 13*, 529–548.

Morgan, R.D., Gendreau, P., Smith, P., Gray, A.L., Labrecque, R.M., MacLean, N., … Mills, J.F. (2016). Quantitative syntheses of the effects of administrative segregation on inmates' well-being. *Psychology, Public Policy, and the Law, 22*, 439–461.

Motiuk, L. (2016). Performance outcomes in the delivery of the Integrated Correctional Program Model (ICPM) to federal offenders (RIB 16-01). Ottawa: Correctional Service Canada.

Nafekh, M., Allegri, N., Stys, Y., & Jensen, T. (2009). Evaluation report: Correctional Service Canada's correctional programs. Retrieved from http://www.csc-scc.gc.ca/text/pa/cop-prog/ cp-eval-eng.shtml.

National crime bill adds $2M to N.B. budget. (2012, January 31). *CBC News*. Retrieved from http://www.cbc.ca/news/canada/new-brunswick/national-crime-bill-adds-2m-to-n-b -budget-1.1147972.

Pate, K. (2016, Spring). How Canada's prisons are failing women (and everyone else). *Herizons*, 24–30.

Perreault, S. (2014). *Adult correctional statistics in Canada: 2011/2012*. Ottawa: Canadian Centre for Justice Statistics.

Petersilia, J., & Turner, S. (1989). Comparing intensive and regular supervision of high-risk probationers: Early results from an experiment in California. *Crime and Delinquency, 36*, 87–111.

Pomerance, R.M. (2013). The new approach to sentencing in Canada: Reflections of a trial judge. *Canadian Criminal Law Review, 17*, 305–326.

Public Health Agency of Canada. (2015). *Summary: Estimates of HIV incidence, prevalence and proportion undiagnosed in Canada, 2014*. Ottawa: Author.

Public Health Agency of Canada. (2016). *Report on Hepatitis B and C in Canada, 2013*. Ottawa: Author.

Public Safety Canada. (2016). *Corrections and conditional release: Statistical overview, 2015*. Ottawa: Public Works and Government Services. Retrieved from https://www.publicsafety. gc.ca/cnt/rsrcs/pblctns/ccrso-2015/ccrso-2015-en.pdf.

Reitano, J. (2016). *Adult correctional statistics in Canada: 2014/2015*. Ottawa: Canadian Centre for Justice Statistics.

Ricciardelli, R. (2014). *Surviving incarceration : Inside Canadian prisons*. Waterloo, ON: Wilfred Laurier University Press.

Romani, C.J., Morgan, R.D., Gross, N.R., & McDonald, B.R. (2012). Treating criminal behavior: Is the bang worth the buck? *Psychology, Public Policy, and Law, 18*, 144–165.

Rudin, J. (2013). There must be some kind of way out of here: Aboriginal over-representation, Bill C-10, and the Charter of Rights. *Canadian Criminal Law Review, 17*, 349–363.

Sapers, H. (2015). *Annual report of the Office of the Correctional Investigator, 2014–2015.* Ottawa: Her Majesty the Queen in Right of Canada.

Sapers, H. (2016). *Annual report of the Office of the Correctional Investigator, 2015–2016.* Ottawa: Her Majesty the Queen in Right of Canada.

Scharff-Smith, P. (2006). The effects of solitary confinement on prison inmates: A brief history and review of the literature. In M. Tonry (Ed.), *Crime and justice: A review of research* (vol. 34, pp. 441–528). Chicago, IL: University of Chicago Press.

Smith, H.P., & Kaminski, R.J. (2010). Inmate self-injurious behaviors: Distinguishing characteristics within a retrospective study. *Criminal Justice and Behavior, 37*, 81–96.

Smith, P., Gendreau, P., & Goggin, C. (2007). What works in predicting psychiatric hospitalization and relapse: The specific responsivity assessment dimension of effective correctional treatment for mentally disordered offenders. In R. Ax & T. Fagan (Eds.), *Corrections, mental health, and social policy: International perspectives* (pp. 209–233). Springfield, IL: Charles C. Thomas.

Smith, P., Goggin, C., & Gendreau, P. (2002). *The effects of prison sentences and intermediate sanctions on recidivism: General effects and individual differences (2002–3).* Ottawa: Solicitor General Canada.

Statistics Canada. (2015). *Adult correctional statistics in Canada: 2013/2014.* Ottawa: Canadian Centre for Justice Statistics.

Stewart, L., Nolan, A., Sapers, J., Power, J., Panaro, L., & Smith, J. (2015). Chronic health conditions reported by male inmates newly admitted to Canadian federal penitentiaries. *Canadian Medical Association Journal Open, 3*, E97–E102.

Trudeau, J. (2015, November). Minister of justice and attorney general of Canada mandate letter. Retrieved from http://pm.gc.ca/eng/minister-justice-and-attorney-general-canada-mandate-letter.

United Nations Office on Drugs and Crime. (2015). *The United Nations standard minimum rules for the treatment of prisoners.* Vienna: Justice Section.

Vantour, J.A. (1975). *Report of the study group on dissociation.* Ottawa: Solicitor General Canada.

Walmsley, R. (2015). *World prison population list.* London: Institute for Criminal Policy Research.

Webster, C.M., Doob, A.N., & Meyers, N.M. (2009). The parable of Ms Baker: Understanding pre-trial detention in Canada. *Current Issues in Criminal Justice, 21*, 79–102.

Webster, P.C. (2012). Former Supreme Court justice blasts minimum sentences for marijuana users. *Canadian Medical Association Journal, 184*, E391–E392.

Weinrath, M. (2013). Probation. In J. Winterdyk & M. Weinrath (Eds.), *Adult corrections in Canada* (pp. 86–110). Whitby, ON: de Sitter.

Weinrath, M. (2016). *Behind the walls: Inmates and correctional officers on the state of Canadian prisons.* Vancouver, BC: UBC Press.

White, M. (2011, December 8). Controversial crime bill to cost Canadians $19 billion: Study. *Vancouver Sun.* Retrieved from http://www.vancouversun.com/Controversial+crime+bill+cost+Canadians+billion+study/5832700/story.html.

World Prison Brief. (n.d.). Highest to lowest—Prison population rate. Retrieved from http://www.prisonstudies.org/highest-to-lowest/prison_population_rate?field_region_taxonomy_tid=All.

Yalkin, T.R., & Kirk, M. (2012). *The fiscal impact of changes to eligibility for conditional sentences of imprisonment in Canada.* Ottawa: Office of the Parliamentary Budget Officer.

Conditional Release in Canada

LEARNING OUTCOMES

After reading this chapter, students will be able to:

- Explain the purposes of conditional release programs in Canada.
- Describe the types of conditional release that are used in Canadian correctional systems.
- Describe the conditional release experience for Indigenous offenders.
- Describe the conditional release process, and the nature of supervision and enforcement.
- Discuss how conditional release contributes—or does not contribute—to public safety.
- Discuss the major challenges and controversies surrounding conditional release.

Introduction

This chapter describes conditional release programs in Canada and examines whether they reduce recidivism. It also considers whether they reduce the number of people incarcerated and the associated costs of incarceration.

There are numerous conditional release laws, regulations, programs, and practices in Canada. It is beyond the scope of this chapter to address them all. Instead, this chapter will discuss the following key questions related to conditional release:

- What assumptions and purposes underlie conditional release?
- What types of conditional release are used with offenders?
- How are conditional release decisions made?
- What principles and practices guide the supervision and enforcement of those who are conditionally released?
- Do conditional release programs reduce crime?
- What challenges and controversies surround conditional release?

Owing to space limitations, greater emphasis will be placed on how conditional release is used within the federal correctional system, which administers prison sentences of two or more years. Sentences of less than two years' incarceration are administered by the provinces and territories. While provincial and territorial prison admissions far outnumber those of federal penitentiaries (225,776 compared with 8,323 in 2010, respectively; Statistics Canada, 2012), their conditional release practices vary from one another, precluding discussion here. It is worth noting that with the exception of Ontario and Quebec, which maintain their own independent provincial parole boards, conditional release decisions are made by the Parole Board of Canada (PBC) (formerly the National Parole Board) for inmates under both provincial and federal jurisdictions. As a result, with the exception of Ontario and Quebec, provincially sentenced offenders who are granted parole are supervised by Correctional Service Canada (CSC).

What Is Conditional Release?

conditional release
The lawful release of an inmate from prison before the expiry of the sentence, subject to conditions set by the releasing authority.

Conditional release is the lawful release of an inmate from prison, subject to specific conditions, before the full expiry of a custodial sentence (the "warrant expiry date"). The release of the inmate is conditional upon terms imposed by the releasing authority. Moreover, while some conditions apply to all inmates, special conditions are applied to each individual and tailored to his or her specific risk and needs profile. For example, a person may be required to wear an electronic monitoring bracelet, abstain from consuming alcohol or other intoxicants, participate in certain rehabilitative programs, refrain from associating with certain individuals, or adhere to any other conditions that are deemed reasonable and necessary to protect society.

For those who receive a determinate sentence, release conditions remain in effect until the sentence expires. Conditions placed on someone serving a life or indeterminate sentence apply until the individual dies, because those sentences never expire. Conditional release does not reduce the length of the sentence imposed by the court. Rather, it provides a mechanism for some offenders to serve a portion of their prison sentence in the community, subject to conditions, under the supervision of a parole officer.

The nature of the conditions and the intensity of supervision vary among individuals on conditional release and may change over time, but any offender can be returned to prison at any time and for any reason that causes the parole board to believe that his or her risk of committing another crime has increased. Conditional release is intended to reduce recidivism and enhance public safety by addressing the person's criminogenic *risks* through monitoring and supervision, while also addressing the person's criminogenic *needs* through appropriate intervention, including treatment, programs, and support.

Does Conditional Release Undermine Punishment?

For some, the notion of early release conflicts with what they consider to be "just" punishment imposed by the court. They find it difficult to understand that someone sentenced to a prison term might be released before the full period of imprisonment has been served.

Conditional release programs provide a restricted re-entry into society, and except in specific circumstances ordered by the court, there is no provision that would allow for a federal offender to serve his or her entire sentence in prison and then be released under community supervision. The exceptions are long-term supervision orders and probation ordered in conjunction with a jail term of two years or less. Barring these exceptions, once a person's jail term expires, no mechanism exists to allow him or her to be supervised in the community. The central questions one must consider when evaluating the merits of conditional release are these: Does society benefit more by keeping individuals in prison for the entirety of their sentence, recognizing that there will be no monitoring, supervision, or conditions to restrict their freedom after their release? Or, is society better served by an arrangement where most offenders serve a portion of their sentence in prison followed by a portion in the community under specific conditions and the supervision of a parole officer? Except in the circumstances mentioned above, there can be one or the other, but not both.

Before attempting to reconcile whether conditional release undermines punishment, it is worth examining the purpose of the correctional system and the purpose of conditional release.

The purpose of the correctional system is set out in the *Corrections and Conditional Release Act* (CCRA) (see "Sidebar—Purpose of the Correctional System").

The purpose of the correctional system is to ensure that the sentence ordered by the court is carried out and to help prepare inmates for their release back into the community, which is where conditional release options are leveraged. It is important to note that only the courts can determine punishment and set the maximum term of loss of freedom. It is not the role of the correctional system to determine the punishment, so it is not mentioned as a purpose in the CCRA. Indeed, as it is clearly stated in s 3.1 of the CCRA, "The protection of society is the paramount consideration for the Service in the corrections process." This principle guides all aspects of correctional decision-making.

One cannot consider the purposes of the correctional system without examining the purpose of conditional release, as the latter contributes to how the former can be achieved. The purpose of conditional release is also set out in the CCRA (see "Sidebar— Purpose of Conditional Release").

Kelly Ellard was convicted in the brutal 1997 murder of BC teenager Reena Virk. In February 2017, Ellard was granted temporary escorted absences from prison to attend medical appointments and programs with the baby she gave birth to in prison. Ellard says the baby has been a very therapeutic part of her rehabilitation.

SIDEBAR

Purpose of Conditional Release
Section 100 of the CCRA states the following:

The purpose of conditional release is to contribute to the maintenance of a just, peaceful and safe society by means of decisions on the timing and conditions of release that will best facilitate the rehabilitation of offenders and their reintegration into the community as law-abiding citizens.

Clearly, the purpose of the correctional system and the purpose of conditional release are aligned in terms of their shared goal of protecting society by assisting with the rehabilitation and reintegration of offenders into the community as law-abiding citizens.

Since the inception of the penitentiary in North America at the beginning of the 19th century, the management of inmates has depended primarily on the use of force and coercion to maintain control. Initially, authorities relied entirely on measures such as the "silent system," which mandated inmate silence, hard labour, floggings, isolation, and other forms of deprivation (all with a smattering of religious instruction) on the basis that these measures would reform inmates by making them "penitent" (hence the name "penitentiary"). Instead, inmates were more likely to become broken, humiliated individuals who were driven to insanity, self-mutilation, and suicide (Jackson, 2002). It slowly became clear that relying entirely on force and intimidation to maintain control was of limited effect and created circumstances that were inhumane and counterproductive. Prison officials came to recognize that the most powerful motivator for the vast majority of inmates was the prospect of earlier release from custody.

In 1868, Canada introduced a system of "remission" through which inmates could reduce their time in custody by up to one-third through good behaviour. While the practice of granting remission for good behaviour was abolished in the federal correctional system in 1969, it is still a significant feature of provincial and territorial corrections today.

A few decades later, in 1899, *The Ticket of Leave Act: An Act to Provide for the Conditional Liberation of Convicts* introduced the first a form of conditional release, which was referred to as a "ticket of leave." The *Parole Act* of 1959 abolished the ticket of leave, replacing it with "parole," which became the responsibility of the newly created National Parole Board. The Act set out the purpose of parole and the criteria for release. In 1992, the laws relating to all forms of conditional release were revised and included in the CCRA.

Types of Conditional Release

There are several types of conditional release—each with its own purpose, eligibility period, and granting criteria. Decisions regarding applications for conditional release are the responsibility of the PBC, which considers a host of factors in granting parole. These factors include (1) the nature of the index offence, particularly whether it involved violence; (2) offender risk level; (3) treatment progress during imprisonment; (4) any history of offender non-compliance (i.e., escape attempts, etc.); (5) physical and mental health status and specific needs in those areas; (6) drug or alcohol issues; (7) the nature and extent of the offender's community support network; and (8) the offender's degree of insight regarding his or her ability to manage in the community.[1]

Temporary Absences

As the term implies, **temporary absences** from prison last a limited period of time. There are three types:

- An *escorted temporary absence (ETA)* may be granted to an offender at any time during his or her sentence, but it requires that the offender be accompanied by an escorting officer and may include conditions to protect society. ETAs may be provided for medical treatment, community service, family contact, rehabilitation, or compassionate reasons (Correctional Service Canada [CSC], 2016). The number of offenders released on ETAs decreased by 7.7 percent from 2013–14 to 2014–15 (i.e., from 2,734 to 2,524 offenders) (Public Safety Canada, 2016).
- An *unescorted temporary absence (UTA)* is a release of limited duration and it requires that the offender have served a specified portion of his or her sentence (one-sixth of the sentence) before becoming eligible. UTAs are granted for a particular purpose, similar to ETAs. Various conditions may also be attached to the release to mitigate risk and protect society. Maximum security inmates are not eligible for UTAs (CSC, 2016). The number of offenders released on UTAs decreased by 9.6 percent from 2013–14 to 2014–15 (i.e., from 447 to 404 offenders) (Public Safety Canada, 2016).
- A *work release* of a specified duration may be granted to an offender for the purpose of work or community service. Offenders who are eligible for UTAs are also eligible to apply for a work release (CSC, 2016).

temporary absence
A type of conditional release that allows an offender to be absent from prison for a temporary, defined period of time.

Day Parole

Day parole is granted at the discretion of the parole board and allows offenders to leave the institution during the day for the purposes of participating in community activities or programs such as job searches, employment, or school, in preparation for full parole or statutory release. Among other conditions, offenders are required to return to the institution at night. Eligibility criteria are outlined in the CCRA. Except for those serving indeterminate or life sentences, offenders are eligible six months prior to their full parole date or after serving six months of their sentence, whichever is longer (CSC, 2016). Approximately one-quarter (26.8 percent) of offenders released in 2014–15 were granted day parole, which represents a slight decrease as compared with 2004–5 (30.1 percent) (Public Safety Canada, 2016).

day parole
A type of conditional release that allows an offender to be out of prison during the day and requires him or her to return at night.

Full Parole

Full parole is granted at the discretion of the parole board, with eligibility criteria set out in the CCRA. Most offenders are eligible for this type of release after serving one-third of sentence, or seven years, whichever is less. For offenders serving a life sentence, parole eligibility is set by the court at the time of sentencing. For first-degree murder, eligibility is automatically set at 25 years, and for second degree murder, eligibility may be set at between 10 and 25 years. Offenders on full parole are permitted to reside in the community, under the supervision of a parole officer. Full parole, like the other types of conditional release discussed so far, is a privilege and not a right, and most offenders who apply for it are denied. In 2014–15, 45.1 percent of women applicants and 29.5 percent of men applicants were granted full parole (Public Safety Canada, 2016). The provincial full parole grant rate was 32 percent, and the federal full parole grant rate was 30 percent (Parole Board of Canada [PBC], 2015b).

full parole
A type of conditional release that allows an offender to reside in the community for the remainder of his or her sentence, subject to conditions of the parole board.

Statutory Release

The law requires the release of an offender after two-thirds of a determinate sentence has been served. Offenders on **statutory release** are those who either did not apply for parole, or were denied it. Offenders on statutory release are supervised by a parole officer for the remainder of their sentence and may have, among other restrictions, a condition to reside in a community-based residential facility or **halfway house**. Not everyone is freed on statutory release, as there are provisions that allow for some individuals to be detained until their warrant expiry date. The parole board may order **detention** on the basis that there are reasonable grounds to believe the offender is likely to commit an offence causing death or serious harm to another person, a sexual offence involving a child, or a serious drug offence before the end of his or her sentence (*Corrections and Conditional Release Act*, s 129(2)).

The differences between the various conditional release programs centre on the earliest possible date that a person can be considered for release (the "eligibility date"), the criteria that must be met before the person can be released, and the extent of the liberty granted for each type of release. Applications are reviewed and may be granted or denied, or the person may be required to meet specific objectives, such as completing a program, before the case will be reviewed again.

Figure 10.1 shows the usual conditional release eligibility dates for those serving fixed sentences.

statutory release
A type of mandatory release for most federal offenders at two-thirds of their sentence.

halfway house
A residential setting within the community that is staffed by professional workers who support offenders released on parole with the process of returning to the community.

detention
Incarceration in prison that, in certain circumstances, may extend until the end of the sentence.

FIGURE 10.1   Conditional Release Eligibility Dates

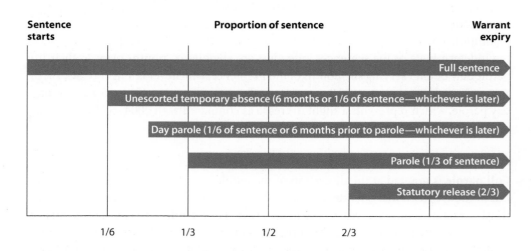

Notes: Applies only to those serving fixed terms—not those serving life or indefinite sentences. Parole eligibility can be set at 50 percent of sentence by the court at time of sentencing for some offenders. Does not include court-ordered post-sentence supervision for certain high-risk offenders.

Source: Parole Board of Canada (2016c).

IN-CLASS EXERCISE

Conditional Release

An offender has a fixed-term sentence of six years. Identify when the offender would be eligible for each type of conditional release listed below and the purposes of each release:

- escorted temporary absence (ETA)
- unescorted temporary absence (UTA)
- day parole
- full parole
- statutory release

The Special Case of Statutory Release

Statutory release differs from other types of release and deserves greater attention here because it accounted for 70.8 percent of all releases from federal prisons in Canada in 2014–15 (Public Safety Canada, 2016) and demonstrates one of the greatest conflicts relating to the purpose of conditional release. Unlike the other forms of conditional release, where inmates must convince the parole board that they deserve to be released, with statutory release, the parole board must show why certain inmates (owing to specific criteria) should remain in prison until their sentence expires. As a result, the majority of inmates eligible for statutory release are indeed released (National Parole Board, Performance Measurement Division, 2010, Tables 92 and 93, p. 105).

The Ouimet Committee's Report on Corrections

Without some understanding of how statutory release developed, it is easy to criticize a system that releases those who were denied or did not apply for other forms of conditional release. In 1969, the Ouimet committee, in its *Report of the Canadian Committee on Corrections*, reviewed Canada's experience during the first decade after the *Parole Act* came into force. The committee noted that, while the lowest-risk offenders were being released to community supervision through parole, those who had not been granted parole were being released directly into the community without supervision or assistance. In other words, those who would likely have the most difficulty reintegrating were left to make it on their own (Ouimet, 1969).

The logic of supervised release was compelling to the Ouimet committee, but, at the same time, it also understood that it involved a trade-off between short-term risk and long-term benefits:

> As has been pointed out repeatedly, … from many sources in many countries and jurisdictions, there are risks in any form of treatment of the offender. The short-term risks of parole are calculated risks and in the opinion of the Committee are less than the risks in the alternative of sudden and dramatic contrast between incarceration and total [unsupervised] freedom. …
>
> Increasingly, however, it is being pointed out that the practice of parolling only the better risks means that those inmates who are potentially the most dangerous to society are still, as a rule, being released directly into full freedom in the community without the intermediate step represented by parole. (Ouimet, 1969, pp. 331, 348)

The Ouimet committee chose to recommend a system "under which almost everyone would be released under some form of supervision" (Ouimet, 1969, p. 350). However, members of the committee were also aware of the political implications of releasing the most difficult and potentially dangerous inmates. To address this problem, they proposed that the period of supervision occur during what had been until then known as "remission." At that time, remissions allowed for the release, free and clear of any legal restraint or conditions, of all inmates serving a fixed sentence when they had reached the remission point in their sentence—typically, when two-thirds of their sentence had been served (the maximum remission that could be earned was one-third of the sentence).

Remission was replaced with "mandatory supervision," later changed to "statutory release." Despite often being referred to as "early release," no one has served less time in prison, many have served more time, and all have been subjected to the loss of freedom through supervision because of it.

What Do You Think?

Is community supervision best used for low-risk "deserving" individuals, or can it be used to reduce the risk of all inmates regardless of their likelihood to reoffend? Can it do both?

In terms of its justification, statutory release is markedly different from the other forms of release in that it is granted on the basis that the person needs supervision and support after release, as opposed to the person deserving early release because of his or her risk profile, progress, and reintegration plan. The individual being released on statutory release has not earned the trust of correctional officials by demonstrating a low risk to reoffend. Quite the contrary, because the person appears much more likely to reoffend, the supervision is imposed as a means to manage risk.

Many other important questions arise with statutory release: Is conditional release about rewarding good behaviour, or is it about maximizing the potential for successful reintegration? Should inmates be granted conditional release because their risk is low, because it is high, or both? If the answer is "both," then the criteria and eligibility dates for conditional release would need to be reconsidered to reconcile the two seemingly contradictory purposes. Perhaps the most important change, however, would be in relation to the role and authority of parole boards.

As the data on conditional release outcomes in Figure 10.2 show, more individuals on parole complete their sentences successfully than do those on statutory release. Most of the difference in the success rates between parole and statutory supervision relates to breaches of the conditions of release, while differences in criminal activity account for much less. Although more individuals committed a violent offence on statutory release than on parole (0.9 percent versus zero, respectively, in 2014–15), the percentage of non-violent and violent offences committed under both types of release is low and declining (Public Safety Canada, 2016, Tables D9 and D10).

A report published in 2007 by the Correctional Service of Canada Review Panel proposed that statutory release be abolished (Sampson, 2007), having concluded that compared with parole, recidivism under statutory release was excessive. The report was criticized for ignoring the fact that a higher failure rate was an expected outcome from the time of its design and for not addressing the more relevant question of whether the statutory release group's recidivism rate would be lower in the future if released on warrant expiry without supervision (Jackson and Stewart, 2009).

Although some individuals progress through the various conditional release programs to parole before their warrant expiry date sets them free, most are released only when

FIGURE 10.2   Conditional Release Outcomes, 2010–11 to 2014–15

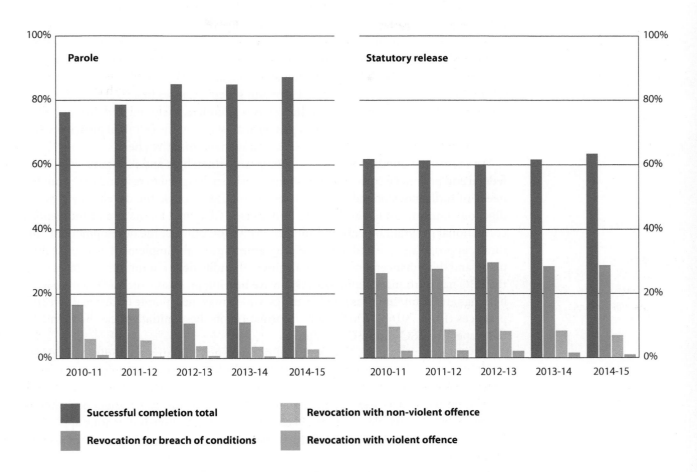

Notes: Excludes offenders serving indeterminate sentences because they do not have a warrant expiry date and can only successfully complete full parole by dying. Revocation for breach of conditions includes revocation with outstanding charges. Violent offences include murder and Schedule I offences (listed in the *Corrections and Conditional Release Act*) such as assaults, sexual offences, arson, abduction, robbery, and some weapon offences.

Source: Public Safety Canada (2016, Tables D9 and D10).

they reach their statutory release date. Although legally eligible for different types of conditional release, some serve their sentences in full, after which they enter the community free of any conditions, which include reporting to and being supervised by a parole officer, and clear of any obligations to report. In rare cases, the court can order a person to be supervised after the determinate term of custody expires, for a period of up to ten years ("long-term supervision orders"); that individual remains under the supervision of a parole officer during the additional time.

Conditional Release: The Indigenous Experience

As discussed in other chapters of this text, Indigenous people are overrepresented in the criminal justice system. According to the Office of the Correctional Investigator, in 2014–15, 4 percent of the overall Canadian population were Indigenous, while 24 percent of incarcerated federal offenders and 17 percent of federal offenders on conditional release were Indigenous (Office of the Correctional Investigator [OCI], 2016). The *Criminal Code* (s 718.2(e)) and the CCRA (ss 81–84) contain specific clauses intended to address the unique needs and circumstances of Indigenous offenders, including but not limited to the overrepresentation of Indigenous people at all stages of the criminal justice system. It is beyond the scope of this chapter to examine these initiatives here.

An increasing number of services, supports, partnerships and programs within the federal and provincial correctional systems have been designed to respond to the unique needs of Indigenous offenders. Initiatives by the CSC include the development of Indigenous housing units and Healing Lodges (see Chapter 11); the use of Indigenous correctional program officers and Indigenous liaison officers; the development of culturally appropriate core and non-core programming and the implementation of healing plans; and the enhancement of relationships with Indigenous communities. For its part, the PBC has introduced culturally responsive hearing processes such as Elder-assisted hearings and community-assisted hearings, which may incorporate traditional spiritual practices (PBC, 2016b). Much more information on these initiatives can be found on the respective CSC and PBC websites.

It is important to note, however, that despite such initiatives, conditional release grant rates for Indigenous offenders continue to be lower compared with rates for non-Indigenous offenders. In 2014–15, 68.2 percent of applications by Indigenous offenders for federal day parole were granted versus 72.0 percent for non-Indigenous offenders. Similarly, full parole was more likely to be granted to non-Indigenous applicants (19.4 percent versus 32.4 percent). Further, in the same time period, 84 percent of releases for Indigenous offenders were at statutory release compared with 66 percent of releases for non-Indigenous offenders (Public Safety Canada, 2016).

While culturally responsive strategies at the correctional stage of the criminal justice system should be commended, it is important to recognize that such initiatives are reactive by design, implemented only after harm has been caused and an offender is within the correctional system. In that regard, and as has been pointed out by Patenaude-Harris (2013), such "strategies do not address the much broader underlying social and economic inequalities and systematic discrimination" experienced by Indigenous people.

Efforts to resolve macro-level issues of inequality and systemic discrimination will need to take place in a bigger arena than the criminal justice system or, in this case, the correctional system. Further, such efforts will need to include proactive measures designed to *prevent* crime, rather than to only respond to crime via the courts and correctional system. The 2015 report by the Truth and Reconciliation Commission of Canada aimed to redress injustices by formalizing calls to action on several macro-level social issues including child welfare, education, youth, equality, health, language, and culture (Truth and Reconciliation Commission of Canada, 2015). In addition, several recommendations were made in the arena of criminal justice specifically, including calls to reduce the overrepresentation of Indigenous people in custody; fund the evaluation of community sanctions that are reasonable alternatives to custody; and amend the *Criminal*

Code to allow judges to depart from mandatory minimum sentences and restrictions on the use of conditional sentences (Truth and Reconciliation Commission of Canada, 2015). Time will show the impact that these calls to action will have on Canadian society and, specifically, within the contexts of criminal justice and correctional services.

The Conditional Release Process

For the purposes of this section, the steps involved in applying for parole will be discussed based on the provincial correctional system in Ontario. As mentioned earlier, Ontario and Quebec are the only provinces that maintain their own provincial parole boards. Conditional release decisions for those sentenced to less than two years of imprisonment are made by the PBC in all other jurisdictions.

As previously discussed, offenders are entitled to a parole hearing after serving one-third of their sentence. They can waive this right, but if they choose to apply for parole, they will complete an application that includes several components that cumulatively represent how they intend to successfully reintegrate into the community as law-abiding citizens. In the formal request, the applicant will identify a parole sponsor, who is the person with whom he or she plans to reside. The sponsor is expected to report any concerns or violations of conditions, and be a reliable collateral contact for the parole officer. The applicant will also provide a verifiable residence, along with plans for treatment and/or counselling following release, as well as plans to secure employment and/or attend school.

All aspects of the applicant's plan are investigated and verified by a parole officer as part of a pre-parole investigation, including a visit at the proposed residence. Victims are contacted by the parole officer, and they are given the opportunity to make submissions (either in person or in writing) to the parole board for the purposes of expressing how they have been affected by the crime, along with any safety concerns related to the release of the offender (Ontario Parole Board [OPB], 2016).

After the pre-parole investigation is complete, a report is prepared for the parole board that provides an analysis of the plan and applicant, including an expression of the applicant's risk for recidivism based on the results of an **actuarial risk assessment**. The parole officer is required in the report to take a position on whether conditional release is supported, and to include any recommended special conditions, should the board grant release.

actuarial risk assessment
A statistical evaluation of offender risk; it measures variables that research has shown are predictive of recidivism.

The Parole Hearing

The parole board is an administrative tribunal that has absolute discretion to grant or deny parole (OPB, 2016). The parole hearing takes place within the institution where the offender is housed and is an intensive interview where no topic or question is off limits. Equipped with the offender's file (which includes the criminal record, police occurrence reports, victim impact statements, pre-sentence reports, social history, institutional conduct, program participation, various actuarial risk assessments, and the release plan), the board conducts an intensive interview with the offender to decide whether to grant release. The board will ask questions that probe the offender's level of insight into the offence, level of responsibility, and empathy and remorse. The board will also examine the offender's progress, relapse prevention strategies, and the proposed release plan.

In making its decision, the parole board is guided by the principles of conditional release in the CCRA:

The protection of society is the primary consideration for the Board and the provincial parole boards in determination of all cases. (s 100.1)

According to s 102, "Criteria for granting parole," the board *may* grant parole to an offender if, in its opinion,

>   (a) the offender will not, by reoffending, present an undue risk to society before the expiration according to law of the sentence the offender is serving;
>   *AND*
>   (b) the release of the offender will contribute to the protection of society by facilitating the reintegration of the offender into society as a law-abiding citizen. [Emphasis added.]

In other words, the board *may* release the offender if it believes not only that the individual will not pose an undue risk to society but also that the release will contribute to the protection of society through a comprehensive reintegration plan. After the interview process is completed, the offender along with any observers and/or assistants are required to leave the room while the parole board deliberates. Once the board's decision is made, everyone returns to hear the decision, along with the reasons for it.

Parole Board Decisions: From the Field

In June 2016, the *Toronto Star* published an article by a former parole board member, Lubomyr Luciuk, who reflected on his experience making conditional release decisions. In the article, he wrote: "Bottom line: if you get it wrong someone could be hurt, or worse. If that happens, you, as the decision-maker, will be held accountable, publicly .... I did my best. I pray I made the right choices. Only time will tell. And, like every other board member who came before me, and every one who'll follow, I live with that" (Luciuk, 2016).

For the full text of the article, see www.thestar.com/opinion/commentary/2016/06/23/making-parole-decisions-is-one-tough-job.html or search online for "Making Parole Decisions Is One Tough Job" by Lubomyr Luciuk.

For a detailed explanation of what to expect at a parole board hearing, search online for "Virtual Tour of a Hearing Room," created by the PBC. For videos produced by the PBC, visit the PBC YouTube channel at www.youtube.com/user/PBCclcc/videos.

What Do You Think?

Examine the release criteria in s 102 of the CCRA, noted previously. Now, put yourself in the position of a parole board member. What would you like to see in a parole plan?

Parole Supervision and Enforcement

Those granted release are subject to conditions imposed by the parole board as well as monitoring, intervention, and supervision by a parole officer that is tailored to their individual criminogenic risks and needs. Conditions may include abstention from drugs and alcohol, restrictions on movement or travel, attendance at specified treatment programs, psychological counselling, work, attendance at school, and non-association with victims. These conditions are intended to manage risk; address social, emotional, or psychological difficulties related to the person's criminal behaviour; and deal with barriers to successful reintegration into the community. The individual is supervised by a parole officer whose role is to ensure compliance with those rules and expectations, and to provide support, guidance, and referrals to other resources.

An individual can be returned to prison at any time if the parole board concludes that he or she has become an unacceptable risk based on its belief that the person has violated any conditions of the release, or anything else that, in its opinion, reflects an increased risk to public safety. The authority of the parole board is substantial and subject only to internal review. The most common reason for revoking a conditional release is for a breach of the conditions that were set, rather than for committing another criminal offence (Public Safety Canada, 2010).

MINI CASE STUDY

Should Parole Be Revoked?

Tabatha is a single mother of three young children (two of whom have been diagnosed with attention deficit hyperactivity disorder) and is currently on full parole, having served eight months in custody for cheque fraud. She receives no support from the children's father, despite numerous attempts to have his pay garnished for child support. Her own mother wants nothing to do with her or her children, claiming that her troubles are rooted in her lack of remorse.

Tabatha works part-time as an exotic dancer. She has sought out other work, but with no education and no discernible employment skills, she cannot find a job that will pay her as well. Given the problems that her children are experiencing, she has become actively involved in their school and assists with extracurricular activities in the community. She works with her children on their homework before going to work and volunteers as a hot lunch coordinator at their school.

Although there have been no reports of alcohol or substance abuse, she has been seen smoking marijuana with her friends. A prohibition on alcohol and drug use is part of her conditions of release, and smoking marijuana is a breach of these conditions.

What Do You Think?

As Tabatha's parole officer, would you breach her? What would be the ramifications for her children? What are the reasons for your decision? (Remember to articulate your reasons in terms of public safety.)

Premises for Conditional Release

Relatively few inmates die in jail; the vast majority are released into the community on or before their warrant expiry date. The period during which the person is most at risk for reoffending is during the first few months after release. The results of an analysis of cumulative recidivism in 2007 showed a high recidivism rate occurring immediately after release, but then flattening quickly after the first 12 months. After seven years of crime-free life, ex-inmates reoffend at a rate that is no greater than those who have no criminal record (Centre of Criminology, 2007, p. 7). Again, conditional release is premised on the principle that public safety is enhanced by the gradual release of eligible offenders to the community when timing and circumstances are appropriate (PBC, 2016a).

Many assume that "tough on crime" measures and, in particular, longer prison sentences will increase public safety. In reality, though, because the risk of reoffending decreases with time, it is not all ex-offenders in the community that present a risk, but rather the number that have been released *recently*. It is true that a longer sentence postpones release and can interrupt the recidivism of very active repeat offenders, but after a period of adjustment, the number of inmates actually being released in any given year returns to the same level as before the longer sentences were imposed. The net safety benefit to the community therefore evaporates, while the cost of holding a larger prison population increases—often dramatically (Rajekar & Mathilakath, 2010). In fact, longer periods in prison tend to be related to slightly higher rates of recidivism (French & Gendreau, 2003). Long prison terms also result in the incarceration of many individuals who no longer pose a serious risk of reoffending.

There are potentially huge social and economic benefits to developing initiatives that would reduce the risk of reoffending while also reducing the size of prison populations. Indeed, that is the premise on which programs of support, treatment, and supervision immediately following release were developed in Canada over the last century and even earlier.

Does Conditional Release Reduce Crime?

According to the RCMP, about 4 million Canadians have a criminal record (Royal Canadian Mounted Police, 2012). That amounts to more than 10 percent of the adult population, of which about 14 to 18 percent are adult males. In 2014–15, there were 39,623 people in custody in federal and provincial prisons on any given day (Reitano, 2016). That means that about 0.01 percent of all those with criminal convictions are in jail. Research by the Centre of Criminology (2007) showed that recidivism drops to an insignificant level over seven years. Therefore, it is reasonable to surmise that a large portion of these people have probably given up their criminal activity. Figure 10.3 shows how criminal activity is tied closely to age; relatively few individuals continue committing crimes as they grow older.

The task of conditional release is to help offenders reintegrate successfully into the community as law-abiding citizens. You might think that proving that conditional release is effective would not be difficult to do. In fact, it is not easy, as Griffiths, Dandurand, and Murdoch (2007) found in *The Social Reintegration of Offenders and Crime Prevention*:

FIGURE 10.3   Persons Accused of Crime, by Age, Canada, 2014

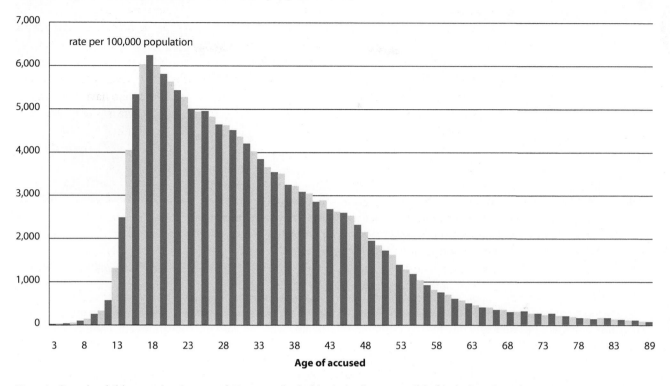

Note: In Canada, children under the age of 12 cannot be held criminally responsible for their actions, but they can be identified by police as accused. There were approximately 5,400 "child accused" in 2014.

Source: Allen and Superle (2014, Chart 4).

While there is an abundance of ideas as to what, in theory, should work, the findings of program evaluations are often disconcerting. Further, the majority of reintegration programs have not been subjected to controlled evaluations, and successful approaches remain to be identified and articulated. (p. 2)

To understand how conditional release promotes public safety, one must look beyond the warrant expiry date. When a person is released before warrant expiry, clearly that person can reoffend before his or her sentence expires—and some do. If the purpose of corrections and conditional release is to reduce the incidence of reoffending over the long term, then the short-term risk of early release needs to be balanced against the long-term benefits of lower criminal recidivism. The important question is not whether some reoffend under conditional release, but whether those released through such programs are less likely to reoffend over the longer term.

Conditional release has a compelling logic, but research and data are also needed to assess its effectiveness in practice and, therefore, to be able to judge whether the benefits of conditional release outweigh the costs—particularly with respect to recidivism. The best way to evaluate conditional release and to determine whether and for whom it is effective would be to randomly assign inmates to conditional release and follow up with

CAREER PROFILE

Nicole Cordingley

Nicole Cordingley is a probation and parole officer with the Ministry of Community Safety and Correctional Services in Kingston, Ontario.

How did you first become interested in criminal justice and corrections?
While working as a veterinary assistant, I began reading true crime books and watching documentaries. The individuals, their backgrounds, and the factors that led to the crime fascinated me. The psychological aspect was extremely interesting as well. The more books I read and conversations I had with family and friends, the more exciting the idea of studying this field became.

How did you become a probation and parole officer?
Following a conversation I had with a professor while at Loyalist College, I decided to apply for the Community and Justice Service Worker program. I was extremely nervous but very excited, as I was a mature student changing my career path. Throughout college, I had spoken to a few of my professors regarding university. Through their inspiring words and encouragement, I was accepted into the Bridge Program at the University of Ontario Institute of Technology. During my fourth year, I completed a placement within a probation and parole office, where I was able to connect with managers from different offices across the province for upcoming contract opportunities. One month after graduating, I began working.

Describe a typical day for you. What are some of your most important duties?
A typical day is not usually what you planned for! I may have a few clients booked and be hoping to complete administrative duties, but then crises may arise with some of my clients—homelessness, relationship problems, mental health issues, or a relapse.

I tend to have several clients booked throughout the day. We discuss their concerns, any questions that may arise, their goals, and any programming or counselling they are involved in.

Once I have finished appointments, I complete my administrative duties: case notes and collateral contacts

to any counsellors, victims, doctors, police, and family. I make referrals to several different programs in the area that are best suited to the client, and speak with the program coordinators about clients. At times, I have court-ordered reports, which must be completed in a certain time frame.

What are the most rewarding and most challenging aspects of your job?
The most rewarding aspects of my career so far are the ongoing challenges and the daily learning experiences. I enjoy working with my colleagues each and every day, and learning from their experiences with difficult situations. It makes me want to be a better probation and parole officer. Another rewarding aspect is seeing my clients succeed. My clients tend to be placed on probation orders from 12 months to three years, so seeing them staying sober, completing programs, or accomplishing goals is very rewarding.

Hearing clients' stories is very challenging. These are often very sad stories and can result in compassion fatigue or vicarious trauma. Unfortunately, a lot of my clients were often exposed to substance abuse and physical abuse. I also speak with victims of domestic violence and sexual abuse. At times, I may be the only person in their life helping them find a positive path. As well, I also work with those who are suffering from mental illness. These illnesses can be very complex, and some clients aren't willing to receive the help offered.

How does parole help offenders reintegrate into the community?
Probation comes with several conditions they must abide by—abstaining from drugs and/or alcohol, no weapons, no association with specific individuals, and rehabilitative programming or counselling, to name a few. If the client is released from custody and has a probation order to follow, it gives me an opportunity to work with that

person's top priority, whether it's finding housing or providing a referral to a rehabilitation program. Probation and parole officers can help offenders make positive changes by guiding and supporting their efforts.

How does an inmate's behaviour change if they believe they might be granted parole? What is your role in the process? An inmate may show the desire to attend programming or counselling, attend schooling, or seek employment upon their release. If released, they may gain the support of friends and loved ones that are willing to help and guide them. During the pre-parole investigation, I visit the proposed parole sponsor's home to confirm the address, see who all lives there, discuss their expectations of the parolee, and see whether or not they are prepared to work with me to support the parolee. I also consult with the police, as well as any victims or employers. My report to the Parole Board includes a recommendation of whether the offender is a manageable risk in the community. I also include conditions that would assist in the supervision of the offender should he or she be released.

them for years afterward. For both legal and ethical reasons, such studies are not possible, and other forms of research and analysis must be relied on. For many years, CSC has had an active research program dedicated to determining the most effective ways to reduce recidivism. In 2005, CSC summarized its findings in the document *The Safe Return of Offenders to the Community* (Motiuk, Cousineau, & Gileno, 2005), which states:

> There is solid evidence to support the premise that the gradual and structured release of offenders is the safest strategy for the protection of society against new offences by released offenders.
> … [R]ecidivism studies have found that the percentage of safe returns to the community is higher for supervised offenders than for those released with no supervision. (p. 3)

Some studies, however, are less certain about the impact of supervised release on reoffending. An extensive review of recidivism data in the United States was unable to identify any indication that post-release supervision had an effect on lowering recidivism (Solomon, Kachnowski, & Bhati, 2012). The authors acknowledged that the nature of their study made it impossible to sort out whether the lack of data about specific programs might hide good results.

It should not be surprising that community supervision is less effective when caseloads are very high, support services are minimal, supervision is preoccupied with surveillance and apprehension, and the programs are not evidence-based in their design or implementation. Based on a review of the literature, Griffiths et al. (2007) identified 11 characteristics of successful reintegration programs. Such programs

1. focus on a specific target group of offenders and their specific challenges;
2. rely on sound methods for assessing the needs and risk factors of offenders;
3. hold the offenders accountable and responsible for their own choices and their actions;
4. begin while the offender is in prison and continue throughout the offender's transition to, and stabilization in, the community (throughcare);
5. strike a balance between surveillance and control on the one hand, and support and assistance on the other;

6. offer assistance in an integrated and comprehensive manner and address the many inter-related challenges faced by offenders (e.g., wrap-around interventions);

7. are offered as a coordinated effort of all the agencies involved and are supported by strong agency cooperation ... ;

8. are supported by sound case management practices and adequate information management systems;

9. reflect the public safety priorities of the community in which they are developed;

10. engage the community in both the planning and the delivery of the intervention and foster strong community ownership;

11. have a robust evaluation component that allows the program to evolve, self-improve, and remain accountable to the community for crime reduction results. (p. 41)

Applying the research on effectiveness in the real world is difficult. Even when adequate resources are available (and putting aside politics), ensuring that parole supervisors are adequately trained is a problem. Research by Bonta, Wallace-Capretta, and Rooney (1999) for the Solicitor General Canada demonstrated that when probation officers were put through just three days of training on effective supervision practices, the recidivism rate of those being supervised dropped by 15 percent.

Blanket statements that conditional release "works" or "does not work" are not helpful or accurate. It is important to know what evidence shows it is effective, for whom, and when. With that information, programs and resources can be developed and targeted to where the best results can be achieved. Otherwise, the promise of conditional release may be defeated because of bad or inadequate practices.

Over the last few decades, a collection of works has emerged showing that programs are most effective when based on the three principles of the Risk-Need-Responsivity (RNR) model, discussed in Chapter 9.

> Developed in the 1980s and first formalized in 1990, the risk-need-responsivity model has been used with increasing success to assess and rehabilitate offenders in Canada and around the world. As suggested by its name, it is based on three principles: 1) the *risk principle* asserts that criminal behaviour can be reliably predicted and that treatment and monitoring should focus more heavily on higher risk offenders; 2) the *need principle* emphasizes the importance of addressing criminogenic needs [needs that are correlated to criminal behaviour] in the design and delivery of treatment; and 3) the *responsivity principle* describes how the treatment should be provided. (Bonta & Andrews, 2007, p. i)

Of particular interest is the finding that programs based on RNR principles were effective in reducing recidivism for higher risk offenders (Bonta, Wallace-Capretta, & Rooney, 2000). After all, low-risk individuals are, by definition, less likely to reoffend whether engaged in programs or not. This finding suggests that restricting conditional release to low-risk offenders makes sense if the intention of the program is only to reduce the immediate costs associated with imprisonment. However, according to the findings, ignoring moderate- and high-risk individuals will likely mean little if any reduction in recidivism rates, especially among those for whom reoffending is most serious.

MINI CASE STUDY

Kirk Clark: An Offender Applying for Day Parole

Criteria Considered by the Parole Board

In making a decision whether to grant parole, the members of the parole board will assess the following:

- the offender's criminal, social, and conditional release history
- factors affecting the offender's self-control
- the offender's response to programming and interventions
- the offender's institutional and community behaviour
- the offender's change and progress in addressing his or her correctional plan and crime-cycle indicators
- the release plan and community management strategies (Government of Canada, 2016).

With these criteria in mind, consider the case of Kirk Clark, an offender applying for day parole.

Clark is 42 years old and has served 13 years of a life sentence for second-degree murder. The victim was a taxicab driver, murdered during a robbery that went wrong. This is Clark's first federal sentence, but he also has served three provincial sentences of less than 18 months for crimes including driving while intoxicated, two assaults, two robberies, possession of stolen property, possession of drugs, and two breaches of a recognizance while on bail. His employment history has been sporadic; he has taken jobs, only to quit or be fired within a very short time. His average length of employment is about two months. Drug and alcohol abuse is a common theme, mentioned in pre-sentence reports and in most of his crimes. He began abusing alcohol at age 10 and drugs at age 12. His first conviction was as a youth, at age 14. Kirk currently resides in a minimum-security penitentiary.

The particulars of the case for which Kirk is being considered for release are that, while under the influence of drugs, he planned to rob a taxicab. He called for a cab and took a knife with him when he entered the cab. The initial police report indicated that Kirk said he did not want to be identified, so he killed the driver. He stole $253 from the driver.

Kirk describes his entire life as one filled with chaos, anti-social friends and peers, and chronic substance abuse. Various reports from psychologists, front-line staff, and counsellors note his remorse regarding the offence.

Given the charge and his previous offence history, Kirk was referred for a psychological assessment. He was rated in the moderate range on the **PCL-R** (see "Key Terms," which follows). The reports noted his overall good institutional record and his successful completion of various programs (cognitive living, substance abuse, violence prevention). He was also assessed as a moderate–high recidivism risk, based on his **SIR-R** score of −8.

In the first couple of years of incarceration, Kirk had some minor adjustment difficulties, as shown in the institutional charges. One charge was for possession of "brew," and two incidents were noted of disrespectful language to staff. For the past ten years, his institutional behaviour has been very good. He has been active in the Lifers Group and has participated in the **LifeLine Program**. He has actively participated in chaplaincy programs, and he reports that he feels he has been re-born. While attending programs inside the institution, he met his current girlfriend, a volunteer with Alcoholics Anonymous and the chaplaincy programs.

Kirk has never been married and has no children. Other than his girlfriend, he has no family or community support.

He has continued to attend a substance abuse program and Alcoholics Anonymous while in minimum security. He feels he has his drinking under control, but would be willing to see a psychologist in the community while on day parole.

The community assessment report notes that his girlfriend seems fully aware of his background and that she is a tremendous support for Kirk. He has met the minister of her church, and he plans to join the congregation and volunteer in the church when granted release.

Staff at the halfway house that has accepted Kirk have had frequent contact with him and fully support his release into their care. They have already tentatively found him employment in the local community.

What Do You Think?

If you were a member of the parole board, would you release Kirk on day parole? What would your reasons be? How does your decision reflect the research presented in this chapter related to parole and ultimately the long-term protection of society?

Key Terms

PCL-R (Psychopathy Checklist-Revised): A 20-item scale used to assess the core elements of a psychopathic character. This instrument was developed by Robert Hare in the 1990s for use with adult males in prison. Symptoms of psychopathy include the following: lack of conscience or sense of guilt, lack of empathy, egocentricity, pathological lying, repeated violations of social norms, disregard for the law, shallow emotions, and a history of victimizing others.

SIR-R (Statistical Information on Recidivism-Revised): A statistical tool for predicting recidivism; originally developed by Joan Nuffield in the Ministry Secretariat of the Solicitor General of Canada in the 1970s, and introduced as a diagnostic tool for the Parole Board and Correctional Service Canada in 1988. The scale combines 15 static factors related to criminal activity and social functioning. The factors include current offence, age of admission, age of adult conviction, previous incarceration, previous convictions, employment status, and marital status.

LifeLine Program: A partnership between Correctional Service Canada, the National Parole Board, and non-governmental agencies (e.g., St. Leonard's Society). Under the program, paroled offenders returned to an institution to work with fellow convicts and to assist in their successful release. The program was cut in 2012 by the federal government.

Source: Adapted from a National Parole Board case study; courtesy Brian Chase.

Who Benefits from Conditional Release?

As long as conditional release is seen as an act of mercy that benefits only the inmate, the issue of whether the person "deserves" conditional release will be foremost in people's minds. In fact, the idea that a person should deserve conditional release is and always has been a common theme in the public discourse.

With the introduction of the *Parole Act* in 1959 and statutory release in 1969, the notion of parole as a form of mercy was rejected in official policy and regulations. Today, conditional release is not intended to benefit the inmate so much as it is intended to benefit the community through lower rates of reoffending and reduced costs of prison systems. Recall the principles that guide parole boards when deciding whether to grant release: the primary consideration is public safety.

A study commissioned by the John Howard Society of Toronto on the costs and benefits of providing housing for ex-inmates was very careful to frame the analysis in terms of the benefits to the public:

> If supports and housing are conceived as interventions on behalf of the public (i.e., a public service), the beneficiary is the community itself. Then the issue of deservedness is really a question of whether the community deserves to be safe, deserves another functioning member, to incur lower costs, and whether the community deserves to have lower incidence of crime. The cost–benefit analysis concerns itself with the question of whether the intervention achieves these goals. (Stapleton, Pooran, & Doucet, 2012, p. 4)

Without clear public benefit, there is little likelihood of the service ever being supported through government funding and cooperation.

When a person successfully reintegrates into society, the community benefits by no longer being victimized by that person and no longer having to pay the bills for a very expensive criminal justice system. However, the individual also benefits from living a lawful life through restored relationships with family and the community, and from being free and self-sufficient.

Often there is strong public resistance to rehabilitative measures that appear to result in the offender being treated leniently. The problem is that there are no purely painful ways to rehabilitate. It is very difficult to be both harsh and helpful at the same time. Helping one become a better person is accomplished through learning, and that involves being exposed to positive influences of pro-social people, ideas, and opportunities. Isolating a person in an austere and often anti-social environment such as prison, and restricting access to positive learning opportunities such as school, as well as to social events and family visits, can be counterproductive to someone developing the knowledge needed to become a better citizen. Likewise, treatment can only be helpful in an environment where the person is treated respectfully by the therapist.

The only model of sentencing that tries to justify pain as rehabilitation is the deterrence model (see Chapter 8). Deterrence allows us to be punitive—often harshly so—on the ground that harsh treatment prevents further crime by convincing a rational decision-maker that crime is not worth the pain of punishment. While deterrence might be a convenient approach, it is difficult to confirm through research that sentence severity reduces crime rates (Doob & Webster, 2003).

It is perhaps more important to know what factors make crime attractive in spite of any perceived deterrence. For example, a person acting out of fear or the need to be accepted into a social structure—even if it is a gang—or who has a mental illness, or an addiction, might not consider any consequences relating to criminal activity, because any one of these factors, let alone in combination, might undermine the deterrent effect.

What Risks Are Being Balanced?

Recall the article by the former parole board member discussed in "Sidebar—Parole Board Decisions: From the Field." Those responsible for correctional policy and release decisions know that there are potentially great costs to the community and to them personally when a person reoffends. The regret that comes from making a decision that leads to serious harm, and then being subjected to investigation and appearance at an inquest along with difficult media scrutiny, can result in an intensely painful experience. These same individuals rarely receive recognition or praise when good decisions are made, so it should be no surprise that their decisions by default are as cautious as possible. Their decisions seek to balance personal risk and public risk.

Incidents of failure have far greater impact on public policy than do success rates. It takes a well-informed, principled, and courageous politician or correctional official to stand against this pressure. Consequently, with few exceptions, since the 1970s there has been movement toward increasingly restricting and limiting the use of conditional release, and toughening supervision.

Conclusion

PBC data appear to illustrate encouraging success rates for conditional release, including a recent finding that "100% of releases on parole that ended in 2014–15 did not result in a conviction for a new violent offence prior to warrant expiry" (PBC, 2015a, p. 19). Despite such data, it only takes one incident of violent offending by an offender while on conditional release to curb public support for such programs. Strong differences of opinion exist about what the purpose of conditional release should be and how it should operate. Attempts to accommodate these conflicting views have resulted in a system that is, at times, in conflict with the evidence on effective reintegration. The fact remains that the vast majority of inmates will be released, and the time when interventions have the best likelihood of reducing recidivism is immediately following discharge from prison. The challenge then is to use evidence-based practices in order to maximize opportunities to enhance public safety.

IN-CLASS EXERCISE

Day Parole

Review the scenario in "Mini Case Study—Kirk Clark: An Offender Applying for Day Parole," and then answer the following questions:

1. In preparing for the day parole hearing, what components should be included in Kirk Clark's plan to manage risk and promote success? As you reflect on his plan, remember to consider the purposes of the correctional system and conditional release, as well as the RNR principles.
2. Were any components of the release plan missing in the mini case study? Explain.
3. What release conditions would you recommend to the parole board? Again, remember to justify these according to the principles mentioned in question 1.
4. Suppose that you denied Clark's request for day parole. How would you suggest that he prepare for the next hearing?
5. Suppose that Clark was granted day parole. What would you do if he violated a condition by missing an appointment with his psychologist? Explain your decision.

DISCUSSION QUESTIONS

1. Is the purpose of a sentence undermined or complemented by conditional release? Explain.
2. Should programs of conditional release be used for those who are low risk, for those who present the greatest needs and risks, or for both?
3. How might conditional release be changed and/or explained so that its benefits might be better understood by the public?

NOTE

1   Some of the material in the section on Types of Conditional Release is contributed by Claire Goggin.

SUGGESTED FURTHER READINGS

For detailed background information on conditional release, see the Parole Board of Canada website: https://www.canada.ca/en/parole-board.html.

For an alternative approach to conditional release decision-making, see John Howard Society of Canada. (2007). *Presumptive gradual release*. Kingston, ON: Author. Retrieved from http://www.johnhoward.ca/document/presumptive/presumptive.pdf.

For key policy papers that informed the development of the *Corrections and Conditional Release Act*, see Solicitor General Canada. (2002). *Influences on Canadian correctional reform: Working papers of the Correctional Law Review, 1986 to 1988*. Ottawa: Author. Retrieved from http://www.naacj.org/en//pdf/res_influences_canadian_correctional_reform.pdf.

REFERENCES

Allen, M.K., & Superle, T. (2014). Youth crime in Canada, 2014. Retrieved from http://www.statcan.gc.ca/pub/85-002-x/2016001/article/14309-eng.htm.

Bonta, J., & Andrews, D.A. (2007). *Risk-need-responsivity model for offender assessment and rehabilitation: 2007-06*. Ottawa: Her Majesty the Queen in Right of Canada. Retrieved from https://www.publicsafety.gc.ca/cnt/rsrcs/pblctns/rsk-nd-rspnsvty/rsk-nd-rspnsvty-eng.pdf.

Bonta, J., Wallace-Capretta, S., & Rooney, J. (1999). *Electronic monitoring in Canada*. Ottawa: Public Works and Government Services Canada. Retrieved from https://www.publicsafety.gc.ca/cnt/rsrcs/pblctns/lctrnc-mntrng-cnd/lctrnc-mntrng-cnd-eng.pdf.

Bonta, J., Wallace-Capretta, S., & Rooney, J. (2000). A quasi-experimental evaluation of an intensive rehabilitation supervision program. *Criminal Justice and Behavior, 27*, 312–329.

Centre of Criminology. (2007). Offenders who have gone six or seven years without committing a new offence are only slightly more likely to offend than are people who have no criminal record at all. *Criminological Highlights, 8*(4), 7.

Correctional Service Canada. (2016). Types of release. Retrieved from http://www.csc-scc.gc.ca/parole/002007-0003-eng.shtml.

Corrections and Conditional Release Act, SC 1992, c. 20.

Doob, A.N., & Webster, C.M. (2003). Sentence severity and crime: Accepting the null hypothesis. *Crime and Justice, 30*, 143–195.

French, S., & Gendreau, P. (2003). *Safe and humane corrections through effective treatment*. Ottawa: Correctional Service of Canada. Retrieved from http://www.csc-scc.gc.ca/research/092/r139_e.pdf.

Government of Canada. (2016). Parole decision-making. Retrieved from https://www.canada.ca/en/parole-board/services/parole/parole-decision-making.html.

Griffiths, C.T., Dandurand, Y., & Murdoch, D. (2007). *The social reintegration of offenders and crime prevention* (Report No. 2007-2). Ottawa: National Crime Prevention Centre, Public Safety Canada. Retrieved from https://www.publicsafety.gc.ca/cnt/rsrcs/pblctns/scl-rntgrtn/scl-rntgrtn-eng.pdf.

Jackson, M. (2002). *Justice behind the walls: Human rights in Canadian prisons*. Vancouver: Douglas & McIntyre.

Jackson, M., & Stewart, G. (2009). A flawed compass: A human rights analysis of the roadmap to strengthening public safety. Retrieved from http://www.justicebehindthewalls.net/resources/news/flawed_Compass.pdf.

Luciuk, L. (2016, June 23). Making parole decisions is one tough job. *Toronto Star*. Retrieved from https://www.thestar.com/opinion/commentary/2016/06/23/making-parole-decisions-is-one-tough-job.html.

Motiuk, L., Cousineau, C., & Gileno, J. (2005). *The safe return of offenders to the community: Statistical overview*. Ottawa: Correctional Service of Canada. Retrieved from http://www.csc-scc.gc.ca/research/092/sr2005-safe_return2005_e.pdf.

National Parole Board, Performance Measurement Division. (2010). *Performance monitoring report: 2009–2010*. Ottawa: Author.

Office of the Correctional Investigator. (2016). Backgrounder: Aboriginal offenders—A critical situation. Retrieved from http://www.oci-bec.gc.ca/cnt/rpt/oth-aut/oth-aut20121022info-eng.aspx.

Ontario Parole Board. (2016). Victims and the Ontario Parole Board. Retrieved from http://www.slasto.gov.on.ca/en/OPB/Pages/Victims-and-the-Ontario-Parole-Board.aspx.

Ouimet, R. (1969). *Report of the Canadian Committee on Corrections: Toward unity: Criminal justice and corrections*. Ottawa: Queen's Printer.

Parole Board of Canada. (2015a). *2014–15 Department performance report*. Ottawa: Her Majesty the Queen in Right of Canada. Retrieved from https://www.canada.ca/content/dam/canada/parole-board/migration/005/008/093/005008-2000-2015-en.pdf.

Parole Board of Canada. (2015b). 2014–2015: Performance monitoring report. Retrieved from https://www.canada.ca/en/parole-board/corporate/transparency/reporting-to-canadians/performance-monitoring-report/2014-2015.html.

Parole Board of Canada. (2016a). 2016–2017: Report on plans and priorities. Retrieved from https://www.canada.ca/en/parole-board/corporate/transparency/reporting-to-canadians/report-on-plans-and-priorities/2016-2017/report.html.

Parole Board of Canada. (2016b). Community-assisted hearings. Retrieved from https://www.canada.ca/en/parole-board/corporate/publications-and-forms/fact-sheets/community-assisted-hearings.html.

Parole Board of Canada. (2016c). Types of conditional release. Retrieved from https://www.canada.ca/en/parole-board/services/parole/types-of-conditional-release.html.

Patenaude-Harris, L. (2013). Parole and conditional release. In J. Winterdyk & M. Weinrath (Eds.), *Adult corrections in Canada*. Whitby, ON: de Sitter Publications.

Public Safety Canada. (2010). *Corrections and conditional release statistical overview: Annual report 2010*. Ottawa: Public Works and Government Services Canada. Retrieved from https://www.publicsafety.gc.ca/cnt/rsrcs/pblctns/ccrso-2010/2010-ccrs-eng.pdf.

Public Safety Canada. (2016). *Corrections and conditional release statistical overview: 2015 annual report*. Ottawa: Public Works and Government Services Canada. Retrieved from https://www.publicsafety.gc.ca/cnt/rsrcs/pblctns/ccrso-2015/ccrso-2015-en.pdf.

Rajekar, A., & Mathilakath, R. (2010). *The funding requirement and impact of the "Truth in Sentencing Act" on the correctional system in Canada*. Ottawa: Office of the Parliamentary Budget Officer. Retrieved from http://www.parl.gc.ca/PBO-DPB/documents/TISA_C-25.pdf.

Reitano, J. (2016). *Adult correctional statistics in Canada: 2014/2015*. Ottawa: Canadian Centre for Justice Statistics.

Royal Canadian Mounted Police. (2012). Quick facts in Canadian Criminal Real Time Identification Services (CCRTIS).

Sampson, R.C. (2007). *Report of the Correctional Service of Canada Review Panel: A roadmap to strengthening public safety*. Ottawa: Public Works and Government Services Canada. Retrieved from http://publications.gc.ca/collections/collection_2008/ps-sp/PS84-14-2007E.pdf.

Solomon, A.L., Kachnowski, V., & Bhati, A. (2012). *Does parole work? Analyzing the impact of postprison supervision on rearrest outcomes.* Washington, DC: Urban Institute. Retrieved from http://www.urban.org/sites/default/files/publication/51536/311156-Does-Parole-Work-.PDF.

Stapleton, J., Pooran, B., & Doucet, R. (2012). *Making Toronto safer: A cost–benefit analysis of transitional housing supports for men leaving incarceration.* Toronto: The John Howard Society of Toronto.

Statistics Canada. (2012). Adult correctional services, admissions to provincial, territorial and federal programs (provinces and territories). Retrieved from http://www.statcan.gc.ca/tables-tableaux/sum-som/l01/cst01/legal30b-eng.htm.

Truth and Reconciliation Commission of Canada. (2015). *Honouring the truth, reconciling for the future: Summary of the final report of the Truth and Reconciliation Commission of Canada.* n.p.: Author. Retrieved from http://www.trc.ca/websites/trcinstitution/File/2015/Findings/Exec_Summary_2015_05_31_web_o.pdf.

Prison Populations in Focus

LEARNING OUTCOMES

After reading this chapter, students will be able to:

- Understand the challenges faced by older incarcerated offenders.

- Understand the challenges faced by women inmates.

- Understand the concerns of transgender inmates.

- Explain how the use of alcohol and substances in correctional facilities can affect staff and inmates.

- Describe the "dangerous offender" designation and critically evaluate its effect on the offender's experience in incarceration.

- Describe the unique challenges faced by sex offenders during incarceration and when they reintegrate into the community.

- Understand the prevalence of mental disorders among offender populations and be able to differentiate between suicide and self-injurious behaviour.

- Explain some of the reasons why Indigenous offenders are overrepresented in the correctional system.

- Describe the challenges faced by correctional staff and management in meeting the needs of a diverse population of inmates.

Introduction

In this chapter, we will briefly outline specific populations within the Canadian correctional landscape: older offenders, female offenders, offenders who do not identify as heterosexual or who have a non-conforming gender identity, offenders with a substance abuse problem, dangerous offenders, sex offenders, offenders with mental disorders, Indigenous offenders, and ethnoculturally diverse offenders. It is important to keep in mind that many incarcerated individuals fall into more than one of these categories, which means that the issues they face will often be much more complex than those discussed here.

Subpopulations of inmates deserve special consideration because they face unique challenges in relation to how they cope with incarceration. Moreover, although these subpopulations may be small (e.g., transgender inmates), they can nonetheless pose significant challenges for corrections with respect to the resources and the staffing necessary to meet their unique needs. The goal of this chapter is to call attention to the diversity of the offender population and the need to recognize the varied kinds of challenges confronting them and those who work with them in the prison environment.

Older Offenders

Correctional Service Canada (CSC) considers any offender aged 50 years or over to be an "older" offender.[1] Evidence to date suggests that this group of inmates is growing in number. The percentage of federal inmates over the age of 50 has doubled from about 12 percent in 2000 to 24 percent in 2014 (Correctional Service Canada [CSC], 2009a, 2014a). Researchers attribute this growth to an increase in the percentage of non-Indigenous men aged 50 to 64 in custody (CSC, 2014b). Regionally, the highest proportion (26 percent) of offenders over the age of 50 is in Quebec, and the lowest proportion is in the Prairie region, where older offenders constitute only 13 percent of the federal inmate population. Overall, the growth in the proportion of older offenders is not really surprising, given that since the 1970s, the Canadian population has been aging, and is expected to continue to do so into the near future. As crime tends to be a "young man's game," it stands to reason that as the relative proportion of young people in Canada declines and the relative size of the older cohort increases, there should be an overall decline in the crime rate (all other factors being equal).

SIDEBAR

Crime Rates and Age

Professor Peter Carrington used statistics to forecast the relationship between population age and crime rates. According to his estimations, there should be a reduction in Canada's overall crime rates from 2000 to 2041 (Carrington, 2001). However, Carrington noted that the crime rates for offences that are more typical of older adults (e.g., sexual assault, and drinking and driving) would be less affected by the aging of the country's population.

When their incarceration history is considered, the Canadian population of older offenders is not homogeneous. One group of older offenders consists of those who were young when they were first incarcerated and have grown older in prison while serving a lengthy sentence (often for a homicide). These individuals tend to be model inmates and pose a relatively low risk to reoffend. About 24 percent of older male inmates fit into this category (CSC, 2014a). A second group of older offenders consists of those who have been in and out of prison all of their lives. Estimates suggest that 45 percent of older male offenders are recidivists. These individuals are sometimes referred to by criminologists as "career criminals" because they tend to view prison as part of their lifestyle. Compared with other groups of older offenders, recidivists pose the highest level of risk for reoffending, are more involved in institutional misconduct, and have a history of being held in segregation (CSC, 2014a). The final group of older offenders consists of those who are serving their first prison sentence as older adults. Approximately 28 percent of

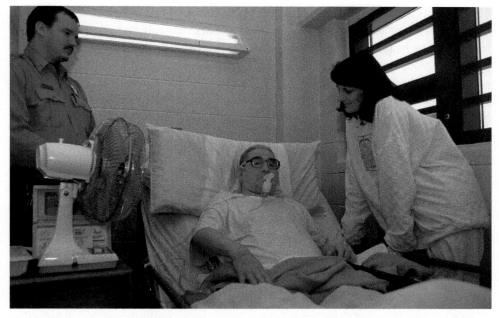

Older offenders make up the fastest growing segment of the prison population, which is leading to an increasing emphasis on the need to address health care concerns.

older male offenders fall into this category (CSC, 2014a). Individuals in this category are more likely than younger offenders to be serving a sentence for a sexual offence. Also, compared with younger offenders, they are less likely to have a substance abuse problem or be involved in institutional misconduct (CSC, 2014a). However, compared with other older offenders, individuals in this category are likely to have the hardest time coping with institutional life.

The issues associated with incarcerated older offenders are well known in the United States, where research on older offenders and their unique needs has been undertaken for a number of years. In the United States, older offenders make up the fastest-growing population among state prisons, increasing 203 percent in a ten-year period (Ortiz, 2000). Between 1999 and 2009, the percentage of older inmates (who were aged 50 or older at the end of 2009) on death row more than doubled to 29.3 percent (Snell, 2000, 2010). By 2014, the percentage had risen again: 39.1 percent of those on death row were over the age of 50. Clearly, the mean age of those who remain on death row is increasing. In 1999, the average age of a death row inmate was 38. In 2014, it was 47 (Snell, 2014). American researchers have noted that older inmates have more significant health issues than do their younger counterparts, thus increasing the cost of incarcerating them, given that they require additional medical and dietary considerations. Correctional systems face a number of challenges as they prepare to meet the unique needs of this growing population.

One of these challenges is the physical health of older inmates. The aging process during incarceration is accelerated for many. Some have suggested that factors such as lifestyle choices, socio-economic status, and poor access to medical care lead certain incarcerated individuals to appear ten years older than non-incarcerated individuals in the same age group (Office of the Correctional Investigator [OCI], 2011. This suggestion is especially significant given that almost one in four incarcerated offenders in Canada is

50 or older (CSC, 2014b). Factors such as poor diet, smoking, drug and alcohol abuse, and limited access to dental and health care have undoubtedly had an overall negative impact on the health of those entering correctional facilities (OCI, 2011). As such, inmates as a group are more likely to face the effects of aging and chronic health problems earlier in life than the general population. Cancer, emphysema, diabetes, cardiovascular disease, and various types of dementia are all chronic conditions that require inmates to be treated in-house. Treatments may include continuous monitoring of an individual's condition while incarcerated; frequent appointments with a variety of health care staff (nurses, doctors, physiotherapists, dentists, psychiatrists); and outside trips to consult with specialists in the community.

SIDEBAR

Managing Older Offenders

The challenges associated with incarcerating older offenders in Canadian prisons and the lack of a national strategy by CSC to deal with the needs of older inmates have caught the attention of the OCI. The Correctional Investigator is mandated by legislation (*Corrections and Conditional Release Act*) to be an **ombudsman** for all federal offenders. In addition to investigating complaints by individual offenders, the OCI is responsible for reviewing CSC policies and procedures and for making recommendations specific to its areas of concern.

A fairly extensive report on older Canadian offenders was produced by CSC's research branch in 1998 (Uzoaba, 1998). Following this report, CSC created an Older Offender Division in 2000, and a policy group was formed to make recommendations at the national level. Apparently, however, these initiatives have been abandoned, and none of the recommendations have been implemented (OCI, 2011).

In the OCI's 2010–11 annual report, Correctional Investigator Howard Sapers (2011) made four recommendations pertaining to the management of older offenders within CSC:

- that more appropriate programming be developed to better meet the needs of older offenders, including physical fitness programs;
- that more staff with training and experience in gerontology and palliative care be hired;
- that when new buildings are planned, the physical needs of older offenders be taken into consideration (e.g., accessible living arrangements); and
- that the CSC develop a national older-offender strategy that will include not only a geriatric release policy, but also improved post-release supports for older offenders.

In the OCI's 2014–15 annual report, Sapers (2015) reiterated that it is imperative that CSC develop a chronic/long-term care model that is responsive to the needs of incarcerated older offenders.

ombudsman
A government official whose role is to hear and investigate complaints made by citizens (in this case, federal inmates) about government officials or government agencies (in this case, Correctional Service Canada).

The physical health challenges faced by older offenders include not only chronic illness but also mobility issues and sensory impairments that may necessitate providing inmates with hearing aids, eyeglasses, canes, walkers, wheelchairs, and prostheses. Additional accommodations may also need to be made to the inmate's physical environment.

Because traditionally prisons have not been built with the needs of older inmates in mind, there are often accessibility challenges when it comes to meeting older inmates' daily needs (bathing, toileting, feeding). Many of the prisons that house federal inmates are in desperate need of retrofitting in order to meet these needs. A number of penitentiaries have been designated as heritage buildings, and five are more than 100 years old, thus making modernizing these facilities a very expensive endeavour (Sapers, 2011).

Social and Safety Challenges

Older offenders also face considerable challenges when it comes to coping with the stress of incarceration. Issues of safety may be a factor. Older offenders may feel threatened by younger members of the general population, and this feeling can be made worse by mobility concerns (e.g., not being able to fend off or flee from a physical attack). Similarly, older inmates may be the target of bullying. The fact that they often have very little social status within the institution and have limited physical strength can make them an easy target for younger and stronger inmates. In addition to safety concerns, older offenders may find it challenging to access recreational activities that could help them lower their stress levels. This may have a harmful effect on their ability to cope (Sapers, 2011).

Correctional institutions must also provide appropriate programming options for older offenders, who have different needs from younger offenders. Programs that deal with employment or vocational training may be of little relevance to the older offender who is of retirement age. Very few aging inmates typically access the kinds of rehabilitation and reintegration services that are needed to successfully return to the community (Sapers, 2011). They may require special accommodations to be able to fully participate in programs offered in an institution. For example, they may need shorter program sessions, more bathroom breaks, various aids, or material presented in a more accessible format in order to fully benefit from a program.

Ultimately, prisons are faced with having to offer palliative care to terminally ill inmates. Across Canada, 43 deaths from natural causes took place in federal prisons in 2014–15 (Sapers, 2015). In a review of natural deaths in prison from 2011 to 2015, the leading cause of death was cancer, followed by cardiovascular disease. The average age of inmates who die as a result of natural mortality in a federal prison is 60. This age is much lower than the life expectancy of Canadian men (78.3 years) and women (83 years), which is a cause for concern. Sapers has called for CSC to explore options that will allow those who are terminally ill to complete their sentences in a community hospice or long-term care facility. He has also emphasized the need for more applications of "parole by exception" to the Parole Board of Canada on behalf of terminally ill inmates. Such alternatives to incarcerating elderly and terminally ill inmates are humane and make financial sense.

Female Offenders

Women make up a small percentage of those who commit crimes. While they constitute about 15 percent of overall admissions to provincial or territorial correctional services, they account for about 11 percent of those in sentenced custody, 20 percent of those under community supervision, and 13 percent of those admitted on remand. Women make up far less of the federally incarcerated population—about 7 percent—than men do (Reitano, 2016). In recent decades, however, the percentage of women being admitted to federal programs has been slowly increasing (Statistics Canada, 2007). Prior to the building of five new regional correctional facilities across Canada in the 1990s, most federally sentenced women were incarcerated at the Prison for Women in Kingston, Ontario. This prison was officially closed on July 6, 2000.

In a 2008–9 "snapshot" of inmates in Canadian adult correctional institutions, Hotton Mahony (2011) reported that incarcerated women were, "on average[,] younger, more likely to be single, less likely to have a high school diploma, and more likely to be unemployed" than women in the general population (p. 33). About one-half of all provincial and territorial female inmates had not completed high school.

As of April 2014, among federally sentenced women in custody, 56 percent were serving time for committing a violent offence, and 26 percent were sentenced for a serious drug offence (CSC, 2014c). Moreover, in 2014, 123 women made up only 3.5 percent of those serving a life or indeterminate sentence (Public Safety, 2015). Notably, between 1998 and 2009, the number of women serving a life sentence increased by 37 percent.

Women's offences are varied, but they have historically centred around crimes related to prostitution, theft, and drug use. A 1999 Statistics Canada snapshot of female inmates, Indigenous inmates, and inmates serving life sentences found that women were serving time for fewer offences than were men, had less extensive criminal histories, and shorter **aggregate sentences** (Finn, Trevethan, Carrière, & Kowalski, 1999). A more recent study (in 2003–4) found that men were more likely to face multiple charges, and women were more likely to be one-time offenders (Kong & AuCoin, 2008). In almost half (46 percent) of the cases where women have been charged with a violent offence, the victim of the crime was an intimate partner or spouse, whereas for men, the victim of the crime was more often an acquaintance (Caya & Stuart, 2012).

Indigenous women continue to be overrepresented across provincial, territorial, and federal correctional facilities. In 2014–15, approximately 31 percent of women in federal sentenced custody and 38 percent of women in provincial/territorial sentenced custody

aggregate sentences
The combined total of all sentences being served by an individual.

Edmonton Institution for Women is a multi-level security facility with three types of living units, including residential houses.

were Indigenous women (Reitano, 2016). The rate of admission to provincial/territorial sentenced custody for Indigenous women is slightly higher than the rate for Indigenous men (24 percent in provincial/territorial sentenced custody and 22 percent in federal sentenced custody). Indigenous women represent the fastest-growing segment of the federal offender population (Beaudette, Cheverie, & Gobeil, 2014).

Incarcerated women face a host of stressors associated with their lives both inside and outside the prison walls. Although many cope adequately, some turn to strategies that have worked for them in the past, but that are ultimately problematic, such as drinking and using drugs, eating disorders, self-injury, and attempts at suicide. Aside from possibly causing serious injury or death, these behaviours may lead to correctional sanctions (e.g., being placed in segregation for intoxication).

Many women in prison are mothers and often the primary caregivers for their children. One of their biggest issues is the care of their children. In some cases, the children have been made wards of the court, effectively eliminating any future contact with their mothers. When children themselves start having trouble with the law, mothers in prison may face a double dose of guilt for "not being there" for their children and for "setting a bad example."

The Task Force on Federally Sentenced Women

In 1989, the Task Force on Federally Sentenced Women was established with a mandate to assess the correctional management of women sentenced to federal prison in Canada—from initial processing to warrant expiry—including the need to develop a strategic plan to guide and direct this process in a way that was respectful of women's needs (Task Force on Federally Sentenced Women, 1990). The CSC faced some clear difficulties when it came to the operation of new regional facilities for women. The task force's report, *Creating Choices*, and the implementation of its recommendations were met with a number of criticisms (Hannah-Moffat, 2000). As Hannah-Moffat (1995) noted:

> Perhaps one of the most profound difficulties is that feminists have failed to adequately define the meaning and criteria of woman centeredness. The implementation of the task force's recommendations and the definition of *woman centered* have been left to Corrections Canada with little external (feminist) input. (p. 141)

When the new regional facilities were opened, they were not able to accommodate the needs of maximum-security women.[2] This failure to balance the practical aspects of implementing a woman-centred philosophy against the systemic demands inherent in managing violent offenders was glaring. As Shaw (1999) pointed out:

> It is unfortunate that the model of the women-centred prison developed in *Creating Choices* failed to take account of the fact that women can be perpetrators of violence as well as victims. The failure to confront the issue of women's use of violence other than as a response to continued partner violence is not restricted to the Task Force alone, but has been characteristic of feminist accounts of women and violence within criminology more generally. (p. 258)

Few would disagree that societal issues such as classism, sexism, and racism have had an impact on who becomes criminalized in Canada. Generally, it is a subset of women— those most negatively affected by these issues in our society—who become criminalized.

Offenders' Gender Identity and Sexual Orientation

There are considerable additional challenges for individuals living in a prison environment who do not identify as heterosexual or who have a non-conforming gender identity. The reality is that society is sexually diverse, and by extension, prison populations are also sexually diverse. In addition to the heterosexual majority, there are individuals who identify as homosexual, lesbian, gay, intersex, transsexual, transgender, queer, questioning, two-spirited, bisexual, pansexual, polysexual, omnisexual, and asexual. However, in prison, sexual diversity is not often acknowledged or accepted. For example, the coalition fighting Lisa Neve's dangerous offender designation (see "Mini Case Study—Lisa Neve," later in this chapter) noted that the psychiatric evidence used against Neve relied on aspects of her sexual orientation as an indicator of pathology. A thorough discussion of the marginalization of sexually diverse groups in society is beyond the scope of this text. However, this section will focus on the realities that some individuals in the correctional system face as a result of their gender identity and sexual orientation.

In the past, institution-wide homophobic practices such as segregating homosexuals (under the guise that it was for their own safety) were not unusual, and were an early target for gay prison advocates. The evidence to date suggests that coerced or forced sexual activities are more common in male correctional facilities than in female facilities, but coercive sexual activities do occur in female facilities (Hensley & Tewksbury, 2002). In a recent study, 9 percent of a sample of female inmates reported being sexually coerced in prison, and 22 percent responded that they had been forced into a sexual experience in prison (Walsh, Gonsalves, Scalora, King, & Hardyman, 2012). Further, what may appear at first to be consensual sexual activity between male inmates may, on closer examination, actually have an element of coercion or manipulation fuelled by concerns over safety, security, and financial support (Hensley & Tewksbury, 2002).

In Ontario, a total of 63 individuals identified as transgender at intake in provincial custody between April 2014 and March 2015. In November 2015, Alberta had 16 people in custody who identified as transgender, and Saskatchewan had one person in custody who identified as transgender (Lupick, 2015). To date, empirical research on transgender inmates is lacking. A 2010 study of transgender inmates in California showed that these inmates are more likely to experience a high unemployment rate, be 36 to 45 years old, homeless, incarcerated for a property crime, housed in secure facilities, and classified as sex offenders (Sexton, Jenness, & Sumner, 2010). While they are less likely to be gang members, they are more likely to be identified as having a mental disorder, to suffer from alcohol and drug abuse, and to have a history of suicidal thoughts or attempts; more than 40 percent have previously worked in the sex trade. Staggeringly high estimates of HIV infection (60 to 80 percent of transgender inmates are HIV-positive) have also been reported. In sum, the demographic profile of transgender inmates is different from that of the general inmate population.

In a recent exploration of how transgender inmates experience being imprisoned in a male institution, Jenness and Fenstermaker (2014) noted that "transgender prisoners engage in a set of activities that together constitute what we refer to as a pursuit of gender authenticity" (p. 22). The transgender inmates described the desire to be viewed by other inmates as a "real girl," and this led to practices within the prison that were gendered and embraced "male dominance, heteronormativity, classed and raced gender ideals, and a daily acceptance of inequality" (p. 23).

Transgender inmates have likely experienced rampant **homophobia**, extensive harassment, and verbal, physical, and sexual assaults during their lives. They are also more likely than other inmates to spend time in protective custody—sometimes for their own protection; however, extended periods in isolation are clearly harmful. Depending on the jurisdiction, transgender inmates may have additional health care concerns associated with their transition (e.g., hormones, surgery) that are not met. Where prison officials have denied the requests of inmates to access specific transgender health care, cases of self-castration and **penectomy** have been documented (Brown, 2010).

Transgender inmates face issues with correctional procedure as well. Canada is one of the few countries that actually has a formal correctional policy on **gender dysphoria**. Transgender inmates may be recognized as such by CSC if they have been assessed and diagnosed by an expert in gender dysphoria. They may initiate or continue with hormone therapy while incarcerated and are allowed to wear clothing consistent with their self-identified gender. If they are pre-operative, they will be held in an institution consistent with their birth sex (i.e., someone who is physically male and has not had sex reassignment surgery yet would be held in a male facility). Sex reassignment surgery may be available to an inmate, and paid for by CSC, if the person meets a number of conditions.

Recently, a complaint was filed with the Canadian Human Rights Commission on behalf of transgender inmates in an attempt to bring about a change in CSC policy. The complaint was filed by the West Coast Prison Justice Society and alleged that CSC policy "fails to accommodate transgender prisoners" (Lupick, 2015, para. 10). The claim is supported by evidence provided by a transgender inmate in a federal prison by the name of Nastasia Laura Bilyk, who reported that she had been raped repeatedly in prison and had to be held in protective custody in a male institution (Lupick, 2015). She requested that the CSC recognize her gender and allow her to reside in a female institution.

In 2015, a new admission and placement policy for transgender inmates was implemented by the Ministry of Community Safety and Correctional Services in Ontario. Transgender inmates in Ontario Correctional Services are no longer assigned to institutions consistent with their biological sex, but are instead admitted to institutions consistent with their gender identity and preferences (Strapagiel, 2015). Further, they will be referred to by their preferred name and gender pronoun (i.e., he, her, or ze [gender neutral pronoun]), and will also be permitted to choose the gender of the staff who search them.

Offenders Who Abuse Drugs and Alcohol

In 2013, 76 percent of Canadians reported drinking alcohol in the past year, and nearly 11 percent reported using cannabis over the same time period (Government of Canada, 2013). Research has shown that offenders, as a group, appear to "mirror the general population's usage patterns of alcohol and other drugs," but problems from their substance use are much more frequent and serious (Begin, Weekes, & Thomas, 2006, p. 18). The link between crime and the use of alcohol and drugs has been well demonstrated in the literature. In a 2011 study, almost half (49 percent) of 10,264 male federal offenders reported that they were under the influence of alcohol or drugs on the day of their offence (Ternes & Johnson, 2011).

homophobia
Negative attitudes, including hatred, fear, and/or contempt, directed toward people who do not identify as heterosexual.

penectomy
Amputation of the penis.

gender dysphoria
Where there is a conflict between the person's physical gender and his or her self-perceived gender (e.g., a person who is born physically male, but believes she is really female). Specific diagnostic criteria for gender dysphoria are outlined in the *Diagnostic and Statistical Manual of Mental Disorders* (DSM-5).

What Do You Think?

1. Even though there is a formal CSC policy on how transgender inmates are to be treated, might there still be serious safety concerns for these individuals?

2. Can you think of any challenges to placing a pre-operative transgender inmate in an institution consistent with his or her birth sex?

3. Can you think of any challenges to placing a pre-operative transgender inmate in an institution consistent with his or her gender identity?

Substance abuse and crime may have a *direct* link (a person may only become violent and commit assault when under the influence of alcohol) or an *indirect* link (a mother steals food to bring home for her kids because she spent the last of her money on crack cocaine). Substance abuse is considered to be one of the top eight predictors of recidivism and is one factor that seems to be interconnected with other types of criminogenic needs. So, while substance abuse may have a negative impact on a person's ability to finish school or hold down a job, it may also interfere with family and marital relations and negatively affect finances. Further, substance abuse may lead individuals to become involved with others who are antisocial, thus exposing users to antisocial attitudes (Andrews & Bonta, 2010). All of these factors have been found to be related to recidivism.

Because of the link between substance abuse and crime, identifying alcohol and/or drug abuse is part of the intake procedure for new inmates (Kunic, 2006). In a recent study of 13,081 federally incarcerated male offenders, approximately 72 percent acknowledged that they had a substance abuse problem. In all, 25 percent of individuals in the sample had a severe problem, were aware of their problem, and were ready for treatment. In addition, 31 percent of individuals in the sample had a low-level substance abuse problem, and 16 percent had a moderate-level problem (CSC, 2014d). A national substance abuse programming strategy has been employed across the Canadian federal prison landscape, and outcome studies have shown that it has had some success (Doherty, Ternes, & Matheson, 2014; Ternes, Doherty, & Matheson, 2014).

Substance Use in Prison

detoxification

A process of cleansing the bloodstream of toxins. For the alcoholic or drug addict, it may include abstention from alcohol or drugs as well as medical intervention.

Numerous issues arise from substance use and abuse in correctional settings. Initially upon intake, an inmate may have physical health issues associated with **detoxification**. While such issues are more likely something local jails and holding facilities have to deal with, it is also possible that an inmate returning from a pass or an inmate who is new to a federal institution may arrive under the influence. In these situations, ensuring that the inmate has proper medical care is essential. The use of substances within institutions is not unusual and leads to issues around treatment, security, and safety for both inmates and staff. Results from a study of random urine testing among federal offenders showed that about 11 percent of offenders tested positive for drug use, suggesting that certain offenders continued to use substances while incarcerated and while on conditional release in the community (MacPherson & Fraser, 2006). Participants in treatment programs who are under the influence of drugs or alcohol can be disruptive to other program participants. Further, users are unlikely to gain much from the program while under the influence. While there are always concerns about violence in institutions, an increased risk of violence is possible when inmates are high and/or involved in the drug trade in prison.

Apart from homemade alcohol (known as "brew") and the misuse of prescribed medications, any substances that are circulating within an institution had to have been brought there by inmates, staff, or visitors. The smuggling of substances into an institution is a major concern for security personnel. Plastic bottles of alcohol thrown over walls, substances smuggled in body cavities, and drugs sent over fences in tennis balls comprise just a few of the ways that this contraband enters institutions. Once these substances are inside an institution, their effects on the people who ingest them can quickly wreak havoc on institutional order (McVie, 2001). Although it is a priority for correctional officials to prevent the smuggling of banned substances into prisons, the reality is that some substances make it in, and inmates do use them.

Because of the myriad health concerns associated with substance use, a harm-reduction approach must be taken when dealing with certain aspects of substance abuse. For example, the rates of HIV and hepatitis C are much higher in inmate populations than the general population (CSC, 2011a). Various programs (e.g., Reception Awareness Program, Choosing Health in Prisons, National HIV/AIDS Peer Education and Counselling Program, Circles of Knowledge Keepers, and Chee Mamuk) provide education to inmates about infectious diseases and how to reduce their risk of infection (Zakaria, Thompson, & Borgatta, 2010, p. 5). In addition, access to bleach kits (to clean needles), condoms, and dental dams is now standard in Canadian federal institutions, and the availability of **methadone** maintenance programs ensures that opiate addicts have a medical alternative to injecting heroin (CSC, 2011b). All of these practices are aimed at harm reduction. However, needle exchange is not available to inmates, despite recommendations from the Canadian Human Rights Commission, the Correctional Investigator, and the Canadian HIV/AIDS Legal Network (Chu, 2009). While CSC (2005) has stated that it is committed to working with public health agencies to explore whether needle exchanges will fit within prison health care initiatives, to date there has been no significant progress made, and no needle exchange programs are in operation in any Canadian prisons (Chu, 2009; van der Meulen & Ka Hon Chu, 2015).

methadone
A synthetic narcotic that is orally administered and is used in the treatment of opiate (e.g., heroin) addiction.

Dangerous Offenders

When the term *dangerous offender* (DO) is mentioned, Clifford Olson, Paul Bernardo, and Robert Pickton likely come immediately to mind. However, there are other, lesser-known DOs, such as Lisa Neve, a former DO (featured in "Mini Case Study—Lisa Neve"). Interestingly, Neve could be included in a number of the groups referred to in this chapter: Indigenous women; substance abusers; psychiatric survivors; sex trade workers; dangerous offenders; and lesbian, gay, bisexual, transgender, questioning, and two-spirited (LGBTQ2) people.

It is important to distinguish between DOs who are likely to remain incarcerated for an indefinite period of time and DOs who will be released but whose past violence necessitates the issuance of a long-term supervision order when they leave prison.

For a DO who is likely to remain incarcerated, correctional management must consider issues related to both the nature of the DO's offence and the indefinite length of his or her sentence. For some DOs, the heinous nature of their crimes necessitate that they be housed separately from the general prison population. Convicted killers Paul Bernardo and the late Clifford Olson are examples of DOs who had to be held in segregation at various points in their sentence for the safety of themselves and others (Hewitt, 2010). In fact, Olson was held in a super-maximum-security Special Handling Unit (SHU), a type of facility reserved for Canada's most violent, difficult-to-manage inmates. Programming issues arise from their segregation and their long sentences. DOs held in segregation are not able to attend regularly scheduled programming with other offenders. Moreover, given the indeterminate nature of DO sentences, the programming that is offered to DOs must be tailored to take into account that DOs are unlikely to be released in the foreseeable future. According to CSC (2007), programs such as "sexual deviance treatments, intensive violence prevention programs, mental disorder treatments, and educational programs" have been developed specifically for DOs.

Lisa Neve

In 1994, at the age of 21, Lisa Neve became the second woman in Canadian history to be declared a DO. The first female DO was Marlene Moore, who committed suicide in 1988 at the age of 31 while incarcerated at the infamous Prison for Women in Kingston, Ontario. Neve was similar to Moore in a number of ways; however, Neve's DO designation was eventually overturned and she was subsequently released from prison.

Lisa Colleen Neve was born in December 1972, and her biological mother was Indigenous. Neve was adopted at the age of three months by Jim and Colleen Neve. The family, who lived in Calgary, included two other adopted children: an older brother and a younger sister. Neve's developmental history was initially unremarkable. She was described as an "outwardly loving, trusting child" (Yeager, 2000, p. 10). However, it was not long before problems started to emerge. Neve experienced learning and behavioural difficulties in school, which the media later speculated may have been caused by fetal alcohol syndrome (Jimenez, 1999). Over the years, her parents hired tutors and referred her to mental health professionals in an attempt to address these issues, but by the time she was 13, her acting out had escalated to the point where she was expelled from school for being disruptive and drinking alcohol. It was around this time that she began working in the sex trade, and her drug and alcohol abuse increased.

Neve came to the attention of a variety of child welfare agencies as a youth. She would routinely run away from these facilities and return to either her parents' home or the street. Under the *Young Offenders Act*, she was found guilty of a total of 15 offences, including carrying a concealed weapon (knife), failing to appear in court, soliciting, escape from custody, failure to comply, uttering death threats, assault with a weapon, and forcible confinement. Neve was sentenced to periods in secure youth custody and was admitted on numerous occasions to the Alberta Hospital, where she first engaged in self-injury.

As an adult, Neve was convicted of seven criminal offences, including assault with a weapon, uttering threats, robbery, and aggravated assault. The aggravated assault charge was a serious one in which Neve used an exacto knife to slash the neck of her victim. She reported that she had problems recalling the event, as she was drunk and high on cocaine at the time. In another serious offence, she and a co-accused convinced a woman (who they alleged had been involved in an assault on a friend of Neve's) to go out for a ride. They took her to a field in a rural area and stripped her of her clothes and, in so doing, cut the victim. The pair took the victim's belongings and money and left her naked in the field; it was only 5°C at the time. For her role in this robbery, Neve was declared a DO in November 1994 and sentenced to an indeterminate term of imprisonment. At that time, about a month shy of her 22nd birthday, she was the youngest offender ever to be designated as a DO.

The DO hearing took three weeks to complete, with the Crown's evidence focusing on police testimony and notes written by Neve both in and out of custody. The police testified that she was a heavy user of cocaine and alcohol, and that she was known as an "enforcer" on the street and "someone not to be messed with" (Yeager, 2000, p. 12). The Crown also focused on her hospitalization records, which described numerous instances of "violence, aggressive behaviour, threats of violence to both staff and other patients, and an alarmingly negative attitude toward life in general and the well-being of others" (Yeager, 2000, p. 12). The Crown also identified portions of her own diaries where she described acts that she said she had committed that were sadistic and violent. Neve claimed that she had not committed any such acts, and later explained that she was simply trying to divert attention away from her real issues.

A coalition (made up of the Canadian Association of Elizabeth Fry Societies, the Disabled Women's Network Canada, the Women's Legal Education and Action Fund, and the Native Women's Association of Canada) fought to have Neve's DO designation overturned. They asserted that the designation was made based on myths and stereotypes about women who are involved in the criminal justice system, and who are Indigenous, lesbian, and working in the sex trade. They noted that the decision to declare Neve a DO was made without any consideration of the context in which a woman commits crimes, the realities that face sex trade workers, and women's strategies of survival employed in both community and custodial settings. Further, the use of the Hare Psychopathy

Checklist-Revised was heavily criticized for its application in this case, given the lack of published norms for female offender populations. Lastly, the coalition pointed out that a good deal of the Crown's psychiatric evidence relied on Neve's sexual orientation as an indicator of pathology when it described her as "homosexual and sadistic." It was also noted that the problem with the psychiatric evidence was compounded by the fact that it did not seem to adequately consider her extreme alcoholism and dependence on drugs (Yeager, 2000).

The Alberta Court of Appeal reversed Neve's DO designation on June 28, 1999. This decision was made for a number of statutory reasons, including the recognition that the robbery was not serious enough to warrant the DO application in the first place. Moreover, the Court of Appeal determined that the psychiatric evidence that had been relied upon was tainted. It also stressed that the sentencing judge must consider the "context in which the criminal conduct occurred" (Yeager, 2000, p. 18).

In July 1999, Neve was released from prison. In a CBC television interview, she commented:

> Every day I have to deal with part of my dangerous offender sentence and stuff, "cause it's still a big part of me and it depresses me and it hurts me. It's hard just to forgive and forget." (Stewart, 2000, p. 5)

SIDEBAR

The "Dangerous Offender" Designation

Individuals are designated as DOs if it can be shown that they pose a significant risk of committing a future violent or sexual offence. The DO provision is found in s 753 of the *Criminal Code*. In order to be "DO'd," an individual must be convicted of a serious personal injury offence and be deemed a threat to others. This must be evidenced by one of the following: (1) a pattern of repetitive behaviour that the offender is unable to control and that will likely cause death or serious injury to others; (2) a pattern of persistent, aggressive behaviour in which the offender is indifferent to the consequences to others; or (3) behaviour associated with the offence that is so brutal that the offender is believed unlikely to be able to be inhibited by normal types of behavioural restraint. The long-term offender provisions address concerns about those who do not meet the criteria for DO designation, but who nonetheless pose a significant risk to society. Under a long-term supervision order, an individual may be supervised for up to ten years following the custodial sentence (Public Safety Canada, 2011a).

According to a recent estimate, there are 622 DOs in Canada, with 36 in supervised care in the community and the rest incarcerated (Sapers, 2016). From 2004 to 2008, there was a 20 percent increase in the number of offenders with a DO designation (CSC, 2009b). Seventy-two percent of DOs have at least one current conviction for a sexual offence (Public Safety Canada, 2015). The vast majority of DOs are male; at the end of 2014, there were only four women designated as DOs. One of these women, Renée Acoby, was originally sentenced to three and a half years in prison, but received an additional 18 years for crimes committed while incarcerated, culminating in an indefinite sentence as a result of a successful DO application. A similar pattern of an ever-increasing sentence as a result of convictions incurred during incarceration was also experienced by Ashley Smith (see the case study that begins Part Five of this text). In 2005, Acoby and another inmate, while serving time at Grand Valley Institution for Women in Kitchener, Ontario, took two staff members hostage and threatened and tortured them for more than three hours. Interestingly, of the three female DO cases mentioned in this chapter (Marlene Moore, Lisa Neve, and Renée Acoby), none had been convicted of a sexual offence or of taking anyone's life, and all three had a history of convictions that included forcible confinement or hostage takings. Without minimizing the trauma that these women caused their victims, it is noteworthy that their crimes are not really comparable to the levels of violence commonly associated with infamous male DOs like Bernardo or Olson. In fact, convicted double murderer Russell Williams (who pleaded guilty to a total of 88 charges) was handed two life sentences, but the Crown attorney in that case did not pursue a DO designation because he believed Williams would never be paroled, given the facts outlined at trial (CBC, 2010).

Sex Offenders

In 2008–9, 4.3 percent of those in provincial custody and 10.4 percent of those in federal custody had committed a sexual assault as their most serious offence. That amounts to 3,167 and 2,348 offenders, respectively (Calverley, 2010). At the federal level, approximately 13 percent of new admissions are for a sexual offence (CSC, 2015). In their analysis of 95 studies of more than 31,000 sex offenders, Hanson and Morton-Bourgon (2004) identified that the observed sexual recidivism rate was 13.7 percent, the violent recidivism rate (including both sexual and non-sexual violence) was 25 percent, and the general recidivism rate was almost 37 percent. The average follow-up period for these studies was five to six years.

SIDEBAR

Recidivism Rates

Recidivism rates will vary for a couple of reasons. Rates depend on how researchers define the term *recidivism* (e.g., Does it include rearrest, reconviction, or revocation of release?). They also depend on the follow-up period that researchers use; longer follow-up periods are associated with higher rates of recidivism. It has been suggested that a reconviction rate range between 41 and 44 percent is a reasonably good estimate for Canadian federal offenders, and it can serve as a measure against which to evaluate the success of rehabilitative programs both over time and with one another (Bonta, Rugge, & Dauvergne, 2003).

National Sex Offender Programs

The CSC offers a variety of programs for sex offenders, including the High Intensity National Sex Offender Program, Moderate Intensity National Sex Offender Program, and National Sex Offender Maintenance Program. These programs provide group sessions targeted to high- to low-risk sex offenders and are intended to assist offenders in developing self-management skills. These programs also target "cognitive distortions [e.g., a sex offender thinking that it is normal to have sex with children], deviant arousal and fantasy, social skills, anger and emotion management, empathy, and victim awareness" (Cortoni & Nunes, 2007, p. iii). A 2007 study of the Canadian low and moderate intensity national sex offender programs found that those who participated in the programs had a lower rate of recidivism than those who did not. As Cortoni and Nunes (2007) noted, this finding is consistent with various research that has found sex offender treatment programs to be effective in reducing recidivism.

Female Sex Offenders

The vast majority of sex offenders are male. However, interestingly, a recent meta-analysis of sexual offences across 12 countries revealed that while only a small proportion (about 2 percent) of sexual offences reported to police identify a woman as the perpetrator, victimization surveys reveal a higher proportion (12 percent) of sexual offences committed by females (Cortoni, Babchishin, & Rat, 2016). In the past, the approach to assessing and treating female sex offenders tended to mirror the approach that had been developed for men. However, as Cortoni (2009) noted, this approach has not been without criticism. According to Nathan and Ward (2002), the treatment for female sex offenders must be "tailored to their distinct needs and characteristics rather than proceed on the assumption that all individuals should receive exactly the same interventions" (p. 20).

Comparatively speaking, the recidivism rates for female sex offenders are much lower. In their review of the recidivism rates of adult female sex offenders across five countries, Cortoni and Hanson (2005) found a sexual recidivism rate of 1 percent, a violent recidivism rate (including sexual) of just over 6 percent, and a general recidivism rate (including violent and sexual) of just over 20 percent. The average follow-up period was five years.

Segregating Sex Offenders

Some sex offenders can request to be placed in administrative segregation for their own safety. As a group, sex offenders are viewed by other inmates as being very low in the inmate hierarchy, and can be subject to abuse. In 1996, a riot at Headingley Correctional Centre in Manitoba saw presumed sex offenders attacked by other inmates, resulting in genital mutilation and three inmates having fingers cut off with exacto knives. In a riot at Mountain Institution in British Columbia, Michael Andrew Gibbon, a notorious sex offender, died from wounds inflicted upon him by other inmates. While Gibbon was residing among the general prison population when he was killed, most of the inmates attacked during the Headingley riot were living in protective custody—which rioting inmates gained access to by taking a set of keys from a guard (Matas, 2008; Roberts, 1996).

A study of administrative segregation in federal corrections found that more offenders placed in administrative segregation have been identified in their correctional plan as having sexual behaviour issues than those who have not been identified as such (OCI, 2015). This finding is consistent with a previous study that found that those who were voluntarily segregated were significantly more likely to have a previous conviction for a sexual offence (27 percent) compared with inmates who were involuntarily segregated (18 percent) for disciplinary reasons (Motiuk & Blanchette, 1997). These data are particularly noteworthy, since it has been found that offenders who request to be voluntarily segregated stay segregated twice as long (average length of stay is 68 versus 35 days) as those who are segregated involuntarily (Bottos, 2007). In a review of the literature on the administratively segregated population, Bottos (2007) noted that some evidence indicates that administrative segregation may negatively impact "individuals' well-being, their security reclassification status, program participation, discretionary release decisions, and conditional release outcomes" (p. 17). This evidence is significant given the disproportionate number of sex offenders who voluntarily seek out protective custody.

Reintegrating Sex Offenders

Reintegration issues must be considered as part of release planning for sex offenders. Sex offenders have to deal with not only the barriers and stigma common to most former inmates when looking for employment upon release, but also the barriers and stigma specific to the nature of their offence. As a result of policies and procedures put in place to protect members of society, some sex offenders need to consider the likelihood that they cannot return to their previous employment and must therefore look into retraining to find suitable employment upon release. In addition to facing employment challenges, sex offenders are also subject to community notification and to sex offender registration laws (Harris & Hanson, 2010; Manitoba Department of Justice, 2011; Public Safety Canada, 2011b).

Offenders with Mental Disorders

Mental disorders are considered health conditions. They can include changes in mood, behaviour, or thinking (or all three) that affect how a person functions and may be associated with distress (Health Canada, 2011). In a review of the literature, McGuire (2000) noted that "globally, there is little evidence to suggest that a diagnosis of mental disorder in itself is clearly linked to increased occurrence of any specific type of crime" (para. 22). Although there may not be a direct link between the two areas, studies have shown that a significant proportion of inmates meet the criteria for a diagnosis of a mental disorder. (See Chapter 6 for a discussion of the not criminally responsible on account of mental disorder designation.)

Collaboration between correctional and mental health systems is essential because some individuals with a mental disorder will find themselves detained in correctional facilities. In a recent study on the national prevalence of mental disorders among incoming federal male offenders, over 70 percent of male offenders were found to meet the criteria for a mental disorder (Beaudette, Power, & Stewart, 2015). The most common was alcohol/substance use disorder, at 49.6 percent. With this diagnosis excluded, 40 percent of incoming male offenders met the criteria for at least one mental disorder (Beaudette et al., 2015). Compared with community samples, both male and female incarcerated offenders appear to have considerably higher lifetime prevalence rates of mental disorder (Folsom, 2009). As you may recall from the case study, Lisa Neve had a history of interactions with the mental health system in addition to correctional systems.

Protocols for mental health assessment in Canadian corrections have been in place for a number of years. All federal institutions are required, under Commissioner's Directive 840, to provide psychological services, including assessment, to offenders as needed (CSC, 1994). An initial screening of offenders during the intake process is done to determine who may require further assessment and possible treatment. Psychological assessments must address mental health needs; those done for the purposes of pre-release must also include reference to the inmate's level of risk. Mental health assessments must be culturally and gender-sensitive. A mental health strategy for female offenders in CSC facilities has also been developed, and recommendations have been made that specifically address the needs of incarcerated women with mental disorders (Laishes, 2002).

Safety and Suicide Concerns

Issues of safety are of paramount importance to correctional officials. Two behaviours related to psychological functioning are of particular concern: self-injury and suicide. On average, there are ten suicides in federal corrections each year, accounting for approximately 20 percent of all deaths in custody (OCI, 2014). Although self-injury and suicide can appear similar (i.e., some instances of self-injury may be misinterpreted as a suicide attempt), the intent of each is different. The Correctional Investigator noted that a quarter of the female offender population has a history of self-injury (OCI, 2012). Such behaviour can take many forms, including hanging, cutting, scratching, reopening wounds, head banging, biting, swallowing non-food items (such as glass), and inserting objects into the skin. It has been pointed out repeatedly that self-injurious behaviour must be considered a mental health concern and not be treated as a matter of security (Heney, 1990; Sapers, 2010). Historically, this has not been the case, and even today, the OCI has documented cases where CSC has shown an overreliance on the use of seclusion and restraints to manage self-injury (OCI, 2012; Sapers, 2011). Individuals in federal prison are more at risk for killing themselves than being murdered (Larivière, 1997). The most likely method of suicide in federal institutions is hanging, and suicides most often occur in the inmate's general population cell. Suicide rates for prison populations are about seven times higher than in the wider population (OCI, 2014).

Directives for prison staff specify that all inmates must be screened for **suicidal ideation** within the first 24 hours of being admitted to an institution,[3] when placed in administrative segregation (whether voluntary or for disciplinary reasons), and when staff have reason to believe an inmate is at risk for suicide. Whenever possible, a mental health professional is expected to assess the inmate and assign him or her to a suicide watch level.

suicidal ideation
Thoughts, either fleeting in nature or well-thought-out, that a person has about killing himself or herself.

Psychologists, psychiatrists, and psychiatric nurses are a few of the professionals employed in corrections to address the mental health needs of offenders. Therapeutic and crisis interventions are two types of psychological services available to federal inmates. However, in many institutions, insufficient resources are available to carry out these interventions. The following quote, from the 2007 report of the CSC Review Panel, summarizes the state of psychological services for federal inmates:

> Most penitentiaries have a limited number of psychologists on staff, and mental health care is usually limited to crisis intervention and suicide prevention. Psychologists spend a significant percentage of their time preparing risk assessments intended to assist the National Parole Board in making decisions regarding conditional release. The primary and intermediate mental health care provided to offenders is insufficient. Offenders with mental health problems usually do not receive appropriate treatment unless their needs reach crisis levels. Many are segregated for protection because of their inability to cope in regular penitentiary settings, and therefore they have limited access to programming or treatment. (Sampson, Gascon, Glen, Louie, & Rosenfeldt, 2007, p. 55)

CSC has not escaped criticism for its handling of individuals with severe forms of mental disorder. While exchange of service agreements exist with some secure psychiatric facilities, inmates can still end up bouncing between correctional facilities and psychiatric facilities, or between their home institution and regional psychiatric correctional institutions. In some instances, inmates have been transferred to give staff relief. Cases such as that of Ashley Smith, who died in segregation at Grand Valley Institution for Women, bring public attention to the plight of those who are incarcerated and shuffled from institution to institution, all the while trying to cope with serious mental illness.

Indigenous Offenders

Former Assembly of First Nations National Chief Shawn Atleo stated that "First Nations children are more likely to go to jail than to graduate from high school" (Therien, 2011, para. 1). This statement speaks volumes about the continued marginalization of Indigenous people in Canada. Indigenous people are over-represented in the correctional system, making up 25 percent of federally sentenced offenders but only 3 percent of the country's adult population (Sapers, 2016; Reitano, 2016). Seventy percent of Indigenous men in federal custody identify as First Nations, 25 percent as Métis, and 4 percent as Inuit (Farrell MacDonald, 2014). Overrepresentation also occurs at the provincial level, where 26 percent of those in custody and 24 percent of those under community supervision are Indigenous people (Reitano, 2016). There is every indication, based on the youthful demographics of the growing Indigenous population, that this over-representation will get worse, not better, over time (Mann, 2009). Further, the number of Indigenous inmates grew by 50 percent between 2005 and 2015 while the corresponding increase in the number of non-Indigenous inmates was 10 percent. Indigenous incarceration rates vary per region but are particularly high in the Prairie region, where they represent almost 50 percent of all inmates (Sapers, 2016).

Colonialism can be viewed as a major contributor to this over-representation. It has been defined as a "systematic oppression of a people through a variety of assimilationist measures that are intended to eradicate the peoples and/or their sense of individual and cultural identity" (Restoule, 2009, p. 272). Colonialist practices continue to exert an influence in Canada, although more subtly than in previous eras.

In a study of case management practices, assessments for decisions relating to offender security classification (i.e., minimum, medium, or maximum security) and release were examined to determine the extent to which Indigenous social history factors were considered (Keown, Gobeil, Biro, & Beaudette, 2015). Indigenous social history factors were documented in 98 percent of the assessments reviewed in the study. Notably, the researchers did not find any evidence to suggest that Indigenous social history factors were misconstrued as risk factors.

Passed in 1992, the *Corrections and Conditional Release Act* (CCRA) was the first piece of legislation to give Indigenous peoples some involvement in the development of services, policies, and programs in corrections, as well as to ensure that the correctional environment provided opportunities for Indigenous spirituality and cultural practices. One of the principles in the CCRA is as follows: "correctional policies, programs and practices respect gender, ethnic, cultural and linguistic differences and are responsive to the special needs of women, aboriginal peoples, persons requiring mental health care and other groups." (s 4(g)).

Introduced in 1995, Commissioner's Directive 702 outlined CSC's policy to accommodate Indigenous cultural and spiritual practices within federal prisons. The use of ceremonial medicines (e.g., sweetgrass, sage, cedar, and tobacco), ceremonial and personal spiritual objects (e.g., medicine bags, smudge bowls, and feathers), traditional foods, and the practice of ceremonies (e.g., smudging, sweat lodge, pipe ceremonies, and potlatches) are all covered under this directive (CSC, 2008).

CSC has developed programs that target the needs of specific groups of Indigenous offenders, such as Inuit sex offenders, violent females, and substance abusers. CSC has attempted to offer culturally sensitive programming, while still adhering to the principles of effective correctional treatment. It also established nine Aboriginal Healing Lodges across Canada, which are either operated by CSC and its staff or funded by CSC and managed by community partner organizations (CSC, 2016b). The first healing lodge for female offenders (Okimaw Ohci Healing Lodge) was opened in Maple Creek, Saskatchewan in 1995, and the first healing lodge for male offenders (Pê Sâkâstêw Centre) was opened in Maskwacis, Alberta in 1997. These facilities are staffed primarily by people of Indigenous descent and are geared to minimum/medium-security female offenders and minimum-security male offenders. In 2003, CSC established an Aboriginal Corrections Continuum of Care model, which includes Elders and Indigenous correctional staff, to address the needs of Indigenous offenders (CSC, 2006).

According to some, Indigenous corrections is at a crossroads, with an urgent need for action on the part of CSC to translate "good intentions" into results that will lessen the existing gap between Indigenous and non-Indigenous offenders (Mann, 2009, p. 5). Indigenous inmates are overrepresented in segregation, are more likely to be classified as high needs and high risk, are released at later points in their sentences, and are more likely to serve full sentences, to have their conditional release revoked, and to have had a previous youth or adult sentence (Mann, 2009; Therien, 2011). Factors such as "substance abuse, intergenerational abuse, and residential schools, low levels of education, employment, and income, and substandard housing and health care" have been identified as likely playing a role in this overrepresentation (Mann, 2009, p. 4). Although CSC developed a strategic plan for Indigenous corrections that included almost 200 actionable items, a review of the plan by the OCI found that very few of these "promising and ambitious undertakings" have been accomplished (p. 4). In the decision of *Ewert v Canada* (2015), the court found that the use by the CSC of certain psychological risk assessment tools (including the Hare Psychopathy Checklist-Revised, discussed in Chapter 5) in an Indigenous offender's psychological evaluation violated the offender's "right to life, liberty and security of the person" (s 7 of the *Canadian Charter of Rights and Freedoms*). Ewert, a Métis, argued that these measures were not reliable for Indigenous persons on account of the cultural bias of the tests. This decision has called into question the validity of the use of non-Indigenous risk assessment tools on Indigenous offenders.

Diversity in Corrections

It is important to acknowledge that the offender population is becoming more diverse, and correctional practices must be responsive to this change. In fact, Commissioner's Directive 767 was put in place to "ensure that the needs and cultural interests of offenders belonging to ethnocultural minority groups are identified and that programs and services are developed and maintained to meet those needs" (CSC, 2016a). A study of ethnic diversity in new admissions to federal institutions found that the number of Southeast Asian, Chinese, and Latin American offenders increased significantly between 2000 and 2009 (Gottschall, 2012). It also found that black offenders and Southeast Asians are overrepresented in federal institutions compared with their representation in the general population.

The OCI reported that black[4] inmates are one of the fastest-growing groups in federal corrections (OCI, 2013b). Specifically, from 2002–3 to 2011–12, the number of black inmates in federal corrections increased by 75 percent (i.e., from 767 to 1,340). In 2011–12, black inmates accounted for 9.3 percent of those incarcerated federally, while only 2.9 percent of the Canadian population identified as black (OCI, 2013b). As is the case with Indigenous people (and echoing the findings of Gottschall [2012]), black offenders are overrepresented in federal corrections (OCI, 2013b). Gottschall (2012) reported that

Pê Sâkâstêw Centre in Maskwacis, Alberta is a minimum security facility that promotes a healing process based on Indigenous culture.

male black offenders had the lowest (average) age upon admission and had the highest percentage of admissions to maximum-security institutions. In terms of risk–needs assessment at intake, black offenders were most likely to be assessed as having need in the areas of attitudes and associates.

In terms of offence type, the percentage of male offenders serving a sentence for a violent offence was highest among Indigenous male offenders (69.8 percent), Latin American male offenders (60.4 percent), black male offenders (57.3 percent), and white male offenders (53.5 percent). The percentage of male offenders serving a sentence for a drug-related offence was highest among Southeast Asian male offenders (62.2 percent), Chinese male offenders (58.3 percent), Latin American male offenders (39.0 percent), and black male offenders (38.6 percent) (Gottschall, 2012).

When involvement in incidents in federal institutions was examined, Indigenous, black, and South Asian male offenders had the highest involvement as perpetrators or associates (Gottschall, 2012). Gang involvement was also higher among visible minority male offenders than it was for white male offenders.

A diverse correctional population has implications for correctional management. With awareness of the changing demographics of institutional populations, Correctional Services Canada should be in a position to take the steps necessary to ensure that Commissioner's Directive 767 is adhered to, and that appropriate services and programs are in place to meet the needs of such a diverse population. In 2013, the OCI published a report on the black inmate experience in federal penitentiaries (OCI, 2013b). While the OCI acknowledged that the CSC has instituted a number of measures[5] to address the needs of a more diverse population, the OCI identified the ongoing need for CSC to be able to better accommodate these needs. Based on its research, the OCI noted that the cultural needs of black inmates were not being met in three key areas: correctional programs were not culturally relevant, cultural products (e.g., hair and skin care products, cultural food) were often not available, and relevant community help was limited or non-existent (OCI, 2013b). The OCI (2013a) concluded that correctional programs need to be reviewed and updated based on a diversity perspective. It also recommended hiring more diverse security and program staff, especially in those areas where diversity of the inmate population is greatest (OCI, 2013a). The CSC notes on its website that training on diversity is part of the Correctional Training Program, Parole Officer Training Program, and New Employee Orientation Program.

Conclusion

What should be clear after reading this chapter is that Canada's correctional population is very diverse. When considering the needs of the offender population, marginalized groups are of prime importance—the focus should not be solely on the majority.

The discussion of special subpopulations in this chapter was not meant to be exhaustive. It was meant to highlight the diversity within the larger correctional population. The Mini Case Study of Lisa Neve was chosen because of the complexities of her case; she herself could be classified as a member of several subpopulations. Her case reminds us that people cannot be neatly classified using one label or another, nor should they be. The reality is that each individual serving time in a custodial setting has a distinctive story and life. While it is useful to consider some of the challenges inmates face as subpopulations, it is imperative that the individuals themselves not be forgotten. Keep this in mind as you read the next section (Part Five), and the tragic case of Ashley Smith.

IN-CLASS EXERCISE

The Impact of Being Incarcerated

Take five to ten minutes and jot down the impact that being incarcerated would have on aspects of your life (such as family, work, and school).

- What are some of the practical arrangements you would need to make if you faced a prison sentence? What would you do with your apartment, or your pet?
- What three key concerns would you have about being in prison? How might these concerns create challenges for the CSC staff who develop correctional programming? How do your concerns inform your reflections on the correctional experience?

Regardless of what people are incarcerated for, they are going to face similar kinds of concerns. As a student, trying to imagine just how many aspects of your life would change as a result of being incarcerated, and acknowledging your fears, will help you to realize just how overwhelming a period of incarceration can be.

IN-CLASS EXERCISE

The "True Grit" Facility

View the following excerpt from a CBC feature on a Nevada prison called "True Grit," which was designed specifically for older offenders: www.cbc.ca/player/play/2212854897.

After watching the CBC clip, break into small groups and answer the following questions:

1. What aspects of the "True Grit" facility seem to speak to the specific needs of older inmates in ways that are different from the general population prison environment?
2. Do you think specialized facilities such as "True Grit" are warranted? Or should older and younger inmates be housed in the same institution? Why or why not?

DISCUSSION QUESTIONS

1. If you were a prison warden and you were approached by a local AIDS organization to pilot a needle exchange program in your prison, how would you decide whether your facility would participate (assuming that you were the final decision maker)? What are the pros and cons of instituting a prison needle exchange program? Be sure to include the issues of security, health care, and the concerns of staff and non-using inmates in your answer.

2. You are out with a friend for dinner when your friend comments on a recent case in which a 67-year-old male was sent to prison for life. Your friend jokes that the inmate will probably have a better life at "Club Fed" than he would in the community. How would you respond to the comment? What points would you make to educate your friend on the status of older offenders in Canadian prisons?

3. Do you agree with the provisions for transgender inmates as outlined in Commissioner's Directive 800-5 (available at http://www.csc-scc.gc.ca/politiques-et-lois/800-5-gl-eng.shtml)? Do you think that pre-operative transgender inmates should be housed in an institution consistent with their sex at birth? Why or why not?

4. Of the subpopulations that were discussed in this chapter, can you identify a single challenge that they all pose with respect to prison management? From an operational perspective, what common issues affect some of these subpopulations? How would you address these issues with staff to ensure the smooth operation of the facility?

NOTES

A portion of this chapter was adapted from Barker, J. (Ed.). (2008). *Women and the criminal justice system: A Canadian perspective.* Toronto: Emond Montgomery.

1   Because Chapter 12 discusses the unique challenges inherent in dealing with youth in conflict with the law, this chapter will only cover the topic of age as it relates to the older offender.

2   Most of the regional women's institutions can now accommodate maximum security women in a secure unit.

3   The OCI noted that as of April 2014, CSC was not conducting suicide risk screens on first-time federal offenders who were being transferred from provincial remand to federal corrections.

4   The OCI uses the term *black* to be consistent with CSC's collection and reporting of race data.

5   CSC has established various committees (e.g., National and Regional Ethno-Cultural Advisory Committees, National Advisory Council on Diversity, and National Diversity Committee), cultural programs and awareness activities, diversity and sensitivity training, staffing initiatives (including targeted recruitment as well as mentoring and leadership programs) to increase staff representation among employment equity groups (OCI, 2013b).

SUGGESTED FURTHER READINGS

Andrews, D., & Bonta, J. (2010). *The psychology of criminal conduct* (5th ed.). New Providence, NJ: LexisNexis.

Sapers, H. (2008). A preventable death. Retrieved from http://www.oci-bec.gc.ca/cnt/rpt/pdf/oth-aut/oth-aut20080620-eng.pdf.

Sapers, H. (2011). *Annual report of the Office of the Correctional Investigator 2010–2011*. Ottawa: Her Majesty the Queen in Right of Canada. Retrieved from http://www.oci-bec.gc.ca/cnt/rpt/pdf/annrpt/annrpt20102011-eng.pdf.

Sapers, H. (2015). *Annual report of the Office of the Correctional Investigator 2014–2015*. Ottawa: Her Majesty the Queen in Right of Canada. Retrieved from http://www.oci-bec.gc.ca/cnt/rpt/pdf/annrpt/annrpt20142015-eng.pdf.

Yeager, M.G. (2000). Ideology and dangerousness: The case of Lisa Colleen Neve. *Critical Criminology, 9*(1–2), 9–21. doi:10.1007/BF02461035.

REFERENCES

Andrews, D., & Bonta, J. (2010). *The psychology of criminal conduct* (5th ed.). New Providence, NJ: LexisNexis.

Beaudette, J., Cheverie, M., & Gobeil, R. (2014). Aboriginal women: Profile and changing population (Research report R-341). Ottawa: Correctional Service Canada. Retrieved from http://www.csc-scc.gc.ca/005/008/092/R-341-eng.pdf.

Beaudette, J.N., Power, J., & Stewart, L.A. (2015). National prevalence of mental disorders among incoming federally-sentenced men offenders (Research report R-357). Ottawa: Correctional Service Canada. Retrieved from http://www.csc-scc.gc.ca/005/008/092/005008-0357-eng.pdf.

Begin, P., Weekes, J., & Thomas, G. (2006). The Canadian addiction survey: Substance use and misuse among the Canadian population. *Forum on Corrections Research, 18*(1), 12–18. Retrieved from http://www.csc-scc.gc.ca/text/pblct/forum/e181/e181d_e.pdf.

Bonta, J., Rugge, T., & Dauvergne, M. (2003). *The reconviction rate of federal offenders* (User report 2003-02). Ottawa: Public Works and Government Services Canada. Retrieved from https://www.publicsafety.gc.ca/cnt/rsrcs/pblctns/rcnvctn-rt-fdrl/rcnvctn-rt-fdrl-eng.pdf.

Bottos, S. (2007). Profile of offenders in administrative segregation: A review of the literature (Research brief B-39). Ottawa: Correctional Service Canada. Retrieved from http://www.csc-scc.gc.ca/research/b39-eng.shtml.

Brown, G. (2010). Autocastration and autopenectomy as surgical self-treatment in incarcerated persons with gender identity disorder. *International Journal of Transgenderism, 12*, 31–39. doi:10.1080/15532731003688970.

Calverley, D. (2010). Adult correctional services in Canada, 2008/2009. *Juristat, 30*(3), 1–32. Catalogue No. 85-002-X. Retrieved from http://www.statcan.gc.ca/pub/85-002-x/2010003/article/11353-eng.pdf.

Carrington, P.J. (2001). Population aging and crime in Canada, 2000–2041. *Canadian Journal of Criminology, 43*(3), 331–356.

Caya, S., & Stuart, P. (Eds.). (2012). Canada Year Book. Ottawa: Statistics Canada. Retrieved from http://www.statcan.gc.ca/pub/11-402-x/2012000/pdf/crime-eng.pdf.

CBC. (2010, October 21). Williams gets 2 life terms for "despicable crimes." *CBC News*. Retrieved from http://www.cbc.ca/news/canada/story/2010/10/21/russell-williams-day-four.html.

Chu, S. (2009). Clean switch: The case for prison needle and syringe programs. *HIV/AIDS Policy & Law Review, 14*(2), 86–92. Retrieved from http://sagecollection.ca/en/system/files/policy_law_review_142.pdf.

Correctional Service Canada. (1994). Commissioner's Directive 840: Psychological services. Retrieved from https://www.publicsafety.gc.ca/lbrr/archives/cd-840-cd.pdf.

Correctional Service Canada. (2005). CSC action plan in response to the report of the Canadian Human Rights Commission. Retrieved from http://www.csc-scc.gc.ca/ publications/fsw/gender4/CHRC_response-eng.shtml.

Correctional Service Canada. (2006). *Strategic plan for Aboriginal corrections: Innovation, learning and adjustment, 2006–07 to 2010–11.* Ottawa: Author. Retrieved from http://www.csc-scc.gc.ca/aboriginal/092/002003-1000-eng.pdf.

Correctional Service Canada. (2007). A program for every inmate: Meeting specific needs [Education module]. Retrieved from http://www.csc-scc.gc.ca/ educational-resources/005005-3040-eng.shtml.

Correctional Service Canada. (2008). Commissioner's Directive 702: Aboriginal offenders. Retrieved from http://www.csc-scc.gc.ca/acts-and-regulations/702-cd-eng.shtml.

Correctional Service Canada. (2009a). Creating better relations: Aging offenders—Aging community.

Correctional Service Canada. (2009b). Dangerous offender designations: A five-year offence profile. *Research Snippet*, Number RS-09-03. Retrieved from http://www.csc-scc.gc.ca/ research/rs09-03-eng.shtml.

Correctional Service Canada. (2011a). Infectious disease surveillance in Canadian federal penitentiaries 2005–2006. Retrieved from http://www.csc-scc.gc.ca/publications/ infdscfp-2005-06/tb-eng.shtml.

Correctional Service Canada. (2011b). Specific guidelines for methadone maintenance treatment.

Correctional Service Canada. (2014a). A brief profile of incarcerated older men offenders. *Research Snippet*, Number 14-2. Ottawa: Author. Retrieved from http:// www.csc-scc.gc.ca/005/008/092/rs14-02-eng.pdf.

Correctional Service Canada. (2014b). Older offenders in the custody of the Correctional Service Canada. *Research in Brief*, Number 14-21. Retrieved from http:// www.csc-scc.gc.ca/005/008/092/rs14-21-eng.pdf.

Correctional Service Canada. (2014c). *Research results: Women offenders.* Ottawa: Author. Retrieved from http://www.csc-scc.gc.ca/publications/092/005007-3014-eng.pdf.

Correctional Service Canada. (2014d). Substance abuse problem severity, treatment readiness, and response bias among incarcerated men. *Research Snippet*, Number 13-5. Ottawa: Author. Retrieved from http://www.csc-scc.gc.ca/005/008/092/rs13-05-eng.pdf.

Correctional Service Canada. (2015). Federal offender population—2013: Warrant of committal admissions—All offenders. Retrieved from http://www.csc-scc.gc.ca/ research/092/005008-3002-eng.pdf.

Correctional Service Canada. (2016a). Commissioner's Directive 767: Ethnocultural offenders—Services and interventions. Retrieved from http://www.csc-scc.gc.ca/acts-and-regulations/767-cd-eng.shtml.

Correctional Service Canada. (2016b). Correctional Service Canada healing lodges. Retrieved from http://www.csc-scc.gc.ca/aboriginal/002003-2000-eng.shtml.

Corrections and Conditional Release Act, SC 1992, c 20.

Cortoni, F. (2009). Violence and women offenders. In J. Barker (Ed.), *Women and the criminal justice system: A Canadian perspective* (pp. 175–200). Toronto: Emond Montgomery.

Cortoni, F., Babchishin, K.M., & Rat, C. (2016). The proportion of sexual offenders who are female is higher than thought: A meta-analysis. *Criminal Justice and Behavior, 44*(2), 145–162. Retrieved from http://journals.sagepub.com/doi/pdf/10.1177/0093854816658923.

Cortoni, F., & Hanson, K. (2005). A review of the recidivism rates of adult female sexual offenders. Ottawa: Public Safety and Emergency Preparedness Canada. Retrieved from http://www.csc-scc.gc.ca/research/r169-eng.shtml.

Cortoni, F., & Nunes, K. (2007). *Assessing the effectiveness of the National Sexual Offender Program* (Research report R-183). Ottawa: Correctional Service Canada. Retrieved from http://www.csc-scc.gc.ca/research/r183-eng.shtml.

Doherty, S., Ternes, M., & Matheson, F.I. (2014). *An examination of the effectiveness of the National Substance Abuse Program High Intensity (NSAP-H) on institutional adjustment and post-release outcomes* (Research report R-290). Ottawa: Correctional Service Canada.

Ewert v Canada, 2015 FC 1093 (CanLII).

Farrell MacDonald, S. (2014). *Profile of Aboriginal men offenders: Custody and supervision snapshots* (Research report R-321). Ottawa: Correctional Service Canada. Retrieved from http://www.csc-scc.gc.ca/005/008/092/r321-eng.pdf.

Finn, A., Trevethan, S., Carrière, G., & Kowalski, M. (1999). Female inmates, Aboriginal inmates, and inmates serving life sentences: A one day snapshot. *Juristat, 19*(5). Catalogue No. 85-002-XIE. Retrieved from http://publications.gc.ca/Collection-R/Statcan/85-002-XIE/0059985-002-XIE.pdf.

Folsom, J. (2009). Women offenders and mental health. In J. Barker (Ed.), *Women and the criminal justice system: A Canadian perspective* (pp. 175–200). Toronto: Emond Montgomery.

Gottschall, S. (2012). *Ethnic diversity in Canadian federal offender admissions* (Research report R-263). Ottawa: Correctional Service Canada. Retrieved from https://www.publicsafety.gc.ca/lbrr/archives/cn21498-eng.pdf.

Government of Canada. (2013). Canadian Tobacco, Alcohol and Drugs Survey (CTADS). Summary of results for 2013. Ottawa. Retrieved from http://healthycanadians.gc.ca/science-research-sciences-recherches/data-donnees/ctads-ectad/summary-sommaire-2013-eng.php.

Hamilton, G. (2016, April 6). "Collateral victim" of residential schools gets 15 months for burning child 27 times with cigarette, lighter. *National Post*. Retrieved from http://news.nationalpost.com/news/canada/collateral-victim-of-residential-schools-gets-15-months-for-burning-child-27-times-with-cigarette-lighter

Hannah-Moffat, K. (1995). Feminine fortresses: Woman-centered prisons? *The Prison Journal, 75*(2), 135–164.

Hannah-Moffat, K. (2000). Re-forming the prison: Rethinking our ideals. In K. Hannah-Moffat & M. Shaw (Eds.), *An ideal prison? Critical essays of women's imprisonment in Canada* (pp. 30–40). Halifax: Fernwood.

Hanson, R.K., & Morton-Bourgon, K. (2004). *Predictors of sexual recidivism: An updated meta-analysis*. Ottawa: Public Safety and Emergency Preparedness Canada. Retrieved from https://www.publicsafety.gc.ca/cnt/rsrcs/pblctns/2004-02-prdctrs-sxl-rcdvsm-pdtd/2004-02-prdctrs-sxl-rcdvsm-pdtd-eng.pdf.

Harris, A., & Hanson, K. (2010). Clinical, actuarial and dynamic risk assessment of sexual offenders: Why do things keep changing? *Journal of Sexual Aggression, 16*(3), 296–310.

Health Canada. (2011). *Mental health: Mental illness. It's your health*. Ottawa: Author. Retrieved from http://hc-sc.gc.ca/hl-vs/alt_formats/pacrb-dgapcr/pdf/iyh-vsv/diseases-maladies/mental-eng.pdf.

Heney, J. (1990). Report on self-injurious behaviour in the Kingston Prison for Women. Ottawa: Correctional Service Canada. Retrieved from http://www.csc-scc.gc.ca/text/prgrm/fsw/selfinjuries/toce-eng.shtml.

Hensley, C., & Tewksbury, R. (2002). Inmate-to-inmate prison sexuality: A review of empirical studies. *Trauma Violence Abuse, 3*, 226–243. doi:10.1177/15248380020033005.

Hewitt, P. (2010, October 24). Russell Williams enters a "grim" existence in Kingston Penitentiary. *Toronto Star*. Retrieved from http://www.thestar.com/news/canada/article/880485—russell-williams-enters-a-grim-existence-in-kingston-penitentiary.

Hotton Mahony, T. (2011). *Women and the criminal justice system*. Ottawa. Statistics Canada. Retrieved from http://www.statcan.gc.ca/pub/89-503-x/2010001/article/11416-eng.pdf.

Jenness, V., & Fenstermaker, S. (2014). Agnes goes to prison: Gender authenticity, transgender inmates in prisons for men, and pursuit of "the real deal." *Gender and Society, 28*(1), 5–31. doi:10.1177/08912343213499446.

Jimenez, M. (1999, April 3). The law, violence, and Lisa Neve: Is this the most dangerous woman in Canada? *National Post*. Retrieved from http://business.highbeam.com/435424/article-1G1-54483432/law-violence-and-lisa-neve.

Keown, L.A., Gobeil, R., Biro, S., & Beaudette, J.N. (2015). Aboriginal social history factors in case management (Research report R-356). Ottawa: Correctional Service Canada. Retrieved from http://www.csc-scc.gc.ca/005/008/092/r356-eng.pdf.

Kong, R., & AuCoin, K. (2008). Female offenders in Canada. *Juristat, 28*(1). Catalogue No. 85-002-X. Retrieved from http://www.statcan.gc.ca/pub/85-002-x/2008001/article/10509-eng.htm.

Kunic, D. (2006). The computerized assessment of substance abuse (CASA). *Forum on Corrections Research, 18*(1), 19–23. Retrieved from http://www.csc-scc.gc.ca/text/pblct/forum/e181/e181e_e.pdf.

Laishes, J. (2002). The 2002 mental health strategy for women offenders. Retrieved from http://www.csc-scc.gc.ca/text/prgrm/fsw/mhealth/3-eng.shtml.

Larivière, M. (1997). *The Correctional Service of Canada 1996–97 retrospective report on inmate suicides*. Ottawa: Correctional Service of Canada. Retrieved from https://www.publicsafety.gc.ca/lbrr/archives/hv%206545.6%20l37%201996-97-eng.pdf.

Lupick, T. (2015, December 13). Living nightmare for transgender inmate at all-male prison. *Toronto Star*. Retrieved from https://www.thestar.com/news/canada/2015/12/13/living-nightmare-for-transgender-inmate-at-all-male-prison.html.

MacPherson, P., & Fraser, C. (2006). Random urinalysis testing in federal corrections. *Forum on Corrections Research, 18*(1), 33–37. Retrieved from http://www.csc-scc.gc.ca/text/pblct/forum/e181/e181h_e.pdf.

Manitoba Department of Justice. (2011). Safer communities: Sex offender notifications. Retrieved from http://www.gov.mb.ca/justice/notification/index.html.

Mann, M. (2009). *Good intentions, disappointing results: A progress report on federal Aboriginal corrections*. Ottawa: Office of the Correctional Investigator. Retrieved from http://www.oci-bec.gc.ca/cnt/rpt/pdf/oth-aut/oth-aut20091113-eng.pdf.

Matas, R. (2008, April 3). Ottawa orders full review of prison riot. *Globe and Mail*, p. A6.

McGuire, J. (2000). Treatment approaches for offenders with mental disorder. In L. Motiuk and R. Serin (Eds.), *Compendium 2000 on effective correctional programming*. Retrieved from http://www.csc-scc.gc.ca/005/008/compendium/2000/chap_16-eng.shtml.

McVie, F. (2001). Drugs in federal corrections: The issues and challenges. *Forum on Corrections Research, 13*(3), 7–9. Retrieved from http://www.csc-scc.gc.ca/text/pblct/forum/e133/133c_e.pdf.

Motiuk, L., & Blanchette, K. (1997). *Case characteristics of segregated offenders in federal corrections* (Research report R-57). Ottawa: Correctional Service Canada. Retrieved from http://www.csc-scc.gc.ca/research/092/r57_e.pdf.

Nathan, P., & Ward, T. (2002). Female sex offenders: Clinical and demographic features. *Journal of Sexual Aggression, 8*(1), 5–21. doi:10.1080/13552600208413329.

Office of the Correctional Investigator. (2011). Backgrounder: Summary of issues and challenges facing older and aging offenders in federal custody. Retrieved from http://www.oci-bec.gc.ca/cnt/comm/presentations/presentationsAR-RA0911info-eng.aspx.

Office of the Correctional Investigator. (2012). Backgrounder: Summary of issues and challenges in the management of prison self-injury. Retrieved from http://www.oci-bec.gc.ca/cnt/comm/presentations/presentationsAR-RA1112Info-eng.aspx.

Office of the Correctional Investigator. (2013a). Backgrounder: Ethno-cultural diversity in corrections: A summary of issues and challenges. Retrieved from http://www.oci-bec.gc.ca/cnt/comm/presentations/presentationsar-ra1213info-eng.aspx?texthighlight=diversity.

Office of the Correctional Investigator. (2013b). *A case study of diversity in corrections: The black inmate experience in federal penitentiaries*. Ottawa, Her Majesty the Queen in Right of Canada. Retrieved from http://www.oci-bec.gc.ca/cnt/rpt/pdf/oth-aut/oth-aut20131126-eng.pdf.

Office of the Correctional Investigator. (2014). *A three year review of federal inmate suicides (2011–2014)*. Ottawa: Her Majesty the Queen in Right of Canada. Retrieved from http://www.oci-bec.gc.ca/cnt/rpt/pdf/oth-aut/oth-aut20140910-eng.pdf?texthighlight=suicide.

Office of the Correctional Investigator. (2015). *Administrative segregation in federal corrections: 10 year trends*. Ottawa: Her Majesty the Queen in Right of Canada. Retrieved from http://www.oci-bec.gc.ca/cnt/rpt/pdf/oth-aut/oth-aut20150528-eng.pdf.

Ortiz, M.M. (2000). Managing special populations. *Corrections Today, 62*(7), 64–68.

Public Safety Canada. (2011a). Long term offender designation. Retrieved from https://www.publicsafety.gc.ca/cnt/cntrng-crm/crrctns/protctn-gnst-hgh-rsk-ffndrs/lng-trm-ffndr-dsgntn-eng.aspx.

Public Safety Canada. (2011b). National Sex Offender Registry. Retrieved from https://www.publicsafety.gc.ca/cnt/cntrng-crm/crrctns/protctn-gnst-hgh-rsk-ffndrs/ntnl-sx-ffndr-rgstr-eng.aspx.

Public Safety Canada. (2015). *Corrections and conditional release statistical overview: 2014 annual report*. Ontario: Public Works and Government Services Canada. Retrieved from https://www.publicsafety.gc.ca/cnt/rsrcs/pblctns/ccrso-2014/2014-ccrs-eng.pdf.

R v Gladue, [1991] 1 SCR 688.

Reitano, J. (2016). Adult correctional statistics in Canada, 2014/15. *Juristat, 36*(1). Catalogue No. 85-002-X. Retrieved from http://www.statcan.gc.ca/pub/85-002-x/2016001/article/14318-eng.pdf.

Restoule, B. (2009). Aboriginal women and the criminal justice system. In J. Barker (Ed.), *Women and the criminal justice system: A Canadian perspective* (pp. 257–287). Toronto: Emond Montgomery.

Roberts, D. (1996, April 27). Police end riot at Manitoba jail; 8 guards injured, several prisoners attacked by other inmates. *Globe and Mail*, p. A1.

Sampson, R., Gascon, S., Glen, I., Louie, C., & Rosenfeldt, S. (2007). *Report of the Correctional Service of Canada Review Panel: A roadmap to strengthening public safety*. Ottawa: Minister of Public Works and Government Services Canada. Retrieved from http://www.johnhoward.ca/media/A%20Roadmap%20to%20Strengthening%20Public%20Safety%20-%20English%20Report.pdf.

Sapers, H. (2010). *Annual report of the Office of the Correctional Investigator 2009–2010*. Ottawa: Her Majesty the Queen in Right of Canada. Retrieved from http://www.oci-bec.gc.ca/cnt/rpt/pdf/annrpt/annrpt20092010-eng.pdf.

Sapers, H. (2011). *Annual report of the Office of the Correctional Investigator 2010–2011.* Ottawa: Her Majesty the Queen in Right of Canada. Retrieved from http://www.oci-bec.gc .ca/cnt/rpt/pdf/annrpt/annrpt20102011-eng.pdf.

Sapers, H. (2015). *Annual report of the Office of the Correctional Investigator 2014–2015.* Ottawa: Her Majesty the Queen in Right of Canada. Retrieved from http://www.oci-bec.gc .ca/cnt/rpt/pdf/annrpt/annrpt20142015-eng.pdf.

Sapers, H. (2016). *Annual report of the Office of the Correctional Investigator 2015–2016.* Ottawa: Her Majesty the Queen in Right of Canada. Retrieved from http://www.oci-bec.gc .ca/cnt/rpt/annrpt/annrpt20152016-eng.aspx.

Sexton, L., Jenness, V., & Sumner, M. (2010). Where the margins meet: A demographic assessment of transgender inmates in men's prisons. *Justice Quarterly, 27*(6), 835–866. Retrieved from http://ucicorrections.seweb.uci.edu/files/2013/06/A-Demographic -Assessment-of-Transgender-Inmates-in-Mens-Prisons.pdf.

Shaw, M. (1999). "Knowledge without acknowledgement": Violent women, the prison and the cottage. *The Howard Journal, 38*(3), 252–266.

Snell, T.L. (2000). Capital punishment 1999. *Bureau of Justice Statistics Bulletin* (NCJ 184795). Washington, DC: U.S. Department of Justice. Retrieved from http://bjs.ojp.usdoj.gov/ content/pub/pdf/cp99.pdf.

Snell, T.L. (2010). Capital punishment, 2009—Statistical tables. *Bureau of Justice Statistics: Statistical Tables* (NCJ 231676). Washington, DC: U.S. Department of Justice. Retrieved from http://bjs.ojp.usdoj.gov/content/pub/pdf/cp09st.pdf.

Snell, T.L. (2014). Capital punishment, 2013—Statistical tables. *Bureau of Justice Statistics: Statistical Tables* (NCJ 248448). Washington, DC: U.S. Department of Justice. Retrieved from http://www.bjs.gov/content/pub/pdf/cp13st.pdf.

Statistics Canada. (2007). *Table 385-0002 Federal, provincial and territorial general government revenue and expenditures for fiscal year ending March 31* (table), CANSIM. Retrieved from http://www5.statcan.gc.ca/cansim/pick-choisir?lang=eng&p2=33&id=3850002.

Stewart, B. (2000, January 3). *The National Magazine—CBC Television* [Transcript]. Toronto: CBC.

Strapagiel, L. (2015, January 26). Ontario will now assess transgender inmates based on identity, not anatomy. *Financial Post.* Retrieved from http://news.nationalpost.com/news/ canada/ontario-will-now-assess-transgender-inmates-based-on-identity-not-anatomy.

Task Force on Federally Sentenced Women. (1990). *Creating choices: The report of the Task Force on Federally Sentenced Women.* Ottawa: Correctional Service Canada.

Ternes, M., Doherty, S., & Matheson, F.I. (2014). *An examination of the effectiveness of the National Substance Abuse Program Moderate Intensity (NSAP-M) on institutional adjustment and post-release outcomes* (Research report R-291). Ottawa: Correctional Service Canada.

Ternes, M., & Johnson, S. (2011). *Linking type of substance use and type of crime in male offenders.* Ottawa: Correctional Service Canada.

Therien, E. (2011, July 20). The national shame of Aboriginal incarceration. *Globe and Mail.* Retrieved from http://www.theglobeandmail.com/news/opinions/opinion/the-national -shame-of-aboriginal-incarceration/article2102814/.

Truth and Reconciliation Commission of Canada. (2015). *Honouring the truth, reconciling for the future: Summary of the final report of the Truth and Reconciliation Commission of Canada.* n.p.: Author. Retrieved from http://www.trc.ca/websites/trcinstitution/File/2015/ Findings/Exec_Summary_2015_05_31_web_o.pdf.

Uzoaba, J.H. (1998). *Managing older offenders: Where do we stand?* (Research report R-70). Ottawa: Correctional Service Canada. Retrieved from http://www.csc-scc.gc.ca/ research/092/r70_e.pdf.

van der Meulen, E., & Ka Hon Chu, S. (2015, Spring). Harm reduction behind bars: Prison-based needle and syringe programs. *Prevention in Focus: Spotlight on Programming and Research*. Retrieved from http://www.catie.ca/en/pif/spring-2015/harm-reduction-behind-bars-prison-based-needle-and-syringe-programs#bios.

Walsh, K., Gonsalves, V., Scalora, M., King, S., & Hardyman, P. (2012). Child maltreatment histories among female inmates reporting inmate on inmate sexual victimization in prison: The mediating role of emotion dysregulation. *Journal of Interpersonal Violence, 27*(3), 492–512. doi:10.1177/0886260511421670.

Yeager, M.G. (2000). Ideology and dangerousness: The case of Lisa Colleen Neve. *Critical Criminology, 9*(1–2), 9–21. doi:10.1007/BF02461035.

Zakaria, D., Thompson, J.M., & Borgatta, F. (2010). *The relationship between knowledge of HIV and HCV, health education, and risk and harm-reducing behaviours among Canadian federal inmates*. Ottawa: Correctional Service Canada. Retrieved from http://publications.gc.ca/collections/collection_2011/scc-csc/PS83-3-195-eng.pdf.

PART FIVE

Youth Justice

Ashley Smith: A Preventable Prison Homicide

Susan Reid and Rebecca Bromwich

In 2007, 19-year-old Ashley Smith died alone in a solitary confinement cell in an adult penitentiary in Ontario. Had Ashley committed a heinous offence that warranted transfer to an adult institution? No. Media sources have insisted that the index offence for which she was originally sent to prison was a charge for throwing crab apples at a Canada Post worker while she was on probation. Ashley had been remanded to the secure custody and detention facility for 30 days because of her behavioural issues associated with a psychological assessment ordered for her at a treatment centre. The crab apple incident followed a series of convictions for minor offences, for which she received terms of probation and a **deferred custody and supervision order**. It was her defiance while on probation that led to her committal to closed custody at the New Brunswick Youth Centre (NBYC) in Miramichi. She often ended up in solitary confinement at the NBYC due to a snowballing series of hundreds of administration of justice charges and disciplinary sanctions laid against her while she was in custody.

The public's imagination was captured by the death of Ashley Smith. Her story was twice featured on CBC's *the fifth estate*. An episode called "Out of Control," which aired in 2010, introduced viewers to her life and death. A second episode called "Behind the Wall" aired the following year.

Trajectory: From Disruptive Teen to Victim of Prison Homicide

Ashley was often disciplined for being defiant and disruptive in ways that are statistically unusual for a girl. While girls are widely assumed to be more compliant, overall, than boys, Ashley often did not comply with orders, directions, or expectations. However, she had never stolen anything more valuable than a CD and never hurt anyone except herself.

We cannot know what Ashley's mental health would have been like had she not been kept away from human contact during her adolescent development. However, it is not unreasonable to wonder whether Ashley's mental health issues at the time of her death might have been exacerbated by four years mostly spent in solitary confinement. Before she was incarcerated, Ashley was directed to mental health professionals who were unable to accurately assess her mental health due to her age and her behavioural outbursts requiring her to be removed from the assessment centre. What is clear is that

deferred custody and supervision order
A community-based alternative to a custodial sentence. A judge may order a youth to be placed in custody but then defer custody and release the youth into the community subject to conditions and supervision. The order must not exceed six months. If the youth breaches any of the conditions, he or she may be placed back in custody to complete the remainder of the sentence.

her rights while incarcerated were violated and that the systems in place, particularly in the adult correctional system, dealt very harshly with her disruptive behaviour.

After she was adopted as a baby, Ashley reportedly had a happy childhood. However, in her early teens, she starting getting into trouble. The incidents were all minor in themselves, but taken together they became a serious concern for her teachers and her family. Once Ashley started getting into trouble at school, her mother sought the help of a private psychologist, who found that Ashley showed no signs of mental illness.

From age 12 to 13, Ashley was repeatedly suspended from school. In a single semester in 2002, she was written up for allegedly committing 17 infractions of school rules. According to school forms, Ashley was disciplined for bullying, verbal threats, a disrespectful attitude, and non-compliance. She was also alleged to have stalked one of her teachers. Ultimately, Ashley was removed from the regular school system and sent to an alternative high school. Her parents reported that their relationship with Ashley had become strained; she defied their rules, viewing inappropriate content on the Internet, speaking with strangers in chat rooms, and racking up long-distance charges of up to $1,600 a month.

Ashley's trouble with the law began when she was 14 with a string of minor offences. She was arrested for making harassing telephone calls, for assaulting strangers on the street, and for insulting a parking attendant, bus passengers, and bus drivers. A youth court ordered a one-year probation and a referral to the province's Intensive Support Program (ISP), which provides supplementary guidance for youth assessed to be at high risk for reoffending. Nonetheless, Ashley was subsequently charged multiple additional times.

New Brunswick's Youth Treatment Program team sent Ashley for a 34-day residential assessment at the Pierre Caissie Centre in Moncton. Ashley underwent psychological and psychiatric assessments, and a doctor stated that Ashley suffered from a "learning disorder, ADHD, borderline personality disorder," and "narcissistic personality traits" (Ombudsman and Child and Youth Advocate [Ombudsman], 2008, p. 39). Notably, these are all personality disorders, not psychoses that would put a person out of touch with reality. According to the *Diagnostic and Statistical Manual of Mental Disorders*, fifth edition (DSM-5), *personality disorder* "is a way of thinking, feeling and behaving that deviates from the expectations of the culture, causes distress or problems functioning, and lasts over time" (American Psychiatric Association, 2013). The psychological assessment recommended that Ashley's parents receive counselling in how to cope with an "oppositional defiant youth" and that the parents, school, and community work together to deal with Ashley's behaviour. While she was at the Pierre Caissie Centre, the police were called twice in relation to allegations that Ashley was assaulting staff. Staff leadership decided that Ashley's outbursts were negatively affecting assessments of other residents at the facility, and her stay was reduced to 27 days. She was remanded back to the NBYC for one month. Within a few weeks at NBYC, Ashley was formally disciplined for over 30 infractions, ranging from refusing staff orders to being aggressive to making threats of self-injury. These infractions resulted in additional charges being laid against Ashley. Ashley was often placed in isolation ("therapeutic quiet"), and, in many instances, held in restraints.

The incident with the crab apples followed this initial period of incarceration. Rather than putting Ashley back into secure custody, the court ordered open custody in a foster home environment. Over the course of two weeks, Ashley was moved to three different foster homes. At the third placement, she was removed after locking herself in a bathroom and threatening self-injury with a broken light bulb. After this incident, she was returned to the NBYC. From this point on, the pattern of Ashley being incarcerated, released on community supervision, and then further remanded continued. She incurred additional charges for breach of probation, common assault, trespassing, and causing a disturbance.

Within three months, Ashley was in and out of the NBYC five times. Her lengthiest sentence of incarceration began at the end of December 2003 and lasted until February 2004. Hours after her February release, she was arrested for pulling a fire alarm and breaching probation. She was remanded to the NBYC for an additional 75 days. Further criminal charges were filed, and more time was added to the sentence she was already serving. The upshot was a sentence of 14 months, to be served at the NBYC.

Ashley then spent approximately three years in custody at the NBYC, where staff filed over 800 incident reports about her. The institution laid charges in relation to over 500 of these incidents. As reported by the New Brunswick ombudsman (Ombudsman, 2008), "it was nothing out of the ordinary for Ashley to have anywhere from one to five reported and documented incidents per day" (p. 19). Staff documented 158 self-injurious incidents by Ashley while she was at the NBYC. In addition, staff complaints resulted in 50 further criminal charges being laid against her. Correctional staff and health professionals repeatedly laid new charges during their efforts to prevent or stop her from engaging in self-injurious behaviours.

In January 2006, Ashley turned 18, which meant that if she committed any new offences, she would be treated as an adult. Very soon after, further charges were laid.

On Ashley's 18th birthday, the superintendent of the NBYC, acting in his role as provincial director, filed an application under s 92 of the *Youth Criminal Justice Act* to have Ashley transferred to the adult system. Section 92 provides that the judge responsible for deciding on a transfer must consider whether such a move is in the best interests of the young person or of the public. During the transfer hearing, the judge heard testimony that the adult system would provide Ashley with the opportunity to attend rehabilitation programs. Ashley opposed the transfer, stating by affidavit:

> Although I know that my record looks bad, I would never intentionally hurt anyone. I am really scared about the thought of going to an adult facility with dangerous people. It has occupied my mind for a long time. I have wanted to behave to ensure that I would not ever go to adult and was sure that I would succeed. (Ombudsman, 2008, p. 26)

Ashley's affidavit also indicated her belief that she could "get better and do something productive with [her] life" (Ombudsman, 2008, p. 25). However, the judge decided that Ashley should be transferred. Within a few hours of her transfer to the Saint John Regional Correctional Centre (SJRCC), an adult correctional facility, Ashley was sent to segregation and threatened with both pepper spray and a Taser for not complying with institutional rules.

Staff filed 34 incident reports against Ashley over her 26 days at the SJRCC. As at NBYC, she spent most of her time in segregation. Her behaviour disqualified her from the programs that had been identified as a benefit of her transfer to the adult system. During her short stay, she was threatened with a Taser seven times and with pepper spray twice. However, according to reports made by the New Brunswick Child and Youth Advocate, the mobile mental health team was not called in. The advocate was told that the team was reserved for situations in which the individual was "really very distraught … really out of control … and we really couldn't get a handle on it" (Ombudsman, 2008, p. 26). In other words, the correctional staff felt that they had and were implementing the necessary and appropriate correctional tools to handle Ashley's behaviour.

On October 24, 2006, Ashley appeared in adult court to answer to criminal charges laid against her while she was at NBYC. She was remanded for an additional 348 days of custody. The judge approved the application to have her youth sentences treated as adult sentences. When the new custodial time was added to her existing 1,455 days, the total exceeded the 729-day maximum allowed for individuals to serve their sentence in an adult provincial institution. Ashley had to be transferred to a federal correctional facility. In 2006, at the age of 18, on what would be her last Halloween, she entered the federal penitentiary Nova Institution for Women, in Nova Scotia.

In 11 months in federal custody, Ashley was moved 17 times between three federal penitentiaries, two treatment facilities, two external hospitals, and one provincial correctional facility. She was transferred across four of the five Correctional Service Canada (CSC) regions (Nova Scotia, Quebec, Ontario, Saskatchewan). Howard Sapers, the Correctional Investigator at the time, told the *Toronto Star* that senior corrections officials had read the many reports concerning Ashley: "In the last 11 months of her life, her name appeared on at least 150 'situation reports' filed by federal penitentiaries detailing Smith's attempts to hurt herself or others" (Zlomislic, 2009). Ashley was continuously housed in administrative segregation (solitary confinement), as she had been at the NBYC. During her short stays in the Regional Psychiatric Centre in Saskatchewan and in a provincial mental health centre in Montreal, she was isolated from other patients.

CSC assigned Ashley administrative segregation status for her entire period of incarceration without first assessing her. CSC officials knew that Ashley had never received a full psychological and psychiatric assessment, but no assessment was ever completed. Sapers (2008) explained that because Ashley was constantly transferred between institutions, she was never in one place long enough for an assessment to be completed or a treatment plan to be developed. According to Sapers, because administrative segregation is highly restrictive, it is subject to review every 60 days. In the case of Ashley, however, corrections officials "lifted" her status whenever she was physically moved from one institution to another, circumventing the required 60-day review. As a result, Ashley spent all of her time in federal penitentiaries alone. A psychologist who examined the case interpreted Ashley's self-injurious behaviour as a means of drawing the staff into her cell "in order to alleviate the boredom, loneliness and desperation she had been experiencing as a result of her prolonged isolation" (Sapers, 2008, p. 8).

Ashley Smith took her life in the early morning hours of October 19, 2007, slightly less than one year from the date she was placed in the adult correctional system. Sapers (2008) wrote the following about her death:

> With misinformed and poorly communicated decisions as a backdrop, Ms. Smith died—wearing nothing but a suicide smock, lying on the floor of her segregation cell, with a ligature tied tightly around her neck—under the direct observation of several correctional staff. (p. 8)

In 2011, Ashley's family launched an $11 million lawsuit against CSC for wrongful death. This case was settled out of court for an undisclosed amount of money.

The Inquests

Complex inquest proceedings arose from Ashley's death. Given that Ashley was serving time in an Ontario penitentiary for women, the province's coroner had to investigate the cause of her death. An inquest is a medico-legal inquiry into the cause of death of a person. An inquest jury cannot lay charges against individuals. It can only make recommendations. Further, an inquest does not inquire into the whole history of an inmate who dies in prison. The question for the inquest jury is simply what caused a death.

The inquests into Ashley's death were controversial and fraught with procedural objections brought by CSC and others, including physicians who treated her while she was in custody. A first inquest was terminated in 2011 after Ashley's family demanded a mistrial. After a series of contested motions, the scope of the inquest was expanded beyond the day of her death to the entire 11 months she was in adult custody. A second inquest was convened in 2012. It received daily media coverage on a national level.

After several months of proceedings, in a shocking and unprecedented verdict rendered in December 2013, the inquest jury ruled that, despite Ashley having died by her own hand, her death was neither a suicide nor an accident but a homicide (*Smith (Re)*, 2013). The homicide verdict meant that the jury determined Ashley had been killed by the system itself. This verdict placed blame for her death on the institutions in which she was held and generally implicated the actions of those many individuals who had been involved directly and indirectly in her treatment. Before this case, no Canadian inquest verdict had ruled a prisoner's death a homicide unless the death was caused by another inmate. In this case, the jury made 104 recommendations for changes to the operations of the correctional system in Canada in conjunction with the verdict (Correctional Service Canada [CSC], 2013).

A response to these recommendations from CSC (2014) claimed that appropriate changes had already been made and was generally dismissive of the recommendations. Technically, this closed the case as a legal matter. However, Ashley's case became an issue in the 2015 federal election. The 2015 mandate letter of then newly elected Prime Minister Justin Trudeau to the minister of justice directed the attorney general to take another look at the recommendations from the inquest and make changes to address the problems faced by Ashley Smith.

The very first of the 104 recommendations made by the jury in the Ashley Smith inquest was that her death should be taught as a case study to all CSC management and staff at all levels.

What Went Wrong?

What went wrong in the case of Ashley Smith? It is perhaps dangerous to look for a single, simple answer. Media coverage (and much advocacy) overwhelmingly portrayed Ashley as someone who was mentally ill and suggested that her case demonstrates that our criminal justice and correctional systems deal poorly with people with mental illness. However, while our systems may indeed fail people with mental illness, questions have been raised about whether or not Ashley was mentally ill before her time in prison. Further, the limited scope of the inquests, which could only inquire into her time in adult prison, have focused attention only on her experience within the adult correctional systems.

In Ashley's life, administrative rules and laws that set forth how prisoners are to be treated were routinely violated in letter and in spirit by CSC, and, before that, by other authorities. Under the UN *Convention on the Rights of the Child*, her rights were violated long before the time of her death. Article 40 of the convention requires that children who have violated the penal law be treated in a manner consistent with their age and with the goal of promoting the child's reintegration and constructive participation in society. The hundreds of convictions that Ashley received from the youth criminal justice courts in New Brunswick as a result of her time at NYBC are very problematic from the perspective of this right.

By the time she died, Ashley was clearly in mental distress. It is also clear that she was in segregation for an appallingly long period of time, in direct violation of the treatment of prisoners as outlined by the UN rules related to the treatment of prisoners adopted by the General Assembly in December 1990. However, it is also significant that she was a youth for legal purposes during the course of much of her experience with the education system, child welfare system, courts, and correctional system in New Brunswick, and during this time, there were a number of violations of her rights under the UN Convention on the Rights of the Child, related to education, care, and imprisonment. It is also important to consider the impact on her mental health of the hundreds of institutional charges she was given during her time in both youth and adult custody. We cannot know, but should wonder, how Ashley might have been treated if she had been a similarly defiant adolescent male. Did her defiance, combined with her tall stature and her gender, create a "perfect storm" of socially unusual, or at least not stereotypical, traits and behaviours that affected the way she was treated in incarceration and ultimately led to her death? In the end, it is clear that a lot went wrong in Ashley Smith's case, and that serious, difficult work must be done by many social systems, including health, education, and both youth and adult, to prevent future prison homicides.

Chapter 12 will consider the history and evolution of youth justice policy in Canada, outlining the key legal distinctions in the way young people are dealt with in contrast to adults. As this chapter will note, the Canadian justice system has always recognized that the inexperience of young persons reduces their accountability. Juvenile courts at the turn of the century focused on preventing misguided and misdirected children from entering adult lives of crime and on protecting them from the harshness of the adult penitentiary system. Think about the recent case of Ashley Smith as you read Chapter 12 and ask yourself whether her situation would likely have been better or worse during earlier periods of our youth criminal justice system.

What Do You Think?

Consider how our system could be improved to prevent similar deaths in the future, and how the current federal ministers of Justice and Public Safety should best answer the call put forward in the 2015 mandate letter from Prime Minister Justin Trudeau to rectify the problems revealed by Ashley Smith's case. How should we as Canadians deal equitably with diverse and disruptive children and youth? How can deaths like Ashley Smith's be prevented?

REFERENCES

American Psychiatric Association. (2013). What are personality disorders? Retrieved from https://psychiatry.org/patients-families/personality-disorders/what-are-personality-disorders?_ga=1.92034771.831945319.1485551284.

Bromwich, R.J. (2015). *Looking for Ashley: Re-reading what the Smith case reveals about the governance of girls, mothers, and families in Canada.* Toronto: Demeter.

Correctional Service Canada. (2013, December 19). Coroner's inquest touching the death of Ashley Smith: Verdict and recommendations. Retrieved from http://www.csc-scc.gc.ca/publications/005007-9009-eng.shtml.

Correctional Service Canada. (2014). Response to the coroner's inquest touching the death of Ashley Smith. Retrieved from http://www.csc-scc.gc.ca/publications/005007-9011-eng.shtml.

Ombudsman and Child and Youth Advocate. (2008). *The Ashley Smith report.* Fredericton: Office of the Ombudsman & Child and Youth Advocate. Retrieved from http://www.gnb.ca/0073/PDF/AshleySmith-e.pdf.

Sapers, H. (2008). *A preventable death.* Ottawa: Office of the Correctional Investigator of Canada. Retrieved from http://www.oci-bec.gc.ca/cnt/rpt/pdf/oth-aut/oth-aut20080620-eng.pdf.

Smith (Re), 2013 CanLII 92762 (Ont OCCO).

Trudeau, J. (2015, November). Minister of justice and attorney general of Canada mandate letter. Retrieved from http://pm.gc.ca/eng/minister-justice-and-attorney-general-canada-mandate-letter.

United Nations. (1989, November 20). *Convention on the Rights of the Child,* 1577 UNTS 3, Can TS 1992 No 3 (entered into force September 2, 1990).

Zlomislic, D. (2009, October 10). From generous girl to "caged animal." *Toronto Star.* Retrieved from http://www.thestar.com/news/canada/article/708429—from-generous-girl-to-caged-animal.

Thinking About Youth Criminal Justice

LEARNING OUTCOMES

After reading this chapter, students will be able to:

- Understand the ways in which young people who commit crime have been dealt with throughout history and compare current approaches to youth justice practice.

- Describe the philosophical orientation to youth criminality of the *Juvenile Delinquents Act, the Young Offenders Act,* and the *Youth Criminal Justice Act* (YCJA).

- Describe the overriding principles in the Declaration of Principle of the YCJA.

- Describe the procedures related to arrest, questioning, and detention by the police when dealing with young persons.

- Explain the principles of sentencing specific to young offenders.

- Outline the impact of youth mental illness on youth criminality.

- Describe the approach of correctional programs that have proven to be most successful in reducing recidivism among high-risk young offenders.

Introduction

Historically, in Canada, young criminals have been treated in a way that recognizes their age and stage of maturity, and their sentencing has been approached with a view to providing them with as much guidance as possible to help them avoid a lifetime of crime. Many young people commit offences as part of a process of growing up and taking risks. As a society, we recognize that fact and look upon minor misbehaviour as a valuable lesson that may prevent young people from engaging in more serious criminal activity in the future. Ashley Smith (the subject of Part Five's opening case study) began offending with minor misbehaviour, but her behaviour escalated into a pattern of repeat offending with continual behavioural outbursts. This chapter will explore the conflicting societal demands to treat youth with care and support as a form of prevention, and to punish youthful offenders who violate the criminal law.

This chapter provides an historical overview of approaches that have been used to deal with young offenders in Canada and then contrasts them with the current law that governs the youth criminal justice system: the *Youth Criminal Justice Act* (YCJA). Over the past decade in Canada, reliance on alternatives to the formal youth criminal justice system has increased to avoid the entrenchment of young people in custodial settings, which was common at the time Ashley Smith was incarcerated. Recognizing that young people lack the same level of maturity as adults, the penalties and sentences meted out in youth justice court are designed, in legislative intent, to provide young people with meaningful consequences. Further, the courts recognize that developmentally, youth do not have the same perception of time and consequence, which has led the courts to consider sentences commensurate with their age and stage of maturity.

In addition, this chapter explores police procedures for dealing with youth as well as the types of correctional interventions available for young people. This chapter includes an overview of the UN *Convention on the Rights of the Child* and how these rights are expressed in the YCJA. Further, it includes a number of mini case studies that explore the application of the law in cases that involve young offenders.

Throughout this chapter, you will be asked to consider how information that you learned about the adult criminal justice system in preceding chapters relates to the youth criminal justice system. To this end, the five models of criminal justice discussed in Chapter 1 will be reviewed in relation to the youth criminal justice system. In addition, the adult sentencing principles outlined in Chapter 8 will be compared with the youth sentencing principles provided in the YCJA. We begin by considering why young people, have historically been and continue to be, viewed differently from adults in the criminal justice system. Throughout this chapter, "young offenders," defined as "young persons" under the present legislation, will be used interchangeably with "young person," "young offender," and "youthful offender."

Do Young People Know Right from Wrong?

As the next section shows, the general view that children and young people should be treated differently than adults under the law has a long history. Presently in Canada, youth justice court has jurisdiction over young persons who are at least 12 but under 18 years old. Young people under 12 who commit offences are dealt with by child welfare authorities as children in need of protection, in much the same way that they were under the *Juvenile Delinquents Act* (JDA).

> ### What Do You Think?
>
> Think about the current age jurisdiction of youth justice court. Are the lower and upper limits too high, too low, or just right?

A review of the psychosocial literature shows convincing evidence of changes in a person's moral and cognitive reasoning through the adolescent years (Monahan, Steinberg, Cauffman, & Mulvey, 2009; Umbach, Berryessa, & Raine, 2015). Before the age of ten, children lack the capacity to make moral judgments because they have no awareness of the impact of their actions on others. Children up to the age of 13 lack moral independence from adults, and some research has shown that moral discernment continues to develop up to the age of 17. Both cognitive and moral development continues into the early 20s, with the brain not fully developing until age 25 (Fine, Steinberg, Frick, & Cauffman, 2016). Adolescents have been found to be more impulsive, short-sighted, and less able to resist the influence of their peers (Farrington, Loeber, & Howell, 2012; Gardner & Steinberg, 2005). Research suggests that the apex of risk taking occurs around the age of 18, with rates of unintended pregnancy and binge drinking peaking between ages 19 to 2 (Green et al., 2017). Based on a longitudinal study of anatomical and functional markers of brain development, evidence supports a lack of mature decision-making among young adults (Giedd, 2008). Research has also shown that based on neurological development, youth are not well equipped cognitively to consider in a mature manner the possible adverse consequences of their risky behaviours (Luciana, Wahlstrom, Porter, & Collins, 2012).

With these findings in mind, consider the data regarding the peak age of criminal behaviour, shown in Figure 12.1. When the psychosocial literature and data on youth criminal behaviour are viewed in tandem, it is understandable why the youth criminal justice system is separate from the adult justice system.

FIGURE 12.1   Persons Accused of Crimes, Age 12 to 65, Canada, 2011

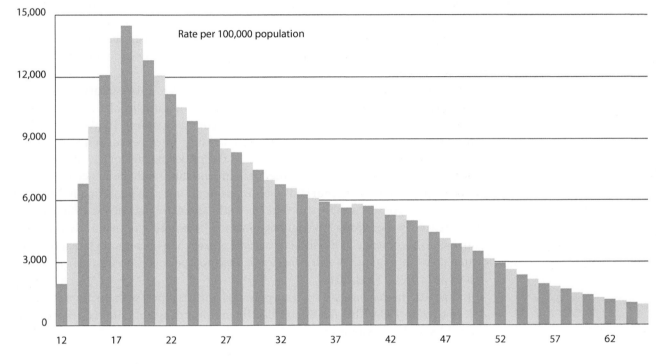

Source: Source: Brennan (2012, chart 15).

Historical Underpinnings of Youth and Justice

The "Good and Evil" Test

As far back as Hebrew law and the writing of Greek philosophers, there is evidence that children were not held to the same degree of responsibility for the commission of crimes as their adult counterparts. According to Aristotle, children were seen as being able to act voluntarily, but like animals and the insane, children were not capable of premeditation and so could not be considered morally responsible for their acts. The legal doctrine of *mens rea* (guilty mind) can be traced to the moral philosophy of these early writers, as was discussed in Chapter 6. The concept

What Do You Think?

In light of evidence that the brain is not fully developed until age 25, should the age at which a young person can be charged with committing a crime be increased? If the age of criminal responsibility were increased to 25, what would be the implications for university and college students? What age do you think is the most appropriate age of criminal responsibility? Why?

of "free will," or the ability to make one's own choices, is the cornerstone of the issue surrounding responsibility for crime. You may recall that the crime-control and justice models, discussed in Chapter 1, both rely on the notion that individuals commit crimes based on free will as opposed to deterministic factors outside their control.

The 13th-century medieval Italian philosopher St. Thomas Aquinas wrote of the distinction between children and adults, arguing that there are many things that are allowed in the young for which older people are punished or at least blamed (Davis-Barron, 2009, p. 7). Throughout history, there are many accounts of children not having the ability to form intent in the same manner in which "fools" could not be held responsible because of their inability to choose the "good" from the "evil" (*conisaunt de bien ne de mal*). The ***doli incapax* doctrine** applied to children under the age of seven, who were considered incapable of evil intent. At this time, males were deemed to have reached puberty at age 14; females, at age 12. Children between the ages of seven and 14 were considered accountable for their actions, but only if the proof of their intention to act was clear and certain.

By the time of the reign of Queen Elizabeth I in the late 16th century, children and the insane were excluded from criminal responsibility because they failed to possess the necessary mental capacity to form the intent to commit a crime. They were treated as "non-persons" because of their lack of understanding, intelligence, and moral discretion. In cases of children above the age of 14 but under the age of 21, the "good and evil" test was used to determine whether such individuals should be subjected to capital punishment, as would others of "full age." The test continued to be the main assessment of criminal responsibility through the17th, 18th, and early part of the 19th centuries, but increasingly the expression "right from wrong" was used synonymously with "good from evil." This practice in English law became entrenched in common law and became criminal law throughout North America. It was incorporated into Canada's first *Criminal Code* in 1892 (Reid, 2011).

In Canada, the *doli incapax* doctrine prevailed until its repeal with the *Young Offenders Act*, enacted in 1984. This Act established the minimum age of criminal responsibility at age 12 and the maximum age at 17.

***doli incapax* doctrine**
Belief that a child of tender years is incapable of an unlawful act.

SIDEBAR

"Good and Evil" Test

A child could be found guilty only if the state could establish that the child was able to distinguish between the concepts of good and evil. If a reasonable doubt were raised concerning the ability to perceive the difference, the child could not be punished.

Early History of Youth Justice in Canada

One of the earliest issues facing colonial Canada in the late 1800s was how to deal with the large numbers of orphans who were left to fend for themselves in the new country. While numerous families crossed the Atlantic Ocean from the British Isles, many of the adults died en route. The Irish famine brought additional numbers of orphaned children during the 1840s. Between 1873 and 1903, under the sponsorship of child immigration agencies, more than 95,000 "at-risk" children came to Canada (Department of Justice Canada [DOJ], 2004, p. 1).

The majority of crime that was documented for young people during these early settlement years was minor in nature. It was becoming common knowledge that children who were committing offences were more often than not victims of poor living conditions and parental neglect. During this time, in any large community, youth could be "found loitering around the streets, idle, neglected and undisciplined" (DOJ, 2004). Many of them "suffered from a lack of proper diet, malnutrition, unsanitary living conditions, drunken and dissolute parents and inadequate or no medical care" (DOJ, 2004). In addition to youth crime, these young people were not interested in the newly developed public schools and were often charged with truancy (i.e., not being in school) (DOJ, 2004). According to Boudreau (2012, p. 121), the number of young people who sold newspapers and engaged in other street trades was an influential factor in the insistence that young people get off the streets and attend school. The idea was that if young people were not visible as "street urchins," the general population would feel safer from the perceived concern of rising youth crime. Lobby groups of middle- and upper-class college-educated reformers became known as the Child Savers, raising awareness about the need to do something for these children by creating policies for compulsory education, child labour laws, and juvenile justice (DeTardo-Bora, 2014). This period was the beginning of a new era in thinking about youth in conflict with the law.

SIDEBAR

Child Savers

Child Savers were white, college-educated members of the middle and upper classes who, during the late 19th and early 20th centuries, established informal charities and grassroots organizations that led to the creation of a juvenile court as well as reform in compulsory education, child labour, juvenile institutions, and juvenile probation.

The Juvenile Delinquents Act

Beginning in the early 1900s, the focus of the legislation governing children and youth at risk was their state of delinquency as opposed to the criminal act itself (which was the focus of legislation for adults accused of a crime). Section 2(2) of the JDA, enacted in 1908, read as follows:

> Where a child is adjudged to have committed a delinquency he shall be dealt with, not as an offender, but as one in a condition of delinquency and therefore requiring help and guidance and proper supervision.

Because of its welfare focus, the youth criminal justice system created by the JDA was closely tied to social services. The line between redress for adolescent offending and provision of social services for youth in need was blurred. The court's role was similar to that of a parent, intervening in the place of parents who were not able to effectively guide the child into adulthood. Section 38 stipulated that

> the care and custody and discipline of a juvenile delinquent shall approximate, as nearly as may be that which should be given by his parents, and that as far as practicable every juvenile delinquent shall be treated, not as a criminal, but as a misdirected and misguided child.

Unlike legislation that would follow (the *Young Offenders Act* and the *Youth Criminal Justice Act*), direction on the philosophy and principles of the JDA did not appear until s 38.

The idea of the state providing assistance and guidance to a child in the same manner as a parent is known as the doctrine of ***parens patriae***. The focus of intervention for youth was no longer punishment, but treatment. There was no need for formal court hearings, legal safeguards, or defined sentences because the young person was not before the court to be corrected. Instead, a young person's appearance at youth justice court was seen as an opportunity to save him or her from a life of neglect, poverty, and dysfunction, and to provide him or her with help from those who were in attendance.

In recognition of the importance of preventing the young person from entering a life of crime as an adult, the proceedings were confidential (*in camera*) and the disposition was that the young person was in a "state of delinquency." There were no specified sentences or sentence length (i.e., **indeterminate**). The staff of the court, including the judge, probation officers, and others focused on looking after the **best interests of the child**, and would provide guidance and assistance. "Delinquents" would receive as much treatment and intervention as was necessary to ensure that they were no longer victimized by neglectful parents. Young persons became wards of the state in the same way that children who are in need of protection in cases of child abuse are removed from the custody of their parents. When the state, under the doctrine of *parens patriae*, took over the responsibility of rearing a delinquent child, it meant that the young person would be in state care until the age of 21 years (the legal age of majority).

It is important to note that many youth who were found guilty under the JDA experienced injustices, such as being "treated" for offences that would not have yielded significant sanctions had they been adults. Further, the status offences (e.g., curfew violation and truancy) contained in the JDA meant that young people were being brought to youth criminal court for a whole host of behaviours that may or may not be deemed criminal.

---

parens patriae ("parent of the nation")
The principle that the state acts as a "kindly parent" to dependent delinquents.

indeterminate
A disposition for juveniles that was not fixed in length. A young person could be held in custody until the youth was deemed by correctional authorities to no longer be seen as a threat to society or to be rehabilitated.

best interests of the child
The principle that the interests of a young person are paramount in decision-making regarding his or her experience in the criminal justice system.

SIDEBAR

Status Offences

Status offences are acts that are considered illegal only because of the age status of the offender. Examples of juvenile status offences include truancy, incorrigibility, and sexual precociousness (i.e., early interest in sexual activities).

Youth Justice in Canada, 1982–2003

With the proclamation of the *Canadian Charter of Rights and Freedoms* in 1982 came great criticism for the provisions of the JDA that denied children basic rights of due process. After almost 25 years of discussion and debate, the *Young Offenders Act* (YOA) was proclaimed in 1984.

The Young Offenders Act

As was the case prior to enacting the JDA, the discussion and debate that led to the YOA centred on the philosophical orientation of the law and such issues as punishment versus treatment, flexible adjudication versus procedural rights, and federal versus provincial jurisdiction (Reid & Reitsma-Street, 2001). Trying to satisfy competing interests, the drafters of the 1984 statute set out a series of principles that were to govern the philosophical direction of the new legislation. The YOA was an attempt to balance the social responsibility that young persons must bear for their criminal conduct (ss 3(1)(b), (c), (d)) against their special needs (ss 3(1)(a), (c), (f)) and the rights of individual youth (ss 3(1)(a), (d), (f), (g)). Further, the YOA acknowledged the responsibility of the community to take reasonable measures to prevent and control youth crime (s 3(1)(b)). The YOA marked a shift from the historical child welfare model of the JDA to more of an adult criminal law model (Reid & Zuker, 2004).

The YOA, which was a compromise of ideological preferences of all three federal parties, reflected an internally contradictory Declaration of Principle (s 3) that set the stage for abuse of judicial discretion. The Declaration of Principle allowed judges to use their discretion in interpreting the YOA in a way that suited their own ideological preferences and values. For example, a judge who was biased toward "protecting society" might impose a lengthy custodial sentence in the name of "rehabilitation." By contrast, a judge who was biased toward "minimal intrusion" in a youth's life might rely on s 3(f) to justify no custody at all for a similar conviction (Reid, Bromwich, & Gilliss, 2015).

Ironically, the YOA was widely accepted by all major political parties, academics, criminal justice officials, and the public at its inception in 1984. However, shortly after its proclamation and for the ensuing years until its ultimate repeal, it attracted continual calls for reform from two major schools of opposition. On the one hand, the "punitive response" critics argued that young offenders were getting away with overly lenient sentences. On the other hand, the "rehabilitation" critics argued that the legislation did not go far enough in providing for meaningful rehabilitation and called for a return to legislation similar to the JDA (Bala, 2015).

The punitive response critics argued that crime had increased since the enactment of the YOA and sought reform, calling for tougher, longer sentences and provisions. However, many "get tough" advocates failed to acknowledge that, under the YOA, there was actually a substantial increase in custodial sentences (although typically for shorter durations than those ordered under the JDA). Moreover, the prevailing criminological research demonstrated that a more punitive approach to youth criminality would not likely act as an effective deterrent. The rehabilitation critics, on the other hand, argued that since the enactment of the YOA, the rehabilitation ideal had been forgotten (Reid et al., 2015).

The implementation of the YOA, with its conflicting goals of rehabilitation and the protection of society, led to an increased use of the youth justice court and, as mentioned above, an even greater use of custodial sanctions than had been experienced under the JDA. Many judges, guided by the YOA's philosophy of crime control and attention to deterrence, imposed short sentences in custody that came to be referred to as a "short, sharp shock" (Doob & Cesaroni, 2004).

On February 14, 2001, the minister of justice at the time, Anne McLellan, rose in the House of Commons to speak on the first reading of Bill C-7, the proposed *Youth Criminal Justice Act* (YCJA):

> [T]he existing YOA has resulted in the highest youth incarceration rate in the western world, including our neighbours to the south, the United States. Young persons in Canada often receive harsher custodial sentences than adults receive for the same type of offence. Almost 80% of custodial sentences are for non-violent offences. (Canada, House of Commons, 2001, p. 1,530)

The focus on deterrence, within the crime-control model, meant that youth who violated their conditions of probation or who showed a similar lack of respect for the law were likely to find themselves serving a short term of custody. These youth would have formerly been seen as "misguided and misdirected" under the JDA; however, under the YOA, such behaviour was criminalized and youth were charged with administration of justice offences. These offences included failure to comply with a disposition (i.e., sentence), failure to appear in court, breach of probation conditions, and contempt against the youth justice court.

The preponderance of administration of justice offences leading to a custodial placement was raised in a series of roundtables hosted by the federal Department of Justice in various cities across Canada in 1997. A number of experts present at these roundtables stressed that using the provisions in the YOA related to **diversion** and community-based sanctions should be a priority to combat the rising rates of youth custody (DOJ, 1998). Several academics asserted, as Anne McLellan had, that Canada had the dubious distinction of having one of the highest youth incarceration rates among westernized countries (Bala, Carrrington, & Roberts, 2009; Doob & Sprott, 2007), even surpassing the United States (Hogeveen, 2005). At the same time, general population surveys in the 1990s showed increasing public demand for even tougher measures against youth crime. This public reaction was significant because for the first time in Canadian history, youth justice became an important national political issue (Alain, Corrodo, & Reid, 2016).

Even though there had been numerous amendments to the YOA between 1984 and 1998, the federal government decided to scrap the legislation and begin anew with the introduction of *Bill C-7, The Youth Criminal Justice Act*, in 2001. The YCJA received royal

diversion
A sentencing approach in which offenders are given an opportunity to perform some community service or are referred to a community agency to better address their needs instead of being processed through the youth justice court system. In the *Youth Criminal Justice Act*, "extrajudicial measures" and "extrajudicial sanctions" are forms of diversion.

One of the core principles of the YCJA is to avoid an overreliance on incarceration for youth convicted of non-violent crimes, in favour of other sentencing options.

assent on February 19, 2002 and was proclaimed in force as of April 2003. The YCJA underwent substantial amendments in 2012 under the *Safe Streets and Communities Act*. As will be noted later in this chapter, these amendments added the principles of denunciation and deterrence as considerations for youth sentencing that had not been part of the sentencing decision-making process under the previous legislation.

The Youth Criminal Justice Act

The YCJA is distinct from most legislation because it provides a great deal more information than most legislation to guide its interpretation. Specific provisions on dealing with youth are outlined in its articles, preamble, Declaration of Principle (s 3), and sentencing principles (s 38).

Preamble

The preamble to a piece of legislation serves as a guide to the statute's legal intention and includes information to help those responsible with interpreting and implementing the statute. The preamble to the YCJA includes statements that relate to how the rest of the legislation is to be interpreted, including the following: "[the YCJA] reserves its most serious intervention for the most serious crimes and reduces the over-reliance on incarceration for non-violent young persons." This statement responds specifically to criticisms of the former YOA and signals the legislation's intended effect to reduce the incarceration of young people. The remainder of the preamble focuses on the responsibility of society to "address developmental challenges and the needs of young persons" and the requirement to "foster responsibility and [ensure] accountability through meaningful consequences and effective rehabilitation and reintegration."

Protecting the rights and freedoms of young persons is an inherent goal of the YCJA. This goal is reflected in the inclusion of the UN *Convention on the Rights of the Child* in the preamble.

SIDEBAR

The UN Convention on the Rights of the Child

In 1985, the UN *Standard Minimum Rules for the Administration of Juvenile Justice*, known as "the Beijing Rules," recognized the special needs of young people and promoted the diversion of young people away from the more formal criminal justice system. Further, the Beijing Rules underscored the principle that custody should be used as a last resort for young people and that all proceedings against young people should be anonymous in order to protect young people from lifelong stigma. The UN *Convention on the Rights of the Child* (UNCRC), which expanded on these rules, was proclaimed in 1989. The convention has been ratified by Canada and more than 190 countries and affirms that children have a right to be protected from degrading and cruel punishment and to receive special treatment in the justice system. Further, it states that children below a minimum age shall be presumed to lack the capacity to infringe the penal law. The convention promotes the principle that all children have the right to a basic quality of life. Its 54 articles address matters such as the right to be protected from abuse and exploitation; the right to education and health care; and the right of children to have a voice in matters that concern them. The convention has four guiding principles: non-discrimination; devotion to the best interests of the child; the right to life, survival, and development; and respect for the views of the child.

There have been some improvements in the implementation of the convention in Canada with respect to policies affecting youth in the criminal justice system, such as ensuring that they understand their rights and the further assurance of having their parents involved, as well as the option of an additional "responsible person" to assist the lawyer to explain these rights. However, the reservation to article 37(c) with respect to housing youth and adult offenders in the same facilities remains a concern. It has been argued that due to the geographical size of the country, from time to time it is necessary to have youth held in pre-trial detention facilities where adults are also housed. This argument has been used by the government to allow the reservation of keeping youth and adult offenders separate to continue despite its contravention with the nature and principle of the UNCRC.

What Do You Think?

1. Why is it important for the UNCRC to be included in the YCJA? What safeguards does the UNCRC provide youth beyond the rights they have under the Charter?

2. What provisions within the UNCRC would you expect to be most relevant to youth justice?

3. What is your opinion about the Canadian government's argument that the country is too big to allow for enough detention facilities to detain youth separately from adults?

The rest of the preamble refers to general principles, such as the protection of society and "effective rehabilitation." It also refers to holding young people accountable through "meaningful consequences." This principle suggests that while young people are not held to the same level of accountability as adult offenders, nonetheless they must be answerable for their wrongdoings. The sanctions that are meted out to youth must provide more than a punishment but strive to deliver a consequence that would be meaningful to the young person. Given that the majority of young offenders are most likely to commit non-violent property-related offences, having a young person complete restitution or some form of compensation to the victim for the loss or damages caused to their property could be seen as a meaningful consequence.

Declaration of Principle

Section 3 of the YCJA, the Declaration of Principle, is a statement of the overriding principles that are meant to inform each provision in the Act. The Declaration of Principle was amended by the 2012 *Safe Streets and Communities Act* to highlight the protection of the public as a key goal of the youth criminal justice system and to underscore the principle of diminished moral blameworthiness (culpability) of young persons.

Statements in the Declaration of Principle that are indicative of the five models of criminal justice discussed in Chapter 1 are listed in Table 12.1.

TABLE 12.1   Models of Criminal Justice Reflected in the Principles of the Youth Criminal Justice Act

Restorative justice	[T]he measures taken against young persons who commit offences should reinforce respect for societal values [and] encourage the repair of harm done to victims and the community	YCJA ss 3(1)(c)(i), (ii)
Community change	[T]he measures taken against young persons who commit offences should … where appropriate, involve the parents, the extended family, the community and social or other agencies in the young person's rehabilitation and reintegration	YCJA s 3(1)(c)(iii)
Welfare	[T]he criminal justice system for young persons must be separate from that of adults and emphasize … rehabilitation and reintegration	YCJA s 3(1)(b)(i)
Justice	[Y]oung persons have rights and freedoms in their own right, such as a right to be heard in the course of and to participate in the processes, other than the decision to prosecute, that lead to decisions that affect them, and young persons have special guarantees of their rights and freedoms	YCJA s 3(1)(d)(i)
Crime control	[T]he criminal justice system for young persons must … emphasize … timely intervention that reinforces the link between the offending behaviour and its consequences	YCJA s 3(1)(b)(iv)

What Do You Think?

Read the provisions in the Declaration of Principle of the YCJA that are not listed in Table 2.1. Under what models of criminal justice do these provisions fit? Do some of the provisions fall under more than one model? If so, how does this provide judges with direction on how to proceed?

Myths and Facts About Youth Crime

How we come to understand youth crime is dependent on a number of factors. As was discussed in Chapter 1, one of the most important factors that affects our understanding of how much crime exists is our own awareness of the media reporting of sensational cases, which may skew our perceptions. Moreover, the crime reported in the American media may also draw our attention away from the reality of crime in Canada. Several myths about youth crime have been circulating for a number of years and have been used to justify tougher penalties for youth accused of crime. Table 12.2 presents some of these myths and the research evidence that negates them.

What Do You Think?

What are some additional "common sense" myths associated with youth and youth crime that you have heard? How would you go about debunking these myths and sharing more accurate information?

TABLE 12.2   Myths and Facts About Youth Violence

Myth	Fact
The increase in the crime rate in Canada is directly related to the increase in youth crime.	The police-reported youth crime rate has been on a general downward trend since peaking in 1991. The rate of youth accused of crime has fallen 40 percent since 2005. The rate of youth accused of crime by police (including youth charged and not charged) continued to decline in 2015. The rate of youth charged with a criminal offence in 2015 declined 1 percent, while the rate of adults charged increased 2 percent.
Locking up all young offenders is the smartest way to deal with juvenile crime.	While it is necessary for some young persons to serve some time in custody, ultimately all young persons are going to return to their communities. It is essential that these offenders are provided with appropriate opportunities for their rehabilitation early on so as to reduce the difficulties experienced when reintegrating into their communities. Research has shown that less juvenile justice processing is more likely to be successful in preventing future criminality.
Just keeping kids in at night would take care of most crime, certainly most violence.	Contrary to what most people think, the peak times for the commission of crime by young persons is between 2 and 6 p.m., the after-school hours when they are left on their own to pursue "leisure" interests. Most drug sales, assaults, and other offences occur during this period. It should be noted that this is also the time of day where there is no municipally imposed curfew. In those cities that have one, the results have shown that a curfew may inadvertently increase youth crime. Part of the problem is that a curfew may further marginalize young persons, and place additional emotional and financial stress on parents or guardians, leading to more conflicts between parents and children.
It is cheaper to lock kids in jail than to try to treat them in the community.	Many programs that prevent youth crime or assist youth in the community are far less expensive than incarceration. The average annual cost of detaining an adult offender in a federal institution is $110,320, while the estimated annual cost of detaining a young offender is almost twice that cost. Youth require additional programming under the YCJA, as well as the provision of education as mandated provincially. The cost of programs in the community is significantly less expensive even when considering those programs that supply incentives.
There is nothing you can do to prevent youth crime.	Many programs have been proven to be effective in curbing the conditions that lead young persons toward crime (criminogenic risk factors), to strengthen the aspects of their lives that tend to keep them from becoming involved with crime (protective factors), and to work with the community to strengthen capacity to effectively deal with young persons.

Sources: Allen (2016); Petrosino, Guckenburg, and Turpin-Petrosino (2010); Reid (2010); Reid, Bromwich, and Gilliss (2015); Reid and Gilliss (2016); Vissing (2011).

A Profile of Young Persons in Conflict with the Law in Canada, 2014–2015

Contrary to media accounts and popular belief, the rate of youth accused of crime declined by 2 percent between 2014 and 2015 (Allen, 2016). This reduction included both violent and property crimes. In 2015, less than half (45 percent) of youth accused of crime were formally charged by police, which represents a 1 percent decline from the previous year. By contrast, the rate of adults charged with a crime increased by 2 percent from 2014 to 2015. In total, about 92,000 youth were accused of a criminal offence in 2015, about 2,700 fewer than in the previous year. Of the youth accused of a criminal offence in 2015, 55 percent were dealt with by other means (i.e., diversion, such as the use of extrajudicial measures and sanctions).

In 2014–15, 70 percent of completed youth justice court cases involved non-violent offences (Miladinovic, 2016). In the same period, five *Criminal Code* offences made up 40 percent of all completed youth justice court cases:

- theft (11 percent)
- common assault (8 percent)
- break and enter (8 percent)
- failure to comply with an order (7 percent)
- mischief (6 percent)

These five offences have been the most frequent offence types in youth justice court cases for the past decade. Mischief and theft of $5,000 and under were the most frequent property crimes among youth, while 58 percent of all violent crimes consisted of common assault and uttering threats (Miladinovic, 2016). Only 7 percent of guilty cases involving common assault received a custodial sentence, while 16 percent of guilty cases involving failure to comply with an order were sentenced to custody.

In 2014–15, probation continued to be the preferred sentence for young people and was handed out in 57 percent of all guilty cases (Miladinovic, 2016). The median length of probation was 360 days. The median length of a custodial sentence was 40 days. Attempted murder had the longest median custody length (585 days), and administration of justice offences had the shortest median custody length (20 days). Only 2 percent of youth received custody sentences of more than a year, with almost half (44 percent) receiving custody sentences of one month or less.

As you consider the provisions in the YCJA, keep in mind that the majority of young persons who are charged commit non-violent offences and that the likelihood of them being sent to custody is far lower than what one might anticipate for an adult offender. Recall the discussion of the crime funnel in Chapter 1, and the reduction in the number of cases that make their way through the criminal justice system. This reduction is even more prevalent for youth who are governed under legislation that is designed to keep them out of the formal court process in order to divert them from a life of crime in the adult system.

Youth Diversion: Meaningful Consequences and Accountability

The YCJA knowledge of the academic literature that has clearly shown that more intensive interventions should be reserved for the highest risk, highest need youth offenders (see Chapter 9).

extrajudicial measures (EJM)
Informal ways in which the
police may keep a young person
out of the youth criminal justice
system. They can include
warnings, cautions, or referrals to
a community agency for help.

extrajudicial sanctions (EJS)
More formal ways of handling
a youth case outside of court
when extrajudicial measures
are not sufficient. They can
include community service,
compensating the victim, and
attending rehabilitation programs.

Diversion programs were developed in response to research that suggested that keeping youth in their families and communities, supported by a package of services aimed at their individual needs—including family treatment and restorative justice practices—has a positive effect and is successful in reducing recidivism (Latimer, 2001; Moyer, 1980; Schwalbe, Gearing, MacKenzie, Brewer, & Ibrahim, 2012; Ungar, 2004; Whitaker, Severy, & Morton, 1984). Keeping youth in their community allows for a "holistic intervention approach" focused on identifying individual, family, and community risks and strengths, and treating them comprehensively (Sullivan, Veysey, Hamilton, & Grillo, 2007). A meta-analysis of diversion programs conducted by Wilson and Hoge (2013) found that programs that were primarily police caution programs were most effective in reducing recidivism for low-risk offenders compared with programs that provided some form of intervention. They reported that "low-risk youth referred to caution programs were 2.44 times less likely to reoffend than the comparison group" (p. 507), while the same low-risk youth that were referred to an intervention program were only "1.49 times less likely to reoffend" (p. 507). For these reasons, the YCJA places emphasis on **extrajudicial measures (EJM)** by the police (e.g., warnings and cautions) and more intensive options such as referrals to community agencies. If an extrajudicial measure is not sufficient to hold a young person accountable through meaningful consequences, then an **extrajudicial sanction (EJS)** can be considered by the Crown. Both of these options are aimed at diverting the young person away from the formal youth criminal justice system and dealing with minor misbehaviour outside of the formal court process.

While the Declaration of Principle of the YCJA states that the measures taken against youth who commit offences should be "meaningful," the concept of meaningful consequence is ambiguous and may be taken by some judges as a justification for more punishment. Although the desired outcome may be that the young person does not offend in the future, other considerations may point to the success of a "meaningful consequence." For example, a young person who has a pattern of offending may have a reduction in the frequency and severity of offending as a result of the imposition of a "meaningful consequence." The concept itself can be defined differently, depending on the individual. For example, what may be interpreted as a meaningful consequence by a young person may not be interpreted as a meaningful consequence by the police and Crown. When holding a young person accountable for his or her actions, all measures taken against him or her must be proportionate to the seriousness of the offence, as outlined in the Declaration of Principle. As Hyde, Marinos, and Innocente (2016) indicate, holding a young person accountable might be interpreted as any or all of the following:

- the youth taking responsibility for his or her actions,
- admitting guilt,
- communicating remorse,
- completing the requirements of the "measure" they receive, or
- learning a lesson about their behaviour. (p. 199)

As you read the next two sections, think about how a young person might respond to the imposition of an extrajudicial measure or an extrajudicial sanction. We will return to this question in "Sidebar—What Young People Have Said About Extrajudicial Sanctions," later in the chapter.

Police and Extrajudicial Measures

Before starting any judicial proceeding against a young person, a police officer is *required* by the YCJA (s 6(1)) to consider whether it would be sufficient to:

1. *Take no further action.* Generally, the police officer decides that it is not necessary to do anything further because the parents, school officials, and in some cases the victim have taken measures to hold the young person accountable.
2. *Warn the young person.* Usually this is a one-to-one lecture by the officer, who explains the possible outcomes if the behaviour is repeated and comes to the attention of the police again.
3. *Administer a caution.* This is a more formal warning by the police, generally put in writing in a letter that may be issued in person in the presence of the parents so that they are aware of the caution. The letter advises the youth that the police believe that he or she has committed a crime but that he or she is not going to be charged at this time; however, if the youth is found committing similar conduct in the future, he or she could be charged.
4. *Make a referral to a community program.* Police may refer the young person, with his or her consent, to a program (e.g., drug addiction program, homework program) that may help the youth not to commit further offences.

Extrajudicial Sanctions

If the police believe that a warning, caution, or referral is not sufficient to hold the young person accountable through meaningful consequences, the case will be referred to the Crown, who will then have the option of using extrajudicial sanctions that have been developed as part of a program authorized by the province, outside of the formal court system. The YCJA requires that parents be notified if such a sanction is used, and victims have the right to be informed of the sanction that was given to the offender. Extrajudicial sanctions may be administered either pre-charge or post-charge, and they require the young person to accept responsibility for the behaviour that led to police involvement. Accepting responsibility is not the same as pleading guilty, but the police must show that there is sufficient evidence to proceed with a charge.

> **What Do You Think?**
>
> Jordan, 14, has been warned once before, for a prank that he and another young person played when they threw eggs at a house one early summer morning. He has come to the attention of the police again for spray-painting a rude message under a bridge. What would you do as the police officer attending this case?

Hyde et al. (2016) reported that in Ontario, when a young person accepts an extrajudicial sanction under s 10 of the YCJA, he or she may be required to complete one or more of the following:

- make a written or verbal apology,
- write an essay,
- make a poster,
- complete community service,
- attend counselling,
- attend an education/information session,
- make a charitable donation,
- accept a referral to a specialized crime prevention program, or
- attend peer mediation.

If the young person fails to complete the requirements set out in the extrajudicial sanction, the case may continue to court.

The police are required to keep records of a youth's participation in extrajudicial measures and sanction programs. A young person's participation in an extrajudicial sanction program may have implications for him or her in later court proceedings. Failure to complete an extrajudicial sanction program can result in a charge, and evidence of any participation is admissible in court for certain purposes—for example, sentencing for a later offence. Pursuant to s 123 of the YCJA, records relating to extrajudicial sanctions are kept for two years from the date that the young person consents to become involved in the program.

SIDEBAR

What Young People Have Said About Extrajudicial Sanctions

As noted earlier, a person's definition of meaningful consequence is dependent upon personal interpretation. Hyde et al. (2016) asked youth who were referred to an extrajudicial sanction program from a courthouse in Ontario to participate in a research interview to discuss their understanding of meaningful consequences and fair and proportionate accountability.

The young people indicated that a consequence was deemed meaningful depending on the time spent fulfilling its requirements and depending on whether the content of the program attended was perceived as helpful. They also indicated that their experience was meaningful "if they learned something on a more personal level as opposed to only in relation to the offence" (Hyde et al., 2016, p. 206). Some respondents indicated that there had been lessons learned as a result of the sanction either through the counselling attended or through participation in a program. One young person commented on the significance of knowing that, had he not been involved in an extrajudicial sanction, he could have been found guilty of the offence in question and would as a consequence have had a criminal record:

> A criminal record could affect your life, um, it affects your freedom because you can't leave the country if you have a criminal record, um … also being labelled as this bad person because what you have or what you have done for the mistakes you've made … like you know just also people treating you differently and just not getting the same—the respect you would normally get because of the consequences of what you did. (Hyde et al., 2016, p. 206)

The young people were also able to address what programs and sanctions were not effective in holding them accountable. Writing an essay was consistently reported as being ineffective, with respondents commenting that very little time and effort was required to complete the task. However, one participant indicated that writing an apology letter was the best part of the extrajudicial sanction as it did not require much time (Hyde et al., 2016, p. 207).

In terms of holding young people accountable, some respondents commented on the process of going to court as being the most useful:

> [Y]eah, even this process, I would never do it again … it's scary, to learn that oh this is the same courtroom that a killer would come into, it's like scary … like you don't know what to say, like you stand up front … it's just, they all just look you in your eye … it's not cool. (Hyde et al., 2016, p. 209)

Others reported that coming to court was effective because it cut into their day and was a "waste of time":

> [Y]eah time commitment, I don't like my time getting wasted, like I don't want to go waste my time when I could be doing other things right … I would say that the most time consuming this is what I would say would go at the top … the most meaningful. (Hyde et al., 2016, p. 209)

What Do You Think?

Given what you have read about the importance of keeping young people out of the formal court system, what evidence is presented for or against the effectiveness of extrajudicial sanctions by the young people in Hyde et al. (2016)'s study? Do you think that extrajudicial sanctions are helpful in the prevention of further criminal involvement? What other types of programs might you suggest that could be developed to assist young people to understand the impact of their offending behaviour without proceeding to a formal youth justice court?

Formal Processing of Young Persons

The detention, questioning, and arrest of adolescents suspected of committing criminal offences in Canada is governed by three main sources of legislation: the Charter, the *Criminal Code*, and the YCJA. As has already been discussed in preceding chapters, the Charter and the Code provide rights that apply to both adults and young persons. However, the YCJA prescribes rights and protections to young persons in addition to those that apply to adults. These additional rights are guaranteed for youth based on the evidence that youth are more vulnerable and less mature than adults. Further, young persons accused of crime are not as well informed about their procedural rights or the justice system in general. Besides enhanced procedural rights, the YCJA encourages the involvement of parents and other responsible persons to assist youth throughout formal processing.

The YCJA makes it clear that being under 18 years of age triggers special requirements for handling suspects and witnesses. With young people, police must be mindful not only of s 9 (the right not to be arbitrarily detained) and s 10(b) (the right to retain and instruct counsel) of the Charter but also of additional safeguards required because of the age and stage of maturity of the young person.

MINI CASE STUDY

R v E.(M.) (2006)

In the case of *R v E.(M.)*, a 17-year-old male accused was found by three police officers asleep at a computer in an Internet café. He was told that he was going to be charged with trespassing. One of the officers asked the accused his name and date of birth, and whether he was wanted on any charges. One of the officers told the young person that if he did not provide this information, he would be arrested. The youth complied with the request and answered the questions.

The police then ran a Canadian Police Information Centre (CPIC) search, which resulted in them learning that the youth was wanted on a warrant. He was arrested and searched, and found to be in possession of the drugs marijuana and ecstasy.

The question during trial was whether the youth had been arbitrarily detained.

Justice Murray ruled that the officers involved did not have grounds to ask the youth for information to run a CPIC and could have written a ticket for trespassing with less information. Further, by telling the youth that he would be arrested if he did not provide the information, the officers created a scenario in which the youth would have felt "psychologically compelled to submit to the officers' questioning."

What had occurred had constituted detention and, moreover, the youth had not been granted his s 10 Charter right to know the reasons for detention.

Justice Murray excluded the evidence and the youth was acquitted.

What Do You Think?

1. What mistakes were made in this investigation?
2. What does *psychologically compelled* mean?

Once the police have made a decision to charge a young person, protecting the value of investigative evidence, especially statements by the accused, becomes extremely important. Interviewing young suspects requires careful compliance with the protective provisions of the YCJA, such as confirming the youth's age and informing him or her about the right to retain and instruct counsel without delay, the right to silence (and waivers to give up that right), and the right to consult with parents and/or another responsible person.

In most cases in which the police initiate a formal process against a young person (as opposed to using extrajudicial measures), the young person is released on an **appearance notice**; he or she may also be released on a summons, a promise to appear, an **undertaking**, or a recognizance. The young person is released to the care of his or her parents or a **responsible person**. If the youth has been arrested, the provisions in ss 497 to 498 of the *Criminal Code* apply. That is, the youth must be released unless his or her identity is in question, evidence must be preserved, or the young person must be detained for the safety and security of the community. You will recall a discussion of this Chapter 7 earlier in this book.

The provisions regarding judicial interim release (bail) for adults also apply to youth. A youth can be denied bail on three grounds: (1) the primary ground that if not detained, the accused would not attend court; (2) the secondary ground that if not detained, the accused would commit further offences or interfere with the administration of justice; and (3) the tertiary ground that the release of the accused would lead to a lack of confidence in the administration of justice. In the case of young persons being considered for release under s 515 of the *Criminal Code*, the judge is required to consider releasing the young person into the care of a responsible person as an alternative to being held in pre-trial detention. The release of a young person into the care of a responsible person allows more youth to be released into the community awaiting trial and is in keeping with one of the cornerstones of the legislative principle to use the least restrictive alternative for low-risk, low-need offenders.

In addition, a **youth justice conference** (YCJA, s 19) may be called to assist with the bail process. The involved parties (defence counsel, Crown, judge, parents, and sometimes child welfare workers) can work together at finding an appropriate placement for an at-risk young person. The parties can also suggest measures to stabilize the young person's life and ensure that he or she will not reoffend while awaiting trial. Conferences at the bail stage can be particularly valuable for brainstorming creative solutions for runaways, those who have had placement problems, or those who find it hard to follow court orders to the point where further charges are laid against them. Further, in allowing for the prospect of release to a responsible person, the conference encourages community involvement, which is consistent with restorative justice–based approaches (Reid et al., 2015, p. 135).

The YCJA contributed to a reduction in the number of young people held in pre-trial detention (see Figure 12.2). However, the number of young people that were required to be detained in remand pending trial remains high compared to the rate of youth in sentenced custody. Bala (2015) suggested that part of the reason for this outcome was related to the lack of guidance that was provided to judges about the restrictions on the use of pre-trial remand. Continuing reliance on pre-trial remand custody became apparent after amendments were made to the YCJA in 2012, as a result of the Nunn Commission

appearance notice
A form given to the accused by police after being charged that tells him or her to appear in court on a specific day and time to answer to a criminal charge.

undertaking
A document that sets out the conditions for the release from police detention of a person charged with an offence. Conditions typically include a curfew, parental supervision, and attendance at school.

responsible person
An adult (other than a parent or guardian) who is willing and able to exercise control over a young person in order for him or her to be released prior to trial.

youth justice conference
A group of people (e.g., family, clinicians, teachers, community members, and the young person) who are asked by a decision-maker (such as a judge) to come together to give advice on a young person's case. The format may include a youth justice committee, a professional case conference, or a family group conference.

of Inquiry (2006). Given the tragic death of McEvoy by a motor vehicle crash with a youth driving after having been released from remand custody just a few days prior, the Nunn Commission tightened the provisions regarding the release of young people from detention. These provisions led to the dramatic increase in the use of pre-trial detention following the 2012 amendments.

The Nunn Commission

In the fall of 2004, a high-speed police chase involving a young offender in a stolen vehicle led to the tragic death of 52-year-old Theresa McEvoy when the car she was driving was struck by a vehicle driven by the fleeing youth. Given the prior youth record of the young person and the fact that he had been released on judicial interim release two days prior to the fatal incident, the Nova Scotia government called for a public inquiry and appointed a retired justice of the Nova Scotia Supreme Court, the Honourable D. Merlin Nunn, as the commissioner. The Nunn Commission resulted in a 381-page report that provided a series of 34 recommendations with respect to youth justice administration and accountability, youth crime legislation, and the prevention of youth crime.

One recommendation was that the Department of Education should provide additional training and adequate funding for assessment and early intervention of students with learning disabilities and other mental and psychological disabilities that may increase the likelihood of their coming into conflict with the law (Nunn Commission of Inquiry, 2006, p. 269). This recommendation was based on research presented to the commission that found that approximately 80 percent of repeat young offenders are living with disabilities, including mental health disabilities.

The 2012 amendments to the YCJA included provisions that were taken directly from the recommendations of the Nunn Commission. The provisions for pre-trial detention under s 29(2) were clarified such that in cases where a young person has been charged with a serious offence or has a criminal history that shows a pattern of either outstanding charges or findings of guilt, those factors will be grounds to hold the young person in pre-trial detention.

What Do You Think?

What are the important considerations regarding the granting or denying of bail that you would want the judge to take into account? If judges followed your advice and concerns, would that mean that there would be an increase or a decrease in the number of youth held in pre-trial detention?

FIGURE 12.2   Youth Pre-trial Detention, 2001–2 to 2014–15

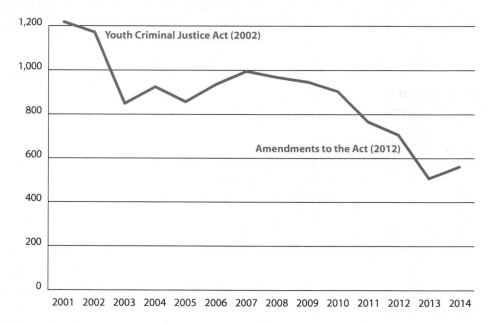

Source: Statistics Canada (2016).

Being held in pre-trial remand is highly stressful for most detainees and particularly so for young people. The fear of the unknown, uncertainty about how long he or she will be required to stay in detention, and the outcome of his or her case all add to the young person's stress. Research has shown that distrust of an authoritarian environment, lack of control, and being isolated from family and friends is particularly problematic for young people (Fagan & Guggenheim, 1996; Freeman & Seymour, 2010). Pre-trial detention may lead to negative psychological outcomes. Wasserman, McReynolds, Schwalbe, Keating, and Jones (2010) noted that, compared with those in custodial corrections, "detainees reported significantly higher rates of both affective and anxiety disorders, along with higher rates of recent suicide attempts" (p. 1,369). Moreover, youth held in pre-trial detention are more likely to plead guilty, to be convicted if tried, and to receive a custodial sentence than youth who are released on conditions of bail (Cesaroni & Peterson-Badali, 2016).

Youth Sentencing

Principles of Sentencing

Section 38 of the YCJA states that the purpose of sentencing is to hold a young offender *accountable* for his or her crime through the imposition of just sanctions that have meaningful consequences for the young person and that promote rehabilitation and reintegration into society, which thereby contributes to the long-term protection of the public. In addition to the principles outlined in the Declaration of Principle of the YCJA, the following sentencing principles also apply:

- *No greater than adult punishment.* In the handing out of a sentence, a young person shall not receive a punishment that would be greater than the punishment for an adult who has been convicted for the same offence committed in similar circumstances.
- *Regional consistency.* The sentence must be similar to the sentences imposed in the region on similar young persons found guilty of the same offence committed in similar circumstances.
- *Proportionate to offence and responsibility.* The sentence must be proportionate to the seriousness of the offence and the degree of responsibility of the young person for the offence.
- *Priority to non-custodial.* All available sanctions other than custody are to be considered for all young persons. Particular attention should be paid to using non-custodial sentences for Indigenous youth.
- *Rehabilitation/reintegration.* The sentence is to be one that is likely to rehabilitate the young person and reintegrate him or her into society and promote a sense of responsibility in him or her, and an acknowledgement of the harm done to victims and the community.
- *Denunciation and deterrence.* The 2012 amendments to the YCJA added these two principles, which are contained in adult sentencing principles. The principles of denunciation and deterrence are only to be considered within the context of the degree of responsibility of the young person for the offence and proportionate to the seriousness of the crime.

> **What Do You Think?**
>
> 1. Which models of criminal justice (restorative justice, community change, welfare, justice, crime control) are represented in the sentencing principles of the YCJA?
>
> 2. How are the sentencing principles for youth different from those for adults, described in Chapter 8? What is the rationale for the differences? Would the arguments made for the age and stage of development also apply to sentencing as it did to the minimum and maximum age jurisdiction of the court? Why or why not?

Factors to Consider in Sentencing Youth

The YCJA requires the court to also take into account the following when determining a youth sentence:

- the degree of participation by the young person in the offence
- the harm done to victims and whether it was intentional or reasonably foreseeable
- any reparations made by the young person to the victim or the community
- time already spent in custody for pre-trial detention
- previous findings of guilt
- any other aggravating and mitigating circumstances related to the young person or the offence that are relevant to the purpose and principles

> **What Do You Think?**
>
> How do the factors considered in youth sentencing compare with the factors considered in adult sentencing, described in Chapter 8?

Indigenous Youth and Sentencing

The Declaration of Principle of the YCJA includes the requirement to respect and respond to the needs of Indigenous young persons, which means that the sentence must also respond to their needs. The circumstances of young Indigenous offenders must be taken into account at the time of sentencing, according to this principle. This principle is similar to the provision for adults in the *Criminal Code* that was a result of the Supreme Court of Canada decision in *R v Gladue* (1999) (see Chapter 11). By way of review, the Supreme Court endorsed the concept of restorative justice and the use of community-based alternatives to imprisonment in the *Gladue* decision. The Supreme Court was asked to consider the meaning of s 718.2(e) of the *Criminal Code*, which states that judges are to consider all reasonable alternatives to incarceration for all offenders, but "with particular attention to the circumstances of Aboriginal offenders." The court ruled that this passage imposes a duty upon judges to recognize factors that affect offenders (particularly Indigenous offenders), such as poverty, substance abuse, and lack of education or employment opportunities, and to consider the role these factors might play in bringing the offender before the courts.

In the *Gladue* decision, the Supreme Court remarked on the overrepresentation of Indigenous people in penal institutions. It noted that in 1997, Indigenous people made up about 3 percent of the population but amounted to 12 percent of federal adult inmates. In 1995–96 in Manitoba, Indigenous adult offenders accounted for 55 percent of admissions to provincial correctional facilities; in Saskatchewan, that figure was 72 percent.

Indigenous communities in Canada tend to have relatively high birth rates and large youth populations. As a result, there is profound concern that these communities will suffer long-term consequences if their young members grow into adult offenders rather than productive, contributing adults. Indigenous communities are also anxious about youth crime issues because members of their communities are the most frequent victims of this type of offending, bearing its immediate costs (Bala, 2015, p. 170).

The historic and contemporary traumas experienced by Indigenous youth, their families, and their communities have been well documented. Moreover, extensive research exists on the overuse of custody that has been linked to past and present inequality (Alain et al., 2016). Manitoba and Saskatchewan have a particularly high prevalence of Indigenous young offenders in their youth criminal justice systems, which points to the vulnerability of this population (Hogeveen, 2005). Section 38(2)(d) of the YCJA underscores the importance of utilizing alternatives to custodial sanctions for Indigenous youth. However, while there is a legislative mandate and case law precedent, the disproportionate overrepresentation of Indigenous youth in the youth criminal justice system remains.

MINI CASE STUDY

R v J.T.S. (2007)

Jonathon Tyrone Slippery (J.T.S.) was convicted of second-degree murder when he was 15. Slippery, accompanied by two other males, got involved in a heated discussion with a couple of individuals over the repayment of a drug debt that led to the stabbing of the victim, who died shortly thereafter. The trial judge determined that Slippery should receive an adult sentence and serve his sentence in an adult facility, despite his young age at the time of the offence. The case ultimately went to the Court of Appeal for Saskatchewan. The Court of Appeal considered a number of factors in addition to the offender's cultural heritage and the provisions with regard to the treatment of First Nations peoples. As was provided under *R v Gladue* (1999), the court is required to consider the role that factors such as poverty, substance abuse, and lack of education for Aboriginal people play in brining the offender to court. Why were these not addressed in Slippery's case? The defence counsel detailed Slippery's troubled past, including his transfer to 16 different foster homes and 11 different schools. However, the lack of an appropriate program to reduce Slippery's risk of re-offending, coupled with a high risk for reoffending, led the appellate judge to concur with the trial judge.

Savarese (2016) noted a number of issues raised by Slippery's case: "ongoing social justice challenges include poverty, educational achievement deficits, intergenerational trauma, inadequate pro-social supports that may precipitate gang involvement, and other psychophysical challenges such as fetal alcohol syndrome." She added that the lack of supports in dealing with these issues may have been the reason behind the insistence on an adult sentence for Slippery. Citing court documents that called for high-intensity programming, Savarese (2016, p. 352) reported that because there was no appropriate program to reduce his risk to reoffend, a youth sentence was deemed unsuitable. By the time Slippery's case was concluded in the Court of Appeal, he had already spent many years in prison (at the maximum-security unit at Prince Albert Penitentiary, Saskatchewan) and was 20 years old, no longer a youth.

What Do You Think?

1. Under s 38(2)(d) of the YCJA, judges are required to consider all sanctions other than custody that are reasonable under the circumstances for Aboriginal young persons. Where should this have applied in Slippery's case?

2. Considering the case study at the beginning of the book and the case study of Ashley Smith, what might have been different for Slippery if he had remained in the youth criminal justice system to serve his sentence?

Community Sanctions for Convicted Youth

In keeping with its goal of reducing the number of youth who are sentenced to custody, the YCJA authorizes the use of non-custodial sentences for youth who commit less serious offences (the majority of young offenders), while reserving custody for the small number of youth who commit serious offences.

Section 42 of the YCJA provides a youth justice court that finds a young person guilty of an offence with the option to impose one of the following non-custodial sentences (listed from the least to the most onerous):

1. A *judicial reprimand* (i.e., a stern warning from the judge) means that a finding of guilt is entered, but it is as if the sentence has already been served, in the belief that the processing of the young person before the court is a sanction in itself.

2. An *absolute discharge* is like a reprimand in that the processing of the young person through the formal court system is the sentence.

3. A *conditional discharge* adds a series of conditions that the court considers appropriate, and may include reporting to a probation officer. Once the conditions have been satisfied, the young person will be discharged. However, if a young person does not fulfill the conditions, the youth can be charged with another criminal offence (failure to comply with the sentence, YCJA, s 137).

4. Although a *fine* of up to $1,000 is an option, some courts are hesitant to give fines as a sentence because they are punitive with very little rehabilitative value, which is seen as contrary to the principle of the legislation. Further, fines may be viewed as unfair for those young persons who have parents with the ability to pay, even though the judge must ask about the young person's present and future ability to pay the fine on his or her own.

5. A young person may be ordered to make *compensation* (payment) or *restitution* (services) for personal injury, for loss of or damage to property, or for loss of income or support. The judge cannot order personal service without the consent of the victim to be compensated, because not all victims may want to have contact or involvement with the young person. An order to perform personal service cannot exceed 240 hours and must be completed within one year of the date of the order.

6. A *community service order* may be issued, which includes personal or community service if the judge deems the young person a suitable candidate and the service does not interfere with the young person's normal work or educational hours. Again, the community service hours may not exceed 240 hours and must be completed within one year of the date of the order.

7. Order of *prohibition, seizure,* or *forfeiture* for at least two years; this order may relate to items such as firearms or other dangerous weapons.

8. *Probation* has been a preferred sanction since the inception of the JDA. Under the YOA, many young persons breached their conditions of probation, which would result in another criminal charge that often put them into custody. The YCJA provides for probation conditions to be reviewed and altered if breached, rather than have a breach always lead to the laying of a new charge. Probation includes the requirement to report periodically to a probation officer, to avoid contact with known offenders, and to meet other conditions that are meant to address the offence committed and respond in a meaningful manner. Community service may also be part of a probation order.

9. *Intensive Support and Supervision Program* (ISSP) is a provision in the YCJA that calls for a more intensive probation order in those provinces where it is available. Rather than the young person having to serve a term in custody, an ISSP keeps youth in the community and adds support in the form of intensive monitoring, additional resources, and referrals to community-based agencies as a condition of the order; and, like probation orders, participation in an ISSP cannot exceed two years.

10. *Attendance at non-residential centres* is a provision to keep young persons out of custody. In addition to reporting to a probation officer, the young person is required to attend a centre that offers programs and services for up to 240 hours for a maximum of six months. This option allows the judge an opportunity to address some of the risk factors that the young person presents by ordering, for example, attendance at a drug and alcohol treatment centre after school. Attendance centre programs are not available in all provinces.

CAREER PROFILE

Carol Skacel

Carol Skacel is a program coordinator at a centre in downtown Toronto that provides counselling and legal services for young offenders.

How did you first become interested in youth justice?
Initially, I wanted to work in the adult justice system. However, experiences and education steered me in a different direction. I wanted to help people make positive changes in their lives and realized that young people may have more of a chance of implementing change. During and after completing college practicum, I realized that I had the ability to empathize, listen, and help people facilitate change.

How did you reach your current position?
I began my career in 1998, working in a secure detention facility for youth in Kingston. In 2000, I moved to Toronto and worked in a secure facility for youth located in the downtown area. I realized that I was very limited in the impact and change I could help facilitate with youth in these environments and, in 2007, I began working in a bail support program for youth. This program provided outreach services to youth that would otherwise not be granted bail. Services included advocacy, individual counselling, assessment and planning, case management, group facilitation, and family support. I recently moved to another program within the agency and now help youth in open detention/custody facilities across the Greater Toronto Area, Peel, and Halton to access mental health supports. While working, I completed my bachelor of social work at Ryerson University. I am also currently a part-time faculty member at Humber College, teaching a course on youth in conflict with the law.

What are some of your most important duties?
Creating an initial rapport and building a relationship is crucial. Doing so leads to effective, client-centred service planning. Clients will only "buy into" a plan that they feel is relevant to them. Assessing the immediate and longer-term needs of a young person while maintaining a strength-based approach provides an opportunity for a young person to experience some successes. Outreach and advocacy are important. Meeting young people in their communities (such as at home or school) enables a less punitive and more collaborative approach to youth justice services. This kind of approach can also lead to a more trusting and open rapport between the young person and the social worker.

What are the most challenging and the most rewarding aspects of your job?
This is a population of young people in conflict with the law, and it can be challenging to gain the trust needed to provide meaningful and effective services. Some of the young people have had prior unsuccessful experiences with service providers and various systems. Navigating the systems themselves can also be challenging. Restrictions placed on the young people by the courts and/or probation may hinder the effectiveness of a service plan. Another challenge is accessing additional supports to augment the service plan, due to wait lists and a lack of resources, particularly in smaller communities.

Witnessing the changes a youth makes, no matter how small, is very rewarding. Building a trusting relationship with a youth and having him or her understand that you are a positive and supportive adult is gratifying. So too is being a part of that youth's story and experiencing growth with him or her. As well, on occasion, you may hear from previous clients who want to let you know that they have maintained positive changes and are pursuing a post-secondary education and a career.

What are some of the main reasons young people find themselves involved in the justice system?
A number of the youth grow up in poor, marginalized communities and subsequently face multiple layers of oppression and systemic barriers. For example, some youth grow up with poverty, racism, discrimination, community disorganization, safety concerns, and a lack of school success. We also see many young people living with mental health concerns. Many youth have experienced trauma, have diagnosed or undiagnosed learning disabilities, Fetal

Alcohol Spectrum Disorders, or other forms of mental health concerns. Family and peer factors can also play a role in risk for involvement in the justice system.

What can be done to stop youth from becoming involved in the criminal justice system?
Preventive measures need to be available at a much younger age. There needs to be more structure for children's time, and an increase in accessible resources for children and youth. Families also need readily available advocacy and support. Schools need to be better edu-

cated on identifying children at risk, and plans to address those risks need to be implemented. Building on strengths and allowing children and youth to experience tangible success is critical. On a systemic level, we need to do more to address oppression and barriers that increase a young person's risk of becoming involved in the youth justice system. Service providers need to work more collaboratively with one another and with systems such as the courts and educational institutions to address the multiple layers of needs this population has.

MINI CASE STUDY

R v S.L.S. (2016)

As noted earlier, probation is the most common sentence handed out in youth justice court. In the case of *R v S.L.S.*, a sentence of 12 months' probation plus 20 hours of community service was given to S after she, at age 15, pleaded guilty to two counts of assault and six counts of breach of an undertaking. At the time of the offence, S was having an argument with her mother regarding a young male visiting with her in the early morning hours. S's mother told the young man to leave and S indicated that she would leave as well. When the mother attempted to prevent her from leaving, S assaulted her. She grabbed her mother's hair, kicked her, and bit her, resulting in a large bruise on the mother's thigh. When S's brother arrived home later in the morning, he found his mother crying, and when he spoke to S, she assaulted him by hitting him in the back of his head and trying to bite him. S was arrested and released on an undertaking that had conditions of a curfew and attending school. Prior to the sentencing hearing, S had breached the school and curfew conditions six times.

In making his determination, Justice Gorman indicated that the assault, having left a bruise on S's mother's thigh, would meet the threshold for a violent offence and therefore open the gate to the possibility of a custodial sentence. However, in considering that this was a first-time offence for S, that S had been bullied in grade

seven, that S had moved to a new school where she was not adapting to the change very well, and that there were problems related to family dysfunction, Justice Gorman chose to impose probation instead.

The court heard that when S was released on an undertaking, she was required to live with her father because of the assaults on her mother and brother. After two days, her father reported that he could not handle her, stating, "She is the worst daughter anyone could have." He signed a voluntary care agreement for her to return to Corner Brook, Newfoundland and be looked after in foster care.

At the sentencing hearing, Justice Gorman was reluctant to impose an order that S stay away from her mother and brother and commented on the value of leaving it open for S to reconcile with the family.

What Do You Think?

1. Given the details of this case, would you have come to the same conclusion about sentencing?

2. What were the risk factors?

3. What are the aggravating factors and mitigating factors in this case?

4. Would an adult have received the same kind of sentence?

More Intensive Interventions: Custodial Sanctions

As previously noted, one of the main purposes of the YCJA was to reduce the use of custodial sentences for young people (something that had become common practice under the YOA). Section 39(1) of the YCJA states that the youth justice court must not commit a young person to custody unless

> (a) the young person has committed a violent offence;
> (b) the young person has failed to comply with non-custodial sentences;
> (c) the young person has committed an indictable offence for which an adult would be liable to imprisonment for more than two years and has a history that indicates a pattern of either extrajudicial sanctions or of findings of guilt or of both under this Act or the *Young Offenders Act* … ; or
> (d) in exceptional cases where the young person has committed an indictable offence, the aggravating circumstances of the offence are such that the imposition of a non-custodial sentence would be inconsistent with the purpose and principles set out in section 38.

Confinement of youth in correctional facilities has a high economic cost as well as other social costs. What evidence there is suggests that custodial sentences have a weak deterrent effect on youth and, in many cases, the impact of incarceration actually increases the likelihood of reoffending (Black, 2016; Mears, 2017). In calculating the costs and benefits of a custodial policy for young persons, it must be kept in mind that almost all young offenders will be released into the community, and there we run the risk of a huge social cost to youth when they "grow up" in jail.

In the correctional system, correctional officers, whose main job is to maintain security, often have impersonal, authoritarian, and hostile relationships with the young offenders in their charge (Schubert, Mulvey, Loughran, & Losoya, 2012). The lack of pro-social peers further complicates the situation for young persons who do not have a caring adult to help them develop social skills, improve relationships, or deal with problems. While some opportunities for education and extracurricular activities exist within youth custodial facilities, young people spend much of their time in cells or in the prison yard under the watchful surveillance of guards. This social context is not conducive to the healthy development of youth or to a successful transition to young adulthood. Upon release, the stigma of having been in custody can thwart efforts to seek out legal and meaningful employment or education. Further, the lack of opportunity to develop social skills can make it very difficult to establish stable pro-social relationships in the community. Research shows that the two most important factors related to no longer engaging in crime are marriage or a stable intimate relationship and meaningful employment (Reid, 2010). Hindering the natural development of significant relationships and the acquiring of skills necessary for meaningful employment through the use of custody jeopardizes young people's successful transition to adulthood (Skeem, Scott, & Mulvey, 2014).

In this context, it is important to recognize the integral role of the community supervision portion of a custodial sentence. During the community reintegration phase of a young person's custodial sentence, it is vital that youth have opportunities to interact with and participate in educational, extracurricular, and employment activities that will introduce them to pro-social peers.

Youth Records

When a young person is found guilty of a criminal offence, the individual will receive a youth record. The period of time that a youth record may be accessed after a finding of guilt varies, depending on the type of sentence (YCJA, s 119(2)). Generally, the more severe the offence, and therefore the more severe the sentence, the longer the access period to the record by police, victims, judges, courts of review, and persons carrying out a criminal record check. Consider the following examples:

- An extrajudicial sanction can be accessed for two years from the time that the young person consented to the sanction.
- A judicial reprimand can only be accessed for two months.
- An absolute discharge can be accessed for a year.
- A conditional discharge can be accessed for three years.
- All other summary conviction offences can be accessed for three years from the time the young person completes the sentence.
- Indictable offences can be accessed for five years from the time the young person completes the sentence.

If a young person is convicted of a subsequent offence, the access period is recalculated. Youth records are not protected from adult proceedings while the access period is still open, which means that a youth record can be brought forward at a time of sentencing as an adult; the fact that a young adult before the court has a youth record can also be published.

What Do You Think?

1. What do you think about the length of time records are kept for extrajudicial sanctions? What are the implications?
2. What do you think about the length of time records are kept for conditional discharge, summary conviction offences, and indictable offences? What are the implications?

The Imposition of an Adult Sentence on a Young Offender

In accordance with the provisions in s 72(1) of the YCJA, an adult sentence can be imposed on a young person if the crime he or she committed is so serious that the sentences available in youth justice court are not sufficient to hold the young person accountable. For an adult sentence to be imposed, the court must be satisfied that the presumption of diminished moral blameworthiness or culpability of the young person is rebutted. This provision has always been available as an "escape hatch" for very serious crimes committed by young people, as far back as the JDA. There have been a series of amendments since the YOA and then the YCJA were enacted, which have systematically addressed the amount of time that is most effective for sentencing a young person given their age and stage of maturity. The youth sentences imposed have been deemed to hold the majority of young persons accountable for their offences. In those cases where the crime is so heinous that an adult sentence is required to hold the young person accountable, adult sentences are available for the small number of youth that may be affected.

MINI CASE STUDY

R v A.O. (2007)

In the case of *R v A.O.*, two 16-year-olds, A.O. and J.M., were convicted of committing six armed robberies at convenience stores. The crimes happened late at night when the store clerks were alone with the youth, who used knives or an imitation handgun. Four of the victims received knife wounds, another was seriously beaten and stabbed, and all six were "traumatized."

The Crown successfully argued that both young persons accused should receive adult sentences of eight years in prison (later reduced to five because they had already spent two-and-a-half years in remand awaiting trial). Both youth appealed, but the Ontario Court of Appeal upheld the ruling, saying that an adult sentence was necessary in order to hold both young persons accountable for their actions and the length of the maximum youth custodial sentence would not be sufficient.

What Do You Think?

Think about young people's view of accountability and meaningful consequences, as discussed in "Sidebar—What Young People Have Said About Extrajudicial Sanctions." In what way(s) does an adult sentence address the issues of accountability and meaningful consequence in this case?

Youth with Mental Health Challenges

Statistics on children and youth with mental health challenges indicate that between 10 and 20 percent of youth are affected by a mental illness or disorder (Canadian Mental Health Association, 2016). Estimates suggest that more than 3.2 million youth between the ages of 12 and 19 in Canada are at risk for developing depression. In Canada, only one in five children who need mental health services receives them, and the majority of young adults living with mental illness report that their problems began in childhood. Indeed, research has shown that young offenders experience high levels of mental health problems (Kapp, Petr, Robbins, & Choi, 2013). However, evidence suggests that the mental health treatment needs of young offenders are not being met (Liebenberg & Ungar, 2014; Whitted, Delavega, & Lennon-Dearing, 2013). A study of 152 youth who were involved with either the youth justice system or the mental health system found that youth in mental health programs had significantly higher contact with health care and mental health services as well as school support services than their youth justice counterparts (Liebenberg & Ungar, 2014). Youth diagnosed with multiple mental health disorders are more likely to offend in the first place and reoffend at greater rates than their peers who do not suffer from mental health challenges (Espinosa, Sorensen, & Lopez, 2013; Hoeve, McReynolds, & Wasserman, 2014).

Section 42(2)(r) of the YCJA provides for an **intensive rehabilitative custody and supervision (IRCS)** option, which is available to young people with mental health challenges who have committed a serious offence that would lead to a custodial disposition. Section 42(7) states that an IRCS order can be made if

(a) either

(i) the young person has been found guilty of a serious violent offence, or

(ii) the young person has been found guilty of an offence, in the commission of which the young person caused or attempted to cause serious bodily harm and for which an adult is liable to imprisonment for a term of more than two years, and the young person had previously been found guilty at least twice of such an offence;

(b) the young person is suffering from a mental illness or disorder, a psychological disorder or an emotional disturbance;

(c) a plan of treatment and intensive supervision has been developed for the young person, and there are reasonable grounds to believe that the plan might reduce the risk of the young person repeating the offence or committing a serious violent offence; and

(d) the provincial director has determined that an intensive rehabilitative custody and supervision program is available and that the young person's participation in the program is appropriate.

The IRCS program, which is specially funded by the federal government, is meant to provide specialized treatment to those youth most in need of rehabilitation due to their risk factors. What is most notable about the IRCS program is its focus on a "wrap-around approach" to meet specific needs in all areas of the individual's life, helping the youth to develop pro-social behaviours that will support his or her reintegration back into society. An IRCS order includes a treatment plan in which the young person must participate while in custody and while being supervised during the community-based reintegrative portion of the sentence.

Correctional Programs that Reduce Recidivism and Prevent Crime

Although a disproportionate number of young people within the criminal justice system have mental health challenges, this does not mean that mental illness *causes* criminal behaviour that results in incarceration. While individual psychological conditions are related to the poor functioning of those who struggle with mental illness in the community, we cannot say that mental disorders cause crime. The main predictors of criminal behaviour and violence in youth are criminal history, anti-social personality, anti-social cognitions, and anti-social peers. Individuals with mental illness and those who do not suffer from mental illness may equally possess these risk factors (Skeem, Manchak, & Peterson, 2011; Skeem et al., 2014).

In order to understand youth offending, one must look at a range of factors at individual, family, school, and broader community levels. Individual factors include impulsivity, anti-social attitudes, continued contact with anti-social peers, and alcohol and other drug abuse. Family factors include parenting style, inconsistent and harsh discipline, parental criminality, and poor parental supervision. School factors include truancy, poor academic performance, a lack of school engagement, and aggressive behaviour at school. Finally, disorganized communities, the availability of drugs and alcohol in the community, and a lack of amenities such as access to sports, leisure, and other activities are factors that contribute to a lack of belonging at the community level and lead to an increased risk for youth crime. It is not uncommon for a youth to have multiple risk factors, and the more problems a youth has, the more difficult it is to address them. In order to address multiple risk factors, it is important to first identify potential sources of problem behaviour and then address these problems with a package of services aimed at the individual's needs (Reid & Gilliss, 2016). For example, if a young person has criminal peers and family problems but holds a steady job, then an employment program would not be suitable. The needs identified are pro-social peers and some form of family intervention.

Research evidence shows that an increase in the severity of punishment does not reduce recidivism in young people (Lipsey & Cullen, 2007; MacKenzie, 2006, 2013). In fact, aversive sanctions and supervision programs may increase future criminal behaviour, as studies of Scared Straight programs (Guerra & Williams, 2012; Petrosino, Turpin-Petrosino, & Buehler, 2003) and boot camps (Cullen, Blevins, Trager, & Gendreau, 2005; Meade & Steiner, 2010) have shown.

The Risk-Need-Responsivity (RNR) model (Andrews & Bonta, 2010) discussed in Chapter 9 suggests that programs should be delivered in a manner that addresses the specific risk level of the offender, targets his or her specific criminogenic needs, and takes into account his or her unique learning styles and capabilities or responsivity to the program being offered. In a study of young offenders in Europe, when cognitive behavioural and behavioural treatment had high adherence to RNR principles, there was a significant reduction in reoffence (Koehler, Lösel, Akoensi, & Humphreys, 2013). Research has shown that programs that target high-risk young offenders (the risk principle) and focus on changing empirically established risk factors (the need principle) through an intervention that maximizes engagement in the treatment process (the responsivity principle) are most successful in reducing recidivism (Brogan, Haney-Caron, NeMoyer, & DeMatteo, 2015; Vieira, Skilling, & Peterson-Badali, 2009).

Even though strong evidence suggests that criminogenic risk can be reduced, there is some hesitation among practitioners with regard to the treatment of high-risk young offenders because the process of treating them is often difficult. The very characteristics that foster involvement in crime, such as non-compliance, negative attitudes, and disruptive behaviour, are all present during the therapeutic treatment regime (Frick, Ray, Thornton, & Kahn, 2014). In other words, the very risk factors that promote offending are also the ones that make treatment difficult, and when youth find the treatment hard, they are much more likely to give up. It is these young people who present the highest risk and who are responsible for the most amount of crime and the greatest impact of crime, not only in their own lives but also in the lives of their families, their victims, and victims' families, and in the broader society. In 2009, Cohen and Piquero estimated that if we were able to prevent one 14-year-old very high-risk youth from becoming a career criminal, we would save between $2.7 and $4.8 million.

IN-CLASS EXERCISE

Crime Prevention Initiatives

Given your understanding of crime prevention from Chapters 2 and 5 and your knowledge of youth justice, what kinds of initiatives for youth might you recommend for the following?:

1. *Primary crime prevention*, which attempts to alleviate known risk factors that contribute to crime before a crime occurs.

2. *Secondary crime prevention*, which addresses behaviour that is known to be linked to future criminal behaviour.

3. *Tertiary crime prevention*, which comprises criminal justice responses and rehabilitation programs after a crime has been committed; its goal is to deter an offender from engaging in future criminal behaviour.

Conclusion

Inevitably, a portion of the crime committed in any society is attributable to young people. On the one hand, the law recognizes that young people between the ages of 12 and 17 proceed through evolving stages of moral and cognitive reasoning on their way to adulthood and must be protected from undue punishment for minor misbehaviour. On the other hand, when young people commit violent or dangerous crimes, there is keen public pressure not to allow them to "get away with" crime simply because they have not yet turned 18.

Legislation around youth criminal justice—from the *Juvenile Delinquents Act* to the *Young Offenders Act* to today's *Youth Criminal Justice Act*—reflects the ongoing development in our understanding of youth and strives to achieve the best possible balance between these competing interests. Justice, in this context, aims to reduce the involvement of youth with the criminal justice system, to prevent the likelihood of recidivism, and to provide proper support programs for young offenders in especially vulnerable groups—while at the same time holding them accountable for their actions. High profile cases like that of Ashley Smith serve as a haunting reminder of the stakes involved in youth criminal justice, and the intolerable cost of getting things wrong.

DISCUSSION QUESTIONS

1. Discuss what might have been the outcome for Ashley Smith had she been living during the time of the JDA. What positive and negative outcomes might there have been for Ashley when the JDA was in effect?

2. The YOA and YCJA represent a number of the philosophical models of criminal justice outlined in Chapter 1. What are some of the positive and negative features of having more than one model represented in youth justice legislation?

3. Have a look at your local newspaper and see how youth crime is depicted. Do you think that the media present one or more of the myths outlined in this chapter? What myths are promoted in the media about young persons and young persons in conflict with the law? In what way(s) can you change how society views young persons who become enmeshed in the youth criminal justice system?

SUGGESTED FURTHER READINGS

Alain, M., Corrodo, R., & Reid, S. (Eds.). (2016). *Implementing and working with the Youth Criminal Justice Act across Canada.* Toronto: University of Toronto Press.

Reid, S., Bromwich, R., & Gilliss, S. (2016). *Youth and the law: New approaches to criminal justice and child protection* (3rd ed.). Toronto: Emond.

Winterdyk, J., & Smandych, R. (Eds.). (2016). *Youth at risk and youth justice.* Toronto: Oxford University Press.

REFERENCES

Alain, M., Corrodo, R., & Reid, S. (Eds.). (2016). *Implementing and working with the Youth Criminal Justice Act across Canada.* Toronto: University of Toronto Press.

Allen, M. (2016). Police-reported crime statistics in Canada, 2015. *Juristat, 36*(1). Retrieved from http://www.statcan.gc.ca/pub/85-002-x/2016001/article/14642-eng.pdf.

Andrews, D., & Bonta, J. (2010). *The psychology of criminal conduct* (5th ed.). New York: Routledge.

Bala, N. (2015). Changing professional culture and reducing use of courts and custody for youth: The *Youth Criminal Justice Act* and Bill C-10. *Saskatchewan Law Review, 78,* 127–180.

Bala, N., Carrington, P., & Roberts, J. (2009). Evaluating the *Youth Criminal Justice Act* after five years: A qualified success. *Canadian Journal of Criminology and Criminal Justice, 51*(1), 131–167.

Black, J.M. (2016). *Understanding the effectiveness of incarceration on juvenile offending through a systematic review and metaanalysis: Do the "get tough" policies work?* (Doctoral dissertation). Nova Southeastern University. Retrieved from http://nsuworks.nova.edu/cahss_jhs_etd/2.

Boudreau, M. (2012). *City of order: Crime and society in Halifax, 1918–35.* Vancouver: UBC Press.

Brennan, S. (2012). *Police-reported crime statistics in Canada, 2011. Juristat.* Catalogue No. 85-002-X. Ottawa: Minister of Industry. Retrieved from http://www.statcan.gc.ca/pub/85-002-x/2012001/article/11692-eng.pdf.

Brogan, L., Haney-Caron, E., NeMoyer, A., & DeMatteo, D. (2015). Applying the Risk-Needs-Responsivity (RNR) model to juvenile justice. *Criminal Justice Review, 40*(3), 277–302.

Canada, House of Commons. (2001, February 14). *Debates: Edited Hansard*, No. 013. Retrieved from http://www.parl.gc.ca/HousePublications/Publication.aspx?Language=E&Mode=1&DocId=2332075.

Canadian Mental Health Association. (2016). Fast facts about mental illness. Retrieved from http://www.cmha.ca/media/fast-facts-about-mental-illness/#.VJHpUzHF9ws.

Cesaroni, C., & Peterson-Badali, M. (2016). The role of fairness in the adjustment of adolescent boys to pretrial detention. *The Prison Journal, 96*(4), 534–553.

Cohen, M.A., & Piquero, A.R. (2009). New evidence on the monetary value of saving a high risk youth. *Journal of Quantitative Criminology, 25*(1), 25–49.

Cullen, F.T., Blevins, K.R., Trager, J.S., & Gendreau, P. (2005). The rise and fall of boot camps: A case study in common sense corrections. *Journal of Offender Rehabilitation, 4*(3–4), 53–70.

Davis-Barron, S. (2009). *Canadian youth and the criminal law.* Toronto: LexisNexis.

Department of Justice Canada. (1998). *A strategy for the renewal of youth justice.* Ottawa: Author.

Department of Justice Canada. (2004). The evolution of juvenile justice in Canada. Retrieved from http://www.justice.gc.ca/eng/rp-pr/csj-sjc/ilp-pji/jj2-jm2/sec01.html.

DeTardo-Bora, K.A. (2014). Child Savers. *The encyclopedia of criminology and criminal justice.* London: Blackwell.

Doob, A., & Cesaroni, C. (2004). *Responding to youth crime in Canada.* Toronto: University of Toronto Press.

Doob, A., & Sprott, B.J. (2007). Punishing youth crime in Canada: The blind men and the elephant. *Punishment & Society, 8*(2), 223–233.

Espinosa, E.M., Sorensen, J.R., & Lopez, M.A. (2013). Youth pathways to placement: The influence of gender, mental health need and trauma on confinement in the juvenile justice system. *Journal of Youth and Adolescence, 42*(12), 1824–1836.

Fagan, J., & Guggenheim, M. (1996). Preventive detention and the judicial prediction of dangerousness for juveniles: A natural experiment. *The Journal of Criminal Law and Criminology, 86*, 415–448.

Farrington, D.P., Loeber, L., & Howell, J.C. (2012). Young adult offenders: The need for more effective legislative options and justice processing. *Criminology & Public Policy, 11*(4), 729–750.

Fine, A., Steinberg, L., Frick, P.J., & Cauffman, E. (2016). Self-control assessments and implications for predicting adolescent offending. *Journal of Youth and Adolescence, 45*(4), 701–712.

Freeman, S., & Seymour, M. (2010). "Just waiting": The nature and effect of uncertainty on young people in remand custody in Ireland. *Youth Justice, 10*(2), 126–142.

Frick, P.J., Ray, J.V., Thornton, L.C., & Kahn, R.E. (2014). Can callous-unemotional traits enhance the understanding, diagnosis, and treatment of serious conduct problems in children and adolescents? A comprehensive review. *Psychological Bulletin, 140*(1), 1–57.

Gardner, M., & Steinberg, L. (2005). Peer influence on risk taking, risk preference, and risky decision making in adolescence and adulthood: An experimental study. *Developmental Psychology, 41*(4), 625–635.

Giedd, J.N. (2008). The teen brain: Insights from neuroimaging. *Journal of Adolescent Health, 42*(4), 335–343.

Green, K.M., Musci, R.J., Matson, P. A., Johnson, R.M., Reboussin, B.A., & Ialongo, N.S. (2017). Developmental patterns of adolescent marijuana and alcohol use and their joint association with sexual risk behavior and outcomes in young adulthood. *Journal of Urban Health, 1*, 1–10.

Guerra, N.G., & Williams, K.R. (2012). Implementing evidence-based practices for juvenile justice in communities. In E.L. Grigorenko (Ed.), *Handbook of juvenile forensic psychology and psychiatry* (pp. 297–307). New Haven, CT: Springer.

Hoeve, M., McReynolds, L.S., & Wasserman, G.A. (2014). Service referral for juvenile justice youths: Associations with psychiatric disorder and recidivism. *Administration and Policy in Mental Health and Mental Health Services Research, 41*(3), 379–389.

Hogeveen, R.B. (2005). "If we are tough on crime, if we punish crime, then people get the message": Constructing and governing the punishable young offender in Canada during the late 1990s. *Punishment & Society, 7*(1), 73–89.

Hyde, C., Marinos, V., & Innocente, N. (2016). What do meaningful consequences and fair and proportionate accountability mean to youth offered extrajudicial sanctions in Ontario? *Canadian Journal of Criminology and Criminal Justice, 58*(2), 194–220.

Kapp, S.A., Petr, C.G., Robbins, M.L., & Choi, J.J. (2013). Collaboration between community mental health and juvenile justice systems: Barriers and facilitators. *Child and Adolescent Social Work Journal, 30*(6), 505–517.

Koehler, J.A., Lösel, F., Akoensi, T.D., & Humphreys, D.K. (2013). A systematic review and meta-analysis on the effects of young offender treatment programs in Europe. *Journal of Experimental Criminology, 9*(1), 19–43.

Latimer, J. (2001). A meta-analytical examination of youth delinquency, family treatment, and recidivism. *Canadian Journal of Criminology, 43*(2), 237–253.

Liebenberg, L., & Ungar, M. (2014). A comparison of service use among youth involved with juvenile justice and mental health. *Children and Youth Services Review, 39*, 117–122.

Lipsey, M.W., & Cullen, F.T. (2007). The effectiveness of correctional rehabilitation: A review of systematic reviews. *Annual Review of Law and Social Science, 3*(1), 297–320.

Luciana, M., Wahlstrom, D., Porter, J.N., & Collins, P.F. (2012). Dopaminergic modulation of incentive motivation in adolescence: Age-related changes in signaling, individual differences, and implication for the development of self-regulation. *Developmental Psychology, 48*(3), 844–861.

MacKenzie, D.L. (2006). *What works in corrections? Reducing the criminal activities of offenders and delinquents*. Cambridge: Cambridge University Press.

MacKenzie, D.L. (2013). First do no harm: A look at correctional policies and programs today. *Journal of Experimental Criminology, 9*(1), 1–17.

Meade B., & Steiner, B. (2010). The total effects of boot camps that house juveniles: A systematic review of the evidence. *Journal of Criminal Justice, 38*(5), 841–853.

Mears, D.P. (2017). Assessing the effectiveness of juvenile justice reforms. *Law and Policy, 22*(2), 175.

Miladinovic, Z. (2016). Youth court statistics in Canada, 2014/2015. *Juristat, 36*(1). Catalogue No. 85-002-X. Retrieved from http://www.statcan.gc.ca/pub/85-002-x/2016001/article/14656-eng.pdf.

Monahan, K.C., Steinberg, L., Cauffman, E., & Mulvey, E.P. (2009). Trajectories of antisocial behavior and psychosocial maturity from adolescence to young adulthood. *Developmental Psychology, 45*(6), 1654–1662.

Moyer, S. (1980). *Diversion from the juvenile justice system and its impact on children: A review of the literature*. Ottawa: Queen's Printer.

Nunn Commission of Inquiry. (2006). Spiralling out of control: Lessons learned from a boy in trouble—Report of the Nunn Commission of Inquiry. Halifax: Government of Nova Scotia. Retrieved from https://novascotia.ca/just/nunn_commission/_docs/Report_Nunn_Final.pdf.

Petrosino, A., Guckenburg, S., & Turpin-Petrosino, C. (2010). Formal system processing of juveniles: Effects on delinquency. *The Campbell Collaboration Library of Systematic Reviews*. Retrieved from http://campbellcollaboration.org/lib/project/81/.

Petrosino, A., Turpin-Petrosino, C., & Buehler, J. (2003). Scared Straight and other juvenile awareness programs for preventing delinquency: A systematic review of randomized experimental evidence. *The Annals of the American Academy of Political and Social Science, 589*(1), 41–62.

R v AO, 2007 ONCA 144, 84 OR (3d) 561.

R v E (M), 2006 ONCJ 146, OJ No 1657 (Ct J).

R v Gladue, [1999] 1 SCR 688.

R v JTS, 2007 SKCA 84, SJ No 424.

R v SLS (2016), 2016 CanLII 57608 (NL PC).

Reid, S., Bromwich, R., & Gilliss, S. (2015). *Youth and the law: New approaches to criminal justice and child protection* (3rd ed.). Toronto: Emond.

Reid, S.A. (2010). The untapped potential in our communities to assist youth engaged in risky behavior. *International Journal of Child, Youth and Family Studies, 1*(2), 179–203.

Reid, S.A. (2011). Age of responsibility. In W.J. Chambliss (Ed.), *Juvenile crime and justice* (pp. 4–13). Thousand Oaks, CA: Sage.

Reid, S.A., & Gilliss, S. (2016). Key challenges in hearing the voice of youth in the youth justice system. In J. Winterdyk & R. Smandych (Eds.), *Youth at risk and youth justice* (2nd ed.). Toronto: Oxford University Press.

Reid, S.A., & Reitsma-Street, M. (2001). Assumptions and implications of new Canadian legislation for young offenders. In T.A. O'Reilly-Fleming (Ed.), *Youth injustice: Canadian perspectives* (pp. 49–73). Toronto: Canadian Scholars' Press.

Reid, S.A., & Zuker, M.A. (2004). A conceptual framework for understanding youth justice in Canada. In K. Campbell (Ed.), *Youth justice in Canada*. Toronto: Pearson.

Savarese, J.L. (2016). Moving forward and standing still: Assessing restorative-based justice in Saskatchewan after the *Youth Criminal Justice Act*. In M. Alain, R. Corrodo, & S. Reid (Eds.), *Implementing and working with the Youth Criminal Justice Act across Canada* (pp. 331–358). Toronto: University of Toronto Press.

Schubert, C.A., Mulvey, E.P., Loughran, T.A., & Losoya S.H. (2012). Perceptions of institutional experience and community outcomes for serious adolescent offenders. *Criminal Justice and Behaviour, 39*(1), 71–93.

Schwalbe, C.S., Gearing, R.E., MacKenzie, M.J., Brewer, K.B., & Ibrahim, R. (2012). A meta-analysis of experimental studies of diversion programs for juvenile offenders. *Clinical Psychology Review, 32*(1), 26–33.

Skeem, J.L., Manchak, S., & Peterson, J.K. (2011). Correctional policy for offenders with mental illness: Creating a new paradigm for recidivism reduction. *Law & Human Behavior, 35*(2), 110–126.

Skeem, J.L., Scott, E., & Mulvey, E.P. (2014). Justice policy reform for high-risk juveniles: Using science to achieve large-scale crime reduction. *Annual Review of Clinical Psychology, 10,* 709–739.

Statistics Canada. (2016). Table 251-0008—Youth correctional services, average counts of youth in provincial and territorial correctional services, annual (persons unless otherwise noted), CANSIM (database). Retrieved from http://www5.statcan.gc.ca/cansim/a26?lang=eng&retrLang=eng&id=2510008&&pattern=&stByVal=1&p1=1&p2=-1&tabMode=dataTable&csid=.

Sullivan, C.J., Veysey, B.M., Hamilton, Z.K., & Grillo, M. (2007). Reducing out-of-community placement and recidivism: Diversion of delinquent youth with mental health and substance use problems from the justice system. *International Journal of Offender Therapy and Comparative Criminology, 51*(5), 555–577.

Umbach, R., Berryessa, C.M., & Raine, A. (2015). Brain imaging research on psychopathy: Implications for punishment, prediction, and treatment in youth and adults. *Journal of Criminal Justice, 43*(4), 295–306.

Ungar, M. (2004). Resilience among children in child welfare, corrections, mental health and educational settings: Recommendations for service. *Child and Youth Care Forum, 34*(6), 445–464.

United Nations. (1985, November 29). *Standard Minimum Rules for the Administration of Juvenile Justice* ("The Beijing Rules"), Resolution 40/33.

United Nations. (1989, November 20). *Convention on the Rights of the Child*, 1577 UNTS 3, Can TS 1992 No 3 (entered into force September 2, 1990).

Vieira, T.A., Skilling, T.A., & Peterson-Badali, M. (2009). Matching court-ordered services with treatment needs: Predicting treatment success with young offenders. *Criminal Justice and Behavior, 36*(4), 385–401.

Vissing, Y. (2011). Curfews. In W.J. Chambliss (Ed.), *Juvenile crime and justice* (pp. 59–72). Thousand Oaks, CA: Sage.

Wasserman, G.A., McReynolds, L.S., Schwalbe, C.S., Keating, J.M., & Jones, S.A. (2010). Psychiatric disorder, comorbidity, and suicidal behaviour in juvenile justice youth. *Criminal Justice and Behaviour, 37*(12), 1361–1376.

Whitaker, J., Severy, L., & Morton, D. (1984). A comprehensive community based youth diversion program. *Child Welfare, 63*(2), 175–181.

Whitted, K.S., Delavega, E., & Lennon-Dearing, R. (2013). The youngest victims of violence: Examining the mental health needs of young children who are involved in the child-welfare and juvenile justice systems. *Child and Adolescent Social Work Journal, 30*(3), 181–195.

Wilson, H.A., & Hoge, R.D. (2013). The effect of youth diversion programs on recidivism: A meta-analytic review. *Criminal Justice and Behavior, 40*(5), 497–518. Retrieved from http://users.soc.umn.edu/~uggen/Wilson_CJB_13.pdf.

You Be the Judge Revisited

Have a look back at the opening case study of Part One. Do you remember what sentence you thought Matt should receive? Can you recall your reasons for choosing that sentence? Now that you have had a chance to consider the many agencies, approaches, and guiding principles involved in Canada's criminal justice system, has your view of Matt's case changed in any way? Considering what you now know about the correctional system, would you make any changes to the sentence you initially suggested for Matt?

The Sentence

Matt's case was heard in 2013 by Judge John Joy of the Provincial Court of Newfoundland and Labrador (*R v Dicker*, 2013). Judge Joy sentenced Matt to a total of seven months in prison—six months for the aggravated assault charge and one month for having breached his previous probation order. The judge ordered that these terms of imprisonment be served consecutively (i.e., one after the other) for a total of seven months of incarceration. Because Matt had spent 66 days in jail on remand, the judge awarded him 99 days of time served (using a 1.5:1 ratio). As a result, Matt was left with a total of 101 remaining days in jail. In addition, Judge Joy issued a DNA order, requiring Matt to provide blood and saliva samples for the RCMP database, and a ten-year firearms prohibition order.

Judge Joy also set out a number of probation conditions that Matt would have to follow after his release from jail:

You have to keep the peace and be of good behaviour. You have to appear in court when the court wants you here. You have to tell your probation officer if you change your address or you get work. You have to report to the probation officer within two working days of your release from jail and on other days that she sets for you. You are not to contact or communicate in any way, directly or indirectly, with Robbie Rich, and you are to stay away from where he lives and works.

You have to attend counselling that your probation officer recommends for anger management. I am also requiring that you continue your counselling with … the Healing Lodge." (*R v Dicker*, 2013, paras. 194–95)

What Do You Think?

What do you think of Judge Joy's decision in this case? Do you agree with it? How different is his decision from the one you reached?

Judge Joy's decision began by noting the seriousness of his role as a sentencing judge. "We are not playing a game in sentencing hearings," he wrote, "and certainly the Lamer Inquiry should have taught us a lesson requiring us to consider all relevant facts not only in trials, but also in sentencing hearings" (*R v Dicker*, 2013, para. 11). He then discussed a number of aggravating and mitigating factors that influenced his decision, including the role the victim played in the altercation. Consider the following passage from the judgment. How many different sentencing principles can you identify?

> I take into account your record …. Prior to the date of this particular offence … you had 16 convictions and all of them were minor offences. None of them involved jail time, all of them resulted in periods of probation. They were all break and enter charges, breaches of court orders and there was one assault. You were also a youth for most of this record. …
>
> I have to take the victim impact statement into account against you, and certainly I condemn you for what you did. I denounce this type of behaviour. You had no right to defend yourself with a knife in these circumstances. I also have to develop a sentence that is going to discourage you and others from committing similar offences. …
>
> I also have to take into account proportionality and that means I have to take into account how serious the offence was and of course stabbing a person in the left chest is a very serious matter. At the same time, however, I also have to take into account your degree of responsibility. I find that is not at the highest level because of the provocation and the self-defence element. …
>
> The words Robbie Rich said to you at the beginning of this incident were serious. He should never have said them, but, at the same time, that set up the initial contact between the two of you. What really happened at that initial contact was very minor. You pushed the bike into him, and you had a scuffle. You may have struck him once and he took a couple of swings at you but did not make any contact.
>
> According to the evidence, you tried to escape. … You were running away, he grabbed you. If he had not grabbed you, you would not be here. You certainly had the right to defend yourself, but the problem was you used excessive force. If you had swung around and struck him with your fist, you would have been fine. You, however, struck him with a knife or with some object that made a hole in his chest. (*R v Dicker*, 2013, paras. 157–66)

In his decision, Judge Joy also referred to the pre-sentence report that was prepared for the sentencing hearing, as well as specific information that it included about Matt, his upbringing, and his plans for the future:

> When I look at the pre-sentence report I find a young man of 20 years of age. … Your mother is Mushuau Innu and your father is a settler or possibly a Métis. You identify yourself as Mushuau Innu, and your first language is Innu-aimun, yet you do speak reasonable English.
>
> The pre-sentence report states that your parents drank heavily and that there was lots of fighting and yelling in the home. When the probation officer looked at your circumstances, she found you were often held back in school, and that you eventually left school at grade 8. …
>
> The report refers to the false charges of sexual assault that relate to the provocation that you suffered in this particular incident. It was clear that you had spent some considerable time as a result of those false charges in the group home in Sheshatshiu …. This had a major effect on your life, and continues to have a major effect on your life.
>
> The pre-sentence report says that you have not had much employment, yet you have filed with the court an offer of work from the Mushuau Innu First Nation, the Facility Management Department …. They are prepared to provide you with work.

The Lamer Inquiry was an investigation of the Newfoundland and Labrador justice system that was conducted in 2006 by former Supreme Court of Canada Chief Justice Antonio Lamer. It was prompted by three wrongful convictions in Newfoundland murder cases.

Which of the *Criminal Code*'s sentencing principles (see Chapter 8) does your initial judgment reflect?

When the probation officer asked you about your plans for the future, she wrote that you would like to finish school but you would also like to get a job eventually coaching hockey.

You expressed to the probation officer your remorse for stabbing Robbie Rich and she has put that in the pre-sentence report. The report, however, also documents that there is a long history of arguments and trouble between yourself and Robbie Rich.

The probation officer said that you were cooperative with her in preparing the report. She also referred to the support that you have from … your sister, who wants you to live with her when you are released from jail. She has also been an advocate for you. She has almost been like a lawyer for you in helping you arrange counselling at the healing lodge …. She says that you need treatment for anger management and domestic violence but I think she really means [that you require this treatment] as far as this charge is concerned. (*R v Dicker*, 2013, paras. 173–80)

How much of Matt's background did *you* consider when you reached your initial decision? Do you think background information on the offender in the pre-sentence report is useful to judges when sentencing an offender? Determining the relevance of an offender's background when handing down a sentence relies a great deal on how we define the purpose of the criminal justice system. What is the role of a criminal sentence? Is it punishment? Rehabilitation? Reintegration? Reconciliation? Finding the "right" sentence depends on how this question is answered.

Judge Joy's decision also specifically noted a trial judge's responsibility "to find a sentence that is fit for the offender, for the offence, for the complainant, and for the community" (*R v Dicker*, 2013, para. 25). Matt's case was heard in the remote Innu community of Natuashish by a circuit court. Judge Joy (and members of his court staff) would have travelled to Matt's community to hear the case. Census data from 2011 recorded the Natuashish population at 931. What do you imagine it is like for a community of this size to experience a "fly-in" criminal justice system? One author described the setting in this way:

On this bright Thursday in October, thirty-two people are scheduled to appear in the makeshift courtroom in the … school gym. Virtually everybody in town has a stake.

[The accused] takes a seat on one of the plastic folding chairs facing Madam Justice Beverley Browne, who will preside from a dusty table directly below the basketball net. At another table, two legal aid lawyers, one in high-heeled boots and a power suit, shuffle files. The Crown prosecutor looks more relaxed in tweed and sneakers—the black-soled kind that, according to a sign on the door, are not allowed in the gym. Groups of people of varying degrees of familiarity settle in around [the accused]. A baby dressed in a hot pink ski suit is passed along a row of women, while school-aged children peer into the room from the hallway through a series of open windows. Justice Browne closes her paperback and puts on her robe. Court is in session. (Minogue, 2012)

The use of circuit courts in Indigenous communities in Canada has not been without its difficulties. Often, there is a clash of both customs and values. As Colin Samson (2003) remarked:

Underneath all the symbolism of *Akaneshau* [Innu word for English Canadian] power—the crucifixes, the armed and uniformed officers, even a portrait of Queen Elizabeth II … —there are no concessions to the people who are being judged. With no introductions made, no names announced, no explanations of either the people or the processes involved, it is as if this were a part of their lives, as though there had never been a time when the Innu were not judged by foreigners. (p. 298)

Often, court proceedings take place in English, leaving many Indigenous people in attendance uncertain about what is taking place. Moreover, criminal proceedings that might seem commonplace to a visiting judge can be confusing or misunderstood by those unfamiliar with the common law system. Many communities are not afraid to take matters into their own hands when this clash in customs goes too far. The Innu community at Davis Inlet went without a visit from the circuit court for almost two years after the Innu "were so insulted by their treatment at the hand of [a judge] that they evicted him and his court by calling a halt to the proceedings and escorting [him] and his entourage to the airstrip" (Samson, 2003, pp. 296–297). Interestingly, in the first circuit court hearing held after this eviction, the lawyer for the Innu defendants (who unsuccessfully requested that a court interpreter be provided so that members of the community could understand the proceedings) was John Joy—the person who would later go on to serve as a circuit court judge himself.

In his decision in the *Dicker* (2013) case, Judge Joy remarked on the historical discrimination and mistreatment of the Innu people:

> It is obvious to everyone that the Mushuau Innu were a nomadic people with very limited contact with settler society. …
>
> The settlers, of course, did not really show, or very few of them showed, any respect for your language, your customs and your way of life. There was, as a result, a lot of trouble in the community with alcohol, domestic violence, suicide and gas sniffing. There was poor housing. It was hard to get back on the mainland, particular[ly] in the spring from the island. (*R v Dicker*, 2013, paras. 168–69)

These historical circumstances were a key component of the judge's decision in Matt's case. Recall that s 718.2(e) of the *Criminal Code* requires that the courts use jail as a last resort for Indigenous offenders, calling upon judges to consider the role of systemic racism in Canada's criminal justice system. Given the overrepresentation of Indigenous men and women in this country's prisons, this consideration is all the more pressing. As the Supreme Court of Canada stated in its decision in *R v Gladue* (1999):

> Sentencing judges are among those decision-makers who have the power to influence the treatment of aboriginal offenders in the justice system. They determine most directly whether an aboriginal person will go to jail, or whether other sentencing options may be employed which may play perhaps a stronger role in restoring a sense of balance to the offender, victim, and community, and in preventing future crime. (para. 65)

This passage speaks to the power of Canada's criminal justice officials in determining the future of Indigenous communities. It also addresses the need to consider how the criminal law and its court system can work toward healing communities.

This is the call to action that the Truth and Reconciliation Commission of Canada (2015) issued after listening to the stories of many Indigenous people who survived the residential school system:

> Reconciliation is going to take hard work. People of all walks of life and at all levels of society will need to be willingly engaged.
>
> Reconciliation calls for personal action. People need to get to know each other. They need to learn how to speak to, and about, each other respectfully. They need to learn how

"The world is a dangerous place, not because of those who do evil, but because of those who look on and do nothing."
—Albert Einstein

to speak knowledgeably about the history of this country. And they need to ensure that their children learn how to do so as well. …

Laws must change.

Policies and programs must change.

The way we educate our children and ourselves must change.

The way we do business must change.

Thinking must change.

The way we talk to, and about, each other must change. (p. 364)

Take the Truth and Reconciliation Commission of Canada's reading challenge pledge at trcreadingchallenge.com!

As this text has sought to demonstrate, successful crime prevention and community restoration requires many hands, including strong family supports, educational programs, successful labour markets, and healthy communities. The challenges facing each of you as students of criminal justice are both daunting and numerous. Where do you see your place in Canada's criminal justice world? How will you meet its future challenges? What call to action will you answer?

DISCUSSION QUESTIONS

1. When delivering his sentence, Judge Joy remarked on the principles of sentencing that are set out in the *Criminal Code*. He described them in detail in his judgment:

> I am well aware of the purposes and principles of sentencing in the *Criminal Code* and these cases contributing to respect for the law and the maintenance of a just, peaceful and safe society with one or more of the following objective[s]:
>
> (1) the purposes to condemn illegal acts, to discourage offenders and others from committing crimes, to jail offenders, to assist in their rehabilitation, to have them pay for the harm they do to victims and their community, and to encourage them to accept responsibility for that harm;
>
> (2) the fundamental principle of establishing the right balance between the gravity of the offence and the offender's degree of responsibility. This balancing does not necessarily mean a judge must provide equal weight to each factor. The facts may well determine that one or the other might be more important;
>
> (3) considering factors against the accused including domestic violence, child abuse and breach of trust;
>
> (4) making similar sentences for similar offenders, offences and circumstances;
>
> (5) not issuing sentences for a series of offences so that the total is too long or harsh;
>
> (6) not imposing a jail sentence if another sentence is appropriate under the circumstances; and
>
> (7) considering all other reasonable sentences under the circumstances besides jail for all offenders, "with particular attention to the circumstances of aboriginal offenders." (para. 26)

How well do you think the judge addressed these principles in the sentence he delivered in Matt's case? Do certain principles seem to have had more influence on his sentence than others?

2. Thinking back on the five models of criminal justice discussed in Chapter 1 (i.e., the crime-control model, welfare model, justice model, community change model, and restorative justice model), which model do you think best explains Judge Joy's approach to crime and its punishment? Is it the same as your own?

3. The altercation between Matt and the victim in this case was a factor that Judge Joy remarked on a number of times in his judgment. He is clear about how it influenced the sentence when he noted the following:

> Both the provocation and the self-defence elements mean that the sentence should be lower than it might otherwise be, if the assault was unprovoked and had no self-defence element. If you had not been provoked and there was no issue of self-defence at all, then the sentence would be much higher. It might be higher too … if you broke into somebody's house and stabbed them. That would make the crime more serious. In your case, however, you do have these aspects of provocation and self-defence that should have the effect of lessening the sentence. (para. 156)

Do you agree with Judge Joy's assessment of what took place between Matt and Robbie? Was the altercation a factor in the sentence you reached when reading this case? Do you think it is fair that an offender might get a more lenient sentence because of something that the victim did? Why or why not?

REFERENCES

Minogue, S. (2012, September 12). Flyby justice: A day in Nunavut's circuit court. *The Walrus.* Retrieved from https://thewalrus.ca/flyby-justice/.

R v Dicker, (2013) CanLII 13200, 280 CRR (2d) 68 (Nfld Prov Ct).

R v Gladue, [1999] 1 SCR 688.

Samson, C. (2003). *A way of life that does not exist: Canada and the extinguishment of the Innu.* London: Verso Books.

Truth and Reconciliation Commission of Canada. (2015). *Honouring the truth, reconciling for the future: Summary of the final report of the Truth and Reconciliation Commission of Canada.* n.p.: Author. Retrieved from http://www.trc.ca/websites/trcinstitution/File/2015/ Findings/Exec_Summary_2015_05_31_web_o.pdf.

Legislation

Anti-terrorism Act, 2015, SC 2015, c 20.

British North America Act, see *Constitution Act, 1867*.

Canada Evidence Act, RSC 1985, c C-5.

Canadian Charter of Rights and Freedoms, Part I of the *Constitution Act, 1982*, being Schedule B to the *Canada Act 1982* (UK), 1982, c 11.

Canadian Security Intelligence Service Act, RSC 1985, c C-23.

Canadian Victims Bill of Rights, SC 2015, c C-13.

Constitution Act, 1867 (UK), 30 & 31 Vict, c 3.

Controlled Drugs and Substances Act, SC 1996, c 19.

Corrections and Conditional Release Act, SC 1992, c 20.

Crimes Against Humanity and War Crimes Act, SC 2000, c 24.

Criminal Code, RSC 1985, c C-46.

Federal Courts Act, RSC 1985, c F-7.

Highway Traffic Act, RSO 1990, c H.8.

Indian Act, RSC 1985, c I-5.

Juvenile Delinquents Act, RSC 1970, c J-3 [repealed, 1984].

Police Act, RSBC 1996, c 367.

Royal Canadian Mounted Police Act, RSC 1985, c R-10.

Safe Streets and Communities Act, SC 2012, c 1.

Strengthening Military Justice in the Defence of Canada Act, SC 2013, c 24.

Young Offenders Act, RSC 1985, c Y-1 [repealed, 2002].

Youth Criminal Justice Act, SC 2002, c 1.

Glossary

abet: To offer encouragement or advice to a person during the commission of a criminal offence.

absolute discharge: A finding of guilt without a conviction. It is imposed when considered to be in the best interests of the accused and not contrary to public interest. Offenders given an absolute discharge cannot be charged and retried for the offence.

absolute jurisdiction: The exclusive authority of a court to try an offence, established by statute or by the classification of an offence. Also referred to as *exclusive jurisdiction*.

accessory after the fact: A person who aids another person they know has committed an offence; assistance includes helping the offender evade capture.

actuarial risk assessment: A statistical evaluation of offender risk; it measures variables that research has shown are predictive of recidivism.

actus reus: Latin for "guilty act"; used in law to refer to the physical acts and circumstances that must be proven to have occurred and been present during the commission of an offence.

adversarial system: System of justice in which cases are argued by two opposing sides, the prosecution and the defence, both of which are responsible for fully and forcefully presenting their respective positions; cases are heard and decided by an impartial judge.

aggravating circumstances: Factors of the crime or life circumstances of the accused, which may permit the judge to allocate a more severe disposition, including specifying a length of time in prison before the offender is eligible to apply for release.

aggregate sentences: The combined total of all sentences being served by an individual.

aid: In law, to do something or fail to do something with the purpose of helping another person commit a criminal offence.

ancillary powers doctrine: The process through which new police powers can be created by way of common law (also known as case law or precedent). Common law is developed by judges through decisions of the courts rather than through legislative action by Parliament.

appearance notice: A form given to the accused by police after being charged that tells him or her to appear in court on a specific day and time to answer to a criminal charge.

arraignment: A court hearing where the accused is called by name before the court, read the charges he or she is accused of, and asked to submit a plea.

arrest: Taking or keeping of a person in custody by legal authority, especially in response to a criminal offence.

arrest warrant: A document signed by a judge or a justice of the peace authorizing a police officer to apprehend a specific person for a specified reason and bring that person before a justice of the peace.

attrition: The filtering process that criminal cases undergo as they move through the criminal justice system.

automatism: A state of impaired consciousness wherein a person's actions are not voluntary.

autrefois acquit: The accused has been acquitted of the same *Criminal Code* offence in a prior criminal case.

autrefois convict: The accused has been convicted of the same *Criminal Code* offence in a prior criminal case.

best interests of the child: The principle that the interests of a young person are paramount in decision-making regarding his or her experience in the criminal justice system.

beyond a reasonable doubt: The standard of proof in criminal cases; it requires believing the accused is guilty beyond any doubt that a reasonable person, having heard all of the same evidence, would have.

bobby: A British slang word (like *peeler*) for policeman, in reference to Sir Robert Peel.

burden of proof: The responsibility to prove the allegations at issue in a trial.

calibre: The width of a gun barrel before rifling is added.

capital murder: A homicide where the victim is a peace officer (including police and other law enforcement officers, sheriffs, prison wardens, guards, and correctional officers).

causal link: An established connection between an accused's conduct (act or omission) and a prohibited legal consequence; also known as *causation*.

challenge for cause: A challenge to the choice of a potential juror on the grounds of ineligibility or impartiality.

change of venue: A court order (applied for under s 5991 of the *Criminal Code*) that transfers jurisdiction over a case to another court within the province for reasons of prejudice or unfairness to the accused.

charge to the jury: The trial judge's instructions to the jury about how the relevant law applies to the case at hand.

child savers: White, college-educated members of the middle and upper classes who, during the late 19th and early 20th centuries, established informal charities and grassroots organizations that led to the creation of a juvenile court and reform in compulsory education, child labour, juvenile institutions, and juvenile probation.

civilianization: The process of transferring non-core police functions from police officers to civilian employees.

class characteristics: Characteristics that allow an exhibit to be associated with a group, but not a single source.

coach officer: An experienced officer who works with a new constable, also called a field training officer.

codified: Written down and collected; for example, the *Criminal Code*, which contains a written record of all of Canada's criminal laws, is a codified law.

coerced-compliant false confession: When a suspect confesses because he or she wishes to escape from the stress of the interrogation, to avoid a threat of harm or punishment, or to gain a promised or implied reward.

coerced-internalized false confession: When a suspect who is coerced, tired, and highly suggestible confesses because the suspect actually comes to believe that he or she committed the crime.

cognitive interview: A method of interviewing witnesses to enhance the correct recall of information.

collective efficacy: The willingness of individuals in a neighbourhood to work together toward a common goal, such as crime control.

colourability: A legal doctrine referring to disguised attempts by a legislature to introduce a law that it does not have the authority or jurisdiction to enact.

common law: Law that is developed by judges when deciding cases, rather than through legislative enactments.

comparison microscope: Two light microscopes connected by an optical bridge that allows the examiner to see two separate objects on different stages, in the same field.

concurrent sentence: A sentence that allows the convicted offender to serve two or more sentences simultaneously; the total time the offender serves is equal to the longest sentence.

conditional discharge: Similar to an absolute discharge, a finding of guilt without conviction. It is imposed when an accused is found guilty for a summary offence with no mandatory minimum punishment, and when it is considered to be in the accused's best interest and not contrary to the public's interest. Conditional discharges are accompanied by rules that must be followed.

conditional release: The lawful release of an inmate from prison before the expiry of the sentence, subject to conditions set by the releasing authority.

conditional sentence: A prison sentence that is served in the community, under certain restrictions, the primary goal of which is to reduce judicial reliance on incarceration.

confirmatory test: A test that identifies a substance conclusively. It has no false positives. However, it is often expensive, so presumptive tests are used to focus the confirmatory test required.

consecutive sentence: A sentence in which the convicted offender serves two or more sentences one after the other; the total time the offender serves is equal to the total time of the sentences imposed.

consent committal: The accused's agreement to proceed to trial; it stops or bypasses the preliminary inquiry.

conspiracy: An agreement between two or more persons to commit a criminal offence.

contemporary community policing: The police and community working together to identify, prioritize, and solve local crime and disorder issues that impact the quality of life in neighbourhoods and business districts. It embraces the concept of policing through crime prevention, and community safety and well-being from holistic and root cause perspectives.

contempt of court: Canada's only common law offence, it consists of deliberately disobeying a court order or showing disrespect to the court process.

continuity of evidence: The chronological record of everyone that handles an exhibit and everything that is done to it, such as analyses, from the moment that it is seized to its final disposition. Also called *chain of custody*.

counsel: In law, to recommend, incite, or repeatedly request that a person commit a criminal offence.

crime rate: A measure of how much crime is known about for any given region or population, calculated by adding up all of the criminal incidents that have been reported to the police and dividing by the population. In Canada, these data are taken from the Uniform Crime Reporting (UCR) Survey.

criminogenic: Producing or tending to produce crime or criminal behaviour.

criminogenic risk factors: Characteristics of the offender or his or her circumstances (such as anti-social attitude, anti-social personality, anti-social associates) that increase criminal potential. When these risk factors are reduced through appropriate treatment, the risk for continued criminal behaviour is reduced.

Crown disclosure: The ongoing legal obligation of the Crown to turn its case (including all evidence and relevant information) over to the accused; this legal right is protected in sections 7 and 11(a) of the Charter, which recognizes the accused's right to make a full answer and defence to a criminal charge.

dangerous offender: A designation that can be applied to an offender who has repeat convictions that shows a failure of restraint, a pattern of offending, and a demonstrable likelihood of causing death or injury to another person. If so designated, the sentence of incarceration imposed can be indeterminate.

dark figure of crime: A term used in criminology and criminal justice studies to refer to the vast amount of criminal activity that is not reported to police, leaving the total amount of crime in any given society impossible to know.

day parole: A type of conditional release that allows an offender to be out of prison during the day and requires him or her to return at night.

deferred custody and supervision order: A community-based alternative to a custodial sentence. A judge may order a youth to be placed in custody but then defer custody and release the youth into the community subject to conditions and supervision. The order must not exceed six months. If the youth breaches any of the conditions, he or she may be placed back in custody to complete the remainder of the sentence.

denounce: Condemn or criticize another's actions.

deterrence: Disincentive to commit a crime, controlled by the person's fear or threat of getting arrested and incarcerated.

detoxification: A process of cleansing the bloodstream of toxins. For the alcoholic or drug addict, it may include abstention from alcohol or drugs as well as medical intervention.

discretion: The decision-making process and judgment police officers use when determining how best to deal with a situation they encounter. Other branches of the criminal justice system, including the courts and corrections, also have discretionary powers that can influence the outcome of cases.

disparity: A difference or inconsistency in rulings and/or dispositions among judges.

disposition: A judicial determination or sentence that is given to a person who has been convicted of an offence.

diversion: A sentencing approach in which offenders are given an opportunity to perform some community service or are referred to a community agency to better address their needs instead of being processed through the youth justice court system. In the *Youth Criminal Justice Act*, "extrajudicial measures" and "extrajudicial sanctions" are forms of diversion.

***doli incapax* doctrine:** Belief that a child of tender years is incapable of an unlawful act.

duty counsel: A lawyer paid by the government to provide legal advice and services to individuals who come to court unrepresented.

election: The accused's choice about which court and trial proceeding will be used; it is available for certain offences only.

elements of the offence: The components of a crime that a Crown must prove to obtain a conviction; that is, the *actus reus* (guilty act) and *mens rea* (guilty mind).

environmental design: Fashioning and developing the physical and built landscape, most often in an urban or suburban setting.

***esprit de corps*:** A spirit of loyalty and enthusiasm among members of a group for the group.

etiological theories of crime: Theories dealing with the causes of crime.

exhibit: An individual piece of evidence.

exigent circumstances: Situations in which people are in imminent danger of bodily harm or death, in which there is risk of imminent loss or destruction of evidence, or in which a suspect will escape.

extrajudicial measures (EJM): Informal ways in which the police may keep a young person out of the youth criminal justice system. They can include warnings, cautions, or referrals to a community agency for help.

extrajudicial sanctions (EJS): More formal ways of handling a youth case outside of court when extrajudicial measures are not sufficient. They can include community service, compensating the victim, and attending rehabilitation programs.

factual guilt: The accused's actual guilt.

faint hope clause: Found in section 745.6 of the *Criminal Code*, it provides persons convicted of the country's most serious offences (i.e., murder or high treason) and who have been sentenced to life imprisonment without the eligibility for parole the opportunity to apply for parole after they have served 15 years of their sentence. It is not permitted in cases where persons have committed more than one murder and is called the "faint hope" clause because of how few applications made under this clause have been successful.

false confession: When individuals confess to a crime they did not commit or exaggerate involvement in a crime they did commit.

federal paramountcy: The principle that when there is a conflict between federal and provincial laws, the federal legislation will succeed and the provincial law will be considered invalid (insofar as it conflicts with the federal law).

fine: Paid by the offender directly to government; the money collected is used to pay for various judicial services and resources.

forensic psychology: The application of psychological research, methods, theories, and practices to a task faced by the legal system.

frankpledge system: A system of law enforcement in medieval England in which all men who were not part of the nobility were formed into groups and bound by a sworn pledge to ensure each other's good conduct.

full parole: A type of conditional release that allows an offender to reside in the community for the remainder of his or her sentence, subject to conditions of the parole board.

"good and evil" test: Used to determine whether a child could be found guilty based on their ability to distinguish between the concepts of good and evil. If a reasonable doubt were raised concerning the ability to perceive the difference, the child could not be punished.

gap principle: A term used to describe how much time (in days, months, or years) has passed from the offender's last conviction (not arrest) to the current conviction.

gender dysphoria: Where there is a conflict between the person's physical gender and his or her self-perceived gender (e.g., a person who is born physically male, but believes she is really female). Specific diagnostic criteria for gender dysphoria are outlined in the *Diagnostic and Statistical Manual of Mental Disorders* (DSM-5).

general intent offence: A crime that involves a minimal level of mental activity or a *mens rea* that only pertains to the performance of the illegal act and not a further objective (e.g., assault).

generalists: Front-line officers who are expected to have a wide range of community resources, skills, and connections to prevent, respond to, and intervene in a variety of calls for service.

gentrification: The changes that result when middle-class or upper-middle-class individuals acquire and upgrade property in low-income and working-class neighbourhoods.

***Gladue* decision:** A 1999 landmark ruling where the Supreme Court of Canada determined that it was imperative that the court system take into account the colonialist actions targeted at Indigenous people in Canada, based on the case of Jamie Lynn Gladue, who was found guilty of murdering her common law husband while under the influence of alcohol. Gladue successfully appealed her sentence of federal custody by arguing that the court had not taken into account distinct cultural issues affecting Indigenous people. As a result, courts must now consider culture-specific and gender-specific issues to better understand who the offender is as a person.

homophobia: Negative attitudes, including hatred, fear, and/or contempt, directed toward people who do not identify as heterosexual.

hung jury: A jury that is unable to reach a unanimous verdict, resulting in a mistrial.

ideology: A system of beliefs or assumptions about the correct or proper order of things, particularly with respect to morality and political arrangements; a value system that shapes a person's position on specific issues.

indeterminate: A disposition for juveniles that was not fixed in length. A young person could be held in custody until the youth was deemed by correctional authorities to no longer be seen as a threat to society or to be rehabilitated.

indictable offence: A serious offence such as murder, with longer periods of imprisonment and more complex prosecution procedures than those for summary conviction offences. Some offences have a minimum term and a maximum term of incarceration; others have no minimum term, but have a maximum term of incarceration; and still others carry the maximum sentence possible, which is life imprisonment.

indictment: A formal accusation of an offence that is presented to a superior court by the Crown (as an agent of the attorney general) to serve as a statement of the charges at issue in a criminal trial.

individual characteristics: Characteristics that allow an exhibit to be associated with a single source.

informal social control: The development, observance, and enforcement of local norms for appropriate public behaviour.

information: A written complaint, sworn under oath by a citizen or more typically a police officer, alleging that the accused has committed a specific criminal offence.

information to obtain a search warrant (ITO): A document prepared and sworn by the person seeking a search warrant (usually a police officer) specifying the offence alleged, the place(s) to be searched, and the specific item(s) to be seized.

insanity defence: A defence to a crime based on an argument that the individual was not responsible for his or her actions at the time of the crime due to his or her mental state.

intensive rehabilitative custody and supervision (IRCS): A sentence available for young persons who suffer from a mental illness, a psychological disorder, or an emotional disturbance and who are convicted of murder, attempted murder, manslaughter, or aggravated sexual assault, or who have been convicted for the third time of a violent offence that caused or attempted to cause serious bodily harm. It involves an intensive treatment and reintegration plan believed to reduce the risk of reoffence.

intermittent sentence: A prison sentence served at designated times (usually weekends), with the offender residing in the community the rest of the time under certain conditions as set out in a probation order.

intervening act: An event or act that occurs between the accused's actions and the victim's injury that is significant enough to break the causal link between the conduct of the accused and the law's prohibited consequence.

interventions: Strategies, such as treatment programs, job training, or upgrading education that are used to help an offender learn alternatives to criminal behaviour.

juror card: A ballot that contains the name, address, and occupation of the person summoned to jury duty that is entered into the lottery drum during a jury selection.

juror summons: A court order that requires a person to appear before a superior court on a specified day as a member of a jury array or jury panel.

jury array: The group of persons summoned to court for jury duty from which the jury is selected. It is also referred to as a *jury panel*.

jury roll: A jurisdiction's list of eligible jurors (from which the jury array or jury panel is summoned).

kin police: Adherents of an informal system of mutual protection wherein law enforcement fell to the citizenry who were responsible for their tribe, family, or kin.

leave to appeal: Permission to bring a case to an appellate court.

legal aid: A collaboratively funded project between the federal and provincial governments to provide legal services to those who cannot afford them.

legal guilt: The accused's guilt that is provable in a court of law.

Locard's exchange principle: A basic principle of forensic science introduced by Edmond Locard who recognized that every contact involves an exchange of physical materials that can be later analyzed scientifically.

locus (pl. loci): A site on a chromosome, almost like the address of an area of the chromosome.

mandatory minimum punishments: Proscribed minimum penalties for certain offences (see Chapter 8 for a full discussion).

manner of death: The classification of death. It can be natural, accidental, suicide, homicide, or undetermined.

maximization: An interrogation strategy whereby an interrogator uses "scare tactics" designed to intimidate a suspect into a confession.

mens rea: Latin for "guilty mind"; used in law to refer to the mental state the Crown must prove the accused had during the commission of an offence.

methadone: A synthetic narcotic that is orally administered and is used in the treatment of opiate (e.g., heroin) addiction.

minimization: An interrogation strategy whereby an interrogator provides suspects with a false sense of security by offering face-saving excuses, moral justification, blaming a victim or accomplice, or playing down the seriousness of the charges to encourage a suspect to make a confession.

mitigating circumstances: Factors of the crime or life circumstances of the accused that may permit the judge to allocate a more lenient disposition in keeping with the parameters outlined in the *Criminal Code.*

M'Naghten standard: The historical standard for insanity that allowed a defendant to be acquitted if he or she did not know what he or she was doing or that it was wrong.

modified objective standard: The consideration of the accused's personal circumstances and knowledge when assessing whether a reasonable person would have acted differently.

motive: A person's reason for committing an offence (which is distinct from the accused's intent).

negligent: Failing to take proper care when acting; in a criminal law context, it is the marked departure from the standard of a reasonable person.

neighbourhood watch: A structured program that involves a group of neighbours organized to prevent crime and disorder problems within a residential neighbourhood or apartment building. Residents are trained to keep an eye out for suspicious individuals or activities and to call police when such circumstances are spotted. Also referred to as *block watch* or *crime watch.*

net widening: A term used to describe the effects of providing alternatives to incarceration that deal with offenders outside the court system in order to reduce the numbers of people going to court, and ultimately entering correctional systems. Rather than decreasing the number of offenders in custody, net widening has increased the total number of offenders under the control of the state.

non-offence factors: Factors that are not directly a part of the offence, but which could impact the type and length of a sentence; for example, whether the offender has a lengthy criminal record or is a first-time offender, or hindered the police investigation.

not criminally responsible on account of mental disorder (NCRMD): A legal finding that an accused person is not criminally responsible on account of a mental disorder.

Oakes test: The framework used by the courts to determine whether a Charter right violation can be justified under s 1 of the Charter.

objective liability: Criminal responsibility for having acted in a negligent way; that is, failing to meet the standard of a reasonable person.

objectively reasonable: Where a person's thoughts or actions, measured by the "objective standard" used in courts to establish criminal responsibility, are deemed to be those that a reasonable person would have in a similar situation.

ombudsman: A government official whose role is to hear and investigate complaints made by citizens (in this case, federal inmates) about government officials or government agencies (in this case, Correctional Service Canada).

omission to act: The failure to act in circumstances where there is a legal obligation to do so.

ordeal: An ancient criminal trial method that involved subjecting the accused to a painful or dangerous test (e.g., holding a hot iron) as a means of seeking an answer from the divine about the accused's guilt or innocence.

parens patriae ("parent of the nation"): The principle that the state acts as a "kindly parent" to dependent delinquents.

parole: A type of conditional release from a federal penitentiary such as escorted temporary absence, day parole, full parole, or statutory release. Just because an offender is eligible to apply for parole does not guarantee that it will be granted.

party to an offence: A person involved in a criminal offence and subject to criminal liability.

pathology: The study of disease.

penal code: A compilation of the laws that establish a jurisdiction's criminal law; also referred to as a *criminal code.*

penectomy: Amputation of the penis.

penology: The multidisciplinary study of the justifications of penalties and social sanctions that seek to understand broader questions concerning who we punish, for what offence, when, and why. The penologist seeks to understand the deployment of penalties within their social, historical, economic, and political contexts.

peremptory challenge: A challenge to a potential juror for which no reason need be provided; it is available to both the Crown and the defence on a limited basis.

perimeter search: A search of the outside of a dwelling and its surroundings; it is used as a method of acquiring sufficient information on which to base a search warrant application to search inside the dwelling.

police subculture: Values, beliefs, and approaches to policing shared by members of the profession.

pre-trial conference: A meeting between the Crown and the accused that takes place before a superior court judge prior to the beginning of a trial; it is referred to as a *trial confirmation hearing* in provincial court cases.

preferring an indictment: The Crown's act of presenting or submitting a statement of the charges it is laying against the accused to a superior court judge.

preliminary inquiry: A court hearing (held before a trial in a superior court) to determine whether the Crown has sufficient evidence to proceed to trial.

presumptive test: An analysis of a sample that indicates whether a substance (e.g., semen) may be present. This test does not prove that a substance is present, as the test has been subject to false positives. If the test result is positive, further confirmatory tests are required. If the test result is negative, the substance is not present and no further testing is required. Such tests eliminate a large number of substances and narrow down the type of confirmatory test required.

prima facie: Legal presumption meaning "on the face of it" or "at first sight." It refers to a matter that appears to be self-evident from the facts. The term denotes evidence that, unless contested, would be sufficient to prove a particular fact in issue; the evidence need not be conclusive.

primary prevention: Interventions that take place before a problem develops; they are directed at a general population rather than specific individuals.

principal: In law, the person who actually commits the offence in question.

principle of simultaneity: A criminal law requirement that the *actus reus* and *mens rea* occurred at the same time or were part of the same chain of events during the commission of a crime.

private prosecution: A criminal trial or proceeding that is brought by a private citizen, rather than a publicly appointed official (e.g., Crown attorney, public prosecutor).

private security personnel: Private security personnel have the same "arrest and detain" powers as an ordinary citizen. While they perform some duties with regard to property protection that are similar to those of the public police, they are often paid by an employer to tend to security needs that are not in the public interest realm, such as controlling property and access to property.

privilege: A legal doctrine that protects certain pieces of evidence from having to be disclosed to opposing counsel on the basis of a legally recognized relationship of confidentiality.

probation: A disposition that is served within the community. Probation orders come with mandatory conditions (e.g., regular check-in with a probation officer; keeping the peace) and often additional restrictions and conditions (e.g., avoidance of certain geographical areas; addiction treatment).

probative value: The ability of a piece of evidence to prove or assist in proving something to the trier of fact.

problem-oriented policing: A proactive policing strategy whereby police focus on the problems that form the basis of crime.

promise to appear: A notice to appear in court on a specified date that is given to an accused (charged with a summary conviction, hybrid, or s 553 offence) upon release by police.

protective factors: Positive conditions, influences, or interventions that can increase the health and well-being of children and families by counteracting risk factors.

provision: In law, it refers to a specific section of a statute; an article or clause in a piece of legislation.

psychopathy: A personality disorder describing individuals who show a blatant disregard for others, both behaviourally and emotionally.

punishment provision: The *Criminal Code* section that describes the classification and eligible penalties for an offence. Also referred to as a *charging section*.

quasi-criminal law: Regulations and statutes pertaining to legal activities that create offences and penalties that are not enacted under the federal government's criminal law power. (See also regulatory offences.)

racial profiling: The act or tendency of law enforcement officers and others to consider people suspicious or more likely to commit crime based on the colour of their skin or their ethnicity.

rank and file: A term used in military and paramilitary organizations to denote the general membership of the organization as set apart from the commanders and leaders.

recidivism: Relapsing into criminal behaviour after treatment and/or sentencing within the criminal justice system. Most simply, it can be thought of as "reoffending."

recklessness: A form of subjective *mens rea* where the accused was aware of the risks created by his or her conduct but chose to proceed in the face of them anyway.

recognizance: A sum of money that is deposited with the court upon the accused's release and forfeited should the accused fail to show up for trial.

reference: An application by the Governor General to have the Supreme Court of Canada issue an interpretation of a federal or provincial law, often in relation to its constitutionality.

regulatory offences: Violations of legal rules or guidelines pertaining to legal activities (e.g., drinking). Also known as *quasi-criminal law*.

reintegrate: The return of offenders to society as law-abiding and productive citizens.

remand: The holding of an accused in custody while the person waits for trial (as opposed to being granted bail, which would allow the individual to live in the community while awaiting trial).

responsible person: An adult (other than a parent or guardian) who is willing and able to exercise control over a young person in order for him or her to be released prior to trial.

restitution order: An order for the offender to pay money directly to the victim(s) of the crime for financial losses incurred as a result of the offender's crime.

reverse onus: A shift in the burden of proof onto the accused; in a bail hearing setting, the requirement that the accused prove why he or she should be released from custody.

rifling: Spiral grooves cut into the barrel of a gun that engage the bullet and put a spin on it, so that it flies straight and does not yaw.

risk assessment: An assessment approach based on the identification of factors shown to predict future delinquent or criminal behaviour.

risk factors: Factors that increase the risk of criminal or delinquent behaviour.

root causes of crime: Social factors in our societies, cultures (family values), economy, and systems that are more likely to lead an individual to commit crime. Examples include peer influence, poverty, unemployment, poor neighbourhoods, and poor literacy.

rule of law: The principle that no one is above the law and that each person, regardless of political or economic position, should be subject to the same law (rather than the arbitrary decisions of the powerful).

safety and security web: A source of specialized knowledge, skills, and resources that can assist police in responding to internal and external trends and challenges in policing.

sanction: A penalty, such as a fine, probation, or incarceration, imposed on a person found guilty of a criminal offence.

secondary prevention: Interventions directed at specific high-risk individuals; the intervention takes place before more serious problems have developed.

sequestered: To keep the jury isolated from the public and any news media about the case so as to preserve impartiality.

show cause hearing: A court hearing to determine whether the accused should be released or held in custody awaiting trial; also known as a *bail hearing*.

specific intent offence: A crime that requires a higher level of thought or reasoning to carry out, such as having knowledge of certain circumstances or an intention to bring about a particular consequence (e.g., murder).

stare decisis: Latin for "to stand by things decided"; used in law to refer to the common law principle that judges must respect and follow decisions made by higher courts.

state of jeopardy: The accused's position of being in danger of criminal conviction and punishment.

status offences: Acts that are considered illegal only because of the age status of the offender.

statutory: Given power by statute, meaning a piece of legislation that is passed by Parliament and becomes law.

statutory release: A type of mandatory release for most federal offenders at two-thirds of their sentence.halfway houseA residential setting within the community that is staffed by professional workers who support offenders released on parole with the process of returning to the community.detentionIncarceration in prison that, in certain circumstances, may extend until the end of the sentence.

stay of proceedings: A court order that suspends (temporarily or permanently, depending on the order) a criminal trial.

suicidal ideation: Thoughts, either fleeting in nature or well-thought-out, that a person has about killing himself or herself.

summary conviction offence: A less serious offence that is tried using a simplified set of rules of procedure. The maximum term of incarceration is six months.

summons: A court order to appear before a judge on a specified date.

surety: A person (usually known to the accused) who agrees to pay a certain sum of money to the court if the accused fails to attend at trial.

talesman: In a jury, a person immediately summoned to court to join a jury panel after the initial array has been exhausted; this person is usually from a place or community near the courthouse.

temporary absence: A type of conditional release that allows an offender to be absent from prison for a temporary, defined period of time.

tertiary prevention: Interventions for individuals usually long after the initial problem developed, with the goal of preventing further criminal behaviour.

thin blue line: A symbolic representation of the police as a protective barrier between the general public and its crime and violence.

thin blue thread: A symbolic representation of the police as a thread woven thorough the communities they serve—a thread that helps hold those communities together; put forth as an alternative to the thin blue line metaphor Philadelphia Police Commissioner Charles Ramsey.

tithings: Among the common citizens of Anglo-Saxon England, groups of ten families who were collectively responsible for each other's behaviour.

trace evidence: Any small piece of evidence that is left behind and/or picked up at a crime scene. This can include just about anything, such as fingerprints, fibres, hair, soil, blood, semen, and paint.

transit police: Specialized police officers or special constables tasked exclusively with maintaining law and order on public transit such as trains, ferries, and buses.

trial committal: An order by a provincial court judge to send an accused to trial, usually issued after a preliminary inquiry.

tribunal: Decision-making body that adjudicates matters that affect a person's legal rights.

trier of fact: Judge and/or jury.

ultra vires: Latin for "beyond the power of"; used in law to refer to legislation that is enacted outside the jurisdiction of the governing body that issued it and is, therefore, invalid.

undertaking: A document that sets out the conditions for the release from police detention of a person charged with an offence. Conditions typically include a curfew, parental supervision, and attendance at school.

use of force: The amount of effort required by police to compel compliance by an unwilling subject.

victim surcharge: A monetary penalty paid by an offender to the province or territory where sentencing occurs; the money collected is used to support victims of crime in the jurisdiction.

vigiles: Watchmen and firefighters in ancient Rome.

voir dire: A court hearing that takes place within a trial in the absence of the jury to determine a legal issue, often the admissibility of evidence.

voluntary false confession: When an innocent person confesses to a crime without being prompted by the police.

waiver: The giving up of a right; it may be done expressly, or it may be implied from the circumstances.

waiver of charges: A court order (applied for by the accused under s 478(3) of the *Criminal Code*) that allows an offence to be tried in a jurisdiction other than the one in which the crime was committed.

watch and ward: Continuous vigilance by constables by night (watch) and day (ward).

white-collar crime: A term initially coined by sociologist Edwin Sutherland in 1939 to refer to the illegal and fraudulent activities of corporate executives, business personnel, and other persons of high social status that are committed for the purposes of financial gain.

Wigmore criteria: Four conditions upon which the doctrine of privilege can be extended to relationships outside the recognized forms of legal privilege; also known as *case-by-case privilege* or *class privilege*.

wilful blindness: A form of subjective *mens rea* where the accused deliberately chose not to see the risks created by his or her conduct.

youth justice conference: A group of people (e.g., family, clinicians, teachers, community members, and the young person) who are asked by a decision-maker (such as a judge) to come together to give advice on a young person's case. The format may include a youth justice committee, a professional case conference, or a family group conference.

youth record: When a young person is found guilty of a criminal offence, the individual will receive a youth record. The period of time that a youth record may be accessed after a finding of guilt varies, depending on the type of sentence. If a young person is convicted of a subsequent offence, the access period is recalculated.

zero tolerance: A disciplinary approach that advocates automatic punitive responses to all types of disorder and crime problems, no matter how minor, with the intention of eliminating undesirable conduct through punishment and deterrence. For example, fighting in school means an automatic suspension. Also sometimes called *order maintenance policing*.

Index

legal components of a crime, 176–185
mens rea, see mens rea
modes of participation, 185–190
parties to an offence, 185–187
primary sources, 172–176
principle of simultaneity, 177
statutory sources and the division of powers, 173–175
criminal mind, 8
criminal pardons, 211–212
criminal participation
incomplete offences, 188–190
parties to an offence, 185–187
criminal procedure, 199
arraignment, 207
burden of proof, 219–220
jury trials, *see* jury trials
pre-trial procedures, *see* pre-trial procedures
trial procedures, 215–220
voir dire, 219
criminal public purpose, 174
criminal responsibility, 152–154
criminals, 20–25; *see also* prison populations
definition, 20
identification of, 23–24
criminogenic, 46
criminogenic risk factors, 274
criminologists, 8
criminology, 8–9, 11
Crown attorneys, 173, 207
Crown disclosure, 214
cruel and unusual punishment, 261, 282
CSIS, *see* Canadian Security Intelligence Service (CSIS)
custodial interviewing and interrogation, 109–110
cybersecurity, 95

dangerous offender, 250, 271–272, 330, 333–336
dark figure of crime, 16–18
day parole, 301, 315–316
de-institutionalization, 94
death investigations, 148–150
deceit, 110
defences
automatism, 190–193
intoxication, 194–195
missing *actus reus* components, 190–193
missing *mens rea* components, 193–195
mistake of fact, 193
not criminally responsible on account of mental disorder, *see* not criminally responsible on account of mental disorder (NCRMD)
delay, 204–205
denounce, 230
dentists, 149
denunciation model, 230–231
Dérôme, Wilfred, 140
detention, 102–103, 302, 380–382
deterrence, 27, 231, 317, 370
deterrence model, 231–232
detoxification, 332
disciplinary segregation, 262, 283

discretion
Crown, 207
judicial discretion, 235
police, 119
discrimination, 220
disorder, 43
disparity, 235
dispositions, 230; *see also* sentencing
absolute discharge, 246, 385
community-based sentences, 278–280, 385–386
community service orders, 280, 386
conditional discharge, 247, 385
conditional sentence, 248–249, 249, 280
dangerous offender designation, 250
fines, 247–248, 386
imprisonment, 250
indeterminate, 368
Intensive Support and Supervision Programs (ISSPs), 279–280, 386
intermittent sentence, 248
judicial reprimand, 385
long-term offender designation, 251
not criminally responsible on account of mental disorder (NCRMD), 246
probation, 250, 279, 386
restitution, 247–248, 386
suspended sentence, 247
types of dispositions, 245–251
young offenders, *see* youth sentencing
diversion, 26, 370, 375–376
diversity in offender population, 342–343
division of powers, 173–175
DNA
CODIS (Combined DNA Index System), 145
databases, 142–143, 145
evidence, 114, 142–145
familial, 143–144
locus/loci, 142
mitochondrial DNA (mtDNA), 145
profiling, 142, 144
short tandem repeats (STRs), 142
doli incapax doctrine, 366
domestic violence, 45
domestic violence courts, 255
Dominion Police, 73
Doob, Anthony, 20
Dorchester Penitentiary, 269
double jeopardy, 211
drug treatment courts, 254
dual offences, 207
Durkheim, Émile, 7
duty counsel, 10, 208
Dziekański, Robert, 118, 119–120, 127

ecological theory of crime, 35
economic development, 51
Edmonton Police Service, 81
Edwards, Henrietta Muir, 201
Edwards v Attorney General of Canada, 201
election, 212, 213

Credits

Part One

Page 3 (photo): Peter Power/ZUMA Press/Newscom

Chapter 1

Page 8 (photo): TinkerSailorSoldierSpy/iStock
Page 14 (Figure 1.1): The Canadian Press. Reprinted with permission.
Page 15 (Figure 1.3): The Canadian Press. Reprinted with permission.
Page 19 (cartoon): Reprinted with the permission of Jeff Parker.
Page 29 (Table 1.2): Reid, Susan A. & Zuker, Marvin A. (2005). Conceptual frameworks for understanding youth justice in Canada: From the Juvenile Delinquents Act to the Youth Criminal Justice Act. In Kathryn M. Campbell (Ed.), *Understanding youth justice in Canada*. Toronto: Pearson. Reprinted with permission.

Chapter 2

Page 36 (photo): Dean2/iStock
Page 49 (photo): Peel Regional Police. Reprinted with permission.
Page 52 (photo): Toronto Police Service. Reprinted with permission.

Part Two

Page 65 (photo): Odd Squad. Reprinted with permission.

Chapter 3

Page 72 (photo): Wikipedia
Page 75 (photo): Chris Bolin. Reprinted with permission.
Page 76 (Figure 3.1): Waterloo Regional Police Service. Reprinted with permission.
Page 77 (Table 3.1): Reprinted with the permission of the RCMP.
Page 79 (Figure 3.2): Reprinted with the permission of Rick Ruddell.
Page 88 (Figure 3.4): Reprinted with the permission of the RCMP.

Chapter 4

Page 100 (photos): CP PHOTO/Fred Chartrand; CP Photo/Paul Chiasson
Page 106 (photo): REUTERS/Alamy Stock Photo
Page 108 (photo): Yafet Tawelde. Reprinted with permission.
Page 112 (photo): CP Photo/Scott Cook
Page 118 (photo): The EditPlayer. Reprinted with permission.
Page 119 (photo): CP Photo-Ho/Paul Pritchard
Page 123 (Figure 4.1): Reprinted with the permission of the Canadian Association of Chiefs of Police.
Page 125 (Table 4.1): Reprinted with the permission of David MacAlister.

Chapter 5

Page 135 (photo): stevanovicigor/Thinkstock
Page 141 (photo): Shawn Hempel/Thinkstock
Page 143 (photo): CP Photo/Nick UT
Page 149 (photos): REUTERS/Alamy Stock Photo; Gail Anderson
Page 150 (photo): Wikipedia
Page 158 (photo): CP Photo/Winnipeg Free Press/Wayne Glowacki

Part Three

Page 167 (photo): CP Photo/Andrew Vaughan

Chapter 6

Page 172 (photo): EmmePi Travel/Alamy Stock Photo
Page 183 (cartoon): CALVIN AND HOBBES © 1993 Watterson. Reprinted with permission of ANDREWS MCMEEL SYNDICATION. All rights reserved.

Chapter 7

Page 200 (Figure 7.1): Department of Justice Canada. (2015). *Canada's court system*. Ottawa: Her Majesty the Queen in Right of Canada. Retrieved from http://www.justice.gc.ca/eng/csj-sjc/ccs -ajc/pdf/courten.pdf. Reproduced with the permission of the Department of Justice Canada, 2017.
Page 200 (photo): Themightyquill/Wikipedia
Page 201 (photo): Library and Archives Canada, PA-195432
Page 210 (photo): CP Photo/Andrew Vaughan
Page 216 (cartoon): www.CartoonStock.com

Chapter 8

Page 231 (photo): AndreyPopov/Thinkstock
Page 252 (Figure 8.1): Department of Justice Canada. (2016a). The appeal process in Canada. Retrieved from http://justice.gc.ca/eng/ csj-sjc/just/appeal2-appel2.html. Reproduced with the permission of the Department of Justice Canada, 2017.

Part Four

Page 261 (photo): PaulFleet/iStock
Pages 261, 262, 263–264 (Literary): Jackson, M. (2015). Reflections on 40 years of advocacy to end the isolation of Canadian prisoners. *Canadian Journal of Human Rights*, 4(1), 57–87. Reprinted with permission.